Evening by Evening

Classic Devotionals by Jim Reimann

Evening by Evening: The Devotions of Charles Spurgeon
(expanded, indexed, and updated in today's language by Jim Reimann),
the companion volume to *Morning by Morning: The Devotions of Charles Spurgeon*

Morning by Morning: The Devotions of Charles Spurgeon
(expanded, indexed, and updated in today's language by Jim Reimann),
the companion volume to *Evening by Evening: The Devotions of Charles Spurgeon*

My Utmost for His Highest by Oswald Chambers
(updated by Jim Reimann)

Streams in the Desert: 366 Daily Devotional Readings by L. B. Cowman
(updated by Jim Reimann)

Streams for Teens by L. B. Cowman
(updated by Jim Reimann)

Streams in the Desert for Graduates by L. B. Cowman
(updated by Jim Reimann)

Evening by Evening

The Devotions of
CHARLES SPURGEON

EXPANDED, INDEXED & UPDATED EDITION IN TODAY'S LANGUAGE

JIM REIMANN

Editor of Updated Editions of *Streams in the Desert*®,
My Utmost for His Highest, and
Morning by Morning: The Devotions of Charles Spurgeon

ZONDERVAN.com/
AUTHORTRACKER
follow your favorite authors

ZONDERVAN

Evening by Evening: The Devotions of Charles Spurgeon
Copyright © 2010 by James G. Reimann

This title is also available as a Zondervan ebook.
Visit www.zondervan.com/ebooks.

Charles Spurgeon's original book is formerly published as *Evening by Evening*

Requests for information should be addressed to:

Zondervan, *Grand Rapids, Michigan 49530*

Library of Congress Cataloging-in-Publication Data

Spurgeon, C. H. (Charles Haddon), 1834–1892.
    Evening by evening : the devotions of Charles Spurgeon / expanded, indexed, and updated in
today's language by Jim Reimann.
       p. cm.
    Includes index.
    ISBN 978-0-310-28388-1 (softcover, gatefold)
    1. Devotional calendars—Baptists. I. Reimann, James. II. Title.
BV4811.S665 2010
242'.2—dc22   2010009000

Cover design: Michelle Lenger
Cover photography: Veer®
Interior design: Beth Shagene

Printed in the United States of America

10 11 12 13 14 15 16 /DCI/ 27 26 25 24 23 22 21 20 19 18 17 16 15 14 13 12 11 10 9 8 7 6 5 4 3 2 1

I think of you through the watches of the night.

Psalm 63:6

The History behind *Evening by Evening*

I think of you through the watches of the night.

Psalm 63:6

"Sell all [the books] you have ... and buy Spurgeon"

These are the words of the noted twentieth-century German theologian Helmut Thielicke (1908 – 86). Including Spurgeon's 140 books and 25,000 sermons, he has some 25 million words in print, more than any other Christian author, living or dead.

Spurgeon's conversion

Charles Haddon Spurgeon (June 19, 1834 – January 31, 1892) finished writing *Morning by Morning* when he was only thirty-one years of age in 1865, and followed it with *Evening by Evening* only three years later — two amazing works for such a young man! By 1868, however, he had been a pastor faithfully expositing God's Word for half of his life, for he was called to the ministry at the early age of seventeen. Ultimately, he would leave this earth at the age of fifty-seven, having spent forty years as a preacher, pastor, and author, as well as a founder of a pastor's college and an orphanage.

The Lord saved him at the age of fifteen on January 6, 1850. The following is his salvation account in his own words:

It pleased God in my childhood to convict me of my sin. I lived as a miserable creature, finding no hope or comfort; thinking, surely God would never save me. But I resolved to visit every place of worship in town to find the way of salvation. I was willing to do anything, and be anything, if God would only forgive me.

I set off, going to all the places of worship, and though I dearly venerate the men who occupy those pulpits now, and did so then, I must honestly say I never heard

them once fully preach the gospel. I mean by that, they preached truth, great truths, many good truths that were fitting to many of their congregation — spiritually-minded people — but what I wanted to know was, "How can I get my sins forgiven?" And they never told me that. I wanted to hear how a poor sinner, under conviction of sin, might find peace with God.

At last, one snowy day — it snowed so much I could not go to the place I had determined to go — I was forced to stop along the road, and it was a blessed stop to me. I found an obscure street and on that street was a little chapel — a place I did not know. I entered and sat down, but no minister came. Finally, a very thin-looking man came to the pulpit and opened his Bible and read these words: "Look unto me, and be ye saved, all the ends of the earth" (Isa. 45:22 kjv). Then, setting his eyes upon me, as if he knew my heart, he said: "Young man, you are in trouble." Well, I was, sure enough. He continued, "You will never get out of it unless you look to Christ." And then, lifting up his hands, he cried out, "Look, look, look! It is only look!" I saw at once the way of salvation. Oh, how I did leap for joy at that moment! I don't know what else he said — I did not take much notice of it, for I was so possessed with that one thought. I had been waiting to do fifty things, but when I heard this word "Look!" what a charming word it seemed to me. Oh, I looked until I could almost have looked my eyes away! And in heaven I will look on still in my joy unspeakable.

I now think I am bound never to preach a sermon without preaching to sinners. I do think that a minister who can preach a sermon without addressing sinners does not know how to preach.

Thus began a life fully surrendered to the Lord and His Word.

Spurgeon's love of education

Although Spurgeon never finished college or attended seminary, it would be a mistake to consider him uneducated. His personal library consisted of more than 12,000 books, most, if not all, he had read, typically reading six books per week. He shares his lack of formal seminary training with the likes of Augustine (354 – 430), John Calvin (1509 – 64), Dwight L. Moody (1837 – 99), Arthur Pink (1886 – 1952), D. Martyn Lloyd-Jones (1899 – 1981), Billy Graham (1918-), and many other renowned preachers. Spurgeon's own writings have been so widely read and distributed that there are few pastors or seminarians around that world who do not own at least one of his books.

This is not intended to cast aspersions on formal theological training, for Spurgeon surely supported it — as long as it was biblically sound. Nevertheless, the church should remain open to Spurgeon's brand of training, or we may miss the next preacher with an exceptional insight into God's Word. In fact, Spurgeon spent much of his life training new candidates for the pastorate through the Pastor's College, which he founded in 1856, early in his career. He once described the professors of the college in these words: "The Lord has sent us tutors who are lovers of sound doctrine and zealous for the truth. Heresy in colleges means false doctrine throughout the churches, for to defile the fountain is to pollute the streams."

Why "From the pen of Jim Reimann" daily segments

Expanding and updating the writings of Charles Spurgeon is a humbling experience — something I readily admit. Yet my purpose is the same as my purpose in previously updating *My Utmost for*

His Highest (Oswald Chambers) and *Streams in the Desert* (Lettie Cowman) — to make these great works from the nineteenth and early twentieth centuries accessible to today's readers.

In *Evening by Evening*, however, I also have added my own comments to supplement Spurgeon's thoughts. One purpose is to shed further light on the Scriptures based on my own life-long study of the Scriptures. The Lord called me to teach His Word more than twenty-seven years ago, and twelve years ago led me into a Bible-teaching ministry offering pilgrimages to Israel. Since then my wife Pam and I have been privileged to travel there more than twenty times, studying and teaching. Many of my comments have come from insights gleaned in what I consider to be the world's greatest seminary — Israel.

My primary purpose is to get people into God's Word itself, not simply another devotional book, for the true power lies there. You will soon discover that most of my comments consist of sharing additional verses of Scripture to consider, or giving the reader the context of Spurgeon's text. By design, one year in *Evening by Evening* will take the reader to every book of the Bible — a claim few devotionals can make.

Spurgeon's influence on Oswald Chambers and Lettie Cowman

There can be no doubt that the writers of the bestselling devotionals of all time, *My Utmost for His Highest* (Chambers) and *Streams in the Desert* (Cowman), were greatly influenced by the ministry of Charles Spurgeon. In fact, Oswald Chambers was saved as a fourteen-year-old teenager immediately after hearing Spurgeon preach at his church in London, while visiting there with his father, Clarence. Hannah, Oswald's mother, also was converted to Christ under the preaching of Spurgeon, and she and Oswald's father were both baptized by the great preacher. And Clarence Chambers was one of the first students to enroll in Spurgeon's Pastor's College. After spending many years reading *Morning* by *Morning*, *Evening by Evening*, and *My Utmost for His Highest*, I can attest personally to the strong influence Spurgeon had on Oswald Chambers, as evidenced by his writings.

Lettie Cowman appears to have been greatly influenced by Spurgeon as well. Her *Streams in the Desert* is a compilation of more than 250 contributors who influenced her life, and Spurgeon is quoted thrity times, far more than any other contributor. And as I said in the introduction to the updated edition of *Streams in the Desert*, there is also a tie between Oswald Chambers and Lettie Cowman, because the Cowmans, who were missionaries to the Orient, once invited Oswald Chambers to minister with them in Japan.

There is thus a historic tie between all four of these enduring devotionals: *My Utmost for His Highest*, *Streams in the Desert*, *Morning by Morning*, and *Evening by Evening*.

Spurgeon's enduring legacy

Spurgeon once described his approach to preaching with these words: "I take my text and make a beeline to the cross" — making his message timeless! A personal friend of his once wrote:

The work done by C. H. Spurgeon cannot die, for I once heard him say, "I beseech you to live not only for this age, but also for the next. I would fling my shadow through the eternal ages if I could." He has done it. His work is an imperishable as the truth of God. His memory shall not fade like a vanishing star, nor his works be forgotten like a dying echo. He will shine on, never ceasing to brighten human lives by the truth he preached, the work he accomplished, and the stainless life he lived.

Spurgeon has been called the greatest preacher since the apostle Paul and has come to be known as "the prince of preachers." My prayer is that you, the reader, will gain insight into God's Word through Spurgeon's work, expanded, indexed, and updated in *Evening by Evening*, and that new generations of readers will discover the timeless truths brought together by Spurgeon — God's uncompromising servant.

Like Abel, Charles Spurgeon "offered God a better sacrifice," and although he passed into glory 118 years ago, "by faith he still speaks, even though he is dead" (Heb. 11:4).

"May the glory of the Lord be praised in his dwelling place!" (Ezek. 3:12).

Jim Reimann
September 2010
(Reader's comments are welcome at *JimReimann.com*.)

EXCERPT FROM SPURGEON'S ORIGINAL PREFACE, MAY 1868

When the noise and turmoil of the day are over, it is a sweet blessing to commune with God — the cool and calm of evening delightfully agree with prayer and praise. The hours of the declining sun are so many quiet alleys in the garden of time where we may find our Maker waiting to commune with us, even as in ages past the Lord God walked with Adam in Paradise "in the cool of the day" (Gen. 3:8).

Having had the seal of our Master's blessing on the previous volume, *Morning by Morning*, I felt encouraged to focus my attention on this present series of brief meditations, and send them out with the persistent prayer that a blessing will rest upon every reader. If they lead one heart upward, which otherwise may have drooped, or sow in a single mind a holy purpose never before conceived, I will be grateful … and the Lord shall be praised.

The longer I live, the more deeply I am conscious that the Holy Spirit alone can make truth profitable to the heart. Therefore, in earnest prayer, I commit *Evening by Evening* and its companion volume, *Morning by Morning*, to His care.

January

JANUARY 1

We rejoice and delight in you.

Song of Songs 1:4

From the pen of Charles Spurgeon:

"We rejoice and delight in you." We should open the gates of this new year, not to the mournful sounds of trombones, but to the sweet strains of harps of joy and cymbals of gladness. "Come, let us sing for joy to the LORD; let us shout aloud to the Rock of our salvation" (Ps. 95:1). We, the called, the faithful, and the chosen should be determined to drive our grief away and to set up our banners of confidence in the name of our God. Let others lament over their troubles, but we who have the "piece of [sweet] wood" (Ex. 15:25) to throw into Marah's bitter pool will joyfully "glorify the LORD" (Ps. 34:3).

"Eternal Spirit" (Heb. 9:14) and our effective Comforter, we who are the temples in whom You dwell will never cease from adoring and blessing the name of Jesus.

"We rejoice and delight in you." We are resolved to do so. Jesus must be the crown of our heart's delight, for we will not dishonor our Bridegroom by mourning in His presence. We who have been ordained ultimately to be the chorus of the skies, let us rehearse our everlasting anthem here before we sing it in the halls of "the new Jerusalem" (Rev. 21:2).

"We *rejoice* and *delight* in you." These two words, *rejoice* and *delight*, have one sense: double joy and blessedness upon blessedness. Thus, does there need to be any limit to our rejoicing in the Lord now? Don't people of grace find their Lord to be "henna and nard ... calamus and cinnamon" (Song 4:13 – 14) even now? What better fragrance will they have in heaven itself?

"We rejoice and delight in *you*." The last word, *you*, is like the meat of the dish, the kernel of the nut, the soul of the text. What heavens are found in Jesus! What rivers of infinite bliss have their source, their end, and every drop of their fullness in Him!

O sweet Lord Jesus, since You are the present portion of Your people, favor us this year with such a sense of Your preciousness that from its first day to its last, "we [may] rejoice and delight in you."

May January open with joy in the Lord, and may the year close in December with gladness in Jesus.

From the pen of Jim Reimann:

This is a difficult time of year for many people. Though it begins with a time of celebration, it is easy to slip into a state of sadness or depression. Shorter days, cold temperatures, and gray skies often lead people to feel sad during this season. Those in business often have a sense of having to start over again to reach new and higher goals. But the Lord would not have us linger here.

Paul said, "I have learned to be content whatever the circumstances. I know what it is to be in need, and I know what it is to have plenty. I have learned the secret of being content in any and every situation, whether well fed or hungry, whether living in plenty or in want. I can do everything through him who gives me strength" (Phil. 4:11 – 13). And Nehemiah said on a day of celebration in Israel's history, "Go and enjoy choice food and sweet drinks, and send some to those who have nothing prepared. *This day is sacred to our Lord. Do not grieve, for the joy of the LORD is your strength*" (Neh. 8:10).

January 2

Let the nations renew their strength!

Isaiah 41:1

From the pen of Charles Spurgeon:

Everything on earth needs renewal from time to time, for no created thing continues forever by itself. The psalmist said to the Lord, "You renew the face of the earth" (Ps. 104:30). Even trees, which never have to worry about daily care nor shorten their lives through difficult work, must drink in the rain of heaven and absorb the hidden treasures of the soil. "The cedars of Lebanon that [God] planted" (Ps. 104:16) live only because they are full of sap freshly drawn day by day from the earth.

Neither can human life be sustained without renewal from God. Just as it is necessary to restore the body's energy with frequent meals, we must reenergize the soul by feeding on God's Book, by listening to the Word being preached and by observing the soul-strengthening sacraments. How weak our spiritual gifts become when we neglect these means of renewal. What poor starving saints some believers are who neglect the diligent use of the Word of God and times of secret prayer. If our spirituality can survive without God, it is not of divine creation — it is nothing but a dream. If it has been born of God, it will look to Him as flowers look to the dew of heaven.

Without constant renewal and restoration, we are not ready for the perpetual assaults of hell, the afflictions of heaven, or even the stresses and strains within us. When the whirlwind is unleashed, woe to the tree that has not absorbed fresh sap from the earth and grasped the rock below with many intertwined roots. When fierce storms arise, woe to mariners who have not strengthened their mast, dropped anchor, or sought a safe haven.

If we allow the good among us to grow weaker, the evil ones will surely gather strength and will struggle to gain control over us, and perhaps then a time of painful desolation or a disgraceful sin may follow. Instead, may we draw near to the footstool of divine mercy in humble prayer, for only then will we realize the fulfillment of the promise: "Those who hope in the LORD will renew their strength" (Isa. 40:31).

From the pen of Jim Reimann:

In this life we certainly need continual renewal of mind, body, and spirit; but there is a future renewal coming that will be lasting and eternal. As we begin this new year, may we reflect on these words of Jesus with hope and expectancy:

> I tell you the truth, *at the renewal of all things,* when the Son of Man sits on his glorious throne, you who have followed me will also sit on twelve thrones, judging the twelve tribes of Israel. And everyone who has left houses or brothers or sisters or father or mother or children or fields for my sake will receive a hundred times as much and will inherit eternal life. But many who are first will be last, and many who are last will be first.
>
> Matthew 19:28 – 30

And may we all say, along with Job, although hopefully with a bit more patience than he had at the time, "I will wait for my renewal to come" (Job 14:14). Yet if we recognize we are harboring any sin in our lives, we should pray as David did,

> *"Create in me a pure heart, O God, and renew a steadfast spirit within me"* (Ps. 51:10).

Finally, may our prayer at the beginning of this year be:

> *"Restore us to yourself, O Lord ...; renew our days as of old"* (Lam. 5:21).

January 3

A voice of one calling in the desert,
"Prepare the way for the Lord, make straight paths for him."

Luke 3:4

From the pen of Charles Spurgeon:

The "voice ... calling in the desert" demanded a "way for the Lord," a way prepared, and one specifically prepared in the desert. I must be attentive to my Master's proclamation and allow Him a road into my heart, one actually prepared by His gracious work through the desert of my nature. Our text today is a quote from Isaiah 40:3, and the four directives from Isaiah 40:4 must be given my serious attention:

"Every valley shall be raised up." Low, shallow thoughts of God must be given up, doubting and despairing must be removed, and self-seeking and sinful delights must be forsaken. Across these deep valleys a glorious causeway of grace must be raised.

"Every mountain and hill [shall be] made low." Proud self-sufficiency and boastful self-righteousness must be leveled to make a highway for "the King of kings" (1 Tim. 6:15). God's divine fellowship is never granted to haughty, high-minded sinners. "The LORD ... looks upon the lowly" (Ps. 138:6) and dwells "with him who is contrite and lowly in spirit" (Isa. 57:15), but He "detests all the proud of heart" (Prov. 16:5). My soul, petition the Holy Spirit to set your heart right in this.

"The crooked shall be made straight" (KJV). A wavering heart must have a straight path of decision for God, one of holiness "marked out" (Heb. 12:1) for it. "A double-minded man [is] unstable in all he does" (James 1:8) and is a stranger to "the God of truth" (Ps. 31:5). My soul, take heed that in all things you are honest and true, "for the LORD searches every heart" (1 Chron. 28:9).

"The rugged places [shall be] a plain." Stumbling blocks of sin must be removed, and "thorns and thistles" (Heb. 6:8) of rebellion must be uprooted. Our great Visitor must not find muddy paths and rock-covered roads when He comes to honor His favored ones with His presence.

Oh, may the Lord find in my heart today a highway made ready by His grace, one upon which He may make triumphal progress to the very limits of my soul from the beginning of this year to its very last day!

From the pen of Jim Reimann:

As believers we have often been taught it was John the Baptist's role to "prepare the way for the Lord." Of course, that is true, but what a profound thought Spurgeon shared that as believers we must keep that way open to Him, not allowing sin to block His path.

One way we block His path into our hearts is by neglecting to spend quality time with Him. Obviously, by reading this devotional book, you have committed to spend time with Him at least today. But will your commitment last throughout the new year? Or will Jesus be the Lord only of the beginning of your year?

May we commit every day this year to God by starting each one with Him. May we follow the example of our Lord who daily spent time with His heavenly Father, for "very early in the morning, while it was still dark, Jesus got up, left the house and went off to a solitary place, where he prayed" (Mark 1:35).

JANUARY 4

Although Joseph recognized his brothers,
they did not recognize him.

Genesis 42:8

From the pen of Charles Spurgeon:

We often consider the need for growth in our knowledge of the Lord Jesus, but let us now consider a related topic, namely, the knowledge our heavenly "Joseph" has of us. Actually, His knowledge of us was absolutely perfect long before we had even the slightest knowledge of Him. "Your eyes saw my unformed body. All the days ordained for me were written in your book before one of them came to be" (Ps. 139:16).

Before we had a place in the world, we had a place in His heart. When we were still His enemies, He knew us; He knew our misery, our madness, and our wickedness. When we wept bitterly in despairing repentance and saw Him only as a judge and ruler, He viewed us as His well-beloved family and His heart yearned for us. He never mistook His chosen ones for others, but always beheld them as objects of His infinite affection. "The Lord knows those who are his" (2 Tim. 2:19) is as true of a prodigal who "feed[s] pigs" (Luke 15:15) as a child who sits at His table (see Luke 22:30).

Alas, we did not know our royal Brother, and out of this ignorance grew a multitude of sins! We withheld our hearts from Him and allowed Him no entrance to our love. We mistrusted Him and gave no credence to His words. We rebelled against Him and paid Him no loving honor. "The sun of righteousness" (Mal. 4:2) shone forth, but we could not see Him. Heaven came down to earth, but earth did not perceive it.

May God be praised that those days are over for us, although even now we know so little of Jesus compared with what He knows of us. We have only begun to study Him, while He knows us completely. It is a blessing, however, that the ignorance is not on His part, for then we would be a hopeless case indeed. As His children, He will never say to us, "I never knew you" (Matt. 7:23), but instead will "acknowledge [our] name" (Rev. 3:5) on the day of "his appearing" (2 Tim. 4:1). And meanwhile He will reveal Himself to us in ways He will never do for the world.

From the pen of Jim Reimann:

Spurgeon quotes from one of David's psalms today, further revealing God's omniscience regarding us. Here is more of that psalm for us to consider as we pray:

"O Lord, you have searched me and you know me. You know when I sit and when I rise; you perceive my thoughts from afar. You discern my going out and my lying down; you are familiar with all my ways. Before a word is on my tongue you know it completely, O Lord. You hem me in — behind and before; you have laid your hand upon me.... For you created my inmost being; you knit me together in my mother's womb. I praise you because I am fearfully and wonderfully made; your works are wonderful, I know that full well. My frame was not hidden from you when I was made in the secret place. When I was woven together in the depths of the earth, your eyes saw my unformed body. All the days ordained for me were written in your book before one of them came to be. How precious to me are your thoughts, O God! How vast is the sum of them!" (Ps. 139:1 – 5, 13 – 17).

JANUARY 5

God saw that the light was good.

Genesis 1:4

From the pen of Charles Spurgeon:

Today let us consider the special view God had of the light He created. "God saw … the light." He looked at it with a sense of satisfaction, gazed on it with pleasure, and saw that it "was good." And if the Lord has given you light, dear reader, He looks on that light with special interest, for it is dear to Him because it is His handiwork and because it is like Him, for "God is light" (1 John 1:5).

It is pleasing to know God's eyes tenderly observe the work of grace He has begun in us, and to know He never loses sight of "this treasure" He has placed in us, who are "jars of clay" (2 Cor. 4:7). Sometimes we cannot see the light in us, but God always sees it, and that is much better. It is better for the Judge to see my innocence than for me to think I see it. It brings me great comfort to know I am one of God's people. But whether I know it or not, as long as the Lord knows it, I am safe. The foundation of this truth is this: "The Lord knows those who are his" (2 Tim. 2:19).

Perhaps you weep with regret over your sinfulness and mourn over your inner darkness, but remember, the Lord sees light in your heart because He placed it there, and all the cloudiness and gloom of your soul cannot hide your light from His gracious eyes. You may have sunk into despondency, even despair, but if your soul has any longing for Christ and if you are truly seeking to rest in His finished work, God sees the light.

In fact, He not only sees it but He also preserves it in you. "I, the LORD, watch over it…. I guard it day and night" (Isa. 27:3). What a precious thought to those who, after anxiously attempting to watch over and guard themselves, feel their powerlessness to do so. This light, thus preserved by His grace, God will someday develop into the brilliance of the noonday sun and the fullness of His glory. The light with us is simply the dawn of the eternal day.

From the pen of Jim Reimann:

"You may be sure that your sin will find you out" (Num. 32:23). Believing we can keep our sins hidden is nothing but foolishness. In fact, there is something therapeutic in exposing our sins to the light. Jesus came to earth not only to expose sin but to be the remedy for its darkness. In the following passage, however, notice the reaction of the chosen, versus the lost, to the light:

> This is the verdict: Light has come into the world, but men loved darkness instead of light because their deeds were evil. Everyone who does evil hates the light, and will not come into the light for fear that his deeds will be exposed. But whoever lives by the truth comes into the light, so that it may be seen plainly that what he has done has been done through God.
>
> John 3:19 – 21

As Spurgeon said, the followers of Christ will have His light and will be like Him. This is also an Old Testament truth, for David wrote the following:

> When one rules over men in righteousness, when he rules in the fear of God, he is like the light of morning at sunrise on a cloudless morning, like the brightness after rain that brings the grass from the earth.
>
> 2 Samuel 23:3 – 4

"The man who walks in the dark does not know where he is going" (John 12:35). "But if we walk in the light, as [God] is in the light … the blood of Jesus, his Son, purifies us from all sin" (1 John 1:7).

JANUARY 6

Now the evening before the man arrived,
the hand of the LORD was upon me.

Ezekiel 33:22

From the pen of Charles Spurgeon:

"The hand of the LORD" may come upon me as a work of His judgment, and if this is the case, it would be wise for me to consider the reason for such a visitation and then submit to the rod of correction and Him who ordained it. Surely I am not the only person to be chastened in the dark "evenings" of life, so may I cheerfully submit to the affliction and seek to profit from it.

"The hand of the LORD," however, may come upon me in another manner, strengthening my soul and lifting my spirit upward to eternal things. Oh, that I may experience the Lord dealing with me in this way! A sense of His divine presence and indwelling Spirit lifts the soul toward heaven, causing it to "soar on wings like eagles" (Isa. 40:31). At such times we are filled with spiritual joy and forget the cares and sorrows of earth; the invisible is so near that the visible loses its power over us; our fleshly body lingers at the foot of the hill, while our spirit worships atop the summit in the presence of the Lord.

Oh, that such a blessed holy time of divine communion may be granted me even now! The Lord knows I severely need it, for my gifts are withering, my depravity rages within me, my faith is weak, and my devotion is cold — all reasons why I need His healing hand upon me. His hand can cool the heat of my burning brow and calm the turmoil of my pounding heart. His glorious right hand that molded the world can recreate my mind, the untiring hand that holds "the pillars of the earth" (1 Sam. 2:8 KJV) can sustain my spirit, the loving hand that embraces all the saints can cherish me, and the mighty hand that breaks the enemy into pieces can subdue my sins. Why shouldn't I feel that hand touching me even now?

Come, my soul, address your God with a powerful plea, asking that you may sense the same hands that were pierced for your redemption being laid upon you. Ask to feel the same hand upon you that once touched Daniel and sent him to his knees that he might see visions of God.

From the pen of Jim Reimann:

True believers will sense a difference when God's hand is upon them. Moses certainly did, especially when he prayed, "O Sovereign LORD, *you have begun to show to your servant your greatness and your strong hand.* For what god is there in heaven or on earth who can do the deeds and mighty works you do? Let me go over and see the good land beyond the Jordan" (Deut. 3:24 – 25). Yet the Lord denied his request to enter the promised land, saying, "That is enough. Do not speak to me anymore about this matter" (v. 26).

Isaiah also knew the difference, for he wrote, "The LORD spoke to me *with his strong hand upon me,* warning me not to follow the way of this people" (Isa. 8:11). And five times in Ezekiel's ministry, from its very beginning to its very end, we are told "the hand of the LORD was upon him" (see Ezek. 1:3 and 40:1, for examples).

As God's hand was upon Ezekiel, and upon the early Christians, may His hand be upon us and our ministries today, for "*The Lord's hand was with them,* and a great number of people believed and turned to the Lord" (Acts 11:21).

JANUARY 7

… my sister, my bride.

Song of Songs 4:12

From the pen of Charles Spurgeon:

Notice the sweet titles our heavenly Solomon uses with such intense affection to address His bride, the church. In essence, He is describing us as: "My sister," you who are close to Me by virtue of the bonds of nature and who partake of the same feelings and emotions; "My bride," nearest and dearest to Me, united by the most tender "ties of love" (Hos. 11:4); My sweet companion, who is a part of My own self; "My sister," by virtue of My incarnation, which makes Me "bone of [your] bones and flesh of [your] flesh" (Gen. 2:23); "My bride," by heavenly engagement, whereby I have betrothed you to Myself in righteousness; "My sister," whom I knew from days of old and have protected from your earliest days of infancy; "My bride," taken from among the daughters of earth, embraced in the arms of love, and married to Me forever.

See how true it is that our royal Kinsman is not ashamed of us, for He dwells with obvious delight on this twofold relationship. In today's verse we see the word *my* used twice, as though Christ is filled with rapture over the possession of His church. In fact, through Solomon, He says, "I was … delighting in mankind" (Prov. 8:30 – 31), because those of the church are His chosen ones. Christ the Shepherd sought the sheep because they were His sheep, "for the Son of Man came to seek and to save what was lost" (Luke 19:10). And He did so because those who were lost were His long before they were lost to themselves or to Him. The church is the exclusive inheritance of her Lord; no one else may claim a partnership with her or presume to share her love.

Lord Jesus, Your church delights that this is true! May every believing soul drink comfort from these wells. Dear soul, Christ is close to you through the ties of a family relationship and through the bonds of a marriage covenant. You are dear to Him, for see how He is grasping both your hands with His own, saying, "My sister, my bride." Notice the two sacred firm grips by which your Lord takes such a double hold of you that He neither will, nor can, ever let you go.

Thus, O beloved, don't be slow to return to the holy flame of His love.

From the pen of Jim Reimann:

It is indeed a beautiful thought that Jesus, the omnipotent Creator of the universe, not only considers you to be family but has made you His bride. Marriage is the closest of all earthly relationships, and when your Lord speaks of marriage, you can know it is a union that will never be broken, "for the Lord, the God of Israel, says: I hate divorce and marital separation" (Mal. 2:16 Amplified). His love for you is based on His eternal covenant, for He tells you, "I will make an everlasting covenant with you, my faithful love promised to David" (Isa. 55:3).

And His Word is replete with confirmations of this covenant of love with you; for example: "From everlasting to everlasting the Lord's love is with those who fear him" (Ps. 103:17) and "I have loved you with an *everlasting* love; I have drawn you with loving-kindness" (Jer. 31:3).

In light of "his great love" (Eph. 2:4) for you, why not recommit yourself this new year to "love the Lord your God with all your heart and with all your soul and with all your strength" (Deut. 6:5). After all, "We love him, because *he first loved us*" (1 John 4:19 KJV).

JANUARY 8

Your love is more delightful than wine.

Song of Songs 1:2

From the pen of Charles Spurgeon:

Nothing gives a believer as much joy as fellowship with Christ. A Christian can have as much enjoyment of the everyday common things of life as anyone else, and he can take pleasure in God's gifts and works. But in each of these separately, or in all of them added together, he will not find as great a delight as in the matchless person of his Lord Jesus Himself. Christ has wine unlike any vineyard on earth has ever produced and bread unlike all the cornfields of Egypt could ever yield. Where else could such sweetness be found as we have tasted in our communion with our Beloved?

The joys of earth should be considered little better than husks for swine compared to Jesus, the heavenly manna. We should more desire one morsel of Christ's love, or even one sip of His fellowship, than a whole world full of earthly delights. What is chaff compared to wheat? Or sparkling gems of paste compared to a true diamond? What is a dream compared to the glorious reality? Or the happiness of this life, even in the most beautiful setting, compared to our Lord Jesus, even in His most despised condition on earth?

If you know anything of the inner spiritual life, you will confess that our highest, purest, and most enduring joys are the fruit "from the tree of life, which is in the paradise of God" (Rev. 2:7). No stream yields water as sweet as the well of God dug by the soldier's spear (see John 19:34). All earthly joy is still just that — earthly, but the joys and comforts of Christ's presence are like Himself — heavenly!

When we consider our communion with Him, we will never find any regrets of emptiness there, no dregs in His wine, no flies in His ointment. "The joy of the LORD" (Neh. 8:10) is solid and enduring. Vanity will never consider His fellowship, but discretion and wisdom will testify it endures the test of years, and that in the test of time and eternity, it is worthy to be called the only true delight.

When it comes to nourishment, comfort, exhilaration, and refreshment, no wine can rival the love of Jesus. May we drink of His love to the full today.

From the pen of Jim Reimann:

How long before we admit that Jesus is all we truly need, that "God will meet all your needs according to his glorious riches in Christ Jesus" (Phil. 4:19)? So many of us pour our lives into amassing great wealth, yet King Solomon, one of the wealthiest men who ever lived, revealed this:

> I thought in my heart, "Come now, I will test you with pleasure to find out what is good." But that ... proved to be meaningless.... I undertook great projects: I built houses for myself and planted vineyards. I also owned more herds and flocks than anyone in Jerusalem before me. I amassed silver and gold for myself, and the treasure of kings and provinces. I acquired men and women singers, and a harem as well — the delights of the heart of man. I became greater by far than anyone in Jerusalem before me. I denied myself nothing my eyes desired; I refused my heart no pleasure. My heart took delight in all my work, and this was the reward for all my labor. Yet when I surveyed all that my hands had done and what I had toiled to achieve, everything was meaningless, a chasing after the wind; nothing was gained under the sun.

Ecclesiastes 2:1, 4, 7 – 11

JANUARY 9

Serve the LORD with gladness.

Psalm 100:2 KJV

From the pen of Charles Spurgeon:

Delighting in serving the Lord is a sign of our acceptance of His will for us. Those who serve Him with a sad countenance, doing what is unpleasant to them, are actually not serving Him at all. They simply have the form of honoring Him, but there is no life in what they do. Our God requires no slaves to grace His throne, for He is Lord of the empire of love and desires His servants to be clothed in His official robes of joy. The angels of God serve Him with songs, not with groans, for a murmur or a sigh would indicate mutiny within their ranks. Obedience that is not voluntary is disobedience, for "the LORD looks at the heart" (1 Sam. 16:7), and if He sees we are only serving out of compulsion, not because we love Him, He will reject the offering of our service.

Conversely, service coupled with cheerfulness is heart-service and is therefore real. Remove joyful willingness from a Christian and you will have removed the test of his sincerity. A man forced into battle is no patriot, but he who marches into the fray with eager eyes and a beaming face, singing, "It is sweet to die for one's country," proves himself sincere in his patriotism.

Cheerfulness is the support of our strength, "for the joy of the LORD is your strength" (Neh. 8:10) and it acts as the remover of difficulties. It is to our service what oil is to the wheels of a railroad car, for without oil the axle will soon grow hot and an accident may soon result. Likewise, if there is not holy cheerfulness to oil our spiritual wheels, our spirits will become bogged down by weariness. A person who is cheerful in his service to God proves that obedience is his motive and thus can sing:

> Make me to walk in Your commands,
> 'Tis a delightful road.
>
> Isaac Watts, 1674 – 1748

Dear reader, Do you "serve the LORD with gladness"? May we show the people of the world who think our faith is nothing but slavery that it is actually a delight and a joy to us! May our gladness proclaim that we serve a good Master.

From the pen of Jim Reimann:

The Lord takes our service to Him quite personally. He desires we serve Him joyfully and gladly from a sense of obedience to Him. He even pronounced a whole host of curses that would come upon Israel if they refused to do so. For a list of those, read Deuteronomy 28:15 – 68, especially noticing these verses:

> Because you did not serve the LORD your God joyfully and gladly in the time of prosperity, therefore in hunger and thirst, in nakedness and dire poverty, you will serve the enemies the LORD sends against you.
>
> Deuteronomy 28:47 – 48

Notice God's people will either serve the Lord or "serve the enemies the LORD sends against [them]" — but we *will* serve! Thus, may each of us ask ourselves today, "Who would I rather serve?" May we take these words to heart:

"Serve the LORD with gladness," for "nothing is better for a man under the sun than to eat and drink and be glad. Then joy will accompany him in his work all the days of the life God has given him under the sun" (Eccl. 8:15).

JANUARY 10

In my flesh I will see God.

Job 19:26

From the pen of Charles Spurgeon:

Notice the object of Job's reverent anticipation: "I will see *God.*" He does not say, "I will see *saints,*" though he will see saints and that itself would bring him untold joy. Nor does he say, "I will see the 'gates ... made of ... pearl'" (Rev. 21:21) or "the wall ... made of jasper" (Rev. 21:18), or gaze upon "crowns of gold" (Rev. 4:4). No, he says, "I will see *God.*" Job is expressing the sum and substance of heaven, the hope of all believers. Here in this life, believers take delight in seeing the Lord by faith through the sacraments, and we love to behold Him by fellowshipping with Him in prayer; but in heaven we will have a full, unclouded view, "for we shall see him as he is" and "we shall be like him" (1 John 3:2).

Likeness to God! Who could wish for more? Seeing God! What could we desire that would be better? Some believers see the words "In my flesh I will see God" as alluding to Christ as "the Word [who] became flesh" (John 1:14), or to the glorious beholding of Him in the splendor of "the last days" (Hos 3:5). Whether these interpretations are correct or not, one thing is certain: Christ will be the object of our eternal vision and we will never desire any joy beyond seeing Him.

As you consider this, never think it is some small thing for the mind to dwell upon. It may be only one source of a believer's delight, but that source in infinite. All His attributes will be subjects for our consideration, and since He is infinite in each of these attributes, there should be no fear of ever exhausting our examination of them. His works, His gifts, His love for us, and His glory through His every purpose and in each of His actions, will all be themes to consider that will always remain new.

Job, the suffering patriarch, looked forward to seeing God as a personal enjoyment of Him, saying, "I myself will see him with my own eyes — I, and not another" (Job 19:27). Imagine being able to see heaven's glory firsthand! Yet someday "your eyes will see the king in his beauty" (Isa. 33:17). At that moment all earthly brightness will fade as we gaze upon His glory — a glory that can never fade. "I will see God"!

From the pen of Jim Reimann:

King David, like Job before him, looked forward to seeing the Lord in His glory. In fact, it was the priority of his spiritual life, for he wrote:

> One thing I ask of the LORD, this is what I seek: that I may dwell in the house of the LORD all the days of my life, *to gaze upon the beauty of the LORD* and to seek him in his temple. For in the day of trouble he will keep me safe in his dwelling; he will hide me in the shelter of his tabernacle and set me high upon a rock. Then my head will be exalted above the enemies who surround me; at his tabernacle will I sacrifice with shouts of joy; I will sing and make music to the LORD. Hear my voice when I call, O LORD; be merciful to me and answer me. My heart says of you, "Seek his face!" Your face, LORD, I will seek. I am still confident of this: I will see the goodness of the LORD in the land of the living. Wait for the LORD; be strong and take heart and wait for the LORD.

> Psalm 27:4 – 8, 13 – 14

JANUARY 11

I have prayed for you.
Luke 22:32

From the pen of Charles Spurgeon:

What an encouragement to know of our Redeemer's never-ceasing intercession for us! When we pray, He pleads our case, and even when we are not praying, He is advocating our cause and through His supplications He shields us from unseen dangers. Notice the words of comfort spoken to Peter: "Simon, Simon, Satan has asked to sift you as wheat. But …" (Luke 22:31 – 32). But what? "But go and pray for yourself"? Certainly that would be good advice, yet that is not what we read. Nor does Jesus say, "But I will keep you alert, and thus you will be spared." Of course, that would have been a great blessing. What Jesus *did* say was: "But I have prayed for you, Simon, that your faith may not fail."

Actually, we know very little of how much we owe to our Savior's prayers. But once we reach the mountaintops of heaven and look back on the paths the Lord our God has led us, oh, how we will praise Him — He who before His Father's eternal throne thwarted the mischief Satan was doing on earth! Oh, how we will thank Him for never keeping His peace, but instead, day and night, pointing to the wounds in His hands and carrying our names on His breastplate! (See Ex. 28:29.) Even before Satan had begun to tempt us, Jesus obstructed our enemy's way and entered a plea in heaven.

Mercy outran malice! Notice that although He told Peter, "Satan demanded to have you" (Luke 22:31 ESV), Jesus restrained Satan's every desire, nipping them in the bud. He did so, not by saying, "But I have *desired* to pray for you," but by saying, "'I *have* prayed for you'; I have already done it; I have gone to court and entered a counterclaim even before an accusation has been made."

O Jesus, what a comfort to know You have pleaded our cause against our unseen enemies, countermined their landmines, and unmasked their ambushes. Your intercession on my behalf fills me with joy, gratitude, hope, and confidence.

From the pen of Jim Reimann:

We tend to forget the numerous legal terms used in the Scriptures, such as *witness* and *testify*. Spurgeon makes the point that Jesus entered God's "court and entered a counterclaim" on our behalf. We need to remember as well that God is a God of justice and that what He does is done legally and in order. With the "legal-ness" of our God in mind, consider the following passages:

"My dear children, I write this to you so that you will not sin. But if anybody does sin, we have one who speaks to the Father *in our defense* — Jesus Christ, the Righteous One" (1 John 2:1). A number of other translations say, "We have an advocate with the Father." The underlying meaning in the Greek is that Jesus is our defense attorney, which brings to mind the verse where He refers to the Holy Spirit as "the Counselor" (John 14:26), another term for *advocate* or *attorney*.

Thus, when Satan comes accusing us of sin, our defense Attorney in heaven "speaks to the Father in our defense," saying, in essence, "Don't look at his sin, look at My cross where I paid the price for his sin." After all, "[Jesus] is the atoning sacrifice for our sins" (1 John 2:2).

January 12

From the pen of Charles Spurgeon:

We should never seek publicity for our own virtue or notoriety for our own zeal, but it is a sin to continually seek to hide what God has bestowed on us for the good of others. A Christian is not to be a village hidden in a valley, but "a city on a hill"; not "a lamp ... put ... under a bowl," but "put ... on its stand" so "it gives light to everyone" (Matt. 5:14 – 15). Intentionally withdrawing has its place at times, and hiding one's self is no doubt modest, but the hiding of Christ in us can never be justified, and holding back truth that is precious to us is a sin against others and an offense against God.

If you tend toward shyness, be careful you don't indulge your trembling tendency too much lest you become useless to the church. Instead, in the name of Him who was not ashamed of you, seek to do some "violence" to your own feelings and be determined to tell others what Christ has taught you. You don't have a booming voice? Then use "a still small voice" (1 Kings 19:12 KJV). You don't have a pulpit and are never quoted by the media? Then say with Peter, "Silver or gold I do not have, but what I have I give you" (Acts 3:6). If you can't preach a sermon on a mountain, speak to the "Samaritan woman" (John 4:7) by the well; if not in the temple, declare the praises of Jesus in a house; if not in the marketplace, in a field; if not in the middle of the masses, in your own household.

From the hidden springs within you, allow the sweetly flowing streams of testimony to flow, giving drink to every passerby. Never hide your talents, but "trade" them in the marketplace and you will bring a good return to your Master. Speaking for God is refreshing to ourselves, encouraging to His saints, useful to sinners, and honoring to the Savior. A mute child is an affliction to his parents.

Lord, unloose Your children's tongues.

From the pen of Jim Reimann:

There is such a thing as false humility, which reveals itself through refusing to use our God-given talents and gifts. Recognizing our gifts and using them to God's glory is not being proud, but is doing exactly what the Lord intends. Yet we should be careful to remember the Source of those gifts at all times. Paul has often been accused of boasting, but he always gave credit to the Lord for his gifts and the fruit they produced. He said:

> If I must boast, I will boast of the things that show my weakness.
>
> 2 Corinthians 11:30

> Even if I should choose to boast, I would not be a fool, because I would be speaking the truth. But I refrain, so no one will think more of me than is warranted by what I do or say. To keep me from becoming conceited ... there was given me a thorn in my flesh, a messenger of Satan, to torment me. Three times I pleaded with the Lord to take it away from me. But he said to me, "My grace is sufficient for you, for my power is made perfect in weakness." Therefore I will boast all the more gladly about my weaknesses, so that Christ's power may rest on me.
>
> 2 Corinthians 12:6 – 9

Remember — Paul also said, "I am not ashamed of the gospel" (Rom. 1:16).

JANUARY 13

Elisha cut a stick and threw it there,
and made the iron float.

2 Kings 6:6

From the pen of Charles Spurgeon:

"The iron axhead" (v. 5) in this story seemed hopelessly lost, and since it had been borrowed, the reputation of "the company of the prophets" (v. 1) was at stake and the name of their God likely to be dishonored. But contrary to human expectations, the iron was made to rise from the depths and to float, for "what is impossible with men is possible with God" (Luke 18:27).

Likewise, I once knew a believer called to undertake a work far exceeding his strength. To human eyes, it seemed so difficult as to be absurd to even attempt it. But God had called him and his faith rose to the occasion. Thus, the Lord honored his faith, unexpected help was sent, and iron was made to float. Another child of God was in dire financial straits, unable to meet all his obligations. Consumed with financial stress he sought help from friends, but in vain. Finally, faith led him to the unfailing Helper, and his trouble was averted and "iron was made to float." A third Christian was dealing with a sad case of depravity in a friend. He had taught, reproved, and warned the friend, all to no avail. "The old Adam" was too strong for the young Melanchthon, and his spirit would not submit. [Editor's note: Philipp Melanchthon, 1497–1560, was a German theologian mentored by Martin Luther.] But once the believing man agonized in prayer for his friend, a blessed answer was sent from heaven, a hard heart was broken, and "iron was made to float."

Beloved reader, what desperate situation are you facing? What heavy matter has you in its grasp? Bring it here, for the God of the prophets lives, and He lives to help His saints. "Those who seek the LORD lack no good thing" (Ps. 34:10). Believe in "the LORD Almighty" (Ps. 24:10). Approach Him while pleading the name of Jesus and "iron will float," and you too will see the finger of God working miracles for His people. "According to your faith will it be done to you" (Matt. 9:29), and yet again "iron will float."

From the pen of Jim Reimann:

Today's truth that believers who walk in faith will see biblical miracles is much akin to the words of Jesus, who said, "I tell you the truth, anyone who has faith in me will do what I have been doing. *He will do even greater things than these*, because I am going to the Father" (John 14:12). And just because Jesus left this earth doesn't mean He took all His miracle-working power with Him. This is one reason He sent His Holy Spirit. Thus, the "one who is in you is greater than the one who is in the world" (1 John 4:4).

This is why James could say, "The prayer offered in faith will make the sick person well; the Lord will raise him up. If he has sinned, he will be forgiven.… The prayer of a righteous man is powerful and effective" (James 5:15–16). But we must remember to always pray, as Jesus did, according to God's will. Here is how He prayed: "*Your will be done* on earth as it is in heaven" (Matt. 6:10) and "Father, if you are willing, take this cup from me; *yet not my will, but yours be done*" (Luke 22:42). And if Jesus had not submitted to His Father's will, we would still be lost!

Lord, thank You for His example. May we pray, and submit, just as He did.

JANUARY 14

Beginning to sink, [Peter] cried out,
"Lord, save me!"
Matthew 14:30

From the pen of Charles Spurgeon:

Sinking times are praying times for the Lord's servants. Peter neglected to pray before stepping out of the boat on his adventurous journey, but once he began to sink, the danger turned him instantly to prayer; his cry, though late, was not too late. In our times of bodily pain and mental anguish, we find ourselves as naturally driven to prayer as a shipwreck is driven to shore by the waves. Foxes scurry to their holes for protection, birds fly to the forest for shelter, and believers experiencing trials should hasten to God's "mercy seat" (Ex. 25:17 KJV) for safety. The name of heaven's great harbor of refuge is Prayer, the place thousands of weather-beaten vessels have found a haven, and the place to which we should set sail the moment a storm begins.

Short prayers are long enough — Peter's petition was only three words, but they were sufficient for his purpose. Strength, not length, is important, and a sense of need is a mighty teacher of brevity. If our prayers had fewer tail feathers of pride and more feathers on their wings, they would be much better. Wordiness is to devotion as chaff is to wheat, for precious things come in small packages. All the components of true prayer found in much longer prayers often could have been uttered in ones as short as Peter's three-word petition.

Our adversities are the Lord's opportunities. Once a strong sense of danger forces an anxious cry from us, the ears of Jesus hear, and because His ears and heart go together, His hand soon follows. Although we may appeal to our Master at the very last moment, His swift hand makes up for our delays with instant and effective action.

Are you nearly swamped by the raging waters of affliction? Then lift your soul to your Savior and rest assured He will not allow you to perish, for when you can do nothing, Jesus "can do all things" (Job 42:2). May you enlist His powerful aid to your side, and all will be well.

From the pen of Jim Reimann:

When Peter needed the Lord's help to keep him from drowning, he almost instinctively knew what to pray as well as to whom he should pray. And as Spurgeon said, his simple three-word prayer was sufficient.

Have you ever experienced a difficulty where you were at a total loss for words? Even then our Lord understands and intercedes for us. Paul wrote, "The Spirit helps us in our weakness. We do not know what we ought to pray for, but the Spirit himself intercedes for us with groans that words cannot express. And he who searches our hearts knows the mind of the Spirit, because the Spirit intercedes for the saints in accordance with God's will" (Rom. 8:26 – 27).

Thus, even when we don't know how to pray, when we don't know what to ask the Lord to do and have no idea what God's will is in a particular situation, we can trust the Spirit of the Lord to intercede with the Father on our behalf and know it will be "in accordance with His will" each time. Remember: Jesus is our high priest, He "always lives to intercede for [us]" (Heb. 7:25), and "we do not have a high priest who is unable to sympathize with our weaknesses, but we have one who has been tempted in every way, just as we are — yet was without sin" (Heb. 4:15).

January 15

But I am a man of prayer.

Psalm 109:4

From the pen of Charles Spurgeon:

"Lying tongues" (v. 2) were busily engaged in attempting to destroy David's reputation, but he did not defend himself. Instead he moved his case to a higher court and pleaded it before the great King himself. Prayer is the safest method of responding to words of hatred. In this psalm, David did not pray in a cold-hearted manner; he totally gave himself to the exercise, throwing his whole heart and soul into it and straining every sinew and muscle, as Jacob did when wrestling with the angel of God (see Gen. 32:24–32).

This, and only this, is the way to make any progress before the throne of grace. Just as a shadow has no power because it has no substance, a petition in which the person's total self is not completely present, agonizingly earnest, nor vehemently desirous of an answer is utterly ineffective, for it lacks what gives it power. As an old saint once said, "'Fervent prayer' (James 5:16 KJV), like a cannon stationed at the gates of heaven, makes them fly open."

Yet the common fault with most of us when it comes to prayer is our readiness to yield to distractions. Our thoughts wander hither and yon, and thus we make little progress toward our desired end. Like quicksilver, our minds will not stay together, but roll this way and that. What a great evil this is! It not only injures us but, what is worse, it also insults our God. What should we think of a petitioner who, while being blessed by an audience with the King is then so unfocused as to be playing with a feather or chasing a fly?

The context of today's verse shows the importance of continuing and persevering in prayer. David did not simply cry out one time and then fall silent. No, his holy "uproar" continued until it brought down the blessing. Prayer must not occur by happenstance, but should be our daily habit, business, and vocation. Just as artists focus themselves completely on their models and poets commit themselves to their classical pursuits, we must become addicted to prayer. We must be immersed in prayer until it becomes as natural as breathing; until we "pray without ceasing" (1 Thess. 5:17 KJV).

"Lord, teach us to pray" (Luke 11:1) so that petitioning You may have more and more power in our lives.

From the pen of Jim Reimann:

Psalm 109, from which we draw our text today, is a foreshadowing of how our Messiah Himself would be treated a thousand years later. Verse 25 says, "I am an object of scorn to my accusers; when they see me, they shake their heads." David's treatment found its ultimate fulfillment in Jesus "the son of David" (Matt. 1:1) on the cross, as we see from the following:

Those who passed by hurled insults at him, shaking their heads and saying, "You who are going to destroy the temple and build it in three days, save yourself! Come down from the cross, if you are the Son of God!" In the same way the chief priests, the teachers of the law and the elders mocked him. In the same way the robbers who were crucified with him also heaped insults on him.

Matthew 27:39–41, 44

But what was Jesus' response to this injustice? It was prayer! "Father, forgive them, for they do not know what they are doing" (Luke 23:34).

JANUARY 16

The Anointed One will be cut off
and will have nothing.

Daniel 9:26

From the pen of Charles Spurgeon:

Blessed be the name of Jesus, "the Anointed One," for there was no cause for His life to "be cut off." He was not born with original sin, nor had actual sin defiled Him, thus death had no claim on Him. No one could have taken His life from Him justly, for He had done wrong to no one, and no one could have taken His life from Him by force unless He had chosen to submit Himself to die.

Amazingly, one person sinned and Another suffered, for justice was offended by us, but found its satisfaction in Him. Rivers of tears, mountains of offerings, seas of the blood of bulls, and hills of incense could not have been sufficient for the removal of sin. But Jesus was "cut off" for us, and the cause of God's wrath thereby was cut off immediately as well, for sin was put away forever.

This is wisdom, that through substitution the sure and swift way of atonement was devised and accomplished. This is condescension, which caused the Messiah — the Prince — to stoop to wearing a crown of thorns and to die upon the cross. "This is love" (1 John 4:10), which led the Redeemer to "lay down his life for his" enemies (John 15:13).

It is not enough, however, to simply admire the scene of the Innocent bleeding for the guilty, for we must make sure of our interest in His death. The sole object of the Messiah's death was the salvation of His church, so ask yourself if you are among those for whom He gave "his life as a ransom" (Matt. 20:28). Did the Lord Jesus stand in your place as your representative? Are you healed "by his wounds" (Isa. 53:5)? It would be a terrible thing indeed if someone finds he has no inheritance in Christ's sacrifice; "it would be better for him if he had not been born" (Mark 14:21).

As solemn as these questions may be, it is a joyful thing that they may be answered clearly and without mistake. "Everyone who believes that Jesus is the Christ is born of God" (1 John 5:1), He is their Savior now, and the blood of reconciliation has been sprinkled upon them. Thus, let everyone who trusts in the merit of the Messiah's death be joyful upon every remembrance of Him, and may their holy gratitude lead them to the fullest consecration to His cause.

From the pen of Jim Reimann:

Today's devotion ends with a plea for us to be fully consecrated to the cause of Christ. Therefore, let us take a moment to consider the meaning of consecration, for it is actually a part of the believer's sanctification process.

Sanctification is the ongoing process in the life of a believer that leads to more holy living. Many Christians know that sanctification includes *separation*, or *being set apart*, yet that is only half its meaning, for it also includes *consecration* — or *dedication* — to what is holy. What will we accomplish if we simply are set apart from sin, but are not dedicated to serve in Christ's kingdom?

"The grace of God ... teaches us to say 'No' to ungodliness and worldly passions, and to live self-controlled, upright and godly lives in this present age" (Titus 2:11 – 12). "For we are God's workmanship, created in Christ Jesus to do good works, which God prepared in advance for us to do" (Eph. 2:10). "May God himself, the God of peace, sanctify you through and through (1 Thess. 5:23).

JANUARY 17

One evening David got up from his bed
and walked around on the roof of the palace.

2 Samuel 11:2

From the pen of Charles Spurgeon:

That very moment, David saw Bathsheba. Whether at home or abroad, we are never out of the reach of temptation and are liable to face the allurements of evil, for our morning opens in its danger, and the fading light of evening still finds us in its jeopardy. Those whom God protects, He protects well, but woe to those who go forth into the world, or who even dare to walk in their own home unarmed. And those who think of themselves as the most secure are actually those who are the most vulnerable to danger, for the armor-bearer of sin is self-confidence.

The king should have been engaged in fighting the Lord's battles, "but David remained in Jerusalem" (v. 1), giving himself to the luxurious living in which he walked that evening. Idleness and luxury are the Devil's jackals, finding abundant prey for him, for stagnant water breeds noxious creatures and neglected soil soon yields a dense tangle of weeds and thorns.

Oh, may I be granted the constraining love of Jesus to keep me active and useful. And when I see even the king of Israel drowsily leaving his bed at the end of the day and immediately falling into temptation, may I take warning and may holy watchfulness guard my door.

Of course, it is entirely possible King David went to his palace roof for a time of devotion, and if that is the case, we should be all the more cautious to never think of any place, however secret, as a sanctuary from sin. Since our hearts are such a tinderbox and sparks so plentiful, we must use all diligence wherever we are to prevent a blazing fire. Satan walks on rooftops and enters prayer closets, and even if we could shut out that foul fiend, our own inner corruptions are enough to work our ruin unless God's grace prevents it.

Dear reader, beware of every temptation, especially those of the evening. The sun may have set, but sin is still up and about, so don't think you are secure. You need a watchman for the night as well as a guardian for the day.

O blessed Spirit, keep us from all evil today, and tonight. Amen.

From the pen of Jim Reimann:

This story of David's sin should be a sobering reminder that regardless of how long we have been a believer or how intimate our relationship with the Lord, we still have a body of flesh and are vulnerable to temptation. And, if we think we are above being tempted by a particular sin, we should be very careful, for that is nothing short of the sin of pride. Remember what Solomon wrote regarding pride: "Pride goes before destruction, a haughty spirit before a fall" (Prov. 16:18).

Paul warned the church of this potential trap as well, saying, "These things happened to [our forefathers] as examples and were written down as warnings for us, on whom the fulfillment of the ages has come. So, if you think you are standing firm, be careful that you don't fall!" (1 Cor. 10:11 – 12).

May this be our prayer:

"Lead us not into temptation, but deliver us from the evil one" (Matt. 6:13).

And may we also recall that "when [we] are tempted, [God] will also provide a way out so that [we] can stand up under it" (1 Cor. 10:13).

JANUARY 18

He explained to them what was said in all the Scriptures
concerning himself.

Luke 24:27

From the pen of Charles Spurgeon:

The two disciples on the Emmaus road had a very profitable journey. Their traveling companion and teacher was the best of tutors and the greatest interpreter of the Scriptures "in whom are hidden all the treasures of wisdom and knowledge" (Col. 2:3). Jesus Himself condescended to become a preacher of the gospel and was not ashamed to exercise His calling before an audience of only two people, just as He now never refuses to teach only one. May we seek the company of such an excellent instructor, for until He "has become for us wisdom from God" (1 Cor. 1:30), we will never be "wise for salvation" (2 Tim. 3:15).

This unequaled tutor used the best of books as His textbook, and although able to reveal new truth, He preferred to explain the old. Through His omniscience He knew the most instructive method of teaching, and thus He turned immediately to "Moses and all the Prophets" (Luke 24:27), showing us that the surest road to wisdom is not speculation, reasoning, or reading books by people, but meditation upon the Word of God. The quickest way to be spiritually rich in heavenly knowledge is to dig in this diamond mine — to gather pearls from this heavenly sea. When Jesus Himself sought to enrich others, He quarried the Holy Scriptures.

This favored pair was led by Him to consider the very best of subjects, for Jesus spoke of Jesus, only expounding things concerning Himself. What could be better than this: the diamond cutting the diamond. The Master of the house unlocked His own doors, invited His guests to His table, and set His very best food before them. He who Himself had "hidden [the treasure] in a field" (Matt. 13:44) guided the two disciples straight to it. Naturally our Lord would discuss the best of topics, and He could find nothing better than His own person and work. With these two topics in mind, we too should continually search the Word.

Grant us the grace, O Lord, to study the Bible with Jesus as both our Teacher and our Lesson.

From the pen of Jim Reimann:

It is interesting that these disciples, although discussing Jesus and His recent death, did not recognize Him as they walked. And notice the sovereignty of God in the following context of today's verse; notice that these two did not open their own eyes to recognize Him, but notice that "their eyes were opened":

> When he was at the table with them, he took bread, gave thanks, broke it and began to give it to them. *Then their eyes were opened and they recognized him*, and he disappeared from their sight. They asked each other, "Were not our hearts burning within us while he talked with us on the road and opened the Scriptures to us?"
>
> Luke 24:30 – 32

In the same way, we must rely on God's sovereignty to enlighten our eyes to His truth, for Paul prayed these words for the believers in Ephesus: "I pray also that *the eyes of your heart may be enlightened* in order that you may know the hope to which he has called you, the riches of his glorious inheritance in the saints, and his incomparably great power for us who believe" (Eph. 1:18 – 19).

"Open my eyes that I may see wonderful things in your law" (Ps. 119:18).

January 19

Then he opened their minds
so they could understand the Scriptures.

Luke 24:45

From the pen of Charles Spurgeon:

As we saw yesterday, He who opened the Scriptures to His two followers in Emmaus now opened their understanding of those Scriptures. Our Lord has many fellow laborers who can open the Scriptures to others, taking it to their minds, but He alone can prepare the minds to actually receive them. Jesus differs from all other teachers in this, for others reach the ear, but He instructs the heart; others deal with the outer letter of the law, but He imparts an inner thirst for the truth by which we perceive its true spirit and flavor. Even the most unlearned can become mature scholars in His school of grace when the Lord Jesus, through His Holy Spirit, unfolds the mysteries of His kingdom to them and grants His divine anointing by which they are enabled to see the invisible.

How blessed we are if we have had our understanding clearly given and strengthened by the Master Himself. Just think of how many people of profound learning are ignorant of eternal things. They may know the killing letter of the law, but can never discern its spirit; they have a veil over their hearts that the eyes of carnal reason can never penetrate. And such was our situation not long ago, for we who now see were once utterly blind, and truth was simply beauty in the dark, unnoticed and neglected. If not for the love of Jesus, we would have remained in ignorance, for without His gracious opening of our understanding, we could no sooner have attained spiritual knowledge than an infant could climb the Pyramids or an ostrich could soar to the stars.

Jesus' college is the only one in which God's truth can truly be learned. Other schools may teach us the truths to be believed, but Christ's school alone can show us how to believe it. Thus, may we sit at the feet of Jesus, and through earnest prayer seek His blessed help that our dull minds may grow brighter and that our feeble understanding may receive heavenly things.

From the pen of Jim Reimann:

Spurgeon himself is a wonderful example of the truth of today's devotion, for although he had little formal education, never even attending college or seminary, he was considered to be "the prince of preachers." It has been said that any preacher "worth his salt" has a library with at least one Spurgeon book in it. In fact, the noted German pastor and theologian Helmut Thielicke (1908 – 1986) once said, "Sell all [the books] you have ... and buy Spurgeon."

Another great preacher, the apostle Paul, never went to seminary, but said, "I want you to know, brothers, that the gospel I preached is not something that man made up. I did not receive it from any man, nor was I taught it; rather, *I received it by revelation from Jesus Christ....* But when God, who set me apart from birth and called me by his grace, was pleased to reveal his Son in me so that I might preach him among the Gentiles, I did not consult any man, nor did I go up to Jerusalem to see those who were apostles before I was" (Gal. 1:11 – 12, 15 – 17).

Paul, noting God's work in him also said, in the verse Spurgeon alluded to today, "[God] has *made us competent as ministers* of a new covenant — not of the letter but of the Spirit; for the letter kills, but the Spirit gives life" (2 Cor. 3:6).

JANUARY 20

Turn my eyes away from worthless things;
preserve my life according to your word.

Psalm 119:37

From the pen of Charles Spurgeon:

There are many kinds of "worthless things," such as the actions of court jesters and the drunkenness and debauchery of the world. The self-absorbed people who practice these things are proud of their vanity, living up to their foolish names and titles. Yet far more treacherous are these equally "worthless things": "the worries of this life [and] the deceitfulness of wealth" (Mark 4:19), for a person may trust in them as easily in an accounting office as on a theater stage. And if someone spends his life simply to amass great wealth, he squanders his days in worthless displays of vanity.

Unless we follow Christ, making Him the one great object of our life, we will only differ outwardly from the most frivolous among us. Thus, there is clearly a great need for today's prayer: "Preserve my life according to your word." The psalmist is confessing his weariness, faintness, and the fact he feels all but dead.

Dear reader, perhaps you feel the same — so unmotivated and lifeless that even the best of motives will not move you; that nothing apart from the Lord Himself will revive you. Won't thoughts of sinners perishing in hell awaken and stir you? What about heaven? Won't thoughts of the reward awaiting the righteous spur you to action? What about death? Can you think of dying, and then standing before your God, and remain slothful in your Master's service? Won't "Christ's love [compel you]" (2 Cor. 5:14) to service? Can you think of His precious wounds or sit at the foot of His cross and not be stirred with fervency and zeal for Him?

Actually, none of this will work, for nothing can motivate us to zealous action but God Himself. Hence the desperate cry: "Preserve my life." The psalmist breathes his entire being into his passionate pleading, uniting his body and soul in prayer. His body prays, "Turn my eyes away," while his soul pleads, "Preserve my life." What a fitting prayer for every day of life.

O Lord, hear this prayer from me today.

From the pen of Jim Reimann:

When we consider the prayer "Turn my eyes away from worthless things," perhaps we should further consider where our eyes should turn instead. First, let us remember this truth:

God chose the foolish things of the world to shame the wise; God chose the weak things of the world to shame the strong. He chose the lowly things of this world and the despised things — and the things that are not — to nullify the things that are, so that no one may boast before him.

1 Corinthians 1:27-29

Of course, everything our eyes see is only temporary, while eternal things remain invisible to our physical eyes. Yet they are "clearly seen" with spiritual eyes, as the following verse attests: "Since the creation of the world God's invisible qualities — his eternal power and divine nature — have been *clearly seen*, being understood from what has been made" (Rom. 1:20). Like Moses, may we see with spiritual eyes, for "he persevered because he saw him who is invisible" (Heb. 11:27). And may this prayer of David be true in you and me:

"My eyes are ever on the LORD" (Ps. 25:15).

January 21

Because he was very thirsty, he cried out to the Lord,
"You have given your servant this great victory. Must I now die of thirst?"
Judges 15:18

From the pen of Charles Spurgeon:

In this story Samson was so thirsty he feared he would die. This particular difficulty was totally different from any the hero had encountered previously. Yet needing to have his thirst satisfied was certainly nothing as great as being delivered from a thousand Philistines. Even so, when the thirst first came upon him, Samson felt that small difficulty was more weighty than the great predicament from which he had just been so miraculously delivered.

Actually, it is quite common for God's people, when they have just experienced a great deliverance, to feel even a small problem is too much for them. "With a donkey's jawbone" (v. 16) Samson had just killed a thousand men, and now he nearly faints for a little water. Jacob wrestled with God at Peniel, overcoming Omnipotence Himself, then limped away because the Lord "touched the socket of Jacob's hip" (Gen. 32:25). How strange it is that our courage shrinks away whenever we win the day. It's as though the Lord must remind us of our smallness — our nothingness — in order to maintain our humility. Samson loudly boasted, "I have killed a thousand men" (Judg. 15:16), but almost immediately his boastful throat grew hoarse with thirst, moving him to prayer. God has many ways of humbling His people.

Dear child of God, if you feel down and depressed after some great work of God's mercy in your life, your situation is not unusual. When David ascended to the throne of Israel he said, "Though I am the anointed king, I am weak" (2 Sam. 3:39). Thus, you too should expect to feel the weakest when you are enjoying your greatest

triumph. If God has delivered you and given you great victories in the past, then your present difficulty is simply like Samson's thirst. Your Lord will not let you faint, nor allow the daughter of the uncircumcised to triumph over you (see Judg. 16:18 – 30).

The road to heaven is one of sorrow, but there are wells of refreshing water all along the way. So, tested Christian, cheer your heart with Samson's story, and rest assured God also will deliver you before long.

From the pen of Jim Reimann:

The story of Elijah's victory over the 850 prophets of Baal and Asherah is another example of great deliverance followed by deep depression. The mighty prophet of God had just experienced his greatest victory, but then ran in fear for his life, crying out to the Lord, "I have had enough, Lord.... Take my life" (1 Kings 19:4). Then two more times he mistakenly told God, "I am the only one left, and now they are trying to kill me too" (vv. 10, 14). The truth was, however, that there were "seven thousand in Israel ... [who had] not bowed down to Baal" (v. 18).

This should be a sobering lesson for us, because after Elijah had complained three times to the Lord, it was as though God had also "had enough." God is long-suffering, but after Elijah complained the third time, the Lord told him, "Go back the way you came ... and anoint Elisha ... to succeed you as prophet" (vv. 15 – 16). Thus, Elijah's work as God's prophet neared its end.

There may come a time when the Lord's patience comes to an end with me as well. Do I really want to hear him say, "Go back the way you came"?

JANUARY 22

Does Job fear God for nothing?

Job 1:9

From the pen of Charles Spurgeon:

This wicked question is what Satan asked the Lord regarding Job, the righteous man of old. But there are many people today of whom it might be asked quite justly, for they exhibit some love toward God when He appears to prosper them, yet as soon as things become difficult for them, they walk away from their boastful, professed faith in Him. As long as they experience worldly prosperity after their so-called conversion, they love the Lord in their own worldly way, but as soon as they experience adversity, they rebel against Him. Their love is simply for the food on the table, not love for the Host — love for what's in the cupboard, not love for the Master of the house.

A true Christian, however, expects to have his reward in the next life and to endure hardship in this one. The promise of the old covenant was prosperity, but the promise of the new covenant is adversity. Remember Christ's words: "Every branch that does bear fruit ..." How does He finish His statement? "... he prunes so that it will be even more fruitful" (John 15:2). Thus, if you "bear fruit," you will have to endure affliction.

Do you then complain, "What a terrible prospect!" Yet remember, these afflictions work amazingly precious results. Thus, we as Christians who are the recipient of these trials must learn to rejoice in them, for as our tribulations abound, so does our comfort abound in Christ Jesus. If we are truly children of God, we may rest assured we will be no stranger to His rod of discipline (see Prov. 13:24), for sooner or later every bar of gold must pass through the refiner's fire.

"Be not afraid," but rather "be glad and rejoice" (Joel 2:21) that such fruitful times are ahead for you, for through those times you will be weaned from earth and made ready for heaven; you will be delivered from clinging to the present and made to yearn for eternal things that will soon be revealed to you.

Thus, when you are tempted to complain that you presently serve the Lord for nothing, remember that soon you will rejoice in the infinite reward of eternity.

From the pen of Jim Reimann:

I should continually ask myself: "Do I serve the Lord for what He gives me or because I truly love Him?"

Listen to what the Lord says to His people:

> Love the LORD your God with all your heart and with all your soul and with all your strength. These commandments that I give you today are to be upon your hearts. Impress them on your children. Talk about them when you sit at home and when you walk along the road, when you lie down and when you get up. Tie them as symbols on your hands and bind them on your foreheads. Write them on the doorframes of your houses and on your gates.
>
> Deuteronomy 6:5 – 9

It is quite obvious from this that our loving Lord desires our love in return and wants us to be people of His Word. Yet, because we cannot outgive God, neither can we serve or "fear God for nothing," as our text verse asks today. May we remember Paul's encouragement: "Let us not become weary in doing good, for at the proper time we will reap a harvest if we do not give up" (Gal. 6:9).

But remember: our reward will come "at the proper time" — in God's time.

January 23

We will remember your love more than wine.

Song of Songs 1:4 NKJV

From the pen of Charles Spurgeon:

Jesus will not allow His people to forget His love, for if they come to the point of nearly forgetting, He will revisit them with fresh love. He says, in essence, "If you forget my cross, I will cause you to remember it, for at My table — the Lord's table — I will reveal Myself anew to you. If you forget what I did for you before God's eternal court, I will remind you, for you will need an advocate and will always find Me ready when you call." Nor does a mother allow her child to forget her, for if her child has traveled to a distant country without writing home, she will write, asking, "Have you forgotten your mother?" Soon thereafter she will receive a letter, proving the gentle reminder was not in vain. It is much the same with Jesus, who says to us, "Remember me."

In the words of our text, our response to Him will be:

"We will remember your love." Then we will go on to say, "'We will remember your love' and its matchless history. It is as ancient as 'the glory [You] had with [Your Father] before the world began' (John 17:5). O Jesus, 'we will remember your [eternal] love' when You pledged Yourself to us as Your bride. 'We will remember your love' which suggested the sacrifice of Yourself; the love which pondered that sacrifice through the ages, and the love which longed for the time when the words 'I have come' that were 'written about [You] in the scroll' (Ps. 40:7) would find their fulfillment. 'We will remember your love,' O Jesus, as it was revealed to us by Your holy life, from the manger in Bethlehem to the Garden of Gethsemane. As we examine Your life from cradle to grave, we rejoice in Your love, for Your every word and deed was love. Thus, we rejoice in Your love — love that death did not exhaust; love that blazed so brilliantly in Your resurrection. 'We will remember [that burning fire of] your love' which will never allow You to rest until Your chosen ones are all safely home, until Zion is glorified, and until Jerusalem is established on her everlasting foundations of light and love in heaven."

From the pen of Jim Reimann:

Because "God is love" (1 John 4:8), defining and personifying it Himself, it is impossible to find a greater love than His. Jesus said, "Greater love has no one than this, that he lay down his life for his friends" (John 15:13), then, as the most precious example possible, laid down His life for His chosen ones. To remind us of His willingness to do so, and that His sacrifice was an act of His love, He said, "No takes [My life] from me, but I lay it down of my own accord. I have authority to lay it down and authority to take it up again" (John 10:18).

As Paul considered the great love of our Lord, which he described as being beyond our capacity to fully understand, his heart began to praise the Savior. The following is how he described it. May it be the desire of our hearts today.

"I pray that you, being rooted and established in love, may have power, together with all the saints, to grasp how wide and long and high and deep is the love of Christ, and to know this love that surpasses knowledge.... *To him be glory in the church and in Christ Jesus throughout all generations, for ever and ever! Amen*" (Eph. 3:17 – 19, 21).

January 24

Martha was distracted by all the preparations
that had to be made.

Luke 10:40

From the pen of Charles Spurgeon:

Martha's mistake was not that she was serving, for the attitude of a servant is becoming to every Christian. In fact, "I serve" (Rom. 1:9) should be the motto of every prince and princess of the royal family of heaven. Nor was she at fault for taking care of "all the preparations," for we cannot do too much. May we do all we possibly can; may our head, heart, and hands be fully engaged in the Master's service. Thus, she was not at fault for busily preparing a feast for the Master. Actually, Martha was privileged to have the opportunity of entertaining such a blessed Guest, and privileged as well to have the attitude of throwing her entire soul so heartily into the preparation.

Martha's mistake, however, was that she "was distracted by all the preparations." She forgot Jesus Himself, being solely focused on her service for Him. She allowed it to take priority over her communion with Him, staining one duty with the blood of another or, in other words, sacrificing one for the other.

We should be Martha and Mary in one, doing much service for Jesus while at the same time still having much communion with Him. But to do so we need a great deal of God's grace, for it is much easier to serve than to commune. For example, it wasn't Joshua who became weary when fighting the Amalekites, it was Moses on top of the mountain whose "hands grew tired" (Ex. 17:12) and who needed the help of two men to keep them lifted in prayer. Thus, the more spiritual the task, the sooner we grow weary. The best fruit is the most difficult to produce, just as the most heavenly gifts are the most difficult to cultivate.

Beloved Christian, don't neglect the external things needed for life, for they have their purpose, but be determined to continually enjoy vital, personal fellowship with Jesus. Make sure you never neglect sitting at the Savior's feet, even if it appears to give others the misleading idea it is service to Him you are neglecting. The first priority for our soul's health, the first priority for His glory, and the first priority for our own usefulness is to keep ourselves in continual communion with the Lord Jesus and to see that the vital spirituality of our faith is maintained over and above everything else in the world.

From the pen of Jim Reimann:

In the fast-paced societies of today, it is easy to become overwhelmed with too many options and too much information. Even in the church we can be bombarded with so many areas of service that we take on too much until what suffers most is our own personal communion with the Lord Jesus.

Yet because we are the only ones who know of our personal quiet time with the Lord, it is often easier to let that time slip away, rather than our public service to Him. But the Bible sees it differently, as does the Lord — who, by the way, also sees our lack of time alone with Him.

Jesus had a beautiful way of cutting through the complexities of life. Here is how He addressed the issue with Martha, quickly showing her the "one thing" she dearly needed: "Martha, Martha,... you are worried and upset about *many things,* but *only one thing is needed.* Mary has chosen what is better" (Luke 10:41 – 42).

JANUARY 25

Do we, then, nullify the law by this faith?
Not at all! Rather, we uphold the law.

Romans 3:31

From the pen of Charles Spurgeon:

When a believer is adopted into the Lord's family, his relationship to the old Adam and the law ceases immediately, because he is now under a new authority and "a new covenant" (Heb. 9:15). Dear believer, you are a child of God and your first responsibility is to obey your heavenly Father. Have nothing to do with a groveling, self-abasing spirit, for you are not a slave. You are a child and, as a beloved child, you are obligated to obey your Father's faintest wish or the least suggestion of His will.

Is He leading you to fulfill a sacred ordinance? If so, you neglect it at your own peril, for you will be disobeying your Father. Has He commanded you to seek the face of Jesus? Isn't it your joy to do so? Hasn't Jesus told you, "Be perfect ... as your heavenly Father is perfect" (Matt. 5:48)? Then you should work to be perfectly holy, not because the law commands it, but because your Savior asks it of you. Does He encourage His saints to love one another? Then do it, not because the law says, "Love your neighbor" (Lev. 19:18), but because Jesus says, "If you love me, you will obey what I command" (John 14:15), and He has given you the command to "Love one another" (John 13:34). Have you been told to give to the poor? Then do it, not because charity is a burden you dare not neglect, but because Jesus taught, "Give to the one who asks you" (Matt. 5:42). Does the Word say, "Love the LORD your God with all your heart" (Deut. 6:5)? Then look at that commandment and reply, "Dear commandment, Christ has fulfilled you already. Therefore, I have no need to obey you for my salvation, but I rejoice to yield in obedience to you, because God is now my Father and He has a claim upon me I will not dispute."

May the Holy Spirit make your heart obedient to the power of Christ's love, so that your prayer may be:

"Direct me in the path of your commands, for there I find delight" (Ps. 119:35).

Grace is the parent and nurse of holiness — not the defender of sin.

From the pen of Jim Reimann:

Spurgeon's statement that "grace is ... not the defender of sin" refers to the fact that after salvation, we should never use God's grace as an excuse to continue to walk in willful sinfulness. Paul said, "Shall we go on sinning so that grace may increase? By no means! We died to sin; how can we live in it any longer?" (Rom. 6:1 – 2).

If we think of God's grace as "the defender of sin," we cheapen that grace which cost the Lord the life of His Son, not to mention the fact that it destroys our witness before the lost of the world. Nothing in the Scriptures can be construed to justify a license to sin simply because we are already saved. In fact, Jude gives us this warning: "Certain men whose condemnation was written about long ago have secretly slipped in among you. *They are godless men, who change the grace of our God into a license for immorality and deny Jesus Christ our only Sovereign and Lord"* (Jude 4).

"Who may ascend the hill of the LORD? Who may stand in his holy place? He who has clean hands and a pure heart" (Ps. 24:3 – 4).

JANUARY 26

All who heard it were amazed
at what the shepherds said to them.
Luke 2:18

From the pen of Charles Spurgeon:

We must never cease to be amazed at the great wonders of our God. Yet it is very difficult to know where wonder ends and true worship begins, for when the soul is overwhelmed with the majesty of God's glory — although it may not express itself in song or even raise its voice with bowed head in humble prayer — still it silently worships Him. Our incarnate God is to be worshiped as "the Wonder-full."

The fact that God would even consider us, instead of simply sweeping His fallen creatures away with the broom of destruction, and that He would take upon Himself to pay the price to become our Redeemer is indeed miraculous. But for believers, redemption is the most miraculous when they view it in relation to themselves. Thus, personalize this truth: it is a miracle of God's grace that Jesus relinquished His throne and royalty above to suffer so humiliatingly here below for you. Allow your soul to lose itself in wonder, for wonder in this case is a very practical emotion that will lead you to grateful worship and heartfelt thanksgiving. It will also produce a godly watchfulness within you, causing you to fear sinning against such a love as this. As you feel the presence of the all-powerful God through the gift of His dear Son, you will automatically "take off your sandals, for the place where you are standing is holy ground" (Ex. 3:5).

At the same time you will sense a glorious hope, for if Jesus has done such miraculous things on your behalf, you will know that heaven itself is not too great a hope for you. Can you really be astonished at anything, once you have been amazed at Jesus' manger and His cross? Can there be anything more wonderful than having seen the Savior?

Dear believer, it may be that you have a rather quiet and lonely existence, scarcely able to imitate the shepherds of Bethlehem who "spread the word concerning what had been told them" (Luke 2:17) and what they had seen. Nevertheless, you can at least join the throng of worshipers before God's throne by being filled with wonder for what He has done.

From the pen of Jim Reimann:

Today's devotion brings to mind the proper reaction to God's miraculous works, which is worship. Never think, however, that everyone will react the same way, for unbelievers see miracles daily, yet continue to walk in sin. For example, consider the reaction of the Jewish leadership to Jesus' miracles. In light of His wonders, "the chief priests and the Pharisees called a meeting of the Sanhedrin. 'What are we accomplishing?' they asked. 'Here is this man performing many miraculous signs. If we let him go on like this, everyone will believe in him, and then the Romans will come and take away both our place and our nation'" (John 11:47 – 48). Notice they knew He was "performing many miraculous signs," which is exactly what the Jews demanded, for Paul once said, "Jews demand miraculous signs" (1 Cor. 1:22). Yet they did not believe!

Father, deliver us from ever becoming desensitized to Your miracles of grace. "Great [are You] LORD and most worthy of praise; [Your] greatness no one can fathom" (Ps. 145:3).

JANUARY 27

But Mary treasured up all these things
and pondered them in her heart.

Luke 2:19

From the pen of Charles Spurgeon:

This event in the life of this blessed young woman points to three aspects of her being: (1) Her memory: she remembered "all these things." (2) Her affections: she kept them "in her heart." (3) Her intellect: she "pondered them." Thus, her memory, affections, and intellect were all employed in all she had seen and heard.

Dear believer, remember what you have heard about your Lord Jesus, and ponder what He has done for you. Make your heart "the gold jar of manna" (Heb. 9:4) that preserves the memory of the heavenly bread which has fed you in the past. Allow your memory to treasure everything about Christ you have either felt, known, or believed, and then let your fond affections hold Him close forever.

Love the person of your Lord. Bring forth the "alabaster jar" (Luke 7:37) of your heart, even though it is broken, and let the precious perfume of your affections flow over His pierced feet.

Then use your intellect regarding the Lord Jesus. Meditate upon His Word, not simply stopping at the surface, but dive into its depths. Never be like a swallow that barely touches the stream with her wing, but be like a fish that penetrates its deepest flow. Abide with your Lord; don't let Him be to you like a traveler who stays only one night, but plead with Him, saying, "Stay with [me], for it is nearly evening; the day is almost over" (Luke 24:29). Hold on to Him, never letting Him go. The word *ponder* means to weigh something in your mind, so prepare the scales of judgment. But where are scales sufficient to fully weigh the Lord Christ? "He weighs the islands as though they were fine dust" (Isa. 40:15), but who can hold Him? He "weighed the mountains on the scales" (Isa. 40:12), but on what scales will we weigh Him?

Even so, if your understanding cannot fully comprehend Him, let your affections do so; and if your spirit cannot fully grasp the Lord Jesus with complete understanding, let it embrace Him with your arms of affection.

From the pen of Jim Reimann:

Who of us can comprehend the Lord Jesus in His full majesty and glory? "Who can proclaim the mighty acts of the LORD or fully declare his praise?" (Ps. 106:2).

Who has measured the waters in the hollow of his hand, or with the breadth of his hand marked off the heavens? Who has held the dust of the earth in a basket, or weighed the mountains on the scales and the hills in a balance? Who has understood the mind of the LORD, or instructed him as his counselor? Whom did the LORD consult to enlighten him, and who taught him the right way? Who was it that taught him knowledge or showed him the path of understanding? Surely the nations are like a drop in a bucket; they are regarded as dust on the scales; he weighs the islands as though they were fine dust."

Isaiah 40:12 – 15

"O LORD, what is man that you care for him, the son of man that you think of him?" (Ps. 144:3). *And although Your greatness is impossible for me to fully grasp, may I be like Jacob who wrestled with You and said, "I will not let you go unless you bless me"* (Gen. 32:26).

JANUARY 28

The shepherds returned, glorifying and praising God
for all the things they had heard and seen,
which were just as they had been told.

Luke 2:20

From the pen of Charles Spurgeon:

Why do we see the shepherds praising God in this verse? They did so because of what they had heard — for the "good news of great joy that ... a Savior [had] been born to [them]" (Luke 2:10 – 11). And because we too have heard of Jesus and His salvation, we should imitate them, raising a song of thanksgiving to God. The shepherds also praised God for what they had seen, for the sweetest music comes from what we have personally experienced, what we have felt in our inner being, and what we have made our own. As the psalmist said, "I speak of the things which I have made touching the king" (Ps. 45:1 KJV).

It is not enough simply to hear about Jesus. Hearing may help tune the harp, but it takes the fingers of living faith to create the music. And if you have ever seen Jesus through the eyes of faith, you will never allow cobwebs to linger on the harp's strings, but will instead loudly praise the Sovereign of grace, saying, "Awake, harp and lyre!" (Ps. 57:8).

Another reason for their praise was the perfect agreement between what they heard and what they saw. Notice the verse says, "All the things ... *were just as they had been told*." Haven't you found the gospel to be in you exactly what the Bible said it would be? Jesus said, "I will give you rest" (Matt. 11:28), and haven't you enjoyed the sweetest peace in Him? He said you would have joy, comfort, and life by believing in Him, and haven't you received each of these? Aren't His ways the most pleasing and His paths the ways of peace?

I can truly say with the queen of Sheba, "Indeed, not even half was told me.... You have far exceeded the report I heard" (1 Kings 10:7). I have found Christ to be sweeter than His servants said He would be. I have looked on the likeness they painted for me, but found it to be a mere dab of paint compared with Jesus Himself, for "the king in his beauty" (Isa. 33:17) outshines all loveliness I can imagine. Surely what I have "seen" keeps pace with what I have "heard." No! It far exceeds it!

Thus, may I glorify and praise God for a Savior so precious and satisfying.

From the pen of Jim Reimann:

Imagine being among the first to see the Christ Child. How magnificent that scene must have been! Yet because He had set His glory aside, making "himself nothing" (Phil. 2:7), as Paul said, that first view of Him may actually pale in comparison to when we will behold Him in all His glory. Someday "the LORD will ... appear in his glory" (Ps. 102:16), and "we know that when he appears, we shall be like him, for we shall see him as he is" (1 John 3:2).

At His first coming, "He had no beauty or majesty to attract us to him, nothing in his appearance that we should desire him" (Isa. 53:2), but "when the Son of Man comes in his glory, and all the angels with him, he will sit on his throne in heavenly glory" (Matt. 25:31). "And when the Chief Shepherd appears, you will receive the crown of glory that will never fade away" (1 Peter 5:4).

"One thing I ask of the LORD, this is what I seek: that I may dwell in the house of the LORD all the days of my life, to gaze upon the beauty of the LORD and to seek him in his temple" (Ps. 27:4).

January 29

The dove returned to him in the evening.

Genesis 8:11

From the pen of Charles Spurgeon:

"Blessed be the LORD" (Gen. 9:26) for a new day of mercy even though I grow weary from its work. Unto the "preserver of men" (Job 7:20 KJV) I lift my song of gratitude. And just as the dove found no rest outside the ark of Noah and returned, my soul has learned that there is no satisfaction found in earthly things. God alone can give rest to my spirit. I am thankful for my family, my business, my possessions, and my attainments, but they cannot fulfill the desires of my eternal nature. "Be at rest once more, O my soul, for the LORD has been good to you" (Ps. 116:7).

It was at the close of the day that the dove wearily winged her way back to her master. *Thus, O Lord, enable me to return to Jesus this evening after a weary day of work.* The dove could not survive a night hovering over the restless sea, nor can I bear even one hour away from Jesus — the place of rest for my heart and the home of my spirit. And notice she did not merely come to rest on the roof of the ark, but instead "returned to him." Oh, that my longing spirit would also desire "the secret of the LORD" (Ps. 25:14 KJV), pierce His deeper truth, enter "the inner sanctuary behind the curtain" (Heb. 6:19), and reach out to "my beloved" (Song 1:14 KJV) through my every action. I must go to Jesus, for my panting spirit will find no rest anywhere short of intimate fellowship with Him.

Blessed Lord Jesus, be with me, reveal Yourself to me, and abide with me, not only today but also throughout tonight, so that when I awake tomorrow I am still with You. I notice, O Lord, that the dove brought Noah an olive branch in her mouth — a memorial plucked from the past and a promise of the future. But do I have anything to bring You, any pledge or deposit of loving-kindness yet to come? Yes, my Lord, I present You my grateful acknowledgments for Your "great love" and "compassions" that "are new every morning" (Lam. 3:22 – 23) and fresh every evening. Even now, Lord Jesus, reach forth Your hands and take me, Your dove, into Your loving embrace.

From the pen of Jim Reimann:

As believers we fight spiritual battles day after day, and often night after night. When we are tempted to give up, may we remember the words of David, especially noticing how he turned first to his Lord:

> Deliver me from my enemies, O God; protect me from those who rise up against me. Deliver me from evildoers and save me from bloodthirsty men. See how they lie in wait for me! Fierce men conspire against me for no offense or sin of mine, O LORD. I have done no wrong, yet they are ready to attack me. Arise to help me; look on my plight!
>
> Psalm 59:1 – 4

David was forced to deal with the enemy at night as well, for he continued: "[My enemies] return at evening, snarling like dogs, and prowl about the city. They wander about for food and howl if not satisfied" (vv. 14 – 15).

Finally, in spite of David's ongoing battles, notice how he turned to a beautiful exercise of praise, trusting the Lord to be his strength: "But I will sing of your strength, in the morning I will sing of your love; for you are my fortress, my refuge in times of trouble. O my Strength, I sing praise to you; you, O God, are my fortress, my loving God" (vv. 16 – 17).

January 30

In Christ ... we have obtained an inheritance.

Ephesians 1:10 – 11 KJV

From the pen of Charles Spurgeon:

When Jesus gave Himself for us, He also gave us all His rights and privileges. Of course, as the eternal God, He has some rights which no human can claim or possess; yet as Jesus, our Mediator and the central head of the covenant of grace, He has no heritage or inheritance He does not share with us. All the glorious benefits of His being "obedient to death" (Phil. 2:8) are the riches shared in common by all who are in Him — those for whom He accomplished God's divine will. He entered into glory, but not for Himself alone, for we are told, "Jesus, who went before us, has entered on our behalf" (Heb. 6:20). "He entered heaven itself, now to appear for us in God's presence" (Heb. 9:24).

Consider this, dear believer: You have no right to heaven within yourself, for your right lies solely in Christ. If you have been pardoned, it was by His blood; if you have been justified, it was by His righteousness; if you are being sanctified, it is because "Christ Jesus ... is made unto [you] ... sanctification" (1 Cor. 1:30 KJV); if you are kept "from falling" (Jude 24), it is because you are preserved in Him; and if you are ultimately made perfect, it is because "you have been given fullness in Christ" (Col. 2:10). Thus, Jesus is glorified, for all this is found only in Him and accomplished solely by Him. And due to this, our inheritance is guaranteed to us, for it is obtained by being in Him. Therefore, each blessing is sweeter and even heaven itself is brighter because it is Jesus our "beloved, in whom" (Matt. 12:18 KJV) we have obtained all this.

Where is someone capable of valuing our divine inheritance? Who can weigh the riches of Christ on the scales or His treasures on the balances — all of which belong to His saints? Plumb the depths of Christ's sea of joy, and then only hope to fully conceive of the happiness "God has prepared for those who love him" (1 Cor. 2:9). It is impossible to find the boundaries of Christ's possessions or to even dream of a limit to the glorious inheritance of the elect, "for all things are yours ... and you are Christ's, and Christ is God's" (1 Cor. 3:21, 23 ESV).

From the pen of Jim Reimann:

After our text today, Paul goes on to say that "having believed, you were marked in him with a seal, the promised Holy Spirit, who is a deposit guaranteeing our inheritance until the redemption of those who are God's possession — to the praise of his glory" (Eph. 1:13 – 14). Thus, not only has the Lord given His saints an eternal inheritance but He also has guaranteed it by giving us a "down payment" — the very life of His Son through the indwelling power of the Holy Spirit.

Paul then takes a stab at describing our inheritance by saying,

> I pray also that the eyes of your heart may be enlightened in order that you may know the hope to which he has called you, the riches of his glorious inheritance in the saints, and his incomparably great power for us who believe. That power is like the working of his mighty strength, which he exerted in Christ when he raised him from the dead and seated him at his right hand in the heavenly realms, far above all rule and authority, power and dominion, and every title that can be given, not only in the present age but also in the one to come.

Ephesians 1:18 – 21

January 31

Then Ahimaaz ran by way of the plain
and outran the Cushite.

2 Samuel 18:23

From the pen of Charles Spurgeon:

How fast we run is not nearly as important as the path we select, for a fast runner who runs over hills and valleys will not keep pace with a slower runner on level ground. The same is true in my spiritual journey. Am I laboring up hills of my own works and down through the ravines of my own humiliations and resolutions, or am I running across the level way of simply living by faith?

How blessed are "those who hope in the LORD" by faith, for "they will run and not grow weary, they will walk and not be faint" (Isa. 40:31). Christ Jesus is the way of life — the level and pleasant way, a way suitable for the unstable feet and feeble knees of trembling sinners. Is this the way I am traveling, or am I searching for another path, such as one of trusting in witchcraft or metaphysics and what they may offer me?

In God's Word I read of "the Way of Holiness" (Isa. 35:8), a way that is unerring even for a traveler who otherwise might be considered a fool. Thus, may I be delivered from proud reasoning and be brought down to the level of a little child to rest in Jesus' love and trust in His blood. Then by God's grace, I will outrun even the strongest runner who chooses any other path. To my profit, may I remember this truth in all my daily cares and needs, for my wisest course is to go immediately to my God and not wander round and round, going to this friend and then the other. He knows my wants and needs and can meet them. Who but Him should I run to with my direct appeal of prayer, remembering the argument that the best runner runs straight ahead. Thus, I will not linger with the servants, but will run straight to the Master.

If people compete with each other in the common matters of life, how much more important is it to run well in spiritual matters? I should run in solemn earnestness and "run in such a way as to get the prize" (1 Cor. 9:24).

Lord, help me "prepare [my mind] for action" (1 Peter 1:13) to run well and to "press on toward the goal to win the prize for which God has called me heavenward in Christ Jesus" (Phil. 3:14).

From the pen of Jim Reimann:

Throughout the New Testament, the Christian life is compared to running a race. One of the most beautiful of these passages is this selection from Hebrews. As you read, remember that the "great cloud of witnesses" are the Old Testament saints listed in the previous chapter — those who ran so well that we are told: "The world was not worthy of them" (Heb. 11:38).

Therefore, since we are surrounded by such a great cloud of witnesses, let us throw off everything that hinders and the sin that so easily entangles, and let us run with perseverance the race marked out for us. Let us fix our eyes on Jesus, the author and perfecter of our faith, who for the joy set before him endured the cross, scorning its shame, and sat down at the right hand of the throne of God. Consider him who endured such opposition from sinful men, so that you will not grow weary and lose heart.

Hebrews 12:1 – 3

"I have chosen the way of truth.... I run in the path of your commands" (Ps. 119:30, 32).

February

FEBRUARY 1

Your love for me was wonderful.

2 Samuel 1:26

From the pen of Charles Spurgeon:

Our text verse speaks of David's love for his friend Jonathan, but, dear believer, may each of us speak for ourselves today of the wonderful love of Jesus. May we not share simply what we have been told of Him, but only what we have personally tasted and experienced of Christ's love.

"Your love for me was wonderful," O Jesus, even when I was a stranger wandering far from You, fulfilling my own ideas and fleshly desires. Your gracious love kept me from the "sin that leads to death" (1 John 5:16), and You protected me from self-destruction. Your love restrained the axe when justice demanded, "Cut it down! Why should it use up the soil?" (Luke 13:7). Your love drew me into the wilderness, stripped me of myself, and made me feel the guilt of my sin and the burden of my iniquity. And once I was totally dismayed, Your love spoke these words of comfort to me, "Come to me ... and I will give you rest" (Matt. 11:28).

Oh, how matchless Your love that in an instant washed my sins away, and which took my polluted soul, crimson with the blood of my own nature and black with the filth of my transgressions, and made it as white as driven snow and as pure as the finest wool (see Isa. 1:18). Oh, how You proved Your love when You whispered in my ear, "I am yours and 'you are mine'" (Isa. 43:1). How kind were Your words when You said, "The Father himself loves you" (John 16:27). And how precious the times when You declared to me "the love of the Spirit" (Rom. 15:30). My soul will never forget those moments of intimate fellowship when You revealed Yourself to me.

Moses had his "cleft in the rock" (Ex. 33:22) where he saw the Lord's glory pass by, but we too have our clefts in the rock where we behold the full splendor of the Godhead in the person of Christ. Just as the psalmist remembers "the high mountains ... [of] the wild goats" (Ps. 104:18), and David declares, "I will remember you from the land of the Jordan, the heights of Hermon" (Ps. 42:6), we too can cherish those places that are equally blessed of the Lord to us.

Precious Lord Jesus, grant us a fresh measure of Your wondrous love to begin this month. Amen.

From the pen of Jim Reimann:

The love between David and Jonathan reveals one of mankind's greatest friendships. Yet some in the world today attempt to convey the idea that it was more than platonic. To paraphrase C. S. Lewis, however, someone who says that has never had a true friend.

Yet we must be careful who our friends are, because God's Word warns: "Anyone who chooses to be a friend of the world becomes an enemy of God" (James 4:4). We have also been given this admonition: "Do not be yoked together with unbelievers. For what do righteousness and wickedness have in common? Or what fellowship can light have with darkness?" (2 Cor. 6:14).

But there is Someone who "is a friend who sticks closer than a brother" (Prov. 18:24), and He has said, "I no longer call you servants, because a servant does not know his master's business. Instead, I have called you friends, for everything that I learned from my Father I have made known to you" (John 15:15).

FEBRUARY 2

These records are from ancient times.

1 Chronicles 4:22

From the pen of Charles Spurgeon:

The records mentioned in today's verse, although ancient, are not nearly as ancient as those precious things that are the primary delight of our souls. Let's consider them for a moment, recounting them as a miser would count his gold.

The sovereign choice of the Father that elected us to eternal life is an event of great antiquity, occurring before the earth came into being, and a date so long ago the human mind cannot conceive of it. "He chose us in him before the creation of the world" (Eph. 1:4), and eternal love went along with His choice, for it was not simply an act of His divine will by which we were set apart to salvation, but His divine affections were involved as well. The Father has loved us from the beginning, something that should be a daily theme for our thoughtful consideration. God's eternal purpose to redeem us from our inevitable ruin, to cleanse and sanctify us, and finally to glorify us is a purpose of infinite antiquity and runs side by side with His immutable love and absolute sovereignty.

The covenant is always described as being eternal, and Jesus, the second party to the promise, has existed since eternity past. He signed this sacred agreement long before the first stars ever began to shine, and it was in Him the elect "were appointed for eternal life" (Acts 13:48). Thus, through God's divine purpose, a blessed covenant union was established between the Son of God and His elect people, and it is this union that will forever be the foundation of their security when time is no more.

The church should be more conversant about these ancient truths. It is shameful that they are so neglected, and even rejected, by the majority of professing believers. If these professing Christians knew more of their own sin, then they would be much more apt to love God's electing grace. Thus, may we both admire and adore it today, as we sing:

> A monument of grace,
> A sinner saved by blood;
> The streams of love I trace
> Up to the Fountain, God;
> And in His sacred shelter see
> Eternal thoughts of Love to me.
>
> John Kent, 1766 – 1843

From the pen of Jim Reimann:

Eternity is something our finite minds cannot fathom. In fact, many of us have an errant definition of eternal life itself, believing that at the moment of our salvation the Lord took our physical life, and somehow miraculously transformed it, causing it to live forever.

Yet, based on the true definition of the word *eternal*, that is incorrect, for it means "without beginning and without end." Thus, since the Lord's life is the only life without beginning and without end, what we have been given is His spiritual life, which has existed since eternity past, and which will exist into eternity future.

"The Son of God has come and has given us understanding, so that we may know him who is true. And we are in him who is true — even in his Son Jesus Christ. *He is ... eternal life*" (1 John 5:20).

FEBRUARY 3

Tell me ... where you graze your flock
and where you rest your sheep at midday.

Song of Songs 1:7

From the pen of Charles Spurgeon:

These words express the desire of every follower of Christ and their longing for daily communion with Him. Lord, where do You feed Your flock? In Your house? Then I will go if I will find You there. In private times of prayer? Then I will "pray without ceasing" (1 Thess. 5:17 KJV). In Your Word? Then I will read it diligently. In Your sacraments? Then I will walk in them with all my heart. "Tell me ... where You graze Your flock," for wherever You stand as my Shepherd is where I will lie down as Your sheep, for no one but You can satisfy my needs. My soul hungers and thirsts for the refreshment found only in Your presence.

"Tell me ... where you rest your sheep at midday," for whether at dawn or at noon, my only rest is found with You and Your beloved flock. My soul's rest is a gift of Your grace and thus can be found solely in You. Where is "the shadow of [that] great rock" (Isa. 32:2)? Why shouldn't I find rest beneath it? "Why should I be like a veiled woman beside the flocks of your friends?" (Song 1:7). Certainly You have friends, so why shouldn't I be one?

Satan tells me I am unworthy, but I was always unworthy, and yet You chose to love me long ago. Therefore, my unworthiness cannot be a barrier to my having fellowship with You today. Yes, it is true I am weak in faith and prone to fall, but my feebleness is all the more reason why I should always be where You feed Your flock so that I may be strengthened and protected "beside quiet waters" (Ps. 23:2).

Why should I turn away from my Shepherd? There is no reason why I should, but there are a thousand reasons why I should not, for Jesus invites me to come. And even if He should withdraw Himself somewhat, it would only serve to make me value His presence all the more. Then once I became grieved and distressed at being away from Him, He would graciously lead me again to that hiding place where the lambs of His fold are sheltered from the burning sun.

From the pen of Jim Reimann:

Surely Psalm 23 is among everyone's favorite Bible passages, a song written by a shepherd about the Shepherd of believers. As you read this precious psalm today, think of how the Lord so lovingly cares for us, His sheep.

> The LORD is my shepherd, I shall not be in want. He makes me lie down in green pastures, he leads me beside quiet waters, he restores my soul. He guides me in paths of righteousness for his name's sake. Even though I walk through the valley of the shadow of death, I will fear no evil, for you are with me; your rod and your staff, they comfort me. You prepare a table before me in the presence of my enemies. You anoint my head with oil; my cup overflows. Surely goodness and love will follow me all the days of my life, and I will dwell in the house of the LORD forever.

> Psalm 23:1 – 6

Finally today, remind yourself that David looked forward to Jesus, the Good Shepherd, who said of Himself, "I am the good shepherd; I know my sheep and my sheep know me — just as the Father knows me and I know the Father — and I lay down my life for the sheep" (John 10:14 – 15).

Lord, I thank You for "the good shepherd."
Help me to be a good sheep.

FEBRUARY 4

Anyone ... may flee there and
find protection from the avenger of blood.

Joshua 20:3

From the pen of Charles Spurgeon:

Cities of refuge were placed across the land of Canaan so that anyone might reach one within half a day at the most. In a similar fashion, the gospel is always near us, for the way to Jesus is short, requiring simply a renunciation of our own merit and to take hold of Him as our "all in all" (1 Cor. 15:28). God's Word tells us that the roads to the cities of refuge were strictly maintained, with every river bridged and every obstacle removed, so that anyone who fled there would find easy passage to it. And once a year the elders of Israel were to examine the roads so that nothing would impede anyone fleeing for refuge, causing him to be overtaken and killed. Likewise, the promises of the gospel graciously remove stumbling blocks from the path of sinners.

Whenever there were intersections or forks in the road, signs were in place with inscriptions directing people to the city of refuge. This is nothing but a foreshadowing of the road to Christ Jesus. It is not some maze of roads of following the law, demanding that we obey this, or that, or the other; it is simply a straight road — believe and live! It is a road so difficult that no self-righteous person can ever travel it, yet so easy that everyone who admits he is a sinner can easily find his way to heaven.

And as soon as a fugitive reached the outskirts of the city of refuge, he was safe, for it was not necessary for him to fully enter within the city walls. Thus, just as the suburbs themselves were sufficient protection for him, simply touching "the edge of [Christ's] cloak" (Matt. 9:20) will make us whole; taking hold of Him with "faith as small as a mustard seed" (Matt. 17:20) will make us safe.

> A little genuine grace ensures
> The death of all our sins.
>
> Author unknown

Remember, however: don't loiter or waste any time, for "the avenger of blood" is swift of foot and may be close upon your heels even at this moment.

From the pen of Jim Reimann:

If you have never run to Jesus for refuge, claiming Him as your own, don't delay. As the old adage goes, none of us is promised tomorrow. Remember the words of Paul, who said, "Now is the time of God's favor, now is the day of salvation. We put no stumbling block in anyone's path" (2 Cor. 6:2 – 3).

Therefore, drop your self-confidence and self-righteousness, and run to Jesus in repentance and humility, and He will welcome you with open arms, for He says, "Come to me, all you who are weary and burdened, and I will give you rest" (Matt. 11:28).

Consider the Jews of Jerusalem who listened to Peter's sermon. When they were convicted of their sins, they asked, "What shall we do?" (Acts 2:37). He gave them these simple instructions: "Repent and be baptized ... in the name of Jesus Christ for the forgiveness of your sins" (v. 38).

"The name of the LORD is a strong tower; the righteous run to it and are safe" (Prov. 18:10). Why not run to Jesus today in faith?

FEBRUARY 5

At that time Jesus answered....
Matthew 11:25 KJV

From the pen of Charles Spurgeon:

These words are an unusual way to begin a verse, especially when you consider the context, for no one had asked Jesus a question or was involved in a conversation with Him. Yet the passage says, "At that time *Jesus answered* and said, I thank thee, O Father" (v. 25 KJV), indicating His Father was speaking to Him, for a person can only "answer" when someone has first spoken to him. But God's Word does not specifically tell us this, which should teach us that Jesus was in constant fellowship with His Father, and that God spoke so continually to His heart that it was not a circumstance unusual enough for Matthew to even record it.

It was Jesus' habit and life itself to talk with His Father. Jesus was in the world then just as we are today, thus may we learn the lesson this simple statement about Him teaches us. May we as well have silent fellowship with the Father so continually that we will answer Him often, even though the world may not understand with whom we speak. May we respond to that secret Voice, unheard by others, but recognized with joy by our own ears that the Spirit of God has opened. God speaks to us, thus let us speak to Him — to affirm that He is true and faithful to His promise, to confess a particular sin over which the Spirit of God has brought conviction, to acknowledge the mercy His providence has given, or to express agreement to the great truths that God the Holy Spirit has opened to our understanding.

What a privilege is the intimate communion with the Father of our spirit. It is a secret hidden from the world, and a joy that even our closest friend cannot interrupt. But if we truly desire to hear God's quiet whispers of love, our ears must be cleansed and conditioned to listen to His voice. May our hearts this very day be in such a condition, like that of Jesus, that when God speaks to us, we will be prepared to answer Him.

From the pen of Jim Reimann:

Every true believer longs to hear the Lord speak to him, particularly when we are seeking direction for an important decision in our lives. So often, however, we want him to write His will on the wall for us, in the way He did in the book of Daniel, where we are told, "Suddenly the fingers of a human hand appeared and wrote on the plaster of the wall" (Dan. 5:5). Or we want Him to perform a miracle or speak through some great natural wonder. But as you read the following Scripture passage, consider how the Lord spoke to Elijah at a time when he dearly needed a word from Him, for he was severely depressed and despondent:

A great and powerful wind tore the mountains apart and shattered the rocks before the LORD, but the LORD was not in the wind. After the wind there was an earthquake, but the LORD was not in the earthquake. After the earthquake came a fire, but the LORD was not in the fire. And after the fire came a gentle whisper. When Elijah heard it, he pulled his cloak over his face and went out and stood at the mouth of the cave. Then a voice said to him, "What are you doing here, Elijah?"

1 Kings 19:11 – 13

Dear Father, may my heart be conditioned to hear Your "gentle whisper," and may I always be ready to respond in complete obedience to Your voice.

FEBRUARY 6

Pray for each other.

James 5:16

From the pen of Charles Spurgeon:

Remember, as an encouragement to offer intercessory prayer cheerfully, this kind of prayer is the sweetest God ever hears, for Christ's prayers are this type. Also consider that of all the incense our Great High Priest continually places in "the golden altar of incense" (Heb. 9:4), not a single grain is for Himself. Surely Christ's intercession is the most acceptable of all prayers, thus the more our prayers are like His, the sweeter they will be. Although petitions for ourselves will be accepted, our pleadings for others, which exhibit more of "the fruit of the Spirit" (Gal. 5:22) — more love, kindness, and faithfulness — will be the sweetest sacrifice we can offer to God. And solely due to the merits of Jesus, these prayers will be to the Lord the very "fat of the fellowship offering" (Lev. 4:26). Also remember that intercessory prayer and its miraculous results are quite prevalent throughout the Word of God. What wonders it has accomplished.

Dear believer, you have a mighty force within your hand, so use it well, constantly, and by faith; and you will undoubtedly be a true benefactor to the family of Christ. Since you have the King's ear, speak on behalf of the suffering members of His body. When He favors you, allowing you to come very close to His throne, and saying, "Ask and it will be given to you" (Matt. 7:7), then let your petitions not only be for yourself but also for the many who need His help.

If you have any of God's grace at all and are not an intercessor, then the grace you have must be "as small as a mustard seed" (Matt. 17:20), just enough to float your own soul from the quicksand. But if you have deep floods of God's grace, you will carry in your joy-filled ship a heavy cargo of the needs of others and will bring back from your Lord rich blessings for them, which, if not for your intercession, may not have been obtained.

> Oh, let my hands forget their skill,
> My tongue be silent, cold, and still,
> This bounding heart forget to beat,
> If I forget God's "mercy seat"! (Ex. 25:17 KJV).
> Hugh Stowell, 1799 – 1865

From the pen of Jim Reimann:

True intercession is not only the willingness to lift another's needs to the Lord in prayer but is also being willing to put yourself in the place of that person. Loving parents, for example, would willingly take upon themselves the illness or suffering of their child if it meant the child would no longer suffer. Of course, the Lord doesn't actually move the affliction from one person to another, but intercession is an attitude of the heart — a sincere willingness to take someone's suffering upon oneself. This kind of sincerity then leads to fervent prayer and supplication, and we know "the effective, fervent prayer of a righteous man avails much" (James 5:16 NKJV). We also know that "Jesus lives forever.... Therefore he ... always lives to intercede for [us]" (Heb. 7:24 – 25). Thus, may we intercede for others.

Christ Jesus, You are indeed the greatest example of true intercession, for You took my place on the cross. O Lord, make me more like You. Help me take my eyes off myself and be truly willing to intercede for others, as You do for me.

FEBRUARY 7

Then they heard a loud voice from heaven saying to them,
"Come up here."
Revelation 11:12

From the pen of Charles Spurgeon:

Let us consider these words as an invitation from our great Forerunner as His sanctified people, taking them for a moment from their prophetic context. In due time every believer will hear "a loud voice from heaven," saying, "Come up here," which should be a subject of joyful anticipation for the saints. Instead of dreading the time when we will leave this world to go to the Father, we should be longing for the hour when we will be set free from earth. Our song should be:

> My heart is with Him on His throne,
> And scarce can stand delay;
> Each moment listening for His voice,
> "Rise up and come away."
> Robert Cleaver Chapman, 1803 – 1902

Remember, He is not calling us down to the grave, but up to the skies. Thus our heaven-born spirits should yearn to breathe their native air. Yet we should await that celestial summons with patience, for our God knows what time is best to call to us, "Come up here." Therefore, we should not wish to leave before His timing for our departure. Still, I know our strong love will make us cry,

> O Lord of Hosts, the waves divide,
> And land us all in heaven.
> John Wesley, 1703 – 1791

"But … patience [must] have her perfect work" (James 1:4 KJV), for God has ordained in His matchless wisdom the precise amount of time for His redeemed to abide here below. Surely, if it were possible to have regrets in heaven, it would be that the saints would mourn they were not here longer to do more good. Oh, for more wheat for His barn (see Matt. 3:12), more jewels for His crown. Yet this will require more work.

There is also another side to this, for if we live a shorter life, our sins will be fewer. Yet when we are fully dedicated to serving God, scattering His precious seed and reaping "a hundred times more than was sown" (Luke 8:8), we will know it is better to stay where we are. Thus, whether your Master tells you to come or to stay, be equally pleased, as long as He blesses you with His presence.

From the pen of Jim Reimann:

Do you yearn to go on to glory, especially during difficult times? It is only human to want to leave suffering behind, and as the Puritans taught, we should have heaven in our eyes throughout our earthly pilgrimage.

Yet learning to be patient regardless of our plight is one of the hardest lessons for us to learn. But we should always recognize that our precious Savior indeed knows best and has everything in control. He is our sovereign God and has predetermined how many days each of us will live in these mortal bodies, for David tells us, "All the days ordained for me were written in your book before one of them came to be" (Ps. 139:16).

FEBRUARY 8

He will save his people from their sins.

Matthew 1:21

From the pen of Charles Spurgeon:

Many people, if asked what it means to be saved, will respond, "To be saved from hell and taken to heaven." This is certainly one result of salvation, but is not even one-tenth of what this great blessing holds. It is true our Lord Jesus Christ has redeemed all His people and "rescue[d] us from the coming wrath" (1 Thess. 1:10), and He saves us from the fearful condemnation our sins brought upon us, but His triumph is far more than that.

Christ saves His people "from their sins." Oh, how sweet the deliverance from our worst enemies. Where He accomplishes a work of salvation, He casts Satan from his throne, not allowing him to be the master any longer. Thus, no one is a true Christian if "sin reign[s] in [his] mortal body" (Rom. 6:12). Sin will be in us, not being totally expelled until our spirit enters glory, but it will never have dominion over us. There will be struggle for control, a striving against the new law and new spirit God has put within us, but sin will never get the upper hand, becoming the sovereign ruler of our nature. Christ *will* be the Master of our heart, and sin must be put to death. "The Lion of the tribe of Judah" (Rev. 5:5) will prevail, while "the great dragon [will be] cast out" (Rev. 12:9 KJV).

Professing Christian, is sin subdued in you? If your life is not holy, your heart is not changed; and if your heart is not changed, you are not saved. If the Savior has not sanctified you, renewed you, and given you a hatred of sin and a love of holiness, then He has done nothing in you of a saving nature. So-called grace that does not make a person better than others is nothing but a worthless counterfeit, for Christ does not save His people *in* their sins, but *"from"* their sins."

"Without holiness no one will see the Lord" (Heb. 12:14). "Everyone who confesses the name of the Lord must turn away from wickedness" (2 Tim. 2:19). Thus, if we are not saved from sin, how can we hope to be counted as one of His people?

Lord, save me now from all evil and enable me to honor my Savior.

From the pen of Jim Reimann:

There is at least one Christian denomination that teaches that Christians have reached a point of perfect sanctification and holiness in this life. However, one day of even casual scrutiny belies that belief. The Scriptures teach that we will occasionally sin, for John wrote the following to believers: "I write this to you so that you will not sin. *But if anybody does sin*, we have one who speaks to the Father in our defense—Jesus Christ, the Righteous One" (1 John 2:1). Thus, when it comes to sin, the difference between unbelievers and believers is not that we never sin, but that our lives will not be characterized by continual, ongoing sin, for John goes on to say in the same letter: "*No one who is born of God will continue to sin*, because God's seed remains in him; he cannot go on sinning, because he has been born of God" (1 John 3:9).

Remember the words of Jesus to Paul, "I am sending you to [the Gentiles] ... so that they may receive forgiveness of sins and a place among those who are sanctified by faith in me" (Acts. 26:17 – 18).

Therefore, if you are among the sanctified, praise the Lord! If not, why not ask Him to save you today?

FEBRUARY 9

Lead us not into temptation
[but deliver us from the evil one].
Luke 11:4 and NIV footnote

From the pen of Charles Spurgeon:

What we are taught to pursue or to avoid in prayer, we should also pursue or avoid in our actions. Therefore, we very earnestly should avoid temptation and walk cautiously in the path of obedience, so that we may never tempt the Devil to tempt us. We should never enter the woods in search of the lion, for we might pay dearly for such arrogance. He may cross our path or pounce upon us from the woods, but we should have nothing to do with hunting him. Whoever does face him will have a fierce battle on his hands, even though he may ultimately defeat the lion. Thus, Christians should pray to be spared an encounter with him. This is why our Savior, who experienced temptation Himself, earnestly admonished His disciples: "Pray that you will not fall into temptation" (Luke 22:40).

No matter what, however, we will be tempted, which is why we have the prayer: "Deliver us from the evil one." God had one Son "without sin" (Heb. 4:15), but He has no son without temptation. The natural man is born to trouble as surely as sparks fly upward, and Christians are born to temptation just as certainly. We always must be alert, because Satan is like a thief, giving no hint of his approach.

Mature believers who have experienced the ways of Satan know there are certain times when he probably will attack, just as at certain seasons cold winds may be expected. Thus, Christians are put on a double alert by the fear of danger at those times, and the danger is averted by properly preparing to meet it. Prevention is better than the cure, for it is better to be so well armed that the Devil will not attack you, than to endure the dangers of a fight even though you may come away as a victor.

Pray first today that you will not be tempted, and next that if temptation is allowed, you may be "deliver[ed] ... from the evil one."

From the pen of Jim Reimann:

"No temptation has seized you except what is common to man. And God is faithful; he will not let you be tempted beyond what you can bear. But when you are tempted, he will also provide a way out so that you can stand up under it" (1 Cor. 10:13).

It's so easy to claim a verse like this one for ourselves, but first we should consider its context. What is the "way out" it mentions? The preceding verses refer to the stories of the children of Israel that "were written down as warnings for us" (1 Cor. 10:11). Thus, it is through studying, knowing, and applying the Word of God we find the "way out" of temptation.

We should prepare to do battle with the Devil and his temptations just as David did in his youth. Here is what he wrote:

How can a young man keep his way pure? By living according to your word. I seek you with all my heart; do not let me stray from your commands. *I have hidden your word in my heart that I might not sin against you.* Praise be to you, O LORD; teach me your decrees. I delight in your decrees; *I will not neglect your word.*

Psalm 119:9 – 12, 16

FEBRUARY 10

I have swept away your offenses like a cloud,
your sins like the morning mist.
Return to me, for I have redeemed you.

Isaiah 44:22

From the pen of Charles Spurgeon:

Notice from our text that our sins are like a cloud. And just as clouds have many shapes and shades, so do our transgressions. As clouds obscure the light of the sun and darken the landscape below, our sins hide the light of Jehovah's face from us and cause us to "sit in darkness and in the shadow of death" (Ps. 107:10 KJV). Our sins are earth-born things that rise from the miry places of our nature and, if allowed to accumulate, threaten us with fierce storms. Unfortunately, unlike clouds, our sins do not provide any pleasant rain showers for us, but only threaten to deluge us with a fiery flood of destruction. O you black clouds of sin, how can there be fair weather in our souls while you remain?

May my eyes joyfully dwell on the glorious act of God's divine mercy "blot[ting] out my transgressions" (Ps. 51:1). God Himself appeared on the cloudy scene, and with divine gentleness instead of anger, revealed His grace. He once and for all effectively removed my sins, not by simply blowing away the clouds, but by blotting them out of existence forever. Thus, sins no longer stand against me; I have been justified, for the great legal transaction of the cross has eternally removed my transgressions from me. On Calvary's summit, the great achievement whereby the sin of all the chosen of God was put away forever was completely and effectively performed.

May I also obey God's gracious command in our text: "Return to me." Why, after being pardoned, should I live at a distance from Him? If all my sins have been forgiven, may I never allow any fear to prevent me from boldly approaching the Lord. May I truly regret my backslidings and

be determined not to persevere in them. Thus may I strive to return to Him in the power of the Holy Spirit to the place of the closest communion possible.

O Lord, restore me even now.

From the pen of Jim Reimann:

Throughout the Old Testament, the Lord encourages His people with the words "Return to me." Israel, as God's bride, often "prostituted themselves to other gods and worshiped them" (Judg. 2:17). Still, the Lord always stood ready to restore His people to His fellowship if they would only return to Him in repentance and humility. Here is how Joel declared this truth to God's people:

"'Even now,' declares the LORD, 'return to me with all your heart, with fasting and weeping and mourning.' Rend your heart and not your garments. Return to the LORD your God, for he is gracious and compassionate, slow to anger and abounding in love, and he relents from sending calamity. Who knows? He may turn and have pity and leave behind a blessing — grain offerings and drink offerings for the LORD your God" (Joel 2:12 – 14).

We as Christians are often unfaithful to the Lord as well. Yet we should remember that our gracious God is a God of restoration, for He went on to say through His prophet Joel: "I will repay you for the years the locusts have eaten. You will have plenty to eat, until you are full, and you will praise the name of the LORD your God, who has worked wonders for you; never again will my people be shamed" (Joel 2:25 – 26).

FEBRUARY 11

You have forsaken your first love.

Revelation 2:4

From the pen of Charles Spurgeon:

We should always remember that greatest of all hours — the moment we first saw the Lord, laid down our burden of sin, received His promise, rejoiced in our complete salvation, and then went our way in peace. It was like springtime to our soul, with winter suddenly gone. The rumble of Mount Sinai's thunder was hushed, the flash of its lightning was seen no longer, reconciliation with God was at hand, His law threatened no vengeance, and justice demanded no punishment.

Then the flowers of hope, love, peace, and patience sprang from our hearts, as well as the hyacinth of repentance, the snowdrop of pure holiness, the crocus of golden faith, and the daffodil of early love — all adorning the garden of our soul. The time of the singing of birds had come, and we rejoiced with thanksgiving, magnifying the holy name of our forgiving God. Our resolve was:

Lord, I am Yours — wholly Yours. All I am and all I have I devote to You. With Your blood You purchased me, so may I be spent in Your service. In life and in death may I be consecrated to You.

But how have we kept this resolution? Our early love burned with a holy flame of devotion to Jesus, but does it burn as brightly today? Couldn't Jesus say to us as well, "I hold this against you: You have forsaken your first love" (Rev. 2:4). Regrettably, we have done very little for our Master's glory. Our winter has lasted far too long, for we are cold as ice when we should be feeling a summer glow and should be blooming with sacred flowers. We offer Him pennies when He deserves dollars — even more, He deserves our heart's blood, which should be invested in the service of His church and His truth. How can we continue like this!

O Lord, after You have so richly blessed us, forgive us for being so ungrateful and for becoming so indifferent to Your will and Your work. Awaken us to return to our "first love" and to "the things [we] did at first" (Rev. 2:5). Send the warmth of spring to our hearts, O "sun of righteousness" (Mal. 4:2).

From the pen of Jim Reimann:

Jesus begins His letter to the church in Ephesus in Revelation 2 with a commendation: "I know your deeds, your hard work and your perseverance. I know that you cannot tolerate wicked men, that you have tested those who claim to be apostles but are not, and have found them false. You have persevered and have endured hardships for my name, and have not grown weary" (vv. 2–3).

Next He follows His commendation with a complaint: "Yet I hold this against you: You have forsaken your first love" (v. 4).

Finally, He offers His words of correction: "Remember the height from which you have fallen! Repent and do the things you did at first" (v. 5).

As His people, we must be careful not only to do the "hard work" of Christ, as the Ephesians were doing, but also to do whatever we do in the right way — in love, and certainly without forgetting our "first love."

Jesus, may I never forget You — my "first love." And may I never need to hear Your complaints and correction, but only Your commendations, such as, "Well done, good and faithful servant!" (Matt. 25:21).

FEBRUARY 12

He will give you another Counselor
to be with you forever.

John 14:16

From the pen of Charles Spurgeon:

The Father revealed Himself to believers of old before the coming of His Son, and was known to Abraham, Isaac, and Jacob as God Almighty. Then Jesus came to earth in the person of the Son and was the delight of His people's eyes. Next, at the time of the Redeemer's ascension to heaven, the Holy Spirit became the head of the current church age, and His power was gloriously revealed at Pentecost and after. Thus, Christ's Spirit remains with His people today and is "'Immanuel' — which means, 'God with us'" (Matt. 1:23), dwelling in and with His people, giving them life, guiding them, and ruling in their midst.

But do we acknowledge His presence as we should? We cannot control the Holy Spirit, for He is completely sovereign in all He does. Nevertheless, are we sufficiently desirous of His help and careful lest we provoke Him to withdraw His aid? Without Him we can do nothing, but by His almighty power, extraordinary results can be produced. Yet each result is completely dependent upon the Spirit either revealing or concealing His power. Are we continually looking to Him for our inner life and outward service, offering Him the respectful dependence He is due? Don't we often go before He calls and act independently of His help?

Thus, let us humble ourselves today for our past neglect of Him, and pray for His heavenly dew to fall upon us, His sacred oil to anoint us, and His celestial flame to burn within us. The Holy Spirit is not a temporary gift, for He ever abides with His saints. All we must do is seek Him in the proper way and He will be found by us. Yes, He is a "jealous God" (Ex. 20:5), but He is also "full of compassion" (Ps. 86:15 KJV), and if He leaves in anger, He will return in mercy. In humility and tenderness, He never wearies of us, but always waits to be gracious.

> Sin has been hammering my heart
> Into a hardness, void of love;
> Let supplying grace to cross his art
> Fall from above.
>
> George Herbert, 1593 – 1633

From the pen of Jim Reimann:

In Old Testament times, the Holy Spirit would come upon people for a special work for the Lord and would later depart once that work was accomplished. The Word even says "the Spirit of God came upon" men such as Balaam (Num. 24:2), who was nothing but a pagan sorcerer, thus showing God's complete sovereignty over even the ungodly among us. Later we see that "the Spirit of the LORD came upon" Gideon (Judg. 6:34), Samson (Judg. 15:14), Saul (1 Sam. 10:10), and Ezekiel (Ezek. 11:5), just to name a few.

The only exception we see in the Old Testament, one where God's Spirit continually remained on someone, is in the life of David. When the Lord selected him to be the next king of Israel, we are told: "Samuel took the horn of oil and anointed him in the presence of his brothers, and *from that day on the Spirit of the LORD came upon David in power*" (1 Sam. 16:13). What a beautiful foreshadowing of the indwelling life of Christ, through the power of His Holy Spirit, in the life of the very king of Israel through whom the Messiah would ultimately come.

FEBRUARY 13

Therefore, there is now no condemnation.

Romans 8:1

From the pen of Charles Spurgeon:

Come, dear soul, and think of this. As a believer in Jesus, you are actually and effectively cleared from all guilt; you have been freed from prison. Thus, you are no longer in the bonds of slavery, you have been delivered from the bondage of the law, you are freed from sin, and you may walk as freely as anyone, for your Savior's blood has bought your full release and freedom. You now have the right to approach your Father's throne without fearing any flames of vengeance or fiery swords, for Justice cannot strike the innocent. All your disabilities have been taken away as well, for once you were unable to see your Father's face, but today you are fully able. Once you could not speak with Him, but now you may approach His throne with boldness. Once the fear of hell hung over you, but now you have no fear of it whatsoever, for how can there be punishment for the guiltless?

"Whoever believes ... is not condemned" (John 3:18), and thus cannot be punished. Even more, all the privileges you might have enjoyed if you had never sinned are yours now that you are justified. All the blessings you would have had if you had kept the law, and more, are yours because Christ has kept it for you. All the love and acceptance that perfect obedience could have obtained from God belongs to you, because Jesus was perfectly obedient on your behalf. He has imputed all His worthiness to your account, so that you may be exceedingly rich through Him, who for your sake became exceedingly poor.

Oh, how great is the debt of love and gratitude I owe my Savior!

A debtor to mercy alone,
Of covenant mercy I sing;
Nor fear with Your righteousness on,
My person and offerings to bring:
The terrors of law and of God,
With me can have nothing to do;
My Savior's obedience and blood
Hide all my transgressions from view.

Augustus Montague Toplady, 1740 – 78

From the pen of Jim Reimann:

Our topic today is justification, the act by which God declares believers in Christ to be righteous in His sight in spite of their sin. It is a once-for-all change in one's legal standing before God. As believers, we have been declared "not guilty" in His court of law. This is why "there is now no condemnation."

Some teach that *justified* means "just as if I'd never sinned." From our perspective, that appears to be true, but that view alone cheapens God's grace. We should view justification, and its cost, from God's perspective. From eternity past, He has viewed His Son as "the Lamb that was slain from the creation of the world" (Rev. 13:8). Then John, who was being shown the future, described Jesus as follows: "I saw a Lamb, looking as if it had been slain, standing in the center of the throne" (Rev. 5:6).

Thus, Jesus has borne the marks of our sin since eternity past, and He will continue to bear them throughout eternity future. Never forget the price He paid.

FEBRUARY 14

The woman ... had been instantly healed.

Luke 8:47

From the pen of Charles Spurgeon:

This is one of the most touching and instructional of the Savior's miracles. This woman believed that the "power [had] gone out from [Christ]" (v. 46) through some law of necessity, without His knowledge or direct will. She knew nothing of the generosity of Jesus' character, or she would not have gone behind Him to "steal" a cure He was so ready to bestow. Yet misery should always place itself directly in the face of mercy. If she had known of the love of Jesus' heart, she would have said, "I only have to get where He can see me, for His omniscience will teach Him of my problem, and His love will immediately work a cure for me."

We admire her faith, but we marvel at her ignorance, for as soon as she obtained her cure, she rejoiced in trembling fear. She was glad Christ's power had worked a miracle in her, but she feared He might withdraw the blessing of His grace. Little did she comprehend the fullness of His love.

None of us has as clear a view of Him as we might wish. We don't fully "grasp how ... high and deep is the love of Christ" (Eph. 3:18), yet we do know for certain He is too good to withdraw a gift from a trembling soul. But here is the true miracle: although she had such little knowledge, her faith was real faith, which not only saved her but saved her "instantly," as our text declares. There was no wearisome delay — faith's miracle was instantaneous — for "if you have faith as small as a mustard seed" (Matt. 17:20), salvation is your immediate and eternal possession. As long as we are listed among the Lord's children, even though we may be the weakest of the family,

we are His heirs by faith, and no power, whether human or demonic, can remove our salvation. We may not be as bold as John, "who had leaned back against Jesus at the supper" (John 21:20), but if we will dare to press in "behind him and [touch] the edge of his cloak" (Luke 8:44), we will be "made whole" (Matt. 9:22 KJV).

Take courage, timid one. "Your faith has saved you; go in peace" (Luke 7:50). "Therefore, since we have been justified through faith, we have peace with God through our Lord Jesus Christ" (Rom. 5:1).

From the pen of Jim Reimann:

Though trembling, this poor woman boldly touched the Lord, believing if she could touch "the edge of his cloak," she would be healed. How did she come by that belief? Jesus said to her, "Daughter, your faith has healed you" (Luke 8:48). But in what or in whom was her faith?

Here was a Jewish woman, who may not have had full understanding of Jesus' true character, but she undoubtedly believed He was the Messiah of the Old Testament prophesies. She apparently knew the Messiah, or "the sun of righteousness," would come "with healing in [His] *wings*" (Mal. 4:2), for in Hebrew, the word for *wing* is "*kanaph*." It is no coincidence the same word is used for *corner* in the words Ruth spoke to Boaz: "Spread the *corner* of your garment over me, since you are a kinsman-redeemer" (Ruth 3:9).

Thus, this woman was placing her faith in Jesus not just for physical healing, but was trusting Him as the Messiah. She touched the hem of His garment because, as the Messiah, He alone would come with healing in His "*kanaph*."

FEBRUARY 15

They have made You glad.

Psalm 45:8 NKJV

From the pen of Charles Spurgeon:

Who are those privileged enough to make the Savior glad? Is it possible they are His church — His people? He makes us glad, but how can we make Him glad? The answer is this: by our love. Yet we think of our love as somewhat cold and weak, and unfortunately we must sorrowfully confess that often is true. Nevertheless, our love is very sweet to Christ. Listen to His tribute of that love in this joyful song: "How delightful is your love, my sister, my bride! How much more pleasing is your love than wine!" (Song 4:10).

Loving believer, see how He delights in you. When you lean your head on His shoulder, you not only receive from Him, but you also give Him joy; when you lovingly gaze on His glorious face, you not only receive comfort, but you also impart delight. Our praise gives Him joy, not simply from the lyrics on our lips but also the melody of our heart's deep gratitude. Our gifts are very pleasing to Him too, for He loves to see us lay our time, talents, and possessions upon the altar, not because of the value of what we give, but because of the loving motive behind the gifts. Even modest offerings from His saints are more pleasing to Him than mountains of gold and silver.

Holiness is like frankincense and myrrh to him. Forgive your enemy and you make Christ glad; give of your possessions to the poor and He rejoices; be the vessel for the saving of souls, and you give Him the gift of seeing "the travail of his soul" (Isa. 53:11 KJV); proclaim His gospel and you are "a pleasing aroma" (Ex. 29:18) to Him; and share with those who have never heard of His cross, and you have given Him honor.

It is in your power even now to break the "alabaster jar" (Matt. 26:7) of "the oil of gladness" (Isa. 61:3) in order to pour it upon Jesus' head, just as the woman did of whom He said, "Wherever this gospel is preached … what she has done will also be told, in memory of her" (Matt. 26:13). Will you hesitate? Or will you offer the fragrance of "myrrh and aloes and cassia" (Ps. 45:8) of your heart's praise to your beloved Savior?

Yes Lord, "from palaces adorned with ivory" (Ps. 45:8) You will hear the songs of the saints.

From the pen of Jim Reimann:

Isn't it amazing that our actions can bring great joy to our almighty God. As we walk in obedience, we exhibit our love for Him and make His heart glad. May the following words of David and the writer of Hebrews express the attitude of our hearts today:

Let the heavens rejoice, let the earth be glad; let them say among the nations, "The LORD reigns!" Let the sea resound, and all that is in it; let the fields be jubilant, and everything in them! Then the trees of the forest will sing, they will sing for joy before the LORD, for he comes to judge the earth. Give thanks to the LORD, for he is good; his love endures forever.

1 Chronicles 16:31 – 34

Here we do not have an enduring city, but we are looking for the city that is to come. Through Jesus, therefore, let us continually offer to God a sacrifice of praise — the fruit of lips that confess his name. And do not forget to do good and to share with others, for with such sacrifices God is pleased.

Hebrews 13:14 – 16

FEBRUARY 16

You gave your good Spirit to instruct them.

Nehemiah 9:20

From the pen of Charles Spurgeon:

All too common is the sin of forgetting the Holy Spirit, which is nothing less than foolishness and ingratitude. Certainly He deserves much more from us, for He is good — supremely good, good in His essence. The Spirit shares in the threefold attribution of the words "Holy, holy, holy" (Isa. 6:3; Rev. 4:8) that ascend to the triune Jehovah. He is undiluted purity, truth, and grace. He is lovingly kind, tenderly withstands our waywardness, strives with our rebelliousness, bestows life from our death in sin, and finally prepares us for the heavens above as a loving mother nurtures her child.

How generous, forgiving, and tender is this patient Spirit of God. But not only is He good in His attributes, He is also good in His actions, for all His works are good to the highest degree possible. He suggests good thoughts, prompts good actions, reveals good truths, applies good promises, assists in good accomplishments, and leads to good results. He is the author and sustainer of all spiritual good in the entire world, and heaven itself owes the perfect character of its redeemed inhabitants to His work. By holy authority the Spirit is officially good, whether as Comforter, Instructor, Guide, Sanctifier, Life-Giver, or Intercessor. He executes His office well and His every work is filled with the highest good for God's church. In fact, they who yield to His influences become good, they who obey His promptings do good, and they who live under His power receive good.

Thus, let us respond to the Spirit with the proper gratitude His goodness dictates. Let us revere, adore, and bless Him forever as God over all. Let us appropriate His power and recognize our need of Him by waiting upon Him in all our spiritual endeavors. Let us continually seek His help, never grieve Him, and give Him praise at every opportunity.

The church will never thrive until it more reverently believes in the Holy Spirit. He is so good and kind that it is quite sad indeed that He should ever be grieved by our inattention and outright neglect.

From the pen of Jim Reimann:

The Holy Spirit plays several important roles in the lives of God's people. The context of today's verse tells of the people of Nehemiah's day recounting their ancestors' deliverance from Egypt, and from this we know that even the people of the Old Testament knew of the Spirit's role as our Teacher. Of course, Jesus taught that once He ascended to heaven, His Holy Spirit would indwell His people forever, but that the Spirit's role would be essentially the same as in days of old. He said, "The Holy Spirit ... will teach you all things and will remind you of everything I have said to you" (John 14:26), and "The Spirit of truth ... will guide you into all truth" (John 16:13). He also said that when we stand trial for our faith, "The Holy Spirit will teach you at that time what you should say" (Luke 12:12).

But for the Spirit to do His work in us, we must be teachable. It is normal to resist a "know-it-all," and this is true of the Lord as well, for "God opposes the proud" (James 4:6). Thus, may we humble ourselves before Him and be ready to learn from His Holy Spirit — our Teacher. May this be our prayer even now:

"Teach me to do your will, for you are my God; may your good Spirit lead me on level ground" (Ps. 143:10).

FEBRUARY 17

... even though I the LORD was there.

Ezekiel 35:10

From the pen of Charles Spurgeon:

Edom's princes saw both Israel and Judah "laid waste" (v. 12), and thus counted on an easy conquest. But there was one great obstacle in their way that was unknown to them — "the LORD was there" — and it was His presence that gave security to His chosen land. Whatever secret schemes and devices the enemies of God's people may have, this same effective barrier of His presence is always there to thwart their plans. The saints are God's heritage, He is always in their midst, and He will protect His own.

What great comfort this assurance yields to us through our troubles and spiritual conflicts. We are constantly opposed — yet perpetually preserved. Satan attacks our faith, but our faith defies the power of "the flaming arrows of the evil one" (Eph. 6:16). And not only are they turned aside, but they also are quenched upon "the shield of faith" (Eph. 6:16), for "the LORD is there." Our good works are targets of Satan's attacks. In fact, there is nothing — whether a saint's works, gifts, or virtues — not targeted by hellish bullets. Whether our hope, bright and shining; our love, warm and fervent; our all-enduring patience; or our zeal, flaming with coals of fire; the ancient enemy of everything good attempts to destroy it. But remember, the only reason anything virtuous or pleasing remains in us is this — "the LORD is there."

And if the Lord is with us through life, we need never fear a lack of confidence at our death, for when it is our time to die, we will find "the LORD is there" as well. Even when the waves are the most stormy and the water the most freezing, our feet will touch bottom and we will know

things are still good, for our feet will stand upon the Rock of Ages when time is slipping away.

Beloved saint, from the beginning of a Christian's life to its very end, the only reason you do not perish is — "the LORD is there." Not until the God of everlasting love changes, leaving His elect to perish, will His church be destroyed. Yet that will happen then, and only then, because it is written in His Word, Jehovah-Shammah — "the LORD is there."

From the pen of Jim Reimann:

It is comforting to know that the eventuality Spurgeon mentions in his closing today — that we as His people will be destroyed only if God changes — is an utter impossibility! His Word says, "I the LORD do not change. So you ... are not destroyed" (Mal. 3:6), and "He who is the Glory of Israel does not lie or change his mind; for he is not a man, that he should change his mind" (1 Sam. 15:29).

We are also told, "The LORD himself goes before you and will be with you; he will never leave you nor forsake you. Do not be afraid; do not be discouraged" (Deut. 31:8). Thus, we can be ever thankful that not only will He never change, but also that "the LORD is [always] there."

In fact, one of the Lord's names, as Spurgeon mentioned, is Jehovah-Shammah, which is Hebrew for "the LORD is there." It is the symbolic title given by Ezekiel to Jerusalem, which he saw in a vision. This is what he wrote: "And the name of the city from that time on will be: THE LORD IS THERE" (Ezek. 48:35).

"O LORD, do not forsake me; be not far from me, O my God" (Ps. 38:21).

FEBRUARY 18

Father, I have sinned.

Luke 15:18

From the pen of Charles Spurgeon:

Those whom Christ has washed in His precious blood need never confess their sins as guilty criminals before God the Judge, for Christ legally has removed their sins from them forever. Therefore they no longer stand where they can be condemned, for they are once for all "accepted in the beloved" (Eph. 1:6 KJV). Having become His children, but nevertheless children who continue to offend, shouldn't they daily go before their heavenly Father to confess their sins?

Human nature teaches erring children it is their duty to confess their sinfulness to their earthly father, and God's grace in the heart of His children teaches us that we as Christians owe our heavenly Father the same honor. We sin each day and should never rest without seeking His daily pardon. If the sins against our Father are not taken immediately to Him to be washed away by the cleansing power of the Lord Jesus, what will be the consequence? If we do not seek forgiveness and are not washed from these offenses against our Father, we will feel we are some distance from Him. We will doubt His love for us, will be fearful of Him, and will be afraid to pray to Him. Ultimately, we will become like the prodigal, who, although he was still the father's child, was far from him.

But if we will go to Him as His child with the attitude of true sorrow for having offended such a gracious and loving Parent, confessing all our sins and not resting until we realize we are forgiven, we will feel the holy love of our Father. Then we will walk through the Christian life not only saved but also enjoying peace in God through Jesus Christ our Lord.

There is a vast difference between confessing sin as a guilty criminal and confessing sin as a child, and the Father's embrace is the place for repentant children to confess. Christians have been cleansed once and for all, but our feet still need to be washed from the defilement of our daily walk as children of God.

From the pen of Jim Reimann:

"We have been made holy through the sacrifice of the body of Jesus Christ once for all" (Heb. 10:10), but as Paul said, in essence, we are all still in process. He wrote, "Not that I have ... already been made perfect, but I press on to take hold of that for which Christ Jesus took hold of me" (Phil. 3:12).

Yes, the Lord "chose us in him before the creation of the world to be holy and blameless in his sight" (Eph. 1:4), and that is how He sees us. God views us through the precious blood of His Son, and thus sees us as perfect. However, we do continue to sin in this life, which is why John wrote the following: "If we claim to be without sin, we deceive ourselves and the truth is not in us" (1 John 1:8). But then he goes on to describe the process of the daily washing we all need, saying, "If we confess our sins, he is faithful and just and will forgive us our sins and purify us from all unrighteousness" (v. 9). Thus, may this be our daily prayer:

> "Good and upright is the LORD; therefore he instructs sinners in his ways. He guides the humble in what is right and teaches them his way. All the ways of the LORD are loving and faithful for those who keep the demands of his covenant. For the sake of your name, O LORD, forgive my iniquity, though it is great" (Ps. 25:8 – 11).

FEBRUARY 19

The first thing Andrew did
was to find his brother Simon.

John 1:41

From the pen of Charles Spurgeon:

Andrew's story is one of the greatest examples of a healthy spiritual life, for as soon as He found Christ, he began to find others. No one will believe you have truly tasted of the honey of the gospel if you eat it all yourself, for true grace puts an end to spiritual monopolies. Andrew first found his own brother Simon, and then found others, indicating our relationships have a strong bearing on our initial individual efforts.

Andrew did well to begin with Simon, for there are doubtless many Christians who would more quickly give away gospel tracts at other people's houses than their own. No doubt there are also many people engaged in useful mission work abroad, but who are neglecting their own particular sphere of usefulness at home. You may or may not be called to evangelize people in a particular place, but certainly you are called to see to your own employees, friends, and family members. Let your faith begin at home.

Many business people export their best products, but a Christian should not. Regardless of where he is, especially in his own family, he should take care to put forth the sweetest fruit of his spiritual life and testimony. When Andrew went to find his brother, he could never have imagined how influential and prominent Simon ultimately would become. Simon Peter was worth ten Andrews, at least from what we gather from history, and yet it was Andrew who was instrumental in bringing Simon Peter to Jesus. You may be somewhat lacking in talent yourself, but you may be the means the Lord uses to bring someone to Christ who will become quite prominent in God's grace and service.

Dear friend, you know very little of the possibilities that lie within you. Perhaps you will only speak a word to a child, but within that child may be a slumbering, yet impressive, heart that may stir God's church in the years to come.

Andrew may have had only "two talents" (Matt. 25:15), but he found Peter.

"Go and do likewise" (Luke 10:37).

From the pen of Jim Reimann:

Remember how excited you were when Jesus saved you? Remember how you couldn't keep the good news of the gospel to yourself? If you took an honest look at your life today, however, would you be forced to confess that "you have forsaken your first love" (Rev. 2:4)?

Paul is a great example of someone who never lost his "first love." And he encouraged other believers, and us today, saying, "Never be lacking in zeal, but keep your spiritual fervor, serving the Lord" (Rom. 12:11). Here is what he said to Timothy, "I give you this charge: Preach the Word; be prepared in season and out of season" (2 Tim. 4:1 – 2).

Do we understand what the words "in season and out of season" truly mean? They mean to be prepared to share the gospel when it is popular or fashionable, and when it is not; when conditions are favorable, and when they are not. Who of us is ready to respond to God's call to share our faith at all times, even if it means sharing with the members of our own family?

Can I say with unwavering zeal, "Here am I. Send me!" (Isa. 6:8)?

FEBRUARY 20

Then Jesus was led by the Spirit into the desert
to be tempted by the devil.

Matthew 4:1

From the pen of Charles Spurgeon:

Being holy does not prevent temptation, for Jesus was tempted. When Satan tempts us, his sparks fall on tinder, but in Christ's case, it was like sparks falling into water. Even so, the enemy persisted in his evil work. Thus, if the Devil continued to strike when there was no result, consider how much more he will do when he knows the flammable framework of our hearts. Although you are in the process of becoming perfectly sanctified by the Holy Spirit, you can still expect the great dog of hell to continue to bark at you in the meantime. On this earth we should expect to be tempted, and we should realize that taking precautions such as secluding ourselves from others will not protect us. Jesus Christ was led away from human contact into the wilderness but still was tempted by the Devil. Solitude has its place and benefits, and may be useful in keeping "the lust of the eyes, and the pride of life" (1 John 2:16 KJV) in check, but remember that the Devil will follow us into the most beautiful places of retreat as well.

And never suppose it is only the most worldly minded among us who have terrible thoughts and blasphemous temptations, for even the most spiritually minded people must endure them, and it is when we are in the most holy of places that we may suffer the darkest temptations. Nor will being fully consecrated or dedicated to the holy things of God insure you against satanic temptation, for Christ was consecrated through and through. He said, "My food ... is to do the will of him who sent me" (John 4:34), and yet He was tempted.

Your heart may have the glow of an angelic flame of love for Jesus, but the Devil will still attempt to bring you down to the lukewarmness of Laodicea (see Rev. 3:14 – 16). There will never be a time when God will allow Christians to lay their armor aside until Satan ceases to tempt us. Thus, in this life, like the knights of old in times of war, we must sleep with our "helmet of salvation" (Eph. 6:17) and "breastplate of righteousness in place" (Eph. 6:14), for the archdeceiver will seize our first unguarded moment to make us his prey.

Lord, keep me watchful at all times, and, as You did for David, "[deliver] me from the paw of the lion and the paw of the bear" (1 Sam. 17:37).

From the pen of Jim Reimann:

The story of Jesus' temptation in the wilderness highlights the importance of knowing the Word of God and its context. Just as Satan did in tempting Eve in the Garden of Eden, he quoted God's Word in tempting Jesus. In Eve's case, he changed and twisted God's words; in Jesus' case, he lifted a verse from its context and added words to it.

We should always beware, knowing that Satan knows God's Word and will tempt us to question it. That is why it is essential for us to know precisely what the Lord has said. This knowledge will only be gleaned, however, by "diligently study[ing] the Scriptures" (John 5:39), and "by constant use," thereby "train[ing] [our]selves to distinguish good from evil" (Heb. 5:14).

Always remember how Jesus overcame Satan's temptation: "It is written ..." (Matt. 4:4), "It is also written ..." (v. 7), and finally, "For it is written ..." (v. 10).

FEBRUARY 21

"Do you understand what you are reading?"
Philip asked.
Acts 8:30

From the pen of Charles Spurgeon:

Like Philip, we should be competent teachers of others. And if we have a more informed understanding of the Word of God, we will be less likely to be "blown here and there by every wind of teaching" (Eph. 4:14). The Holy Spirit is the Author of the Scriptures, and it is He alone who can enlighten us to understand them correctly. Thus, we should constantly ask for His teaching and His guidance "into all truth" (John 16:13).

When the prophet Daniel sought to interpret Nebuchadnezzar's dream, what did he do? He dedicated himself to earnest prayer, asking God to reveal the dream and its interpretation to him (see Dan. 2). The apostle John in his vision on the Isle of Patmos "saw ... a scroll ... sealed with seven seals" with "no one ... worthy to open the scroll or look inside" (Rev. 5:1, 4). Soon, however, "the Lion of the tribe of Judah" who "[had] triumphed" was "able to open the scroll" (v. 5). But this happened only after John had "wept and wept" (v. 4). His tears had become liquid prayers, and as far as he was concerned, they were the sacred keys to unseal the scroll.

Therefore, if you desire to be filled "with the knowledge of [God's] will through all spiritual wisdom and understanding" (Col. 1:9) for the benefit of yourself and others, remember that prayer is your best means of "study." Like Daniel, you will understand the dream and its interpretation when you have sought it through the Lord in prayer; and like John, you will see the "seven seals" after you have "wept and wept." Stones are not broken except through the earnest use of a hammer, and often the stonemason must go down on his knees to accomplish his task.

In the same manner, you must use the hammer of diligence and employ the knees of prayer in order to unlock God's truth. There is no hard doctrine of His revelation that is important for you to understand that will not be shattered into pieces by the exercise of prayer and faith. The power of prayer allows you to force your way through anything, for ideas and reason are like steel wedges that give you a hold upon truth, but prayer is the lever that forces the iron chest of sacred mystery wide open so you may discover its hidden treasure.

From the pen of Jim Reimann:

Job asked, "Where then does wisdom come from? Where does understanding dwell? ... God understands the way to it and he alone knows where it dwells, for he views the ends of the earth and sees everything under the heavens.... He looked at wisdom and appraised it; he confirmed it and tested it. And he said to man, 'The fear of the Lord — that is wisdom, and to shun evil is understanding'" (Job 28:20, 23 – 24, 27 – 28).

Seeking wisdom is a worthy pursuit, but finding it requires diligence, for Solomon wrote:

My son, if you accept my words and store up my commands within you, turning your ear to wisdom and applying your heart to understanding, and if you call out for insight and cry aloud for understanding, and if you look for it as for silver and search for it as for hidden treasure, then you will understand the fear of the LORD and find the knowledge of God. For the LORD gives wisdom, and from his mouth come knowledge and understanding.

Proverbs 2:1 – 6

FEBRUARY 22

The LORD is slow to anger
and great in power.

Nahum 1:3

From the pen of Charles Spurgeon:

Jehovah "is slow to anger." When the Lord sends mercy into the world, it streaks to earth on winged steeds, with the wheels of its chariot red hot; but when He sends forth His wrath, it slowly plods along with unhurried steps, for God takes no pleasure in a sinner's death. The Lord's rod of mercy is continually in His outstretched hands, while His sword of justice is kept in its sheath, held down by His pierced hand of love that bled for the sins of men.

"The LORD is slow to anger" because He is "great in power." Someone who is truly "great in power" has power over himself. Thus, when God restrains Himself, He exhibits true power, for power that can suppress omnipotence surpasses omnipotence. A person who has a strong mind can bear insults for a very long time and will only resent the wrong when a sense of right demands his action. A weak mind is quickly irritated, while a strong mind bears wrongdoing like an unmovable rocky shore easily absorbs a thousand waves breaking upon it — waves which simply cast their pitiful malicious spray upon its summit.

The Lord takes note of His enemies, but He holds His anger. If He were less than the Divinity He is, He long ago would have sent forth the full force of His thunder and emptied the artillery of heaven. He would have blasted the earth with the astounding fires of its lower regions, totally destroying mankind. But the greatness of His power has granted us mercy instead.

Dear reader, what is your position today? Can you in humble faith look to Jesus and say, "You are my substitute, my rock, and the one in whom I trust"? If so, beloved Christian, don't be afraid of God's power, for by faith you have fled to Christ for refuge, and thus the power of God need no longer terrify you any more than the sword and shield of a warrior need terrify those whom He loves. Rejoice instead that He who is "great in power" is your Father and Friend.

From the pen of Jim Reimann:

Today's verse is taken from the following context:

> The LORD is a jealous and avenging God.... The LORD takes vengeance on his foes and maintains his wrath against his enemies. *The LORD is slow to anger and great in power;* the LORD will not leave the guilty unpunished.
>
> Nahum 1:2 – 3

Though these verses do not include the word *justice*, God's justice is its underlying theme. Notice that "the LORD is slow to anger," yet He "will not leave the guilty unpunished." In fact, the Lord *cannot* leave sin unpunished and remain just and holy. Paul taught this truth in the following way:

> God presented [Christ Jesus] as a sacrifice of atonement, through faith in his blood. *He did this to demonstrate his justice,* because in his forbearance he had left the sins committed beforehand unpunished — *he did it to demonstrate his justice at the present time, so as to be just* and the one who justifies those who have faith in Jesus.
>
> Romans 3:25-26

Yes, "the LORD is slow to anger," but "He has set a day when he will judge the world with justice" (Acts 17:31). Yet as Spurgeon said, Christians need never fear God's power or justice, for "since we have been justified through faith, we have peace with God through our Lord Jesus Christ" (Rom. 5:1).

Lord, "You are my refuge in the day of disaster" (Jer. 17:17).

FEBRUARY 23

Take up the cross,
and follow me.
Mark 10:21 KJV

From the pen of Charles Spurgeon:

You did not make your own cross, although unbelief is a master carpenter when it comes to making crosses. Nor are you permitted to choose your own cross, although self-will desires to do so and thereby make you your own lord and master. No, your cross is prepared and ordained for you by God's divine love, and you are to accept it with cheerfulness; you are to "take up [your] cross" as your appointed badge and burden, not to idly stand by objecting over it.

Jesus invites you to submit your shoulder to His easy yoke today, "for [His] yoke *is* easy" (Matt. 11:30). Do not resist it in anger, trample it in pride, fall under it in despair, or run from it in fear; but "take up the cross" like a true follower of Jesus. He was a cross-bearer Himself and leads the way through the path of sorrow, so you could not desire a better guide. And if He carried a cross, what more honorable burden could you desire? The Via Crucis (the Way of the Cross) is the way of safety, so never fear to tread its difficult paths.

Beloved Christian, the cross is not made of feathers or lined with velvet, but is heavy and hard to disobedient shoulders. But for those who are obedient, remember, it is not an iron cross, though your fears may have pictured it as such. It is a wooden cross, one a person *can* carry, for the "man of sorrows" (Isa. 53:3) tested the load. Thus, "take up [your] cross" and through the power of the Spirit of God you will soon be so in love with it that, like Moses, you would not exchange "disgrace for the sake of Christ" for all "the treasures of Egypt" (Heb. 11:26).

Remember, Jesus carried it, giving it a sweet aroma. Also remember that it will soon be followed by a crown. Therefore, the thought that it is "achieving for us an eternal glory" (2 Cor. 4:17) will greatly lighten the current heaviness of trouble. May the Lord help you bow your spirit in submission to His divine will. And may you willingly carry today's cross with the holy and submissive spirit that truly becomes a follower of the Crucified.

From the pen of Jim Reimann:

The "health-wealth" theology of today, though prevalent, is unbiblical. This so-called "Word of Faith" teaching is actually based on anything but faith, for the burden lies with the believer rather than recognizing faith as God's gift. Reduced to its essence, faith then becomes works dependent on the person, not the Lord.

A biblical walk of faith is never easy, indeed requiring a believer to carry his cross. Paul tied the truth that faith is a gift of God to suffering, saying, "It has been granted to you on behalf of Christ not only to believe on him, but also to suffer for him" (Phil. 1:29).

In fact, today's text is from the story of the rich man who treasured his wealth more than Christ, which is why Jesus told him, "Sell everything you have and give to the poor, and you will have treasure in heaven" (Mark 10:21). The man's problem wasn't his wealth, but the emphasis he placed on it. Consider these words of Jesus:

The pagans run after all these things, and your heavenly Father knows that you need them. *But seek first his kingdom and his righteousness*, and all these things will be given to you as well.

Matthew 6:32 – 33

FEBRUARY 24

Then the angel of the LORD said,
"LORD Almighty, how long will you withhold mercy from Jerusalem …?"
So the LORD spoke kind and comforting words to the angel who talked with me.

Zechariah 1:12 – 13

From the pen of Charles Spurgeon:

What a precious response to a question rising from distress. Dear church, let us rejoice in it today. "O Zion" (Zech. 2:7), there are good things in store for you, your trial will soon be over, your children will soon be brought forth, and your captivity will end. Patiently submit to the Lord's "rod of correction" (Prov. 29:15) for a season, and though enduring a time of darkness, maintain your trust in God, for His love still burns brightly toward you. God loves His church with a love much deeper than human comprehension, for He loves her with His whole infinite heart.

Thus, may Zion's children be of good courage, for God's church cannot be far from flourishing when He speaks "kind and comforting words." What are these words? They are these: "I am very jealous for Jerusalem and Zion" (Zech. 1:14). The Lord loves His church so much He grieves when she strays to others, yet even then He cannot stand for her to suffer too harshly or for too long. He protects her from His enemies and is displeased with them when they increase her misery.

Even when God seems to have withdrawn from His church the most, His heart remains warm toward her. History tells us that whenever God uses His rod to chasten His servants, He always breaks it afterwards, as though He loathes the rod that caused His children pain. "As a father has compassion on his children, so the LORD has compassion on those who fear him" (Ps. 103:13). God has not forgotten us just because He strikes us in discipline; His blows are not evidence of a lack of love. And if this is true of His church collectively, it is also true for each individual member. You may fear the Lord has passed you by, but that is not true, for "He [who] determines the number of the stars and calls them each by name" (Ps. 147:4) is in no danger of forgetting His own children. He knows your situation as thoroughly as though you were the only creature He ever made or the only saint He ever loved. Therefore, approach Him and be at peace.

From the pen of Jim Reimann:

Today's Scripture means even more when we understand it was written during the time of Judah's return after seventy years of Babylonian captivity. God's people were experiencing deliverance once again. Yes, they had been severely disciplined for following other gods, but the true God had not forgotten or forsaken them. Here is another sampling of His "kind and comforting words" through His prophet Zechariah:

"Shout and be glad, O Daughter of Zion. For I am coming, and I will live among you," declares the LORD. "Many nations will be joined with the LORD in that day and will become my people.… The LORD will inherit Judah as his portion in the holy land and will again choose Jerusalem. Be still before the LORD, all mankind, because he has roused himself from his holy dwelling."

Zechariah 2:10 – 13

Zechariah expressed God's great love for His people by referring to them in these beautiful terms: "Whoever touches you touches *the apple of his eye*" (Zech. 2:8).

Jonah ran away from the LORD and headed for Tarshish.
He went down to Joppa … to flee from the LORD.

Jonah 1:3

From the pen of Charles Spurgeon:

Instead of going to Nineveh to preach the Word as God had commanded him, Jonah "went down to Joppa" to escape what he considered an unpleasant task. There are occasions when God's servants shrink from their duty, but there is always a consequence. Consider what Jonah lost because of his conduct.

He lost the sense of God's abiding presence and the comfort and enjoyment of His love. When we serve our Lord Jesus as believers should do, God is with us, and even though the whole world may be against us, it doesn't matter. But the moment we head away from Him to seek our own plans, we are like a ship without someone at the helm. Thus, when we turn away, may we bitterly regret our actions and cry out, "O God, where have You gone? How could I have been so foolish as to have run from serving You, and thereby to have lost the bright shining rays of Your face? The cost is too high. Allow me to return to a place of obedience that I may rejoice in Your presence."

Jonah not only lost the sense of God's presence but also his peace of mind. Sin quickly destroys a believer's comfort. It is like the sap of the upas tree of Southeast Asia, which was once used to make deadly arrows, for sin oozes deadly drops that destroy the joy and peace of life. Jonah lost everything from which he may have otherwise drawn great comfort. He no longer could claim the promise of God's divine protection, for He ran from His will and His ways. Nor could he say, "Lord, I came by these difficulties through the normal discharge of my duties, therefore help me through them." Jonah reaped what he had sown, for he was filled with his own ways, not God's.

Dear Christian, never be like Jonah unless you want the waves of the sea to crash over you. The road of running from God's work and His will is far more difficult than the one of obedience to Him. Jonah wasted his time, for he ultimately had to go to Nineveh.

It is difficult to fight against God. Let us yield ourselves to Him now.

From the pen of Jim Reimann:

Obedience is a matter of faith. Thus, only believers are able to walk in it — as difficult as that often may be. Paul was an apostle "to call people … to *the obedience that comes from faith*" (Rom. 1:5). After the fall of Adam and Eve in the Garden of Eden, all people became slaves to sin, but the ability to be obedient has been restored through faith in Christ. Paul put it this way:

> Thanks be to God that, though you used to be slaves to sin, you wholeheartedly obeyed the form of teaching to which you were entrusted. You have been set free from sin and have become slaves to righteousness.
>
> Romans 6:17 – 18

And as Jonah quickly learned, the principle of reaping what we sow is true for believers and unbelievers alike. "The one who sows to please his sinful nature, from that nature will reap destruction; the one who sows to please the Spirit, from the Spirit will reap eternal life" (Gal. 6:8).

> This is love: that we walk in obedience to his commands. As you have heard from the beginning, his command is that you walk in love.
>
> 2 John 6

Where will I walk today? In sin or obedience?

FEBRUARY 26

If the disease has covered his whole body,
he shall pronounce that person clean.

Leviticus 13:13

From the pen of Charles Spurgeon:

As strange as this teaching in our text may appear, there is wisdom in it, for it indicates the disease has run its course and the person's body was strong enough to withstand it. But what is the application of such an unusual verse?

We too are lepers, and as such, we may apply this law concerning lepers to ourselves. When someone sees himself as totally lost and ruined, completely covered with the defilement of sin and without one part of his life free from its pollution, when he renounces all righteousness of his own and pleads guilty before the Lord, he is then made clean through the blood of Jesus and the grace of God. It is actually the hidden, unrecognized iniquity that is the true leprosy. But when sin is felt and acknowledged, it receives its deathblow, and the Lord looks with eyes of mercy on the soul afflicted with it.

Nothing is more deadly than self-righteousness or more hopeful than true contrition. We must confess that we are "nothing else but sin" (John Calvin, 1509 – 64), for no confession short of this will be the whole truth. And if the Holy Spirit is truly at work in us, convicting us of sin, then there will be no difficulty in making such an acknowledgment. In fact, it will spring spontaneously from our lips.

Yet what comfort does today's text bring to the newly awakened sinner? It is this: the very circumstance that so grievously discouraged the sinner is suddenly turned into a sign and symptom of a hopeful condition. Sinners must be stripped of their rags before they can be properly clothed, just as the first thing that must be done to build a house is to dig out the dirt for the foundation. Thus, a thorough sense of sin is one of the earliest works of God's grace in the human heart.

Oh, poor leprous sinner, utterly devoid of even one clean spot in your life, take heart from today's verse, and then come as you are to Jesus.

> For let our debts be what they may,
>   however great or small,
> As soon as we have naught to pay,
>   our Lord forgives us all.
> 'Tis perfect poverty alone
>   that sets the soul at peace:
> While we can call one cent our own,
>   we have no full release.
>
> Joseph Hart, 1712 – 68

From the pen of Jim Reimann:

Today's devotion alludes to a doctrine of grace commonly called "the total depravity of man." This teaching is confusing to some, because in error they believe it means "utter depravity," meaning people are always as wicked as they possibly can be. But total depravity simply means there is not one part of our being, whether spiritual, physical, or emotional, that is not fallen and thereby unaffected by sin.

Because of the fall of mankind, we were born with original sin. David knew this, for he wrote: "Surely I was sinful at birth, sinful from the time my mother conceived me" (Ps. 51:5). He also knew the necessity of confession and contrition for forgiveness, for he continued: "The sacrifices of God are a broken spirit; a broken and contrite heart, O God, you will not despise" (v. 17).

FEBRUARY 27

Bethlehem Ephrathah,
… out of you will come for me one who will be ruler over Israel,
whose origins are from of old, from ancient times.

Micah 5:2

From the pen of Charles Spurgeon:

The Lord Jesus had dealings before God's throne as our representative long before people appeared on the stage of time. It was "from ancient times" in eternity past that He signed the covenant with His Father that He would pay the price of suffering, agony, and death on behalf of His people. And it was "from ancient times" that He would give Himself up without "open[ing] his mouth" (Isa. 53:7) to speak even one word of complaint; that from the crown of His head to the soles of His feet He would "sweat … drops of blood" (Luke 22:44); that people would "mock him and spit on him, flog him and kill him" (Mark 10:34), cutting and crushing Him beneath the pains of death. Yes, His "origins are from of old, from ancient times" — from eternity past — as our Guarantee of God's covenant.

"O my soul" (Ps. 103:2), pause in wonder for a moment, for through the person of Jesus I have "origins … from ancient times." Christ did not begin to love me when I was born into the world, but He has been "rejoicing in his whole world and delighting in mankind" (Prov. 8:31) since before there was mankind. He continually has thought of me and has "set his affection on [me]" (Deut. 7:7) "from everlasting to everlasting" (Ps. 103:17).

What, my soul, do I think Christ who so long ago planned my salvation will fail to accomplish it? Will He who has gone forth to save me since eternity past, lose me now? Will He who has carried me in His hand as His precious jewel now let me slip through His fingers? Will He who chose me before the mountains were created or before the channels of the deep were dug, reject me now? Impossible! I can be sure He would not have loved me so long if He were not changeless, for if it were possible, He would have grown weary of me long before now. If He had not loved me with a love as deep as hell and as strong as death itself, He would have turned from me long ago.

Oh, joy above all joys to know I am His everlasting and inalienable inheritance, given to Him by His Father before the earth was created. When I rest from today's work, may His "everlasting love" (Jer. 31:3) be my pillow tonight.

From the pen of Jim Reimann:

Peter confirmed the truth of Jesus being chosen as our Savior before He became the creator of the world, saying,

> You know that it was not with perishable things such as silver or gold that you were redeemed from the empty way of life handed down to you from your forefathers, but with the precious blood of Christ, a lamb without blemish or defect. *He was chosen before the creation of the world*, but was revealed in these last times for your sake.
>
> 1 Peter 1:18 – 20

Although the Father chose Him to die for us, never think we were the only ones God loved, for John shared with us the following prayer of Jesus regarding the Father's love for Him: "Father, I want those you have given me to be with me where I am, and to see my glory, the glory you have given me because *you loved me before the creation of the world*" (John 17:24).

Finally, we see the confirmation of how much, and how long, He has loved us, "*for he chose us in him before the creation of the world* to be holy and blameless in his sight" (Eph. 1:4). Consider that amazing truth for a moment and rejoice!

FEBRUARY 28

The jar of flour was not used up and the jug of oil did not run dry,
in keeping with the word of the LORD spoken by Elijah.

1 Kings 17:16

From the pen of Charles Spurgeon:

This verse shows the faithfulness of God's love. The widow in the story had many daily needs, including feeding her son and herself in a time of famine, and now she had the prophet Elijah to feed as well. But in spite of the fact that she now had three mouths to feed, she suddenly had a constant supply of flour. She checked on the amount in the jar every day, but the level remained the same.

Dear reader, you too have daily needs, and because your needs come so frequently, you are apt to fear that "the jar of flour" will one day be empty and "the jug of oil" will fail you. But rest assured that, according to God's Word, this will not be your experience. Though each day brings new trouble, it also brings new help, for even if you should outlive Methuselah [who "lived 969 years" (Gen. 5:27)], and though your needs are as many as the sands on the seashore, God's grace and mercy will be sufficient for your needs; you will never be in true want.

In the time of this widow, the skies had not seen one cloud nor had the stars wept one holy tear of dew on the wicked earth for three long years. Famine, devastation, and death made the land a distressing wilderness. Yet this woman never went hungry, and, in fact, she always had an abundant supply of food.

It will be the same with you. Though you will see a sinner's hope perish, for he trusts in his own strength; though you will see a proud Pharisee's confidence crumble, for he builds his hope "upon the sand" (Matt. 7:26 KJV); and though you will see even your own plans wither and die, your place of "refuge will be [a] mountain fortress. [Your] bread will be supplied, and water will not fail [you]" (Isa. 33:16).

It is better to have God as your guardian than to possess all the money of the Bank of England. Ultimately you might be able to spend "the wealth of the Indies," but you will never be able to exhaust the infinite riches of God.

From the pen of Jim Reimann:

Spurgeon's phrase "the wealth of the Indies" may be a phrase unfamiliar to some. It dates to the days of Marco Polo (c. 1254-1324), whose journeys turned the eyes of much of Europe to the Indies, which included the Orient, namely, China, Japan, Indonesia, India, and Southeast Asia. His stories of its riches led many explorers, such as Christopher Columbus (1451 – 1506), to brave the high seas to find a more direct route there. Today, however, much of this area's inhabitants go to bed hungry. Thus, it is sobering to imagine that not so long ago, they fared much better than the people of western Europe.

"Cast but a glance at riches, and they are gone, for they will surely sprout wings and fly off to the sky like an eagle" (Prov. 23:5), "for riches do not endure forever" (Prov. 27:24), "but whoever trusts in the LORD is kept safe" (Prov. 29:25).

Remember David's words: "I was young and now I am old, yet I have never seen the righteous forsaken or their children begging bread" (Ps. 37:25).

O Lord, "give me neither poverty nor riches, but give me only my daily bread" (Prov. 30:8).

FEBRUARY 29

We have ... received ... the Spirit who is from God,
that we may understand what God has freely given us.

1 Corinthians 2:12

From the pen of Charles Spurgeon:

Have you "received ... the Spirit who is from God" in your soul? The necessity of the work of the Holy Spirit in my heart may be clearly seen by this fact: all that God the Father or God the Son has accomplished will remain totally ineffective in me until the Spirit works in my soul and reveals His truth to me. What effect does the doctrine of election have on anyone until the Spirit of God enters him? Election is like an undelivered letter in the soul until God's Spirit calls a person "out of darkness into his wonderful light" (1 Peter 2:9). Only after having been called by God to salvation will I see my election; and then, knowing I am called by Him, I will know I have been chosen in His eternal purpose.

A covenant was made between the Lord Jesus Christ and His Father to accomplish salvation for His chosen ones, but what good does that covenant do until the Holy Spirit brings it to us, opening our hearts to receive its blessings? The blessings of Jesus Christ hung from the nails of His cross, but humankind is much too short to reach them. Only the Spirit of God is able to take those blessing from the cross, hand them to us, and make them ours. Covenant blessings by themselves are like manna high in the sky, far out of our reach, but the Spirit of God opens the windows of heaven and scatters the living bread around the camp of spiritual Israel (see Num. 11:9).

Christ's finished work is like wine stored in a vat. Unbelief keeps us from being able to access the wine. But the Holy Spirit dips the vessel of our soul into this precious wine and enables us to drink. Without the Spirit we remain as truly dead in sin as though the Father had never elected us to salvation, and as dead as though the Son had never bought us with His blood. Thus, the Holy Spirit is absolutely necessary to our well-being.

May we walk in love toward Him and tremble at the thought of ever grieving Him.

From the pen of Jim Reimann:

Luke, in the book of Acts, gives us a perfect example of the sovereign work of the Lord in salvation through the working of His Holy Spirit:

On the Sabbath we went outside the city gate to the river, where we expected to find a place of prayer. We sat down and began to speak to the women who had gathered there. One of those listening was a woman named Lydia, a dealer in purple cloth from the city of Thyatira, who was a worshiper of God. *The Lord opened her heart to respond to Paul's message.*

Acts 16:13 – 14

Of course, Lydia became the first European convert to Christianity. Although Luke referred to her as "a worshiper of God," she was not yet saved. She was a believer in the God of the Jews, and thus a convert to Judaism, but she had not yet heard the gospel of Jesus Christ. Hearing, however, was still not enough, for what was needed was the opening of her heart by the Spirit so she could "respond to Paul's message."

As a believer in Jesus Christ, your salvation is solely a work of His grace, for His Spirit has opened your heart and enabled you to believe and to respond. Why not thank the Lord today for the miraculous work of His Spirit in you?

March

MARCH 1

He is precious.

1 Peter 2:7 KJV

From the pen of Charles Spurgeon:

Just as all rivers run to the sea, all true delights in life are centered in our beloved Savior. A simple glance from His eyes outshines the sun, the beauty of His face is more appealing than the most exquisite flowers, and no perfume is as fragrant as His breath. The rarest of gems from the earth or pearls from the sea are worthless when compared to Jesus' preciousness. Peter tells us, "He is precious," but he did not say, nor could he tell us, just how precious Jesus is, for who could compute the value of God's "indescribable gift" (2 Cor. 9:15)? Words cannot fully express how precious the Lord Jesus is to His people, nor can words fully explain just how essential He is to their satisfaction and happiness.

Believer, even in times of plenty, if your Lord was absent, wouldn't you experience a famine? If the sun was shining but He was hidden from your view, wouldn't the entire world be dark to you? And at night, if "the bright Morning Star" (Rev. 22:16) was gone, wouldn't it seem as though no other star was emitting as much as a ray of light?

What a desolate wilderness this world would be without our Lord! If He ever once hid Himself from us, the flowers of our garden would wither, the fruit of our trees would spoil, the birds would cease their singing, and a severe storm would blow our hopes away. All the candles of earth could never make daylight if "the sun of righteousness" (Mal. 4:2) was eclipsed, for He is the soul of our soul, the light of our light, and the life of our life.

Dear reader, what would you do without Him? What would you do if you awoke to face the day's battles alone? And what would you do at night, after a stressful day, if there were no hope of fellowship between you and Christ?

"Let the name of the Lord be praised" (Ps. 113:2). Jesus will never allow us to live without Him, for He never forsakes His own. Nevertheless, may the thought of what life would be like without Him enhance His preciousness to us.

From the pen of Jim Reimann:

Everyone knows the pain of betrayal by a friend or loved one. Consider how you felt when you were betrayed. Not only was there pain but also a sense of helplessness over circumstances beyond your control. Perhaps you had done something to prompt the betrayal — perhaps not — but either way, didn't you grieve over the situation? Remember what Jesus prophesied: "*You will be betrayed* even by parents, brothers, relatives and friends" (Luke 21:16).

Now consider Jesus. He was "tempted in every way, just as we are — *yet was without sin*" (Heb. 4:15). Thus, He did not deserve to be betrayed, although He predicted, "*The Son of Man is going to be betrayed* into the hands of men" (Matt. 17:22). How right He was!

Next consider this: His betrayal continues today at times, even by us to whom He said, "I have called you friends, for everything that I learned from my Father I have made known to you" (John 15:15).

Finally, consider His loving response in spite of our betrayals of Him: "Surely I am with you always, to the very end of the age" (Matt. 28:20), for "I will never leave you nor forsake you" (Josh. 1:5).

No wonder Jesus is so very precious "to [us] who believe" (1 Peter 2:7).

MARCH 2

Although I am less than the least of all God's people, this grace was given me:
to preach to the Gentiles the unsearchable riches of Christ.

Ephesians 3:8

From the pen of Charles Spurgeon:

The apostle Paul believed it was a special privilege to be allowed to preach the gospel. He did not think of his calling as drudgery, but approached it with great delight. Yet while Paul was quite thankful for his role as an apostle, his success in it greatly humbled him. And his humility increased as his responsibilities and success grew, in the same way a ship sits deeper in the water as it carries more cargo.

People who have never had a job may have unjustified pride over their supposed abilities because they are untested, for those who are hard workers soon discover their own weaknesses. Thus, if you desire humility, try hard work. If you desire to know your true nothingness or insignificance, attempt something great for Jesus. If you want to know how utterly powerless you are apart from the living God, take on the great work of proclaiming "the unsearchable riches of Christ," for then you will know, as you have never known before, precisely how weak and unworthy you are.

Although Paul knew and acknowledged his weakness, he was never confused as to the focus of his ministry. From his first sermon to his last, he preached Christ and nothing but Christ. He lifted up the cross and exalted the Son of God who bled upon it. We then should follow Paul's example in all our personal attempts to spread the good news of salvation, making our ever-recurring theme "Jesus Christ and him crucified" (1 Cor. 2:2).

Christians should be like those lovely spring flowers that open their golden blossoms when the sun is shining upon them, as if to say, "Fill us with your rays," but which, when the sun is hidden behind a cloud, close themselves and bow their heads. In the same manner, believers should feel the pleasant influence of Jesus. He must be our sun and we must be the flowers who yield ourselves to "the sun of righteousness" (Mal. 4:2).

Oh, to speak of Christ alone — the subject that is both "seed for the sower and bread for the eater" (Isa. 55:10). He alone is the "live coal" (Isa. 6:6) for the mouth of the speaker and the master key to the heart of the hearer.

From the pen of Jim Reimann:

Spurgeon exhorts us to follow Paul's example in preaching Christ and lifting up His cross. What better example could we ever find than Paul, the great evangelist and apostle. Even Paul encouraged the new believers of Corinth and Philippi to follow his example, for he wrote: "I urge you to *imitate* me" (1 Cor. 4:16). "Whatever you have learned or received or heard from me, or seen in me — put it into practice" (Phil. 4:9).

Who of us would dare make those statements! And who of us *could* make those statements honestly, yet humbly. Nevertheless, Paul spoke these words in true humility. He had the perfect blend of unashamedly knowing his calling as an apostle and true humility, for he said, "I am not in the least inferior to the 'super-apostles,' even though I am nothing" (2 Cor. 12:11).

Lord, may I, like Paul, remember today: "I became a servant of this gospel by the gift of [Your] grace" (Eph. 3:7).

MARCH 3

Jesus ... saw the Spirit of God
descending like a dove and lighting on him.

Matthew 3:16

From the pen of Charles Spurgeon:

Just as the Spirit of God descended upon the Lord Jesus, the head of the church, He descends upon the members of His spiritual body. Thus, His descent falls upon us in the same way and measure as it fell upon our Lord. This often happens so extraordinarily fast, we are unaware of it; we simply are impelled forward and heavenward beyond our greatest expectations. Yet there is none of the hurriedness of earthly haste, for the wings of the dove are as soft as they are swift. Quietness as well appears to be an essential element in the Spirit's work, for the Lord speaks in "a gentle whisper" (1 Kings 19:12), and like dew, His grace is distilled in silence.

A dove has always been the symbol of purity, and the Holy Spirit is holiness itself. Wherever He goes "is pure,... lovely, [and] ... admirable" (Phil. 4:8), and He enables us to "abound in every good work" (2 Cor. 9:8), while sin and uncleanness depart. Peace also reigns wherever the Spirit's power goes, for He carries an "olive leaf" (Gen. 8:11), a symbol that the waters of God's divine wrath have receded. Gentleness is another result of the Sacred Dove's transforming power, for hearts touched by His calm influence are "gentle and humble in heart" (Matt. 11:29) immediately and forever. Harmlessness follows as well, for by nature eagles and ravens hunt their prey, while doves simply endure wrong but cannot inflict it. Thus, we must be "harmless as doves" (Matt. 10:16 KJV).

A dove is also a fitting symbol of love, for its voice is full of affection. Thus, a soul indwelt by the Holy Spirit "abound[s] in love" (1 Thess. 3:12 KJV) to God, to other believers, to sinners, and, above all, to Jesus. "The Spirit of God ... hovering over the waters" (Gen. 1:2) first created order and life, and in our hearts He creates and nurtures new life and light.

Blessed Holy Spirit, as You came to rest upon our precious Redeemer, come to rest upon us today and forever.

From the pen of Jim Reimann:

Today's text is taken from Matthew's account of the baptism of Jesus. This story is one of very few Scriptures where we view all three Persons of the Trinity at once. Here is our verse in its context:

Then Jesus came from Galilee to the Jordan to be baptized by John. But John tried to deter him, saying, "I need to be baptized by you, and do you come to me?" Jesus replied, "Let it be so now; it is proper for us to do this to fulfill all righteousness." Then John consented. As soon as Jesus was baptized, he went up out of the water. At that moment heaven was opened, and he saw the Spirit of God descending like a dove and lighting on him. And a voice from heaven said, "This is my Son, whom I love; with him I am well pleased."

Matthew 3:13 – 17

If it was important for the Holy Spirit to descend upon Jesus, "the Lamb of God, who takes away the sin of the world" (John 1:29), how much more do we who are sinful need His presence! Before you do anything else today, why not thank the Lord for this truth:

God has poured out his love into our hearts by the Holy Spirit, whom he has given us.

Romans 5:5

MARCH 4

They feast on the abundance of your house.

Psalm 36:8

From the pen of Charles Spurgeon:

"When the queen of Sheba saw ... the palace [Solomon] had built, the food on his table, the seating of his officials, the attending servants in their robes, [and] his cupbearers ... she was overwhelmed" (1 Kings 10:4 – 5). But what were Solomon's provisions and hospitality compared to those of the God of grace? Think of the millions who are daily fed by Him. They come to His banquet hungry and thirsty, but not one leaves unsatisfied, for there is always enough for each, enough for all, enough for evermore. Although the multitudes who feed at Jehovah's table are as countless as the stars of heaven, they all have their own portion of food.

Think how much grace just one saint needs. It is so much that nothing but the Infinite Himself could provide it for one day, and yet the Lord spreads His table not just for one saint, but for many. And He does so not for one day, but for years, for generation after generation. Today's text speaks of "the abundance" of the feast that satisfies the guests at the Lord's mercy banquet. Yet it more than satisfies, it abundantly satisfies; and not simply with ordinary fare, but "with the richest of foods" (Ps. 63:5) from God's own house. And this great feast is guaranteed by His faithful promise to "both high and low among men [who] find refuge in the shadow of [Jehovah's] wings" (Ps. 36:7).

I once thought if I could only get the scraps of meat at the back door of God's grace, I would be satisfied, like the woman who said, "The dogs eat the crumbs that fall from their masters' table" (Matt. 15:27). Yet no child of God is ever served leftovers and scraps, for like Mephibosheth, they all eat "at the king's table" (2 Sam. 9:13). When it comes to matters of grace, we all have the appetite of Benjamin, who was "a ravenous wolf" (Gen. 49:27), yet we have ten times more grace than we expect. Though our needs are great, we stand amazed by the miraculous abundance of God's grace that He gives us to experience and enjoy.

From the pen of Jim Reimann:

Believers will feast on "the richest of foods" in heaven, but the food we are talking about today is the spiritual food of God's grace, the only kind of "food" that truly satisfies. And it is a "food" we can enjoy in this life, which is why the prophet Isaiah wrote:

> Come, all you who are thirsty, come to the waters; and you who have no money, come, buy and eat! Come, buy wine and milk without money and without cost. Why spend money on what is not bread, and your labor on what does not satisfy? Listen, listen to me, and eat what is good, and your soul will delight in the richest of fare.
>
> Isaiah 55:1 – 2

Jesus also compared and contrasted physical and spiritual food by saying, "I tell you the truth, you are looking for me, not because you saw miraculous signs but because you ate the loaves and had your fill. Do not work for food that spoils, but for food that endures to eternal life, which the Son of Man will give you" (John 6:26 – 27).

May the prayer of our hearts today be the same as these words of Jesus: "My food ... is to do the will of him who sent me and to finish his work" (John 4:34).

MARCH 5

Say to my soul,
"I am your salvation."
Psalm 35:3

From the pen of Charles Spurgeon:

May this prayer be my petition to God today. But first, may I use it as a meditation to learn what it can teach me. Initially, I learn that David had his doubts, for why would he ask the Lord to "say to [his] soul, 'I am your salvation,'" unless he struggled occasionally with doubts and fears? Thus, may I "be of good cheer" (Matt. 14:27 KJV), for I am not the only saint who suffers weakness of faith from time to time. If David had doubts, then I need not conclude I am not a Christian simply because I have doubts. This verse also reminds me that David was not content as long as he had doubts and fears, but that he went at once to God's "mercy seat" (Ex. 25:17 KJV) to pray for assurance, for he valued it as much as pure gold. I too must seek after an abiding sense of being "accepted in the beloved" (Eph. 1:6 KJV), and should have no joy until I know "God has poured out his love into [my heart] by the Holy Spirit" (Rom. 5:5). And when my Bridegroom is gone from me, my soul must and will fast.

I also learn that David knew where to obtain "full assurance of faith" (Heb. 10:22), for he went directly to his God in prayer, crying, "Say to my soul, 'I am your salvation.'" I must spend a great deal of time alone with the Lord if I am to have a clear sense of Jesus' love, for when my prayers are few, my eyes of faith will grow dim. If I spend much time in prayer, I will spend much time in heaven; but if I am slow to prayer, I will be slow in spiritual growth.

I also notice that David would not be satisfied unless his assurance had a divine source. Thus, his words, "Say to my soul," were addressed to God. *Lord, are You speaking?* This is what we should ask, for nothing short of a divine testimo-

ny in our soul will ever give genuine contentment to a true Christian.

Finally, David could not rest until his assurance was personal. "Say to *my* soul, 'I am your salvation.'"

> *Lord, saying this to all the saints means nothing, unless You say it to me. "Father, I have sinned" (Luke 15:21) and do not deserve Your smile. Thus, I scarcely dare to ask; nevertheless, say to my soul, yes, even to mine, "I am your salvation." Please give me a present, personal, perfect, and indisputable sense that I am Yours and You are mine.*

From the pen of Jim Reimann:

As Spurgeon said, "David had his doubts," which is why he asked God for assurance. Yes, even David, the king through whom the Messiah would ultimately come, had doubts during some difficult times in his life.

And although it may sound strange, faith and doubt can coexist in believers. Consider the man who brought his demon-possessed son to Jesus' disciples for healing. That act alone proved his faith in the Lord. After the disciples were unable to perform the miracle, the man said to Jesus, "If you can do anything, take pity on us and help us," to which Jesus responded, "Everything is possible for him who believes" (Mark 9:22–23). Then we see the coexistence of faith and unbelief when the man exclaims, "I do believe; help me overcome my unbelief!" (v. 24).

Let this be our prayer today:

> *"I do believe; help me overcome my unbelief!" And "Say to my soul, 'I am your salvation.'"*

MARCH 6

Before his downfall a man's heart is proud.

Proverbs 18:12

From the pen of Charles Spurgeon:

There is an old adage: "Coming events cast their shadows before them," and Solomon's wisdom teaches us here that a proud heart is the prophetic prelude of evil. Pride is as dependable a sign of coming destruction as the dropping of pressure in a barometer is a sign of rain; in fact, pride is even more infallible than that, for when people have ridden their high horse, destruction has always overtaken them.

For example, "David was conscience-stricken after he had counted the fighting men" (2 Sam. 24:10), showing an eclipse of man's glory after doting on his own greatness. And Nebuchadnezzar, the mighty builder of Babylon, "ate grass like cattle ... [and] his hair grew like the feathers of an eagle and his nails like the claws of a bird" (Dan. 4:33), for pride turned the boaster into a beast just as it turned Lucifer from an angel into the Devil. "The LORD hates ... haughty eyes" (Prov. 6:16 – 17) and never fails to humble them, for all His arrows are aimed at proud hearts.

Dear Christian, is your heart proud today, for pride can enter a saint's heart as well as a sinner's? And it can delude you into believing you "have acquired wealth and do not need a thing" (Rev. 3:17). Are you taking pride in your own gifts and talents? Are you taking credit for your past spiritual experiences? If so, then mark this down, dear reader, destruction is on its way to you as well. Your proud flowers of self-conceit will be plucked up by their roots, your gifts will wither like new sprigs of grass in the blazing sun, and your self-sufficiency will become like straw thrown on the dunghill.

If you forget to live humbly at the foot of the cross in the deepest lowliness of spirit, God will not forget to bring you pain from His "rod of discipline" (Prov. 22:15). Oh, unduly exalted believer, destruction will come to you. Although there can be no destruction of your soul, you will experience a destruction of your joy and comfort.

Therefore, "Let him who boasts boast in the Lord" (1 Cor. 1:31).

From the pen of Jim Reimann:

Our text today is similar to another passage from Solomon's book of Proverbs: "Pride goes before destruction, a haughty spirit before a fall. Better to be lowly in spirit and among the oppressed than to share plunder with the proud" (Prov. 16:18 – 19). Indeed, the Lord hates pride, the very sin that caused Satan to be cast down and the sin that led to the fall of Adam and Eve. Paul certainly understood this truth, and although he was "not in the least inferior to the 'super-apostles,'" he remained humble, saying, "I am nothing" (2 Cor. 12:11).

If we desire our prayers to be heard in heaven, may we be like Daniel, who was sent a messenger from God with these words: "Since the first day that you set your mind to gain understanding and to humble yourself before your God, your words were heard, and I have come in response to them" (Dan. 10:12).

Thus, may Paul's words be our prayer:

Lord, "If I must boast, I will boast of the things that show my weakness" (2 Cor. 11:30). "Therefore I will boast all the more gladly about my weaknesses, so that [Your] power may rest on me" (2 Cor. 12:9).

MARCH 7

It is better to take refuge in the LORD
than to trust in man.

Psalm 118:8

From the pen of Charles Spurgeon:

There can be no doubt each of us is tempted to rely "on what is seen" (2 Cor. 4:18) rather than trusting solely on "the invisible God" (Col. 1:15). In fact, Christians often look to man for help and counsel, and thereby mar the noble simplicity of exercising sole reliance on their God.

If the topic of today's devotion hits you, as a child of God, between the eyes, then allow me to reason with you. Why are you troubled over temporary things if you trust in Jesus, and only in Jesus, for your salvation? Doesn't God's Word say, "Cast your cares on the LORD" (Ps. 55:22), and "Do not be anxious about anything, but in everything, by prayer and petition ... present your requests to God" (Phil. 4:6)? Can't you therefore trust God for the temporal things of life? And if you can't trust Him for those, how dare you trust Him for spiritual things. If you can trust Him for your soul's redemption, why can't you rely on Him for lesser gifts of His mercy? Isn't God enough to meet your needs, or is His all-sufficiency lacking when it comes to you?

Do you really believe other eyes are needed to view your needs besides those of Him who sees every secret thing? Is His heart weak? Are His arms weary? If so, seek another God! But if He truly is infinite, omnipotent, faithful, true, and full of wisdom, why waste so much effort seeking assurance everywhere else? Why do you continue to comb the earth in hope of uncovering another founda-

tion, when He alone is strong enough to bear all the weight of anything you could ever build?

Dear Christian, just as people do not mix wine with water, never mix the gold of your faith with the dross of human self-confidence. Solely wait upon God, placing all your expectations in Him. Never covet Jonah's gourd (see Jonah 4:6 KJV), but rest in Jonah's God instead. Leave the sandy foundations of worldly trust to the foolish of earth, but when it comes to you, be someone who sees the storm approaching and who prepares an abiding place for yourself on the Rock of Ages.

From the pen of Jim Reimann:

Spurgeon's closing thought brings to mind the beautiful hymn "Rock of Ages," by Augustus Montague Toplady (1740 – 78). Caught in a severe thunderstorm, Toplady hid himself between two massive limestone rocks, where he penned these words:

> While I draw this fleeting breath,
> When mine eyes shall close in death,
> When I soar to worlds unknown,
> See Thee on Thy judgment throne,
> Rock of Ages, cleft for me,
> Let me hide myself in Thee.

Lord, You said to Moses, "There is a place near me where you may stand on a rock. When my glory passes by, I will put you in a cleft in the rock and cover you with my hand" (Ex. 33:21 – 22). "Let me hide myself in Thee." Be my Rock of Ages today!

MARCH 8

As [Rachel] breathed her last — for she was dying —
she named her son Ben-Oni [means "son of my trouble"].
But his father named him Benjamin [means "son of my right hand"].

Genesis 35:18 and NIV footnotes

From the pen of Charles Spurgeon:

There is a bright side and a dark side to everything. In today's text, Rachel was overwhelmed with the sorrow surrounding her own trouble and her impending death; but Jacob, although weeping over the loss of his wife, nevertheless saw God's mercy in the birth of his child. Likewise, when our flesh mourns over the trials of life, our faith should triumph in God's divine faithfulness. The carcass of Samson's lion provided honey for him (see Judg. 14:8 – 9), and so will our adversaries if we view them properly. The stormy sea feeds multitudes of people with its fish, the wild forest blooms with a host of beautiful flowers, the tempestuous wind sweeps away pestilence, and the biting frost loosens the soil. Dark clouds distil bright raindrops, and dark soil produces the most beautiful flowers.

Thus, a vein of good can be found in every mine of evil. Yet, unfortunately, sad hearts have a strange skill of taking the most disadvantageous point of view to gaze upon a trial. If there were only one spot of quicksand in the world, they would soon be up to their necks in it, and if there were only one lion in the desert, they would hear it roar. In each of us lies a hint of this wretched and foolish tendency, and, like Jacob, we are sometimes prone to cry, "Everything is against me!" (Gen. 42:36).

But faith's way of walking is to "cast [all] cares on the LORD" (Ps. 55:22) and to anticipate good results from the worst calamities. Like Gideon's men, faith doesn't fret over a broken jar, but rejoices that the light of the torch blazes forth all the more (see Judg. 7:19 – 20). Out of the rough oyster shell of difficulty, faith extracts a rare pearl of honor, and from the deep ocean caves of distress, she obtains the most priceless coral of experience. When her floods of prosperity begin to ebb, she finds treasure hidden in the sand, and when her sun of delight begins to set, she trains her telescope of hope on the starry promises of heaven. Even when death itself appears on the horizon, faith looks to the light of the resurrection beyond the grave — thus changing our dying Ben-oni into our living Benjamin.

From the pen of Jim Reimann:

Christians who find the bad in everything have been described as having been "baptized in vinegar" and tend to have a draining effect on everyone. Yet the sacrifice of our lives should have an uplifting effect on those we touch.

Consider how God viewed the Old Testament sacrifices. Instead of the burnt offerings filling His nostrils with the smell of death, they became "a pleasing aroma to the LORD" (Ex. 29:25). And Paul described the gifts the church at Philippi sent him as "a fragrant offering, an acceptable sacrifice, pleasing to God" (Phil. 4:18).

Perhaps this is why Paul encourages us to focus on the bright side, with these words:

> Whatever is true, whatever is noble, whatever is right, whatever is pure, whatever is lovely, whatever is admirable — if anything is excellent or praiseworthy — think about such things.

Philippians 4:8

MARCH 9

Abide in me.

John 15:4 KJV

From the pen of Charles Spurgeon:

Communion with Christ is the certain cure for every problem. Whether it is the bitterness of distressing difficulties or the sickening sweetness of excessive earthly delight, close fellowship with the Lord Jesus will take bitterness from one and sweetness from the other. Dear Christian, if you live close to Jesus, it will be a matter of secondary importance whether you live on the mountain of honor or in the valley of humiliation. If you live close to Him, "He will cover you with his feathers, and under his wings you will find refuge" (Ps. 91:4), and "underneath [you will be His] everlasting arms" (Deut. 33:27).

Let nothing keep you from the holy communion of a soul who has the blessed privilege of being married to the "well-beloved" (Song 1:13 KJV). Never be content to spend time with Him now and then, but always seek to be with Him, for only in His presence do you have comfort and safety. Jesus should not be a friend we see only occasionally, but one with whom we walk continually and forever.

Dear traveler to heaven, you have too difficult a road ahead of you to travel it without a guide. You must walk through "the blazing furnace" (Dan. 3:20), so be sure not to enter it unless, like Shadrach, Meshach, and Abednego, you have the Son of God as your companion (see Dan. 3:24 – 25). You must attack the Jericho of your own sins and corruption (see Josh. 6:1 – 5), but never attempt this warfare until, like Joshua, you see the "commander of the army of the LORD" (Josh. 5:14) "with a drawn sword in his hand" (v. 13). You must face the Esau of your many temptations (see Gen. 33:1 – 4), but don't do so until, like Jacob, you have wrestled with the angel by the Jabbok River and prevailed (see Gen. 32:22 – 30).

In every circumstance and in every situation, you will need Jesus, especially when the iron gates of death open before you. Therefore, stay close to your soul's Husband, lean your head on His shoulder, and ask to be refreshed by His "spiced wine" and "the nectar of [His] pomegranates" (Song 8:2). Then ultimately you will be found by Him to be "without stain or wrinkle or any other blemish" (Eph. 5:27).

Remember, you have lived with Him — and in Him — here, and you will abide with Him forever in heaven.

From the pen of Jim Reimann:

Spurgeon said, "You have too difficult a road ahead of you to travel it without a guide." Thankfully, as believers we have a God who is not only with us and in us but also one who has promised to be our guide forever. May these words be our prayer today, as we look to the Lord as our constant guide:

> "Within your temple, O God, we meditate on your unfailing love. Like your name, O God, your praise reaches to the ends of the earth; your right hand is filled with righteousness.... Walk about Zion, go around her, count her towers, consider well her ramparts, view her citadels, that you may tell of them to the next generation. For this God is our God for ever and ever; he will be our guide even to the end" (Ps. 48:9 – 10, 12 – 14).

MARCH 10

Man ... is of few days and full of trouble.

Job 14:1

From the pen of Charles Spurgeon:

Today's text, although a sad truth, is nevertheless a great reminder to us to let loose of earthly things. There is nothing too pleasant in remembering we are not above suffering the rod of adversity, but it may humble us and prevent us from boasting like the psalmist who wrote, "When I felt secure, I said, 'I will never be shaken'" (Ps. 30:6). Perhaps it will keep us from sinking our roots too deeply in this earthly soil, since we are soon to be transplanted to the heavenly garden. May we remember the truly weak grasp we have on the temporal blessings of this life. If we would only remember that all the trees of earth have been marked for the woodman's axe, we would not be so quick to build our nests in them.

We should love others, but with a love that expects death and its ultimate separation, for our loved ones are simply on loan to us, and the hour we must return them to the Lender's hand may be at our door even now. The same is true of our worldly goods and riches, "for they will surely sprout wings and fly off to the sky" (Prov. 23:5). Our health is equally unstable, for we are frail "flowers of the field" (Isa. 40:6) and must not think we will bloom forever. There is a time appointed to us for weakness and sickness when we will have to glorify God by suffering, not by vigorous activity. There is no secure place in this life where we can hope to escape the sharp arrows of affliction, for although our days may be few, not one of them is guaranteed to be exempt from sorrow. Earthly life is a cask full of bitter wine, and whoever looks for joy in it had sooner seek for honey in an ocean of saltwater.

Beloved Christian, "set your minds on things above, not on earthly things" (Col. 3:2), for here on earth the "thief comes near" and the "moth destroys" (Luke 12:33), but in heaven all joys are perpetual and eternal.

Lord, help me remember this truth: The path of trouble is the way home.

From the pen of Jim Reimann:

It is far too easy to read a passage like today's text and become negative and bitter. Remember the words of Solomon, who when focused on earthly things said, "I hated life, because the work that is done under the sun was grievous to me. All of it is meaningless" (Eccl. 2:17). Yet he went on to explain himself, saying,

What does the worker gain from his toil? I have seen the burden God has laid on men. He has made everything beautiful in its time. He has also set eternity in the hearts of men; yet they cannot fathom what God has done from beginning to end. I know that there is nothing better for men than to be happy and do good while they live. That everyone may eat and drink, and find satisfaction in all his toil — this is the gift of God. I know that everything God does will endure forever; nothing can be added to it and nothing taken from it. God does it so that men will revere him.

Ecclesiastes 3:9 – 14

Father, grant me a view of Your sovereignty today through Your words given to Solomon: "There is a time for everything, and a season for every activity under heaven: a time to be born and a time to die, a time to plant and a time to uproot, a time to kill and a time to heal, a time to tear down and a time to build, a time to weep and a time to laugh, a time to mourn and a time to dance" (Eccl. 3:1 – 4).

MARCH 11

You shall be called Sought Out.

Isaiah 62:12 Amplified

From the pen of Charles Spurgeon:

The surpassing grace of God is seen very clearly in the fact that we are not only sought, but "Sought Out" until we are found. People search for something they have lost in their house, but in such a case there is only seeking, not necessarily a "seeking out" until the item is found. The loss is more serious and the search more relentless when an item is "sought out."

When it comes to our spiritual condition, we were mingled with the mire. The Lord sought us out, just as one will search for a precious piece of gold that falls into the sewer, stirring and searching through it, carefully inspecting a horrible amount of filth until the treasure is found. Or, to use another example, we were lost in a maze, wandering here and there. Even when mercy sought us with the gospel, it did not find us at first, but had to search and seek for us. We were sheep so desperately lost, wandering in such a foreign land, that it seemed impossible for even the Good Shepherd to track our hidden, devious paths.

Therefore, glory be to unconquerable grace that we were "Sought Out." No darkness or gloom could hide us, nor any filthiness conceal us, for we were found and brought home. Glory be to infinite love, for God the Holy Spirit restored us. If the lives of some of God's people were written down for us, we would be filled with holy astonishment, for the various ways God has used to find His own are both strange and miraculous.

Blessed be His name, for He never abandons His search until His chosen ones are effectively "Sought Out." Nor does He seek His people today and then cast them away tomorrow, for they are secure in Him. The power and wisdom of the Lord come together for those He has "Sought Out," and He will never experience failure in seeking His own. The fact that anyone is "Sought Out" is evidence of His matchless grace, but the fact that *we* have been "Sought Out" is grace beyond measure! We can find no reason for it except God's sovereign love. We can simply lift our hearts in awe and praise the Lord that we carry the name "Sought Out."

From the pen of Jim Reimann:

Spurgeon stood against the seeker-sensitive movement of his day during what was known as the Down-Grade Controversy. He wrote: "I do not hear [Christ] say, 'Run after these people, Peter, and tell them we will have a different style of service tomorrow, something short and attractive with little preaching. We will have a pleasant evening for the people. Tell them they will be sure to enjoy it. Be quick, Peter, we must get the people somehow.' Jesus pitied sinners, sighed and wept over them, but never sought to amuse them.... The need is biblical doctrine, so understood and felt, that it sets men on fire."

Jesus is the seeker, not us, for He Himself said, "The Son of Man came to seek and to save what was lost" (Luke 19:10). And it is His Spirit who inspired David to write:

> God looks down from heaven on the sons of men to see if there are any who understand, any who seek God. Everyone has turned away, they have together become corrupt; there is no one who does good, not even one.
>
> Psalm 53:2 – 3

MARCH 12

To whom do you belong?

1 Samuel 30:13

From the pen of Charles Spurgeon:

When it comes to faith, there can be no neutrality. We either serve under the banner of Prince Immanuel, fighting His battles, or we are a warrior of the prince of darkness, Satan. "To whom do you belong?"

Dear reader, allow me to assist you in your response. Have you been "born again" (John 3:3)? If so, you belong to Christ, but without new birth you cannot be His. In whom do you trust? Those who trust in Jesus are the "children of God" (1 John 3:2). Whose work are you doing? Each of us serves our true master, for whomever you serve is undeniably your lord. What company do you keep? If you belong to Jesus, you will socialize with those who also wear the "uniform" of the cross, for as the adage goes, "Birds of a feather flock together." What do you discuss? Is your conversation heavenly or earthly? What have you learned about your master? True apprentices learn a great deal from their master, and if you have served your time with Jesus, it will be said of you, as it was of Peter and John, "They took note that these men had been with Jesus" (Acts 4:13).

Again I press the question, "To whom do you belong?" Answer honestly before you begin today's work. If you do not belong to Christ, you are in a place of difficult service, so run away from your cruel master! Instead, enter into the service of the Lord of Love and you will enjoy a life of blessedness.

If, however, you belong to Christ, allow me to advise you to do four things. First, since you belong to Him, let His Word be your law and His desire be your will. Second, since you belong to the Beloved, love Him, let your heart embrace Him, and let your entire soul be filled with Him. Third, since you belong to the Son of God, trust Him and rest nowhere except on Him. Fourth, since you belong to the "King of kings" (Rev. 17:14), be determined to live for Him. If you will do these four things, even without His name branded on your brow, everyone will know you belong to Him.

From the pen of Jim Reimann:

When Jesus redeemed us, He purchased us. Peter wrote, "For you know that it was not with perishable things such as silver or gold that you were redeemed from the empty way of life handed down to you from your forefathers, but with the precious blood of Christ, a lamb without blemish or defect" (1 Peter 1:18–19). Thus, we are His!

Paul agreed, saying, "[God] set his seal of ownership on us, and put his Spirit in our hearts as a deposit, guaranteeing what is to come" (2 Cor. 1:21–22), and, "We are God's workmanship, created in Christ Jesus to do good works, which God prepared in advance for us to do" (Eph. 2:10). David too understood we belong to the Lord. May his words be our closing prayer today:

"Shout for joy to the LORD, all the earth. Worship the LORD with gladness; come before him with joyful songs. Know that the LORD is God. It is he who made us, and we are his; we are his people, the sheep of his pasture. Enter his gates with thanksgiving and his courts with praise; give thanks to him and praise his name. For the LORD is good and his love endures forever; his faithfulness continues through all generations" (Ps. 100:1–5).

MARCH 13

[Noah] reached out his hand and took the dove
and brought it back to himself in the ark.

Genesis 8:9

From the pen of Charles Spurgeon:

Wearied by her long, wandering flight, the dove finally returned to the ark as her only resting place. How heavy she must have felt — ready to drop — as though she would never reach the ark. But she struggled on. Noah had been looking for his dove all day, standing ready to receive her. Yet she had only enough strength remaining to reach the very edge of the ark. She could hardly alight upon it, being totally spent, when Noah "reached out his hand and brought it back to himself."

Carefully notice these words: "brought it back to himself." She did not fly into the ark, because she was either too fearful or too weary to do so. She flew as far as she could and then Noah "reached out his hand and brought it back to himself." This act of mercy was shown to the wandering dove, but notice that she was not scolded for her wanderings and was brought back into the ark just as she was.

You too, backsliding sinner, will be received by the Lord with all your sin — only return. These are God's simple, but gracious words: *only return*. What! Nothing else is required? No, only return. On this flight, the dove had no olive leaf in her mouth, and thus returned from her wanderings with nothing but herself. She simply needed to return and, upon doing so, Noah brought her "back to himself."

Fly, O wanderer; fly, O weary dove that you are! Although you may think of yourself as being as dark as a raven with the mire of sin, return to your Savior. Every moment you delay only increases your misery, and your vain attempts to purify yourself, to make yourself fit for Jesus, are all worthless. Come to Him just as you are. "'Return, backsliding Israel,' says the LORD" (Jer. 3:12 NKJV). Notice He does not say, "Return, *repenting* Israel." Obviously, He desires your repentance, but His first invitation is to you as His backsliding one, inviting you to return with all your backslidings still about you.

Return, return, return! Jesus is waiting for you! And He will reach "out His hand" and take you "back to himself" — your heart's true home.

From the pen of Jim Reimann:

Just as the loving father in Jesus' parable longed for his prodigal son to return home (see Luke 15:11 – 32), the Lord longs for His wayward children to return to Him. Yet He says, "Israel's arrogance testifies against him, but despite all this he does not return to the LORD his God or search for him" (Hos. 7:10).

But listen to this beautiful promise to God's people when they finally do return to Him:

If you return to the Almighty, you will be restored: If you remove wickedness far from your tent and assign your nuggets to the dust … then the Almighty will be your gold, the choicest silver for you. Surely then you will find delight in the Almighty and will lift up your face to God. You will pray to him, and he will hear you, and you will fulfill your vows. What you decide on will be done, and light will shine on your ways.

Job 22:23 – 28

Thank You, heavenly Father, for "the blood of Jesus" that "purifies us from all sin" (1 John 1:7).

MARCH 14

I will watch my ways.

Psalm 39:1

From the pen of Charles Spurgeon:

Fellow pilgrim, never say in your heart, "I will go here and there and will not sin," for you are never so sure to be threatened by the danger of sinning as when you are able to boast about it. A Christian's road is quite miry and it will be difficult to pick your path so as not to muddy your clothing. Our world is one of tar and you will need to watch carefully if you are to keep your hands clean. There is a thief at every turn of the road ready to rob you, a temptation in every mercy, and a snare in every joy. Thus, if you are ever to reach heaven, it will be a miracle of divine grace attributed entirely to your heavenly Father's power.

Be on your guard, for when you carry a bomb in your hand, you must be careful to stay far from the flame. Take care "so that you will not fall into temptation" (Matt. 26:41). Even your everyday actions can be sharp tools, so be careful how you handle them. In fact, nothing in this world fosters a Christian's devotion to God, for worldly things attempt to destroy it instead.

Therefore, how quick you should be to look to Him, that He may keep you. Your prayer should be, "Uphold me, and I will be delivered" (Ps. 119:117). Then having prayed, you must also watch, guarding every thought, word, and action with holy jealousy. Never expose yourself to danger unnecessarily, but if called to go where darts are flying, never venture out without your shield, for if the Devil ever finds you without it, he will rejoice that his time of triumph has come and you will fall prey to his arrows. Although he cannot slay a believer, you can be wounded by him.

"Be self-controlled and alert" (1 Peter 5:8), for danger may come when you feel the most secure. "Therefore be clear minded and self-controlled so that you can pray" (1 Peter 4:7), for no one ever fell into error by being too watchful. May the Holy Spirit guide us in all our ways so that they always please the Lord.

From the pen of Jim Reimann:

The Bible is replete with warnings for us to be watchful at all times and never to let down our guard. In the Garden of Gethsemane, Jesus' disciples had no idea what they soon would be facing. Yet by His omniscience, their Master not only knew of their coming trouble but also warned them, saying, "Watch and pray so that you will not fall into temptation" (Matt. 26:41).

Earlier, His disciples asked Him about the end of time, to which Jesus responded with another warning:

Keep watch because you do not know when the owner of the house will come back — whether in the evening, or at midnight, or when the rooster crows, or at dawn. If he comes suddenly, do not let him find you sleeping. What I say to you, I say to everyone: "Watch!"

Mark 13:35 – 37

Father, may this verse be true of my life today: "As for me, I watch in hope for the LORD, I wait for God my Savior; my God will hear me" (Mic. 7:7). And I thank You for watching over me, for You have said, "The LORD watches over you — the LORD is your shade at your right hand; the sun will not harm you by day, nor the moon by night. The LORD will keep you from all harm — he will watch over your life; the LORD will watch over your coming and going both now and forevermore" (Ps. 121:5 – 8).

MARCH 15

[Hezekiah] ... worked wholeheartedly.
And so he prospered.

2 Chronicles 31:21

From the pen of Charles Spurgeon:

Hezekiah's experience is not unusual, for the general rule of the moral universe is that those who work with all their hearts typically prosper, while those who work only halfheartedly are nearly certain to fail. God does not give harvests to idle people, except a harvest of thistles, nor is He pleased to send wealth to those who refuse to dig in the field to find its hidden treasure. It is universally believed that those who desire to prosper must be diligent in business. And this is as true when it comes to faith as it is in other things.

If you desire to prosper in your work for Jesus, make it the priority of your heart, and then work at it with all your heart. Put at least as much effort, energy, and earnestness into your faith as you put into your business, for, in fact, it deserves far more. "The Spirit helps us in our weakness" (Rom. 8:26), but He does not encourage our idleness, for He loves active believers.

Who are the most useful people in Christ's church? Those who do what they do for God with all their hearts. Who are the most successful Sunday school teachers? Those who are the most talented? No, those who are the most zealous and whose hearts are on fire. The best teachers are those who see their Lord prosperously riding forth in the majesty of His salvation. Wholeheartedness reveals itself through perseverance, for although there may be failure at first, an earnest worker will say, "This is the Lord's work and it must be done. My Lord has called me to do it, and in His strength I will accomplish it."

Dear Christian, is this how you are serving your Master? Are you serving God "with all your heart" (Deut. 6:5)? Remember the earnestness of Jesus. Think of the work of His heart, for truly He could say, "Zeal for your house consumes me" (Ps. 69:9). When He "sweat ... great drops of blood" (Luke 22:44 KJV), it was due to no light burden He had to carry on His blessed shoulders, and when He poured out His heart, it was no weak effort He was making for the salvation of His people.

Was Jesus in earnest? Are we lukewarm?

From the pen of Jim Reimann:

The Zealots of Jesus' day gave the term *Zealot* a bad connotation because they often resorted to violence. But being truly zealous for God is a wonderful thing. In fact, Isaiah tells us "the zeal of the LORD Almighty will accomplish" (Isa. 9:7) the establishing of the Messiah's eternal kingdom.

We too are to be zealous for His kingdom, for Paul tells us, "Never be lacking in zeal, but keep your spiritual fervor, serving the Lord" (Rom. 12:11). And we must be wholehearted in our service. Consider Paul's determination in these words:

> *I press on* to take hold of that for which Christ Jesus took hold of me. Brothers, I do not consider myself yet to have taken hold of it. But one thing I do: Forgetting what is behind and *straining toward what is ahead*, *I press on* toward the goal to win the prize for which God has called me heavenward in Christ Jesus.
>
> Philippians 3:12 – 14

Father, like Jesus, may "zeal for your house [consume] me" as well!

MARCH 16

Keep your servant also from willful sins.

Psalm 19:13

From the pen of Charles Spurgeon:

This verse was the prayer of David — "a man after [God's] own heart" (1 Sam. 13:14). If a person as holy as this needed to pray these words, then how much more do we who are infants in grace. It's as though David prayed, "Hold me back, Lord, or I will rush headlong over the precipice of sin." Our sin nature, like an unbroken horse, is prone to run away, but may the grace of God put a bridle on it and restrain it from rushing into sinfulness. There is nothing even the best of us would not do, if not for the restraints the Lord puts on us through His sovereignty and His grace! The psalmist's prayer is directed against the worst form of sin — that which is done with deliberate willfulness. And even the holiest among us need the Lord to "keep" us, as David prayed, from the vilest transgressions.

It is a sobering thought to see the apostle Paul warning the saints of God against the most loathsome of sins. He wrote, "Put to death, therefore, whatever belongs to your earthly nature: sexual immorality, impurity, lust, evil desires and greed, which is idolatry" (Col. 3:5). What! Do God's saints need to be warned against sins such as these? Yes, for even the whitest robes will be defiled by the darkest spots unless their purity is protected by the Lord's divine grace.

If you are an experienced Christian, never boast in your experience, for you will certainly trip if you look away from "him who is able to keep you from falling" (Jude 24). If your love is fervent, your faith constant, and your hope bright, don't say, "I will never sin," but cry out, "Lead [me] not into temptation" (Matt. 6:13). There is enough kindling in the heart of even the best people to light a fire that will burn to the lowest hell unless God extinguishes the sparks as they fall. For example, who would have dreamed that righteous Lot ever would have become so drunk as to commit incest with his daughters? (See Gen. 19:30 – 38.) And Hazael, when Elisha told him of "the harm [he would] do to the Israelites," including "dash[ing] their little children to the ground, and rip[ping] open their pregnant women" (2 Kings 8:12), questioned, "What is your servant, only a dog, that he should do this monstrous thing?" (v. 13 Amplified). We too are prone to use the same self-righteous question. Thus, may God's infinite wisdom cure us of the insanity of self-confidence.

From the pen of Jim Reimann:

Paul said of the biblical stories: "These things happened to them as examples and were written down as warnings for us.… So, if you think you are standing firm, be careful that you don't fall!" (1 Cor. 10:11 – 12). David, after committing adultery and murder, prayed, "My sin is always before me.… Surely I was sinful at birth" (Ps. 51:3, 5). And Paul said, "I am less than the least of all God's people" (Eph. 3:8), and "I am the worst [of sinners]" (1 Tim. 1:15).

If the great King David and the apostle Paul were so sinful, what hope is there for us! But may the following comfort us, and may we thank God for working in us as He did in David and Paul:

There are different kinds of gifts, but the same Spirit. There are different kinds of service, but the same Lord. There are different kinds of working, but *the same God works all of them in all men.*

1 Corinthians 12:4 – 6

MARCH 17

Blessed are the peacemakers,
for they will be called sons of God.

Matthew 5:9

From the pen of Charles Spurgeon:

This verse is the seventh of the eight beatitudes, with seven being the Hebrew number of perfection. Perhaps the Savior placed "Blessed are the peacemakers" seventh on His list because a peacemaker most nearly resembles the perfect person in Christ. Whoever desires perfect blessedness, at least as much as possible here on earth, must aspire to live according to this beatitude and become a peacemaker.

There is also significance in the placement of this beatitude immediately after "Blessed are the pure in heart, for they will see God" (v. 8). There is value in understanding that first we are to be *pure*, then *peace loving*, for our desire to be a peacemaker should never be at the cost of compromising with sin or tolerating evil. We must set our faces "like flint" (Isa. 50:7) against everything contrary to God and His holiness, for purity must become a settled matter in our souls before we can move on to peacemaking.

The placement of the verse following our text, "Blessed are those who are persecuted because of righteousness, for theirs is the kingdom of heaven" (Matt. 5:10), seems to be significant as well, for despite our peacemaking efforts in this world, at times we will be misunderstood and misrepresented. This should not surprise us, for even the "Prince of Peace" (Isa. 9:6), due to His own peacemaking, brought "fire" to the earth. Although He loved all people and never did any wrong toward them, "He was despised and rejected by men, a man of sorrows, and familiar with suffering" (Isa. 53:3). Again, as peacemakers, we should not be surprised when persecuted by our enemies, yet we should remember that not only has a blessing been pronounced on us — "Blessed are those ..." — but also that we will be surrounded by blessings, "for [ours] is the kingdom of heaven."

Lord, grant us grace to rise to the level of the seventh beatitude! Purify our minds so we may be pure — then peacemaking; and give us strength so our peacemaking will not lead us into cowardice and despair when we are persecuted for Your sake.

From the pen of Jim Reimann:

Again, we should remember the blessings that accompany persecution, for believers have been called to suffer unjustly for righteousness. Peter, like Spurgeon, related the same truth to Isaiah 53, saying:

It is commendable if a man bears up under the pain of unjust suffering because he is conscious of God. But how is it to your credit if you receive a beating for doing wrong and endure it? But if you suffer for doing good and you endure it, this is commendable before God. To this you were called, because Christ suffered for you, leaving you an example, that you should follow in his steps. "He committed no sin, and no deceit was found in his mouth." When they hurled their insults at him, he did not retaliate; when he suffered, he made no threats. Instead, he entrusted himself to him who judges justly.

1 Peter 2:19 – 23

"It is better, if it is God's will, to suffer for doing good than for doing evil" (1 Peter 3:17).

MARCH 18

As the Father has loved me,
so have I loved you.
John 15:9

From the pen of Charles Spurgeon:

As we see from this verse, Jesus loves His people in the same way the Father loves the Son. But what is that divine way? How does He love us?

There was no beginning to the Father's love, and thus Jesus loves His people in the same manner, for the Lord said, "I have loved you with an everlasting love" (Jer. 31:3). When it comes to human affection, we can easily determine its beginning. Each of us easily remembers the beginning of our love for Christ, but His love for us is a stream whose source is hidden in eternity past.

Also, the Father's love for Jesus is unchanging. Therefore, dear Christian, you may take comfort that there is no change in Jesus Christ's love for those who rest in Him. Yesterday you may have been on top of the Mount of Transfiguration and were able to say, "He loves me." Today you may face the valley of humiliation, but He still loves you the same. On "the heights of Hermon" and "Mount Mizar" (Ps. 42:6), you heard His sweet voice in songs of love; and now, whether *on* the sea or even *in* the sea when all the stormy waves are crashing over you, His loving heart is faithful to His ancient choice — His choice to love you.

And just as there was no beginning to the Father's love, He loves the Son without end. Thus, the Son loves His people in the same way. Dear saint, you never need to fear the severing of "the silver cord" (Eccl. 12:6), for His love for you will never cease. Rest assured that Christ will go with you down to the grave and will rise with you from it to be your guide across the heavenly hills.

Finally, the Father loves the Son without measure — the same immeasurable love the Son bestows on His chosen ones. Christ's heart is fully dedicated to His people, for "he loved us" (1 John 4:10) and "gave himself for us" (Titus 2:14) — a "love that surpasses knowledge" (Eph. 3:19).

Indeed, we have an immutable Savior, a precious Savior who loves us without measure, without change, without beginning, and without end — just "as the Father has loved [Him]." There is rich spiritual food in these truths for those who know how to digest it. Thus, let us pray for the Holy Spirit to lead our souls to "be satisfied as with the richest of foods" (Ps. 63:5).

From the pen of Jim Reimann:

Much of the apostle John's gospel and his epistles focus our attention on the topic of love and, in particular, God's love. In the following passage from John's first letter, notice how love is defined and personified in God Himself:

Dear friends, let us love one another, for love comes from God. Everyone who loves has been born of God and knows God. Whoever does not love does not know God, because *God is love.* This is how God showed his love among us: He sent his one and only Son into the world that we might live through him. *This is love: not that we loved God, but that he loved us and sent his Son as an atoning sacrifice for our sins.*

Dear friends, since God so loved us, we also ought to love one another. No one has ever seen God; but if we love one another, God lives in us and his love is made complete in us.

1 John 4:7 – 12

MARCH 19

[Ruth] ate all she wanted
and had some left over.

Ruth 2:14

From the pen of Charles Spurgeon:

Whenever we are privileged to eat of the bread Jesus gives, like Ruth, we are fully satisfied with the meal, for when Jesus is the host, no guest leaves hungry. The precious truth Christ reveals satisfies our head; Jesus, as the "altogether lovely" (Song 5:16) object of our affection, gives contentment to our heart; and He brings satisfaction to our hope, for whom do we have in heaven but Jesus? All our desires are satisfied in Him, for what more could we desire than "the surpassing greatness of knowing Christ Jesus ... and be[ing] found in him" (Phil. 3:8 – 9)? Jesus fills our conscience till it is at "perfect peace" (Isa. 26:3), fills our judgment with the certainty of His teachings, fills our memory with recollections of what He has done, and fills our imagination with the prospects of what He is yet to do.

As Ruth "ate all she wanted and had some left over," so is it with us. Although we have had times of deep feeding on Christ, after thinking we could take Him in and having done our best to do so, we have had to leave a vast amount "left over." We sat at the table of the Lord's love and said, "Nothing but the Infinite can ever satisfy me; I am such a great sinner that I must have the Lord's infinite merit to wash my sin away." But after we have had our sin removed, we have found there is merit to spare; we have had our hunger satisfied at the feast of His sacred love, and then found an abundance of spiritual meat remaining.

There are some sweet things in the Word of God we have not enjoyed yet, things for which we must patiently wait, for we are like the disciples to whom Jesus said, "I have much more to say to you, more than you can now bear" (John 16:12).

Yes, there are gifts of His grace we have not experienced, places of fellowship closer to Christ we have not reached, and heights of communion our feet have not climbed. At every banquet of the Lord's love, there are many "baskets ... left over" (John 6:13). Thus, like Ruth, let us praise the generosity of our glorious Boaz.

From the pen of Jim Reimann:

The Lord has promised to care for His people, and like Boaz, who generously gave to Ruth, we are to care for others if we expect God to care for us. Here is what the Lord told His people through Isaiah:

"If you spend yourselves in behalf of the hungry and satisfy the needs of the oppressed, then your light will rise in the darkness, and your night will become like the noonday. The LORD will guide you always; he will satisfy your needs in a sun-scorched land and will strengthen your frame. You will be like a well-watered garden, like a spring whose waters never fail.... Then you will find your joy in the LORD, and I will cause you to ride on the heights of the land and to feast on the inheritance of your father Jacob." The mouth of the LORD has spoken.

Isaiah 58:10 – 11, 14

David spoke of the abundant love and provision of the Lord as well, for he prayed, "You prepare a table before me in the presence of my enemies. You anoint my head with oil; my cup overflows" (Ps. 23:5).

"How great is the love the Father has lavished on us!" (1 John 3:1).

MARCH 20

Husbands, love your wives,
just as Christ loved the church.

Ephesians 5:25

From the pen of Charles Spurgeon:

What a perfect example Christ has given His followers. Very few teachers could venture to say, "If you desire to follow my teaching, imitate my life," but since Jesus' life was the epitome of virtue, He could point to Himself not only as the teacher of holiness but also as its ideal. Christians should have nothing short of Christ for their model, and under no circumstances should we be content unless we reflect the grace that was in Him.

As a true Christian husband, a man is to look at the portrait of Christ Jesus and then paint his own life according to it. The love of a husband is to be a special love, for the Lord Jesus cherishes the church with a special affection higher than His love for the rest of humanity, for He said, "I pray for them. I am not praying for the world" (John 17:9). The elect church is the favorite of heaven, the treasure of Christ, the crown on His head, the bracelet on His arm, the breastplate over His heart — indeed, the very center and core of His love. Thus, a husband should love his wife with a constant love, for this is how Jesus loves His church. And the level of Christ's affection never varies. Jesus may vary the way He displays His affection, but the level of His love remains the same. A husband should love his wife with an enduring love, for nothing "will be able to separate us from the love of God that is in Christ Jesus our Lord" (Rom. 8:39). A true husband loves his wife with a powerful love, a love filled with passion and intensity, not a love of mere lip service.

Oh, beloved Christian, what more could Christ do to prove His love than what He has already done! His love delights in His spouse, for He cherishes her affection and takes great pleasure in her sweet satisfaction. Dear believer, you may be in awe of Jesus' love and may truly admire it — but are you imitating it? In your family relationships is this — "just as Christ loved the church" — the standard of your love?

From the pen of Jim Reimann:

In the Old Testament, we see the Lord as a loving, faithful, and merciful husband, with Israel as His bride. Yet Israel was an unfaithful bride, for she was told:

> "You have rebelled against the LORD your God, you have scattered your favors to foreign gods ... and have not obeyed me.... Return, faithless people," declares the LORD, "for *I am your husband*. I will choose you ... and bring you to Zion. Then I will give you shepherds after my own heart, who will lead you with knowledge and understanding."
>
> Jeremiah 3:13 – 15

Then, in the New Testament, we see the church as the bride of Christ, for Jesus alluded to Himself as the Bridegroom and His followers as His bride. And the apostle John was given a vision of heaven and wrote: "Blessed are those who are invited to the wedding supper of the Lamb!" (Rev. 19:9). Thus, throughout the Bible, marriage is a picture of the unity we are to have with the Lord.

Father, may our marriages exhibit true oneness — oneness between husband and wife, and oneness with You. And may our love for one another bring You glory.

MARCH 21

Can you bind the beautiful Pleiades?
Can you loose the cords of Orion?

Job 38:31

From the pen of Charles Spurgeon:

If we are ever inclined to boast of our abilities, the grandeur of nature will soon show us just how powerless we are. We cannot move even the least of the twinkling stars or extinguish as much as one little beam of the morning's light. We think we have power, but the heavens laugh us to scorn. When the Pleiades brightly shine in the spring with fresh energy, we cannot restrain their influence; when Orion reigns in the winter sky and the year seems bound by the season's cold fetters, we cannot relax the icy chains. The seasons revolve according to God's divine appointment, something the entire human race is powerless to change. "O Lord, what is man?" (Ps. 144:3).

In the spiritual realm, as in the natural, man's power is limited on every side. When the Holy Spirit pours out His joyful delights in a soul, nothing can come against it, for all the cunning and craftiness of men is ineffective in preventing the miraculous life-giving power of the Comforter. And when He decides to visit a church to revive it, even His most firmly entrenched enemies cannot resist His good work; they may ridicule it, but they can no more restrain it than they can push back the time when the Pleiades rules the skies. If God wills it, it must and will be.

And if the Lord in His sovereignty or justice binds a person so that his soul is in bondage, who can give him liberty? God alone can remove the winter of spiritual death from an individual or a group of people, for He, and He alone, can loosen the cold chains of Orion. And oh, what a blessing that He can do it! Oh, that He would perform that miracle tonight!

Lord, end my winter and let my springtime

begin. *Even with all my yearnings to do so, I cannot raise my soul from her death and darkness, but "everything is possible for you"* (Mark 14:36). *I need Your heavenly power, the bright light of Your love, the shining rays of Your grace, and "the light of your face"* (Ps. 4:6), *for they are like the Pleiades to me. I greatly suffer from sin and temptation; they are the signs of winter in my life — my terrible Orion. Lord, work wonders in me, and for me. Amen.*

From the pen of Jim Reimann:

As we transition from winter to spring, let us consider, as Spurgeon said, just how powerless we are when compared to God. A generation ago, in 1969, man walked on the moon. Then, in 1977, man reached for the stars, launching the *Voyager 2* spacecraft, which 30 years later left our solar system — to date, the only feat of its kind. Yet as great as these accomplishments are, they are nothing compared to the greatness of God and His ability to create all things.

Thus, His Word challenges us, saying:

Lift your eyes and look to the heavens: Who created all these? He who brings out the starry host one by one, and calls them each by name. Because of his great power and mighty strength, not one of them is missing.

Isaiah 40:26

I am the Lord, and there is no other. I form the light and create darkness, I bring prosperity and create disaster; I, the Lord, do all these things.... It is I who made the earth and created mankind upon it. My own hands stretched out the heavens; I marshaled their starry hosts.

Isaiah 45:6 – 7, 12

MARCH 22

Father, I want those you have given me
to be with me where I am.

John 17:24

From the pen of Charles Spurgeon:

O death! Why do you fell the tree beneath whose spreading branches the weary take rest? Why do you snatch away the excellent of the earth, those in whom we all delight? If you must wield your deadly axe, wield it against the trees that bear no fruit, for then you even may be given thanks. But why do you fell the magnificent "cedars of Lebanon" (Ps. 104:16)? Withhold your axe and spare the righteous!

But this is not meant to be. Death strikes the best of our friends, for even the most generous, the most prayerful, the most holy, and the most devoted must die. But why is that true? It is because of Jesus' prevailing prayer: "Father, I want those you have given me to be with me where I am." Christ's prayer carries them "on eagles' wings" (Ex. 19:4) to heaven, for every time a believer rises from this earth to paradise, it is an answer to His prayer.

A godly old believer once remarked, "Jesus and His people often pull against each other in prayer. We bend our knee in prayer, saying, 'Father, I want the saints to stay with me,' while Christ has already prayed, 'Father, I want those you have given me to be with me where I am.'" Thus, Christ's disciples end up at odds with the purpose of their Lord, for a soul cannot be in both places. Our beloved ones cannot be with Christ and with us at the same time.

So which pleader will prevail with the Lord? What if God our King should step from His throne and ask you: "I have two prayers here, but they are in opposition to each other. Which one should I answer?" Realizing that Christ is praying, "Father, I want those you have given me to

be with me where I am," how would you respond? Although I know it would be agonizing for you, surely you would abandon your prayer for your loved one's life and say, "Jesus, 'not my will, but yours be done'" (Luke 22:42).

Lord, You shall have them. Therefore, by faith we let them go.

From the pen of Jim Reimann:

Contrary to the teaching of many so-called TV evangelists today, it is not God's will for everyone to be healed each and every time we pray for healing. If that were truly the case, we would never see a believer die physically, and we know that occurs. Of course, when we see a friend or family member dealing with a difficult illness, our spiritual nature leads us to pray for them. And that is what we should do. Yet we must keep in mind that our will always must be in submission to God's will.

It is inevitable, if we live a long life here on earth, that we will have to deal with the loss of a loved one — perhaps many losses. Although it is not wrong to pray for God's healing, we should always desire that His will be done. And there may come a time when the Lord reveals to you that He wants to take His saint on to glory. At that point, it is not only appropriate but also obedient to release that person through prayer to the Lord. It also may be appropriate to tell the loved one for whom you are praying that it is okay to go on to glory. Remember:

Precious in the sight of the Lord is the death of his saints.

Psalm 116:15

MARCH 23

"I tell you," [Jesus] replied, "if they keep quiet,
the stones will cry out."

Luke 19:40

From the pen of Charles Spurgeon:

The question is: Could the stones really cry out? They could if He who opened the mouth of the mute summoned them to lift up their voices. And if they were to speak, certainly they would have much to proclaim in praise of Him who created them by "his powerful word" (Heb. 1:3), for they could testify to the wisdom and power of their Maker who called them into being. Thus, shouldn't we too speak well of Him who gave us new life — He who out of "stones … [could] raise up children for Abraham" (Luke 3:8)?

The ancient rocks could tell of chaos followed by order and of the handiwork of God in the successive stages of creation's drama, but can't we tell of God's decrees, of His great work in ancient times, and of all He did for His church in days of old? If the stones were to speak, they could tell of their Quarryman, how He broke them, took them from the quarry and made them fit for His earthly temple. But can't we too speak of our glorious Breaker, He who broke our hearts with the hammer of His Word so we might be used as a building block in His spiritual temple?

If the old stones did cry out, they would glorify their Maker who shaped, polished, and used them in His palace. Shouldn't we as well speak of our Architect and Builder who has placed us into the temple of the living God? If the stones cried out, they would be able to tell a long story of old where they were used as pillars of remembrance before the Lord. We as well can testify of Ebenezer stones of help (see 1 Sam. 7:12) and stones of memorial (see Josh. 4:7). The broken stones of the law (see Ex. 32:19) cry out against us, but Christ Himself, who rolled away the stone from the door of His tomb (see Luke 24:2), speaks on our behalf.

Stones may well be able to cry out, but we should not allow them to do so. Let us hush their praise with ours. Let us break forth into sacred song and bless the majesty of the Most High God. Let all our days glorify Him whom Jacob called "the Shepherd, the Rock of Israel" (Gen. 49:24).

From the pen of Jim Reimann:

Have you ever heard the expression "dumb as a rock"? It is never meant as a compliment. Since the word *dumb* not only means stupid but also means mute, ask yourself, "Am I as mute as a rock?" Our text today tells us that if we who are disciples of Jesus "keep quiet, the stones will cry out."

We are not to be cold, dead rocks, never proclaiming or praising our Lord before a dying world. In fact, Peter said we are to be living memorials. Here is how he stated this great truth:

As you come to [Jesus], the living Stone — rejected by men but chosen by God and precious to him — you also, like *living stones*, are being built into a spiritual house to be a holy priesthood, offering spiritual sacrifices acceptable to God through Jesus Christ.

1 Peter 2:4 – 5

Remember the words of Jesus, who said,

If anyone is ashamed of me and my words in this adulterous and sinful generation, the Son of Man will be ashamed of him when he comes in his Father's glory with the holy angels.

Mark 8:38

MARCH 24

At that time Jesus,
full of joy through the Holy Spirit, said ...
Luke 10:21

From the pen of Charles Spurgeon:

Our Savior was "a man of sorrows" (Isa. 53:3), but any thinking person would recognize the fact that down deep in His innermost soul, Jesus possessed an inexhaustible treasury of refined, heavenly joy. Of all the people who have ever lived, there has never been a man who had a deeper, purer, or more abiding peace than our Lord Jesus Christ. God anointed Him "above [His] companions ... with the oil of joy" (Ps. 45:7). From the very nature of things, Jesus' great benevolence must have brought Him the deepest possible delight, for benevolence is joy.

There were, in fact, a number of remarkable moments when His joy was revealed. In Luke we are told, "At that time Jesus, full of joy through the Holy Spirit, said, 'I praise you, Father, Lord of heaven and earth'" (Luke 10:21). Although He faced many dark times, and although His face was marred and had lost the luster of earthly happiness, it nevertheless was sometimes lit with the matchless splendor of unparalleled satisfaction. This is because Christ focused on the ultimate reward, and in the midst of His congregation He sang His songs of praise to God.

Thus, in this way the Lord Jesus is a blessed picture of His church. The church walks in sympathy with her Lord along a thorny road and, "through many hardships," (Acts 14:22), is pressing forward to the reward of her crown. To carry a cross is her calling and duty (see Matt. 16:24), and to be scorned as "an alien [by her] own mother's sons" (Ps. 69:8) is her lot in life. Yet the church has a deep well of joy. There are "storehouses ... of corn, and wine, and oil" (2 Chron. 32:28 KJV) hidden in the midst of our Jerusalem to eternally nourish and sustain the saints of God. And on occasion, as in our Savior's case, we have times of great delight, for "there is a river whose streams make glad the city of God" (Ps. 46:4). Although we are exiles on earth, we "rejoice ... in [our] King" (Ps. 149:2). Indeed, in Him we greatly "rejoice before God" and are "happy and joyful" (Ps. 68:3), while we "lift up our banners in the name of our God" (Ps. 20:5).

From the pen of Jim Reimann:

There is a saying that "your cup of joy is only as deep as your cup of suffering," meaning your capacity for joy is developed by the suffering you endure. This also means that joy and suffering are not mutually exclusive, but can and should coexist in the lives of believers.

Hebrews tells us that "Jesus ... for the joy set before him endured the cross" (Heb. 12:2). Does this mean that dying on a cross was a joyful thing? It was in this respect: Jesus knew His mission was to die for our sins, and that going to the cross was His Father's will. Also, as Spurgeon said, He was focused on His coming reward, that of once again being seated "at the right hand of the throne of God" (v. 2). It is the same for us, for regardless of the suffering we may be forced to endure, we will have tremendous joy when walking in God's will for our lives. In fact, suffering is a gift granted by God. Paul said, "It has been granted to you on behalf of Christ not only to believe on him, but also to suffer for him" (Phil. 1:29).

MARCH 25

…the Son of Man.
John 3:13

From the pen of Charles Spurgeon:

Our Master continually referred to Himself as "the Son of Man." If He had chosen to do so, He could have spoken of Himself instead as "the Son of God" (Luke 1:35), "Wonderful Counselor, Mighty God, Everlasting Father, [or] Prince of Peace" (Isa. 9:6); but look at His humility! He preferred "the Son of Man." May we learn a lesson of humility from our Savior and never seek great titles or prideful recognition for ourselves.

There is another lesson here that is even sweeter: Jesus loved mankind so much that He delighted to honor us. Indeed, the greatest honor to dignify mankind is that Jesus is "the Son of Man," and that He loved using that title. By using that name, it is as though He hung royal stars upon the chest of mankind and poured forth the love of God to "Abraham's seed" (Gal. 3:29). "The Son of Man" — whenever Jesus used that title He placed a halo around our heads as Adam's children.

Yet there is perhaps even a more precious thought: Jesus called Himself "the Son of Man" to express His oneness and sympathy with His people. In this way He reminds us He is the one whom we may approach without fear. Thus, as human beings, we may take all our troubles to Him, knowing He sympathizes, for He has experienced them Himself and is thereby able to aid and comfort us.

O blessed Jesus! We praise You for eternally using the title of "the Son of Man," that sweet name that acknowledges You are our dear brother. May it continually be a sure reminder to us of Your grace, humility, and love.

Oh see how Jesus trusts Himself
Unto our childish love,
As though by His free ways with us
Our earnestness to prove!
His sacred name a common word
On earth He loves to hear;
There is no majesty in Him
That love may not come near.
Frederick William Faber, 1814 – 63

From the pen of Jim Reimann:

Hebrews tells us, in essence, why Jesus had to be "the Son of Man":

Since the children have flesh and blood, he too shared in their humanity so that by his death he might destroy him who holds the power of death — that is, the devil — and free those who all their lives were held in slavery by their fear of death. For surely it is not angels he helps, but Abraham's descendants. *For this reason he had to be made like his brothers in every way*, in order that he might become a merciful and faithful high priest in service to God, and that he might make atonement for the sins of the people. Because he himself suffered when he was tempted, he is able to help those who are being tempted.

Hebrews 2:14 – 18

Consider this wonderful truth: Jesus identified with us in our humanity so we might someday identify with Him in His glory, for Paul said, "We share in his sufferings in order that *we may also share in his glory*" (Rom. 8:17).

MARCH 26

...when he comes in his Father's glory with the holy angels.

Mark 8:38

From the pen of Charles Spurgeon:

If we share with Jesus in His shame, we will also "share in the glory" (1 Peter 5:1) that will surround Him when He returns. But, dear one, are you with Christ Jesus? Do you have a vital, living relationship that has united you with Him? If so, today you share with Him in His shame, you have "take[n] up his cross" (Matt. 16:24), you have gone with Him "outside the camp, bearing the disgrace he bore" (Heb. 13:13), and no doubt you will be with Him when His cross is exchanged for a crown.

Thus, judge yourself even now, for if you are not with Him through regeneration, then neither will you be with Him "when he comes in his Father's glory." If you are walking in darkness, you will not share the bright happiness of communing with the King "when he comes ... with the holy angels." What! Is it only angels who will return with Him? For it is not angels He takes to heaven with Him, "but Abraham's descendants" (Heb. 2:16).

Dear soul, if you are indeed one of His beloved, you will never be far from Him. And if His friends and neighbors are called to see His glory, what about you who are married to Him? Will you be kept at a distance? Although the day of His return will be one of judgment, you will not be far from the heart that, having allowed angels into intimacy, also has brought you into union. After all, hasn't He said to you, "I will betroth you to me forever ... in righteousness and justice, in love and compassion" (Hos. 2:19)? Haven't His own lips declared, "I am your husband" (Jer. 3:14) and "take delight in you" (Isa. 62:4)? If angels who are only His friends and neighbors will be with Him, it is certain that His own beloved

"Hephzibah" (Isa. 62:4), in whom is His total delight, will be near Him and sit at His right hand.

This should be a "bright Morning Star" (Rev. 22:16) of such great brilliance for you that it may well light up even the darkest and most desolate of your experiences.

From the pen of Jim Reimann:

There are many who profess salvation who have no relationship with God. Jesus Himself said,

> Not everyone who says to me, "Lord, Lord," will enter the kingdom of heaven, but only he who does the will of my Father who is in heaven. Many will say to me on that day, "Lord, Lord, did we not prophesy in your name, and in your name drive out demons and perform many miracles?" Then I will tell them plainly, "I never knew you. Away from me, you evildoers!"
>
> Matthew 7:21–23

Perhaps this is why Paul, in his letter to the church in Corinth, said, "Examine yourselves to see whether you are in the faith; test yourselves. Do you not realize that Christ Jesus is in you — unless, of course, you fail the test?" (2 Cor. 13:5).

Jesus said of His return: "At that time men will see the Son of Man coming in clouds with great power and glory" (Mark 13:26). And Paul added these words for true believers: "Brothers, we do not want you to be ignorant about those who fall asleep, or to grieve like the rest of men, who have no hope. We believe that Jesus died and rose again and so *we believe that God will bring with Jesus those who have fallen asleep in him*" (1 Thess. 4:13–14).

MARCH 27

"Yes, Lord," she said,
"but even the dogs eat the crumbs that fall from their masters' table."
Matthew 15:27

From the pen of Charles Spurgeon:

The woman in this story gained comfort in her misery by thinking great thoughts of Christ. The Master had just told her, "It is not right to take the children's bread and toss it to their dogs" (v. 26), but she argued, in essence, "Lord, since You are the Master of the table of grace, I know You are a generous person. Surely there is an abundance of bread on Your table — such an abundance for Your children that there will also be many crumbs thrown to the floor for the dogs, and yet the children will fare none the worse because the dogs are fed." She thought of Jesus as having such an abundance on His table that a crumb would meet her needs. Remember, she was seeking to have a demon cast out of her daughter. This would be a great miracle for her, but because she had such high esteem for Christ, she saw it as nothing but a crumb for Him to give.

The path she took is the royal road to comfort, for focusing your thoughts on your sin alone will drive you to despair, but having great thoughts of Christ will guide you into the haven of peace. In effect, she thought, "I have many sins, but it is nothing for Jesus to take them all away! The burden of my guilt weighs me down as a giant's foot would crush a worm, but it is nothing more than a speck of dust to Jesus, because He has come to bear its curse 'in his body on the tree' (1 Peter 2:24). It would be a small thing for Him to give me total forgiveness, but it would be an infinite blessing for me to receive it!" She thus opened her soul's mouth very wide, expecting great things of Jesus, and He filled it with His love (see Ps. 81:10).

Dear soul, why not do the same? This needy woman acknowledged the hard words Jesus laid at her door, but held fast to Him and drew her arguments from those hard words themselves. She believed great things of Him, and thus by faith, by believing in Him, won her victory. Her story is of the power of prevailing faith, and if we are to be victorious like her, we must imitate her actions.

From the pen of Jim Reimann:

Jesus' response to this Canaanite woman may seem rude initially, but He is simply making the point that the gospel was to be sent first to the Jews. Yet the gospel was never meant to be exclusively for the Jews, for the Old Testament said of the Messiah, "I will also make you a light for the Gentiles, that you may bring my salvation to the ends of the earth" (Isa. 49:6), and Jesus' last words before His ascension were: "You will be my witnesses in Jerusalem, and in all Judea and Samaria, and to the ends of the earth" (Acts 1:8). With this in mind, may the following psalm be our prayer:

> "May God be gracious to us and bless us and make his face shine upon us, that your ways may be known on earth, your salvation among all nations. May the peoples praise you, O God; may all the peoples praise you. May the nations be glad and sing for joy, for you rule the peoples justly and guide the nations of the earth. May the peoples praise you, O God; may all the peoples praise you. Then the land will yield its harvest, and God, our God, will bless us. God will bless us, and all the ends of the earth will fear him" (Ps. 67:1–7).

MARCH 28

I will accept you as fragrant incense.

Ezekiel 20:41

From the pen of Charles Spurgeon:

The merits of our great Redeemer are "as fragrant incense" to "God Most High" (Gen. 14:18). And when it comes to the Christ's righteousness, there is an equal fragrance to His active and His passive righteousness. There was a sweet fragrance to His actions by which He honored the law of God, and thereby caused its every precept to glitter like a precious jewel adorned in the pure setting of His own person. Likewise, His passive obedience was "as fragrant incense," such as when, in uncomplaining, silent submission, He endured hunger and thirst, cold and nakedness, sweat great drops of blood in Gethsemane, suffered horrific scouring and His beard being ripped from His face, and when He ultimately offered Himself to be nailed to the cruel wood so He might suffer the wrath of God on our behalf.

Thus, both His actions and His passiveness are "as fragrant incense" to "God Most High." And as a direct result of His doing and His dying, and His substitutionary sufferings and His vicarious obedience, the Lord our God accepts us. What a preciousness there must be in Him to overcome our complete lack of preciousness. What a "fragrant incense" to defeat our foul stench. What cleansing power in His blood to take away sin such as ours. And what glory in His righteousness to make us — such unacceptable creatures — "accepted in the beloved" (Eph. 1:6 KJV).

Dear believer, consider how sure and unchanging our acceptance must be, since it is in Him. So take care that you never doubt your acceptance in Jesus, for just as you cannot be accepted without Christ, once you have received His merit, you cannot be unaccepted. In spite of all your doubts, fears, and sins, Jehovah's gracious eyes never look on you in anger. Although He sees the sins you commit, when He looks at you through Christ, He sees no sin. You are always accepted in Christ, always blessed and dear to the Father's heart. Therefore, today as you see the smoking incense of the merit of the Savior sweetly rising before the "throne of sapphire" (Ezek. 10:1), let your song of praise be lifted up as well.

From the pen of Jim Reimann:

Incense played a vital role in Israel's worship, from "the offerings ... [of] fragrant incense" (Ex. 25:3, 6) in Exodus to these words of God in Malachi: "In every place incense and pure offerings will be brought to my name, because my name will be great among the nations" (Mal. 1:11). Thus, Moses was told: "Aaron must burn fragrant incense on the altar every morning when he tends the lamps. He must burn incense again when he lights the lamps at twilight so incense will burn regularly before the LORD for the generations to come" (Ex. 30:7 – 8). And as Spurgeon alluded to today, our prayers are to be "as fragrant incense," wafting their way to God's heavenly throne. John, who had a revelation of that very throne, wrote: "The four living creatures and the twenty-four elders ... were holding *golden bowls full of incense, which are the prayers of the saints*" (Rev. 5:8).

I thank You, dear Father, for accepting me "as fragrant incense" in Christ. "May my prayer be set before you like incense; may the lifting up of my hands be like the evening sacrifice" (Ps. 141:2).

MARCH 29

I called him
but he did not answer.
Song of Songs 5:6

From the pen of Charles Spurgeon:

Sometimes we are forced to wait for answers to our prayers, like someone lingering at the gate of the King's palace, waiting for Him to extend blessings to fulfill our requests. When the Lord first gives someone great faith, He has been known to test it through long delays. For example, He has allowed His servants' voices to echo in their ears as though they were bouncing off a brass sky. And they have knocked at His golden gate but have found it immovable, as though it were rusted on its hinges. Like Jeremiah, they have cried, "You have covered yourself with a cloud so that no prayer can get through" (Lam. 3:44).

Thus, even true saints have waited patiently for long periods without reply, not because their prayers were not fervent or because the Lord rejected their requests, but because it pleased Him who is sovereign and who gives according to His own pleasure. After all, if it pleases God to exercise our patience, should He not do as He wills with His own? Should beggars be choosy as to the time, place, or type of test He determines?

In spite of denials or delays to our answers, we must be careful not to delay in praying, for the Lord's seemingly "past-due" bills will be honored in His perfect timing. We must not allow Satan to shake our confidence in the God of truth by pointing to our unanswered prayers, for unanswered petitions are not unheard. God keeps a record of our prayers. They are never blown away by the wind, but are treasured in the King's archives — a registry in the court of heaven where every prayer is recorded.

Dear tested believer, your Lord keeps a tear bottle in which every costly drop of your sacred grief is stored and a book in which your holy groans are numbered. Soon your heavenly court case will prevail, so can't you be content to wait a little longer? Won't the Lord's timing be better than yours? Soon He will appear to your soul's joy and comfort, causing you to put aside the "sackcloth and ashes" (Dan. 9:3) of long periods of waiting, and dressing you instead in the "scarlet yarn and fine linen" (Ex. 25:4) of His perfect answers.

From the pen of Jim Reimann:

There is a distinct dichotomy between answers, or lack of answers, to the prayers of believers and unbelievers. The Lord declines to answer the prayers of those who reject Him and His Word. Here is how Solomon recorded God's thoughts on this truth:

> They will call to me but I will not answer; they will look for me but will not find me. Since they hated knowledge and did not choose to fear the LORD, since they would not accept my advice and spurned my rebuke, they will eat the fruit of their ways and be filled with the fruit of their schemes. For the waywardness of the simple will kill them, and the complacency of fools will destroy them.
>
> Proverbs 1:28 – 32

Thankfully, the circumstance of the righteous is profoundly better, for Solomon went on to say, "But whoever listens to [the LORD] will live in safety and be at ease, without fear of harm" (Prov. 1:33), and "The LORD is far from the wicked but he hears the prayer of the righteous" (Prov. 15:29).

"Praise be to God, who has not rejected my prayer or withheld his love from me!" (Ps. 66:20).

MARCH 30

Let us examine our ways and test them,
and let us return to the LORD.

Lamentations 3:40

From the pen of Charles Spurgeon:

A wife who deeply loves her traveling husband longs for his return, for a lengthy separation from her spouse is like a semi-death to her spirit. And so it is with those who deeply love the Savior. They must see His face and cannot bear for Him to stay away "on the rugged hills" (Song 2:17), where they can no longer commune with Him. His affectionate children are only happy in His smile and are grieved by His critical glance or upraised hand after offending their loving Father.

Beloved Christian, once this was true of you. All it took was a verse of Scripture, a subtle warning, or a simple touch of "affliction by the rod of his wrath" (Lam. 3:1) before you fell at your Father's feet, crying, "Tell me what charges you have against me" (Job 10:2). Are you still like this or are you content to follow Jesus from a distance? Does the idea of broken communion with Him alarm you? Can you bear to have your Beloved oppose you because your walk is contrary to His? Have your sins caused a separation between you and your God? Is your heart at rest?

Allow me to offer a loving warning, for it is a grievous thing to think you are living contentedly without the joy of seeing the Savior's face. Thus, be diligent to learn what an evil thing it is to have such little love for your own Savior, so little joy in your precious Jesus, and so little fellowship with your Beloved. You should hold a season of Lent in your soul, grieving over the hardness of your heart. But do not stop at sorrow. Remember where you received salvation and return at once to the cross, for it is there, and only there, your spirit will be revived. No matter how hard, unthinking, and dead you may have become, return

to the cross in your rags, poverty, and the defilement of your natural condition. Cling to the cross again, look into Jesus' loving eyes, and bathe yourself in that "fountain filled with blood." This will return you to "your first love" (Rev. 2:4), will restore the simplicity of your faith, and will renew the tenderness of your heart.

From the pen of Jim Reimann:

Indeed, a Christian can become cold and unfeeling toward Jesus. A backslider still may outwardly perform, but all to no avail, just as the church in Ephesus, who was told,

> I know your deeds, your hard work and your perseverance. I know that you cannot tolerate wicked men, that you have tested those who claim to be apostles but are not, and have found them false. You have persevered and have endured hardships for my name, and have not grown weary. *Yet I hold this against you: You have forsaken your first love.*
>
> Revelation 2:2 – 4

As we have seen, there is a remedy: to return to the cross and to "confess our sins," for we have a Savior who "is faithful and just and will forgive us our sins and purify us from all unrighteousness" (1 John 1:9). May we remember these words of the beautiful old hymn Spurgeon quoted briefly:

> There is a fountain filled with blood
> Drawn from Immanuel's veins,
> And sinners plunged beneath that flood
> Lose all their guilty stains.
>
> William Cowper, 1731 – 1800

MARCH 31

Rizpah daughter of Aiah took sackcloth and spread it out for herself on a rock.
From the beginning of the harvest till the rain poured down from the heavens
on the bodies [of her two slain sons], she did not let the birds of the air
touch them by day or the wild animals by night.

2 Samuel 21:10

From the pen of Charles Spurgeon:

If a mother's love could cause Rizpah to prolong her mournful vigil such a long time for her sons, should we ever grow weary of considering the sufferings of our blessed Lord? As she drove away the birds of prey, shouldn't we chase from our times of meditation all the worldly and sinful thoughts that defile our minds and the holy themes we are considering? Away, birds of evil! Leave this sacrifice alone!

Rizpah endured the heat of summer and the nights of dew and rain, unsheltered and alone. Sleep as well was chased from her weeping eyes, for her heart was too filled with grief for slumber. Behold how she loved her children. How could she endure so much, when we run at the first hint of a little inconvenience or trial? Are we such cowards that we cannot bear to suffer with our Lord? She even chased away wild beasts, an especially courageous act for a woman. Why are we so seldom prepared to face a foe for Jesus' sake? Her two sons were slain by hands other than hers, and yet she wept and watched in mourning. What then should we do — we who through our own sins crucified our Lord? Our debt is boundless, so our love should be fervent and our repentance complete.

To "watch with [Jesus]" (Matt. 26:38) should be our business, to protect His honor our occupation, and to stand vigil at His cross our comfort. The ghastly corpses of her sons may well have frightened Rizpah, especially at night; but when it comes to our Lord, by whose cross we sit, there is nothing revolting, and everything beautiful. In fact, there has never been anything as beautiful or enchanting as our dying Savior.

Jesus, we will "watch with [You]" now. We ask that You graciously reveal Yourself to us, so that we would not sit beneath sackcloth, but in Your royal house.

From the pen of Jim Reimann:

If you read Rizpah's full story (2 Sam. 21:1 – 14), you may think David's treatment of King Saul's descendants is unjust. But sin has consequences, and Saul had sinned greatly, as made clear from the following:

There was a famine for three successive years; so David sought the face of the LORD. The LORD said, "It is on account of Saul and his blood-stained house; it is because he put the Gibeonites to death." ... (Now the Gibeonites were not a part of Israel but were survivors of the Amorites; the Israelites had sworn to spare them, but Saul in his zeal for Israel and Judah had tried to annihilate them.) David asked the Gibeonites, "What shall I do for you?" ... They answered the king, " ... Let seven of [Saul's] male descendants be given to us to be killed."

2 Samuel 21:1 – 3, 5 – 6

Yet we see God's grace here as well, for "The king spared Mephibosheth son of Jonathan, the son of Saul, because of the oath before the LORD between David and Jonathan" (v. 7).

Jesus, as I "watch with [You]," make me a vessel of Your grace.

April

APRIL 1

It is time to seek the LORD.
Hosea 10:12

From the pen of Charles Spurgeon:

The month of April derives its name from the Latin verb *aperire*, meaning "to open," because all the buds and blossoms are now opening. Thus, we have arrived at the gates of the flowery time of the year.

Dear reader, if you are still unsaved, may your heart, in harmony with the awakening of nature, be opened to receive the Lord. May every blossoming flower warn you "it is time to seek the LORD." Don't be out of tune with nature, but let your heart bud and bloom with holy desires. If you are still in your youth, I plead with you to give your youthful energy to the Lord. I was called to salvation early in my youth, and it has been my unspeakable happiness throughout my life, something for which I praise the Lord every single day. Salvation is priceless, and we must let it come when it may, but early salvation seems to have double value to it. Dear young men and women, it is possible you will die before you reach your prime, so "it is time to seek the LORD."

And to you middle-aged adults who are already experiencing the signs of aging, pick up your pace and let those signs be warnings you must not ignore. "It is time to seek the LORD." Do you see a little gray now mixed into your hair? The years click by and death marches closer, so may the return of spring awaken you to get your spiritual house in order.

Finally, to you readers who are well advanced in age, I plead and implore you to delay no longer. There is a time of grace for you now. Be thankful for that, but remember — it is a limited season, one that grows shorter with every tick of the clock.

To each reader, from my inmost soul as God's servant, I lay before you this warning: "It is time to seek the LORD." I plead with you not to ignore these words, for they may be your last call from destruction, the final syllables from the lips of Grace.

From the pen of Jim Reimann:

Salvation is completely a work of God's grace, and if today's devotion has given you a desire to know Jesus as your Savior, it is an indication the Lord is drawing you to Himself. Jesus said, "No one can come to me unless the Father who sent me draws him" (John 6:44), and later said, "No one can come to me unless the Father has enabled him" (John 6:65).

Why not ask the Lord to enable you to go to Him now, for as His Word says, "Now is the time of God's favor, now is the day of salvation" (2 Cor. 6:2). Ask Him to open your heart to the gospel, just as "the Lord opened [Lydia's] heart to respond to Paul's message" (Acts 16:14).

As Spurgeon said, he was called to salvation early in his youth. At the age of fifteen he heard a sermon on Isaiah 45:22, realized salvation was from God, and that it was as simple as looking to Him: "Look unto me, and be ye saved, all the ends of the earth: for I am God, and there is none else" (Isa. 45:22 KJV).

If you don't know Jesus as your personal Savior, "look unto [Him]" today.

APRIL 2

He [the Messiah] will see his offspring and prolong his days,
and the will of the LORD will prosper in his hand.

Isaiah 53:10

From the pen of Charles Spurgeon:

You who love the Lord, pray for the speedy fulfillment of this promise. When our desires are founded on God's own promises, prayer is easy work, for how can He who gave His word refuse to keep it? The Lord's immutable truthfulness cannot demean itself with a lie, and eternal faithfulness cannot degrade itself by neglect. Thus, God must bless His Son, for His covenant in today's verse binds Him to do so, and that which the Spirit prompts us to ask for Jesus' sake is that which God has decreed to give Him already.

So whenever you are praying for the kingdom of Christ, keep your eyes focused on that blessed day that is drawing near, when the Crucified will be crowned as King in the place where mankind once rejected Him. Take courage, you who prayerfully labor for Christ for even the slightest bit of success, for it will not be like this forever — better times are ahead. Your physical eyes cannot see the bliss-filled future, so borrow the telescope of faith, wipe the misty breath of your doubts from the lens, and then look through it to behold the coming glory.

Dear reader, allow me to ask, "Is it your constant prayer that the Lord's kingdom be expanded?" Remember, the same Christ who instructed us to say, "Give us today our daily bread" (Matt. 6:11), first gave us this petition to pray, "Hallowed be your name, your kingdom come, your will be done on earth as it is in heaven" (Matt. 6:9 – 10). So don't allow your prayers to be only about your own sins, your own wants, your own imperfections, and your own trials. Instead, allow them to climb the heavenly ladder to Christ Himself.

Then, as you draw near to the blood-sprinkled "mercy seat" (Ex. 25:17 KJV), offer this prayer continually, "Lord, enlarge the kingdom of Your dear Son." Such a petition, if fervently prayed, will elevate the spirit of all your devotional times. But be careful to prove the sincerity of your prayer by working to promote the Lord's glory.

From the pen of Jim Reimann:

Indeed, we are to look forward to Christ's eternal kingdom, yet one beautiful aspect of being a believer is this truth that Jesus taught: "The kingdom of God is within you" (Luke 17:21). When He returns to earth to set up His earthly kingdom, He will once again rule and reign over all the nations, but in the meantime His kingdom is a spiritual one — a kingdom in the hearts of those He has chosen and saved.

Thus, as you seek to serve Him in this world, allow Him to fully reign in your heart. Surrender every area of your life to Him, and then seek to expand His kingdom through prayer and by taking His gospel to a world that desperately needs its good news. Work and pray for the expansion of the Lord's kingdom that is "within" while also keeping your eyes focused on His glorious kingdom to come. May this be the prayer of our hearts today:

"All the ends of the world shall remember and turn to the LORD, and all the families of the nations shall worship before You. For the kingdom is the LORD's, and He rules over the nations" (Ps. 22:27 – 28 NKJV). *"Come, Lord Jesus"* (Rev. 22:20)!

APRIL 3

We all, like sheep, have gone astray,
each of us has turned to his own way;
and the Lord has laid on him the iniquity of us all.

Isaiah 53:6

From the pen of Charles Spurgeon:

This verse is a confession of sin common to all of God's elect people. All the elect are fallen and, thus, may sing in unison, from the first who entered heaven to the last who will enter there, "We all, like sheep, have gone astray." This confession, although unanimous, is also an individual one: "Each of us has turned to his own way." Every individual has a unique sinfulness; all are sinful, but each has something not found in others. And although one sign of genuine repentance is relating with other repentant sinners, repentance is also a place of loneliness, for "each of us has turned to his own way." These words are a confession that each person has sinned against light that is distinctly his own or sinned in a way unique to himself — not in a way that he saw in others.

This confession is also an unreserved one, meaning there is not a word to detract from its force nor one syllable uttered as an excuse. It is a true laying down of all claims of self-righteousness. It is a declaration of people who are aware of their guilt, people who are guilty without excuse and who now stand with their weapons of rebellion broken in pieces and cry out, "We all, like sheep, have gone astray, each of us has turned to his own way."

Yet in this Scripture passage there is no long, sorrowful wailing attached to its confession of sin, for the very next phrase nearly turns it into song: "The Lord has laid on him the iniquity of us all." The most grievous phrase of the three, it overflows with comfort. Isn't it amazing that where misery was at its very greatest, mercy reigned; and where sorrow reached its highest possible climax, weary souls find rest. Our bruised Savior is the cure for bruised hearts.

Look at today's text and see how lowly repentance gives way to assured confidence by simply gazing at Christ on the cross.

From the pen of Jim Reimann:

Today's verse is taken from one of the most beautiful prophecies describing our Savior in all of the Scriptures. As you read it in its context, gaze upon your crucified Christ and consider His great love that nailed Him to the cross for you.

> Who has believed our message and to whom has the arm of the Lord been revealed? He grew up before him like a tender shoot, and like a root out of dry ground. He had no beauty or majesty to attract us to him, nothing in his appearance that we should desire him. He was despised and rejected by men, a man of sorrows, and familiar with suffering. Like one from whom men hide their faces he was despised, and we esteemed him not. Surely he took up our infirmities and carried our sorrows, yet we considered him stricken by God, smitten by him, and afflicted. But he was pierced for our transgressions, he was crushed for our iniquities; the punishment that brought us peace was upon him, and by his wounds we are healed.

> We all, like sheep, have gone astray, each of us has turned to his own way; and the Lord has laid on him the iniquity of us all. He was oppressed and afflicted, yet he did not open his mouth; he was led like a lamb to the slaughter, and as a sheep before her shearers is silent, so he did not open his mouth.

Isaiah 53:1-7

APRIL 4

Come, let us go up to the mountain of the LORD.

Isaiah 2:3

From the pen of Charles Spurgeon:

It is extremely beneficial to our souls to climb above this present evil world to something nobler and better. "The worries of this life and the deceitfulness of wealth" (Matt. 13:22) are apt to choke everything good within us, leading us to become fretful, despondent, and perhaps proud and carnal. Thus, it is good for us to chop down these thorns and briers, for heavenly seed sown among them is not likely to yield a bountiful harvest; and where will we find a better sickle with which to remove them than communion with God and the things of His kingdom?

There are some valleys in Switzerland where many of the inhabitants once suffered from miasma, a sickness caused by swamp gases from nearby stagnant water, leading to some deformities and a sickly appearance. But on the mountains just above these valleys, the people were healthy and strong because they breathed the clean fresh air as it blew across the virgin snows of the alpine summits. The people down below would have been much better off had they frequently left their marshes and stale air to inhale the cold air of the hills.

It is an adventure of climbing such as this that I invite you to experience today. May the Spirit of God assist us to rise above the stale air of fear and anxiety, and the ills that gather in this valley of earth, and to climb the mountains of awaiting joy and blessedness. May God the Holy Spirit cut the cords keeping us here below and help us to climb. All too often, however, we sit like eagles chained to a rock, except that, unlike the eagle, we begin to love our chain; and if the truth be known, we would hate to see the chain broken.

Thus, may God grant us grace now. Even if we cannot escape our fleshly chains, may God's grace break the chains of our spirit. Then, leaving the body behind, as Abraham left his servants at the foot of the mountain (see Gen. 22:5), may our soul climb, as Abraham did, to the top of God's mountain to commune with "God Most High" (Gen. 14:18).

From the pen of Jim Reimann:

"The mountain of the LORD" Isaiah refers to in today's verse is Mount Moriah (also known as Mount Zion), or what has become known as the Temple Mount. Although two Islamic mosques sit on the site today, it remains a holy site to the Jews. And because Jesus visited the Temple Mount on many occasions, this relatively small piece of property is revered by Christians as well.

Thus, each of the world's three largest faiths lay claim in one respect or another to this mountain. But what does God say about Mount Zion? In His Word, He refers to this disputed property twelve times as either "my holy mountain" or "my holy hill." For example, David wrote the following in reference to the Messiah who was yet to come: "'I have installed my King on Zion, *my holy hill.*' ... Blessed are all who take refuge in him" (Ps. 2:6, 12).

And by way of fulfillment of today's text, Isaiah later wrote of how the Lord Himself will cause His people to "go up to the mountain of the LORD," saying, "Foreigners who ... love the name of the LORD ... *I will bring to my holy mountain and give them joy in my house of prayer*" (Isa. 56:6 – 7).

Father, make this my abiding passion: "Come, let [me] go up to the mountain of the LORD."

APRIL 5

Humility comes before honor.

Proverbs 15:33

From the pen of Charles Spurgeon:

Humiliation of the soul always comes with a blessing, for if I empty my heart of self, God will fill it with His love. Whoever desires close communion with Christ should remember these words of the Lord: "This is the one I esteem: he who is humble and contrite in spirit, and trembles at my word" (Isa. 66:2). If you truly desire to climb to heaven, first stoop, for don't we know that Jesus first descended so that later He might ascend? (See Eph. 4:9 – 10.) First you must grow downward that you may grow upward, for the sweetest fellowship with heaven is enjoyed by humble souls — and by them alone. There is no blessing God will deny to a fully humbled spirit. "Blessed are the poor in spirit, for theirs is the kingdom of heaven" (Matt. 5:3). God's entire heavenly treasury will be a gift to the soul who is humble enough to be able to receive it without growing proud because of it.

Thus, He blesses each of us to the full measure and limit of what is safe for Him to do. So if you do not get a blessing, it is because it is not safe for you to have it. If your heavenly Father were to let your unhumbled spirit win a victory in His holy war, you would steal the crown for yourself. Then, when you encounter your next enemy, you would fall victim, because He will keep you humble for your own safety. But when a person is sincerely humble, never venturing to touch so much as a grain of praise for himself, there is scarcely any limit to what God will do for him.

Humility prepares us to be blessed by the God of all grace and to deal effectively with others, for true humility is a flower that will enhance and adorn any garden. It is a spice with which you may season every dish of life, improving every situation. Whether it is prayer or praise, whether work or suffering, the genuine salt of humility cannot be used to excess.

From the pen of Jim Reimann:

Humility is a continual theme in God's Word. As the following passage shows, His purpose in taking His children through the wilderness before allowing them to enter the promised land was to humble them. He told them:

> Be careful to follow every command I am giving you today, so that you may live and increase and may enter and possess the land that the LORD promised on oath to your forefathers. Remember how the LORD your God led you all the way in the desert these forty years, *to humble you and to test you* in order to know what was in your heart, whether or not you would keep his commands. *He humbled you*, causing you to hunger and then feeding you with manna, which neither you nor your fathers had known, to teach you that man does not live on bread alone but on every word that comes from the mouth of the LORD.

Deuteronomy 8:1 – 3

Jesus, although He was God's Son, spoke of His own humility, saying, "Take my yoke upon you and learn from me, for *I am gentle and humble in heart*, and you will find rest for your souls. For my yoke is easy and my burden is light" (Matt. 11:29 – 30). Paul too, encouraging us to imitate our Savior, said, "*Be completely humble and gentle*; be patient, bearing with one another in love" (Eph. 4:2).

APRIL 6

In the name of the LORD I cut them off.

Psalm 118:12

From the pen of Charles Spurgeon:

By His death our Lord Jesus did not purchase simply a right to a part of us, but purchased the entire person. He considered in His passion and death our complete sanctification: spirit, soul, and body; and that through this threefold kingdom, He would reign supreme without a rival. In fact, it is the business of the newborn nature that God has given to those He has regenerated to assert the rights of the Lord Jesus Christ.

Dear soul, if you are truly a child of God, you must conquer the areas of yourself that remain unblessed; you must submit all your powers and passions to the silver scepter of Jesus' gracious reign; and you must never be satisfied until He who is King due to His purchase of you also becomes King by your submission to His coronation in your heart, fully acknowledging His supreme reign. Thus, seeing that sin has no right to any part of us, we should wage a good and lawful war to seek to drive it out in the name of God.

Oh, my body, you are a member of Christ's body. Will I tolerate your subjection to the prince of darkness? "O my soul" (Ps. 103:2), Christ has suffered for your sins and redeemed you with His most "precious blood" (1 Peter 1:19). Will I allow my mind to become a storehouse of evil or my passions to be weapons of sin? Will I surrender my godly judgment to be perverted by error or my will to be led astray into the bonds of iniquity? No, my soul, you are Christ's, and sin has no right to you.

Dear Christian, be courageous in this. Don't be disheartened as though your spiritual enemies could never be destroyed. You are able to overcome them — not in your own strength — for even your weakest enemy would be too much for your greatest strength; but you can and will overcome them "by the blood of the Lamb" (Rev. 12:11). Go directly to your powerful God for strength and wait humbly upon Him. Then "the Mighty One of Jacob" (Gen. 49:24) will surely come to your rescue, and you will sing a song of victory through His grace.

From the pen of Jim Reimann:

Paul taught we are already "more than conquerors through him who loved us" (Rom. 8:37). And remember what John said of the redeemed: "They overcame ... by the blood of the Lamb and by the word of their testimony.... Therefore rejoice, you heavens and you who dwell in them!" (Rev. 12:11 – 12). With this in mind, may we prayerfully sing this song of victory to the Lord today:

"Oh, sing to the LORD a new song! For He has done marvelous things; His right hand and His holy arm have gained Him the victory. The LORD has made known His salvation; His righteousness He has revealed in the sight of the nations. He has remembered His mercy and His faithfulness to the house of Israel; All the ends of the earth have seen the salvation of our God. Shout joyfully to the LORD, all the earth; Break forth in song, rejoice, and sing praises. Sing to the LORD with the harp, With the harp and the sound of a psalm, With trumpets and the sound of a horn; Shout joyfully before the LORD, the King" (Ps. 98:1 – 6 NKJV).

APRIL 7

Save me from bloodguilt, O God, the God who saves me,
and my tongue will sing of your righteousness.

Psalm 51:14

From the pen of Charles Spurgeon:

In this solemn confession, it is good to note that David plainly names his sin. He does not lessen it to manslaughter or speak of it as some sort of reckless act or unfortunate accident that happened to a worthy man, but he calls it by its true name: bloodguilt, meaning murder. David did not actually kill the husband of Bathsheba himself; nevertheless, it was planned in his heart for Uriah to be slain, and before the Lord he was Uriah's murderer.

Thus, learn to be honest with God when confessing your sins. Don't assign better-sounding names to your foul-smelling sins, for whatever name you give them, they will smell no sweeter. Whatever God sees them to be is how you should endeavor to see them, and then, with complete openness of heart, acknowledge their true character.

Notice also that David was evidently oppressed with the heinousness of his sin. It is easy to use words, but difficult to feel their meaning, yet Psalm 51 is the perfect picture of a contrite spirit. May we seek after the same kind of brokenness of heart, for however excellent our words may be, if our heart is not fully conscious of the hell-deservingness of our sin, we cannot expect to find forgiveness.

Today's verse is an earnest prayer, addressed to "the God who saves," for it is His prerogative to forgive, and it is His role and His very name to save those who "seek his face" (Ps. 27:8). Better still, David refers to the Lord in our text as "the God who saves *me*," personalizing it. Yes, blessed be His name, for when I go to Him through Jesus' blood, I can rejoice that He is "the God who saves *me*"!

The psalmist David ends today's verse with a commendable vow, saying in essence, "If God will deliver me, I 'will sing.'" The King James Version says it even more strongly, that David will "sing *aloud*," for who can keep silent about such a mercy as this. But be sure to note that the subject of the song is God's righteousness, for he says, "My tongue will sing of *your righteousness.*"

We as well must sing of the finished work of our precious Savior, and those of us who have experienced the most of His forgiving love should sing the loudest.

From the pen of Jim Reimann:

God's Word tells us that "anyone who hates his brother is a murderer" (1 John 3:15). So who of us was not a murderer before Jesus saved us, for who of us has not harbored hate in our heart for someone at some point? Thus, we were under the condemnation of bloodguilt, just as David was. But there is a precious answer to this terrible dilemma, and isn't it interesting that the only solution to the shedding of another's blood through murder was the shedding of the Lord's blood.

Just as David was granted forgiveness for murdering Uriah, God long ago promised forgiveness for bloodguilt to those of us He has chosen. Here is how Joel recorded this beautiful promise:

"Judah will be inhabited forever and Jerusalem through all generations. Their bloodguilt, which I have not pardoned, I will pardon." The LORD dwells in Zion!

Joel 3:20 – 21

APRIL 8

I will fear no evil, for you are with me.

Psalm 23:4

From the pen of Charles Spurgeon:

Isn't it amazing how free the Holy Spirit can make a Christian from outer circumstances? How bright the light that can shine within us when it is so dark without. How steady, calm, happy, and peaceful we can be even when the world around us seems to be shaking to and fro and when "the pillars of the earth" (1 Sam. 2:8 KJV) are removed. Even death with all its terrible strength has no power to interrupt the music in a Christian's heart. Instead it makes the music become more sweet, clear, and heavenly until the final act of kindness that death can do, which makes our earthly song melt into the heavenly chorus, turning our temporal joy into eternal bliss. Thus, let us have confidence in the blessed Spirit's power to comfort us.

Dear believer, are you facing poverty? "Fear not" (Luke 12:32 KJV), for God's divine Spirit can give you, even in your poverty, greater blessings than the rich have in their abundance. You never know what joys may be in preparation for you around your humble earthly cottage, for God's grace may be planting beautiful roses of contentment even now. Are you facing an illness or a decline in your bodily strength, so much so that you are anticipating long nights of suffering and languishing and days of continual pain? Don't be sad. Your bed may become a throne to you, for you have little knowledge of how every pain shooting through your body may "be like a refiner's fire" (Mal. 3:2) to consume your dross — a beam of glory to light up the secret parts of your soul. Are your eyes growing dim? Jesus will be your light. Is your hearing failing you? Jesus' name will be your soul's best music and He Himself your dearest delight.

Greek philosopher Socrates (c. 470 – 399 BC) once said, "Philosophers can be happy without music." And Christians can be happier than philosophers, even when all outward causes or reasons for rejoicing are removed.

In You, my God, my heart will triumph, despite what outward trials I face. By Your power, O blessed Spirit, my heart will be exceedingly glad, though all earthly things may fail me.

From the pen of Jim Reimann:

Learning to be content regardless of our circumstances is difficult. It is easy to find someone who appears to have an easier life than we do, but it also is easy to find someone who is enduring much more troubling circumstances. Yet the Bible encourages us more than once to be content. For example, John the Baptist once responded to the Roman soldiers who had come to him, saying, "Don't extort money and don't accuse people falsely — *be content with your pay*" (Luke 3:14); and Paul told Timothy, "*Godliness with contentment is great gain. For we brought nothing into the world, and we can take nothing out of it. But if we have food and clothing, we will be content with that*" (1 Tim. 6:6 – 8).

The lesson of contentment is just that — a lesson — something that even the apostle Paul had to learn, for he said, "*I have learned* to be content whatever the circumstances" (Phil. 4:11). Finally, the writer of Hebrews tells us, "Keep your lives free from the love of money and *be content with what you have*, because God has said, 'Never will I leave you; never will I forsake you'" (Heb. 13:5).

APRIL 9

Your gentleness has made me great.

Psalm 18:35 NKJV

From the pen of Charles Spurgeon:

Another possible translation of this verse is: "Your *goodness* has made me great." Thus, David attributed all his greatness not to his own goodness, but to the goodness of God. "Your *providence*" is another possible rendering, and providence is nothing more than goodness in action, for goodness is the bud of the flower of providence or, in other words, goodness is the seed of which providence is the harvest. Another translator rendered it "Your *help*," for *help* is a synonym for *providence*, where, in this case, providence means the steadfast ally of the saints, aiding them in their service to the Lord. Still another possible reading is "Your *humility* has made me great."

In fact, it is God's act of humbling Himself that is the cause of our being made great. We are so small that if God should totally reveal His greatness without humbling Himself, we would be trampled under His feet. But our gracious God, who must stoop even to view the sky, and who must bow to see what angels do, turns His eyes still lower to see the lowly and contrite — and then makes them great.

Another rendering from the Septuagint (Greek translation of the Old Testament from the third and second centuries BC) reads, "Your *discipline*" (meaning "Your *fatherly correction*") "has made me great." And the Chaldee paraphrase (Aramaic translation of a portion of the Bible from the second century BC) reads, "Your Word has increased me." Despite all these various translations, the idea is still the same: David at-

tributes every aspect of his own greatness to the humble goodness of his Father in heaven.

May this sentiment be echoed in my heart today as I "lay [my crown]" (Rev. 4:10) at Jesus' feet and cry, "Your gentleness has made me great"! How miraculous has been my experience of God's gentleness. How gentle His corrections have been. How gentle He has been by exercising such patience with me. How gently He has drawn me to Himself and taught me.

Dear believer, meditate on this theme. Let your gratitude be awakened, your humility be deepened, and your love be revived before you end your time alone with God today.

From the pen of Jim Reimann:

Of course, Spurgeon did not have access to the New International Version of the Bible, which renders today's verse: "You stoop down to make me great" — a reading consistent with the others. Isn't it amazing how our omniscient, omnipresent, and omnipotent God was willing to "stoop down" to "make [us] great." Paul expressed this miraculous truth in words as beautiful as those of David, when he wrote:

> Your attitude should be the same as that of Christ Jesus: Who, being in very nature God, did not consider equality with God something to be grasped, but made himself nothing, taking the very nature of a servant, being made in human likeness. And being found in appearance as a man, he humbled himself and became obedient to death — even death on a cross!
>
> Philippians 2:5 – 8

APRIL 10

Last night an angel of the God whose I am and whom I serve
stood beside me.

Acts 27:23

From the pen of Charles Spurgeon:

The crew of the ship in this story from Acts faced "a wind of hurricane force" (v. 14) and a time of prolonged darkness "when neither sun nor stars appeared for many days" (v. 20). Those dangers along with the imminent risk of shipwreck put the crew in a dire situation, but one man among them remained perfectly calm, and it was through his words the rest were reassured. That man was Paul, and he alone was brave enough to say, "I urge you to keep up your courage" (Acts 27:22). There were veteran Roman soldiers and salty old mariners on board, yet this poor Jewish prisoner showed more bravery than all the others, for he had a secret friend who kept his courage strong. The Lord Jesus had dispatched a heavenly messenger to whisper words of comfort into the ear of His faithful servant, thus he was able to have a shining countenance and speak like a man at ease.

If we "fear the LORD" (Deut. 6:13), we may look for His timely intercession when our situation is at its worst. Thankfully, angels are not deterred by storms or kept from us by darkness, nor do seraphim think it a humiliation to visit the poorest of God's heavenly family. Although angel visits may be few and far between during ordinary times, they will be frequent in our nights of struggles and storms. Friends may abandon us during times of great pressure, but our contact with the inhabitants of the angelic world will be more abundant, and their loving message brought to us from God's throne by way of Jacob's ladder (see Gen. 28:12) will give us the strength we need to persevere.

Dear believer, is this a time of distress for you? If so, ask for help specific to your need. Jesus Himself is the angel of God's covenant, and if you earnestly seek His presence, it will not be denied. His presence will cheer your heart, and, like Paul, who had an angel from God standing with him through the storm, you will experience His protection when the anchor of life's ship breaks loose and the rocky shore threatens.

> O angel of my God, be near,
> Amid the darkness hush my fear;
> Loud roars the wild tempestuous sea,
> Your presence, Lord, shall comfort me.
>
> Author unknown

From the pen of Jim Reimann:

We often tend to think that examples of the work of angels in days of old, such as the angel's ministry to Paul in today's verse, is something that doesn't happen today. And although the following passage is typically attributed solely to the Messiah, it is also a promise to us:

> If you make the Most High your dwelling — even the LORD, who is my refuge — then no harm will befall you, no disaster will come near your tent. For he will command his angels concerning you to guard you in all your ways; they will lift you up in their hands, so that you will not strike your foot against a stone.
>
> Psalm 91:9 – 12

By way of confirmation of this truth, remember these words: "Are not all angels ministering spirits sent to serve those who will inherit salvation?" (Heb. 1:14).

APRIL 11

Look upon my affliction and my distress
and take away all my sins.

Psalm 25:18

From the pen of Charles Spurgeon:

It is good when our prayers regarding our sorrows are tied to our prayers regarding our sins — that is, when we are submissive to God's hand and are not totally consumed with our own pain, but remember our offenses against Him. It is good when we take both our sorrow and sin to the same place. It was to God that David took his sorrow, and it was to God that David confessed his sin.

Thus, it is to God that you as well must take your sorrows. Even your smallest sorrows may be rolled onto Him, for "even the very hairs of your head are all numbered" (Matt. 10:30), and your greatest sorrows may be committed to Him, for "who else has held the oceans in his hand?" (Isa. 40:12 NLT). So go to Him, whatever your trouble, and you will find Him willing and able to relieve you of it. But don't forget to take Him your sins as well. You must carry them to Jesus' cross so His blood may fall on them, purging away their guilt and destroying their defiling power.

Yet the special lesson today is this: we are to go to the Lord with our sorrows and sins in the right spirit. Notice, regarding his sorrow, David simply asks, "*Look upon* my affliction and my distress," but also note his next petition is vastly more definite and direct — "*Take away* all my sins." If suffering, most of us would have prayed, "*Take away* my affliction and my distress and *look upon* all my sins." But David does not, for he cries out, saying, in essence, "Lord, as for my affliction and my distress, I will not dictate to Your wisdom and Your will. Lord, look at my troubles. I leave them to You. Although I would be glad to

have my pain removed, do as You will. But as for my sins, Lord, I know exactly what I want done with them. I must have them forgiven, for I cannot endure to remain under their curse another moment."

When Christians weigh sorrow and sin on the scale, they must see sorrow as lighter than sin. And although they do not desire their troubles to continue, there is no way they can continue to support the burden of their sins.

From the pen of Jim Reimann:

From today's text we see that David understood that God could take his sins away, but we may wonder if he fully understood that the Messiah would take the sins of His people, and their sorrows, upon Himself. Of course, David would not have known these beautiful words of Isaiah, for they would not be written until some three hundred years after his death:

> Surely he took up our infirmities and carried our sorrows, yet we considered him stricken by God, smitten by him, and afflicted. But he was pierced for our transgressions, he was crushed for our iniquities; *the punishment that brought us peace was upon him*, and by his wounds we are healed. We all, like sheep, have gone astray, each of us has turned to his own way; and *the LORD has laid on him the iniquity of us all*.
>
> Isaiah 53:4 – 6

Jesus, thank You for taking my sin and sorrows upon Yourself. And help me to carry Your burden, although You said, "My yoke is easy and my burden is light" (Matt. 11:30).

APRIL 12

… the King's Garden.
Nehemiah 3:15

From the pen of Charles Spurgeon:

The mention of "the King's Garden" here by Nehemiah brings to mind the paradise "the King of kings" (1 Tim. 6:15) prepared for Adam and Eve. But sin has totally ruined the most delightful home of all time and forced mankind to till the ground, which yields thorns and briers for them.

Dear soul, remember mankind's fall, for it was your fall as well. Weep and deeply grieve because the Lord of love was so shamefully treated by the head of the human race of which you are a member — a member as undeserving as any. Recognize how many dragons and demons now roam this fair earth, which was once a garden of delight.

But also look back to another "King's Garden" — one that the King watered with His own bloody sweat: Gethsemane, a garden whose bitter herbs are far sweeter to regenerated souls than even the luscious fruits of Eden. It was in Gethsemane that the evil of the serpent in the first garden was undone, there that the curse was lifted from the earth, and there that it was borne by the woman's promised Seed.

Dear believer, deeply contemplate your Lord's agony and passion in Gethsemane. Go often to the garden of the olive press and behold your great Redeemer rescuing you from your lost estate. It is the "Garden of gardens" indeed, where your soul may truly see the guilt of sin and the power of love — two sights that surpass all others.

Is there no other "King's Garden"? Yes, it is the human heart — or it should be. But are the flowers flourishing in my heart? Are any of the finest fruits ripening there? Is the King walking there and finding rest in the orchards of my spirit? Oh, may I take care to see that the plants are pruned and watered, and that I "catch … the little foxes that ruin the vineyards" (Song 2:15)!

Come, Lord Jesus, and let the heavenly wind blow at Your coming, so the fragrance of the spices of Your garden may waft across the land. O Lord, don't let me forget "the King's Garden" of the church. Send her success — rebuild her walls, nourish her plants, ripen her fruit, and from her huge wilderness, reclaim her barren wasteland. Truly make her "the King's Garden."

From the pen of Jim Reimann:

There is another "King's Garden" from the life of our Savior that all believers should remember with thanksgiving in our hearts, for *"at the place where Jesus was crucified, there was a garden, and in the garden a new tomb, in which no one had ever been laid. Because it was the Jewish day of Preparation and since the tomb was nearby, they laid Jesus there"* (John 19:41 – 42). And if not for what happened in this garden — Christ's resurrection — we would all still be hopelessly lost. Here is what Paul taught regarding Jesus' resurrection, and ours:

If Christ has not been raised, our preaching is useless and so is your faith.… And if Christ has not been raised, your faith is futile; you are still in your sins. Then those also who have fallen asleep in Christ are lost. If only for this life we have hope in Christ, we are to be pitied more than all men. But Christ has indeed been raised from the dead, the firstfruits of those who have fallen asleep.

1 Corinthians 15:14, 17 – 20

APRIL 13

He is to lay his hand on the head of the burnt offering,
and it will be accepted on his behalf to make atonement for him.

Leviticus 1:4

From the pen of Charles Spurgeon:

Our Lord being "made ... sin for us" (2 Cor. 5:21) is prefigured in today's text by the very meaningful transfer of the people's sin to "the young bull ... [by] ... the priests" (Lev. 1:5). The laying of the hand on the animal by the one offering the sacrifice was not seen as a mere touch, for other Scriptures define the word as "leaning heavily," as in: "Your wrath lies heavily upon me" (Ps. 88:7). This is indeed the very essence and nature of faith which does not simply put us into contact with Jesus, the great Substitute, but teaches us to lean upon Him with the entire burden of our guilt.

Jehovah God placed upon the head of the Substitute all the offenses of His covenant people, but each of those chosen ones is brought personally to Him to ratify this solemn covenant act, when by grace he is enabled by faith to lay his hand upon the head of "the Lamb that was slain from the creation of the world" (Rev. 13:8).

Dear believer, do you remember that joyous day when you first received your pardon through Jesus the sin-bearer? Can't you make the glad confession, agreeing with the writer who proclaimed:

My soul recalls my day of deliverance with delight. Burdened with guilt and full of fears, I saw my Savior as my Substitute and laid my hand upon Him. Oh, how timidly at first! Yet my courage grew and my confidence was confirmed until I leaned my soul entirely on Him, and now it is my unceasing joy to know my sins are no longer imputed to me, but have been laid on Him. And just as the Samaritan covered the debts of the wounded traveler [see Luke 10:35], Jesus has said of all my future sinfulness, "Charge it to My account."

Author unknown

Blessed discovery! The eternal comfort of a grateful heart!

My numerous sins transferred to Him,
Shall never more be found,
Lost in His blood's atoning stream,
Where every crime is drowned!
Augustus Montague Toplady, 1740 – 78

From the pen of Jim Reimann:

The sacrificial system was only a picture of what was to find its fulfillment in Jesus. He became the sacrificial lamb, taking our sin upon Himself, but He also became "the scapegoat" (Lev. 16:8), taking our sin away forever. "As far as the east is from the west, so far has he removed our transgressions from us" (Ps. 103:12). And when He cried, "It is finished" (John 19:30), the perfect sacrifice had been made, and "by one sacrifice he has made perfect forever those who are being made holy" (Heb. 10:14). With this in mind, may this be our prayer to our eternal Substitute:

"Holy, holy, holy is the Lord God Almighty, who was, and is, and is to come.... You are worthy, our Lord and God, to receive glory and honor and power, for you created all things, and by your will they were created and have their being" (Rev. 4:8, 11).

APRIL 14

Tell the righteous it will be well with them.

Isaiah 3:10

From the pen of Charles Spurgeon:

It will *always* "be well" with "the righteous." If this verse had said, "'Tell the righteous it will be well with them' *in times of prosperity*," we would have to be thankful only during times of great wealth, yet prosperity is often a time of peril, and being spared from its snares is actually a gift from heaven. Or if the verse were written, "'It will be well with them' *when under persecution*," we would have to be thankful only when we are being sustained during times of persecution. But when it says, "It will be well with them," and no time is mentioned, all time is included.

God's use of the word *will* must be understood always in the largest sense. For example, "It will be well with [the righteous]" — from the beginning to the end of the year, from the first of evening shadows until the first light of dawn, in all conditions and under all circumstances. In fact, "it will be [so] well with them," they could never imagine it to be better, for they are well fed, feeding on the flesh and blood of Jesus; they are well clothed, for they wear the imputed righteousness of Christ; they are well housed, for they dwell with God; they are well married, for their souls are joined through the bonds of marriage to Christ; they are well provided for, for "the LORD is [their] shepherd" (Ps. 23:1); and they are well-endowed, for heaven is their inheritance. "It will be well with [the righteous]" by God's divine authority, for it is by the mouth of God we have this comforting assurance.

O beloved, if God declares all "will be well," ten thousand demons may declare all things bad, but we will "laugh them to scorn" (Job 22:19 KJV).

Praise God for a faith that enables us to believe Him when every created being seems to contradict Him. His Word tells us, in essence, "'It will be well with [you],' O righteous one." But if you cannot see it, allow His Word to stand in place of your sight. Yes, believe it on His divine authority with more confidence than if your own eyes and feelings had said it to you. Whom God blesses is blessed indeed, and what His mouth declares to be truth is the most trustworthy and steadfast thing we can know.

From the pen of Jim Reimann:

A word of caution here: Spurgeon is not saying, nor does today's text mean, that everything will always go well *by mankind's definition* for the righteous. What man sees as bad is not always bad, and what man sees as good is not always good, "'For my thoughts are not your thoughts, neither are your ways my ways,' declares the LORD" (Isa. 55:8). God uses all things, whether "good" or "bad," to conform us "to the likeness of his Son" (Rom. 8:29), for as Paul said in the previous verse, "We know that in all things God works for the good of those who love him" (Rom. 8:28).

It is during the difficult times — difficult from our perspective — that we typically are the most profoundly changed. Remember, difficulties are gifts from Him, for Isaiah said, "The Lord *gives* you the bread of adversity and the water of affliction" (Isa. 30:20). We also must remember: "He is the Rock, his works are perfect, and all his ways are just. A faithful God who does no wrong, upright and just is he" (Deut. 32:4).

APRIL 15

Lift them up for ever.

Psalm 28:9 KJV

From the pen of Charles Spurgeon:

God's people need lifting up, for we are heavily burdened by nature. We have no wings, and even if we did, we would be like the soldiers who slept "among the campfires" (Ps. 68:13). We need God's divine grace to make us "mount up with wings" (Isa. 40:31 KJV) "sheathed with silver … [and] feathers with shining gold" (Ps. 68:13). Sparks naturally fly upward, but the sinful souls of mankind fall downward.

O Lord, "Lift them up for ever"! David himself prayed, "To you, O LORD, I lift up my soul" (Ps. 25:1), and in today's text he expressed the necessity for souls other than his to be lifted up as well. Thus, when you ask for this blessing for yourself, don't forget to seek it for others too.

There are three ways in which God's people need to be lifted up. The first is that they need to be elevated in character. *O Lord, "Lift them up." Do not allow Your people to be like the world's people! The world dwells with the wicked one — lift them out of it! The world's people seek after silver and gold, their own pleasure, and the gratification of their own lusts; but, Lord, lift Your people above all this. Keep them from being "muckrakers," as John Bunyan (1628 – 88), in* The Pilgrim's Progress, *called the man who was always scratching after gold. Instead, O Lord, set their hearts upon their risen Lord and their heavenly heritage!*

Believers also need to be lifted up in warfare. *O Lord, if your people seem to be falling in battle, be pleased to give them the victory. If the foot of their foe is upon their neck for even a moment, help them to grasp "the sword of the Spirit"* (Eph. 6:17) *and to win the battle eventually. Lord, lift Your children's spirits in the day of conflict;* *don't allow them to sit in the dust, mourning forever. Don't allow their Adversary to frustrate them greatly or make them fret, but when they have been persecuted, let them sing like Hannah, who sang of the mercy of a God who delivered her.*

Finally, we also may ask our Lord to "raise [us] up at the last day" (John 6:39).

Lord, lift us up by taking us home. Lift our bodies from the grave, and raise our souls to Your eternal kingdom in glory.

From the pen of Jim Reimann:

Hannah, mentioned by Spurgeon, experienced the deliverance of the Lord, for we are told, "Because the LORD had closed her womb, her rival kept provoking her in order to irritate her. This went on year after year. Whenever Hannah went up to the house of the LORD, her rival provoked her till she wept and would not eat" (1 Sam. 1:6 – 7). Ultimately, she was given a son, the prophet Samuel. Thus, she knew something of being lifted up, for she prayed:

My heart rejoices in the LORD; in the LORD my horn is lifted high. My mouth boasts over my enemies, for I delight in your deliverance…. The LORD brings death and makes alive; he brings down to the grave and raises up. The LORD sends poverty and wealth; he humbles and he exalts. He raises the poor from the dust and lifts the needy from the ash heap; he seats them with princes and has them inherit a throne of honor. For the foundations of the earth are the LORD's; upon them he has set the world.

1 Samuel 2:1, 6 – 8

APRIL 16

Moses' hands ... remained steady till sunset.

Exodus 17:12

From the pen of Charles Spurgeon:

Moses' prayer was so powerful that the entire victory depended on it. His petitions unnerved and confused the enemy more than Joshua's fighting, yet both were needed. And when it comes to conflict in the soul, force and fervor, decision and devotion, and valor and vigor must join forces. You must wrestle with your sin, but the most important part of wrestling must be done alone, in private with God.

A prayer like this one of Moses' raises the sign of the covenant to the Lord. His rod represented the emblem of God working with Moses, and thus was also the symbol of God's government in Israel. So learn, O praying saint, to raise the promise and the oath of God to Him, for the Lord cannot deny His own declarations. Raise the rod of His promise and receive what you desire.

When Moses grew weary of holding his hands in the air, his friends assisted him. So when your prayers begin to grow weary, let faith support one hand and holy hope the other. This kind of prayer, securely seated on "the stone of Israel" (Gen. 49:24 KJV) — "the Rock of our salvation" (Ps. 95:1) — will persevere and prevail. We must beware of becoming faint in our devotion, for if Moses felt faint, who of us will escape? It is far easier to fight with sin in public than to pray against it in private. It has been said that Joshua never grew weary in battle, while Moses *did* grow weary in praying, but the more spiritual the exercise, the more difficult it is for flesh and blood to continue it.

Therefore, let us plead with the Lord for extra strength, and may the Spirit of God who "helps us in our weakness" (Rom. 8:26) enable us like Moses to continue with steady hands "till sunset"

— till the evening of life is over; till we come to the rising of a better sun in the land where prayer is "swallowed up" (1 Cor. 15:54) in praise.

From the pen of Jim Reimann:

Today's verse is taken from a story of the Israelites soon after their deliverance from Egypt. Although the Egyptians were no longer a threat, God's people were still far from the Promised Land and they still faced a number of enemies. This miraculous, God-given victory should have provided the Israelites yet another reason to trust the Lord as they entered Canaan, but unfortunately they distrusted Him, bringing upon themselves forty years of wandering in the wilderness. Here is today's verse in its context:

Joshua fought the Amalekites as Moses had ordered, and Moses, Aaron and Hur went to the top of the hill. As long as Moses held up his hands, the Israelites were winning, but whenever he lowered his hands, the Amalekites were winning. When Moses' hands grew tired, they took a stone and put it under him and he sat on it. Aaron and Hur held his hands up — one on one side, one on the other — so that his hands remained steady till sunset. So Joshua overcame the Amalekite army with the sword.

Then the LORD said to Moses, "Write this on a scroll as something to be remembered and make sure that Joshua hears it, because I will completely blot out the memory of Amalek from under heaven."

Moses built an altar and called it The LORD is my Banner. He said, "For hands were lifted up to the throne of the LORD."

Exodus 17:10 – 16

APRIL 17

We would like to see Jesus.
John 12:21

From the pen of Charles Spurgeon:

The world seems to cry out continually, "Who will show us anything good?" The lost soul seeks satisfaction in earthly comfort, enjoyment, and riches. But a sinner whose heart has been quickened by God knows of only one good pursuit: "If only I knew where to find him!" (Job 23:3). Once his soul has been truly awakened to sense his guilt, you could place all the world's gold at his feet and he would say, "Take it away. I want to find Him."

It is a true blessing for someone finally to have all desires brought into focus, centered on one object. With fifty different desires, the heart resembles a stagnant pool of marshy water, breeding stench and pestilence; but when all desires are focused into one flowing channel, the heart becomes a river of pure water, swiftly running to fertilize the fields. Thus, happy is the one who has but one desire, if that desire is focused on Christ, for when the soul begins to focus on Him, it is a blessed sign of God working within the heart. Such a person will never be content with mere religious rituals, but will say, "I want Christ. Mere rituals are of no use to me. I want Jesus Himself, and offering these to me is like offering me an empty pitcher when I am dying of thirst. Jesus is my soul's desire. I 'would like to see Jesus'!"

Dear reader, is this your condition? Do you sense only one desire, the desire for Christ? If so, you are not far from the kingdom of heaven. Do you have but one wish: that you may be washed from all your sins in Jesus' blood? Can you truly confess, "I would give all I have to be a Christian — everything I have and hope for — if I might only sense that I have an inheritance in Christ"? If so, "be of good cheer" (Matt. 9:2 KJV), for the Lord loves you and soon you will come into the daylight and will rejoice in the liberty of being made free in Christ.

From the pen of Jim Reimann:

The context of today's passage is a very interesting one. We are told: "Now there were some Greeks among those who went up to worship at the Feast [of Passover]. They came to Philip … with a request. 'Sir,' they said, 'we would like to see Jesus'" (John 12:20 – 22).

Yet Jesus responds in a way that seems quite strange at first blush. But an understanding of the fuller context of the book of John puts it into perspective. "Jesus replied, 'The hour has come for the Son of Man to be glorified'" (John 12:23). Up to this point John had repeatedly written regarding Jesus — and Jesus Himself had said — that "his time had not yet come" (John 8:20).

What suddenly had changed, causing the Lord to say for the very first time, "The hour has come"? Remember Jesus' earlier words, referring to the Gentiles: "I have other sheep that are not of this sheep pen. I must bring them also. They too will listen to my voice, and there shall be one flock and one shepherd" (John 10:16). Now, Jesus sees the Greeks (or Gentiles) coming to Him — a sign of His ministry on earth nearing its completion — and says, "The hour has come."

Father, may this indeed be the hour You have chosen to awaken the hearts and souls of those we love who don't yet know You. Let them "see Jesus."

APRIL 18

You said, I will surely do you good.

Genesis 32:12 Amplified

From the pen of Charles Spurgeon:

When Jacob was at the Jabbok River, and Esau was headed toward him with armed men, he earnestly sought God's protection. His over-arching reason in his plea to God was: "You said, 'I will surely do you good.'" Oh, the power of that prayer! He was holding God to His word — "You said...." The attribute of God's faithfulness is one of the splendid "horns of the altar" (Ex. 29:12) we may lay our hands on. Jacob not only says "You said," but reminds the Lord of His promise, "I will surely do you good" — something even stronger to hold in our grasp. "Does he speak and then not act?" (Num. 23:19). "Let God be true, and every man a liar" (Rom. 3:4).

Will God not be true to His word? Will not every word that comes from His lips stand firm and be fulfilled? Solomon, at the dedication of the temple, used the same powerful prayer. He pleaded with God to remember the promise He had spoken to his father David and to bless that place (see 1 Kings 8:22 – 30). When some-one gives another person a promissory note, his honor is at stake; he signs his name to the note and must follow through on its terms in a timely manner or risk his credit. But it will never be said that God dishonors His obligations, for the credit of the "God Most High" (Gen. 14:18) has never been impeached, and never will be. He is punctual to the second — never early, never late. If you search His Word and compare it to the ex-perience of His people, you will find the two in perfect agreement from beginning to end. Many a gray-haired patriarch has said with Joshua, "Not one of all the good promises the LORD your God gave you has failed. Every promise has been fulfilled; not one has failed" (Josh. 23:14).

You need not pray a promise of God with an "if," but may plead it with certainty, for the Lord meant to fulfill the promise or He would not have given it. He does not give us His promises simply to keep us quiet or to keep us hopeful for a while with the intention of putting us off in the end. No. When He speaks, it is because He means to do as He says.

From the pen of Jim Reimann:

The Jews have a history of reminding God of His promises, asking Him to fulfill them. Today we have seen Jacob and Solomon take the word of the Lord back to Him in prayer. And there can be no doubt that Solomon learned to do this from his father David, who prayed the same way. As you read the following prayer of David, no-tice how often he reminds the Lord of His own words:

> And now, LORD God, keep forever the promise you have made concerning your servant and his house. Do as you promised, so that your name will be great forever. Then men will say, "The LORD Almighty is God over Israel!" And the house of your servant David will be established before you. O LORD Almighty, God of Israel, you have revealed this to your servant, saying, "I will build a house for you." So your servant has found courage to offer you this prayer. O Sovereign LORD, you are God! Your words are trust-worthy, and you have promised these good things to your servant. Now be pleased to bless the house of your servant, that it may continue forever in your sight; for you, O Sovereign LORD, have spoken.
>
> 2 Samuel 7:25 – 29

APRIL 19

These are the words of the Amen.

Revelation 3:14

From the pen of Charles Spurgeon:

The word *amen* formally confirms "the words" that went before; thus Jesus is the great Confirmer, for He is immutable and is forever "the Amen" of all His promises. Dear sinner, I hope to comfort you with this reflection: Jesus Christ said, "Come to me, all you who are weary and burdened, and I will give you rest" (Matt. 11:28). And if you go to Him, He will say "Amen" in your soul and His promise will be true to you. When He was here in the flesh, He fulfilled the words of Isaiah, who wrote, "A bruised reed he will not break" (Isa. 42:3). O you poor, broken, and bruised heart, if you will only go to Him, He will say "Amen" to you, and what has been true in countless cases in bygone years will be true in your soul too.

And dear Christian, aren't these words comforting to you, that there is not a word that has ever come from the Savior's lips that He has ever retracted? The words of Jesus will stand when "heaven and earth will pass away" (Matt. 24:35). Even if you will take hold of only half a promise, you will find it to be true, but beware of someone such as Mr. Clip-promise (a character in *The Pilgrim's Progress* by John Bunyan, 1628 – 88), who will destroy much of the comfort of God's Word.

Jesus is the "Yes" and the "Amen" (2 Cor. 1:20) in each of His offices, for He was a Priest to offer pardon and cleansing in the past, but is "the Amen" as a Priest still today. He was a King to rule and reign for His people and to defend them with His "mighty arm" (Ps. 89:13 KJV), but is still the same today as an Amen King. And He was a Prophet of old to prophesy of good things to come, but His "lips drop sweetness as the honeycomb" (Song 4:11) still today as the Amen

Prophet. He is also "the Amen" when it comes to the merit of His blood and His righteousness, for His sacred blood-stained robe of righteousness will remain great and glorious long after the earth has decayed.

Therefore, Jesus is "the Amen" in every title He bears. He is "your husband" (Isa. 54:5), never seeking a divorce; your Friend, sticking "closer than a brother" (Prov. 18:24); your Shepherd, walking with you through "the valley of the shadow of death" (Ps. 23:4); your "help and ... deliverer" (Ps. 40:17); your "fortress ... and the horn of [your] salvation" (Ps. 18:2); "[your] security" (Job 31:24); "[your] joy and [your] delight" (Ps. 43:4); your "all in all" (1 Cor. 15:28); and finally, your "Yes" and "Amen" in all things.

From the pen of Jim Reimann:

If you are unfamiliar with Mr. Clip-promise from *The Pilgrim's Progress*, perhaps a word of explanation would be helpful here. In a sermon from 1860, Spurgeon used him as an example, saying:

> Mr. Clip-promise does not doubt God's promise, but only "clips" the edge of it, saying that not all of it will be fulfilled — just a part of it.... And if you have attempted to cut God's promise down, I plead with you to take it as it stands in all of its plenteousness of grace and sufficiency. Never judge it by your own ideas, but take it as it comes from God, shining and glittering from the mint of heaven. Take it at its full current value and you will surely have its equivalent in the fulfillments that God will work for you in His providence and grace.

APRIL 20

Fight the battles of the LORD.

1 Samuel 18:17

From the pen of Charles Spurgeon:

The sacred army of God's elect is still at war upon the earth, with Jesus Christ as the Captain of their salvation, for He said, "Surely I am with you always, to the very end of the age" (Matt. 28:20). Listen to the shouts of war. May the people of God stand fast in their ranks, and may no one's heart fail him.

Even now it is true in England that the battle has turned against us, and unless the Lord Jesus lifts His sword, there is no telling what will become of God's church in this country. But may we "be strong and courageous" (Deut. 31:6). There has never been a time when Protestantism has seemed to tremble more in the scales than now when there is a fierce effort to restore the Roman antichrist to his ancient seat. We greatly need a bold voice and a strong hand to preach and publish the old gospel for which the martyrs bled and the confessors died.

May we take heart with the knowledge that our Savior, through His Spirit, is still on earth. And because He is always in the midst of the battle, the outcome is never in doubt. As the conflict rages, how satisfying it is to know that the Lord Jesus, in His role as our great Intercessor, is powerfully pleading for His people. O you who are fearful, don't gaze so much at the battle here below where you are surrounded by smoke and stunned by so many bloody garments. Instead, lift your eyes above, where your Savior lives and pleads on your behalf, for as long as He "lives to intercede" (Heb. 7:25), the cause of God is safe. Thus, let us fight as if everything depends on us, but let us look up, knowing that everything truly depends on Him.

Now, with the rose of the Savior's atonement and the lily of Christian purity (see Song 2:1), "I charge you" (Song 2:7) who love Jesus to fight valiantly in the Holy War for truth and righteousness. For the sake of His kingdom, fight onward, "for the battle is not yours, but God's" (2 Chron. 20:15).

From the pen of Jim Reimann:

As in Spurgeon's day, the gospel is greatly under attack, even within the organized church. The seeker movement, along with that of the emerging church, has moved the preaching of God's Word to the sidelines instead of making it the holy center of God's church. What we need today are men committed to preaching "the whole counsel of God" (Acts 20:27 NKJV), as Paul said. This means having preachers who exposit the Word of God and allow it to do its work, not simply teach topically or preach with an ulterior motive. Here is a portion of Paul's warning in Acts to God's church:

> I never shrank or kept back or fell short from declaring to you the whole purpose and plan and counsel of God.
>
> Acts 20:27 Amplified

Keep watch over yourselves and all the flock of which the Holy Spirit has made you overseers. Be shepherds of the church of God, which he bought with his own blood. I know that after I leave, savage wolves will come in among you and will not spare the flock. Even from your own number men will arise and distort the truth in order to draw away disciples after them. So be on your guard!

Acts 20:28 – 31

APRIL 21

Christ Jesus … is at the right hand of God.

Romans 8:34

From the pen of Charles Spurgeon:

He who "was [once] despised and rejected by men" (Isa. 53:3) now occupies the esteemed position of a beloved and honored Son, for "the right hand of God" is the place of majesty and favor. And our Lord Jesus is His people's representative — when He died for them they received rest, when He rose again they received liberty, and when He sat down at His Father's right hand they received favor, honor, and dignity. Thus, when Christ is elevated, all His people are raised, accepted, cherished, and glorified, for He is their head and representative. The fact that Jesus is seated "at the right hand of God" should therefore be seen as the acceptance of Him as our Guarantor and our Representative, and as the acceptance of our souls.

Dear saint, look at this truth as the assurance of your freedom from condemnation. "Who is he that condemns" (Rom. 8:34), for who will condemn those who are in Jesus, seated "at the right hand of God"? The right hand is the side of power and authority, and Christ "at the right hand of God" has "all authority in heaven and on earth" (Matt. 28:18). Who will be able to fight against those who have such a powerful Captain? Dear soul, what can destroy you if Omnipotence is your helper? If the shield of the Almighty covers you, what sword can strike you? So rest in the assurance that if Jesus is your all-prevailing King; if He "has put all his enemies under his feet" (1 Cor. 15:25); if He has conquered sin, death, and hell; and if you are represented in Him — there is no possibility whereby you could be destroyed.

> Jesus' tremendous name
> Puts all our foes to flight:
> Jesus, the meek, the angry Lamb,
> A Lion is in fight.
> By all hell's host withstood;
> We all hell's host o'erthrow;
> And conquering them, through Jesus' blood
> We still to conquer go.
>
> Charles Wesley, 1707 – 88

From the pen of Jim Reimann:

Jesus prophesied: "In the future you will see the Son of Man sitting at the right hand of the Mighty One" (Matt. 26:64). Later Paul taught that "the glorious Father … seated [our Lord Jesus Christ] at his right hand in the heavenly realms" (Eph. 1:17, 20). But he went on to teach that "God raised *us* up with Christ *and seated us with him* in the heavenly realms in Christ Jesus" (Eph. 2:6). This is why Paul could also say, "Don't you know that all of us who were baptized into Christ Jesus were baptized into his death? We were therefore buried with him through baptism into death in order that, just as Christ was raised from the dead through the glory of the Father, we too may live a new life" (Rom. 6:3 – 4).

Because "[we] are in Christ Jesus" (1 Cor. 1:30), "we are more than conquerors" (Rom. 8:37). "Let the name of the LORD be praised" (Ps. 113:2).

APRIL 22

You will not fear the terror of night.

Psalm 91:5

From the pen of Charles Spurgeon:

What is "the terror of night"? It may be the fear of a fire or a break-in by thieves or perhaps the fear of sudden sickness or death. We live in a world of death and sorrow and thus may expect difficulties under the stars of night as commonly as beneath the glare of the scorching sun. Yet this should not alarm us, for whatever the terror may be, God's promise is that a believer "will not fear." Why should a believer fear? Or to make it more personal, "Why should *we* fear?" God our Father is always with us, even through the lonely hours of night, for He is an almighty "watcher of men" (Job 7:20), a never-sleeping Guardian, and a faithful Friend. Nothing can happen without His direction, for even hell itself is under His control. Darkness is not dark to Him, and He has promised to be "a wall of fire" (Zech. 2:5) around His people — who can break through such a barrier?

Those in the world, however, should be afraid, for they have an angry God above, a guilty conscience within, and a gaping hell beneath them. Yet we who rest in Jesus are saved from all these by God's rich mercy. But if we give way to the foolishness of fear, we dishonor our confession of faith and lead others to doubt the reality of our godliness in Him. Thus, what we should fear is being afraid, so we "do not grieve the Holy Spirit" (Eph. 4:30) by our foolish distrust.

Away with you, then, you miserable forebodings and groundless fears! God has not forgotten to be gracious or run out of "tender mercy" (Luke 1:78). We may experience a time of night or darkness in our soul, but there is no need to fear, for "the God of love" (2 Cor. 13:11) never changes. "Children of light" (Eph. 5:8) may walk in darkness, but the Lord does not cast them away because of it. Instead, they are enabled to prove their adoption as a child of their heavenly Father by trusting in Him — something hypocrites cannot do.

> Though the night be dark and dreary,
> Darkness cannot hide from Thee;
> Thou art He, who, never weary,
> Watches where Thy people be.
>
> James Edmeston, 1791 – 1867

From the pen of Jim Reimann:

There is no question we are more prone to fear at night. Yet Asaph, one of the psalmists, gives us this beautiful solution — one designed to help us change our thinking:

> I cried out to God for help; I cried out to God to hear me. When I was in distress, I sought the Lord; at night I stretched out untiring hands and my soul refused to be comforted.... I remembered my songs in the night. My heart mused and my spirit inquired: "Will the Lord reject forever? Will he never show his favor again? Has his unfailing love vanished forever? Has his promise failed for all time? Has God forgotten to be merciful? Has he in anger withheld his compassion?" Then I thought, "To this I will appeal: the years of the right hand of the Most High." I will remember the deeds of the LORD; yes, I will remember your miracles of long ago. I will meditate on all your works and consider all your mighty deeds. Your ways, O God, are holy. What god is so great as our God?
>
> Psalm 77:1-2, 6-13

APRIL 23

Then I saw a Lamb, looking as if it had been slain,
standing in the center of the throne.

Revelation 5:6

From the pen of Charles Spurgeon:

Why does our exalted Lord Jesus still carry the evidence of His wounds in glory? It is because His wounds are His glories, His jewels, His sacred adornments. When believers view Jesus, they see Him as white and red, or, as the Scriptures say, "white and ruddy" (Song 5:10 KJV): "white" due to His innocence and purity, and "ruddy," or red, due to His blood. We see Him as the lily of matchless purity and as the crimson rose because of His blood. When we see Him on the Mount of Olives, the Mount of Transfiguration, or by the Sea of Galilee, He is beautiful; but there has never been such matchless beauty as that of our Christ as He hung upon the cross. It was there we beheld the perfection of His beauty, saw all His attributes and character fully developed, and beheld the perfect expression of His love being poured out.

Beloved Christian, the wounds of Jesus are far more beautiful to our eyes than all the splendor and pomp of kings, and His crown of thorns is far more precious than the most bejeweled imperial crown. It is true that today He wields "a measuring rod of gold" (Rev. 21:15), but there was a glory that flashed from His "measuring reed" (Ezek. 40:3 KJV) of old that no golden scepter can ever match. Jesus continues to wear the image of a slain Lamb — the very image He wore as He wooed our souls and redeemed us by His perfect atonement. Yet these are not simply adornments, but are visible trophies of His love and His victory. He has "divide[d] the spoils with the strong" (Isa. 53:12) and has "redeem[ed] as a people for himself" (2 Sam. 7:23) a great multitude no one can number, and His scars are the memorials of the fight.

Oh, if Christ so loves to maintain the thoughts of His suffering on behalf of His people, how much more precious should His wounds be to us.

> Behold how every wound of His
> A precious balm distils,
> Which heals the scars that sin had made,
> And cures all mortal ills.
> Those wounds are mouths that preach
>   His grace;
> The ensigns of His love;
> The seals of our expected bliss
> In paradise above.
>
> Joseph Stennett, 1663 – 1713

From the pen of Jim Reimann:

It may also be argued that not only will Jesus bear the marks of His suffering on our behalf throughout eternity future but also that He has borne those marks since eternity past, for John described Him as "the Lamb that was slain from the creation of the world" (Rev. 13:8). Yet Isaiah saw the coming Messiah as "a glorious crown [and] a beautiful wreath" (Isa. 28:5). Thus, with His sacrifice and His beauty in mind, may these words of David be our prayer:

"One thing I ask of the Lord, this is what I seek: that I may dwell in the house of the Lord all the days of my life, to gaze upon the beauty of the Lord" (Ps. 27:4).

APRIL 24

Flowers appear on the earth; the season of singing has come,
the cooing of doves is heard in our land.

Song of Songs 2:12

From the pen of Charles Spurgeon:

A long, dreary winter helps us appreciate the cheering warmth and sweetness of spring, and spring's promise of summer tends to further enhance our enjoyment of it. Likewise, after periods of spiritual depression, it is wonderful to once again enjoy the light of "the sun of righteousness" (Mal. 4:2), for it is then our sleeping gifts begin to stir from their weariness, just as the crocus and daffodil bloom from their earthly beds. It is then our hearts are made glad with beautiful songs of gratitude far more melodious than the singing of birds. And it is then the comforting assurance of peace is heard within the soul.

Now is the time for our soul to seek communion with our Beloved, time to rise from our inherent lowliness and shame, time to walk away from sinful relationships. And if we don't raise our sails while the wind is favorable, we are to blame; opportunities for refreshing improvement should not be wasted. When Jesus Himself visits us with tenderness and calls us to rise, will we be so insensitive and disobedient as to refuse His request? After all, He Himself has risen that He may raise us as well. His Holy Spirit has revived us "in order that ... we too may live a new life" (Rom. 6:4), ascend to the heavens, and thereby commune with Him. When the Lord creates a season of spring within us, may we let our sap flow with vigor, causing our soul to blossom, and may we resolve to set aside the wintry mix of coldness and indifference.

O Lord, if it is not springtime in my chilly heart, I pray You would make it so, for I am profoundly weary of living at a distance from You. Oh, how long my dreary winter has been! Come, Holy Spirit, and renew my soul! Awaken me, restore me, have mercy upon me! Dear Lord, I implore You to take pity on Your servant and to send me a joyous revival of spiritual life.

From the pen of Jim Reimann:

Charles Spurgeon often suffered bouts of depression, something he called a "darkness of the soul." Long before depression was understood, and was a stigma to many, he was not afraid to disclose his affliction. In fact, Spurgeon once wrote:

> Fits of depression come over most of us. Even if we are usually cheerful we will feel downcast at times. The strong are not always vigorous, the wise not always ready, the brave not always courageous, and the joyous not always happy. Some people may be made of iron and show no perceptible detriment from wear and tear, but surely rust affects even those; and as for ordinary people, the Lord knows, and causes them to know, they are but dust.... "We have [the] treasure" of the gospel "in jars of clay" (2 Cor. 4:7), and if there is a flaw in the jar here and there, no one should be surprised. Our work, when earnestly done, opens us to attacks of depression. After all, who can bear the weight of souls without sometimes sinking to the dust?

Remember — "There is a time for everything, and a season for every activity under heaven: ... a time to weep and a time to laugh, a time to mourn and a time to dance" (Eccl. 3:1, 4).

APRIL 25

If anyone hears my voice and opens the door,
I will come in.
Revelation 3:20

From the pen of Charles Spurgeon:

What is your desire today? Is it set upon heavenly things? Do you desire true freedom to enjoy intimate communion with God? Do you long to know and enjoy just "how wide and long and high and deep is the love of Christ" (Eph. 3:18)? If so, you must draw near to Jesus; obtain a clear view of Him in His preciousness and completeness; and see Him in His work, His various offices, and His person. Christ is the great key to unlock all the various treasures of God, for those who understand Him receive an anointing from the Holy One by which they know all things. There is no treasure house of God that will be closed to a soul who lives near Jesus. Are you yearning for Him to dwell in your heart and make it His dwelling place forever? Then open the door, beloved, and He will come into your soul.

Jesus has long been knocking, all with one goal: that He may "eat with [you], and [you] with [Him]" (Rev. 3:20). Your heart becomes the home where He may eat, but you are able to eat with Him solely because He brings the provisions. If He were not in your heart, you would be unable to eat with Him, for your cupboard would remain bare if He did not bring the spiritual food with Him. Thus, fling wide the portals of your soul, and He will bring you the love you long to feel, the joy you desire for your depressed spirit, and a peace you have never experienced. He will "strengthen [you] with raisins [and] refresh [you] with apples" (Song 2:5), cheering you until you have no "sickness" other than that of God's overpowering love.

Simply open the door to Him, drive out His enemies, give Him the keys of your heart, and He will dwell there forever. Oh, wondrous love that brings such a Guest to dwell in a heart such as yours and mine.

From the pen of Jim Reimann:

Jesus' words: "I stand at the door and knock. If anyone hears my voice and opens the door, I will come in and eat with him, and he with me" (Rev. 3:20), are often mistakenly used as a verse for evangelism, but are instead the words of Jesus to His people — those who are believers already — for He says, "He who has an ear, let him hear *what the Spirit says to the churches*" (Rev. 3:13). In fact, today's verse in its context deals with the repentance of the church. Jesus says, "Remember, therefore, what you have received and heard; obey it, and repent" (Rev. 3:3), and, "Those whom I love I rebuke and discipline. So be earnest, and repent" (Rev. 3:19).

Thus, Revelation 3 is a warning from Jesus never to allow sin to interrupt our fellowship with Him as believers. In today's devotion, Spurgeon encourages us to "fling wide the portals of your soul" — something only a believer is capable of doing. Remember the words of Luke regarding Lydia, the first European convert, and her inability to receive the message of God's salvation through Jesus Christ until "*the Lord opened her heart* to respond to Paul's message" (Acts 16:14).

Salvation is completely a work of God, as we see in the following psalm:

Find rest, O my soul, in God alone; my hope comes from him. He alone is my rock and my salvation; he is my fortress, I will not be shaken. My salvation and my honor depend on God; he is my mighty rock, my refuge.

Psalm 62:5 – 7

APRIL 26

Blessed is he who stays awake.

Revelation 16:15

From the pen of Charles Spurgeon:

The apostle Paul said, "I die every day" (1 Cor. 15:31). This was the life of the early Christians, for everywhere they went, their lives were at risk. Today most of us are not called to experience the same fearful persecution, but if we were, the Lord would give us grace to bear the trial. However, the tests of the Christian life today, though outwardly not as terrible, are even more likely to overcome us than those of the fiery past. We are forced to endure the contempt of the world, with its empty flattery, soft words, slick speeches, and hypocrisy, which are a far worse test.

The danger is that we will grow rich and become proud, thereby giving ourselves over to the trends of this present evil world, and lose our faith. Or if wealth is not our trial, worldly cares and needs may be our test, and they can be just as destructive. If the roaring lion of wealth is unable to tear us to pieces, the bear of worldly needs may attempt to squeeze us to death; but the Devil doesn't care which it is as long as he is able to destroy our love for Christ and our confidence in Him. My concern is that Christ's church is far more likely to lose her integrity in these soft and easy times of today than in those more difficult days of old.

We must be awake, for the delightful ground we walk may lead to our falling asleep and our own undoing — that is, unless our faith in Jesus is a reality and our love for Him is a fervent flame. In fact, in these days of easy "believism," many people are likely to be weeds — not wheat (see Matt. 13:24–30). They are hypocrites wearing lovely masks over their faces, but are not true-born "children of the living God" (Rom. 9:26 KJV).

Dear Christian, never think these are times in which you may dispense with watchfulness or holy zeal, for you need them now more than ever. May God the eternal Spirit display His omnipotence in you that you may be able to say, in easy days or in difficult ones, "We are more than conquerors through him who loved us" (Rom. 8:37).

From the pen of Jim Reimann:

In Gethsemane, Jesus told Peter, James, and John, "Stay here and keep watch with me," but "He returned ... and found them sleeping," and asked, "Could you men not keep watch with me for one hour?" (Matt. 26:38, 40). In spite of Jesus' obvious disappointment, His response was one of understanding and love, for He continued, "Watch and pray so that you will not fall into temptation. The spirit is willing, but the body is weak" (Matt. 26:41).

Today's Christians, however, have something Jesus' disciples were lacking at that time — the indwelling of the Holy Spirit. We share in the promise the Lord made to His early followers: "You will receive power when the Holy Spirit comes on you" (Acts 1:8). And Paul confirmed this truth, writing, "Our gospel came to you not simply with words, but also with power, with the Holy Spirit and with deep conviction" (1 Thess. 1:5).

With this in mind, may these words of the prophet Micah characterize our life today: "As for me, I watch in hope for the LORD, I wait for God my Savior" (Mic. 7:7).

APRIL 27

The LORD is King for ever and ever.

Psalm 10:16

From the pen of Charles Spurgeon:

Jesus Christ is not some tyrant illegally claiming divine right — He is truly the Lord's anointed. "God was pleased to have all his fullness dwell in him" (Col. 1:19) and to give Him all power and "all authority in heaven and on earth" (Matt. 28:18). As the Son of Man He is "head over everything for the church" (Eph. 1:22), and He reigns over heaven, earth, and hell, with the keys of life and death on His sash. Some earthly princes have taken delight by being proclaimed king by the will of their people, and certainly our Lord Jesus Christ is proclaimed as King by His church, for if it could be put to a vote as to whether or not He should be our King, every believing heart would crown Him as such.

But oh, that we could crown Him more gloriously than we do! We would spare no expense if it would glorify Christ. Suffering would be a pleasure, and loss would be gain, if through them we could crown His brow with brighter crowns and thereby make Him even more glorious in the eyes of men and angels. Yes, He shall reign. *Long live the King! All hail to You, King Jesus!* "Bring forth the royal diadem, and crown Him Lord of all" (Edward Perronet, 1726 – 92).

Our Lord Jesus is King in Zion by right of conquest, for He has conquered and carried the hearts of His people by storm, slaying their enemies who held them in cruel bondage. Our Redeemer has drowned the pharaoh of our sins in the Red Sea of His own blood — shall He not be King in Jeshurun? [Editor's note: Jeshurun is a poetic name for Israel. For example, see Deut.

33:5, 26.] He has delivered us from the heavy yoke and iron curse of the law — shall not the Liberator be crowned? We are His inheritance whom He has taken from the hands of the Amorites with His sword and His bow — who shall snatch His conquest from His hand?

All hail, King Jesus! We gladly submit to Your gentle rule. Reign in our hearts forever, You beautiful "Prince of Peace" (Isa. 9:6).

From the pen of Jim Reimann:

Some believers look ahead to the second coming of Christ when He will return as King, but the truth is, as today's text proclaims — "The LORD *is* King for ever and ever." He will not *become* the "King of kings" — He *is* even now "the blessed and only Ruler, the King of kings and Lord of lords" (1 Tim. 6:15). Thus, as His people, we should recognize Him as such, living our lives in complete submission to our only sovereign King.

As we consider these truths today, may these beautiful words of David be our closing prayer:

"The earth is the LORD'S, and everything in it, the world, and all who live in it; for he founded it upon the seas and established it upon the waters…. Lift up your heads, O you gates; be lifted up, you ancient doors, that the King of glory may come in. Who is this King of glory? The LORD strong and mighty, the LORD mighty in battle. Lift up your heads, O you gates; lift them up, you ancient doors, that the King of glory may come in. Who is he, this King of glory? The LORD Almighty — he is the King of glory" (Ps. 24:1 – 2, 7 – 10).

APRIL 28

The whole house of Israel is hardened and obstinate.

Ezekiel 3:7

From the pen of Charles Spurgeon:

Actually, there are no exceptions to being "hardened and obstinate." If God's favored race is described in this way, what about the rest of us? If the best are this bad, then what must the worst of us be like?

Dear heart, consider how much you share in this universal accusation, and while you do so, be ready to accept your proper share of shame where you may be guilty. God's first charge in today's text is that of impudence, or a hardness of head, a lack of holy shame, or an unholy boldness in practicing evil. Before my conversion, I could sin without feeling any misgivings, hear of my guilt yet remain unhumbled, and even confess my iniquity while exhibiting no inward humiliation as a result of it.

For a sinner to go to God's house while pretending to pray to Him and praise Him reveals a brazenness of the worst kind. Regrettably, since the day of my new birth, I have doubted my Lord to His face, unblushingly complained in His presence, worshiped before Him in a slothful manner, and sinned without grieving over it. Obviously, if my head were not so unyielding, harder than flint itself, I would exhibit far more holy fear and a far deeper contrition of spirit. "Woe to me!" (Isa. 6:5), for I am one of the "hardened" of Israel.

God's second charge is one of obstinacy, and I cannot plead innocent here either. Once I had nothing but a "heart of stone," and although by grace I now have a new "heart of flesh" (Ezek. 36:26), much of my former stubbornness remains. I am not as affected by the death of Jesus as I should be; neither am I as moved as I should be by the ruin of my fellow man, the wicked-

ness of our times, chastisement by my heavenly Father, nor my own failures. Oh, that my heart would melt when I consider my Savior's suffering and death. Oh, that God would rid me of this millstone deep within me — this horrid "body of death" (Rom. 7:24).

"May the name of the Lord be praised" (Job 1:21) that my disease is not incurable, for the Savior's precious blood is the universal solvent. It will effectively soften me — yes, even me — melting my heart as wax in the fire.

From the pen of Jim Reimann:

Ezekiel predicted a future humbling of Israel. Consider these words of the Lord to him, especially noticing the response God hopes to elicit from Ezekiel himself:

> Prophesy against the land of Israel and say to her: "This is what the Lord says: I am against you." ... Therefore groan, son of man! Groan before them with broken heart and bitter grief. And when they ask you, "Why are you groaning?" you shall say, "Because of the news that is coming. Every heart will melt and every hand go limp; every spirit will become faint and every knee become as weak as water." It is coming! It will surely take place.
>
> Ezekiel 21:2 – 3, 6 – 7

Yet, as Spurgeon alluded to today, God promises His people, "I will give you a new heart and put a new spirit in you" (Ezek. 36:26). And consider Paul's wondrous answer to the question: "Who will rescue me from this body of death? Thanks be to God — through *Jesus Christ our Lord!*" (Rom. 7:24 – 25).

APRIL 29

The LORD takes delight in his people.

Psalm 149:4

From the pen of Charles Spurgeon:

Oh, how comprehensive is the love of Jesus! There is nothing regarding His people's interests He does not consider, and nothing concerning their welfare that is not important to Him. Dear believer, He doesn't merely think of you as an immortal being, but as a mortal one as well. Therefore, don't deny or doubt it, for "even the very hairs of your head are all numbered" (Matt. 10:30), and "the steps of a good man are ordered by the LORD, and He delights in his way" (Ps. 37:23 NKJV).

It would be a sad thing for us indeed if His mantle of love did not cover all our concerns, for just imagine what problems we might encounter in the areas not coming under our gracious Lord's inspection. You may rest assured, believer, that the heart of Jesus even cares about the simplest details of your life. The breadth of His tender love is such that you may take each and every matter to Him, for in all your afflictions He is afflicted, and just as a father has compassion on his children, He shows you compassion. Yes, even the simplest interests of every saint are carried upon the all-encompassing heart of the Son of God.

Oh, what a heart Jesus has — not one that is simply aware of each of His people, but one that fully comprehends the countless and varying concerns of each person as well. Dear Christian, do you think you can measure the love of Christ? Consider what His love has brought you: justification, adoption, sanctification, eternal life. The riches of His goodness are unsearchable; you will never be able to list them fully, much less fully describe them.

Oh, the breadth of the love of Christ! Should such a love as His have only half our heart? Should His love receive only coldness in return? Should Jesus' miraculous loving-kindness and tender care be met with nothing but faint responses or delayed acknowledgments? "O my soul" (Ps. 103:2), tune your harp to a joyous song of thanksgiving. Rejoice, for you are not a desolate wanderer; you are a beloved child — watched over, cared for, and supplied and defended by your Lord.

From the pen of Jim Reimann:

The love of God is a theme quite prevalent throughout the Scriptures, and, of course, it is due to that great love that He redeemed us. Paul wrote, "Because of his great love for us, God, who is rich in mercy, made us alive with Christ even when we were dead in transgressions" (Eph. 2:4 – 5). And Paul went on to describe Christ's great love as being beyond our capacity to fully comprehend it. Here's how he said it: "I pray that you ... may have power ... to grasp how wide and long and high and deep is the love of Christ, and to know *this love that surpasses knowledge*" (Eph. 3:17 – 19). And as we read the following, we can almost hear how overwhelmed John is by the Father's love: "How great is the love the Father has lavished on us, that we should be called children of God! And that is what we are!" (1 John 3:1).

What should be my response? "I will sing of the LORD's great love forever; with my mouth I will make your faithfulness known through all generations" (Ps. 89:1).

"Love the LORD, all his saints!" (Ps. 31:23).

APRIL 30

How precious to me are your thoughts, O God!

Psalm 139:17

From the pen of Charles Spurgeon:

The Lord's divine omniscience offers no comfort whatsoever to the mind of the ungodly, but to the child of God it overflows with consolation and comfort. He is always thinking of us, for He never turns His thoughts nor His eyes away from us. And this is exactly as we should desire, for it would be dreadful to exist for even a moment beyond the observation of our heavenly Father. His thoughts are always tender, loving, wise, prudent, far-reaching, and bring us countless benefits. It is a delight to remember them.

Since eternity past, the Lord has always thought of His people — hence their election and the covenant of grace by which their salvation is secured. And He will always think of them in the future — hence their ultimate perseverance by which they will be brought safely to their final place of rest. In all our wanderings the watchful eyes of the Eternal Watcher are forever fixed on us — never will we roam beyond our Shepherd's view. In all our sorrows He continually observes us — not one twinge of pain escapes His eye. And in all our toils He notes our weariness — writing each struggle of His faithful ones in His book. These thoughts of the Lord encompass us in all our paths and penetrate the innermost depths of our being, for all the smallest details of our private world are in the thoughts of our great God.

Dear reader, is this precious to you? If so, then cling to it. Never be led astray by those philosophical fools who preach an impersonal God and who speak of our being self-existent and self-governing. The Lord lives and thinks of us! This is a truth far too precious for us to be so easily robbed of it. Society highly values the notice of any nobleman today, but how much greater it is to be thought of by "the King of kings" (1 Tim. 6:15). If the Lord thinks of us, all is well, and we may "be joyful always" (1 Thess. 5:16).

From the pen of Jim Reimann:

Today's text is taken from a psalm of David that focuses on God's sovereignty in every detail of our lives, from our being created by Him to our length of days being numbered by Him. Here is a portion of his beautiful prayer:

"You created my inmost being; you knit me together in my mother's womb. I praise you because I am fearfully and wonderfully made; your works are wonderful, I know that full well. My frame was not hidden from you when I was made in the secret place. When I was woven together in the depths of the earth, your eyes saw my unformed body. All the days ordained for me were written in your book before one of them came to be. How precious to me are your thoughts, O God! How vast is the sum of them! Were I to count them, they would outnumber the grains of sand. When I awake, I am still with you" (Ps. 139:13 – 18).

As you contemplate the truth that your heavenly Father is ever thinking of you with thoughts of love, why not make these verses of David's psalm your prayer today:

"Search me, O God, and know my heart; test me and know my anxious thoughts. See if there is any offensive way in me, and lead me in the way everlasting" (vv. 23 – 24).

May

MAY 1

I am the rose of Sharon.

Song of Songs 2:1 KJV

From the pen of Charles Spurgeon:

Whatever beauty there may be in the material world, Jesus Christ possesses in the spiritual world to an exponential degree. Among earthly flowers the rose is deemed the sweetest, but Jesus is infinitely more beautiful in the garden of the soul than the rose could ever be in the gardens of earth. He is the fairest of ten thousand, and is the sun, while all others are simply stars. The heavens and even daytime itself are dark in comparison to Him, for the King in His beauty far transcends them all.

"I am the rose of Sharon," the best and the rarest of all roses. Notice He is not simply "the rose," but "the rose of Sharon"; just as He refers to His garments of righteousness not simply as "gold," but as the "gold of Ophir" (Ps. 45:9) — the best of the best. He is by far the loveliest.

Yet there is variety in His beauty, for the rose is not only delightful to the eye but also has a refreshing scent. Thus, each of the senses of the soul, whether spiritual taste, touch, hearing, sight, or smell, finds complete gratification in Jesus. For example, simply recalling His love is sweet. Take "the rose of Sharon," pull it apart petal by petal and lay each one in your jar of memory, and you will find each one to remain fragrant long afterwards, filling your spiritual house with its fragrance.

Christ satisfies even the finest taste of the most educated spirit to the fullest extent. From the least amateur in perfumes to the most refined of souls, each will be fully satisfied with "the rose." In fact, not only will each be content, but as the soul matures in its taste, it will grow in its ability to appreciate Him.

Heaven itself possesses nothing that sur-

passes "the rose of Sharon." What symbol could fully represent His beauty? Human speech and earthly things fail to describe Him, for even the best the earth has to offer mixed together is but a feeble picture when compared to His abounding preciousness.

Blessed Rose, bloom in my heart forever!

From the pen of Jim Reimann:

Human language bankrupts itself in attempting to describe our beautiful Savior, who is "altogether lovely" (Song 5:16). The best descriptions come not from us, but from the Lord Himself in His Word. For example, read the description He gave of Himself to the apostle John in the book of the Revelation:

I saw heaven standing open and there before me was a white horse, whose rider is called Faithful and True. With justice he judges and makes war. His eyes are like blazing fire, and on his head are many crowns. He has a name written on him that no one knows but he himself. He is dressed in a robe dipped in blood, and his name is the Word of God. The armies of heaven were following him, riding on white horses and dressed in fine linen, white and clean. Out of his mouth comes a sharp sword with which to strike down the nations. "He will rule them with an iron scepter." He treads the winepress of the fury of the wrath of God Almighty. On his robe and on his thigh he has this name written: KING OF KINGS AND LORD OF LORDS.

Revelation 19:11 – 16

Remember — "In that day the Branch of the LORD will be beautiful and glorious" (Isa. 4:2).

MAY 2

All these people were still living by faith when they died.

Hebrews 11:13

From the pen of Charles Spurgeon:

What a beautiful epitaph for all those blessed saints who fell asleep before the coming of our Lord. It really doesn't matter *how* they died, whether of old age or by violent means, for the most important thing they had in common is that they all "were still living by faith when they died." They had lived "by faith," for it was their comfort, their guide, their motivation, and their support; and it was in the same spiritual blessing they died, ending their life's song with the same sweet strain in which they had walked for so long. They did not die resting in the flesh or resting on their own accomplishments, but firmly holding to the way of faith. They understood it is as precious to die by faith as it is to live by faith.

They realized the link between dying by faith and the past, for they believed the promises that had gone before and were thereby assured that their sins were blotted out through the mercy of God. Yet they understood that dying by faith also is tied to the present, for these saints were confident of their acceptance by God, daily enjoying the rays of His love and resting in His faithfulness to the very end. Finally, they knew that in dying by faith they were looking to the future as well, for they fell asleep affirming the Messiah would surely come, that He would in the last days appear upon the earth, and that they would rise from their graves to behold Him. To these saints the pains of death were but the birth pangs of a better life.

Therefore, take courage, dear soul, as you read this epitaph. Your path through grace is also one of faith. But remember — this has also been the path of the brightest and the best, for the orbit of faith is the path all the brightest of stars traveled while here. Thus, be happy that it is your path. Look anew to Jesus, "the author and perfecter of [your] faith" (Heb. 12:2), thanking Him for giving you the gift of precious faith — faith just like those souls who are now in glory.

From the pen of Jim Reimann:

Paul wrote of living by faith, saying, "In the gospel a righteousness from God is revealed, a righteousness that is by faith from first to last, just as it is written: 'The righteous will live by faith'" (Rom. 1:17). Of course, Paul is quoting the prophet Habakkuk, who said, "The righteous will live by his faith" (Hab. 2:4). Paul later reiterates this truth, by declaring, "Clearly no one is justified before God by the law, because, 'The righteous will live by faith'" (Gal. 3:11). Finally, the writer of Hebrews says, "My righteous one will live by faith. And if he shrinks back, I will not be pleased with him" (Heb. 10:38).

Yet, as we see from today's text, the writer of Hebrews goes on to say: "All these people were still living by faith when they died." This brings to mind the idea that not only should our life bring glory to God, but our death should bring Him glory as well. Perhaps this is why John tells us the following about Peter: "Jesus said this to indicate *the kind of death by which Peter would glorify God*" (John 21:19).

Lord, may the way I live, and the way I die, bring You great glory!

MAY 3

God is our ... ever-present help in trouble.
Psalm 46:1

From the pen of Charles Spurgeon:

Covenant blessings are not meant simply for us to read about, but to be appropriated. Even our Lord Jesus is given to us for our present use. Dear believer, are you making use of Him as you should? When you are in trouble, are you telling Him all about your problems? Don't you know that He has a sympathizing heart and that He can comfort and care for you? Are you going to all your friends, except your best Friend, and sharing your story everywhere except in the arms of your Lord?

Are you burdened with sins committed even today? Then go to the "Fountain filled with blood" (William Cowper, 1731 – 1800) and use it, dear saint, use it! Has a sense of guilt returned to you? Let the pardoning grace of Jesus prove itself to you again and again. Go to Him at once for cleansing. Do you deplore your own weakness? He is your strength — why not lean on Him? Do you feel spiritually naked? Then come, dear soul, and put on the robe of Jesus' righteousness. Don't just stand there, looking at it, but wear it. Strip away your own righteousness, and your own fears as well, and put on His pure white linen, for it was meant to be worn.

Are you sick? Then ring His doorbell through prayer, calling upon the Beloved Physician. He will give you the perfect remedy to revive you. Are you poor? Remember — you have "a kinsman ... a mighty man of wealth" (Ruth 2:1 KJV). What! Will you not go to Him, asking Him to give you from His abundance, even after He has given you His promise that you are "co-heirs with Christ" (Rom. 8:17), offering you all that He is and all that He has?

There is nothing Christ dislikes more than for His people to use Him for "show and tell," but not truly use Him. He loves to be used by us, and the more burdens we put on His shoulders, the more precious He will be to us.

> Let us be simple with Him, then,
> Not backward, stiff, or cold,
> As though our Bethlehem could be
> What Sinai was of old.
> Frederick William Faber, 1814 – 63

From the pen of Jim Reimann:

Our Lord is a personal God and longs to have an intimate, personal relationship with each of us as His child. Perhaps this is why, even though we are indeed His children, Jesus refers to us as his brother, sister, and friend. He said, "Whoever does the will of my Father in heaven is my brother and sister and mother" (Matt. 12:50), and "I no longer call you servants, because a servant does not know his master's business. Instead, I have called you friends, for everything that I learned from my Father I have made known to you" (John 15:15).

In other words, Jesus is not a Lord who "lords" His lordship over us, but a loving, caring Savior who wants us to know Him, to call on Him in our everyday circumstances of life. Why not go to Him now in prayer, taking Him at His word, for as Paul said, "He who did not spare his own Son, but gave him up for us all — how will he not also, along with him, graciously give us all things?" (Rom. 8:32).

MAY 4

You have been born again,
not of perishable seed, but of imperishable.

1 Peter 1:23

From the pen of Charles Spurgeon:

Peter earnestly exhorted "God's elect … [who were] scattered throughout" (v. 1) Asia Minor to "love one another deeply, from the heart" (v. 22), wisely taking his argument to do so not from the law, from nature, or from philosophy, but from that high and divine nature God has placed within His people. God sees His people as heirs of glory, princes of royal blood, descendants of "the King of kings" (1 Tim. 6:15), and earth's truest and oldest aristocracy. Thus, Peter says to them, in essence, "See to it that you 'love one another' because of your noble birth, having been 'born again … of imperishable' seed; because of your pedigree, being descended from God, the Creator of all things; and because of your immortal destiny, for you shall never pass away, although the glory of the flesh will fade and even ultimately cease to exist."

Accordingly, it would be good for us, in the spirit of humility, to recognize the true dignity of our regenerated nature — and to live up to it. Exactly what is a Christian? If you compare him with an earthly king, not only does he have royal dignity but also priestly sanctity. An earthly king's royalty often lies only in his crown, or office, but with a Christian it is infused into his inmost nature. In fact, a Christian is as much above his fellow man, due to his new birth, as mankind is above the beasts of earth that perish. Thus, he ought to conduct himself in all his dealings as someone who is not one of the multitude, but one who is chosen out of the world, distinguished by God's sovereign grace as a person "belonging to God" (1 Peter 2:9), and who therefore cannot wallow in the dust, living like the world's citizens.

Oh, believers in Christ, allow the dignity of your nature and the brightness of your future to compel you to cling to holiness and to "avoid every kind of evil" (1 Thess. 5:22).

From the pen of Jim Reimann:

Jesus said to His disciples, "I confer on you a kingdom, just as my Father conferred one on me, so that you may eat and drink at my table in my kingdom and sit on thrones, judging the twelve tribes of Israel" (Luke 22:29 – 30). Paul too declared that as His people "we will also reign with him" (2 Tim. 2:12). This, of course, is a fulfillment of God's promise to the Israelites just three months after delivering them from Egypt, for He told them, "Although the whole earth is mine, *you will be for me a kingdom of priests and a holy nation*" (Ex. 19:5 – 6).

Remember, however, the kingdom where we will reign with Jesus is a future, heavenly kingdom, for He said, "My kingdom is not of this world…. My kingdom is from another place" (John 18:36). And recall this promise He made to John much later in John's life: "Blessed and holy are those who have part in the first resurrection…. They will be priests of God and of Christ and will reign with him for a thousand years" (Rev. 20:6). What unselfishness — that "the King of kings" desires to share His glorious kingdom with the sinners for whom He died!

Father, may I be a worthy representative of Your kingdom and may "your kingdom come, your will be done on earth as it is in heaven" (Matt. 6:10).

MAY 5

Whoever gives heed to instruction prospers,
and blessed is he who trusts in the LORD.

Proverbs 16:20

From the pen of Charles Spurgeon:

Wisdom is mankind's true strength, and under its guidance we best accomplish the purpose of our being. Wisely handling life is the best use of our power and affords us the richest enjoyment of life itself; hence, by doing so we find good to the fullest extent. Without wisdom mankind is like a wild donkey running to and fro, wasting strength. Wisdom is the compass by which we steer our lives across the wasteland of life, for without it we would be rudderless ships, completely at the will of the wind and the waves. We must be prudent in a world such as this or we will find no good at all and will become prey to countless ills. A spiritual pilgrim will severely wound his feet among the briers of the woods of life if he does not choose his steps with the utmost caution. He who walks through a wilderness infested with gangs of thieves must handle life's matters wisely to travel safely.

If we are trained by the Great Teacher and follow where He leads, we will find good even in this dark world, for there is heavenly fruit to be harvested this side of Eden's orchard and songs of paradise to be sung amid the groves of earth. But where will we find this wisdom? Where will we learn it? The answer is in listening to the voice of the Lord, for He has proclaimed the secret and revealed to mankind where true wisdom lies. In fact, today's text gives us the answer: "Blessed is he who trusts in the LORD."

The proper way to handle a matter wisely is to trust in the Lord. This is the unfailing clue to even the most intricate labyrinths of life, for if we will follow it, we will find eternal blessings. Whoever "trusts in the LORD" receives a diploma of wisdom as a gift of God. He will be blessed here on earth and even more blessed above.

Lord, walk with me this very moment through the garden of life and teach me the wisdom of faith.

From the pen of Jim Reimann:

There is a vast difference between human wisdom and wisdom from God, as we see in Solomon's writings. For example, regarding man's wisdom, he confessed, "I applied myself to the understanding of wisdom, and also of madness and folly, but I learned that this, too, is a chasing after the wind. For with much wisdom comes much sorrow; the more knowledge, the more grief" (Eccl. 1:17 – 18). But regarding godly wisdom, he declared,

Blessed is the man who finds wisdom, the man who gains understanding, for she is more profitable than silver and yields better returns than gold. She is more precious than rubies; nothing you desire can compare with her. Long life is in her right hand; in her left hand are riches and honor. Her ways are pleasant ways, and all her paths are peace. She is a tree of life to those who embrace her; those who lay hold of her will be blessed.

Proverbs 3:13 – 18

Yet I will know I am walking in wisdom only when my life is characterized by these words of James: "The wisdom that comes from heaven is first of all pure; then peace-loving, considerate, submissive, full of mercy and good fruit, impartial and sincere" (James 3:17).

MAY 6

All the days of my appointed time will I wait.

Job 14:14 KJV

From the pen of Charles Spurgeon:

Our short stay here on earth will make heaven more heavenly, for nothing makes rest as sweet as hard work, and nothing causes security to feel as pleasant as exposure to danger. The bitter quassia blossoms of earth will provide a beautiful contrast to the new wine that will sparkle in the golden glasses of glory. And our battered armor and scarred countenances will make our victory above seem even more glorious, when we are welcomed to the seats of those who have "overcome the world" (John 16:33). After all, we would never have perfect fellowship with Christ if not for our journey here below, for He was baptized with a baptism of suffering among mankind, and we must be baptized with suffering as well if we desire to share His kingdom. Yet fellowship with Him is such an honor that even the most severe sorrow is a small price to obtain it.

Another reason for our lingering here on earth is for the good of others. Surely we would not wish to enter heaven until our work here is done, and it may be that the Lord has ordained us to continue to minister light to souls overtaken by the wilderness of darkness and sin.

Also, there can be no doubt that our seemingly prolonged stay here is for God's glory, for a tested saint, like a well-cut diamond, greatly glitters in the King's crown. And nothing reflects as much honor on a worker than triumphantly enduring a lengthy, severe trial in his work without giving in to the ordeal in any respect. "We are God's workmanship" (Eph. 2:10) in whom He will be glorified through our afflictions; consequently it is for the honor of Jesus we endure with sacred joy the trials of our faith.

Thus, may each of us surrender our own desires to the glory of Jesus and say, in essence, "If my lying in the dust would elevate my Lord by as much as an inch, may I lie in the dirtiest place on earth. And if living here forever would make my Lord more glorious, it would be my heaven to be shut out of heaven itself."

Since our time here is fixed by eternal decree, may we not be anxious. Instead, may we patiently wait until the "gate made of … pearl" (Rev. 21:21) stands open.

From the pen of Jim Reimann:

Spurgeon makes an amazing declaration today: "If living here forever would make my Lord more glorious, it would be my heaven to be shut out of heaven itself"! This statement is much akin to that of Paul, when he proclaimed, "I could wish that I myself were cursed and cut off from Christ for the sake of my brothers, those of my own race, the people of Israel" (Rom. 9:3 – 4). Of course, Paul knew it was impossible for him to trade places with an unbeliever, but nevertheless he meant what he said, for he prefaced his words by saying, "I speak the truth in Christ — I am not lying, my conscience confirms it in the Holy Spirit" (Rom. 9:1).

What a testimony of a heart truly bent toward evangelizing the lost!

Father, help me live fearlessly, knowing that "all the days ordained for me were written in your book before one of them came to be" (Ps. 139:16). And may my heart be like Paul's — dedicated to using each day to share the gospel and thereby bring You greater glory.

MAY 7

Then Jesus said to him,
"Get up! Pick up your mat and walk."
John 5:8

From the pen of Charles Spurgeon:

Like many others, the disabled man in this story had been waiting for a miracle or a sign to be given. He wearily watched the pool, but no angel came, or at least did not come for him. Yet, thinking this was his only hope, he continued to wait, not knowing there was Someone nearby whose very word could heal him in an instant.

Many are in the same desperate situation today — waiting for some extraordinary emotion, miraculous event, or heavenly vision — but they wait in vain and watch for nothing. Even if we suppose that remarkable signs are seen in a few cases, these are still rare, and no one has a right to expect one in his own case, especially someone who knows their disability — or lack of power — to take advantage of "the water [miraculously being] stirred" (v. 7), even if that were to happen.

It is very sad that tens of thousands now wait, trusting in their works, religious rites, and vows, and thus mindlessly waste their time utterly in vain. Meanwhile, these poor souls forget the nearby Savior, who bids them, "Look unto me, and be ... saved" (Isa. 45:22 KJV). He could heal them immediately, but they prefer to wait for an angel and a miracle. Trusting Him is the surest way to every blessing, and He is worthy of the most complete confidence, but unbelief causes them to prefer the cold colonnades of the Pool of Bethesda rather than the warm embrace of Jesus' love.

Oh, that the Lord would turn His eyes to the multitudes who are in this condition today! May He forgive their neglect of looking to His divine power, and may He call them with His sweet, compelling voice to rise from their bed of despair and, by the power of faith, to "pick up [their] mat and walk."

O Lord, hear our prayer for all such people even now, and before today is over may they look to You and live.

Dear reader, is there anything in today's devotion for you?

From the pen of Jim Reimann:

As any true Christian can attest, knowing *of* Jesus is not the same as knowing Jesus. And, unfortunately, the simplicity of the gospel is often overcomplicated today. Spurgeon himself, when he was fifteen years old, went from church to church, hoping to hear the way of salvation, until finally he heard the simple truth of Isaiah 45:22 — "Look unto me, and be ye saved" (Isa. 45:22 KJV). The Lord saved him that moment, and he later wrote, "I had been waiting to do fifty things, but when I heard this word 'Look!' what a charming word it seemed to me. Oh, I looked until I could almost have looked my eyes away! And in heaven I will look on still in my joy unspeakable."

In the same way, the Israelites were spared from death in the wilderness by looking to Moses' bronze snake (see Num. 21:8 – 9). In fact, Jesus said, "Just as Moses lifted up the snake in the desert, so the Son of Man must be lifted up, that everyone who believes in him may have eternal life" (John 3:14 – 15). Thus, salvation is not some complicated set of rules, but is simply: "Look unto [Jesus], and be ... saved"!

If you don't yet know Jesus as *your* Savior, why not look to Him today?

MAY 8

Now acquaint yourself with Him,
and be at peace.

Job 22:21 NKJV

From the pen of Charles Spurgeon:

If you desire to properly "acquaint yourself with [God], and be at peace," you must know Him as He revealed Himself — not only in the essence and eternity of His being but also in the three Persons of His being. "God said, 'Let us make man in our image'" (Gen. 1:26), thus you should never be content until you know something of the "us" from whom His being is derived. Endeavor to know the Father. Bury yourself in His embrace in deep repentance, confessing, "I am no longer worthy to be called your son" (Luke 15:21). Then receive the kiss of His love and allow His ring, which is the sign of His eternal faithfulness, to be placed upon your finger. Finally, sit at His table and let your heart be glad in His grace.

Then press ahead, seeking to know as much as possible of the Son of God, who, although He "is the radiance of [His Father's] glory" (Heb. 1:3), for our sakes became man by an act of inexpressibly humble grace. Know Him in the extraordinary complexity of His nature — for He is the eternal God, but became a suffering, finite man — and follow Him as He walks on water with the feet of deity (see Matt. 14:25), but then sits by a well in the tiredness of humanity (see John 4:6). Never be satisfied until you truly know Jesus Christ as your Friend (see John 15:15), Brother (see Matt. 12:50), Husband (see Matt. 25:6 and Jer. 3:14) — your all!

And don't forget the Holy Spirit. Strive to obtain a clearer view of His character, attributes, and works. Behold the Spirit who first "moved upon the face of the waters" (Gen. 1:2 KJV), bringing order out of chaos, and who now visits the chaos of your soul, creating the order of holiness. Behold Him not only as the Lord and giver of spiritual enlightenment (see Eph. 1:17 – 18) and life (see Rom. 8:11), but also as your Instructor and Counselor (see John 14:26), and your Sanctifier (see 2 Thess. 2:13). Behold Him who "is like precious oil poured on the head" of Jesus, and which now rests "upon [you who are] the collar of his robes" (Ps. 133:2).

This type of intelligent, scriptural, and practical belief in the Trinity in perfect unity is yours if you truly know God — that is, if you have truly "acquaint[ed] yourself with Him." Such knowledge brings peace indeed!

From the pen of Jim Reimann:

Of the persons of the Trinity, we relate more readily to Jesus because He became like us through His incarnation. Yet as Spurgeon said today, He is extraordinarily complex, exhibiting amazing contrasts. A few of these contrasts are highlighted in the following quote:

> The Incarnation is a stupendous fact; it is the mystery of godliness, the grand miracle of the Christian faith.... The Eternal entered time and became subject to its conditions; the Infinite became the finite; the Immutable became mutable; the Invisible became visible; the Almighty became the weak and infirm; the Creator became the creature; God became man.*

God, thank You for Jesus, who "humbled himself" to become a man (Phil. 2:8).

---

* "Incarnation: the Fact," *Wycliffe Bible Encyclopedia* (Chicago: Moody Press, 1975) p. 838. Used by permission.

MAY 9

Come, my beloved, let us go out into the fields …
and see whether the vines have budded.

Song of Songs 7:11 – 12 ESV

From the pen of Charles Spurgeon:

Notice how the speaker in this verse does not say, "I will go," but instead, "let us go." The voice represents God's church, about to engage in difficult work, and desiring the Lord's presence in it. What a blessing it is having Jesus at our side when we work!

The business of God's people is to be the trimmers of His vines. Like our first parents, Adam and Eve, God put us in His garden for us to be useful. Therefore, "let us go out into the fields." Today's text reminds us that when the church is thinking properly, she desires the enjoyment of communion with Christ in all her work. Some people imagine they have fellowship with Him while not actively serving Him, but they are mistaken. No doubt it is true we can fritter away our inner life through over-activity in our outward work, and then complain, "They made me the keeper of the vineyards, but I've been unable to maintain my own inner one." But there is no reason why this should be true except for our own laziness and neglect.

Some professing Christians who do nothing, and who are proud of their lack of busyness, may give the impression of communing with Jesus, but they may be as lifeless in spiritual things as those who are the most busy. Mary, Martha's sister, was not praised for simply sitting still, but for sitting at Jesus' feet (see Luke 10:42). In the same way, Christians should not receive praise for neglecting their duties with the pretense of enjoying inner spiritual fellowship with Jesus, for, again, it is not sitting, but sitting at Jesus' feet, that is commendable.

We should never think that active work itself is evil, for it is a great blessing and is often the path whereby God extends His grace to us. Paul said, "This grace was given me: to preach … " (Eph. 3:8), thus every type of Christian service may become a personal blessing to those employed in it.

Believers who have the most fellowship with Christ are not recluses or hermits from society, those with much time to spare, but those untiring laborers who are working for Jesus and who have Him with them in their work, so that they are workers together with God. Thus, let us remember that in anything we do for Jesus, we can do it, and should do it, in close communion with Him.

From the pen of Jim Reimann:

Solomon, again relating his thoughts to the vineyard, wrote,

> I went past the field of the sluggard, past the vineyard of the man who lacks judgment; thorns had come up everywhere, the ground was covered with weeds, and the stone wall was in ruins. I applied my heart to what I observed and learned a lesson from what I saw: A little sleep, a little slumber, a little folding of the hands to rest — and poverty will come on you like a bandit and scarcity like an armed man.
>
> Proverbs 24:30 – 34

Certainly, there is nothing wrong with resting, but we should have balance in our lives between work and rest. Our primary lesson here is this: our Lord must be involved in both. We should remember these words of Solomon: "Commit to the Lord *whatever you do*, and your plans will succeed" (Prov. 16:3).

MAY 10

... the One and Only, who came from the Father,
full of grace and truth.

John 1:14

From the pen of Charles Spurgeon:

Dear believer, as a Christian you can proclaim that Christ is "the One and Only, who came from the Father" and is "the firstborn from the dead" (Rev. 1:5). You may also declare: He is God to me, even if He is considered only human to the world, for He has done for me only what God could do. He has subdued my stubborn will and melted my heart that was "as hard as flint" (Zech. 7:12), "for he breaks down gates of bronze and cuts through bars of iron" (Ps. 107:16). He has turned my mourning into laughter and my despair into joy; He has "filled [my heart] with an inexpressible and glorious joy" (1 Peter 1:8). To me He must be "the One and Only, who came from the Father" — blessed be His name!

In addition, He is "full of grace," and if that were not true, I would never have been saved! He drew me to Himself even when I struggled to escape His grace, and when I finally came like a condemned criminal, trembling before His "mercy seat" (Ex. 25:17 KJV), He said, "Take heart, son; your [many] sins are forgiven" (Matt. 9:2).

He is also "full of ... truth." Each of His promises has been true — not one has failed. I bear witness to the fact that no servant has ever had a master such as I have, no brother as great a family member as He, and no spouse such a husband as Christ has been to my soul. No sinner has ever had a better Savior, and no mourner a better comforter than He has been to my spirit.

Thus, I want no one but Him. In life Christ is my life, and in death He will be the death of death. In poverty He is my riches, in sickness He visits my bed, in darkness He is my shining star, and in brightness He is my sun. He is my manna in the wilderness, and He will be my harvest when I cross the river to Canaan. Jesus is to me all grace and no wrath, all truth and no falsehood, for He is "full of grace and truth" — infinitely full!

My soul, bless your "One and Only" with all your might today.

From the pen of Jim Reimann:

As Spurgeon said, "In life Christ is my life," a truth Paul espoused as well by teaching: "Your life is now hidden with Christ in God. When *Christ, who is your life*, appears, then you also will appear with him in glory" (Col. 3:3–4). Yet the idea of the Lord being our very life is not simply a New Testament concept. For example, Moses told Israel:

This day I call heaven and earth as witnesses against you that I have set before you life and death, blessings and curses. Now choose life, so that you and your children may live and that you may love the LORD your God, listen to his voice, and hold fast to him. *For the LORD is your life.*

Deuteronomy 30:19–20

John, who wrote today's text, agreed with Paul that we are in Christ and He is our life, saying, "We know also that the Son of God has come and has given us understanding, so that we may know him who is true. And we are in him who is true — even in his Son Jesus Christ. He is the true God and eternal life" (1 John 5:20).

"Thanks be to God for his indescribable gift!" (2 Cor. 9:15).

MAY 11

Be strong and very courageous.

Joshua 1:7

From the pen of Charles Spurgeon:

Our God's tender love for His servants makes Him concerned about even our inner feelings. He desires us to "be of good courage" (Ps. 27:14 KJV). Some deem it a small thing for a believer to be filled with doubts and fears, but God disagrees, for today's text makes it clear our Master does not want us to be entangled by fears. He does not think as lightly of our unbelief as we do, and thus desires we remove all worry, doubt, and cowardice.

When we are despondent, we are subject to a serious condition, something not to be trifled with, but something to be taken at once to our beloved Physician. Our Lord does not like to see our countenance sad. King Xerxes made a law that no one should come into the king's court dressed in clothes for mourning (see Est. 4:2), but this is not a law of "the King of kings" (1 Tim. 6:15), for we may approach Him as we are — even in mourning. Yet He would rather that we, "instead of mourning," put on "a garment of praise" (Isa. 61:3), for there are great reasons to rejoice.

Christians ought to have a courageous spirit in order to glorify the Lord by enduring trials in a heroic manner, for if we are fearful and fainthearted, we dishonor Him. Besides, what a bad example we set by our doubting and discouragement, which then becomes an epidemic, soon spreading amongst the Lord's flock. One downcast believer can make twenty souls sad. Additionally, unless your courage is maintained, Satan will be too much for you.

Therefore, let your spirit be joyful in God your Savior, "for the joy of the LORD [shall be] your strength" (Neh. 8:10), and no fiend of hell shall make headway against you. Even difficult work is light to someone with a cheerful spirit, and thus success waits for cheerfulness. The believer who toils, rejoicing in his God and believing with all his heart, is guaranteed success. He who sows in hope "will reap with … joy" (Ps. 126:5), so, dear reader, "Be strong and very courageous."

From the pen of Jim Reimann:

King David fully understood the principle Spurgeon shared with us, as we see in Psalm 21. The following is his prayer, changed in order for each of us to pray it in the first person. Why not make this your prayer even now?

"O LORD, [I rejoice] in your strength. How great is [my] joy in the victories you give! You have granted [me] the desire of [my] heart and have not withheld the request of [my] lips. You welcomed [me] with rich blessings and placed a crown of pure gold on [my] head. [I] asked you for life, and you gave it to [me] — length of days, for ever and ever. Through the victories you gave, [my] glory is great; you have bestowed on [me] splendor and majesty. Surely you have granted [me] eternal blessings and made [me] glad with the joy of your presence. For [I trust] in the LORD; through the unfailing love of the Most High [I] will not be shaken.…

"Though [your enemies] plot evil against you and devise wicked schemes, they cannot succeed; for you will make them turn their backs when you aim at them with drawn bow. Be exalted, O LORD, in your strength; [I] will sing and praise your might" (Ps. 21:1–7, 11–13).

MAY 12

Do not be afraid to go down to Egypt, for I will make you into a great nation there.
I will go down to Egypt with you, and I will surely bring you back again.

Genesis 46:3 – 4

From the pen of Charles Spurgeon:

Jacob must have shuddered at these words and the very thought of leaving the land of his father to dwell among heathen strangers. It was a new scene for him, and one that was likely to be a trying one, for who can venture into the domain of a foreign king without anxiety? Yet it was evident his way was appointed for him by God and thus he resolved to go.

This is often the position of believers today as well. They may be called to face perils and temptations completely new to them, but when they are, may they imitate Jacob's example by offering sacrifices of prayer to God and seeking His direction. May they not take a step until they have waited upon the Lord for His blessing, for then they will have Jacob's Companion as their friend and helper.

What a blessing it is to feel assured the Lord is with us wherever we go, and to know He humbles Himself to enter into our humiliations and banishments with us. Even beyond a dark, unknown ocean, our Father's love shines as brightly as the sun. Thus, we should never hesitate to go where Jehovah promises us His presence, for even the dark valley of death grows bright with the radiance of this assurance.

Believers who march onward with faith in their God have the same promise God made to Jacob. They will be brought "back again," whether it be from the troubles of life or the throes of death. Jacob's ancestors eventually came back from Egypt, and in the same way, all God's faithful will pass unscathed through the tribulation of life and the terror of death.

So let us exercise the confidence of Jacob, to

whom God said, "Do not be afraid." This is the Lord's command and His divine encouragement to those who are launching themselves upon new seas at His bidding, and His divine presence and preservation forbid even as much as one unbelieving fear. Without our God, we should fear to move, but when He bids us to go, it would be dangerous to delay.

Dear reader, go forward and "Do not be afraid."

From the pen of Jim Reimann:

Yesterday's and today's devotions have a common theme: refuse to be fearful. Yet we live in a time when many professing Christians exhibit a great deal of fear. What kind of witness are we to a lost world when we as His followers walk in fear? Thus, let us consider the "so-called" best- and worst-case scenarios. The best case: We have a long life, giving us many years to tell of the Lord and His gospel of grace. Then we die and go to glory for eternity. And the worst case: We die young and go to glory for eternity. Either way — we win!

Therefore, may these determined words of David, written when he "was very much afraid of Achish king of Gath" (1 Sam. 21:12), be our prayer today:

"When I am afraid, I will trust in you. In God, whose word I praise, in God I trust; I will not be afraid. What can mortal man do to me? ... I am under vows to you, O God; I will present my thank offerings to you. For you have delivered me from death and my feet from stumbling, that I may walk before God in the light of life" (Ps. 56:3 – 4, 12 – 13).

MAY 13

You are my portion, O LORD.
Psalm 119:57

From the pen of Charles Spurgeon:

Look at your possessions, believer, and compare your portion with that of your fellowmen. Some have their portion in the fields of the countryside; thus they are rich, and their harvests yield them a golden increase. But what are their harvests compared to your God, the God of the harvests? What are barns bursting with grain compared to Him who is "the gardener" (John 15:1) and who feeds you "with the bread of heaven" (Ps. 105:40).

Others have their portion in cities; their wealth is abundant, flowing to them in continual streams, until they become a veritable repository of gold. But what is gold compared to your God? You cannot live on it, nor can your spiritual life be sustained by it. Try applying it to a troubled conscience or a despondent heart. Does it relieve the pain? Does it stop one solitary groan or lessen any grief? Remember — you have God, and in Him you have more than riches could ever buy.

Still others have their portion in applause and fame. But ask yourself if your God is not more to you than that? What if a myriad of trumpets heralded your acclaim? Would it prepare you to face the judgment? No, there are troubles in life that wealth cannot alleviate, and there is a profound need in our dying hour for which no riches can provide.

But when you have God as your portion, you have more than all else combined. In Him every need is met, whether in life or in death. With God as your portion, you are rich indeed, for "God will meet all your needs" (Phil 4:19), comfort your heart, allay your grief, guide your steps, be with you in a dark valley, and finally take you home to enjoy Him as your portion forever.

Esau said, "I ... have plenty" (Gen. 33:9), which is the best the world can say. But Jacob replied, "I have all I need" (Gen. 33:11) — a truth too lofty for worldly minds.

From the pen of Jim Reimann:

King David lived today's truth, for he prayed,

"I cry aloud to the LORD; I lift up my voice to the LORD for mercy. I pour out my complaint before him; before him I tell my trouble. When my spirit grows faint within me, it is you who know my way. In the path where I walk men have hidden a snare for me. Look to my right and see; no one is concerned for me. I have no refuge; no one cares for my life. I cry to you, O LORD; I say, 'You are my refuge, my portion in the land of the living'" (Ps. 142:1 – 5).

And Asaph, a Levite in the service of temple praise for both King David and King Solomon, agreed, for he declared:

"When my heart was grieved and my spirit embittered, I was senseless and ignorant; I was a brute beast before you. Yet I am always with you; you hold me by my right hand. You guide me with your counsel, and afterward you will take me into glory. Whom have I in heaven but you? And earth has nothing I desire besides you. My flesh and my heart may fail, but God is the strength of my heart and my portion forever" (Ps. 73:21 – 26).

Finally, let these words of Jeremiah be yours today: "The LORD is my portion; therefore I will wait for him" (Lam. 3:24).

MAY 14

He gathers the lambs in his arms
and carries them close to his heart.

Isaiah 40:11

From the pen of Charles Spurgeon:

Who is He of whom such gracious words are spoken? He is "the good shepherd" (John 10:11). Why does He carry "the lambs … close to his heart"? Because He has a tender heart and any weakness in His lambs melts His heart. The sighs, ignorance, and feebleness of the little ones of His flock evoke His compassion, for as their "faithful high priest" (Heb. 2:17), it is His role to consider the weak. After all, He purchased them with His own blood, so they are His property. Thus, He must, and will, care for those who cost Him so much. He is responsible for each lamb due to His covenant promise not to "lose one of them" (Luke 15:4 KJV, also see John 6:39). They are all a part of His glory and reward.

But what is the understanding behind the idea that He "carries" His lambs at all? Sometimes He carries them by not permitting them to endure a difficult trial; thus in His providence, He deals tenderly with them. He carries His lambs by being filled with an unusual degree of love for them, making them able to endure and withstand a trial. And although their knowledge may not be deep, due to His treatment of them they have a profound sweetness in what they do know. He carries His lambs by giving them a very simple faith, one which takes His promises just as they are, and which in basic belief runs directly to Jesus with every trouble. The simplicity of their faith gives them an unusual degree of confidence, which carries them above those in the world.

Look again at the phrase: "He … carries them close to his heart." What limitless affection! Would He carry them "close to his heart" if He did not have great love for them? What tender closeness! They are so close to Him that they could not possibly be closer. What holy fellowship! There is precious communication of love between Christ and His weak lambs. What perfect safety! Who could hurt those in His embrace? To do so, they must hurt the Shepherd first. What perfect rest and the sweetest comfort!

Surely we are not fully aware of the infinite tenderness of Jesus.

From the pen of Jim Reimann:

As we have seen today, God is often called a shepherd in His Word. Just before his death, Jacob referred to the Lord as "the God who has been my shepherd all my life to this day" (Gen. 48:15), and also called Him "the Shepherd, the Rock of Israel" (Gen. 49:24). Yet for thousands of years, even to this day in the Middle East, shepherds have been considered the lowest of society. In fact, as Jacob's household arrived in Egypt, when Joseph was Pharaoh's "second-in-command" (Gen. 41:43), Joseph said to his brothers, "When Pharaoh calls you in and asks, 'What is your occupation?' you should answer, 'Your servants have tended livestock from our boyhood on, just as our fathers did.' Then you will be allowed to settle in the region of Goshen, *for all shepherds are detestable to the Egyptians*" (Gen. 46:33 – 34).

Therefore we should be all the more thankful for Jesus, who "humbled himself and became obedient to death — even death on a cross!" (Phil. 2:8). Let us remember His glorious words of sacrificial love: "I am the good shepherd. The good shepherd lays down his life for the sheep" (John 10:11).

MAY 15

...made perfect.

Hebrews 12:23

From the pen of Charles Spurgeon:

There are two types of perfection the Christian needs: justification in the person of Jesus Christ and sanctification produced in him by the Holy Spirit. Our experience quickly teaches us that corruption still remains in the hearts of those who have been regenerated, for lusts and evil thoughts linger within us. But I rejoice that the day is coming when God will finish His work and will present my soul before His throne, not only perfect in Christ but perfect through the Spirit, "without stain ... or any other blemish" (Eph. 5:27).

Can it truly be that this poor sinful heart of mine will become holy — just as God is holy? Can it be that my spirit, which often cries, "What a wretched man I am! Who will rescue me from this body of death?" (Rom. 7:24), will actually be rid of sin and death — that I will have no evil things to distress my ears and no unholy thoughts to disrupt my peace?

When I finally cross the Jordan, the work of sanctification will be finished — but not until that moment will I begin to claim perfection in myself. Only then will my spirit have its final baptism in the Holy Spirit's fire. Oh, how I look forward to death, when I will receive that last purification that will usher me into heaven! There will not be a heavenly angel more pure than I will be, for I will be able to say — in a double sense — "I am clean," for I will be clean through Jesus' blood and through the Spirit's work.

Oh, how we should exalt the power of the Holy Spirit for making us fit to stand before our Father in heaven! But may the hope of future perfection never make us content with imperfection now, for if that is the case, our hope cannot be genuine; for godly hope is a purifying thing, even now. The work of grace must be abiding and active in us now or it will not lead to perfection then. So let us pray to "be filled with the Spirit" (Eph. 5:18) that increasingly we "may be ... filled with the fruit of righteousness" (Phil. 1:10 – 11).

From the pen of Jim Reimann:

Jesus told His disciples, "You are clean" (John 13:10), and His way of making people clean was always from the inside out. The Jews were obsessed over bodily cleanliness, especially before eating or when entering the temple. They would wash their hands with ceremonial water and would completely immerse themselves in pools known as *mikvahs* before entering the temple. This is why He taught, "Woe to you, teachers of the law and Pharisees, you hypocrites! You clean the outside of the cup and dish, but inside they are full of greed and self-indulgence. First clean the inside of the cup and dish, and then the outside also will be clean" (Matt. 23:25 – 26).

Even from His first miracle in Cana, Jesus showed the importance of being made clean on the inside. It was there He took "six stone water jars, the kind used by the Jews for ceremonial washing" (John 2:6), and had them filled with water, as if to say, "Take me (or My blood, represented by the wine) into yourself, and I will make you clean from the inside out." Do you recall His words, "Whoever eats my flesh and drinks my blood remains in me, and I in him" (John 6:56)?

Remember — "The blood of Christ...cleanse[s] our consciences from acts that lead to death, so that we may serve the living God!" (Heb. 9:14).

MAY 16

[Elisha] said, "This is what the LORD says: Make this valley full of ditches.
For this is what the LORD says: You will see neither wind nor rain, yet this valley will be filled
with water, and you, your cattle and your other animals will drink."

2 Kings 3:16 – 17

From the pen of Charles Spurgeon:

The armies of the kings of Israel, Judah, and Edom "had no more water for themselves or for the animals with them" (2 Kings 3:9), but God was about to provide for them, for in today's text we see God's prophet announcing the blessing. This was a case of human helplessness, for as valiant as these men were, they could not procure a drop of water from the sky or the wells of earth. This is often the situation of the Lord's people; they find themselves at their wits' end, seeing their own helplessness, and thereby learn where help is to be found.

Yet the people were required to prepare for God's blessing in faith by digging the ditches in which the precious water would be held. Likewise, the church, using her various gifts, efforts, and prayer, must make herself ready to be blessed; she must dig the pools, and the Lord will fill them. This must be done in faith, in full assurance that the blessing is about to descend.

God filled the ditches in this case in a very unusual manner, not as in Elijah's case when water poured from the clouds, but in a silent and mysterious way. The Lord has His own sovereign modes of action. He is not tied to a particular way and time as we are, but will do as He pleases. Our role is simply to receive from Him with thanksgiving, not to dictate to Him.

Yet we should also notice in this story the remarkable abundance of His provision, for there was enough to meet the needs of all. And so it is with the gospel blessing; all the needs of the church will be met by His divine power in answer to prayer; and even beyond this — victory will be speedily given to the armies of the Lord.

What am I doing for Jesus? What ditches am I digging?

O Lord, make me ready to receive the blessing You are so willing to bestow.

From the pen of Jim Reimann:

Years ago, the warning parents gave their children was that if they didn't get a good education, they would end up being ditch diggers. Yet, spiritually speaking, in light of today's devotion, that's exactly what we should be. That is why the apostle Paul encouraged us to be involved in the ongoing process of our sanctification, saying, "Therefore, my dear friends,... continue to work out your salvation with fear and trembling" (Phil. 2:12).

Our tendency is to sit back and ask God to work. We even tell Him the various ways He can answer our prayers. But His people are to be involved in the process, and as in today's Scripture, the Lord worked in a way they never could have imagined. God had provided water for His people in the wilderness before, but this time He did it in a way they had never experienced.

Even Nebuchadnezzar, once his "sanity was restored," declared, "The Most High ... does as he pleases with the powers of heaven and the peoples of the earth. No one can hold back his hand or say to him: 'What have you done?'" (Dan. 4:34 – 35).

After all, doesn't God receive more glory when He works in a way we never expected? Doesn't that make you want to start digging?

MAY 17

"You are my servant";
I have chosen you and have not rejected you.

Isaiah 41:9

From the pen of Charles Spurgeon:

If we have truly received the grace of God in our hearts, its practical effect is to make us His servants. We may be unfaithful and "unworthy servants" (Luke 17:10), but, blessed be His name, we are nevertheless God's servants. We bear His image, are fed at His table, and ultimately obey His commands. We were once the servants of sin, but He who made us free has now taken us into His family and taught us obedience to His will. We do not serve our Master perfectly, although we would if we could. Thus, as we hear God's voice saying to us, "You are my servant," we can respond with David: "I am your servant; ... you have freed me from my chains" (Ps. 116:16).

Not only does the Lord call us His servants but also His chosen ones — "I have chosen you." We did not choose Him; He chose us. We have not always been God's servants, and the change can only be credited to God's sovereign grace. The eye of sovereignty singled us out, and the voice of unchanging grace declared, "I have loved you with an everlasting love" (Jer. 31:3). Long before time began or space was created, God wrote the names of His elect people upon His heart, "predestined [them] to be conformed to the likeness of his Son" (Rom. 8:29), and ordained them as heirs of all the fullness of His love, grace, and glory.

What comfort we have in this! Will the Lord who has loved us this long ultimately reject us? He knew how obstinate we would be and understood our hearts were evil, and yet He made the choice. Our Savior is not fickle when it comes to love, for He does not feel enchanted for a while by some gleam of beauty from His church's eye, and then afterwards cast her aside because of her unfaithfulness. No, He married her in eternity past, and it is written of Jehovah, "I hate divorce" (Mal. 2:16).

God's eternal choice is a covenant bond upon our gratitude and upon His faithfulness that neither of us can disown.

From the pen of Jim Reimann:

Jesus confirmed today's truth, saying, "You did not choose me, but I chose you and appointed you to go and bear fruit — fruit that will last" (John 15:16), and "You do not belong to the world, but I have chosen you out of the world" (John 15:19). Again, as we can see from these words, we are not chosen simply to belong to God, but to be His servants as well.

Thus, may we consider the blessings described in the context of today's verse:

I took you from the ends of the earth, from its farthest corners I called you. I said, "You are my servant"; I have chosen you and have not rejected you. So do not fear, for I am with you; do not be dismayed, for I am your God. I will strengthen you and help you; I will uphold you with my righteous right hand.

Isaiah 41:9 – 10

In light of these gracious words, may our closing prayer be:

"Remember me, O Lord, when you show favor to your people, come to my aid when you save them, that I may enjoy the prosperity of your chosen ones, that I may share in the joy of your nation and join your inheritance in giving praise" (Ps. 106:4 – 5).

MAY 18

Later on …
Hebrews 12:11

From the pen of Charles Spurgeon:

How happy tested Christians are — "later on." There is no calm as profound as that which follows a storm. Who has not rejoiced in the bright sunshine after rain? Victory banquets are for well-seasoned soldiers. It is after we kill the lion that we eat the honey (see Judg. 14:5 – 9). It is after climbing the Hill Difficulty that we sit down in the arbor to rest, after traversing the Valley of Humiliation, after fighting with Apollyon, that the Shining One appears with the healing branch from the tree of life. [Editor's note: Hill Difficulty represents the right road for Christian, a character in *The Pilgrim's Progress* by John Bunyan (1628 – 88); Apollyon (literally "Destroyer") is the lord of the City of Destruction, whom Christian battles in the Valley of Humiliation, on the other side of Hill Difficulty; and the Shining One is a messenger or angel of God.]

Our sorrows, like the keels of ships upon the sea, leave a silver line of holy light behind them "later on." That light is peace — sweet, deep peace — that follows the horrible turmoil that once reigned in our tormented, guilty souls. Thus, "later on" we see the happy condition of a Christian. He has his best things last, and therefore, in this world, receives his worst things first. But even his so-called "worst things," are "later on" good things — that is, hard plowings that yield joyful harvests.

Yet even now a believer grows rich through his losses, for he rises by falling, lives by dying, and becomes full by being emptied. Therefore, if his severe afflictions yield such abundant peaceful fruit in this life, what will the full vintage of joy be like "later on" in heaven? If his dark nights here are as bright as the world's days, what will his days in heaven be like? If he can sing in a dungeon now, how sweetly will he sing in heaven. If he can praise the Lord through the testing fires, how much more will he exalt Him before the eternal throne? If evil is good to him now, what will the overflowing goodness of God be to him then?

O blessed "later on"! Who wouldn't desire to be a Christian? Who wouldn't bear today's cross for the crown that comes "later on"? But in this comes the work of perseverance, for our rest is not for today nor the triumph for the present, but "later on." Thus wait, O soul, and let "perseverance … finish its work" (James 1:4).

From the pen of Jim Reimann:

We see today that this life is the worst a believer will ever endure, but it is the best an unbeliever will ever enjoy. So, believer, remember: "Our present sufferings are not worth comparing with the glory that will be revealed in us" (Rom. 8:18).

We also see today the seeming contradictions of the Christian life, such as "living by dying." Jesus confirmed this difficult truth with these words that have a blessing "later on":

Unless a kernel of wheat falls to the ground and dies, it remains only a single seed. But if it dies, it produces many seeds. The man who loves his life will lose it, while the man who hates his life in this world will keep it for eternal life. Whoever serves me must follow me; and where I am, my servant also will be. My Father will honor the one who serves me.

John 12:24 – 26

Lord, grant me the patience to wait for the blessing that comes "later on."

MAY 19

[Elijah] ... prayed that he might die.

1 Kings 19:4

From the pen of Charles Spurgeon:

Isn't it remarkable that the man who would never die — the man for whom God had ordained something infinitely better, the man who would be translated or carried to heaven in "a chariot of fire" (2 Kings 2:11) — never to see death — would pray, "Take my life; I am no better than my ancestors" (1 Kings 19:4). This is a memorable proof that God does not always answer prayer in kind, though He always does in effect; for He gave Elijah something better than what he asked, and thus God really did hear and answer him. It was strange indeed that the lion-hearted Elijah became so depressed by Jezebel's threat (see 1 Kings 19:2) that he asked to die, and it was blessedly kind on the part of our heavenly Father that He did not take His despondent servant at his word.

There is a limit to the doctrine of the prayer of faith. We are not to expect that God will give us everything for which we choose to ask. We know that sometimes we ask and "do not receive, because [we] ask with wrong motives" (James 4:3). If we ask for that which God has not promised, if we ask contrary to His sovereign will, if we ask merely for the gratification of our own ease rather than God's glory, then we must not expect to receive.

However, when we ask in faith, without any doubts, and do not receive precisely what we have asked, then we will receive its equivalent — and more than its equivalent. As someone once remarked, "If the Lord does not pay in silver, He will pay in gold, and if not in gold, He will pay in diamonds." If God does not give you precisely what you ask, He will give you something in lieu of it that will cause you to rejoice greatly.

Therefore, dear reader, be much in prayer. Why not make today a day of earnest intercession? But be careful what you ask.

From the pen of Jim Reimann:

Two of Jesus' most famous prayers are the Lord's Prayer and His prayer in Gethsemane, shortly before His death on the cross. But what these two prayers have in common is directly connected to an important teaching of today's devotion. Jesus prayed in the Lord's Prayer, "Your will be done on earth as it is in heaven" (Matt. 6:10), and in Gethsemane He again prayed, "Not my will, but yours be done" (Luke 22:42). The truth is, because God is sovereign, His will is going to be done — period. No amount of "naming and claiming," so prevalent among many professing believers today, is going to make God do something not in His will.

Remember — God is not at our mercy — we are at His mercy! He does not exist to be a "vending machine in the sky" for us; we exist to glorify Him. With this in mind, may our prayers always be in accordance with His will. And when situations arise when we don't know how to pray, don't know what His will may be, or don't know what to do, may our prayer be akin to that of King Jehoshaphat, who prayed:

"We will stand in your presence before this temple that bears your Name and will cry out to you in our distress, and you will hear us and save us.... We do not know what to do, but our eyes are upon you" (2 Chron. 20:9, 12).

MAY 20

I drew them with gentle cords,
with bands of love.
Hosea 11:4 NKJV

From the pen of Charles Spurgeon:

Our heavenly Father often draws us to Himself "with bands of love," but oh, how reluctant we are to run to Him. How slowly we respond to His gentle nudges. He leads us to exercise a more simple faith in Him, but we have not yet attained the type of confident faith Abraham exhibited. We don't leave our worldly cares with God; instead, like Martha, we encumber ourselves with "over serving." Thus our meager faith brings leanness to our souls; and although He promised, "Open wide your mouth and I will fill it" (Ps. 81:10), we don't open our mouths.

Isn't God even now drawing you to trust Him? Can't you hear Him saying, "Come, my child, and trust Me. 'The curtain of the temple [has been] torn' (Matt. 27:51), so enter into My presence and 'approach [my] throne of grace with confidence' (Heb. 4:16). I am worthy of your complete confidence, so 'cast your cares on [Me]' (Ps. 55:22). 'Shake off your dust' (Isa. 52:2) of cares and put on your beautiful garments of joy." Regrettably, though the Lord calls us with expressions of love to the blessed experience of His comforting grace, we will not go to Him. At other times He draws us to even closer communion. We have been sitting on the doorstep of His house, and He invites us into the banquet hall to dine with Him, but we decline the honor. There are secret rooms we have not yet visited; Jesus invites us to enter them, but we hold back.

Shame on us and our cold hearts for exhibiting such poor love for our sweet Lord Jesus. We are not fit to be His servants, much less His bride, yet He has exalted us to be "bone of [His] bones and flesh of [His] flesh" (Gen. 2:23), married to Him through a glorious marriage covenant. "This is love" (1 John 4:10). But it is a love that will not take "No" for an answer. If we disobey the gentle wooing of His love, He will send affliction to drive us into closer intimacy with Him, for He will have us nearer. What foolish children we are to refuse His "gentle cords ... of love" and thereby bring upon our own backs the scourge of small cords, which Jesus does know how to use.

From the pen of Jim Reimann:

When Israel was unfaithful to the Lord, God said to His people:

> Return, faithless Israel.... I will frown on you no longer, for I am merciful.... I will not be angry forever. Only acknowledge your guilt — you have rebelled against the LORD your God, you have scattered your favors to foreign gods under every spreading tree, and have not obeyed me.... Return, faithless people,... for I am your husband. I will choose you — one from a town and two from a clan — and bring you to Zion. Then I will give you shepherds after my own heart, who will lead you with knowledge and understanding.
>
> Jeremiah 3:12 – 15

This passage testifies to God's great love for His people and the fact that He is always faithful, even when we are not. Paul taught: "If we are faithless, he will remain faithful, for he cannot disown himself" (2 Tim. 2:13). In other words, God's faithfulness has nothing to do with our obedience, for the Lord "cannot disown" His attributes, one of which is His absolute faithfulness.

Thus, as Spurgeon said, "He will have us nearer!" But wouldn't it be much better to willingly respond to His "gentle cords" and "bands of love" out of a deep motivation of love for Him? Believer, how will you respond?

MAY 21

There is grain in Egypt.

Genesis 42:2

From the pen of Charles Spurgeon:

Famine was affecting all the nations, so it seemed inevitable that Jacob and his family would ultimately be in great need. But the God of providence, who never forgets the objects of His electing love, had prepared a granary for His people by giving the Egyptians a warning of the coming scarcity, and thereby leading them to store up grain through the years of plenty. Little did Jacob expect deliverance from Egypt, but it was there the Lord provided grain for him.

Dear believer, although everything may appear to be against you, rest assured that God has made plans on your behalf. Somehow He will deliver you, and somewhere He will provide for you. The place from which your rescue will come may be an unexpected one, but help will come in your time of need, and as a result you will magnify the name of the Lord. If people don't feed you, ravens will (see 1 Kings 17:2 – 6); and if earth doesn't yield wheat for you, God "will rain down bread from heaven" (Ex. 16:4).

Therefore "be strong and take heart" (Ps. 31:24) and rest quietly in the Lord. God can make the sun rise in the west if He pleases, and He can make the source of your distress your channel of delight. All the grain in Egypt was in the hands of the beloved Joseph, and he opened and closed the granaries as he pleased. Likewise, all the riches of Providence are in the absolute power and control of our Lord Jesus, who will dispense them liberally to His people. Joseph was abundantly prepared to come to the aid of his own family, and Jesus is forever faithful to care for His own brothers and sisters as well.

Our part is to go after the help provided for us, to take action and not sit idly by in despondency. Prayer will carry us quickly into the presence of our royal Brother, and once we are before His throne, all we have to do is ask in order to have. His storehouse is never exhausted; there is always grain available. And His heart is never hard; thus He will give the grain to us.

Lord, forgive our unbelief, and cause us even now to draw richly from Your fullness and receive "one blessing after another" (John 1:16).

From the pen of Jim Reimann:

One of the most difficult lessons for God's people to fully comprehend is that God doesn't need what is in our storehouse — we need what is in His! The Lord said:

I have no need of a bull from your stall or of goats from your pens, for every animal of the forest is mine, and the cattle on a thousand hills. I know every bird in the mountains, and the creatures of the field are mine. If I were hungry I would not tell you, for the world is mine, and all that is in it. Do I eat the flesh of bulls or drink the blood of goats? Sacrifice thank offerings to God, fulfill your vows to the Most High, and call upon me in the day of trouble; I will deliver you, and you will honor me.

Psalm 50:9 – 15

We need to give, not because God has needs, but in obedience to Him and to keep the channel of blessings open. Then, as Paul experienced, "God will meet all your needs *according to his glorious riches in Christ Jesus*" (Phil. 4:19).

MAY 22

Behold, you are beautiful, my beloved.

Song of Songs 1:16 ESV

From the pen of Charles Spurgeon:

In every way our Beloved is beautiful, and our various experiences are ordained by our heavenly Father to furnish fresh vantage points from which we may view the beauty of Jesus. Thus our trials seem much more bearable since they offer us clearer views of Him than ordinary life could ever provide. We have seen Him "from the crest of Amana, from the top of Senir, [and] the summit of Hermon," and He has shone His light on us like the sun in His power; but we also have seen Him "from the lions' dens and the mountain haunts of the leopards" (Song 4:8), and even there He has lost none of His beauty. From the suffering of a sick bed to the edge of the grave, we have turned our eyes to our soul's Spouse and never found Him to be anything but beautiful. Many of His saints have gazed upon Him from the gloom of dungeons and from the red flames of being burned at the stake, yet have never uttered an unkind word of Him, but instead have died extolling His surpassing beauty.

Oh, the wonder and grace of gazing forever at our sweet Lord Jesus. Isn't it wonderful to view our Savior in each of His roles, recognizing His matchlessness in each — in essence, turning the kaleidoscope and continuing to find fresh combinations of His unparalleled beauty? In the manger or in eternity, on the cross or on His throne, in the garden or in His kingdom, and between thieves or among angels, "he is altogether lovely" (Song 5:16). Examine every action of His life and every trait of His character, and He will be as lovely in every small detail as in His majesty. Judge Him as you will — you cannot find fault; measure Him as you please — He will not be found lacking.

All of eternity will never reveal even the shadow of an imperfection in our Beloved. To the contrary, as the ages come and go, His hidden glories will shine forth with still more splendor, and His loveliness will more and more overwhelm every heavenly mind.

From the pen of Jim Reimann:

Today we consider the beauty of the Lord Jesus. But didn't Isaiah say of the Messiah, "He had no beauty or majesty to attract us to him, nothing in his appearance that we should desire him" (Isa. 53:2)? Yes, but he also said, "In that day the Branch of the Lord will be beautiful and glorious" (Isa. 4:2), with the word *Branch* referring to the Messiah. (Note: the Hebrew for *branch* is *netzer*, the root word for Nazareth. Thus, Matthew wrote: "He [Joseph] went and lived in a town called Nazareth. So was fulfilled what was said through the prophets: 'He [Jesus] will be called a Nazarene'" [Matt. 2:23].)

The difference between these quotes from Isaiah is that one refers to Christ's first coming, while the next refers to His second advent; for once again, referring to His return, Isaiah prophesied, "In that day the Lord Almighty will be a glorious crown, a beautiful wreath for the remnant of his people" (Isa. 28:5). The Lord also promised through Isaiah, "Your eyes will see the king in his beauty" (Isa. 33:17). With this in mind, may this be our heart's prayer today:

> "One thing I ask of the Lord, this is what I seek: that I may dwell in the house of the Lord all the days of my life, to gaze upon the beauty of the Lord and to seek him in his temple" (Ps. 27:4).

MAY 23

You have not bought any fragrant calamus for me.

Isaiah 43:24

From the pen of Charles Spurgeon:

Worshipers at the temple would customarily bring gifts of perfume to be burned on God's altar; but Israel, during her backsliding, lacked generosity and made very few offerings in keeping with her vows. This was evidence of the coldness of her heart toward God and His house.

Does this ever occur with you? Could the charge of today's text occasionally, if not frequently, be brought against you? Those who are monetarily poor, but rich in faith, will be no less accepted because their gifts are small. If you are poor, are you giving the proper proportion to God, or are you withholding your "widow's mite" (see Mark 12:42 KJV) from His sacred treasury? And if you are rich, be thankful for what He has entrusted to you, but never forget your great responsibility, for "from everyone who has been given much, much will be demanded" (Luke 12:48). Are you mindful of your obligation to give to the Lord according to the benefit received?

Jesus gave His blood for us — what shall we give to Him? We, and everything we have, are His, for He has purchased us for Himself. So how can we act as if we are our own? Oh, how we need more consecration to Him and love for Him.

Blessed Jesus, how good it is of You to accept our "fragrant calamus" bought with money! Nothing would be too costly for us as a tribute to Your unequaled love, and yet You receive with favor even the smallest gifts of our affection! You receive mere tokens of our love as though they were intrinsically precious, receiving them with as much love as a mother accepting a bouquet of wild flowers from her child. May we never grow miserly toward You, and from this moment on, may we never have to hear again Your complaint of us withholding gifts of our love. We will offer You "the firstfruits of all [our] crops" (Prov. 3:9) and tithes on everything, and then will confess that "we have given you only what comes from your hand" (1 Chron. 29:14).

From the pen of Jim Reimann:

Although Israel had now become miserly, they once had given willingly for the building of God's temple. In fact, Spurgeon's closing quote is taken from this prayer of David's on that occasion:

"Wealth and honor come from you; you are the ruler of all things. In your hands are strength and power to exalt and give strength to all. Now, our God, we give you thanks, and praise your glorious name. But who am I, and who are my people, that we should be able to give as generously as this? Everything comes from you, and we have given you only what comes from your hand.... O LORD our God, as for all this abundance that we have provided for building you a temple for your Holy Name, it comes from your hand, and all of it belongs to you" (1 Chron. 29:12 – 14, 16).

Let us remember Moses' words: "You may say to yourself, 'My power and the strength of my hands have produced this wealth for me.' But remember the LORD your God, for *it is he who gives you the ability to produce wealth*" (Deut. 8:17 – 18).

Lord, may David's prayer be true of me: "All these things have I given willingly and with honest intent" (1 Chron. 29:17).

MAY 24

Conduct yourselves in a manner worthy of the gospel of Christ.

Philippians 1:27

From the pen of Charles Spurgeon:

The word *conduct* here does not merely refer to a limited area of our life, but it encompasses the totality of our life and behavior in the world. The Greek word for *conduct* signifies the actions and privileges of citizenship, and thus we as citizens of "the new Jerusalem" (Rev. 3:12) are commanded to act "in a manner worthy of the gospel of Christ." But what sort of conduct is this to be?

In the first place, the gospel is very simple. Thus, Christians should be plain and simple in their ways. When it comes to our manner, speech, and dress — in fact, our entire behavior — we should exhibit a simplicity which is the very soul of beauty.

Next, the gospel is preeminently true. It is gold without dross. Thus, a Christian's life will have no luster or value without the jewel of truth.

The gospel is a fearless gospel. It boldly proclaims the truth, whether people like it or not. Thus, we must be equally faithful, unflinching, and unafraid.

But the gospel is also gentle. We see this spirit in the gospel's Author: "A bruised reed he will not break" (Isa. 42:3). Yet some professing believers are sharper than a thorn bush; such people are not like Jesus. Thus, may we seek to win others by the gentleness of our words and actions.

The gospel is very loving. It is the message of "the God of love" (2 Cor. 13:11) to a lost and fallen human race. Christ's last command to His disciples was, "Love one another" (John 13:34). Oh, how we need more unity among believers, a real and vigorous love for all God's saints, and a more tender compassion for the souls of the worst and vilest of mankind.

Finally, we must never forget that the gospel of Christ is holy. His gospel never excuses sin; it pardons it, but only through the atonement. Thus, if our life is to resemble the gospel, we must shun anything and everything that would hinder our perfect conformity to Christ, not merely what we consider the worst vices.

Therefore, for Jesus' sake, for the sake of others, and for our own sake, we must strive day by day to bring our conduct into greater accordance with His gospel.

From the pen of Jim Reimann:

Another attribute of the gospel is this — it is a *personal* gospel. Consider how Paul described it: "God will judge men's secrets through Jesus Christ, as *my gospel* declares" (Rom. 2:16); "Now to him who is able to establish you by *my gospel* and the proclamation of Jesus Christ ... " (Rom. 16:25); and "Remember Jesus Christ, raised from the dead, descended from David. This is *my gospel* ... " (2 Tim. 2:8). Of course, Paul's primary meaning here is that God showed him aspects of the gospel not yet revealed to others, for he wrote of "the mystery made known to me by revelation.... In reading this, then, you will be able to understand my insight into the mystery of Christ" (Eph. 3:3 – 4).

Yet we know he proclaimed a gospel of personal intimacy with Christ. This is why Paul, though already God's child, could declare: "[For my determined purpose is] that I may know Him [that I may progressively become more deeply and intimately acquainted with Him]" (Phil. 3:10 Amplified).

MAY 25

They got up and returned at once to Jerusalem....
Then the two told what had happened on the way,
and how Jesus was recognized by them.

Luke 24:33, 35

From the pen of Charles Spurgeon:

Once these two disciples reached Emmaus and were refreshing themselves at their evening meal, the mysterious stranger who had so captivated them on the road "took bread ... [and] broke it" (v. 30), revealed Himself to them, and "disappeared from their sight" (v. 31). Earlier they had "urged him strongly" to stay with them "for ... the day [was] almost over" (v. 29); but now, although it was much later, their love for Him became a lamp — even wings — to their feet. They forgot the darkness, their weariness was gone, and they immediately traveled back the "seven miles [to] Jerusalem" (v. 13) to share the joyful news of the risen Lord who had appeared to them along the way. Reaching the Christians in Jerusalem, they were received with a burst of happy news before they could tell their own story.

These early Christians were all on fire to tell of Christ's resurrection and to proclaim what they knew of the Lord, making their experiences the common property of all. May their example make a deep impression upon us that we too must bear witness of Jesus. John's account of the empty tomb needed to be supplemented by Peter, and Mary added further details. Then combined, we have a full testimony from which nothing can be taken away.

God has given each of us specific gifts and insights, but the one common objective He has in mind is the perfecting of the entire body of Christ. Therefore we must bring our spiritual possessions and lay them at the apostles' feet, so what God has shown us may be distributed to all. We must never hold back any portion of God's precious truth, but should tell what we know and testify to what we have seen. We must not allow weariness, darkness, or even the possible unbelief of our friends to be considered for even a moment.

Rise up and march to your place of duty. And once there tell what great things the Lord has shown your soul.

From the pen of Jim Reimann:

Every true believer's encounter with the Lord Jesus, from the shepherds who visited Him at His birth to His post-resurrection appearance to these men on the road to Emmaus, is characterized by the same response — telling others. Concerning the shepherds at His birth, for example, we are told, "They spread the word concerning what had been told them about this child, and all who heard it were amazed at what the shepherds said to them" (Luke 2:17–18). Then forty days after His birth, Anna, the prophetess, had an encounter with Him at the temple; and we are told: "She gave thanks to God and spoke about the child to all who were looking forward to the redemption of Jerusalem" (Luke 2:38).

Paul, who had an encounter with the ascended Christ, proclaimed, "I am compelled to preach. Woe to me if I do not preach the gospel!" (1 Cor. 9:16). This is much akin to the powerful words of Jeremiah, who declared, "If I say, 'I will not mention him or speak any more in his name,' his word is in my heart like a fire, a fire shut up in my bones. I am weary of holding it in; indeed, I cannot" (Jer. 20:9).

Preacher or not, each of us must "always be prepared to give an answer to everyone who asks [us] to give the reason for the hope that [we] have" (1 Peter 3:15).

MAY 26

Remain true to the faith.

Acts 14:22

From the pen of Charles Spurgeon:

Perseverance is the sign of a true saint. The Christian life not only should be a journey in God's ways at its beginning, but should exhibit those ways to the end. The great French conqueror Napoleon (1769 – 1821) once said, "Conquest has made me what I am, and conquest must maintain me." Likewise, dear brothers and sisters, conquest by God's power has made you what you are, and continuing to conquer must sustain you. Your motto must be: *"Excelsior"* — Latin for "ever upward." The only true conqueror is the one who receives a crown at the end — he who perseveres until the war trumpet ceases to blow.

Thus, our perseverance is the target of all our spiritual enemies. The world will not object to your being a Christian for a time if it can tempt you to stop your pilgrimage and, ultimately, get you to trade with it in Vanity Fair. [Editor's note: Vanity Fair is a city in *The Pilgrim's Progress* by John Bunyan (1628 – 1688) where a fair is held.] The flesh will seek to ensnare you and prevent you from pressing on to glory, saying, "It's tiring work being a pilgrim. Give it up! Must I always be put to death and never be indulged? At least allow me a short break from this constant warfare."

Satan himself will make many fierce attacks on your perseverance — it will be the target for each of his arrows. He will strive to hinder you in your service by insinuating you are not accomplishing any good and that you need rest; he will endeavor to make you weary of suffering and whisper to you, "Curse God and die!" (Job 2:9). Or he will attack your steadfastness, saying, "What is the good of being so zealous? Keep quiet like everyone else, sleep as others do, and let your lamp go out as the other virgins do" (see Matt. 25:1 – 13). Or he will assault your doctrine, saying, "Why do you believe these denominational creeds? Sensible people are becoming more liberal and are removing the old fundamentals of the faith. Get with the times!"

Therefore, dear Christian, take up your shield, fasten your armor, and cry out mightily to God, praying that by His Spirit you may endure to the end.

From the pen of Jim Reimann:

Remember those earlier days after you had received the light, when you stood your ground in a great contest in the face of suffering. Sometimes you were publicly exposed to insult and persecution; at other times you stood side by side with those who were so treated. You sympathized with those in prison and joyfully accepted the confiscation of your property, because you knew that you yourselves had better and lasting possessions. So do not throw away your confidence; it will be richly rewarded. You need to persevere so that when you have done the will of God, you will receive what he has promised. For in just a very little while, "He who is coming will come and will not delay. But my righteous one will live by faith. And if he shrinks back, I will not be pleased with him."

Hebrews 10:32 – 38

The truth is — all Christians *will* endure to the end by God's grace and power, for the writer of Hebrews continues: "But we are not of those who shrink back and are destroyed, but of those who believe and are saved" (Heb. 10:39). We, of course, should endeavor to finish well.

MAY 27

Mephibosheth bowed down and said [to King David],
"What is your servant, that you should notice a dead dog like me?"

2 Samuel 9:8

From the pen of Charles Spurgeon:

If Mephibosheth was so greatly humbled by David's kindness, how much more should we be humbled in the presence of our gracious Lord? The more grace we have, the less we will think of ourselves, for grace, like light, reveals our impurity. Even the most renowned saints have scarcely known how to describe themselves. Samuel Rutherford (1600? – 1661), the Scottish Presbyterian preacher, once said, "I am a dry and withered branch, a dead carcass, dry bones, and not able to step over a piece of straw." Another time he wrote, "If not for what the Lord has done in me, I would be no better than Judas or Cain."

A truly humble person even views the lowest objects of nature as better than they are, because those objects have never sinned. For example, a dog may appear greedy, fierce, or filthy, but it has no conscience to violate and no Holy Spirit to resist. A dog may be a worthless animal, yet when shown a little kindness by its master, it soon exhibits great love for that master and will be faithful till death. But we forget the goodness of the Lord and often fail to follow when He calls. To call someone a "dead dog" is one of the strongest terms of contempt, but it is none too strong for a truly humble believer to use for himself in expressing his own self-abhorrence. Such a believer will not exhibit a false modesty, but will mean what he says. He will have weighed himself on God's scales and discovered the vanity of his nature.

At best, we are simply clay, living dust, or walking mounds of dirt; but when viewed as sinners, we are monsters indeed. May heaven itself declare the wonder that the Lord Jesus would set His heart's love upon creatures such as we are.

And although we are only dust and ashes, we must and will praise the exceeding greatness of His grace, for couldn't His heart have found its true rest in heaven? Did He really need to come to the world's "tents of Kedar" (Song 1:5) for a spouse? O heavens and earth, break forth into song and give all glory to our sweet Lord Jesus!

From the pen of Jim Reimann:

Only a fool believes the Lord will tolerate pride in the hearts of His people. If Jesus humbled Himself to the degree He did, can we expect not to be humbled ourselves? The truth is, God will go to extraordinary lengths to humble us. Here is a warning Moses gave the Israelites before they entered the Promised Land:

> Be careful to follow every command I am giving you today, so that you may live and increase and may enter and possess the land that the LORD promised on oath to your forefathers. *Remember how the LORD your God led you all the way in the desert these forty years, to humble you and to test you* in order to know what was in your heart, whether or not you would keep his commands. *He humbled you,* causing you to hunger and then feeding you with manna, which neither you nor your fathers had known, to teach you that man does not live on bread alone but on every word that comes from the mouth of the LORD.

Deuteronomy 8:1 – 3

Then Peter commanded: "Clothe yourselves with humility toward one another, because, 'God opposes the proud but gives grace to the humble'" (1 Peter 5:5).

MAY 28

This I call to mind and therefore I have hope.

Lamentations 3:21

From the pen of Charles Spurgeon:

Our memory frequently becomes a slave to despondency, for a mind filled with despair calls to remembrance every dark fear from the past, and focuses on every gloomy problem of the present. Thus, our memory, dressed in sackcloth, brings to mind only "bitterness and ... gall" (v. 19). This dilemma, however, is unnecessary, for wisdom can quickly transform our memory into an angel of comfort. The same remembrance that brings so many gloomy omens in its left hand can be trained to offer a wealth of hopeful signs in its right. It need not wear a crown of iron, but may encircle its brow with a tiara of gold adorned with diamonds.

This was Jeremiah's experience, for in the previous verses his memory had brought him to deep depression, and he wrote: "I remember my affliction ... and my soul is downcast within me" (vv. 19 – 20). But then the same memory that depressed him restored him to life and comfort: "This I call to mind and therefore I have hope." Like a two-edged sword, his memory first killed his pride with one edge, then slew his despair with the other.

Thus, as a general principle, if we would exercise our memories more wisely during our times of darkest distress, we might strike a match that would instantly light a lamp of comfort. There is no need for God to create some new thing on earth in order to restore believers to joy, for if they would prayerfully rake the ashes of the past, they would find light for the present; and if they would but turn to the Book of Truth and the throne of grace, their candle would soon shine as brightly as in the past.

May it be our pattern to remember the loving-kindness of the Lord and to recall His works of grace. Let us open our mind's book of remembrance that is so richly illuminated with memories of God's mercy, and we will soon be filled with joy. Thus, our memory may be, as Samuel Coleridge (1772 – 1834), the English poet, calls it: "The heart-spring of joy." And when the Divine Comforter bends our mind to His service, it may be preeminent among our earthly comforters.

From the pen of Jim Reimann:

Consistent with today's text, Jeremiah also wrote: "The LORD appeared to us in the past, saying: 'I have loved you with an everlasting love; I have drawn you with loving-kindness'" (Jer. 31:3). Notice how he recalled the past, focusing on God's love. We find this practice in this psalm of Asaph as well:

> When I was in distress, I sought the Lord.... I remembered you, O God, and I groaned; I mused, and my spirit grew faint.... I thought about the former days, the years of long ago; I remembered my songs in the night.... My spirit inquired: "Will the Lord reject forever? Will he never show his favor again?" ... Then I thought, "To this I will appeal: the years of the right hand of the Most High." I will remember the deeds of the LORD; yes, I will remember your miracles of long ago. I will meditate on all your works and consider all your mighty deeds.
> Psalm 77:2 – 3, 5 – 7, 10 – 12

Finally, Paul wrote in agreement: "Whatever is true, whatever is noble, whatever is right, whatever is pure, whatever is lovely, whatever is admirable — if anything is excellent or praiseworthy — think about such things" (Phil. 4:8).

MAY 29

Cursed before the LORD
is the man who undertakes to rebuild this city.
Joshua 6:26

From the pen of Charles Spurgeon:

If the person who rebuilt Jericho was to be cursed, how much more the person who works to restore Popery (Roman Catholicism) among us. In the days of our ancestors, the gigantic walls of Popery fell through the power of their faith, the perseverance of their efforts, and the blast of their gospel "trumpets." But today there are some who would rebuild that accursed system on its old foundation.

> *O Lord, please thwart their unrighteous endeavors, and tear down every stone they build.*

We should make it our serious business to thoroughly purge ourselves from every error that may have a tendency to foster the spirit of Popery. And once we have made a clean sweep of it at home, we should seek in every way possible to oppose its all too rapid spread abroad in the church and the world. Our opposition to it can be done in secret through fervent prayer and in public through bold testimony. With thoughtful boldness we must warn those who are inclined toward the errors of Rome, especially instructing the young in the truth of the gospel and relating to them the dark, sinful deeds of Catholicism in times of old. We must work more diligently to spread the light throughout the land, for Catholic priests, like owls, hate the light.

Are we doing all we can for Jesus and His gospel? If not, our negligence plays directly into the craftiness of the Catholic priests. What are we doing to spread the Bible, which is nothing but a curse and a poison to the Pope? Are we actively involved in spreading sound gospel books abroad? Martin Luther (1483 – 1546; German church reformer and former Catholic monk) once said, "The devil hates goose quills" (pens), and no doubt he has good reason, for authors gifted and blessed by the Holy Spirit have done his evil kingdom great damage.

If the thousands of people who read this devotion today would do all they can to hinder the rebuilding of this accursed "Jericho" of Roman Catholicism, the Lord's glory will quickly spread amongst mankind. Dear reader, what can you do? What *will* you do?

From the pen of Jim Reimann:

Over the last one hundred and twenty years or so since Spurgeon's day, the Roman Catholic Church has somewhat changed its terminology toward more evangelical-sounding verbiage. But don't be fooled! No pope before or since the time of Martin Luther has renounced Rome's works-based system of salvation. Are there saved Catholics? Yes, but they are saved only by God's grace — and in ignorance of their own church's actual doctrine.

True believers must continue to fight against any works-based system of salvation, whether it is Roman Catholicism, Islam, Buddhism, Hinduism, Mormonism, or any other heresy. Remember — this warning from Paul still holds:

> Some people are throwing you into confusion and are trying to pervert the gospel of Christ. But even if we or an angel from heaven should preach a gospel other than the one we preached to you, let him be eternally condemned! As we have already said, so now I say again: If anybody is preaching to you a gospel other than what you accepted, let him be eternally condemned!
>
> Galatians 1:7 – 9

MAY 30

We should no longer be slaves to sin.

Romans 6:6

From the pen of Charles Spurgeon:

Dear Christian, why are you flirting with sin? Hasn't it cost you enough already? Will you continue to play with fire even after being burned? Having once been caught in the jaws of the lion, will you now step a second time into his den? Have you not had enough of "that ancient serpent" (Rev. 12:9)? Hasn't he poisoned all your veins with his venom before? Will you now play near the hole of the asp and put your hand into his nest again?

Don't be so foolish! Did sin ever yield you lasting pleasure? Did you ever find true satisfaction in it? If so, go back to your old drudgery. If it delights you so much, wear its chain again. Yet since sin never really gave you what it promised, but deluded you with lies, don't be snared again by the old fowler's net. Stay free, and let the remembrance of your former bondage forbid you from being trapped again. Sin is contrary to the plan of God's eternal love, which is to lead you to purity and holiness. Therefore, don't run counter to the purpose of your Lord.

Yet there is another thought that should restrain you from sin. It is that Christians can never sin cheaply, for they always pay a heavy price for their iniquity. Transgression destroys peace of mind, obscures fellowship with Jesus, hinders prayer, and brings darkness to the soul. So do not be the servant or slave of sin.

Finally, there is still a higher argument, for each time you "serve sin" (Rom. 6:6 KJV), you "are crucifying the Son of God all over again and subjecting him to public disgrace" (Heb. 6:6). Can you bear that thought? If you have fallen into any sin today, perhaps this devotion is specifically for you. It may be the Master's admonition meant to

bring you back before you have backslidden very far. Turn back to Jesus, for He has not forgotten His love for you and His grace is still the same. With weeping and repentance return to "his footstool" (Ps. 99:5), and He will once again take you to His heart. He will "set [your] feet on a rock and [give you] a firm place to stand" (Ps. 40:2).

From the pen of Jim Reimann:

Today's text is taken from Paul's argument against the following idea some people still espouse: Since believers' past, present, and future sins are forgiven, don't we have the license to sin as much as we desire? But if someone is truly a believer, his life and his desires will be transformed. Therefore, Paul's argument is framed around the idea of leading a new life, as we see from the following context:

> Shall we go on sinning so that grace may increase? By no means! We died to sin; how can we live in it any longer? Or don't you know that all of us who were baptized into Christ Jesus were baptized into his death? We were therefore buried with him through baptism into death in order that, just as Christ was raised from the dead through the glory of the Father, *we too may live a new life.* For we know that our old self was crucified with him so that the body of sin might be done away with, that we should no longer be slaves to sin — because anyone who died has been freed from sin.
>
> Romans 6:1 – 4, 6 – 7

Jude agreed, saying, in essence, that *only* "godless men ... change the grace of our God into a license for immorality" (Jude 4).

MAY 31

Praise the LORD,
who ... heals all your diseases.

Psalm 103:2 – 3

From the pen of Charles Spurgeon:

As humbling as this statement is, one thing is certain: we are all suffering from the disease of sin. But what a comfort to know we have a great Physician who is both willing and able to heal us! Let's think of Him in this regard for a few moments.

His cures are fast, for there is life in simply looking at Him; His cures are thorough, for He strikes the very core of the disease; and thus His cures are sure and certain. He never fails and the disease never returns, for there is no relapse where Christ heals. Therefore His patients should have no fear of simply being patched up temporarily, for He makes new people of them, giving them a new heart and placing "a steadfast spirit within [them]" (Ps. 51:10).

The Lord is well skilled in all diseases, while other physicians have their individual specialty. Although they may know something of most of our pains and ills, there is typically one disease they have studied above all others. But Jesus Christ is thoroughly acquainted with all of human nature. Hence, He is as much at home with one sinner as another and has never been confronted with a case too difficult for Him. He has dealt with extraordinary complications of a host of strange diseases, but with one simple glance He has always known exactly how to treat each patient.

Jesus is the only universal doctor, and the medicine He gives is the only true universal remedy, healing in every instance. Whatever our spiritual malady may be, we should go at once to the Divine Physician. There is no brokenness of heart He cannot heal, for "the blood of Jesus ... purifies us from all sin" (1 John 1:7). If we will only think of the myriads of people who have been delivered from all sorts of diseases through the power and virtue of His touch, we will joyfully put ourselves in His hands.

Trust Him — and sin dies. Love Him — and grace lives. Wait for Him — and grace is strengthened. See Him as He is — and grace is perfected forever!

From the pen of Jim Reimann:

Concerning healing, be careful not to misuse Isaiah 53:5: "By his wounds [or stripes, KJV] we are healed." Certainly all healing comes from the Lord and He can heal, or not heal, as He chooses, for "Our God ... does whatever pleases him" (Ps. 115:3). Notice Spurgeon focuses today on "whatever our *spiritual* malady may be," not our *physical* malady. If God guaranteed physical healing in the atonement of Christ, then no believer would ever die physically — and, of course, we know Christians do die. Yet all believers can thank the Lord that *spiritual* healing *is* in the atonement, for Jesus came to save us from the "sickness" of sin and its penalty of eternal death. He Himself said, referring to the need for the spiritual healing of sinners: "It is not the healthy who need a doctor, but the sick. *I have not come to call the righteous, but sinners*" (Mark 2:17).

Whether physically healed or not, we can be thankful the Lord will accomplish His ultimate purpose for us, which Paul shares in the following blessing: "May God himself, the God of peace, sanctify you through and through. May your whole spirit, soul and body be kept blameless at the coming of our Lord Jesus Christ" (1 Thess. 5:23).

June

JUNE 1

The LORD ... will make her deserts like Eden.

Isaiah 51:3

From the pen of Charles Spurgeon:

This verse brings to mind a vision of a howling wilderness such as the great and terrible Sahara. In the vision I see nothing of relief, only hot and arid sand strewn with ten thousand bleaching skeletons of wretched men who have expired in anguish, having lost their way crossing the pitiless wasteland. What a horribly appalling sight to view a limitless sea of sand without an oasis — a grim graveyard for a forlorn race.

But then suddenly I behold a miracle! I see a beautiful plant springing from the scorching sand, and as it grows it begins to bud. As the bud expands, I see it is a rose, and by its side is a lily, bowing its modest head. Then, miracle of miracles, as the fragrance of those flowers is diffused across the sand, the wilderness itself is transformed into a fruitful field. Flowers begin to bloom everywhere, and the desert begins to glow with "the glory of Lebanon" and "the splendor of Carmel and Sharon" (Isa. 35:2). Thus, we should no longer call it Sahara — call it Paradise. Don't speak of it any longer as the valley of death, where skeletons lie bleaching in the sun. Behold, a resurrection has been proclaimed, and a mighty army filled with immortal life is springing from the dead. Of course, Jesus is that beautiful rose, for His presence "make[s] all things new" (Rev. 21:5 KJV). And the wonder of each individual's salvation is no less miraculous.

Dear reader, I also beheld you from afar, seeing you as a castaway or an infant; unclothed, defiled, and lying in your own blood, left as food for beasts of prey. But look! A Jewel has been placed in your heart by God's divine hand, and for the sake of the Jewel you have been shown pity and care by divine Providence. You have been washed and cleansed from your defilement, adopted into heaven's family, had God's seal of love placed on your forehead, and had His ring of faithfulness placed on your hand. You are now a prince of God, though you were once an orphan and a castaway.

Therefore, greatly prize God's exceedingly matchless power and grace that changes deserts into gardens, and makes barren hearts sing for joy!

From the pen of Jim Reimann:

In the Middle East, sand has always been more abundant than water. No doubt this is why Isaiah spoke of the Messiah's coming in the following ways:

"Water will gush forth in the wilderness and streams in the desert. The burning sand will become a pool, the thirsty ground bubbling springs" (Isa. 35:6 – 7). "See, I am doing a new thing! Now it springs up; do you not perceive it? I am making a way in the desert and streams in the wasteland. I provide water in the desert and streams in the wasteland, to give drink to my people, my chosen" (Isa. 43:19 – 20). "I will pour water on the thirsty land, and streams on the dry ground; I will pour out my Spirit on your offspring, and my blessing on your descendants" (Isa. 44:3).

And let us recall the Messiah's words: "If anyone is thirsty, let him come to me and drink" (John 7:37), while never forgetting He is the "rose of Sharon" and the "lily of the valleys" (Song 2:1).

JUNE 2

Good Master …
Matthew 19:16 KJV

From the pen of Charles Spurgeon:

In every believer's heart there is a constant struggle between the old nature and the new. The old nature is very active and never loses an opportunity to use all its deadly weapons against newborn grace, while the new nature is always on guard to resist and destroy its enemy. Grace within us will use prayer, faith, hope, and love to cast out evil and will earnestly wrestle with it, employing "the full armor of God" (Eph. 6:11). These two opposing natures will never cease their struggle as long as we are in this world.

The battle of Christian with Apollyon in *The Pilgrim's Progress* by John Bunyan (1628 – 1688) lasted only three hours, but the battle of Christian with himself lasted all the way from the Wicket Gate in the river Jordan. [Editor's note: Apollyon is the evil lord of the City of Destruction, while the Wicket Gate is the entry point onto the narrow way to the Celestial City.] The enemy is so securely entrenched within us that he can never be driven out while we are in this earthly body. But though we are so closely attacked and often in severe conflict, we have an almighty Helper — Jesus, "the author of [our] salvation" (Heb. 2:10). He is always with us and assures us that "we are more than conquerors through him" (Rom. 8:37). And with His assistance, our newborn nature is more than a match for its foes.

Are you fighting with the adversary today? Are Satan, the world, and the flesh all against you? "Do not be dismayed" (Isa. 41:10) or discouraged, but fight on! God Himself is with you, Jehovah-Nissi "is [your] Banner" (Ex. 17:15), and Jehovah-Rophi is "the LORD, who heals you" (Ex. 15:26). "Do not be afraid" (Deut. 31:6); you will overcome, for who can defeat Omnipotence? "Fix [your] eyes on Jesus" (Heb. 12:2) and fight on, and although the conflict is long and hard, victory will be sweet and the promised reward will be glorious.

> "From strength to strength" go on; (Ps. 84:7)
> Wrestle, and fight, and pray,
> Tread all the powers of darkness down,
> And win the well-fought day.
> Charles Wesley, 1707 – 88

From the pen of Jim Reimann:

The Christian life was never meant to be an easy one. Remember, this is the training ground for heaven, and the Lord uses the difficulties and struggles of this life to purify us and mold us into "the likeness of his Son" (Rom. 8:29). As Spurgeon said, we should not become discouraged. So before you become too self-focused and dejected, remember you are not alone. Take a moment to consider that even the apostle Paul struggled with sin, for he wrote: "I do not understand what I do. For what I want to do I do not do, but what I hate I do" (Rom. 7:15). Although this may sound rather hopeless, Paul never gave up.

Lord, help me, like Paul, never to give in or give up. May his words be true of me as well: "Forgetting what is behind and straining toward what is ahead, I press on toward the goal to win the prize for which God has called me heavenward in Christ Jesus" (Phil. 3:13 – 14).

JUNE 3

[Christ Jesus] humbled himself.

Philippians 2:8

From the pen of Charles Spurgeon:

Jesus is the greatest example of a humble heart, so let us learn of Him. Look how the Master "wrapped a towel around his waist … and began to wash his disciples' feet" (John 13:4 – 5). After seeing that, follower of Christ, won't you humble yourself? Once you have seen Him as the Servant of servants, surely you cannot be proud.

Isn't today's verse a wonderful summary of His life: "He humbled himself"? While on earth, wasn't He continually stripping away one robe of honor after another until, finally naked, He was nailed to the cross. Even on the cross, didn't He continue to empty out His inmost self, pouring out His lifeblood and giving His all for us until, penniless, they laid Him in a borrowed tomb?

How could our dear Redeemer have been brought any lower! How then can we be proud? Stand at the foot of His cross; count the drops of blood by which you have been cleansed; look at His crown of thorns; observe His scourged shoulders, still gushing with crimson streams. See His hands and feet surrendered to iron spikes; see His entire entity subjected to mockery and scorn; and see His severe suffering, pain, and upheaval of inner grief, finally revealing themselves in His outer frame. Hear His intense cry: "My God, my God, why have you forsaken me?" (Matt. 27:46).

If, after viewing all this, you do not lie prostrate on the ground before His cross — you have never seen it. If you are not humbled in the presence of Jesus — you do not know Him. You were once so lost that nothing but the sacrifice of God's "one and only Son" (John 3:16) could save you. Just think of that! And as Jesus humbled Himself for you, bow yourself in complete humility at His feet, for an awareness of Christ's amazing love for us should have a greater tendency to cause us to humble ourselves than even the consciousness of our own guilt.

May the Lord take us in an attitude of contemplation to Calvary, for then our position will no longer be that of a pompous person of pride. Instead, we will take the humble place of one who loves much because we have been forgiven much (see Luke 7:47). Pride cannot exist at the foot of the cross, so let us sit there and learn the lesson of humility. Then let us rise and put it into practice.

From the pen of Jim Reimann:

When it comes to humility, these words, from which today's text is taken, cannot be improved upon:

> Do nothing out of selfish ambition or vain conceit, but in humility consider others better than yourselves. Each of you should look not only to your own interests, but also to the interests of others. Your attitude should be the same as that of Christ Jesus: Who, being in very nature God, did not consider equality with God something to be grasped, but made himself nothing, taking the very nature of a servant, being made in human likeness. And being found in appearance as a man, he humbled himself and became obedient to death — even death on a cross! Therefore God exalted him to the highest place and gave him the name that is above every name, that at the name of Jesus every knee should bow, in heaven and on earth and under the earth, and every tongue confess that Jesus Christ is Lord, to the glory of God the Father.

Philippians 2:3 – 11

JUNE 4

[Christ Jesus] was taken up in glory.

1 Timothy 3:16

From the pen of Charles Spurgeon:

Yesterday we viewed our beloved Lord during His days on earth, looking at His humiliation and severe distress, for "He was despised and rejected by men, a man of sorrows, and familiar with suffering" (Isa. 53:3). He whose brightness is as the morning sun, was clothed in the sackcloth of sorrow as His daily robe, for shame and reproach were His garments. But now, since He has triumphed over all the powers of darkness upon His blood-soaked cross, our faith beholds our King "coming from Edom ... with his garments stained crimson" (Isa. 63:1), robed in the splendor of victory. And how glorious He must have appeared to the seraphim, when "a cloud hid him from [the] sight" (Acts 1:9) of mortal men, and He ascended into heaven!

Now Jesus wears the glory He had with God before the creation of the world, and even another glory above that — one He earned in His victorious battle against sin, death, and hell. Thus, as Victor He wears the glorious crown He so well deserves. Listen to the sweet refrain of victory. It is this beautiful new song: "Worthy is the Lamb, who was slain" (Rev. 5:12), for "with [His] blood [He has] purchased [us] for God" (Rev. 5:9). He wears the glory of an Intercessor who can never fail, the glory of a Prince who can never be defeated, the glory of a Conqueror who has vanquished every foe, and the glory of a Lord who has the heart's allegiance of His every subject. He wears all the glory the majesty of heaven can bestow upon Him — that which "ten thousand times ten thousand" (Rev. 5:11) angels can administer to Him. Even with the greatest stretch of human imagination, one could never fully conceive of His exceeding greatness. Yet someday there will be a further revelation of it: "When the Son of Man comes in his glory, and all the angels with him, he will sit on his throne in heavenly glory" (Matt. 25:31).

Oh, the splendor of His glory! It will overwhelm His people's hearts. Yet His return is not the end, for eternity will resound with His praise, saying, "Your throne, O God, will last for ever and ever" (Heb. 1:8). But, dear reader, if you plan on rejoicing in Christ's glory in the hereafter, He must be glorious in your sight today. Is He?

From the pen of Jim Reimann:

Indeed, we must view Jesus for who He is — "the Lord of glory" (1 Cor. 2:8). From eternity past to eternity future, He *is* victorious and full of glory. And as we see from Ephesians 4:8 – 13, the early church saw the following psalm as a fore-shadowing of Christ's resurrection, ascension, and reign, now and in the world to come:

> When you ascended on high, you led captives in your train; you received gifts from men, even from the rebellious — that you, O Lord God, might dwell there. Your procession has come into view, O God, the procession of my God and King into the sanctuary. You are awesome, O God, in your sanctuary; the God of Israel gives power and strength to his people. Praise be to God!
>
> Psalm 68:18, 24, 35

Therefore, since "the Son is the radiance of God's glory" (Heb. 1:3), let us "ascribe to the Lord the glory due his name" (Ps. 29:2).

JUNE 5

Whoever does not love
does not know God.

1 John 4:8

From the pen of Charles Spurgeon:

What distinguishes a Christian from others is his confidence in the love of Christ and the yielding of his love to Christ in return. First, faith marks the person with a seal of ownership, thereby enabling the person's soul to say, as Paul did, "The Son of God ... loved me and gave himself for me" (Gal. 2:20). Next, love confirms that seal by stamping gratitude and love for Jesus in return upon the believer's heart. Thus, "We love him, because he first loved us" (1 John 4:19 KJV).

Ages ago, during the early period of the Christian faith, this double seal of love was clearly seen in all believers in Jesus. They were people who knew the love of Christ and rested upon it, just as a shepherd leans upon a staff whose trustworthiness has been fully tried. And the love they had for the Lord was not a silent emotion they hid within themselves in some secret chamber of their soul, spoke of solely in their private meetings on Sundays, or sang of only in hymns honoring Christ Jesus the crucified. No, it was a passion within them of such power and all-consuming intensity that it was visible in all their actions. It came out in their everyday talk and shone from their eyes in their every glance. Love for Jesus was a flame, feeding upon the very heart and soul of their being; and thus, by the force of its own power, it burned its way into the outer man and shone brightly there. Zeal for the glory of King Jesus was the seal and mark of all genuine Christians, and because of their dependence upon Christ's love, they dared much, and because of their love for Christ, they did much.

It is the same today. True children of God are ruled in their inmost being by love, "for Christ's love compels [them]" (2 Cor. 5:14). They rejoice that His divine love is upon them, for they feel "his love" being "poured out ... into [their] hearts by the Holy Spirit, whom he has given [them]" (Rom. 5:5). Then, by the force of their genuine gratitude, they love the Savior with a pure heart — and do so passionately.

Dear reader, do you love Him in this way? Do nothing else before this day ends until you give an honest answer to this important question.

From the pen of Jim Reimann:

John's writings were filled with the idea that the true mark of a believer was love because "love comes from God ... because God is love" (1 John 4:7 – 8). His premise was that it is impossible for an unbeliever to extend true love, and that it is also impossible for a believer not to extend love. With the shallowness of the visible church of Jesus today, perhaps what we are seeing are many professing Christians who really don't know Him. Remember the words of Jesus, addressing this issue:

> Every tree that does not bear good fruit is cut down and thrown into the fire. Thus, by their fruit you will recognize them. Not everyone who says to me, "Lord, Lord," will enter the kingdom of heaven, but only he who does the will of my Father who is in heaven.
>
> Matthew 7:19 – 21

Again, the seal or mark of a true believer is love, and it *will* produce fruit. Akin to Spurgeon's closing plea today, Paul once encouraged his readers to "examine yourselves to see whether you are in the faith" (2 Cor. 13:5).

JUNE 6

Are they Israelites?
So am I.
2 Corinthians 11:22

From the pen of Charles Spurgeon:

Paul makes a personal claim here — one that needs proof. Although the apostle knew his claim was indisputable, there are many people today who have no right to the claim, but who nevertheless claim to belong to the Israel of God. If we confidently declare, "I am an Israelite," we should do so only after a thorough search of our heart in the presence of God. But if we can prove we are truly following Jesus and can say from the heart, "I trust Him completely, trust Him only, trust Him simply, trust Him now, and trust Him forever," then the title claimed by God's saints of old also belongs to us, and everything they enjoyed becomes our possession as well.

We may be "less than the least of all God's people" (Eph. 3:8), yet, since the mercies of God belong to His saints simply by virtue of being a saint — not necessarily mature saints, or well-educated saints — we may proclaim, "'Are they Israelites? So am I.' Therefore the promises are mine, grace is mine, and glory will be mine." This claim, if rightly made, is one that will yield untold comfort. What joy there is, when God's people are rejoicing that they are His, to be able to say, "So am I"! How joyful it is, when they speak of being pardoned, justified, and "accepted in the beloved" (Eph. 1:6 KJV), to respond, "By God's grace, 'So am I'"!

This claim, however, not only has its enjoyments and privileges but also has its duties and responsibilities. For example, we must be willing to declare we belong to God when it is easy to do so — and when it is not. When we hear God's saints spoken of with contempt, and ridiculed simply for being Christians, we must come boldly forward and declare, "So am I." And when we see them working for Jesus, giving their time and talent — in fact, their entire being to Him — we must be ready and able to say, "So do I."

Oh, may we prove our gratitude by our devotion to Christ and live as those who, having claimed a privilege, are also willing to accept the responsibility connected to it.

From the pen of Jim Reimann:

Many Jews take great pride in being known as God's chosen people. Yet they should remember that they were chosen by His grace, not because they were a great nation. In fact, Moses said to Israel, "The LORD did not set his affection on you and choose you because you were more numerous than other peoples, for you were the fewest of all peoples. But it was because the LORD loved you and kept the oath he swore to your forefathers" (Deut. 7:7 – 8).

Later Paul spoke of a "spiritual Israel," as opposed to a "physical Israel," saying, "Not all who are descended from Israel are Israel. Nor because they are his descendants are they all Abraham's children. On the contrary, 'It is through Isaac that your offspring will be reckoned.' In other words, it is not the natural children who are God's children, but it is the children of the promise who are regarded as Abraham's offspring" (Rom. 9:6 – 8). Thus, it is not Jewish blood running in my veins that makes me an Israelite, but being chosen by God's grace to be a member of His family.

I must remember: "By the grace of God I am what I am" (1 Cor. 15:10).

JUNE 7

Be zealous.

Revelation 3:19 KJV

From the pen of Charles Spurgeon:

If you desire to see souls converted, to place crowns on the head of the Savior, to see His throne lifted high, to hear the shout: "The kingdom of the world has become the kingdom of our Lord" (Rev. 11:15), then be filled with zeal. God uses the zeal of the church as a component of His grace in the world's conversion. He uses the believer's various gifts, but zeal must lead the way, followed by watchfulness, knowledge, patience, and courage. It is not the extent of our knowledge, though that is useful; it is not the extent of our talent, though that is not to be discounted; it is our zeal that will accomplish great things.

This zeal is the fruit of the Holy Spirit, drawing its living power from the continual workings of the Spirit in our soul. Thus, if our inner life dwindles or our heart beats slowly for God, we will not "be zealous." But if we are strong and vigorous within, we cannot keep from having a loving zeal to see "[His] kingdom come, [His] will be done on earth as it is in heaven" (Matt. 6:10).

A deep sense of gratitude will nourish a Christian's zeal. If we consider the deep pit from which we were rescued, we will find abundant reason why we should spend and be spent for God. And zeal will be further stimulated by thinking of our eternal future. Zeal looks down with tearful eyes to the flames of hell, and cannot sleep; then zeal gazes up to heaven with eyes of anticipation, and cannot help being stirred. Zeal feels time is short compared to the work yet to be done, and therefore devotes all it has to the cause of its Lord.

Finally, zeal is ever strengthened by remembering Christ's example, for He "wrapped himself in zeal as in a cloak" (Isa. 59:17). His zeal propelled Him as swiftly as chariot wheels, and He allowed no loitering along the way. Thus, may we prove we are His disciples by manifesting the same spirit of zeal.

From the pen of Jim Reimann:

Isaiah says "the zeal of the Lord Almighty will accomplish" the following:

To us a child is born, to us a son is given, and the government will be on his shoulders. And he will be called Wonderful Counselor, Mighty God, Everlasting Father, Prince of Peace. Of the increase of his government and peace there will be no end. He will reign on David's throne and over his kingdom, establishing and upholding it with justice and righteousness from that time on and forever. *The zeal of the Lord Almighty will accomplish this.*

Isaiah 9:6 – 7

What a beautiful gospel message! If God were zealous enough to send us His Son to be our Savior, shouldn't we have enough zeal to tell that story? Shouldn't we be willing to sacrifice like Paul, who said, "I endure everything for the sake of the elect, that they too may obtain the salvation that is in Christ Jesus, with eternal glory" (2 Tim. 2:10).

Thus, may we take these words of Paul to heart: "Never be lacking in zeal, but keep your spiritual fervor, serving the Lord" (Rom. 12:11).

Father, please grant me the zeal to accomplish Your will for my life, and to "press on to take hold of that for which Christ Jesus took hold of me," and to "press on toward the goal to win the prize for which God has called me heavenward in Christ Jesus" (Phil. 3:12, 14).

JUNE 8

You will now see whether or not
what I say will come true for you.

Numbers 11:23

From the pen of Charles Spurgeon:

God had promised Moses He would feed the vast multitude with meat in the wilderness "for a whole month" (v. 20). But Moses, overcome by a bout of unbelief, looked to outward means and was at a loss to know how God's promise could be fulfilled. He doubted because he looked to the creature rather than the Creator.

But does the Creator ever expect the creature to fulfill His promise to him? Of course not, for He who makes the promise always fulfills it by His own unaided omnipotence. If He speaks, it is done — done by Him. His promises do not depend upon the cooperation of the puny strength of mankind for their fulfillment. Thus, we can quickly perceive the mistake Moses made in this case, and yet how often we do the same thing. God has promised to "meet all [our] needs" (Phil. 4:19), but we look to the creature to do what God has promised. Then, because we perceive the creature to be weak and feeble, we indulge in unbelief.

Yet why do we look there at all? Would we look to the North Pole to find fruit ripened by the sun? But doing that is actually no more foolish than looking to the weak for strength, or looking to the creature to do the Creator's work. So let us put the issue on the proper footing, for the foundation of faith is not the sufficiency of the visible means for the performance of the promise, but the all-sufficiency of the invisible God — He who most assuredly will do exactly as He has said.

If we dare to indulge in unbelief after clearly seeing that the burden lies with the Creator and not with the creature, this question of His to Moses should hit powerfully home to us: "Is the LORD's arm too short?" (Num. 11:23). But, in His mercy, may His question also come with a glorious flash across our soul of His blessed promise: "You will now see whether or not what I say will come true for you."

From the pen of Jim Reimann:

The book of Numbers also tells us: "God is not a man, that he should lie, nor a son of man, that he should change his mind. Does he speak and then not act? Does he promise and not fulfill?" (Num. 23:19).

What we struggle with today is that a person's word is no longer his bond. But God cannot be separated from His Word, for what He says, He does. He said, "Let there be light" and it immediately follows "there was light" (Gen. 1:3). Much later, of course, we are told: "When the time had fully come, God sent his Son" (Gal. 4:4), and "The Word became flesh and made his dwelling among us" (John 1:14). Indeed, "the Word became flesh" shows that the Lord cannot be separated from His Word. He is His Word! Therefore, what He says, He does. Period! Why not praise Him even now for His greatness and His faithfulness to His Word?

"By the word of the LORD were the heavens made, their starry host by the breath of his mouth. Let all the earth fear the LORD; let all the people of the world revere him. For he spoke, and it came to be; he commanded, and it stood firm" (Ps. 33:6, 8 – 9).

JUNE 9

Diligently study the Scriptures.
John 5:39

From the pen of Charles Spurgeon:

The Greek word here for *study* signifies a strict and thorough search, such as that of miners seeking gold or that of hunters seeking game. Thus we must never be content with a superficial reading of a chapter or two of Scripture, but must, using the light of the Spirit, deliberately seek out its hidden meaning.

The Scriptures demand searching. Much of God's Word can only be learned through careful study. It has milk for babies but also meat for the mature. Jewish rabbis say that a mountain of truth hangs on its every word, but, in fact, a mountain hangs on its "least stroke of a pen" (Matt. 5:18). Tertullian (c. 155 – 220 AD), an early church theologian, exclaimed, "I adore the fullness of the Scriptures." No one who merely skims the Bible can profit from such a practice, for uncovering its hidden treasure requires digging and searching. The door of the Word can only be unlocked and opened by the key of diligence.

The Scriptures deserve searching. They are the writings of God, bearing His divine authority and imprimatur, so who would dare treat them so flippantly. He who despises the Word despises the God who wrote it. Therefore, God forbid that any of us should neglect our Bible, causing it to become the first witness against us when we give an account on the great day of judgment.

The Scriptures reward searching. The Lord does not call us to sift a mountain of chaff with only a grain of wheat here and there. No, the Bible is sifted grain, and we only have to open the granary door to find it. As we study, the Scriptures grow on us, for God's Word is full of surprises. Under the teaching of the Spirit, our searching eyes begin to widen and glow with the splendor of God's revelation. We begin to see the Word as a vast temple paved with gold and roofed with rubies, emeralds, and every other precious jewel; and we grow to realize that nothing man can purchase is like the "merchandise" of Scripture.

The Scriptures reveal Jesus. He said, "These are the Scriptures that testify about me" (John 5:39). Thus, no more powerful motive can be urged upon Bible readers than this: He who finds Jesus finds life, heaven — everything! Blessed are those who, "diligently study[ing] the Scriptures," discover their Savior.

From the pen of Jim Reimann:

Psalm 138:2 reads: "You have exalted above all things your name and your word," and although this is true, it misses something of the original. A more literal rendering of this verse is: "You have exalted above all else Your name and Your word *and You have magnified Your word above all Your name!*" (Amplified). Think about this — the Lord has magnified His Word even above His name — even the name of Jesus, about which is written: "There is *no other name* under heaven given to men by which we must be saved" (Acts 4:12), and "God ... gave him *the name that is above every name*, that at the name of Jesus every knee should bow" (Phil. 2:9 – 10).

If the Lord places His Word in such a place of honor, what priority does it demand and deserve in my life?

God, grant me Your view of Your Word, for You have said: "It pleased the Lord for the sake of his righteousness to make his law great and glorious" (Isa. 42:21).

JUNE 10

These are the Scriptures that testify about me.

John 5:39

From the pen of Charles Spurgeon:

Yesterday we looked at the first portion of this verse and the importance of "diligently study[ing] the Scriptures"; today we will look at Jesus Christ Himself, who is "the Alpha and the Omega" (Rev. 22:13) of the Bible. He is the constant theme of its holy pages, for from first to last they testify of Him.

At creation we see Him as one of the "us" (Gen. 1:26) of the sacred Trinity; we catch a glimpse of Him in the promise of "the woman, and ... [her offspring]" (Gen. 3:15); we see a type of Him represented by the ark of Noah (see Gen. 7:11 – 23); we walk with Abraham as he sees Messiah's day (see John 8:56); we live "in tents [with] Isaac and Jacob" (Heb. 11:9), feeding upon God's gracious promise; we hear Israel (Jacob) talking of the coming of Shiloh (see Gen. 49:10 KJV); and through numerous types in God's law we see the Redeemer foreshadowed. Prophets and kings, priests and preachers, all did the same — they stood like the cherubim over "the ark of the covenant" (Num. 10:33), desiring to look within to read the mystery of God's great propitiation — Jesus' coming sacrifice that would fully satisfy the wrath of God.

Then in the New Testament we see our Lord even more openly revealed as its one preeminent subject. We don't just see specks of gold dust or a nugget here or there — we stand on a solid floor of gold. The entire substance of the New Testament is "Christ crucified" (1 Cor. 1:23); even its closing sentence (Rev. 22:21) is bejeweled with the Redeemer's name.

We should always read Scripture in this light and should consider the Word to be a two-way mirror through which Christ looks down from heaven. Then as we look in it ourselves, we see His face reflected — as "a poor reflection" it is true — but still in a way that is a blessed preparation for when "we shall see [Him] face to face" (1 Cor. 13:12). This blessed Book contains Jesus Christ's letters to us, scented by the perfume of His love, for its pages are the robes of our King, "fragrant with myrrh and aloes and cassia" (Ps. 45:8). Scripture is the royal chariot in which Jesus rides, and its path is "paved with love, for the daughters of Jerusalem" (Song 3:10 KJV). The Scriptures are the "swaddling clothes" (Luke 2:7 KJV) containing the holy child Jesus. Unwrap them and you will find your Savior, for the essence of God's Word is Christ.

From the pen of Jim Reimann:

Some believers take pride in calling themselves "New Testament Christians," not fully recognizing the fact that Jesus is on every page of the Old Testament as well. The entire Bible is the story of redemption through the work of all three persons of the Trinity, ultimately finding its fulfillment in the death, burial, and resurrection of Jesus. Therefore, all of God's Word demands and deserves our study, our devotion, and our preaching. This is why the apostle Paul proclaimed, "I never shrank or kept back or fell short from declaring to you *the whole purpose and plan and counsel of God*" (Acts 20:27 Amplified).

In using the phrase "the whole ... counsel of God," Paul is referring to God's entire revealed Word — the Bible. And he saw "the whole ... counsel" being only one topic, for he declared: "We preach Christ crucified ... Christ the power of God and the wisdom of God" (1 Cor. 1:23 – 24).

JUNE 11

There he broke the flashing arrows, the shields and the swords,
the weapons of war.

Psalm 76:3

From the pen of Charles Spurgeon:

Our Redeemer's glorious cry of "It is finished" (John 19:30) was the death knell to all the adversaries of Christ's people — the breaking of the "arrows, the shields and the swords, the weapons of war." Behold the hero of Golgotha using His cross as an anvil and His suffering as a hammer, and thereby smashing to pieces bundle after bundle of our sins — those poisoned "arrows." Behold Him trampling every indictment and accusation against us. What glorious blows the mighty Breaker wields with a hammer far more powerful than the fabled weapon of Thor (the mythological Norse god of thunder). Look! He draws from its hellish sheath the dreaded sword of satanic power, breaks it across His knee as a man breaks a dry twig, and casts it into the fire.

Beloved, no longer can any sin of a believer be an arrow to mortally wound him, and "no condemnation" (Rom. 8:1) can ever be a sword to kill him, for the punishment of our sin was borne by Christ, and full atonement was made for all our iniquities by our blessed Substitute and Guarantee (see Heb. 7:22). "Who will bring any charge ...? Who is he that condemns? Christ Jesus [has] died — more than that, [He] was raised to life" (Rom. 8:33 – 34). Jesus has emptied the quivers of hell, has "extinguish[ed] all the flaming arrows of the evil one" (Eph. 6:16), and broken off the head of every arrow of wrath. The ground lies strewn with the splinters and relics of the weapons of hell's warfare, which remain visible only to remind us of our former danger and of our great deliverance. Thus, "sin shall not have dominion over [us]" (Rom. 6:14 KJV), for Jesus has made an end of it, putting it away forever. And the enemy is headed to his eternal destruction.

Therefore, "tell of all [the LORD's] wonderful acts" (Ps. 105:2); "You who make mention of the LORD, do not keep silent" (Isa. 62:6 NKJV), neither by day nor when the sun goes to its rest. "Praise the LORD, O my soul" (Ps. 103:1).

From the pen of Jim Reimann:

The apostle Paul builds his case for the power of sin being broken in a believer's life by comparing it to Jesus' victory over death. For example, he says, "We know that since Christ was raised from the dead, *he cannot die again; death no longer has mastery over him*" (Rom. 6:9). Then, applying this truth directly to believers, he continues,

> *In the same way, count yourselves dead to sin* but alive to God in Christ Jesus. Therefore do not let sin reign in your mortal body so that you obey its evil desires. Do not offer the parts of your body to sin, as instruments of wickedness, but rather offer yourselves to God, as those who have been brought from death to life; and offer the parts of your body to him as instruments of righteousness. For sin shall not be your master.
>
> Romans 6:11 – 14

This is why Paul was able to declare:

> In all these things we are more than conquerors through him who loved us. For I am convinced that neither death nor life, neither angels nor demons, neither the present nor the future, nor any powers, neither height nor depth, nor anything else in all creation, will be able to separate us from the love of God that is in Christ Jesus our Lord.
>
> Romans 8:37 – 39

May these glorious truths lead us to live a holy life of praise to God!

JUNE 12

God ... has saved us
and called us to a holy life.
2 Timothy 1:8 – 9

From the pen of Charles Spurgeon:

Paul uses the perfect tense in this verse, saying "God ... *has* saved us." Believers in Christ Jesus *are* saved; they are not people in some hopeful condition, who ultimately *may* be saved, but *are* saved already. Salvation is not a blessing only to be enjoyed on our deathbed and to be sung about in a future life above; it is enjoyed now. Christians are perfectly saved in God's purpose, for God has ordained them to salvation and His purpose is complete. They are perfectly saved due to the price paid for them, for the cry of the Savior as He died was: "It is finished" (John 19:30).

Believers are perfectly saved due to their covenant Head, for as they all fell in Adam, they all now live in Christ. But their complete salvation is accompanied by a holy calling, for those whom the Savior saved upon His cross are effectively called by the power of God the Holy Spirit to a life of holiness. Thus they leave their sins behind and endeavor to be like Christ. They choose holiness, not out of a sense of compulsion, but by the power of a new nature — one that leads them to rejoice in holiness just as they formerly delighted in sin.

God chose and called them, not because they *were* holy, but that they might *be* holy, for holiness is the beautiful work He produces in them. These perfecting works we see in believers are as much the work of God as the atonement itself, and it is through these works we begin to behold the fullness of the grace of God. In fact, salvation must be by grace because the Lord is its author, for what motive but grace could cause Him to save the guilty? And salvation must be by grace because the Lord works in such a way that our

righteousness is forever excluded as a possible means.

Therefore believers enjoy the privilege of a *present* salvation. And the evidence that they have been called to it is a holy life.

From the pen of Jim Reimann:

The question often is asked, "How can I know for sure I am saved?" Various answers are given. Some people even state that you cannot know for sure, though John declared: "I write these things to you who believe in the name of the Son of God *so that you may know that you have eternal life*" (1 John 5:13).

Spurgeon said "the evidence ... is a holy life." God saves His chosen and gives them life by the power of His Spirit, and Paul addresses the resulting change, saying,

> You ... are controlled not by the sinful nature but by the Spirit, if the Spirit of God lives in you. And if anyone does not have the Spirit of Christ, he does not belong to Christ.... Therefore, brothers, we have an obligation — but it is not to the sinful nature, to live according to it. For if you live according to the sinful nature, you will die; but if by the Spirit you put to death the misdeeds of the body, you will live, because *those who are led by the Spirit of God are sons of God.*
> Romans 8:9, 12 – 14

God has given us a new nature — one that leads to holiness. And He is in the process of perfecting that holiness, for Paul also said, "May God himself, the God of peace, sanctify you through and through.... *The one who calls you is faithful and he will do it*" (1 Thess. 5:23 – 24).

JUNE 13

Keep falsehood and lies far from me.

Proverbs 30:8

Be not far from me, O my God.

Psalm 38:21

From the pen of Charles Spurgeon:

In these verses we have two great lessons — what to deplore and what to implore. The happiest place for a Christian is a place of holiness. Therefore, just as the most heat is nearest to the sun, the most happiness is nearest to Christ. Christians can't experience comfort when their eyes are fixed on the vain things of life; they find satisfaction only when the soul is awakened to the ways of God. I don't blame ungodly people for rushing headlong to their pleasures. Let them have their fill, for that is all they have to enjoy. For instance, a believing wife who despaired over her unconverted husband was very kind to him, for she said, "My concern is that this is the only world in which he will be happy, and I have made up my mind to make him as happy as I can in it."

But Christians must seek their delights in a higher realm than the worthless frivolities of the world. Vain pursuits are dangerous to renewed souls. Christians are not safe when their soul is slothful and their God is far from them. Yes, believers are always safe as to their fundamental standing in Christ, but they are not safe regarding their experience of walking in holiness and in communion with Jesus in this life.

Satan seldom attacks a Christian who is living close to God. It is when the believer departs from God, becomes spiritually starved, and endeavors to feed on the vanities of life that the Devil discovers his opportunity to strike. Sometimes he will stand toe-to-toe with a child of God who is active in the Master's service, but the battle is generally short-lived. Yet he who slips as he goes down into the Valley of Humiliation simply invites Apollyon to attack him every time he takes a false step. [Editor's note: In *The Pilgrim's Progress* by John Bunyan (1628 – 1688), Apollyon is the lord of the City of Destruction, whom Christian battles in the Valley of Humiliation.]

Oh, for grace "to walk humbly with [our] God" (Mic. 6:8).

From the pen of Jim Reimann:

As we see today, David prayed to God, "Do not be far from me." He makes the same plea four times in the Psalms, including: "*Do not be far from me*, for trouble is near and there is no one to help" (Ps. 22:11). Earlier in the same psalm he cried, "My God, my God, why have you forsaken me?" (v. 1) — a foreshadowing of the crucified Messiah, a thousand years before His coming. It depicts Jesus' separation from God on our behalf. Thus, only because He experienced "be[ing] far from" His Father, may we draw near to God.

"Therefore, brothers, since we have confidence to enter the Most Holy Place by the blood of Jesus, by a new and living way opened for us through the curtain, that is, his body, and since we have a great priest over the house of God, *let us draw near to God* with a sincere heart in full assurance of faith" (Heb. 10:19 – 22). "*Come near to God and he will come near to you*" (James 4:8).

Only there will believers find enduring happiness and joy. "As for me, *it is good to be near God*. I have made the Sovereign Lord my refuge" (Ps. 73:28).

JUNE 14

O Lord, we ... are covered with shame
because we have sinned against you.

Daniel 9:8

From the pen of Charles Spurgeon:

The proper view of sin, which includes a deep sense of its wickedness and the punishment it deserves, should make us lie prostrate before God. If only this were always the case, for we have sinned as Christians! As favored and privileged as we have been — far beyond others — we have been ungrateful, not producing fruit in proportion to our blessings. Who of us, though we may have been engaged in Christian warfare many years, will not blush when we consider our past? May the days before we were regenerated be forgiven and forgotten. But since then, though we have not sinned as before, we have sinned against God's light that has penetrated our minds and sinned against His love in which we have rejoiced.

Oh, the atrocity of the sin of a pardoned soul! An unpardoned sinner's sin is cheap compared to the sin of one of God's elect — one who has communed with Jesus and leaned upon His shoulder. Look at David. Many of us speak of his great sin, but I implore you to look at his repentance. Hear his broken bones as each one moans its sorrowful confession. Notice his tears falling to the ground and listen to the deep sighs that accompany the softened music of his harp.

We too have erred. So let us seek the spirit of repentance. Look again at Peter. We often speak of him denying his Master, but remember: "He ... wept bitterly" (Matt. 26:75). Don't we have such times of denial of our Lord to be lamented in tears? Our sins, whether before or after conversion, would condemn us to the place of inextinguishable fire if not for God's sovereign mercy, which has plucked us like burning sticks from the flames.

My soul, bow under a deep sense of your sinfulness and worship God. Admire the grace that saves you, the mercy that spares you, and the love that pardons you.

From the pen of Jim Reimann:

Let us consider Peter's response to denying the Lord. Note that "Peter remembered the word Jesus had spoken" (Matt. 26:75) to him, and that it was only after remembering "the word Jesus had spoken" that he wept bitterly. We too must remember God's Word for repentance to take place. Thankfully, as believers, we have the Holy Spirit within to "convict [us] of guilt" (John 16:8) and to guide us "into all truth" (John 16:13) — the truth of God's Word. And, as Spurgeon pointed out, David's sins were great — sins of adultery and murder — but his repentance also was great. Here is a portion of his prayer after being confronted with his sin:

> Have mercy on me, O God, according to your unfailing love; according to your great compassion blot out my transgressions. Wash away all my iniquity and cleanse me from my sin. For I know my transgressions, and my sin is always before me. Against you, you only, have I sinned and done what is evil in your sight, so that you are proved right when you speak and justified when you judge.... Create in me a pure heart, O God, and renew a steadfast spirit within me.
>
> Psalm 51:1 – 4, 10

O Lord, like David, I pray You would "grant me a willing spirit" (v. 12) that I may humble myself in obedience to You.

JUNE 15

What he opens no one can shut,
and what he shuts no one can open.

Revelation 3:7

From the pen of Charles Spurgeon:

Jesus is the gatekeeper of paradise, and before every believing soul He places "an open door that no one [neither man nor the Devil] can shut" (v. 8). And what joy it is to find that faith in Him is the golden key to those doors of eternity! My soul, do you carry this key in your heart, or are you trusting some deceitful, doomed-to-failure scheme to pick the lock at the last minute?

Read this parable and remember it: The great King has prepared a banquet and has proclaimed to the entire world that no one shall enter but those who bring with them the fairest flower of all. Souls come to the gates, each bringing one flower they esteem to be the queen of the garden. Some clasp the poisonous nightshade blossom of superstition, or the pompous poppies of Rome, or the deadly hemlock of self-righteousness; but these are not dear to the King, so those who hold them are shut out of the pearly gates.

My soul, have you gleaned the "rose of Sharon"? Are you wearing the "lily of the valleys" (Song 2:1)? If so, when you arrive at the gates of heaven, you will know its value, for you only have to show this Flower — the choicest of all — and the Gatekeeper will open the gates. He will not deny you admission, for when that Rose is shown, the gates will always open. With the "rose of Sharon" in your hand, you will find your way to the very throne of God, for heaven itself possesses nothing that excels its radiant beauty; and of all the flowers that bloom in paradise, there is nothing that can rival the "lily of the valleys."

My soul, take Calvary's blood-red Rose into your hand by faith, wear it by love, preserve it by communing with Christ, and through daily watchfulness make it your "all in all" (1 Cor. 15:28). Then you will be blessed beyond all joy and happy beyond all dreams.

Jesus, be mine forever — my God, my heaven, my all.

From the pen of Jim Reimann:

Today's verse is taken from Jesus' words to the church of Philadelphia in the following context: "These are the words of him who is holy and true, who holds the key of David. What he opens no one can shut, and what he shuts no one can open. I know your deeds. See, I have placed before you an open door that no one can shut" (Rev. 3:7 – 8). Of course, this is a fulfillment of the following foreshadowing of Jesus seen in Isaiah: "I will place on his shoulder the key to the house of David; what he opens no one can shut, and what he shuts no one can open" (Isa. 22:22).

Indeed, Jesus is "the fulfillment of the ages" (1 Cor. 10:11). Not only is He "the key to the house of David," but He is also the door itself, for He said, "I am the door" (John 10:9 KJV). Of all His names, however, perhaps there are none more beautiful than those from the Song of Songs: "I am a rose of Sharon, a lily of the valleys" (Song 2:1). With this in mind, may this be our closing prayer today:

"Let the beauty and delightfulness and favor of the Lord our God be upon us; confirm and establish the work of our hands" (Ps. 90:17 Amplified).

JUNE 16

The LORD is my light and my salvation — whom shall I fear?
The LORD is the stronghold of my life — of whom shall I be afraid?

Psalm 27:1

From the pen of Charles Spurgeon:

The phrase "The LORD is my light and my salvation" shows something personal, for He is "*my* light and *my* salvation." Our soul has assurance of it, and therefore declares it boldly. God's divine light is poured into a soul as the precursor to salvation and new birth, and when there is not enough light to reveal our own darkness and to make us yearn for the Lord Jesus, there is no evidence of salvation. Thus, after conversion, God is our joy, comfort, guide, and teacher; and He is in every sense our light — light within us, light around us, light reflected from us, and light being revealed to us. Yet this verse does not merely say that the Lord *gives* light, but He *is* light; nor that He *gives* salvation, but He *is* salvation. Therefore, whoever has taken hold of God by faith has all His covenant blessings in his possession.

After the truth — "The LORD is my light and my salvation" — is stated as fact, the question then follows, "Whom shall I fear?" But the answer is inherent within the verse itself — the powers of darkness are not to be feared, for the Lord, our light, destroys them; and the damnation of hell is not to be dreaded by us, for the Lord is our salvation. In this case, asking "Whom shall I fear?" is quite different from the boastful challenge of Goliath (see 1 Sam. 17), for it rests, not on the conceited strength of "only the arm of flesh" (2 Chron. 32:8) but upon the real power of the omnipotent "I AM" (Ex. 3:14).

"The LORD is the stronghold of my life." This is the third phrase of our text, demonstrating the author's hope was fastened by "a cord of three strands" (Eccl. 4:12) that could not be broken. This should lead us to expressions of praise for the Lord who lavishes His deeds of grace upon His people. And because our life derives all its strength from God, if He chooses to favor us with strength, we can never be weakened by any of the secret cunning of our adversary.

"Of whom shall I be afraid?" This bold question looks to the future and to the present, for, "If God is for us, who can be against us" (Rom. 8:31) — either now or in the time to come?

From the pen of Jim Reimann:

The point has been made today that Jesus not only *gives* light and salvation, He *is* light and salvation. Thus, the converse is also true: without Him there is only darkness and death. The Scriptures are clear that Jesus personifies other major truths typically thought of as events or character traits. Consider these words of Jesus: "I am the resurrection" (John 11:25); and "I am the way and the truth and the life" (John 14:6). Then consider these words of John and Paul: "We are in … Jesus Christ. He is … eternal life" (1 John 5:20); and "You are in Christ Jesus, who has become for us wisdom from God — that is, our righteousness, holiness and redemption" (1 Cor. 1:30). Let us personalize these precious truths today, by praying:

O Lord Jesus, I praise You, for You are my light, salvation, stronghold, resurrection, way, truth, life, eternal life, wisdom, righteousness, holiness, and redemption. Indeed, You are my "all in all" (1 Cor. 15:28).

June 17

Then Israel sang this song: "Spring up, O well! Sing about it."

Numbers 21:17

From the pen of Charles Spurgeon:

The well in the wilderness at Beer was renowned due to the promise God gave there, for it was "the well where the LORD said to Moses, 'Gather the people together and I will give them water'" (v. 16). The people needed water, and it was promised to them by their gracious God; we need fresh supplies of heavenly grace, which He pledged in His covenant to provide according to our need.

The well was the cause of their song. But it was before the water gushed forth that the people sang in joyful faith. Then as they saw the crystal water bubbling up, their song became more joyous. In the same way, we who believe God's promises should rejoice at the prospect of divine revival in our soul, and as we experience it our holy joy should overflow. Are you spiritually thirsty? Don't complain. Sing! Spiritual thirst is difficult to bear, but you don't need to bear it, for God's promise points to His well. So have a cheerful heart and look for it.

Also, the well was the focus of their prayer. "Spring up, O well!" What God has promised to give, you must ask from Him or else you reveal you have neither the desire nor the faith for it. Thus, ask Him today that the Scriptures you read, as well as these devotions, will not become an empty ritual, but a fountain of grace to your soul. Oh, that God the Holy Spirit would work in each of us with all His mighty power, filling us with all the fullness of God.

Finally, the well was the aim of their effort. "The nobles [dug the well] with scepters and staffs" (v. 18), just as the Lord would have us involved in obtaining grace. Our staff is ill equipped for digging a well, but we must learn to use it to the best of our ability. Doing so means prayer must not be neglected, "meeting together" (Heb. 10:25) must not be forsaken, and God's holy ordinances must not be forgotten. The Lord promises to give us His peace abundantly, but not through the path of idleness. So let us stir ourselves to seek Him in whom all our springs are found.

From the pen of Jim Reimann:

Spurgeon's last sentence is a reference to the following: "All my springs are in you" (Ps. 87:7 ESV). Of course, water represents life, which is why we see so many references to it, including: "The poor and needy search for water, but there is none.... But I the LORD will ... make rivers flow on barren heights, and springs within the valleys. I will turn the desert into pools of water, and the parched ground into springs" (Isa. 41:17 – 18); and "They will neither hunger nor thirst.... He who has compassion on them will guide them and lead them beside springs of water" (Isa. 49:10).

These passages find their fulfillment in Jesus, for later we read: "The Lamb at the center of the throne will be their shepherd; he will lead them to springs of living water" (Rev. 7:17); which is why He had previously proclaimed: "If anyone is thirsty, let him come to me and drink. Whoever believes in me, as the Scripture has said, streams of living water will flow from within him" (John 7:37 – 38).

Jesus, I thirst for You, for "the LORD [is] the spring of living water" (Jer. 17:13).

JUNE 18

I have come into my garden, my sister, my bride.

Song of Songs 5:1

From the pen of Charles Spurgeon:

Christ's garden is the heart of believers, for He bought it with His "precious blood" (1 Peter 1:19), and He enters it and claims it as His own. A garden implies separation, for it is not an open wilderness or common ground for everyone to walk across, but is enclosed by a wall or a hedge. If only we could see the wall of separation between the church and the world made wider and stronger! It saddens me to hear Christians say, "There's no harm in this or in that," thereby getting as close to the world as possible. Grace flows at low tide in a soul that even dares to raise the question of how far it may go in worldly conformity. A garden is a place of beauty that far surpasses wild, uncultivated land.

Genuine Christians must seek to be more excellent in their life than the best moralists, because Christ's garden ought to produce the best flowers in the world. Yet even our best is poor compared to what Christ deserves. Therefore, let us not shame Him with small, withering plants; but let us bloom with the rarest, richest, and loveliest lilies and roses in the garden that Jesus calls His own.

A garden is a place of growth, thus saints should not be underdeveloped, always remaining mere buds and small blooms. Instead, we should "grow in the grace and knowledge of our Lord and Savior Jesus Christ" (2 Peter 3:18). Growth should be rapid where Jesus is the Gardener and the Holy Spirit is the dew from above.

A garden is also a place of rest. Thus, the Lord Jesus Christ would have us reserve our heart as a place where He can reveal Himself in a way He does not do for the world. Oh, that Christians would keep their heart reserved for Christ alone! We often worry and trouble ourselves, like Martha, with "much serving" (Luke 10:40 KJV), so that we have no room for Him and do not sit like Mary at His feet as we should.

May the Lord grant us the sweet showers of His grace to water His garden today.

From the pen of Jim Reimann:

Whether it is in the dating life of unmarried believers or other aspects of our daily walk, the question is often asked, "How far is too far to go?" Yet even asking this reveals a spiritual problem. Why is it we often push the limits and desire to live at the edge of the world? We are not to "conform any longer to the pattern of this world, but be transformed by the renewing of [our] mind" (Rom. 12:2), and "be conformed to the likeness of [God's] Son" (Rom. 8:29).

Only then will we "be able to test and approve what God's will is — his good, pleasing and perfect will" (Rom. 12:2). Walking in God's grace demands walking in holiness — something God has promised to bless. But walking a path of compromise with the world leads to disaster, such as we see in the life of Lot, who "pitched his tents near Sodom," while "Abram lived in the land of Canaan" (Gen. 13:12).

Don't you know that friendship with the world is hatred toward God? Anyone who chooses to be a friend of the world becomes an enemy of God.

James 4:4

JUNE 19

My beloved is mine, and I am his. He feeds his flock among the lilies.
Until the day breaks and the shadows flee away, turn, my beloved,
and be like a gazelle or a young stag upon the mountains of Bether.

Song of Songs 2:16 – 17 NKJV

From the pen of Charles Spurgeon:

If there is a joyful verse in the Bible, surely it is: "My beloved is mine, and I am his." It is so full of peace and assurance and overflowing with happiness and contentment that it expresses sentiments much like those of Psalm 23. But although it initially reveals a prospect that is fair and lovely — a beautiful earthly setting — it is not entirely a sunlit landscape, for there is a cloud in the sky casting a shadow over the scene. Notice the writer says, "Until the day breaks and the shadows flee away." He mentions "the mountains of Bether," meaning the mountains of division. And when it comes to love, anything even approaching division brings bitterness.

Beloved, this may be your current state of mind. You don't doubt your salvation; you know Christ is yours, but you are not feasting with Him. You understand your life is in Him, so you don't have even the shadow of a doubt that you belong to Him and that He belongs to you, but still, His "left arm is [not] under [your] head," nor does His "right arm [embrace you]" (Song 2:6). Sadness, perhaps caused by some affliction or the seeming temporary absence of your Lord, darkens your heart. So even while you proclaim, "I am his," you are forced to fall to your knees and pray, "Until the day breaks and the shadows flee away, turn, my beloved."

My soul asks where my Beloved is, and the answer comes: "He feeds his flock among the lilies." So if I desire to find Christ, I must commune with His people, participate in the ordinances with His saints. Oh, for just a glimpse of Him! Oh, to dine with Him today!

From the pen of Jim Reimann:

Two days ago and again today, Spurgeon mentioned the ordinances of God, and the importance of not neglecting them. What he is referring to are the ordinances of believers' baptism and the Lord's Supper. When we come together as God's church to observe and participate in baptisms and communion, we not only fellowship with our Beloved but also with His people. Of course, we are also being obedient to the Lord, for, regarding Communion, He said, "Do this in remembrance of me" (Luke 22:19). The goal is to truly commune with the Lord and His saints, becoming one in the unity of His Spirit. Paul wrote of unity, saying, "Make every effort to keep the unity of the Spirit through the bond of peace" (Eph. 4:3).

Obedience to God's Word is the key to unity. Notice what we are *not* told in 1 John 1:7. It does *not* say, "If we walk in the light, as he is in the light" — we have fellowship *with God*. No, it says, "If we walk in the light, as he is in the light, we have fellowship *with one another.*" Yes, we also fellowship with God, and time alone with Him is critical for every believer, but we should not neglect the fellowship of the saints.

"Let us not give up meeting together, as some are in the habit of doing, but let us encourage one another — and all the more as you see the Day approaching" (Heb. 10:25). And let us thank the Lord that He is in the process of "bring[ing] all things in heaven and on earth together under one head, even Christ" (Eph. 1:10) — our Beloved.

JUNE 20

At once they left their nets and followed him.

Mark 1:18

From the pen of Charles Spurgeon:

When Jesus called Simon and Andrew, they immediately obeyed Him without reservation. And if we would always put into practice what we hear with resolute passion and promptness, or at least at the first fitting opportunity, our following of the ways of grace, and our reading of good books, would never fail to enrich us spiritually. Someone who quickly eats his bread cannot have it taken from him, and neither can believers be deprived of the benefit of a doctrine once they have applied it to their life.

Most readers of books such as this one, and many hearers of the Word, are moved simply as far as purposing to make a change; regrettably, however, their proposal is like a bud that never blooms, and therefore no fruit comes of it. They wait, they waver, and then they simply forget, until, like shallow ponds in winter, they melt by day only to be frozen again by night. Their tomorrows are marked by the deadly, blood-red stains of the murder of their good intentions and resolutions, turning those tomorrows into the slaughterhouse of the innocents.

I am personally concerned over whether this little book of daily readings bears fruit, and therefore I pray that you will "not merely [read] the word" contained in it, but also "do what it says" (James 1:22). Thus, the most profitable way to read it is to put its truth into practice. If God impresses you with any act of duty to Him as you peruse these pages, then quickly fulfill it before the holy glow departs from your soul. Immediately leave your nets and all you have, rather than be found rebellious to the Master's call. Do not give the Devil room to work by delaying. Move quickly while the opportunity and the passion are still blessedly together in your life. Don't get caught in your own nets, but break the webs of worldliness and walk where glory is calling you.

Dear reader, if you will resolve to carry out my teachings in this book, I would be blessed with a hundredfold harvest; but more than that, our Master will receive great honor. That would be reward enough to me for these brief meditations and hurried hints.

May You grant this reward, O Lord, to Your servant.

From the pen of Jim Reimann:

Spurgeon wrote very personally in today's devotion, expressing the heart of every true teacher and preacher of the Word. Dedicated ministers of the gospel desire that their students, listeners, or readers would not only learn the information being presented but also would have the wisdom to apply that truth to their lives.

Of course, each of us should have a desire to imitate Christ, who is the Word Himself. The following Scripture is what He taught His disciples after washing their feet. As you read, note that He is not simply teaching about washing each other's feet, but is exhorting them to obey all He has taught them:

I have set you an example that you should do as I have done for you. I tell you the truth, no servant is greater than his master, nor is a messenger greater than the one who sent him. *Now that you know these things, you will be blessed if you do them.*

John 13:15 – 17

JUNE 21

God's solid foundation stands firm.

2 Timothy 2:19

From the pen of Charles Spurgeon:

The "solid foundation" upon which our faith rests is this: "God was reconciling the world to himself in Christ, not counting men's sins against them" (2 Cor. 5:19). This great fact upon which genuine faith relies is proclaimed in these words: "The Word became flesh and made his dwelling among us" (John 1:14); "Christ died for sins once for all, the righteous for the unrighteous, to bring you to God" (1 Peter 3:18); "He himself bore our sins in his body on the tree" (1 Peter 2:24); and "The punishment that brought us peace was upon him, and by his wounds we are healed" (Isa. 53:5).

The great pillar of the Christian's hope is *substitution*. This fundamental fact of the gospel is also expressed as follows: The vicarious sacrifice of Christ for the guilty; "God [making] him who had no sin to be sin for us, so that in him we might become the righteousness of God" (2 Cor. 5:21); Christ offering up a true and proper atoning and substitutionary sacrifice in the place of as many as the Father gave Him — those who are known to God by name, and who recognize Him in their own hearts by their trust in Jesus. If this foundation were removed, what could we do? Yet we know it stands as firm as the throne of God. Indeed, we know it; we rest on it; we rejoice in it; and our delight is to hold it, meditate upon it, and proclaim it. And thus we desire to be moved to action by gratitude for it in every aspect of our life and conversation.

Yet today there is a direct attack upon the doctrine of the atonement. The world cannot bear the idea of substitution, for they despise the thought of "the Lamb of God" (John 1:29) bearing the sin of man. But we who know by experience the preciousness of this truth will proclaim it confidently in defiance of them. We will neither dilute it, change it, nor whittle it down in any way. The message will remain: Christ, a sure and certain substitute, who bore human guilt and suffering in our stead.

We cannot — we dare not — give it up, for this truth is our very life. And despite every controversy, we know: "God's solid foundation stands firm."

From the pen of Jim Reimann:

The story of Abraham and his son Isaac is a beautiful foreshadowing of the substitutionary sacrifice of Jesus. We are told Isaac asked his father, "The fire and wood are here, but where is the lamb for the burnt offering?" (Gen. 22:7). The NIV renders Abraham's response: "God himself will provide the lamb" (v. 8), but a more literal rendering, such as that from the ASV reads: "God will provide himself the lamb"; as if to say, "God will provide *Himself as the lamb!*"

Next we read: "Abraham looked up and there in a thicket he saw a ram caught by its horns. He ... took the ram and sacrificed it as a burnt offering *instead of his son*" (v. 13) — clearly demonstrating substitutionary sacrifice. Again from the Hebrew, the literal meaning is that the ram caught himself in the thicket, thus offering himself up to be sacrificed — just like Jesus, who said, "No one takes [my life] from me, but I lay it down of my own accord" (John 10:18).

O Lord, enable me, like John the Baptist, to see Jesus for who He is — my substitutionary sacrifice — and thus proclaim: "Behold, the Lamb of God, who takes away [my] sin!" (John 1:29 ESV).

JUNE 22

"Once more I will shake not only the earth but also the heavens."
The words "once more" indicate the removing of what can be shaken —
that is, created things — so that what cannot be shaken may remain.

Hebrews 12:26 – 27

From the pen of Charles Spurgeon:

In this life each of us has many things in our possession that "can be shaken," and it reflects poorly on Christians to be attached to them, for since change is written upon all things, there is nothing stable under the skies. Yet we also have certain things that "cannot be shaken." Consider the fact that if the things that "can be shaken" were all taken away, you still may derive real comfort from the things that "cannot be shaken" — those things that remain.

For example, whatever your losses may have been in the past, or may be in the future, you have the blessing today of salvation. You stand at the foot of Jesus' cross, trusting in the merit of His precious blood alone; and no rise or fall of world markets, no bank failure, nor any bankruptcy can interfere with your salvation in Him.

Also, you are a child of God. God is your Father, and no change in your circumstances can ever rob you of that. Even if stripped bare by financial losses to the point of poverty, you can say, "He is still my Father! 'In my Father's house are many rooms' (John 14:2), and therefore I will not be troubled."

You have another permanent blessing: the love of Jesus Christ. He who is God and Man loves you with all the strength of His loving nature, and nothing can affect that. Fig trees may cease to blossom and flocks may be gone from the fields, but it will not matter to the person who can sing, "My beloved is mine, and I am his" (Song 2:16 NKJV).

You cannot lose your richest heritage and best inheritance. So whatever troubles may come, be strong and show you are not so childish as to be depressed by what happens in the poor, fleeting circumstances of this life. Your country is Immanuel's land, your hope is above the sky, and thus, even if you experience the destruction of everything on earth, may you remain as calm as a summer ocean, rejoicing in "the God of [your] salvation" (Ps. 68:19 KJV).

From the pen of Jim Reimann:

The Christian life is full of difficulties that may shake us emotionally, but our future and our inheritance in Christ "cannot be shaken." No doubt Peter grasped this truth, and there can be no better words than his, inspired by the Spirit, to confirm this teaching. Here is what he penned:

Praise be to the God and Father of our Lord Jesus Christ! In his great mercy he has given us new birth into a living hope through the resurrection of Jesus Christ from the dead, and into an inheritance that can never perish, spoil or fade — kept in heaven for you, who through faith are shielded by God's power until the coming of the salvation that is ready to be revealed in the last time. In this you greatly rejoice, though now for a little while you may have had to suffer grief in all kinds of trials. These have come so that your faith — of greater worth than gold, which perishes even though refined by fire — may be proved genuine and may result in praise, glory and honor when Jesus Christ is revealed. Though you have not seen him, you love him; and even though you do not see him now, you believe in him and are filled with an inexpressible and glorious joy, for you are receiving the goal of your faith, the salvation of your souls.

1 Peter 1:3 – 9

JUNE 23

We wait eagerly for our adoption.

Romans 8:23

From the pen of Charles Spurgeon:

Even in this life, we as saints are God's children, but the world cannot recognize us as such, except by certain moral characteristics. This is because our adoption has not yet been openly declared and fully manifested to the world. Likewise, in ancient Rome, a person might adopt a child but keep it private. Later, there was a second adoption in public when the child was brought before the proper authorities. The child's old garments were removed, and the father who had taken the child to be his would give him new clothing suitable for his new status in life.

"Dear friends, now we are children of God, and what we will be has not yet been made known" (1 John 3:2). Thus, we are not yet arrayed in the garments befitting the royal family of heaven, for we are still wearing the flesh and blood we wore as the children of Adam. "But we know that when he appears" (v. 2) — He who is "the firstborn among many brothers" (Rom. 8:29) — "we shall be like him, for we shall see him as he is" (1 John 3:2). Can't you imagine a child in ancient Rome, having been taken from the lowest level of society and adopted by a Roman senator, saying to himself, "I long for the day when I will be publicly adopted. Then I will leave these common clothes behind and be robed like a senator." Though happy to be privately adopted, he would long to receive the fullness of what had been promised him.

It is the same with us today. We too are waiting to be clothed in our proper garments and to be fully revealed as children of God. We are royalty who has not yet worn our crown. We are young brides awaiting the marriage day to come, and who, because of the great love of our Spouse, yearn for that bridal morning with deep sighs.

It is our very happiness that causes us to groan for more, and our joy, like a rain-swollen stream, longs to leap for the skies like an Icelandic geyser. Yes, it is our joy that heaves and groans within our spirit for the lack of being able to fully manifest itself to the world.

From the pen of Jim Reimann:

Today's verse is taken from this context:

We know that the whole creation has been groaning as in the pains of childbirth right up to the present time. Not only so, but we ourselves, who have the firstfruits of the Spirit, groan inwardly as we wait eagerly for our adoption as sons, the redemption of our bodies. For in this hope we were saved. But hope that is seen is no hope at all. Who hopes for what he already has? But if we hope for what we do not yet have, we wait for it patiently.

Romans 8:22 – 25

Paul addressed today's topic again by writing this to the church in Corinth:

Flesh and blood cannot inherit the kingdom of God, nor does the perishable inherit the imperishable.... When the perishable has been clothed with the imperishable, and the mortal with immortality, then the saying that is written will come true: "Death has been swallowed up in victory."

1 Corinthians 15:50, 54

Jesus, grant me holy patience as I await Your coming and the fulfillment of my adoption. I thank You that You have "destroyed death and ... brought life and immortality to light through the gospel" (2 Tim. 1:10).

JUNE 24

Shadrach, Meshach and Abednego replied to the king,
" … we want you to know, O king, that we will not serve your gods."

Daniel 3:16, 18

From the pen of Charles Spurgeon:

This narrative, the story of the courage and miraculous deliverance of three righteous young men, is well orchestrated to stir the minds of believers to determination and steadfastness in upholding the truth even in the face of tyranny and the very jaws of death. May young Christians especially learn from their example in matters of faith as well as in business, learning to be upright and honest at all times, never sacrificing their consciences, for it is better to lose all things than to lose one's integrity. When all else is gone, may you hold fast to the rarest of jewels that can adorn a person's heart — a clear conscience.

Never be guided by the will-o'-the-wisp whims, but by the polestar or guiding light of God's divine authority. [Editor's note: "Will-o'-the-wisp" refers to the legend of strange, flickering lights appearing over lakes at night. When approached, it is said they disappear.] No matter the danger, do what is right; and though you may not see any advantage, "live by faith, not by sight" (2 Cor. 5:7). Honor God enough to trust Him when it comes to matters of personal loss for the sake of principle, and see if He will be your debtor. See if He doesn't prove His promise even in this life that "godliness with contentment is great gain" (1 Tim. 6:6), and that they who "seek first his kingdom and his righteousness" will have "all these things … given to [them] as well" (Matt. 6:33).

Yet should it happen through God's sovereignty that you lose by refusing to compromise your conscience, and the Lord chooses not to repay you with the silver of earthly prosperity, then He will repay His promise with the gold of spiritual joy. Remember — "a man's life does not consist in the abundance of his possessions" (Luke 12:15). Having a guileless spirit, having a heart devoid of offense, and having the favor and smile of God are greater riches than all the merchandise of Tyre (see Neh. 13:16) or the gold mines of Ophir (see 1 Chron. 29:4) could ever yield. "Better a meal of vegetables where there is love than a fattened calf with hatred" (Prov. 15:17). An ounce of heartsease is worth a ton of gold. [Editor's note: Heartsease is a common wildflower thought to have healing properties.]

From the pen of Jim Reimann:

Spurgeon stated that, among other things, "having a guileless spirit" is of great value. Yet the word *guile* is one that is not commonly used today. In the KJV, when Jesus chose Nathaniel, Jesus said of him: "Behold an Israelite indeed, in whom is no guile!" (John 1:47). And later Peter wrote of Jesus, saying, "Christ … did no sin, neither was guile found in his mouth" (1 Peter 2:21 – 22 KJV). The NIV correctly translates the word *guile* as deceit, which includes falsehood, lies, and trickery.

Today's text is the story of three young men "in whom [was] no guile" as well, for they simply could have lied to survive. Instead, they proclaimed their faith to the king in one of the most extraordinary statements in the Bible: "The God we serve is able to save us from [the blazing furnace],… but even if he does not,… we will not serve your gods" (Dan. 3:17 – 18).

O Lord, I desire that kind of faith. May "no guile" be found in me.

JUNE 25

But the dove could find no place to set its feet.

Genesis 8:9

From the pen of Charles Spurgeon:

Dear reader, like Noah's dove, do you believe you can find rest apart from your ark: Christ Jesus? If so, then be assured your faith is in vain. Are you satisfied with anything short of your conscious knowledge of your union and relationship with Christ? If so, then "woe unto you!" (Matt. 23:13). If you profess to be a Christian, but find full satisfaction in worldly pleasures and pursuits, then your profession of faith in Jesus is false. If your soul can find a bed big enough and blankets warm enough to find rest and be comfortable in the rooms of sin, then you are a hypocrite — far from having any true thoughts of who Christ is or any perception of His preciousness.

On the other hand, if you believe you could indulge in sin without punishment, but that the lack of God's punishment itself would be punishment to you; and if you could own the whole world and live in it forever, but that as well would be misery to you; then God — "your God" (Ps. 45:7) — is what your soul craves. So "be of good courage" (Ps. 31:24 KJV), for you are indeed a child of God. In spite of all your sins and imperfections, take comfort in this: If your soul finds no rest in sin, you are not like worldly sinners. If your soul still yearns for something better, then you have not forgotten Christ — and He certainly has not forgotten you. True believers cannot do without their Lord, and words are inadequate to express their thoughts of Him. As Christians we cannot survive on the sand of the wilderness, for we desire the heavenly manna from above; and the worldly "bottles" of creature self-confidence cannot supply even a drop of moisture, for we drink from the rock who abides with us — and that rock is Christ.

When you feed on Him, your soul can sing: "[He] satisfies [my] desires with good things so that [my] youth is renewed like the eagle's" (Ps. 103:5). But if you don't have Him, even your overflowing wine vats and well-stocked barns cannot afford you any sort of satisfaction. If this is true in your case, you should lament over them with these words of wisdom: "Utterly meaningless! Everything is meaningless" (Eccl. 1:2).

From the pen of Jim Reimann:

Indeed, life itself is meaningless for those without Jesus as their Savior. Like Noah's dove in today's text, they look in vain for rest from their labor, much like the rich man in Jesus' parable, who said to himself, "You have plenty of good things laid up for many years. Take life easy; eat, drink and be merry" (Luke 12:19). But God said to him, "You fool! This very night your life will be demanded from you. Then who will get what you have prepared for yourself?" (v. 20). And Jesus, showing this was not a unique circumstance, went on to say, "This is how it will be with anyone who stores up things for himself but is not rich toward God" (v. 21).

How much better to die in Christ! Remember these words of John:

> Then I heard a voice from heaven say, "Write: Blessed are the dead who die in the Lord from now on." "Yes," says the Spirit, "they will rest from their labor, for their deeds will follow them."
>
> Revelation 14:13

Therefore, let us "rest in the LORD, and wait patiently for him" (Ps. 37:7 KJV).

JUNE 26

You may ... escape the corruption in the world caused by evil desires.

2 Peter 1:4

From the pen of Charles Spurgeon:

Dismiss forever any thought of indulging the flesh if you desire to live in the power of your risen Lord. Nothing good can come from a person who is alive in Christ living in the corruption of sin. Remember what the angel said to Mary Magdalene: "Why do you look for the living among the dead?" (Luke 24:5). Should the living reside in a tomb? Should the divine life God bestows be held captive to the burial chamber of fleshly lust? How can we partake of the cup of the Lord and still drink of the cup of Belial? (See 2 Cor. 6:15.)

Dear believer, God has delivered you from your open lust and sinfulness, but have you also escaped the more secret and deceptive snares of Satan? Have you broken free of the lust of pride? Have you escaped the sin of slothfulness? Have you made a clean break with trusting in worldly things for your security? Are you day by day seeking to live above worldliness, "the pride of life" (1 John 2:16 KJV), and the ensnaring vice of materialism and greed?

Remember — this is why you have been enriched with the treasures of God. If you are truly chosen of God and loved by Him, do not allow all His abundant treasures of grace to be wasted on you by walking in sin. Follow after holiness instead, for it is the Christian's crown and glory. Shall we tolerate an unholy church? It is useless to the world and has no honor among mankind. It is an abomination, the laughingstock of hell, and the abhorrence of heaven! In fact, the worst evils that have ever come upon the world have been brought on her by an unholy church.

O Christian, the vows of God are upon you.

You are God's priest, so act like it! You are God's king, so reign over your lusts! You are God's chosen, so do not associate with Belial! Heaven is your inheritance, so live like a heavenly being, thereby proving that your faith in Jesus is true. Remember — faith cannot abide in the heart unless there is holiness in the life.

> Lord, I desire to live as one
> Who bears a blood-bought name,
> As one who fears but grieving You,
> And knows no other shame.
>
> Charitie Lees Smith (1841 – 1923)

From the pen of Jim Reimann:

Spurgeon's call to holiness is a call God's church desperately needs to hear today — and heed today! Yet there is nothing new in his fervent call. In fact, Isaiah, speaking of the Messiah's day yet to come, said, "A highway will be there; it will be called the Way of Holiness. The unclean will not journey on it; it will be for those who walk in that Way; wicked fools will not go about on it" (Isa. 35:8). Dear church, as you read the following verses, notice the contrast between the sins of man and the love of God. May we be motivated to holiness as we reflect on His great love!

> Concerning the sinfulness of the wicked: There is no fear of God before his eyes. For in his own eyes he flatters himself too much to detect or hate his sin.... *Your love, O LORD, reaches to the heavens, your faithfulness to the skies.... How priceless is your unfailing love!*
>
> Psalm 36:1 – 2, 5, 7

JUNE 27

Each one should remain in the situation which he was in
when God called him.

1 Corinthians 7:20

From the pen of Charles Spurgeon:

Some people have the foolish notion that the only way they can live for God long-term is to become a minister or a missionary. Yet if this were true, just think how many people would be shut out from any opportunity of magnifying the Most High God. Beloved Christian, remember, it is not a person's role, position, or earnestness that enables us to glorify God — it is grace. He is far more glorified by a simple tradesman, plying his trade while singing of his Savior's love, than He is by the highest-ranking religious leader who performs his official duties without proclaiming the Savior. And certainly the name of Jesus is just as glorified by a poor, uneducated cabdriver as he drives and blesses his God or speaks to fellow drivers as He is by a popular preacher who thunders out the gospel like "Boanerges" (Mark 3:17).

God is glorified by our serving Him, regardless of our particular vocation. So take care, dear reader, that you don't abandon your path of duty by leaving your occupation, and take care not to dishonor your profession while you are in it. Yes, think little of yourself, but never minimize your calling to your vocation. Every trade, as long as it is legal, can be sanctified by the gospel to the noblest of ends. In the Bible we find even the most menial forms of labor tied either to people exhibiting the most daring deeds of faith or to those whose lives have been great examples of holiness.

So never be discontented with your vocational calling. Wherever God has called you to work, abide there — unless, of course, you are sure He has called you somewhere else. Let your first priority be to glorify God to the best of your ability where you are. Fully use your present sphere of responsibility and influence to bring Him praise, and if He desires you in another place, He will show you. Determine to lay aside all anxious ambition today and fully embrace His peaceful contentment.

From the pen of Jim Reimann:

Spurgeon begins by sharing the foolish idea some espouse that to live for God they must be a minister or missionary. Yet Paul said "it was [Christ] who gave *some* to be apostles, *some* to be prophets, *some* to be evangelists, and *some* to be pastors and teachers" (Eph. 4:11). Notice he didn't say, "Christ gave *all*" of us to serve in these ways. Perhaps this is why he strongly addressed the issue again, saying:

> The eye cannot say to the hand, "I don't need you!" And the head cannot say to the feet, "I don't need you!" On the contrary, those parts of the body that seem to be weaker are indispensable, and the parts that we think are less honorable we treat with special honor. And the parts that are unpresentable are treated with special modesty, while our presentable parts need no special treatment. But God has combined the members of the body and has given greater honor to the parts that lacked it, so that there should be no division in the body, but that its parts should have equal concern for each other. If one part suffers, every part suffers with it; if one part is honored, every part rejoices with it. Now you are the body of Christ, and each one of you is a part of it.
>
> 1 Corinthians 12:21-27

JUNE 28

Aaron's staff swallowed up their staffs.

Exodus 7:12

From the pen of Charles Spurgeon:

This story is a wonderful example of the sure victory of God's work over all opposition. Although the Devil may produce counterfeits, often attempting to overwhelm us with opponents, whenever God is in the work, you can be sure it will always swallow its foes. As long as God's grace has possession of a person, the world's magicians can throw down their rods all they want, and though every rod may be as cunning and poisonous as a serpent, Aaron's rod will always swallow their rods.

The glorious attraction of the cross will woo and win the believer's heart, and he who once lived only for this deceitful earth will begin to focus on the heavens above, yearning to fly away to those celestial heights. Once God's grace wins its victory, even those in the world begin to look to the world to come. And certainly this is true in the life of the believer. Consider, for example, the multitudes of foes our faith must face. The Devil throws down our old sins before us, turning them into serpents. And how many there are! But the cross of Jesus destroys them all, for faith in Christ quickly removes all our sins. The Devil also throws down numerous serpents in the form of worldly trials, temptations, and unbelief; but faith in Jesus is more than a match for all of them, overcoming them all.

The same "swallowing" principle shines brightly when it comes to faithful service to God. When we have an enthusiastic love for Jesus, our difficulties are surmounted, sacrifice becomes a pleasure, and suffering is an honor. If faith is truly a consuming passion in the heart of the believer, then it follows that there are many people who profess to have faith but do not, for what they have will not pass this test.

So, dear reader, examine yourself in light of this truth. Aaron's rod proved it had the power of heaven. Is your faith doing the same? If Christ is anything to you — He must be everything! Never rest until the reigning passion of your soul is love and faith in Jesus!

From the pen of Jim Reimann:

How do we know if Jesus is the reigning passion of our soul? If He is, His gospel will also be a passion burning within us. Note the response of Peter and John to the Sanhedrin after being commanded "not to speak or teach at all in the name of Jesus" (Acts 4:18). They boldly replied, "Judge for yourselves whether it is right in God's sight to obey you rather than God. For *we cannot help speaking about what we have seen and heard*" (vv. 19 – 20). It is no wonder that even the unbelieving religious leaders of that day knew they were facing something unique, for we are told: "When they saw the courage of Peter and John ... they were astonished and they took note that these men had been with Jesus" (v. 13).

Paul proclaimed much the same sentiment as Peter and John: "I am compelled to preach. Woe to me if I do not preach the gospel!" (1 Cor. 9:16). In the same way, may the words of Jeremiah be true of us as well: "If I say, 'I will not mention him or speak any more in his name,' his word is in my heart like a fire, a fire shut up in my bones. I am weary of holding it in; indeed, I cannot" (Jer. 20:9).

JUNE 29

When envoys were sent by the rulers of Babylon to ask [Hezekiah]
about the miraculous sign that had occurred in the land,
God left him to test him and to know everything that was in his heart.

2 Chronicles 32:31

From the pen of Charles Spurgeon:

Hezekiah had been growing so inwardly great, priding himself due to the favor of God, that self-righteousness had crept in. Thus, because of his carnal self-security, the grace of God, at least in its more outer workings, was withdrawn from him for a season. And if the grace of God were to be withdrawn from one of the best Christians, forcing him to contend with "the Babylonians" on his own, there is still enough sin in his heart to make him the worst of sinners. If left to yourself, even you who are now the warmest for Christ would cool down like Laodicea into sickening lukewarmness (see Rev. 3:14 – 16); you who are now sound in the faith would become white with the leprosy of false doctrine; and you who now walk before the Lord with excellence and integrity would reel to and fro, staggering in the drunkenness of evil passion.

Like the moon, we simply "borrow" our light, for as bright as we may appear when God's grace is shining upon us, we are the epitome of darkness when "the sun of righteousness" (Mal. 4:2) withdraws Himself from us. Therefore let us cry to God to never leave us, praying:

"Do not ... take your Holy Spirit from [us]" (Ps. 51:11) nor withdraw from us Your indwelling grace! Have You not said, "I, the Lord, watch over it; I water it continually. I guard it day and night so that no one may harm it" (Isa. 27:3)? Lord, keep us when we are in the valley, so we will not complain against Your humbling hand; and when we are on the mountaintop, keep us from becoming boastful for being lifted up. Keep us in our youth, when our passions are strong; keep us in our old age, when we may be tempted to become conceited due to our wisdom, and thereby prove to be greater fools than the young and prideful; and keep us at our time of death, lest at the very end, we should deny You. Keep us in life, death, work, suffering, battle, and in rest — keep us wherever we are, for, O our God, we need You everywhere!

From the pen of Jim Reimann:

The writer of Chronicles assumes his reader knows the full story of Hezekiah told in 2 Kings and Isaiah. Here is Isaiah's account of his foolish, prideful actions:

Hezekiah received the [Babylonian] envoys gladly and showed them what was in his storehouses — the silver, the gold, the spices, the fine oil, his entire armory and everything found among his treasures. There was nothing in his palace or in all his kingdom that Hezekiah did not show them. Then Isaiah the prophet went to King Hezekiah and asked, " ... What did they see in your palace?" "They saw everything in my palace," Hezekiah said.... Then Isaiah said to Hezekiah, "Hear the word of the Lord Almighty: The time will surely come when everything in your palace, and all that your fathers have stored up until this day, will be carried off to Babylon.... And some of your descendants, your own flesh and blood ... will be taken away."

Isaiah 39:2 – 7

Finally, note Hezekiah's amazingly selfish reply: "'The word of the Lord you have spoken is good.' ... For he thought, 'There will be peace and security in *my* lifetime'" (v. 8). May God, by His grace, keep us from such pride and arrogance.

JUNE 30

Ah, Sovereign LORD, you have made the heavens and the earth
by your great power and outstretched arm.
Nothing is too hard for you.

Jeremiah 32:17

From the pen of Charles Spurgeon:

At the very time "the king of Babylon was … besieging Jerusalem" (v. 2), when "the sword, famine and plague" (v. 24) had already desolated the country, Jeremiah was commanded by God to purchase a field and to have the deed of sale legally sealed and witnessed. This was indeed a strange purchase for a prudent man to make, for it meant buying property the purchaser probably would not have an opportunity to enjoy. But the fact God commanded him to do so was enough for Jeremiah, for he knew God's ways are always righteous and just with each of His children. Jeremiah reasoned, in essence:

"O Lord God! You can make this plot of ground of use to me. You can rid this country of these oppressors, allow me to sit under my own fig tree and vineyard, and even have a family heritage on this land; for 'you have made the heavens and the earth.… Nothing is too hard for you.'"

This brings a great amount of dignity and splendor to these Old Testaments saints, for they dared to obey God's command even when doing so defied human reason and was often condemned. Whether it was Noah who built a ship on dry land (see Gen. 6:9 – 22); Abraham who offered up his only son (see Gen. 22:1 – 19); Moses who forsook "the treasures of Egypt" (Heb. 11:26); or Joshua who besieged Jericho for seven days, using no weapons but the trumpet blast of rams' horns (see Josh. 6); they all acted at God's command. They obeyed, doing what was contrary to human reason, and the Lord gave them a rich reward as a result of their obedient faith.

Oh, if only believers had a more powerful infusion of this type of heroic faith in God in these modern times! If only we would obediently exercise more trust, venturing out upon the pure promise of God. May Jeremiah's brand of confidence be ours, for "nothing is too hard for [God, who] made the heavens and the earth."

From the pen of Jim Reimann:

It was only *after* Jeremiah's obedience that the Lord revealed His purpose for buying this field. Though Babylon would defeat Judah, carrying it into captivity, the Lord told Jeremiah He would fulfill His covenant and return them to their God-given land. Here is what the Lord revealed to Jeremiah:

"By the sword, famine and plague [this city] will be handed over to the king of Babylon"; but … I will surely gather them from all the lands where I banish them in my furious anger and great wrath; I will bring them back to this place and let them live in safety. They will be my people, and I will be their God. I will give them singleness of heart and action, so that they will always fear me for their own good and the good of their children after them. I will make an everlasting covenant with them: I will never stop doing good to them, and I will inspire them to fear me, so that they will never turn away from me. I will rejoice in doing them good and will assuredly plant them in this land with all my heart and soul.… As I have brought all this great calamity on this people, so I will give them all the prosperity I have promised them.

Jeremiah 32:36 – 42

July

JULY 1

[Adam and Eve] heard the voice of the LORD God
walking in the garden in the cool of the day.

Genesis 3:8 KJV

From the pen of Charles Spurgeon:

Dear believer, "in the cool of the day," relax for a while and hear the voice of your God, for He is always ready to speak to you when you are prepared to hear. If there is any reluctance to commune, it is not on His part, but is totally your own, for He "stand[s] at the door and knock[s]" (Rev. 3:20), and if His people will open the door, He rejoices to enter.

So what is the condition of my heart, which is my Lord's garden? My hope is that it is well trimmed, watered, and bringing forth fruit worthy of Him. If not, He will have much to reprove. Even so, I pray He will come to me, for nothing is as certain to bring my heart into the right condition as the presence of "the sun of righteousness" who brings "healing in [His] wings" (Mal. 4:2).

Come, therefore, O Lord, my God. My soul earnestly invites You and eagerly waits for You. Come to me, O Jesus, "my wellbeloved" (Isa. 5:1 KJV), and plant fresh flowers in my garden — the very kind I see blooming in such perfection in Your matchless character. Come, O "my Father [who] is the gardener" (John 15:1), and deal prudently with me, but with Your tenderness. Come, O Holy Spirit, and refresh my entire nature as the herbs are refreshed with the evening dew. O Lord, speak to me! "Speak, for your servant is listening" (1 Sam. 3:10).

If only He would commune with me. I am ready to give my entire heart and mind to Him. What I am asking of Him is only what He delights to give. Thus I am confident He will condescend to fellowship with me, for He has already given me His Holy Spirit to abide with me forever. It is "in the cool of the day" that the stars seem like the eyes of heaven and the cool breeze as the breath of God's celestial love.

My Father, my older Brother, my sweet Comforter, speak now to me "with lovingkindness" (Jer. 31:3), for You have opened my ears and I am not rebellious.

From the pen of Jim Reimann:

There is a difference between *hearing* and *listening*, for Adam and Eve "heard the voice of the LORD God," but due to their sin, "they hid" from Him (Gen. 3:8). Thus the Lord commands us to do both: "*Listen and hear* my voice" (Isa. 28:23). May we determine to truly listen to our heavenly Father, just as the psalmist, who prayed, "I will listen to what God the LORD will say" (Ps. 85:8). He has promised blessings when we listen, but also promised curses when we do not. Notice the severe contrast in the following passages:

"If you listen carefully to the voice of the LORD your God and do what is right in his eyes ... I will not bring on you any of the diseases I brought on the Egyptians" (Ex. 15:26). But — "If you do not listen ... I will send a curse upon you, and I will curse your blessings" (Mal. 2:2).

Remember — if you won't listen to God, He won't listen to you, for He once said of His people: "They refused to pay attention; stubbornly they turned their backs and stopped up their ears.... So the LORD Almighty was very angry. 'When I called, they did not listen; so when they called, I would not listen,' says the LORD Almighty" (Zech. 7:11 – 13).

JULY 2

UNTO YOU do I cry, O Lord my Rock, be not deaf and silent to me, lest,
if You be silent to me, I become like those going down to the pit [the grave].

Psalm 28:1 Amplified

From the pen of Charles Spurgeon:

Crying out is a natural way to express our sorrow and a suitable utterance when all other methods of appeal have failed. But our cries must be directed to the Lord alone, for crying out to mankind is a waste. When we consider the readiness of the Lord to hear us, plus His ability to help, we see good reason for directing all appeals immediately to "the God of our salvation" (Ps. 68:19 KJV). "Call[ing] to … the rocks" (Rev. 6:16) in the day of judgment will be nothing but vanity, but "our Rock" (Deut. 32:31) listens to our cries.

"Be not … silent to me." People who simply go through the formalities of faith may be content without answers to their prayers, but those with genuine heartfelt pleas will never be. Nor are they satisfied simply with the side benefits of prayer in calming the mind and subduing the will, but feel they must go further, obtaining actual answers from heaven, or they cannot rest. And they yearn to receive those answers immediately, dreading even a little of God's silence. "The voice of the LORD" is often so fearsome that it "shakes the desert" (Ps. 29:8), but His silence is equally full of awe to a troubled petitioner. So when it seems God has closed His ears, we must not close our mouths, but must cry out more earnestly, for when our cry grows piercingly intense with grief, He will not deny us a hearing for long. What a dreadful predicament we would be in if the Lord should become forever silent to our prayers.

"Lest, if You be silent to me, I become like those going down to the pit [the grave]." If deprived of the God who answers prayer, we would be in a more pitiable plight than the dead and would soon sink to the same level as the lost in hell. We must have answers to prayer, for our case is urgent and of dire necessity. Surely the Lord will speak peace to our troubled minds, for He could never find it in His heart to permit His own elect to perish.

From the pen of Jim Reimann:

As you read David's prayer in its context, notice its turn from gloom to glory as he recognizes the Lord has heard him — just as He hears our pleas for help.

To you I call, O LORD my Rock; do not turn a deaf ear to me. For if you remain silent, I will be like those who have gone down to the pit. Hear my cry for mercy as I call to you for help, as I lift up my hands toward your Most Holy Place. Do not drag me away with the wicked, with those who do evil, who speak cordially with their neighbors but harbor malice in their hearts. Repay them for their deeds and for their evil work; repay them for what their hands have done and bring back upon them what they deserve. Since they show no regard for the works of the LORD and what his hands have done, he will tear them down and never build them up again.

Praise be to the LORD, for he has heard my cry for mercy. The LORD is my strength and my shield; my heart trusts in him, and I am helped. My heart leaps for joy and I will give thanks to him in song. The LORD is the strength of his people, a fortress of salvation for his anointed one. Save your people and bless your inheritance; be their shepherd and carry them forever.

Psalm 28

JULY 3

If we suffer, we shall also reign with him.
2 Timothy 2:12 KJV

From the pen of Charles Spurgeon:

We should never assume we are suffering *for* Christ, and *with* Christ, if we are not *in* Christ. Beloved friend, are you trusting solely in Jesus? If not, regardless of what you may have to endure on earth, you are not suffering with Christ and have no hope of reigning with Him in heaven. But neither should we conclude that everything a Christian suffers is suffering with Christ, for it is essential that the person be called by God to suffer.

If we are rash and imprudent, running headlong into situations that neither God's grace nor His providence has prepared us to face, we should question whether we are sinning rather than communing with Jesus. If we allow passion to take the place of good judgment, and self-will to reign in place of scriptural authority, we actually are fighting the Lord's battles with the Devil's weapons, so if we cut our own fingers we should not be surprised. When troubles come upon us as the result of sin, we must not suppose we are suffering with Christ. For example, when Miriam spoke evil of Moses and was therefore stricken with leprosy, she was not suffering for God (see Num. 12).

Furthermore, suffering that God accepts must have His glory as its goal. If I suffer in order to increase my own name or to win the acclaim of others, I will receive no reward other than that of "the hypocrites" (Matt. 6:2). It is also necessary that love for Jesus and His elect be the driving force and motivation behind our endurance of suffering, and that we truly manifest the Spirit of Christ through meekness, gentleness, and forgiveness. So let us examine ourselves to see if we truly suffer with Jesus, and if we find that we indeed are suffering for Him, may we view those

sufferings as "light and momentary" (2 Cor. 4:17) when compared to "reign[ing] with him."

Oh, what a blessing it is to be in the furnace with Christ! (See Dan. 3:25.) And what an honor to stand with Him in the stocks of public humiliation — to the point that even if there were no future reward, we would rejoice in the present honor. But when the reward is eternal, and infinitely more than we have any right to expect, will we not take up the cross with enthusiasm and go on our way rejoicing?

From the pen of Jim Reimann:

An important point to remember regarding suffering is that even when suffering is the consequence of a believer's sin, God uses it to purify His child — and always for His glory! Here is how Isaiah stated this:

> I have refined you, though not as silver;
> I have tested you in the furnace of affliction.
> For my own sake, for my own sake, I do this.
> How can I let myself be defamed? I will not yield my glory to another.
>
> Isaiah 48:10 – 11

Therefore, as God's children, we should attempt to view suffering through His eyes, for Isaiah also said that it is "the Lord [who] gives you the bread of adversity and the water of affliction" (Isa. 30:20). Notice the use of the words *bread* and *water* here — both of which represent two of the necessities of life. Could it be that the Lord is telling us it is essential that we encounter suffering?

Remember — suffering is a gift of God — "For *it has been granted to you* on behalf of Christ not only to believe on him, but also to suffer for him" (Phil. 1:29).

July 4

Who may ascend the hill of the Lord? Who may stand in his holy place?
He who has clean hands and a pure heart,
who does not lift up his soul to an idol or swear by what is false.

Psalm 24:3 – 4

From the pen of Charles Spurgeon:

Outer holiness is a precious sign of God's grace. A fearful position to hold, however, is that of those who profess to know Christ, but who pervert the doctrine of justification by faith in such a way that they actually treat good works with contempt. Yet it is those people who will receive everlasting contempt on the last great day of God's judgment. So if our hands are not clean, let us wash them in Jesus' precious blood, and thereby lift pure hands to God.

Yet "clean hands" alone will not suffice, unless they are connected to a "pure heart," for true faith takes place in the heart. We can "clean the outside of the cup and dish" (Matt. 23:25), but if the inside remains filthy, we are totally filthy in the sight of God, for our heart reflects our true inner self. The very life of our being lies in our inner nature, which is why it is imperative to have purity within. It is "the pure in heart [who] will see God" (Matt. 5:8) — all others remain blind.

A person who has been born for heaven "does not lift up his soul to an idol," which is nothing but a vain pursuit. The people of the world lift up their souls through empty, carnal delights, while God's saints are lifted up by more substantial means. Like Jehoshaphat, their hearts are "lifted up in the ways of the Lord" (2 Chron. 17:6 KJV). Yet, like the prodigal son, he who longs "to fill his stomach with the pods that the pigs [are] eating" (Luke 15:16) is no better than the pigs. Does the world satisfy you? If so, then you "have received [your] reward" (Matt. 6:2) and inheritance in this life. So make the most of it, for you will know no other joy.

Nor does a person born for heaven "swear by what is false," for the saints of God are people of honor. A Christian's word is his oath — something that is equivalent to at least twenty oaths of others. Speaking falsely will keep anyone out of heaven, for liars will not enter God's eternal house, regardless of who that person professes to be.

Dear reader, does today's text condemn you, or do you have the hope to "ascend the hill of the Lord"?

From the pen of Jim Reimann:

Our theme today is one of a life of purity with "clean hands and a pure heart." Paul too addressed purity, including "truthful speech," in the following passage. As you read, notice that a Christian's life is not meant to be easy, but that it is the believer who truly possesses all things.

As servants of God we commend ourselves in every way: in great endurance; in troubles, hardships and distresses; in beatings, imprisonments and riots; in hard work, sleepless nights and hunger; in *purity*, understanding, patience and kindness; in the Holy Spirit and in sincere love; in *truthful speech* and in the power of God; with weapons of righteousness in the right hand and in the left; through glory and dishonor, bad report and good report; genuine, yet regarded as impostors; known, yet regarded as unknown; dying, and yet we live on; beaten, and yet not killed; sorrowful, yet always rejoicing; poor, yet making many rich; having nothing, and *yet possessing everything*.

2 Corinthians 6:4 – 10

July 5

Trust in the LORD forever, for the LORD,
the LORD, is the Rock eternal.

Isaiah 26:4

From the pen of Charles Spurgeon:

Knowing that "the LORD, is the Rock eternal," let us rest on Him with all our weight. Since there is no excuse for fear when God is the foundation of our trust, let us make a determined effort to drive away all unbelief, endeavoring to rid ourselves of all the doubts and fears that so greatly disrupt our stability in life. A loving parent would be terribly grieved if his child did not trust him. Thus, how hurtful and mean-spirited is our conduct when we place so little confidence in our heavenly Father who has never failed us — and who never will.

How wonderful it would be if doubting were banished from the family of God. Yet we should be careful to remember that old "unbelief" is as nimble today as when the psalmist asked, "Will he never show his favor again? Has his unfailing love vanished forever?" (Ps. 77:7 – 8). David did not use Goliath's sword for long or put it through a lengthy test, but later said of it: "There is none like it; give it to me" (1 Sam. 21:9). He used it only once, during his famous victory when he was but a youth, but it had proven to be the right metal then and therefore he praised it later.

In the same way, we should speak well of our God, for "there is no God like [Him] in heaven above or on earth below" (1 Kings 8:23). "'To whom will you compare me? Or who is my equal?' says the Holy One" (Isa. 40:25). Our enemies are forced to admit there is no rock like the Rock of Jacob. Therefore, rather than allowing doubts to live in our hearts, let us take the entire detestable crew and slay them, just as Elijah did with the prophets of Baal at "the brook Kishon" (1 Kings

18:40 KJV). But let us select as our sacred torrent that which flows from our Savior's wounded side.

We all have suffered trials, but we have never been placed in a situation where we could not find all we needed in our God. Let us then be encouraged to "trust in the LORD forever," with the assurance that "the LORD … is the Rock eternal," and that His everlasting strength will be, just as it has always been, our help and support.

From the pen of Jim Reimann:

Deuteronomy 33 "is the blessing that Moses the man of God pronounced on the Israelites before his death" (v. 1). He spoke of the nation of Israel in general, but also gave specific blessings for each tribe. Benjamin's blessing is much akin to today's devotion, and is actually a promise upon which every true believer can rely. Here is what Moses said of him: "Let the beloved of the LORD rest secure in him, for he shields him all day long, and the one the LORD loves rests between his shoulders" (v. 12).

Christians alone are able to truly rest, secure in the knowledge that our God is indeed "the Rock eternal." What a gloriously strong description of our Lord! Moses, who obviously agreed with the psalmist who wrote today's text, went on to say of Israel, and, in fact, of all believers in God's covenant:

> The eternal God is your refuge, and underneath are the everlasting arms.… Blessed are you, O Israel! Who is like you, a people saved by the LORD? He is your shield and helper and your glorious sword.
>
> Deuteronomy 33:27, 29

JULY 6

How many wrongs and sins have I committed?

Job 13:23

From the pen of Charles Spurgeon:

Have you ever really considered how great is the magnitude of the sins of God's people? Consider, for instance, how evil your own transgressions are, and you will see that they begin to pile up like one of the Alps, ultimately being heaped upon one another. Like the giants of Greek mythology who piled Mount Ossa onto Mount Pelion in an attempt to scale Mount Olympus, you will see your sins as being one mountain piled upon another. What a massive amount of sin there is in the life of even the most sanctified of God's children!

Next, attempt to multiply the sins of just one person by the number of God's redeemed, which is "a great multitude that no one could count" (Rev. 7:9), and you will have some idea of the massive guilt of those for whom Jesus shed His blood. Yet a better way to consider the magnitude of our sin is to consider the remedy provided for it — the blood of Jesus Christ, God's only and well-beloved Son.

God's Son! Angels cast their crowns before Him! The choirs and symphonies of heaven surround His throne! "Christ, who is God over all, forever praised! Amen" (Rom. 9:5). Yet He took upon Himself "the very nature of a servant" (Phil. 2:7), was scourged and pierced, bruised and torn, and finally slain, since nothing but the blood of the incarnate Son of God could make atonement for our offenses. No finite human mind can adequately calculate the infinite value of His divine sacrifice, for as great as the sin of God's people may be, the atonement that takes it away is immeasurably greater.

Therefore, a believer — though his sin is as great as a dark, raging flood and remembrance of his past is bitter — may stand before the brilliant light of the throne of the great and holy God and cry out, "Who is he that condemns? [It is] Christ Jesus, who died — more than that, who was raised to life" (Rom. 8:34). Although the remembrance of his sin fills him with shame and sorrow, at the same time it becomes a mirror to reflect the brightness of God's mercy. Thus, guilt is simply the dark night through which the bright star of God's divine love shines in peaceful splendor.

From the pen of Jim Reimann:

We live in a day when many professing believers think far too lightly of their sins, even making such comments as, "It's all under the blood of Jesus anyway." But this attitude cheapens grace and the infinitely great value of Christ's sacrifice. This is why Paul warns of such an attitude, declaring, "What shall we say, then? Shall we go on sinning so that grace may increase? By no means! We died to sin; how can we live in it any longer?" (Rom. 6:1 – 2).

The proper view of sin, as we have seen in today's devotion, is to consider what it cost our Savior and to adopt God's view of our sin. David acknowledged his sin to the Lord, expressing it in a way it would be wise for us to imitate. May his words become our prayer of confession when the Holy Spirit convicts us of sin:

"I know my transgressions, and my sin is always before me. Against you, you only, have I sinned and done what is evil in your sight.... Create in me a pure heart, O God, and renew a steadfast spirit within me" (Ps. 51:3 – 4, 10).

July 7

Then I passed by and … I said to you, "Live!"

Ezekiel 16:6

From the pen of Charles Spurgeon:

Dear saved one, gratefully consider this command of God's mercy. Note that the command is one of majesty, for in it we see a sinner with nothing in him but sin, deserving nothing but God's wrath, but when the eternal Lord passes by in His glory, He looks, pauses, and then pronounces only one solitary, yet royal, word: "Live!" And it was nothing but the voice of God, for who but He could even dare to attempt to dispense life itself with a single syllable?

This command also was diverse, for when God said, "Live!" it included many types of life. For example, it conveyed judicial life. The sinner is about to be condemned, but the mighty One says, "Live!" so the sinner rises, pardoned and cleared of sin. It also conveyed spiritual life. We did not know Jesus — our eyes could not see Him, nor could our ears hear His voice — but Jehovah said, "Live!" and thus we who "were dead in [our] transgressions and sins" were "made … alive" (Eph. 2:1, 5). In addition, it conveyed glory life, which is the perfection of spiritual life. "I said to you, 'Live!'" and the word *live* rolls on through all the years of time until death comes. Then, even amid the shadows of death, the Lord's voice will still be heard: "Live!" Once again, on the morning of the resurrection, it will be that same voice echoed by "the voice of the archangel" (1 Thess. 4:16), saying, "Live!" And as the spirits of God's holy saints rise to heaven to be blessed forever in the glory of their God, it will be by the power of this same word: "Live!"

This command was an irresistible command as well. Consider, for instance, Saul of Tarsus, who was on the road to Damascus to arrest the saints of the living God. He heard a voice from heaven and saw a light brighter than that of the sun; and then we see Saul crying out, "Lord, what do You want me to do?" (Acts 9:6 NKJV).

Finally, this command was one of free grace. When sinners are saved, it is solely because God does so to magnify His free, unearned, and unsought grace.

Therefore, dear Christian, recognize your position as a debtor to God's grace. Then show your gratitude through sincere, Christ-like living. And since God Himself has called you and commanded you to live, see to it that you live your life in earnest — worthy of Him.

From the pen of Jim Reimann:

Once again, Spurgeon highlights the sovereignty of God in salvation, teaching that the Lord has commanded His chosen ones to "Live!" And lest we miss the fact that our spirit was completely dead — that we weren't "nearly" dead, on life support — Paul reiterates this important point again and again in Ephesians 2. For example, he says, "As for you, *you were dead* in your transgressions and sins" (v. 1); then, "God, who is rich in mercy, *made us alive* with Christ even when *we were dead* in transgressions" (vv. 4 – 5); and finally, "God raised us up with Christ" (v. 6) — meaning that just as God resurrected Jesus from the dead, He "made us alive" as well. This is why Paul also declared that "just as Christ was raised from the dead through the glory of the Father, we too may live a new life" (Rom. 6:4).

Surely this is why Jesus told Nicodemus, "You *must* be born again" (John 3:7).

JULY 8

Show me Your ways, O LORD; Teach me Your paths.
Lead me in Your truth and teach me, for You are the God of my salvation;
On You I wait all the day.
Psalm 25:4–5 NKJV

From the pen of Charles Spurgeon:

When a believer takes his first faltering steps in the way of the Lord, he asks to continue to be led forward like a little child held by his parent's helping hand, as one who desperately desires to be further instructed in God's alphabet of truth. Practical teaching is at the heart of this prayer of David, for although he knew much, he was aware of areas of ignorance, and thus desired to continue to stay enrolled in the Lord's school. Notice in these two verses David applies four times for a "scholarship" in God's college of grace. Inquiring about the Lord's own paths of truth and asking the Holy Spirit for sanctified understanding and teachable spirits would be a wonderful thing for every professing believer to pursue, instead of following their own plans or blazing new paths of thought for themselves.

"For You are the God of my salvation." The triune Jehovah is "the author and perfecter" (Heb. 12:2) of salvation for His people. But, dear reader, is He "the God of [your] salvation"? Is the foundation of your eternal hope solely found in the Father's election, the Son's atonement, and in the Holy Spirit's life-giving work? If so, you may use the following argument for obtaining further blessings: If the Lord has ordained to save me, then surely He will not refuse to instruct me in His ways. What a joyous thing when we can address the Lord with the confidence David reveals in these verses — something that will give us great power in prayer and comfort through trials.

"On You I wait all the day." Patience is the beautiful servant and daughter of faith, for we can cheerfully wait when we are certain we will not wait in vain. It is our duty and privilege to "wait for the LORD" (Ps. 27:14) through worship, expectancy, and trust every day of our lives. As we do, our faith will be tested, and if found to be genuine, it will continue to withstand continued trials without compromise. And we will never grow weary of waiting on God if we remember how long and how graciously He waited for us.

From the pen of Jim Reimann:

Today we see David refer to the Lord as "the God of *my* salvation" — indicating the personal nature of a relationship with God. Spurgeon then asks, "Is He 'the God of [your] salvation'"? If this question offends you, perhaps you need to examine your heart, remembering what Paul said: "Examine yourselves to see whether you are in the faith; test yourselves" (2 Cor. 13:5). No one can grow spiritually, or should even ask God to teach them, as David does in today's text, unless that person has a personal relationship with the Lord.

It was David's son Solomon, who wrote, "The reverent and worshipful fear of the Lord is the *beginning* and the principal and choice part of knowledge [its starting point and its essence]" (Prov. 1:7 Amplified). Of course, to reverence and to worship God requires my submission to Him. If that is the beginning of knowing Him, and if I find myself bristling over this truth, I should consider the following passage of Scripture: "During the days of Jesus' life on earth … he was heard because of his reverent submission" (Heb. 5:7).

If Jesus, the perfect Son of God, submitted Himself to the Father in heaven, how much more must I?

July 9

God ... separated the light from the darkness.

Genesis 1:4

From the pen of Charles Spurgeon:

A believer has two forces at work within him. In his natural state he was subject to only one — darkness. But now that light has entered into him, there are two opposing forces at work. Notice Paul's words in Romans:

> I find this law at work: When I want to do good, evil is right there with me. For in my inner being I delight in God's law; but I see another law at work in the members of my body, waging war against the law of my mind and making me a prisoner of the law of sin at work within my members.
>
> Romans 7:21 – 23

How did this dilemma occur? "God ... separated the light from the darkness." Darkness, by itself, was quiet and undisturbed, but when the Lord sent light, conflict began, for the two oppose each other. Thus, in a believer's life, conflict will never cease until he is completely "light in the Lord" (Eph. 5:8). If there is division in the heart of a Christian, there is certain to be division in his outer life as well. But as soon as the Lord gives light to someone, that person immediately begins to separate himself from the darkness around him. He withdraws from a mere worldly practice of outward, ceremonial religion, for nothing short of the gospel of Christ will now satisfy him. He also begins to separate himself from worldly society and seeks the company of God's saints instead, for "we know that we have passed from death to life, because we love our brothers" (1 John 3:14).

Light is drawn to light, darkness to darkness. Therefore, what God has divided, let us never try to reunite. Let us come out from the ungodly and be "a people belonging to God" (1 Peter 2:9).

Jesus was holy, harmless, undefiled, and separate from sinners; and, like Him, we are to be non-conformists in the world, shunning all sin, and markedly different from the rest of mankind by our likeness to our Master.

From the pen of Jim Reimann:

Spurgeon quotes a small portion of Peter's words today worthy of being read in its context. Notice his reference to darkness and light:

> You are a chosen people, a royal priesthood, a holy nation, a people belonging to God, that you may declare the praises of him *who called you out of darkness into his wonderful light....* Dear friends, I urge you, as aliens and strangers in the world, to abstain from sinful desires, which war against your soul. Live such good lives among the pagans that, though they accuse you of doing wrong, they may see your good deeds and glorify God.
>
> 1 Peter 2:9, 11 – 12

Note the words of Paul: "Do not be yoked together with unbelievers. For what do righteousness and wickedness have in common? Or what fellowship can light have with darkness? ... What does a believer have in common with an unbeliever? ... Therefore come out from them and be separate, says the Lord" (2 Cor. 6:14 – 15, 17).

With these truths in mind, may this prayer of David's be mine today:

> *"I will watch my ways and keep my tongue from sin; I will put a muzzle on my mouth as long as the wicked are in my presence.... Hear my prayer, O Lord.... For I dwell with you as an alien, a stranger, as all my fathers were"* (Ps. 39:1, 12).

JULY 10

And there was evening, and there was morning —
the first day.
Genesis 1:5

From the pen of Charles Spurgeon:

Notice that evening is darkness and morning is light, but when the two are combined, they are referred to by the name given to light alone: day. This is remarkable, but even more so when we consider that the exact analogy is also true in our spiritual experience. For example, in every believer there is darkness and light, yet Christians should not be considered sinners because they have some sin in them; they should be considered saints because they possess a degree of holiness. This should be a very comforting thought to those who are currently mourning their weaknesses, and who ask, "Can I be a child of God when there is so much darkness in me?"

The answer is yes, for you, like the day, do not take your name from the evening, but from the morning; you are spoken of in the Word of God as though you were perfectly holy today — just as you will be soon. You are considered a child of light, although there is still some darkness within you. You are named after what God sees as your predominant quality, which someday will be the only one.

We should also notice that the evening came first. In the natural order of time, we come into this world as darkness, and that gloominess is often our first mournful awareness that drives us to cry out in deep humiliation, "God, have mercy on me, a sinner" (Luke 18:13). Morning comes second, for it dawns when grace overcomes our dark nature. John Bunyan (1628 – 88) expressed this blessed truth quite succinctly, saying, "That which is last, lasts forever." That which is first yields in due time to the last — and, of course, nothing comes after the last.

Thus, although you are naturally darkness, once "you are light in the Lord" (Eph. 5:8), there is no evening to follow — "Your sun will never set again" (Isa. 60:20). In this life, your first day had an evening and a morning, but your second day — when you will be with God forever — will be a day without an evening. It will be one sacred, eternal high noon.

From the pen of Jim Reimann:

The fact that evening came before morning highlights a spiritual truth — that we are born into darkness, but when God saves us, we are reborn into light. And, thankfully, as Spurgeon said, we cannot go back to the darkness. Yet we are still capable of sin, which is why Paul encouraged new believers to holy living, saying, "You are all sons of the light and sons of the day. We do not belong to the night or to the darkness" (1 Thess. 5:5). He also said the following, partially quoted above: "For you were once darkness, but now you are light in the Lord. Live as children of light" (Eph. 5:8). Of course, Jesus Himself described His followers in these terms:

You are the light of the world. A city on a hill cannot be hidden. Neither do people light a lamp and put it under a bowl. Instead they put it on its stand, and it gives light to everyone in the house. In the same way, let your light shine before men, that they may see your good deeds and praise your Father in heaven.

Matthew 5:14 – 16

"Blessed are those who have learned to acclaim you, who walk in the light of your presence, O Lord" (Ps. 89:15).

JULY 11

Tell it to your children,
and let your children tell it to their children,
and their children to the next generation.

Joel 1:3

From the pen of Charles Spurgeon:

By God's grace, in this way of simply telling our children, a living witness for truth will always be kept alive. "The beloved of the LORD" (Deut. 33:12) are to hand down their testimony of the gospel and God's covenant to their heirs, and the heirs again to the next generation. This is our primary duty, for a believer who does not begin his ministry at home will have a testimony that is lacking. The lost are to be sought, and "the roads and country lanes" (Luke 14:23) are to be searched, but home holds a prior claim; so woe to those who attempt to reverse the Lord's order of things.

Teaching our children is a personal duty, something we cannot delegate even to Sunday school teachers or family friends. Others may assist us, but they will never deliver us from our sacred obligation. In this case, using substitutes and alternates is a wicked method, for mothers and fathers, like Abraham, are to "direct [their] children and [their] household ... to keep the way of the LORD" (Gen. 18:19). We are to "tell [our children] of all [the] wonderful acts" (Ps. 105:2) of "God Most High" (Gen. 14:18).

Teaching our children is a natural duty, for who is more fit to care for a child's well-being than those responsible for his actual being? Neglecting their instruction is worse than cruel, for family faith is not only necessary for the family itself but also for the nation and God's church. In fact, Popery (Roman Catholicism), using a thousand scheming plots, is covertly advancing across our nation, and one of the most effective means for resisting its inroads has been left nearly neglected — namely, the instruction of our children in the faith.

Oh, that parents would awaken to a sense of the importance of this matter. Speaking of Jesus to our sons and daughters is a pleasant responsibility, even more so when we consider that it has often proven to be the accepted work by which God saved the children through their parents' prayers and admonitions.

May every house into which this devotional book shall come honor the Lord in this responsibility and thereby receive His smile.

From the pen of Jim Reimann:

Moses instructed God's people to make His Word the centerpiece of their lives. As you read his words, notice Moses' emphasis on our children, and on our children's children, just as we have seen in our text from Joel today.

These are the commands, decrees and laws the LORD your God directed me to teach you to observe ... so that *you, your children and their children* after them may fear the LORD your God as long as you live.... Be careful to obey so that it may go well with you and that you may increase greatly.... Hear, O Israel: The LORD our God, the LORD is one. Love the LORD your God with all your heart and with all your soul and with all your strength. These commandments that I give you today are to be upon your hearts. Impress them on your children. Talk about them when you sit at home and when you walk along the road, when you lie down and when you get up. Tie them as symbols on your hands and bind them on your foreheads. Write them on the doorframes of your houses and on your gates.

Deuteronomy 6:1 – 9

JULY 12

The Lord ... will bring me safely to his heavenly kingdom.
2 Timothy 4:18

From the pen of Charles Spurgeon:

The heavenly city of the great King is a place of active service where the ransomed of earth serve Him day and night. They never cease to fulfill the good pleasure of their King, and although they continually rest, at least as far as ease and freedom from worry is concerned, they never rest in the sense of inactivity. The golden Jerusalem of heaven is a place where we will commune in eternal fellowship with all the people of God, including such people as Abraham, Isaac, and Jacob. We will have deep conversations with the righteous multitude of Christ's elect, those who by His love and omnipotence have been brought safely home and who now reign with Him in glory. We will not sing solos, but with the chorus of heaven we will sing praises to our King.

Heaven is also a place of victory realized. Dear Christian, whenever you have achieved a victory over lusts — whenever, after a difficult struggle, you have laid a temptation dead at your feet — at that moment you have experienced only a foretaste of the joy that awaits you when "the God of peace will soon crush Satan under your feet" (Rom. 16:20), and you see that you are "more than [a conqueror] through him who loved us" (Rom. 8:37).

Paradise is a place of security as well. When you enjoy the "full assurance of faith" (Heb. 10:22), you have a promise of the glorious security that will be yours by virtue of being a perfect citizen of the heavenly Jerusalem. O Jerusalem, my sweet home — the happy harbor of my soul! I offer thanks to Him whose great love has taught me to long for you; but I will offer louder thanks throughout eternity, when I will possess you at last.

> My soul has tasted of the grapes,
> And now it longs to go
> Where my dear Lord his vineyard keeps
> And all the clusters grow.
> Upon the true and living vine,
> My famished soul would feast,
> And banquet on the fruit divine,
> An everlasting guest.
>
> John Berridge, 1716 – 93

From the pen of Jim Reimann:

The believer's eternal home is "the new Jerusalem" (Rev. 21:2), which John describes as made "of pure gold, as pure as glass" (v. 18). And though its physical description is beautiful, its spiritual description is even more glorious:

> I did not see a temple in the city, because the Lord God Almighty and the Lamb are its temple. The city does not need the sun or the moon to shine on it, for the glory of God gives it light, and the Lamb is its lamp.... On no day will its gates ever be shut, for there will be no night there. The glory and honor of the nations will be brought into it. Nothing impure will ever enter it, nor will anyone who does what is shameful or deceitful, but only those whose names are written in the Lamb's book of life.
>
> Revelation 21:22 – 23, 25 – 27

JULY 13

Then my enemies will turn back when I call for help.
By this I will know that God is for me.

Psalm 56:9

From the pen of Charles Spurgeon:

It is impossible for human words to express the full meaning of this wonderful phrase: "God is for me." He was "for us" before the creation of the world; He was "for us," or He would not have sent the gift of His well-beloved Son (see Mark 12:6 KJV); He was "for us" when He delivered the death blow to "his only begotten Son" (John 3:16 KJV), laying the full weight of His wrath upon Him; He was "for us" when we were destroyed in the fall, for He loved us in spite of it all; He was "for us" when we were rebelling against Him, defiantly shaking our fists in His face; He was "for us," or He would not have called us humbly to "seek his face" (Ps. 105:4).

God also has been "for us" through all our struggles. We have been called to encounter a host of dangers, and have been attacked by temptations from without and within us. He is "for us" with all the infinity of His being, the omnipotence of His love, and the infallibility of His wisdom. Arrayed in all His divine attributes, He is "for us" — eternally and immutably "for us." He will be "for us" when "the sky [will be] rolled up like a scroll" (Isa. 34:4) or "like a [worn out] robe" (Heb. 1:12) — "for us" throughout eternity. And because He is "for us," the voice of prayer to Him will always ensure His help, as we see in today's text: "Then my enemies will turn back when I call for help." Yet this is not some uncertain hope, but one of well-grounded assurance, for "by this I will know...."

I will direct my prayer unto You, O Lord, and will look above for the answer, assured it will come and that my enemies will be defeated, for "God is for me."

Dear believer, how blessed are you to have "the King of kings" (1 Tim. 6:15) on your side. How safe to have such a Protector! And how victoriously is your case defended by such an Advocate! (See 1 John 2:1 KJV.) "If God is *for us*, who can be against us?" (Rom. 8:31).

From the pen of Jim Reimann:

Paul's question, "If God is *for us*, who can be against us?" closely echoes David's sentiments in Psalm 56, from which Spurgeon chose today's text. As you read more of David's prayer, notice his focus and dependence on God's Word.

When I am afraid, I will trust in you. In God, *whose word I praise*, in God I trust; I will not be afraid. What can mortal man do to me?... Then my enemies will turn back when I call for help. By this I will know that God is for me. In God, *whose word I praise*, in the LORD, *whose word I praise* — in God I trust; I will not be afraid. What can man do to me? I am under vows to you, O God; I will present my thank offerings to you. For you have delivered me from death and my feet from stumbling, that I may walk before God in the light of life.

Psalm 56:3 – 4, 9 – 13

Let us focus today on the fact that the Lord is indeed "for us," as we see again in these words of Paul: "God demonstrates his own love *for us* in this: While we were still sinners, Christ died *for us*" (Rom. 5:8).

O Lord Jesus, like David, I praise You and Your Word, for "[Your] name is the Word of God" (Rev. 19:13).

JULY 14

Early on the first day of the week, while it was still dark,
Mary Magdalene went to the tomb.

John 20:1

From the pen of Charles Spurgeon:

May we learn today from Mary Magdalene how to seek fellowship with the Lord Jesus. Notice that she sought the Savior very "early ... while it was still dark." If you, however, are content to wait for fellowship with Christ or with only the hope of fellowship with Him sometime in the future, then you will never fellowship with Him at all, for a heart suited for communion is one that hungers and thirsts for Him.

Notice too how Mary Magdalene sought Jesus with great boldness. We are told, "The disciples went back to their homes, but Mary stood outside the tomb crying ... [and] bent over to look into the tomb" (vv. 10 – 11). So if you desire to have Christ with you, seek Him boldly, never allowing anything to hold you back. Defy the world and press on when others flee in fear.

Mary Magdalene sought Christ faithfully, for she "stood" at the tomb. Others find it difficult to stand by a living Savior, but she stood by a dead one. Let us, therefore, seek Jesus in this way, clinging to even the very least thing regarding Him and remaining faithful even when all others forsake Him.

Also notice how earnestly Mary Magdalene sought Jesus, for she "stood outside the tomb crying." Her tears were like a mysterious power drawing the Savior, causing Him to come forth and reveal Himself to her. Thus, if you truly desire Jesus' presence, weep for it. If you refuse to be happy until He comes and says to you, "You are my beloved one," then you will soon hear His voice.

Finally, notice that Mary Magdalene sought only the Savior. She did not care about the angels — she was seeking Jesus. We are told that after her encounter with the angels, "she turned around and saw Jesus" (v. 14). If Christ is your one and only love — if your heart has cast aside every rival to Him — you will not lack the comfort of His presence for long. Mary Magdalene sought Jesus in this way because she greatly loved Him. So let us stir ourselves to the same intensity of affection. Let our hearts, like Mary Magdalene's, be full of Christ so that our love, like hers, will be satisfied with nothing short of Jesus Himself.

O Lord, reveal Yourself to us even now.

From the pen of Jim Reimann:

Spurgeon ends today's devotion asking God to reveal Himself to us. Thus, the question arises — how does He reveal Himself? Of course, initially the Lord reveals Himself to us at the moment He saves us, just as Paul said, "God, who set me apart from birth and called me by his grace, was pleased *to reveal his Son in me*" (Gal. 1:15 – 16).

After we are saved, however, the Lord continues to reveal Himself to us through His Word. Therefore, to fellowship with Him, we must spend time in the Bible. The prophet Samuel, a wonderful example of a life fully committed to the Lord, experienced this very thing. Here is what we are told from his life:

The LORD was with Samuel as he grew up, and he let none of his words fall to the ground. And all Israel ... recognized that Samuel was attested as a prophet of the LORD. The LORD continued to appear at Shiloh, and there *he revealed himself to Samuel through his word.*

1 Samuel 3:19 – 21

JULY 15

Jesus ... appeared first to Mary Magdalene,
out of whom he had driven seven demons.

Mark 16:9

From the pen of Charles Spurgeon:

"Jesus ... appeared first to Mary Magdalene," probably not only due to her great love and persistent seeking of Him but also because, as the context of our verse suggests, she was a special trophy of Christ's power of deliverance. The lesson here is that the magnitude of our sin before our conversion should not cause us to think that we will not be favored by the Lord with the very highest level of fellowship with Him. Mary Magdalene had left everything to become a constant servant of the Savior; He was her primary focus. Many others who were supportive of Christ did not take up His cross; she did, and she spent her entire substance to ease His needs.

So if we truly desire to see Christ often, let us serve Him. Show me those who most often sit under His banner of love (see Song 2:4) and who drink most deeply from His cup of communion, and I will show you those who give the most, serve the best, and abide most closely to the pierced and bleeding heart of their precious Lord.

Yet notice how Christ revealed Himself with one word to this sorrowful woman, for "Jesus said to her, 'Mary'" (John 20:16). After hearing Him say that one word, she knew Him immediately and responded with one word herself, for her heart was too full to say more. Her response: "Rabboni; which is to say, Master" (John 20:16 KJV), was the most fitting for the occasion, for it implies obedience. Saying "Master" is a confession of allegiance that never indicates a cold heart. To the contrary, when your spirit is most aglow with heavenly fire, you will say, "I am your servant; ... you have freed me from my chains" (Ps. 116:16).

If you can honestly say "Master," and if His will is your will, then you stand in a blessed, holy place. If this is the case, He has called you by name, or else you could not have responded, "Rabboni." What do we learn from all this? We see that Christ honors those who honor Him, that love draws our beloved Lord to us, that it only takes one word of His to turn our weeping into rejoicing. It is His presence that creates sunshine in our hearts.

From the pen of Jim Reimann:

People have long debated whether the prostitute who anointed Jesus' feet in Luke 7:36 – 50 was Mary Magdalene. Assuming she is not, as most scholars believe, the two women still have much in common. Both were forgiven by Jesus, who said of the prostitute, "I tell you, her many sins have been forgiven — for she loved much. But he who has been forgiven little loves little" (v. 47). And, the fact that "Jesus ... appeared first to Mary Magdalene" highlights the truth that because she had been forgiven much, she greatly loved Him.

Believer, before we think of ourselves as better than these women, let us remember the attitude of Paul, who said: "Christ Jesus came into the world to save sinners — of whom *I am the worst*. But for that very reason I was shown mercy so that in *me, the worst of sinners*, Christ Jesus might display his unlimited patience as an example for those who would believe on him and receive eternal life" (1 Tim. 1:15 – 16).

Lord, I love You greatly, because I too have been forgiven much.

JULY 16

You will arise and have compassion on Zion,
for it is time to show favor to her; the appointed time has come.
For her stones are dear to your servants; her very dust moves them to pity.

Psalm 102:13 – 14

From the pen of Charles Spurgeon:

A selfish person in trouble is extremely difficult to comfort, because his sources of comfort lie entirely within himself, and when he is sad all his springs run dry. But a generous person who is full of Christian charity has other springs from which to draw comfort besides those that lie within himself. For instance, he can go first to God and find abundant help there; and often he can discover places of consolation in this world at large, his country, but above all, his church.

In this same psalm, David reveals his great sorrow, saying, "I am like a desert owl ... among the ruins.... I have become like a bird alone on a roof" (vv. 6 – 7). The only way he could comfort himself was by remembering that God "will arise and have compassion on Zion" (v. 13), for though David was sad, Zion will prosper, and no matter how low his own condition, Zion will be uplifted.

Christians should learn to comfort themselves in this, seeing how God so graciously deals with His church. And though your path may be dark and difficult, can't you gladden your heart by remembering the triumphs of His cross and by spreading His truth? Our own personal troubles are forgotten as we look not only on what God has done in the past, and is now doing for Zion, but also on the glorious things He has yet to do for His church.

O believer, whenever your heart is sad and your spirit is heavy, try this remedy: forget yourself and your small concerns, and seek the welfare and prosperity of Zion instead. And when you bend your knees in prayer to God, do not limit your petition to the narrow circle of your own life, but send out heartfelt prayers for the church's prosperity. "Pray for the peace of Jerusalem" (Ps. 122:6), and your soul will be refreshed.

From the pen of Jim Reimann:

There can be no doubt that looking away from our own problems to what the Lord is doing for us now, and will do in the future, restores our peace. You may ask, however, why should I "pray for the peace of Jerusalem," when we know from Scripture that lasting peace will not come until Jesus returns? Are we being asked to pray for something we know will not happen? Consider this: perhaps that prayer is designed to accomplish the refocusing of our eyes on our Lord's return and is equal to this final prayer in the Bible: "*Come, Lord Jesus*" (Rev. 22:20).

Remember, at Jesus' first coming, He came as a suffering servant; but when He returns, He will come as the conquering "Prince of Peace" (Isa. 9:6). Yes, He will make war against the nations, but quickly will establish everlasting peace. As you read this account from Zechariah, look for His first and second comings, and notice the emphasis on peace:

Rejoice greatly, O Daughter of Zion! Shout, Daughter of Jerusalem! See, your king comes to you, righteous and having salvation, gentle and riding on a donkey.... I will take away the chariots from Ephraim and the war-horses from Jerusalem, and the battle bow will be broken. *He will proclaim peace to the nations.* His rule will extend ... to the ends of the earth.

Zechariah 9:9-10

JULY 17

Elijah commanded them,
"Seize the prophets of Baal. Don't let anyone get away!"
1 Kings 18:40

From the pen of Charles Spurgeon:

Once Elijah received the answer to his prayer, and the fire from heaven consumed the sacrifice in the presence of all the people, he firmly commanded Israel: "Seize the prophets of Baal. Don't let anyone get away!" Then "Elijah had them brought down to the Kishon Valley and slaughtered there" (v. 40).

It must be the same with our sins — they are all doomed — not one must be spared. Even our "pet" sin must die in spite of its continual crying to be spared. And though it may be as dear to you as Isaac was to Abraham, strike it down, for God struck at sin when it was laid upon His own Son for us. With unwavering purpose, you must condemn to death the very sin that was once the idol of your heart.

Do you wonder how you will do this? Jesus will be your power. You have been given grace to overcome sin in God's covenant of grace, and you have strength to win the victory in the war against inner lusts, because Jesus has promised to be "with you always, to the very end" (Matt. 28:20). So if you desire to triumph over darkness, keep yourself in the presence of "the sun of righteousness" (Mal. 4:2), for there is no place as conducive for the discovery of sin and for recovery from its power and guilt as the close presence of God. For example, Job never knew how to rid himself of sin half as well as when his eyes of faith rested upon God, and then he "despise[d] [him]self and repent[ed] in dust and ashes" (Job 42:6).

The gold of Christians too often becomes tarnished. Thus we need God's sacred fire to consume the dross. Let us flee to Him, "for our 'God is a consuming fire'" (Heb. 12:29), yet He will not consume our spirit — only our sins. And let His goodness spur us to a holy jealousy and sacred revenge against our iniquities that are so detestable in His sight. "Now go, attack the Amalekites and totally destroy … them" (1 Sam. 15:3), in God's strength. "Don't let anyone get away!"

From the pen of Jim Reimann:

Some find it difficult to understand why God told His people to completely destroy their enemies and their possessions, such as we see in His command to Saul to destroy the Amalekites. Yet this practice was foreshadowed when God made His covenant with Abram one thousand years before Saul. He told Abram that his descendants would "be enslaved and mistreated four hundred years" (Gen. 15:13), predicting their slavery in Egypt, and then continued, "In the fourth generation your descendants will come back here, *for the sin of the Amorites has not yet reached its full measure*" (Gen. 15:16).

From this we see the patience of God in withholding His judgment from His enemies for hundreds of years, and we see how the Lord used His people as the instrument of that judgment. And just as they were to destroy everything belonging to their enemy in order to be a holy people, we are to destroy every vestige of sin in our lives. Let us remember the words of Paul, who exhorted us with these words:

> Among you *there must not be even a hint* of sexual immorality, or of any kind of impurity, or of greed, because these are improper for God's holy people.
>
> Ephesians 5:3

JULY 18

[Locusts] do not jostle each other;
each marches straight ahead.

Joel 2:8

From the pen of Charles Spurgeon:

Locusts always keep their rank, and though their numbers are legion, they do not crowd each other, which would throw their columns into confusion. This remarkable fact shows how thoroughly God has instilled the spirit of order into His universe, since we see even the smallest living creatures as much controlled by Him as the rotating planets or angelic messengers.

It would be wise for believers to submit to the same influence of God's order throughout their spiritual lives. Regarding various attributes of Christian character, no one virtue should usurp the domain of another or drain the life of the others for its own support. Love must not smother honesty, courage must not elbow weakness aside, modesty must not jostle energy, and patience must not slay determination.

And regarding our Christian duties, one must not interfere with another. Public service must not be at the cost of private devotion, and church work must not push family worship into a corner, for it is wrong to offer God one duty stained with the blood of another. "Everything [is] beautiful in its time" (Eccl. 3:11) does not mean we may neglect important areas, which is why Jesus said to the Pharisee, "You should have practiced the latter without leaving the former undone" (Luke 11:42).

The same principle applies to our personal position. We must take care to know our place, take it, and keep at it. We must minister as the Spirit has gifted us, but must not intrude on our fellow servant's area. Our Lord Jesus taught us not to covet the highest places of service, but to be willing to be the least of His people. May an envious and ambitious spirit be kept far from us.

Let us feel the power of the Master's command, doing His will and keeping rank with the rest of His troops.

Let us examine today whether we are "keep[ing] the unity of the Spirit through the bond of peace" (Eph. 4:3), and let our prayer be that in all the churches of the Lord Jesus, peace and order may prevail.

From the pen of Jim Reimann:

Church unity is a major theme of Ephesians, as we see from the context of Spurgeon's final quote today:

> Be completely humble and gentle; be patient, bearing with one another in love. Make every effort to keep the unity of the Spirit through the bond of peace. There is one body and one Spirit — just as you were called to one hope when you were called — one Lord, one faith, one baptism; one God and Father of all, who is over all and through all and in all. But to each one of us grace has been given as Christ apportioned it.... It was he who gave some to be apostles, some to be prophets, some to be evangelists, and some to be pastors and teachers, to prepare God's people for works of service, so that the body of Christ may be built up until we all reach unity in the faith.
>
> Ephesians 4:2-7, 11-13

Although today we see division, let us persevere, for someday unity will be reality; for it is "his will according to his good pleasure ... to bring all things in heaven and on earth together under one head, even Christ.... God ... appointed him to be head over everything for the church" (Eph. 1:9 – 10, 22).

JULY 19

A bruised reed he will not break,
and a smoldering wick he will not snuff out.

Matthew 12:20

From the pen of Charles Spurgeon:

What could be weaker than "a bruised reed" or "a smoldering wick"? A reed growing in a marsh or on a riverbank will promptly snap when a wild bird lands on it and is quickly bruised and broken when a person's foot simply brushes against it. Plus, every wind blowing across the river moves it to and fro. It is hard to imagine anything more fragile, or something whose existence is more in jeopardy, than "a bruised reed." Yet let's consider "a smoldering wick." It is true it has a spark within, but it is nearly smothered. Since even the breath of a baby could blow it out, nothing could have a more precarious existence than the flame of "a smoldering wick."

Although the weakest of things are described in our text, Jesus says of them, in effect, "I will not break a bruised reed or snuff out a smoldering wick." Some of God's children have been made strong to do mighty works for Him, for He has His Samsons here and there who can pick up Gaza's gates and carry them to the top of the hill (see Judg. 16:3). He has a few amazingly powerful people who are like lions, but the majority of His people are a timid, trembling race. They are like a fearful flock of starlings frightened by every passerby. When temptation comes they are trapped like birds in a net, and when trials threaten they nearly faint. Their frail boat is tossed about by every crest of the waves while they drift along, floating on the tides like a weak seabird — without strength, wisdom, or foresight.

Yet, as weak as they are — and because they are so weak — this promise is made especially for them. What love and kindness! Oh, how it reveals the compassion of Jesus — so gentle, tender, and considerate. Therefore, we need never shrink back from His touch or fear a harsh word from Him, for though He may have every reason to rebuke us for our weakness, He will not. "A bruised reed" need never fear being struck by Him, nor "a smoldering wick" fear His drenching frown.

From the pen of Jim Reimann:

Matthew attributes Isaiah's description of the Messiah to Jesus in today's text. The Lord was healing people of various diseases, proving to Matthew that He was the "chosen one." The following is today's quote in its context from Isaiah:

> Here is my servant, whom I uphold, my chosen one in whom I delight; I will put my Spirit on him and he will bring justice to the nations. He will not shout or cry out, or raise his voice in the streets. *A bruised reed he will not break, and a smoldering wick he will not snuff out.* In faithfulness he will bring forth justice; he will not falter or be discouraged till he establishes justice on earth. In his law the islands will put their hope.... I, the LORD, have called you in righteousness; I will take hold of your hand. I will keep you and will make you to be a covenant for the people and a light for the Gentiles, to open eyes that are blind, to free captives from prison and to release from the dungeon those who sit in darkness. I am the LORD; that is my name! I will not give my glory to another or my praise to idols.

Isaiah 42:1 – 4, 6 – 8

Lord, I thank You that although at times I am as weak as "a bruised reed," You "have drawn [me] with loving-kindness" (Jer. 31:3).

JULY 20

Now why go to Egypt to drink water from the Shihor?

Jeremiah 2:18

From the pen of Charles Spurgeon:

Through numerous miracles, various mercies, and extraordinary deliverances, Jehovah had proved Himself worthy of Israel's trust. Yet they tore down the hedges whereby God had protected and enclosed them as His sacred garden. They forsook their own true and living God and followed after false gods instead. Still, the Lord constantly reproved them for their infatuation with other gods, with today's text being one such instance of His admonishment of them. In effect He asks, "Why go to Egypt to drink water from such a muddy river? Why wander so far away when you have your own cool stream flowing from Lebanon? Why do you forsake Jerusalem to turn aside to 'Memphis and Tahpanhes' (Jer. 2:16) in Egypt? Why are you so extraordinarily focused on mischief that you cannot be content with what is good and healthy, but would rather follow after what is evil and deceitful?" Perhaps there is a word of reason and warning to Christians in this.

O true believer, called by God's grace and washed in "the precious blood of Christ" (1 Peter 1:19), you have tasted something far better to drink — the fellowship of Christ — than the muddy river of this world's pleasure could offer you. You have been given the joy of seeing Jesus and resting your head on His shoulder. Can the trivialities, the music, the recognition, and the revelry of this earth ever bring you contentment after that? After eating "the bread of angels" (Ps. 78:25), can you now be satisfied by the food of pigs? (See Luke 15:16.) As Samuel Rutherford (1600? – 1661), the Scottish Presbyterian preacher, said, "I have tasted Christ's own manna, and it has soured my taste for the bread of this world's joys."

It should be the same with you. If you are wandering after the waters of Egypt, return quickly to the only "spring of living water" (Jer. 2:13). The water of the Shihor (Nile River) may be sweet to the Egyptians, but will be nothing but bitterness to you. Thus Jesus asks you today: "What do you have to do with the 'water' of this world?"

How will you answer Him?

From the pen of Jim Reimann:

When Moses was on Mount Sinai we are told he "was there with the LORD forty days and forty nights without eating bread or drinking water" (Ex. 34:28). Obviously the Lord fully met his needs during that time. The same is true for every believer today. This is why John recorded these life-sustaining words from the life of Christ:

On the last and greatest day of the Feast, Jesus stood and said in a loud voice, "If anyone is thirsty, let him come to me and drink. Whoever believes in me, as the Scripture has said, streams of living water will flow from within him." By this he meant the Spirit, whom those who believed in him were later to receive.

John 7:37 – 39

Again, it was John who recorded these words of our Lord, "Whoever drinks the water I give him will never thirst. Indeed, the water I give him will become in him a spring of water welling up to eternal life" (John 4:14).

Lord Jesus, may I "hunger and thirst for righteousness" (Matt. 5:6), for You alone are my "righteousness, holiness and redemption" (1 Cor. 1:30).

JULY 21

Why must I go about mourning?

Psalm 42:9

From the pen of Charles Spurgeon:

Dear believer, how would you answer this question? Can you find any reason why you so often are mourning instead of rejoicing? Why are you yielding to such gloomy expectations? Who told you that night would never end in day? Who told you that your sea of circumstances would ebb only after there would be nothing left but long miles of the mud of horrible poverty? Who told you that the winter of your discontent would last from frost to frost and from snow, ice, and hail to deeper snow and an even heavier storm of despair?

Don't you know that day follows night, rain follows drought, and spring and summer follow winter? Then have hope! And hope forever! God will never fail you. Don't you know that your God loves you in the midst of all this? Remember, even when darkness hides the mountains, they are still there and are as real as they are during the day, just as God's love is as faithfully yours in your darkest times as it was in your brightest moments. No father exercises correction continually, and your Lord hates "the rod of discipline" (Prov. 22:15) as much as you do. He uses it only in order to make you willing to receive that which is for your eternal good.

Someday you will climb Jacob's ladder with the angels (see Gen. 28:12) and behold Him who sits at its very top — your covenant God. Someday, amidst the splendors of eternity, you will forget the trials of time or you will remember them only to praise God, who led you through them and worked lasting good in you through them. Therefore, come and sing in the midst of tribulation, even while passing through the "fiery furnace" (Dan. 3:17 KJV). Make your "wilderness ... blossom as the rose" (Isa. 35:1 KJV). Cause your desert to resound with your triumphant rejoicing, "for [y]our light and momentary troubles" (2 Cor. 4:17) will soon be over. And then, once you are "with the Lord forever" (1 Thess. 4:17), your joy will never wane.

> Faint not nor fear, His arms are near,
> He changes not, and you are dear;
> Only believe and you shall see,
> That Christ is all in all to thee.
> John Samuel Bewley Monsell, 1811 – 75

From the pen of Jim Reimann:

The composer of the above verse, the Rev. John Monsell (Irish-Anglican poet and hymnist), easily could have asked himself the question of today's text: "Why must I go about mourning?" He outlived his oldest son, who died during the Crimean War at the age of eighteen, and only six years later lost his oldest daughter to death at the age of twenty-eight. Still, as we see from this verse, Christ was his "all in all" (1 Cor. 15:28). He went on to write eleven volumes of poems and some 300 hymns, including "Worship the Lord in the Beauty of Holiness."

No doubt Monsell understood — and lived — these eternal words of David:

> Sing to the LORD, you saints of his; praise his holy name. For his anger lasts only a moment, but his favor lasts a lifetime; weeping may remain for a night, but rejoicing comes in the morning.
> Psalm 30:4 – 5

July 22

Behold the man!
John 19:5 KJV

From the pen of Charles Spurgeon:

If there is one place where our Lord Jesus most fully becomes the joy and comfort of His people, it is where He plunged most deeply into the depths of misery. Gracious souls, come close and "behold the man" in the Garden of Gethsemane, behold His heart so filled with love that He cannot contain it, and so filled with sorrow that it must find an opening of release. Thus behold the bloody sweat as it seeps from every pore of His body and falls to the ground.

"Behold the man" as they hammer the nails into His hands and feet. Look up, repentant sinners, and see the sorrowful figure of your suffering Lord. Pay close attention as the crimson drops begin to bead upon His crown of thorns, adorning with priceless gems the diadem of the King of Misery. "Behold the man" as "[He is] poured out like water, and all [His] bones are out of joint," as He is brought to "the dust of death" (Ps. 22:14 – 15). God has forsaken Him (see Ps. 22:1) and hell has surrounded Him.

"All you who pass by ... look around and see. Is any suffering like [the] suffering ... inflicted on [Him]" (Lam. 1:12). Draw near and behold this amazing display of grief — unique, unparalleled, a wonder to men and angels alike, an unmatched phenomenon. Behold the Emperor of Woe who has no equal or rival in His agony. Gaze on Him, you mourners, for if the crucified Christ is not a source of comfort, there is no joy on earth or in heaven. O harps of heaven, if there is no hope in the ransom price of His blood, there is no joy in you, and those at the right hand of God will have no pleasure throughout eternity.

We need only to sit at the foot of the cross to be less troubled with doubt and despair. We need only to see His sorrows to be ashamed to mention ours. And we need only to gaze at His wounds to heal our own. If we desire to live in the proper way, it must be by the contemplation of His death; and if we desire to rise in dignity, it must be by considering His humiliation and sorrow.

From the pen of Jim Reimann:

Our Savior was willing to humble Himself to identify with mankind, that "we may also share in his glory" (Rom. 8:17). "Being found in appearance as a man, he humbled himself and became obedient to death — even death on a cross!" (Phil. 2:8).

His ministry began with the words of John the Baptist: "Behold! The Lamb of God who takes away the sin of the world!" (John 1:29 NKJV), and neared its end with the words of Pilate: "Behold the man!" As we consider these words, let us remember to take the Father's view of His Son, who from eternity past sees Him as "the Lamb that was slain from the creation of the world" (Rev. 13:8), and who throughout eternity future will see Him as "a Lamb, looking as if it had been slain" (Rev. 5:6).

"I see him, but not now; I behold him, but not near" (Num. 24:17). Someday, however, I will see Him "face to face" (1 Cor. 13:12). "Behold, He is coming with clouds, and every eye will see Him" (Rev. 1:7 NKJV).

JULY 23

The blood of Jesus, his Son,
purifies us from all sin.

1 John 1:7

From the pen of Charles Spurgeon:

Today's text says "purifies" — not "will purify." Yet there are multitudes who hope to be pardoned only once they die. But oh, how infinitely better to be purified *now*, rather than to depend on the mere possibility of forgiveness when I die. Still others believe that a sense of being pardoned is obtainable only after many years of being a Christian. Yet forgiveness of sin is something for the present — a privilege for today, a joy for this very hour — for the moment a sinner trusts Jesus, he is fully forgiven.

Our text, written in the present tense, also indicates continuance: it was "purifies" yesterday, it is "purifies" today, and it will be "purifies" tomorrow. It will always be "purifies" for you, dear Christian, until you cross the river; thus at any hour you may come to this fountain, for it "purifies" still.

Also notice the completeness of the purification: "The blood of Jesus, his Son, purifies us from all sin" — not only from *sin*, but "from *all sin*." Dear reader, I cannot express to you the exceeding sweetness of the word *all*, but I pray that God the Holy Spirit will give you a taste of it. Great are our sins against God, but whether our debt is small or large, the same payment can discharge one as well as the other. "The blood of Jesus, his Son" is as blessed and divine a payment for the transgressions of a blaspheming Peter as it is for the shortcomings of a loving John.

Our iniquity is gone, gone at once, and gone forever. Blessed completeness! What a sweet truth to meditate on today.

Sins against a holy God;
Sins against His righteous laws;
Sins against His love, His blood;
Sins against His name and cause;
Sins immense as is the sea —
From them all He cleanses me.

Joseph Hart, 1712 – 68

From the pen of Jim Reimann:

"Who may ascend the hill of the LORD? Who may stand in his holy place? He who has clean hands and a pure heart" (Ps. 24:3 – 4). And though God's ceremonial law provided purification from sin, it was only temporary. In Hebrews we read:

The law is only a shadow of the good things that are coming — not the realities themselves. For this reason it can never, by the same sacrifices repeated endlessly year after year, make perfect those who draw near to worship.

Hebrews 10:1

Yet Jesus' mission was to provide that perfect purity for His chosen people, for we are told: "After he had provided purification for sins, he sat down at the right hand of the Majesty in heaven" (Heb. 1:3), indicating His mission was fully accomplished. After all, it was Jesus Himself who said, "It is finished" (John 19:30). Thus we may pray with confidence, just as David did: "Create in me a pure heart, O God" (Ps. 51:10), knowing He will do it.

"Blessed are the pure in heart, for they will see God" (Matt. 5:8).

July 24

The [LORD's] ... forces are beyond number.

Joel 2:11

From the pen of Charles Spurgeon:

My soul, consider for a moment the mightiness of the Lord who is your glory and defense. "The LORD is a warrior" (Ex. 15:3) "whose name alone is JEHOVAH" (Ps. 83:18 KJV). The forces of heaven are at His beck and call, as well as legions of angelic "messengers [and all] the holy ones" (Dan. 4:17) — in fact, all "the powers and authorities" (Col. 2:15) — are attentive to His will.

If our eyes were not blinded by the "nearsightedness" of the flesh, we would see "chariot[s] ... and horses of fire" (2 Kings 2:11) encircling the Lord's beloved. All the forces of nature are subject to the absolute control of the Creator: windstorms, lightning, rain, and hail as well as the morning dew and warm sunshine. Each of them come and go at His decree. The stars comprising the bands of Orion are loosened at His command, just as He controls the Pleiades. Land, sea, and air, along with the regions under the earth, are the barracks for Jehovah's great armies. The heavens are His campground, light is His banner of war, and fire is His sword. And when He goes to war, famine ravages the land, pestilence strikes the nations, hurricanes sweep the sea, tornadoes shake the mountains, and earthquakes cause solid ground to tremble.

As for living creatures, they too are all under His dominion, from the "great fish" (Jonah 1:17) that swallowed the prophet to the "swarms of flies" (Ps. 78:45) that plagued "the region of Zoan" (Ps. 78:43). All these are His servants, just as "the cankerworm, and the caterpiller, and the palmerworm [are the squadrons of His] great army" (Joel 2:25 KJV), for "his forces are beyond number."

My soul, make sure you are at peace with this mighty King. Even more than that, be sure to enlist under His banner, for warring against Him is madness, while serving Him is nothing but glory. Jesus — "Immanuel," "God with us" (Matt. 1:23) — is ready to receive recruits for the army of the Lord. If I am not enlisted, let me go to Him at once, pleading to be accepted on His merits alone. But if I am enlisted as a soldier of the cross, as I trust I am, let me "be strong and take heart" (Ps. 27:14), for the Enemy is powerless compared to Him whose "forces are beyond number."

From the pen of Jim Reimann:

The forces referred to in today's text are actually the army of devastating locusts the Lord sent as a consequence of His people's sinfulness. Yet even in this we see the grace of God, for He tells them in the succeeding verse: "Return to me with all your heart, with fasting and weeping and mourning" (Joel 2:12), and goes on to say, "Return to the LORD your God, for he is gracious and compassionate, slow to anger and abounding in love, and he relents from sending calamity" (Joel 2:13).

Note that the Lord sends calamity, but does so in order to cause His people to repent. In fact, later in Joel we see the promise of God's blessing upon the people's repentance: "I will repay you for the years the locusts have eaten.... Then you will know that I am in Israel, that I am the LORD your God, and that there is no other; never again will my people be shamed. And afterward, I will pour out my Spirit on all people" (Joel 2:25, 27 – 28).

JULY 25

In their misery they will earnestly seek me.

Hosea 5:15

From the pen of Charles Spurgeon:

Losses and adversities are frequently the means the great Shepherd uses to bring His wandering sheep home, for like fierce dogs, troubles worry wanderers back to the fold. Just as lions cannot be tamed if too well fed, but must be weakened through their stomachs before they will submit to their tamer, Christians often will be rendered obedient to the Lord only through the discipline of plain bread and hard work. When professing believers are rich and increasing in wealth, they tend to carry themselves too proudly and speak boastfully. Like David, they flatter themselves, saying, "I will never be shaken.... My mountain stand[s] firm" (Ps. 30:6 – 7).

When a believer grows wealthy, is in good social standing, has good health, and has a happy family, he often invites "Mr. Carnal Security" to feast at his table. [EDITOR'S NOTE: Mr. Carnal Security is a character in *The Pilgrim's Progress* by John Bunyan, 1618 – 88.] But if he is a true child of God, a "rod of discipline" (Prov. 22:15) is already being prepared for him. Wait a while, and you may see his material wealth melt away. You may be surprised how quickly the acres of his estate change hands, how soon losses cause mounting debt, seemingly without end.

These embarrassing events, occurring one after another, are actually a blessed sign of God's divine life if they cause him to become distressed over his backsliding and turn back to his God. Blessed are the waves that wash the mariner onto "the Rock of ... salvation" (Ps. 95:1). Losses in business are often sanctified by God for the enrichment of our soul, for if a chosen soul will not come to the Lord with his hands full, he will come to God empty-handed. If God in His grace finds no other means of causing us to honor Him, He will cast us into the deep; if we fail to honor Him while on the pinnacle of riches, He will bring us into the valley of poverty.

Yet "do not lose heart" (2 Cor. 4:16), heir of sorrow, when you are rebuked. Instead, recognize God's loving hand of discipline and say, "I will arise and go to my father" (Luke 15:18 KJV).

From the pen of Jim Reimann:

It often has been said that poverty is easier to handle than great riches, which perhaps is why we see the lives of so many wealthy people end in strife, difficulty, and devastation. After all, as God's Word tells us, "A man's riches may ransom his life, *but a poor man hears no threat*" (Prov. 13:8). Let us remember the words of Jesus: "I tell you the truth, it is hard for a rich man to enter the kingdom of heaven. Again I tell you, it is easier for a camel to go through the eye of a needle than for a rich man to enter the kingdom of God" (Matt. 19:23 – 24).

Before a believer can handle great wealth in a godly fashion, ultimately using it for God's glory, he must go through a time of testing. The key, of course, is the same, whether we are rich or poor, and that is to "fix our eyes on Jesus" (Heb. 12:2). Let us follow the advice of King David, one of the wealthiest men who ever lived: "Though your riches increase, do not set your heart on them" (Ps. 62:10).

May the following words be the prayer of my heart today:

"Give me neither poverty nor riches, but give me only my daily bread" (Prov. 30:8).

JULY 26

The LORD our God ... lifts the needy from the ash heap;
he seats them with princes.

Psalm 113:5, 7 – 8

From the pen of Charles Spurgeon:

As Christians our spiritual privileges are of the highest order, for sitting "with princes" is for the elite of society. And speaking of the elite, "Our fellowship is with the Father and with his Son, Jesus Christ" (1 John 1:3). Nothing could be better! "[We] are a chosen people, a royal priesthood, a holy nation, a people belonging to God" (1 Peter 2:9), and we comprise "the church of the firstborn, whose names are written in heaven" (Heb. 12:23). As princely saints we have an audience with the King, while common people are kept at a distance. Thus the children of God have free access to the inner courts of heaven, "for through [Christ Jesus] we ... have access to the Father by one Spirit" (Eph. 2:18). As the writer of Hebrews said, "Let us then approach the throne of grace with confidence" (Heb. 4:16).

Earthly princes have abundant wealth. But what is that compared to the riches of believers, "for all things are yours.... And you are Christ's, and Christ is God's (1 Cor. 3:21, 23 NKJV). "He who did not spare his own Son, but gave him up for us all — how will he not also, along with him, graciously give us all things?" (Rom. 8:32).

Earthly princes have tremendous power. But a prince of heaven's empire has even more, for he wields a scepter in his own domain and sits on Jesus' throne, for "[He] has made us to be a kingdom and priests to serve his God and Father" (Rev. 1:6), and "[we] will reign for ever and ever" (Rev. 22:5). We will reign over the united kingdom of time and eternity.

To reiterate, God's princes have special honor, for we are privileged to look down upon all earthborn dignity from the eminently high position where God's grace has placed us. For what human earthly grandeur can compare to this: "God raised us up with Christ and seated us with him in the heavenly realms" (Eph. 2:6)? We share the honor of Christ, and compared to that, no earthly splendor is worth a thought. Intimate communion with Jesus is a richer jewel than ever glittered in any imperial crown on earth. Union with the Lord is a crown of beauty far outshining all the blazing glory of any worldly imperial pomp and circumstance.

From the pen of Jim Reimann:

Not only do the Psalms declare: "The LORD ... seats [His people] with princes," but they tell us how gloriously we are crowned. For example, David sang, "Praise the LORD ... who ... crowns you with love and compassion" (Ps. 103:2, 4), while another psalm tells us, "The LORD ... crowns the humble with salvation" (Ps. 149:4).

Remember — our Lord humbled Himself to the point of wearing a crown of thorns that we might be crowned with "the crown of righteousness" (2 Tim. 4:8), "the crown of life" (James 1:12), and "the crown of glory" (1 Peter 5:4). As we have seen today, what earthly crown could compare with one of love, compassion, righteousness, life, and glory — "a crown that will last forever" (1 Cor. 9:25).

And someday we will see our glorious Lord "with a crown of gold on his head" (Rev. 14:14). Even now, "We see Jesus ... crowned with glory and honor because he suffered death" (Heb. 2:9).

July 27

Who shall bring any charge against God's elect?

Romans 8:33 ESV

From the pen of Charles Spurgeon:

What a blessed question! And how unanswerable, for every sin of the elect was laid upon the great Champion of our salvation and was taken away by His atoning death. Thus no sin remains in God's book against His people: He sees no sin in Jacob (see Isa. 27:9), nor any guilt in Israel (see Jer. 50:20), for they are justified in Christ forever. And when the guilt of sin was taken away, the punishment of sin also was removed. A Christian will never receive a slap from God's angry hand nor so much as a single frown of punitive justice.

A believer may be chastened by his heavenly Father, but God the Judge will say nothing, except, in essence: "I have absolved you; you are acquitted." There is no penalty of death in this world for a Christian, much less "the second death" (Rev. 20:6). He is completely freed from the punishment and guilt of sin, and the power of sin is removed as well. Sin may, however, still stand in our way and annoy us with constant warfare; nevertheless, it is a conquered foe for every soul in union with Jesus. Remember, there is no sin a Christian cannot overcome if he will only rely on his God to do it. Those who now wear white robes in heaven "overcame ... by the blood of the Lamb" (Rev. 12:11), and we may do the same. No lust is too mighty, nor any entangling sin (see Heb. 12:1) too strongly entrenched that we are unable to overcome through "the power of Christ" (2 Cor. 12:9 KJV).

Dear Christian, believe it — your sin is a condemned thing. It may still kick and struggle, but it is doomed to die, for God has written its condemnation across its brow. Christ has cruci-

fied it by "nailing it to the cross" (Col. 2:14). So consider sin dead in your life. May the Lord help you live to His glory, for sin — along with all its guilt, shame, and fear — is gone.

> Here's pardon for transgressions past,
> It matters not how black their cast;
> And, O my soul, with wonder view,
> For sins to come here's pardon too.
>
> John Kent, 1766 – 1843

From the pen of Jim Reimann:

"Who shall bring any charge against God's elect?" is, of course, one of Paul's great questions — one for which the answer is obvious: No one! Yet, lest we miss the point anyway, Paul goes on to answer it. As you read his beautiful answer which follows, notice he left no opening for anything to come against us:

> I am convinced that neither death nor life, neither angels nor demons, neither the present nor the future, nor any powers, neither height nor depth, nor anything else in all creation, will be able to separate us from the love of God that is in Christ Jesus our Lord.
>
> Romans 8:38 – 39

As believers, we should remind ourselves that we have been justified — separated from the penalty of sin; that we are being sanctified — separated from the power of sin; and that someday we will be glorified — separated from the presence of sin.

"Praise the Lord, O my soul, and forget not all his benefits" (Ps. 103:2).

JULY 28

Jesus of Nazareth ... went around doing good.

Acts 10:38

From the pen of Charles Spurgeon:

These are only a few words, but they nevertheless are a beautiful depiction in miniature of the Lord Jesus Christ. They are not many strokes, but they are those of a master's brush. And they are true in the fullest, broadest, and most unqualified sense of the Savior, and only of the Savior, that He "went around doing good."

From these words it is evident that He did good personally, for the gospel writers tell us that when "a man with leprosy came and knelt before him ... Jesus reached out his hand and touched the man" (Matt. 8:2 – 3). We are also told that "he anointed the eyes of the blind man" (John 9:6 KJV), and that, in most cases, when asked to speak a word only at a distance, He did not usually comply, but went Himself to the sick and personally performed their cure.

What is the lesson in this for us? It is this: if we truly desire to do good, we should do it ourselves. When you give gifts to the poor, do it with your own hand, along with a kind look or a warm word that will enhance the value of your gift. Personally speak to a friend about his soul, for your loving appeal will have more influence than an entire library of gospel tracts.

We also see that our Lord's method of doing good was through continual activity. He did not only do good when the opportunity was close at hand, but He "went around" on His errands of mercy. In fact, there was scarcely a village or a hamlet in all Judea that was not gladdened by the sight of Him. What a reproof this is to the lazy manner many professing Christians exhibit in serving the Lord. "Therefore, prepare your minds for action" (1 Peter 1:13), "and ... never tire of doing what is right" (2 Thess. 3:13).

Doesn't today's text also imply that Jesus Christ went out of His way to do good? "He went around doing good" and was never deterred by danger or difficulty. He sought out the objects of His gracious intentions. And so must we. And if our old ways do not meet the need, we must try new ones, for fresh experiments sometimes achieve more than our normal methods.

Christ's perseverance and the unity of His purpose are also hinted at in our text. And the practical application for us may be summed up in the words: "Christ ... [left us] an example, that [we] should follow in his steps" (1 Peter 2:21).

From the pen of Jim Reimann:

This closing quote from Peter is much akin to the following words of Jesus: "I have set you an example that you should do as I have done for you. I tell you the truth, no servant is greater than his master, nor is a messenger greater than the one who sent him. Now that you know these things, you will be blessed if you do them" (John 13:15 – 17). Thus, as followers of Jesus, we should strive to be like Him. As we consider this glorious goal, let us also reflect on these words of encouragement:

God is not unjust; he will not forget your work and the love you have shown him as you have helped his people and continue to help them. We want each of you to show this same diligence to the very end, in order to make your hope sure. We do not want you to become lazy, but to imitate those who through faith and patience inherit what has been promised.

Hebrews 6:10 – 12

JULY 29

All that the Father gives me will come to me.

John 6:37

From the pen of Charles Spurgeon:

This declaration involves the doctrine of election — the teaching that there are some whom the Father gave to Christ. It also involves the doctrine of effective calling — that those who are given to Christ must and will come to Him, and that no matter how strongly they may resist, ultimately they will be brought "out of darkness into his wonderful light" (1 Peter 2:9). Still, it teaches the necessity of faith, for even those who are given to Christ are not saved except by coming to Jesus. Again, even the elect must come, for there is no other way to heaven but through the door — Christ Jesus. "All that the Father gives" to our Redeemer must come to Him, thus none can come to heaven except they come to Christ.

Oh, the power and majesty contained in the words "will come." Notice Jesus does not say they have the power to come, nor that they may come if they desire to do so, but that they "will come." The Lord Jesus, through His messengers, His Word, and His Spirit, sweetly and graciously "compel[s] them to come in" (Luke 14:23 KJV) that they may partake of His "wedding supper" (Rev. 19:9); and He does this, not by violating the free agency of mankind, but by the power of His grace. For example, I may exercise power over another person's will, and yet that other person's will may be perfectly free, because the power is wielded in a manner in accordance with the laws of the human mind.

In like manner, Jehovah Jesus knows how to subdue the whole person through irresistible reasons addressed to the person's intellect, through powerful arguments appealing to his affections, and through the mysterious influence of His Holy Spirit working upon all the powers and passions of his soul. In this way, although the person was once rebellious, he now yields cheerfully to Christ's governance, having been subdued by His sovereign love.

Yet how will we recognize those whom God has chosen? Simply by this result: that they willingly and joyfully accept Christ, coming to Him with simple and genuine faith, and that they rest solely upon Him for their salvation and their heart's desire.

Dear reader, have you come to Jesus in this way?

From the pen of Jim Reimann:

The doctrine of election, or predestination, is taught throughout God's Word, but is nevertheless a teaching many reject — often on the basis of "feelings," not facts. Others reluctantly accept it, but only by saying something akin to the following: "I believe in predestination, but only in this sense: because God is omniscient, He foreknew who would ultimately come to Him." Yet Paul separates foreknowledge from predestination as two different works of the Lord. Here is what he taught:

> *Those God foreknew he also predestined*
> to be conformed to the likeness of his Son....
> And those he predestined, he also called;
> those he called, he also justified; those he
> justified, he also glorified.
>
> Romans 8:29 – 30

Thus, from beginning to end, "salvation comes from the LORD" (Jonah 2:9). This is why Jesus said, "No one can come to me unless the Father who sent me draws him, and I will raise him up at the last day.... Everyone who listens to the Father and learns from him comes to me" (John 6:44 – 45).

JULY 30

Whoever comes to me I will never drive away.

John 6:37

From the pen of Charles Spurgeon:

No time limit has been set on this promise. It does not say, "'I will never drive away' a sinner *the first time* he comes to me"; it says, "I will *never* drive [him] away." In fact, the original Greek conveys the meaning as: "I will *not, not* drive [him] away," or "I will *never, never* drive [him] away." This means Christ will not reject a believer at first; and just as He will not reject him at first, He will not reject him to the very last.

Yet what if I sin after coming to Him? "If anybody does sin, we have one who speaks to the Father in our defense — Jesus Christ, the Righteous One" (1 John 2:1). What if I backslide? "I will heal their backsliding, I will love them freely, For My anger has turned away from him" (Hos. 14:4 NKJV). What if I am tempted? "God is faithful; he will not let you be tempted beyond what you can bear. But when you are tempted, he will also provide a way out so that you can stand up under it" (1 Cor. 10:13). But what if I fall into sin as David did? The Lord will "cleanse me with hyssop, and I will be clean; [He will] wash me, and I will be whiter than snow" (Ps. 51:7). For He said, "I will ... forgive all their sins" (Jer. 33:8).

> Once in Christ, in Christ for ever,
> Nothing from his love can sever.
> Anna Temple Whitney (dates unknown)

Jesus said, "I give [My sheep] eternal life, and they shall never perish; no one can snatch them out of my hand" (John 10:28). O weak, trembling soul, how do you respond to this? Isn't this a precious thought to you: that after coming to Christ, He doesn't simply treat you well for a while and send you on your way; but that He receives you, that He makes you His bride, and that you will be His forever!

Therefore, no longer "receive a spirit that makes you a slave again to fear." Instead, receive "the Spirit of sonship. And by him ... cry, '*Abba*, Father'" (Rom. 8:15)! Oh, the grace in these words: "I will never drive away"!

From the pen of Jim Reimann:

Adam and Eve *were* driven from the Garden of Eden as a consequence of their sin. Yes, it was a punishment, but it was also an act of God's grace. Here is the account from Genesis:

> The LORD God said, "The man ... must not be allowed to reach out his hand and take also from the tree of life and eat, and live forever." So the LORD God banished him from the Garden of Eden.... After he drove the man out, he placed on the east side of the Garden of Eden cherubim and a flaming sword flashing back and forth to guard the way to the tree of life.
>
> Genesis 3:22 – 24

Notice the Lord "guard[ed] the way [back] to the tree of life," lest Adam and Eve eat from it in a fallen state. Even prior to this, we see God calling Adam to Himself, for we are told, "The LORD God called to the man, 'Where are you?'" (Gen. 3:9). And what a comfort to know, now that Jesus has provided a way back to "the Garden" that "[He] will never drive [us] away," for now we are His family and "our citizenship is in heaven" (Phil. 3:20).

JULY 31

Those who were musicians …
stayed in the rooms of the temple …
because they were responsible for the work day and night.

1 Chronicles 9:33

From the pen of Charles Spurgeon:

This verse indicates that the sacred music of the temple never ceased, for the singers were to continually sing, "Giv[ing] thanks to the Lord, for his love endures forever" (2 Chron. 20:21). As God's love never ceases by day or by night, neither was the holy ministry of music ever silenced.

My heart, there is a sweet lesson for you in the ceaseless song of Zion's temple, for you too are a constant debtor to the Lord. So take care that your gratitude never ceases, just as "love never fails" (1 Cor. 13:8). In heaven, God's praise is constant, so learn now to practice the eternal hallelujah. As the sun scatters its light around the earth, its rays awaken grateful believers to sing their morning hymn so that through the priesthood of the saints, perpetual praise continues around the clock, adorning the globe with a robe of thanksgiving and a golden sash of song.

The Lord deserves to be praised for who He is, for His works of creation and providence, for His goodness toward His created beings, and especially for the miraculous act of redemption and all the magnificent blessings that flow from it. Praising the Lord is always beneficial, for it cheers the day and brightens the night, just as it lightens our work and softens our sorrow. It casts a sanctifying radiance over earthly gladness, making it less likely to blind us with its glare.

Don't each of us have something to sing about? Can't we weave a song from our present joys, our past deliverances, our future hopes? By this point of the year, the earth is yielding her summer fruit. The hay is in the barn, the golden grain awaits the sickle, and the sun is tarrying long hours to shine upon a fruitful earth, thereby shortening the intervals of night that we may lengthen the hours of our devotion and worship.

Therefore, by the love of Jesus, let us be stirred to end our day with a psalm of sanctified gladness.

From the pen of Jim Reimann:

The Bible tells us seventeen times to "Sing to the Lord." For example, in Psalm 96 alone, we are instructed to do so three times in two verses: "Oh, *sing to the Lord* a new song! Sing to the Lord, all the earth. Sing to the Lord, bless his name; Proclaim the good news of His salvation from day to day" (Ps. 96:1 – 2 NKJV).

Of course, throughout eternity future, we will see the ultimate fulfillment of this psalm and many others. John, who was given "the revelation of Jesus Christ, which God gave him to show his servants what must soon take place" (Rev. 1:1), left us this glorious testimony of what he saw in heaven:

> And they sang a new song [to the Lamb]: "You are worthy to take the scroll and to open its seals, because you were slain, and with your blood you purchased men for God from every tribe and language and people and nation. You have made them to be a kingdom and priests to serve our God, and they will reign on the earth."
>
> Revelation 5:9 – 10

Heavenly Father, just as "Jehoshaphat appointed men to sing to [You] Lord and to praise [You] for the splendor of [Your] holiness," I "give thanks to [You] Lord, for [Your] love endures forever" (2 Chron. 20:21).

August

AUGUST 1

You crown the year with your bounty.
Psalm 65:11

From the pen of Charles Spurgeon:

All year long, every hour of every day, God is richly blessing us; while we sleep, and when we awake, He pours His mercy upon us. The sun may leave us a legacy of darkness each night, but our God never ceases to shine His rays of love upon His children. Like a river, His loving-kindness is ever flowing with a fullness as inexhaustible as His eternal nature. Like the atmosphere that constantly surrounds the earth and that continually supports human life, the benevolence of God surrounds all His created beings. And in His benevolence, just as in their physical environment, "[they] live and move and have [their] being" (Acts 17:28).

As the summer sun gladdens us with rays more warm and bright than other times of the year, as the rivers are swollen by the rain during certain seasons, and as the atmosphere itself is sometimes filled with more fresh, more chilly, or more balmy properties than usual, so it is with the mercy of God. It has its golden hours, and its days of overflow, when the Lord magnifies His grace "in the sight of men" (Ps. 31:19). Among the "special favor[s] ... [of] the lower springs" (Josh. 15:19), the joyous days of harvest are a special season of God's abundant favor, for it is during the glory of autumn that the ripe gifts of His providence are richly bestowed. It is the golden season of realization, whereas the days before were filled with nothing but hope and expectation. The joy of harvest is great. Thus, happy are the reapers who fill their arms with the abundance of heaven.

The psalmist tells us that harvest is the "crown [of] the year," and surely these crowning mercies of God call for crowning thanksgiving. Therefore, let us express it appropriately with in-

ner emotions of true gratitude. Let our hearts be warmed, and let our spirits remember, meditate, and think upon this goodness of the Lord. But let us also praise Him with our mouths, glorifying and magnifying His name, and thanking Him from whose bounty all this goodness flows.

Finally, let us glorify God by yielding our gifts to His cause and His work, for the practical proof of our true gratitude is a special thank offering to "the Lord of the harvest" (Matt. 9:38).

From the pen of Jim Reimann:

Notice how David begins the psalm of today's text with thankfulness for the "harvest" of souls, and only then thanks the Lord for the physical harvest:

> Praise awaits you, O God.... When we were overwhelmed by sins, you forgave our transgressions. Blessed are those you choose and bring near to live in your courts! We are filled with the good things of your house, of your holy temple.... You care for the land and water it; you enrich it abundantly. The streams of God are filled with water to provide the people with grain, for so you have ordained it. You drench its furrows and level its ridges; you soften it with showers and bless its crops. You crown the year with your bounty, and your carts overflow with abundance.
>
> Psalm 65:1, 3 – 4, 9 – 11

O Lord, I thank You for the abundant blessings of this life, but let me not neglect the spiritual "fields [that] are ripe for harvest" (John 4:35). I ask You as "the Lord of the harvest ... to send out workers into [Your] harvest field" (Matt. 9:38).

AUGUST 2

Ruth gleaned in the field until evening.

Ruth 2:17

From the pen of Charles Spurgeon:

What may I learn from Ruth, the gleaner? Just as she went to the field to gather the sheaves of barley, I must go forth into the fields of prayer, meditation, the sacraments, and hearing the Word to gather spiritual food. Just as Ruth gathered stalk by stalk, receiving her portion little by little, I must be content to search for single truths. For just as every stalk helps in making a bundle, every gospel lesson helps in making me "wise for salvation" (2 Tim. 3:15). As Ruth kept her eyes open, lest she stumble among the stubble and thus have no food over which to rejoice in the evening, I must be watchful in my Christian duties lest they be unprofitable for me. In fact, my concern is that I have lost much already — oh, that I may correctly evaluate my opportunities and thereby glean with greater diligence.

Ruth had to stoop for all she found, and so must I. Those with a haughty attitude simply criticize and object, while those with humble, lowly minds glean and receive blessings. Thus, a heart of humility is a great asset toward profitably hearing the gospel, for the soul-saving and permanent indwelling Word of God can only be received with meekness. A stiff-necked person makes a bad gleaner, so I must conquer the vile robber of pride, never tolerating it for a moment.

Ruth was careful to hold on to what she gathered and not drop a single stalk of grain as she picked up another. She was as careful to retain as to obtain so that her gains would be great. But how often I forget what I read or hear, for the second truth pushes the first one from my head, and thus my reading and hearing end in "much ado about nothing." Do I fully understand the importance of storing up the truth? A hungry stomach makes the gleaner wise, for if there is no grain in the hand, there will be no bread on the table. Knowing this, I will work harder under a sense of necessity with a quicker pace to my feet and a firmer grasp to my hands.

Lord, I have an even greater spiritual necessity. Help me to sense it more deeply, that it may spur me onward to glean in Your fields that will yield an abundant reward for true godly diligence.

From the pen of Jim Reimann:

Ruth is a beautiful example of a humble soul eventually being lifted up. Here was a Moabite "gleaner" — a Gentile — living amongst the Jews of Israel. Due to her commitment to her mother-in-law, Naomi, after the death of her own husband, she had no hope of ever finding another husband and having a child. But look how the Lord worked in her life!

Later we see this Gentile, this Moabite woman, become the great-grandmother of King David, the greatest king in Israel; and ultimately see her listed in Matthew 1:5 in the very lineage of Jesus, the Messiah of Israel! Only the Lord God could accomplish such a feat, but a humble heart was the prerequisite for such glory.

Let us remember these words of humility spoken by Ruth to Naomi: "Don't urge me to leave you or to turn back from you. Where you go I will go, and where you stay I will stay. Your people will be my people and your God my God" (Ruth 1:16).

AUGUST 3

As Jesus was on his way ...
Luke 8:42

From the pen of Charles Spurgeon:

In this passage "Jesus was on his way [through] the crowds" to the house of "Jairus, a ruler of the synagogue" (v. 41) to raise the man's daughter from the dead. However, because of His great goodness, Jesus works another miracle while "on his way"—the healing of "a woman ... who had been subject to bleeding for twelve years" (v. 43).

For us, it is enough if we have but one purpose and then focus on accomplishing it, for it would be imprudent to drain our energy on other tasks along the way. For example, in rushing to rescue a drowning friend, we cannot afford to exhaust our strength on someone else in similar danger. It is enough for us to fulfill our one unique calling of God, just as it is enough for a tree to yield one type of fruit.

Yet our Lord knows no limit of power or boundary to His mission. His grace is so abundant that, like the sun which continually shines as it rolls onward in its orbit, His path is radiant with loving-kindness. He is a swift arrow of love who not only reaches His target but perfumes the air through which He flies. Power is continually going out from Jesus (see Luke 8:46), just as sweet fragrances are exhaled from flowers; and power will always be emanating from Him, just as water flows from a sparkling fountain. Jesus, the perfect fulfillment of "the rod of Aaron" (Num. 17:8 KJV), bears the blossoms of miracles and produces the almonds of perfect works of mercy each day.

What joyful encouragement this truth provides us. My soul, if your Lord is so ready to heal the sick and bless the needy, then never be slow to put yourself in His way so that He may smile on you. And if His giving is so abundant, never be hesitant to ask of Him. But be sure to heed His Word now, and always, that He may speak through it to your heart; and since He is found in His Word, make it your priority, turning first to it to obtain His blessing. Then, when He is present to heal, He may heal you as well. But surely Jesus is present even now, for He always comes to the hearts who need Him.

Dear believer, don't you need Him? Only He knows how much.

"Son of David" (Luke 18:39), *turn Your eyes and look on my distress that is now before You, and make Your humble petitioner whole.*

From the pen of Jim Reimann:

A good example of focusing on our one purpose is that of the early church leaders, who said, "It would not be right for us to neglect the ministry of the word of God in order to wait on tables" (Acts 6:2). So they chose "seven men" and turned that "responsibility over to them," so that they could continue to "give [their] attention to prayer and the ministry of the word" (vv. 3 – 4). Yet, as we have seen, Jesus is not limited to a single focus, for He has no restrictions in meeting our needs — but we must go to Him.

The psalmist wrote, "I will not neglect your word" (Ps. 119:16), and since "[Jesus'] name is the Word of God" (Rev. 19:13), may we never neglect going directly to Him. "Let us then approach the throne of grace with confidence, so that we may receive mercy and find grace to help us in our time of need" (Heb. 4:16).

AUGUST 4

I struck all the work of your hands with blight, mildew and hail.

Haggai 2:17

From the pen of Charles Spurgeon:

How destructive hail is to crops, beating the precious grain to the ground. And how grateful we should be when the corn is spared such ruin. So let us give "thank offerings to God" (Ps. 50:14). Even more to be dreaded than hail are those mysterious destroyers of blight and mildew, for they dry the grain to nothing but dust and turn an ear of corn into a mass of rotting fiber; and they do this in a way that is far beyond all human control. The farmer is compelled to cry out, "This is the finger of God" (Ex. 8:19). Were it not for the goodness of God, the famine of the rider on the "black horse" (Rev. 6:5) would spread across the land. The Lord's infinite mercy spares the food of mankind, but in light of the many destructive forces ready to destroy the harvest, we wisely are taught to pray: "Give us today our daily bread" (Matt. 6:11). The curse is widespread, and thus we have constant need for God's blessing. When "blight, mildew and hail" come, they are chastisements from heaven, and mankind must learn to heed "the rod of discipline" (Prov. 22:15) and Him who ordained it.

Spiritual "mildew" is no uncommon evil, and this blight often appears when our work seems most promising. For example, we hope to see many conversions, but see a general apathy, a vast amount of worldliness, or a callous hardening of the heart. There may be no obvious sin in those to whom we are ministering, but there is a lack of sincerity and action on their part that disappoints our desires. From this we learn to depend upon the Lord and learn to pray that no such blight will fall upon our work in the future.

Yet spiritual pride or laziness will soon bring this dreadful evil upon us, and only "the Lord of the harvest" (Matt. 9:38) can remove it. Spiritual "mildew" may even attack our own hearts, shriveling our prayers and acts of devotion. Thus, may it please our Father, who "is the [great] gardener" (John 15:1) to cause us to avoid such a disaster.

Shine, blessed "sun of righteousness" (Mal. 4:2), *and drive the blight away!*

From the pen of Jim Reimann:

Today's text is only a portion of the sentence that reads in full: "I struck all the work of your hands with blight, mildew and hail, *yet you did not turn to me*" (Hag. 2:17). Notice God's purpose in sending the blight: to cause His people to return to Him in repentance. And earlier in Haggai we see the following:

> Give careful thought to your ways. You have planted much, but have harvested little. You eat, but never have enough. You drink, but never have your fill. You put on clothes, but are not warm. You earn wages, only to put them in a purse with holes in it.... You expected much, but see, it turned out to be little. What you brought home, I blew away.
>
> Haggai 1:5 – 6, 9

May these words be a powerful lesson to us! And may we take the words of the following promise to heart, but as we read, let us consider the strong reminder God gives us as to who He is, reiterated more than once: "Tell the people: This is what *the Lord Almighty* says: 'Return to me,' declares *the Lord Almighty*, 'and I will return to you,' says *the Lord Almighty*" (Zech. 1:3).

AUGUST 5

Moses said to the Gadites and Reubenites,
"Shall your countrymen go to war while you sit here?
Numbers 32:6

From the pen of Charles Spurgeon:

Families come with obligations. Thus "the Gadites and Reubenites" would have been unbrotherly if they had claimed the land already conquered east of the Jordan, but then left the rest of the people to fight alone for their portions on the west side. Likewise, we have received much through the efforts and suffering of the saints in years gone by, and if we do not invest in Christ's church by giving her our best efforts and energy, we are unworthy to be enrolled in her ranks. Some are boldly combating the errors of today, while others are excavating the perishing from the ruins of the fall. If we sit on our hands in idleness, we should be warned, lest the curse of Meroz (see Judg. 5:23) fall upon us.

The Master of the vineyard says, "Why have you been standing here all day long doing nothing?" (Matt. 20:6). What is the idler's excuse, when personal service to Jesus, which is the duty of all, is so cheerfully and abundantly accomplished by so few. The difficult work of devoted missionaries and fervent ministers of the gospel shame us if we sit by in idleness. Avoiding trials is the temptation of those who live in ease in Zion; they eagerly escape the cross, yet want to wear the crown. Thus the question of today's devotion is quite applicable to them: "Shall your countrymen go to war while you sit here?"

If the most precious saints of God are "refined in the fire" (Rev. 3:18), should we escape the crucible? If a diamond must be polished on the grindstone, should we be "made perfect" (Heb. 10:14) without suffering? Why should God command the storm to cease from blowing simply because our boat is in deep water? Why should we be treated better than our Lord? If He as God's firstborn suffered the rod, why shouldn't we as His younger siblings?

Only cowardly pride would cause a soldier of the cross to choose a soft pillow and a comfortable couch. Wiser by far is he who, having first resigned himself to God's divine will, grows to be pleased with it through the power of God's grace, and who thereby learns to gather lilies at the foot of the cross, and who, like Samson, learns to find honey in the carcass of a lion (see Judg. 14:8–9).

From the pen of Jim Reimann:

A life of service to the Lord was never meant to be one without difficulties, for God uses these hardships to purify us. This sanctifying work of grace is often compared in the Scriptures to the refining process. For example, Malachi said of the Messiah: "Who can endure the day of his coming? Who can stand when he appears? For he will be like a refiner's fire or a launderer's soap. He will sit as a refiner and purifier of silver" (Mal. 3:2–3). And Isaiah recorded these words of the Lord: "I have refined you, though not as silver; I have tested you in the furnace of affliction" (Isa. 48:10). Finally, Zechariah, in recording God's words, said this: "I will refine them like silver and test them like gold" (Zech. 13:9).

Father, may these words be true of me: "I consider everything a loss compared to the surpassing greatness of knowing Christ Jesus my Lord, for whose sake I have lost all things. I consider them rubbish, that I may gain Christ" (Phil. 3:8).

AUGUST 6

May the whole earth be filled with [God's] glory.
Amen and Amen.

Psalm 72:19

From the pen of Charles Spurgeon:

This is a huge request! To intercede for an entire city requires a stretch of faith, and, in fact, there are times when a prayer for one person is enough to cause us to stagger. But look how far-reaching is this psalmist's intercession! How comprehensive! How magnificent! "May the whole earth be filled with his glory." It does not exclude a single country, regardless of how pagan or uncivilized they may be. It is uttered for all races of people on earth, exempting no descendant of Adam. Yet we must be sincerely working for our Master, or we cannot honestly offer such a prayer. A petition such as this is not asked with a sincere heart unless we endeavor, with God's help, to enlarge the kingdom of our Master.

Dear reader, is it your prayer that "the whole earth be filled with his glory"? Turn your eyes to Calvary and behold the Lord of Life nailed to a cross, with the crown of thorns upon His brow, and with bleeding head, hands, and feet. What! Can you look upon this miracle of miracles, the death of the Son of God, without feeling a miraculous adoration for Him deep within your soul — one which words could never express? And when you experience His blood applied to your conscience, and know He has "blotted out … your sins" (Isa. 44:22 NKJV), you are not human unless you fall to your knees and cry out, "May the whole earth be filled with his glory. Amen and Amen." Can you truly bow before the Crucified in loving honor and not wish to see your King be the master of the world? Shame on you if you can pretend to love your Prince and not desire to see Him as the universal ruler of the earth. Your faith is worthless unless it leads you to desire that the very mercy that has been extended to you may also bless the whole world.

> Lord, "take your sickle and reap, because the time to reap has come, for the harvest of the earth is ripe" (Rev. 14:15).

From the pen of Jim Reimann:

Today Spurgeon challenges us to examine our hearts to see whether we truly desire the lost around the globe to receive the same mercy that has been extended to us. Let us take a moment and do just that. Next let us consider these words of Paul who wrote,

> I have great sorrow and unceasing anguish in my heart. For I could wish that I myself were cursed and cut off from Christ for the sake of my brothers, those of my own race, the people of Israel.
>
> Romans 9:2 – 4

What an amazing statement! Of course, Paul knew he could never be "cursed and cut off from Christ" after the Lord had given him eternal life, but he meant his words nevertheless. In fact, he must have expected us to question this profound statement, because he prefaced it by saying, "I speak the truth in Christ — I am not lying, my conscience confirms it in the Holy Spirit" (Rom. 9:1). Thus, I must ask myself, "How much do I truly care about the salvation of the lost, and that 'the whole earth be filled with [God's] glory'?"

> Holy Lord, may I, like Paul, be willing to "endure everything for the sake of the elect, that they too may obtain the salvation that is in Christ Jesus, with eternal glory" (2 Tim. 2:10).

AUGUST 7

Satan hindered us.
1 Thessalonians 2:18 KJV

From the pen of Charles Spurgeon:

Since the first moment good came into conflict with evil, it has never ceased to be true that Satan attempts to hinder us in our spiritual walk. From every direction on the compass, all along the line of battle, at the line of advance and at the rear and at the dawn of day and at midnight, "Satan hinder[s] us." If we work in the field, he seeks to break our plow; if we build a wall, he works to tear it down; in fact, wherever we desire to serve God in suffering or in conflict — everywhere — "Satan hinder[s] us."

When we first looked to the cross for eternal life, he waged fierce conflicts to hinder us from coming to Jesus Christ. And now that we are saved, he attempts to hinder the process that is perfecting our personal character. Perhaps you are congratulating yourself, saying, "So far my walk has been consistent. No one can challenge my integrity." Beware of boasting, for you are yet to be tested. But it will happen, for Satan will direct his power against your strongest and most well-known virtue. Even if you have been a firm believer thus far, it will not be long before your faith will be attacked. Even if you are as humble as Moses, who was "more humble than anyone else on the face of the earth" (Num. 12:3), expect to be tempted to speak in an unadvised way.

Satan is also sure to hinder us when we are earnestly engaged in prayer. He seeks to stem our insistency and fervency in order that, if possible, we will miss God's blessing. Nor is Satan less vigilant when it comes to obstructing other Christian efforts, for there has never been a revival of faith without a revival of his opposition. For example, as soon as Nehemiah began to "rebuild the wall of Jerusalem" (Neh. 2:17), Sanballat and Tobiah attempted to hinder them.

What should we learn from this? We should not be alarmed because "Satan hinder[s] us," for it is proof we are on the Lord's side and are working for Him. And in His strength we will win the victory and triumph over our adversary.

From the pen of Jim Reimann:

Let us take to heart today's warning to "beware of boasting" over our consistent walk with the Lord, for Satan will attack at our point of pride. We should remember the following verses: "The LORD hates ... haughty eyes" (Prov. 6:16–17); "When pride comes, then comes disgrace, but with humility comes wisdom" (Prov. 11:2); and "Pride goes before destruction, a haughty spirit before a fall" (Prov. 16:18). Paul warned us, saying, "If you think you are standing firm, be careful that you don't fall!" (1 Cor. 10:12). Yes, we must stand firm, but we must avoid pride. Peter wrote of standing firm as well, but also included an admonition about the Enemy. Here is his warning to us as believers:

> Be self-controlled and alert. Your enemy the devil prowls around like a roaring lion looking for someone to devour. Resist him, standing firm in the faith, because you know that your brothers throughout the world are undergoing the same kind of sufferings. And the God of all grace, who called you to his eternal glory in Christ, after you have suffered a little while, will himself restore you and make you strong, firm and steadfast. To him be the power for ever and ever. Amen.
>
> 1 Peter 5:8–11

AUGUST 8

Everything is possible for him who believes.

Mark 9:23

From the pen of Charles Spurgeon:

Many professing Christians are continually walking in doubt and fear, dejectedly thinking this is the necessary condition of believers. They are mistaken, for "Everything is possible for him who believes." Thus it is possible for us to achieve a state in which a doubt or a fear will be only like a bird quickly flitting across the soul, but which never lingers there. Do you read of the sweet communion enjoyed by specially blessed saints of God, only to sigh and complain, "Sadly, this is not meant for me"?

Dear climber, if you only will have faith, you will stand on the sunny "pinnacle of the temple" (Matt. 4:5 KJV), for "Everything is possible for him who believes." Do you hear of the accomplishments great saints of God have done for Jesus, how they have been blessed by Him, how much they have been like Him, and how they have been able to endure harsh persecutions for His sake; but then you say, "Oh, I am only a worm compared to them; I could never attain this"? Yet there is nothing that one saint ever was, which you may not become. There is no level of grace, no attainment of spirituality, no assurance of salvation, and no place of duty which is not open to you as well, if only you have the power to believe.

Lay aside your "sackcloth and ashes" (Est. 4:3) and rise to the dignity of your true position, for you are small in Israel because you desire to be so, not due to some necessity. It is not fitting for you to grovel in the dust, O child of the King. Rise up, for the golden throne of assurance awaits you! The crown of communion with Jesus is ready to adorn your brow. Clothe yourself in "scarlet, and fine linen" (Ex. 25:4 KJV) and eat sumptuously every day, for if you believe, you may eat of "the finest kernels of wheat" (Deut. 32:14), your land will be one "flowing with milk and honey" (Ex. 3:8), and your "soul will be satisfied as with the richest of foods" (Ps. 63:5). So gather the golden sheaves of grace that await you in the fields of faith.

"Everything is possible for him who believes."

From the pen of Jim Reimann:

As we have seen today, we should not look around us at other saints, saying, "I am only a worm compared to them." The truth is, Christ became "a worm" for us so we could be raised up with Him. The Messiah, prefigured in Psalm 22, said this: "*I am a worm* and not a man, scorned by men and despised by the people" (Ps. 22:6). Yes, we should remember who we are and our humble beginnings, but it is also important to remember who we have become in Christ and what our position is today. Paul put this truth in these words:

> He chose the lowly things of this world and the despised things — and the things that are not — to nullify the things that are, so that no one may boast before him. It is because of him that you are in Christ Jesus.
>
> 1 Corinthians 1:28 – 30

Yes, where we are, and who we are, "is because of him"; and if we are in Him, these words of our Lord are as true for us as they were for any of the greatest believers: "My Father will give you whatever you ask in my name.... Ask and you will receive, and your joy will be complete" (John 16:23 – 24). Again — "Everything is possible...."!

AUGUST 9

He appeared first to Mary Magdalene,
out of whom he had driven seven demons.

Mark 16:9

From the pen of Charles Spurgeon:

Mary of Magdala was the victim of a fearsome evil, for she was possessed by not just one demon, but seven. And these dreadful indwelling devils caused much pain and pollution to the poor soul in which they had found lodging. Her situation was hopeless, for she could not help herself, nor could any other human offer relief. Yet the Lord passed her way, and although unsought and probably even resisted by her, He uttered a word of power, and Mary, the poor demoniac, became a trophy of the healing power of Jesus. All seven demons left her, never to return, forcibly ejected by the Lord of all.

What a blessed deliverance! What a joyful change! From delirium to delight, from despair to peace, from hell to heaven! Immediately Mary became a constant follower of Jesus, hanging on His every word, following His every step, and sharing His difficult life. Through this she became His generous helper and was among the first group of grateful "women [who] were helping to support [Him] out of their own means" (Luke 8:3). And when Jesus was lifted up in crucifixion, Mary stayed to share in His shame, for we see her "watching from a distance" (Mark 15:40), but then later at His feet "near the cross" (John 19:25). She could not die on the cross with Jesus, but she stood as close as she could, and when His blessed body was taken from the cross, "Mary Magdalene ... saw where he was laid" (Mark 15:47). She was a faithful and watchful believer, for she was not only the last at the tomb where Jesus' body was placed, but she was also the first at His grave once He arose.

Mary's holy faithfulness and devotion made her the favored one to first behold her beloved "Rabboni" (John 20:16), who called her by name. And she became His messenger of good news to His fearful "disciples and Peter" (Mark 16:7). Thus, Grace found her a madwoman and made her a minister; Grace cast out demons and let her see angels; Grace delivered her from Satan and united her forever to the Lord Jesus.

O Lord, may I too be such a miracle of Your grace!

From the pen of Jim Reimann:

Many believe the woman in Luke 7 who "brought an alabaster jar of perfume" (v. 37) to anoint Jesus' feet was Mary Magdalene, and she is mentioned in Luke 8:2 as one of the women traveling with Jesus. We have just seen how devoted she was to the Lord and how blessed she was as a result. But why was she so devoted? As our text mentions, Jesus had cast seven demons from her. And, assuming she is the woman of Luke 7 (though most scholars disagree), the implication is that she was a prostitute, "a woman who had lived a sinful life in that town" (v. 37). Yet she came to Jesus with tears of regret and anointed Him in a humble act of love. No doubt this is why the Lord said, "I tell you, her many sins have been forgiven — for she loved much. But he who has been forgiven little loves little" (v. 47).

Of course, the converse also is true: "*He who has been forgiven [much] loves [much].*" Thus, may I consider the multitude of my forgiven sins and pray:

"I love you, O LORD, my strength" (Ps. 18:1).

AUGUST 10

The Son of Man has authority on earth to forgive sins.
Matthew 9:6

From the pen of Charles Spurgeon:

Behold one of the great Physician's greatest attributes — He "has authority ... to forgive sins"! While He lived here on earth, even before the ransom had been paid and before His blood was sprinkled on the "mercy seat" (Ex. 25:17 KJV), He had "authority ... to forgive sins."

But does He still have that power to forgive now that He has died? Yes, for what tremendous power and authority must dwell in Him who has so faithfully discharged the sin debt of His people to the very last farthing! [Editor's note: A farthing is a former coin of England worth one quarter of a penny.] In fact, He has unlimited power now that He has conquered sin. If you doubt this, look at His resurrection from the dead! And behold His splendor in ascending to "the right hand of God" (Mark 16:19). Listen to Him pleading our case before His eternal Father, pointing to His wounds and declaring the merits of His sacred passion. What power and authority to forgive! When He "ascended on high" He "received gifts for men" (Ps. 68:18 KJV) — "repentance and forgiveness of sins" (Luke 24:47). Thus, even the most crimson of sins are removed by His crimson blood.

Dear reader, at this very moment, however great your sin, Christ has the authority and power to pardon you — and millions of others like you. And only one word from Him will accomplish it; He has nothing more to do to win your pardon, for all the atoning work has been done. In response to your tears, He can forgive your sin today and give you the assurance to know it. This very moment He can breathe into your soul a "peace [with] God, which transcends all understanding" (Phil. 4:7) — a peace that will flow from the complete forgiveness of your many iniquities.

Do you believe this? I pray that you do, so that even now you may experience the power of Jesus to forgive sin. Waste no time in appealing to the Physician of souls, but quickly go to Him with words such as these:

> Jesus! Master! Hear my cry;
> Save me, heal me with a word;
> Fainting at Your feet I lie,
> You my whispered plea has heard.
> Anna Shipton, 1815 – 1901

From the pen of Jim Reimann:

Our text tells us that Jesus had "*authority ...* to forgive sins," and the issue of authority is an important one. For example, Matthew relates the following: "The chief priests and the elders of the people came to [Jesus]. 'By what authority are you doing these things?' they asked. 'And who gave you this authority?'" (Matt. 21:23). Yet Jesus refused to answer their questions. Later, however, Jesus told those around Him, "All things have been committed to me by my Father" (Matt. 11:27), and after His resurrection He told His disciples, "All authority in heaven and on earth has been given to me" (Matt. 28:18).

With this is mind — that "all authority" is His and that, as a result, "Even the wind and the waves obey him!" (Mark 4:41) — is it too much to believe that He can forgive my sins?

AUGUST 11

Our Lord Jesus Christ Himself …
has … given us everlasting consolation.
2 Thessalonians 2:16 NKJV

From the pen of Charles Spurgeon:

There is music in the word *consolation*, for like David's harp, it drives away the evil spirit of depression (see 1 Sam. 16:23). Thus, it was a special honor for Barnabas to be called "the son of consolation" (Acts 4:36 KJV). Yet it is one of the illustrious names of One greater than Barnabas, for the Lord Jesus is "the consolation of Israel" (Luke 2:25).

"Everlasting consolation"— here is the greatest gift of all, for eternal comfort is God's crowning and glorious gift. But exactly what is this "everlasting consolation"? It includes a sense of pardoned sin, for a Christian has received in his heart the witness of the Spirit that the Lord has "swept away [his] offenses like a cloud, [his] sins like the morning mist" (Isa. 44:22). And if sin forever has been pardoned, isn't that an "everlasting consolation"?

The Lord also gives His people an abiding sense of acceptance in Christ as part of this "everlasting consolation." A Christian thereby knows that God looks on him as standing in union with Jesus; and union with the risen Lord is a consolation of the most enduring kind, for it is, in fact, everlasting.

Even when dealing with a devastating illness, haven't we seen hundreds of believers as happy in the weakness of disease as they once were in the strength of vibrant health? Even when death's arrows pierce us to the heart, our comfort never dies, for haven't our ears often heard the songs of saints as they have rejoiced, "because God has poured out his love into [their] hearts" (Rom. 5:5) in their dying moments?

Yes, a sense of "accept[ance] in the beloved" (Eph. 1:6 KJV) is an "everlasting consolation," for

Christ provides us with the strong assurance of security. God has promised to save those who believe in Christ, so when a person does just that, he may trust that God is as good as His word and will save him. And he may know he is safe by virtue of his being firmly tied to the person and the work of Jesus.

From the pen of Jim Reimann:

The verse preceding our text is: "Stand firm and hold to the teachings we passed on to you, whether by word of mouth or by letter" (2 Thess. 2:15). Then Paul proceeds to share the idea of "everlasting consolation," or comfort. Another of "the teachings [Paul] passed on to [us]" on the same topic is the following:

Praise be to the God and Father of our Lord Jesus Christ, the Father of compassion and the God of all comfort, who comforts us in all our troubles, so that we can comfort those in any trouble with the comfort we ourselves have received from God. For just as the sufferings of Christ flow over into our lives, so also through Christ our comfort overflows. If we are distressed, it is for your comfort and salvation; if we are comforted, it is for your comfort, which produces in you patient endurance of the same sufferings we suffer. And our hope for you is firm, because we know that just as you share in our sufferings, so also you share in our comfort.
2 Corinthians 1:3 – 7

Lord Jesus, thank You for the gift of suffering and the gift of "everlasting consolation." I pray You would use me to bring comfort to others — today.

AUGUST 12

The rainbow shall be seen in the cloud.

Genesis 9:14 NKJV

From the pen of Charles Spurgeon:

The rainbow, the symbol of the covenant God made with Noah, is also representative of our Lord Jesus, who is God's "witness to the peoples" (Isa. 55:4). But when and where may we expect to see this sign of the covenant? "The rainbow shall be seen in the cloud." So when a sinner's conscience is dark with clouds, as he remembers his past sin with mourning and regret before God, Jesus Christ is revealed to him as the covenant Rainbow, displaying all the glorious colors of His divine character and His promise of peace. When a believer is surrounded by trials and temptations, what a blessing it is to behold the person of our Lord Jesus Christ — to see Him bleeding, dying, living, rising, and pleading our case for us.

God's rainbow is hung over the cloud of our sins, our sorrows, and our afflictions in order to prophesy our deliverance. But a cloud alone cannot provide a rainbow, for there must be drops of "crystal" to reflect the light of the sun. Likewise, our sorrows must not only threaten us, but must be falling on us in reality. In other words, if the vengeance of God against sin had been simply a threatening cloud, there would have been no Christ for us, for actual punishment must fall in fearful drops on the one assuming responsibility. So until there is real anguish in a sinner's conscience, there is no Christ for him; until the punishment he feels becomes severe, he cannot see Jesus.

There must also be a sun to form a rainbow, for clouds and drops of rain alone cannot make one unless the sun is shining. Beloved Christian, our God, who is like the sun to us, always shines; but we do not always see Him, for clouds hide His face. Yet no matter how many drops of rain may be falling or how many clouds may be threatening, as soon as His light breaks through, we will see a rainbow. It has been said that once we see a rainbow, the rain shower is over. But one thing is certain — when Christ appears, our troubles are removed; when we behold Jesus, our sins vanish, and our doubts and fears subside. When Jesus walks the waters of our sea, how profound the calm!

From the pen of Jim Reimann:

The rainbow is, of course, a beautiful reminder of God's covenant to mankind: "Never again will all life be cut off by the waters of a flood; never again will there be a flood to destroy the earth" (Gen. 9:11). Perhaps, when we see a rainbow, we also should remember why the Lord destroyed all but Noah and his family:

The LORD saw how great man's wickedness on the earth had become, and that every inclination of the thoughts of his heart was only evil all the time. The LORD was grieved that he had made man on the earth, and his heart was filled with pain.

Genesis 6:5 – 6

Therefore, when we see a rainbow, let us examine our own hearts and lives so as to never again fill the Lord's heart with pain. Let us never again "grieve the Holy Spirit of God, with whom [we] were sealed for the day of redemption" (Eph. 4:30). Let us prepare ourselves for that great day when we "will see the Son of Man coming in a cloud with power and great glory" (Luke 21:27).

"O LORD, our Lord, how majestic is your name in all the earth! You have set your glory above the heavens" (Ps. 8:1).

AUGUST 13

I will remember my covenant.

Genesis 9:15

From the pen of Charles Spurgeon:

Notice the exact words of God's promise. And notice what He does *not* say: "Whenever *you* see the rainbow, *you* will remember my covenant, and then I will not destroy the earth." No, His words are much more glorious and are not dependent upon our memory, which is so fickle and frail; they are dependent on His memory, which is infinite and immutable. The Lord said, "Whenever the rainbow appears in the clouds, *I* will see it and remember the everlasting covenant" (v. 16).

How wonderful that my safety is not based on my remembering God, but on His remembering me; not on my taking hold of His covenant, but on His covenant taking hold of me! Glory to God that the entire fortress of salvation is secured by His divine power. Again, even the remembrance of the covenant is not left to our memories, for we might forget, but our Lord cannot forget the saints He has "engraved ... on the palms of [His] hands" (Isa. 49:16). What was true for Israel in Egypt is also true for us: God did not say, "When *you* 'see the blood on the top and sides of the doorframe,' I 'will pass over' you." No, He said, "When *the LORD* ... will see the blood," He "will pass over [you]" (Ex. 12:23).

My looking to Jesus brings me joy and peace, but it is God's looking to Jesus that secures my salvation and the salvation of all His elect, since it is impossible for our God to look at Christ, our bleeding substitute, and still be angry with us for sins already punished in Him. No, it is not left to us even to be saved by remembering His covenant. There is no "linsey-woolsey" here, for not a single thread of mankind mars the fabric.

It is not *of* mankind, nor *by* mankind, but of the Lord alone. Yes, we should remember the covenant, and we will, by God's divine grace; yet the door of our safety is not hinged there. It hangs on God remembering us, not on us remembering Him; and therefore the covenant is an everlasting covenant.

From the pen of Jim Reimann:

Spurgeon uses an interesting term today, saying, "There is no 'linsey-woolsey' here." The term was common in his time and referred to the mixing of wool or cotton with linen, thus creating an inferior fabric. Its origin and meaning are found in the following instruction of God to the priests for Ezekiel's temple: "When they enter the gates of the inner court, they are to wear linen clothes; they must not wear any woolen garment" (Ezek. 44:17), for the mixing of the fabrics was symbolic of mankind's fickleness and faithlessness. And, since God has promised, "You will be for me a kingdom of priests" (Ex. 19:6), someday we too will be clothed in "fine linen." As you read the following, notice once again that the clothes are God's gift, not something the saved must provide for themselves:

> The wedding of the Lamb has come, and his bride has made herself ready. *Fine linen, bright and clean, was given her to wear.* (Fine linen stands for the righteous acts of the saints).
>
> Revelation 19:7 – 8

Again, let us be thankful for God's eternal memory, for He said, "I will not forget you!" (Isa. 49:15), and on that wedding day, He will clothe us in "fine linen"!

AUGUST 14

I know their sorrows.

Exodus 3:7 KJV

From the pen of Charles Spurgeon:

Just as a child is cheered by singing the words "This my Father knows" (from the nineteenth-century hymn "My Father Knows," composed by Mrs. Maxwell, dates unknown), shouldn't we be comforted to know that our dear Friend and Bridegroom of our soul knows all about us? Let us look at just three of His roles.

1. He is our Physician. And if He knows all things, there is nothing the patient must know. So, nervously pounding heart, hush your silly prying, peeking, and suspecting. What you don't know today, you will know in the hereafter, and meanwhile, Jesus, the beloved Physician, knows your soul and each of its adversities. So why do you as the patient need to diagnose all the symptoms or prescribe all the medicine? This is the Physician's job, not yours, for your role simply is to trust, while His is to prescribe. And you should not be uneasy even if you are unable to read His handwriting on the prescription, but should rely on His unfailing skill to make everything plain in the end, however mysteriously the cure may happen.

2. He is our Master. And unlike our own knowledge, His knowledge is designed to serve us. Thus, we are to obey, not to judge, for, as Jesus said, "A servant does not know his master's business" (John 15:15). Should the architect explain his plans to every bricklayer on the job? As long as he knows his own intent, isn't that enough? The clay sitting on the potter's wheel cannot even imagine into what pattern it will be formed, but if the potter knows his art, does the ignorance of the clay really matter? Therefore my Lord must not be cross-examined any longer by someone as ignorant as I am.

3. He is our Head. And all understanding is centered there. For example, what judgment does an arm have? Or what comprehension does a foot have? If all the power to know lies in the head, why should any other body part have a brain of its own? Isn't the head able to handle the intellectual role for the entire body? Thus a believer, even in sickness, must rest in the comfort that although he himself cannot see the end, Jesus knows all things.

Sweet Lord, now and forever, be my physician, my master, and my head, and let me be content to know only what You choose to reveal.

From the pen of Jim Reimann:

Indeed, we have an all-knowing God. So let us take comfort in these words of His regarding His omniscience:

"The secret things belong to the LORD our God, but the things revealed belong to us and to our children forever, that we may follow all the words of this law" (Deut. 29:29). "'No eye has seen, no ear has heard, no mind has conceived what God has prepared for those who love him' — but God has revealed it to us by his Spirit. The Spirit searches all things, even the deep things of God" (1 Cor. 2:9 – 10). "God is greater than our hearts, and he knows everything" (1 John 3:20). "Great is our Lord and mighty in power; his understanding has no limit" (Ps. 147:5).

I am God, and there is none like me. I make known the end from the beginning, from ancient times, what is still to come. I say: My purpose will stand, and I will do all that I please.... What I have said, that will I bring about; what I have planned, that will I do.

Isaiah 46:9 – 11

AUGUST 15

I will remove from you your heart of stone
and give you a heart of flesh.

Ezekiel 36:26

From the pen of Charles Spurgeon:

"A heart of flesh" is known for its tender pliability when it comes to sin. To indulge an evil thought or desire for even a moment is enough to cause "a heart of flesh" to grieve before the Lord. A "heart of stone" considers great iniquity as nothing, but not so with "a heart of flesh."

> If to the right or left I stray,
> That moment, Lord, reprove;
> And let me weep my life away,
> For having grieved Your love.
>
> Charles Wesley, 1707 – 88

"A heart of flesh" is tender toward God's will, while Lord Will-be-will (a character in *The Pilgrim's Progress* by John Bunyan, 1628 – 1688) is nothing but a braggart and blowhard. It is difficult to subject him to God's will, but once God gives him "a heart of flesh," his will quivers like an aspen leaf at every breath from heaven and bends like a willow in every breeze coming from God's Spirit. A person's natural will is like cold, hard iron, which cannot be easily hammered into shape; but a renewed will, like molten metal, is quickly molded by the hand of grace.

In "a heart of flesh" there is also a tenderness of affections. A hard heart does not love the Redeemer, but a renewed heart burns with affection for Him. A hard heart is selfish and coldly demands, "Why should I weep over sin? Why should I love the Lord?" But "a heart of flesh" says, "'Lord, you know that I love you' (John 21:16). Help me to love you more!"

The privileges of the renewed heart are many, for it is here God's Spirit dwells and where Jesus rests. It is prepared to receive every spiritual blessing, and every blessing comes to it. It is prepared to yield every heavenly fruit to the honor and praise of God, and therefore the Lord delights in it. A tender heart is the best defense against sin and the best preparation for heaven. And, finally, a renewed heart stands on its watchtower looking for the coming of the Lord Jesus.

Do you have "a heart of flesh"?

From the pen of Jim Reimann:

The heart often has been described as "the seat of the affections." Certainly, this agrees with what we see in the Scriptures. And, as we have seen from our text, the idea of a new heart is a critical one for spiritual life. The prophet Ezekiel, in a similar passage, also emphasized the need for "a new spirit," saying: "I will give them an undivided heart and put a new spirit in them; I will remove from them their heart of stone and give them a heart of flesh" (Ezek. 11:19). Later he reiterated the thought with these words: "Rid yourselves of all the offenses you have committed, and get a new heart and a new spirit. Why will you die, O house of Israel?" (Ezek. 18:31).

Thus, "Today, if you hear his voice, do not harden your hearts" (Heb. 4:7). "My flesh and my heart may fail, but God is the strength of my heart and my portion forever" (Ps. 73:26).

AUGUST 16

We ourselves,
who have the firstfruits of the Spirit ...
Romans 8:23

From the pen of Charles Spurgeon:

Notice this truth is declared in the present tense: that at this present moment "we ... *have* the firstfruits of the Spirit." Now — we have repentance, that gem of the baptism "with water for repentance" (Matt. 3:11); we have faith, that "pearl of great price" (Matt. 13:46 KJV); we have hope, that heavenly emerald; and we have love, that glorious ruby. In other words, "in Christ" we are *already* "a new creation" (2 Cor. 5:17) through the effective work of God the Holy Spirit.

This is known as "the firstfruits of the Spirit" because it comes first. Just as the wave-sheaf was the first of the harvest (see Lev. 23:9 – 11), the spiritual life, and all the gifts of God's grace which adorn it are the first operations of the Spirit of God in our soul. The firstfruits represent the promise of the coming harvest.

Therefore, dear brothers and sisters, when God gives us "whatever is pure, whatever is lovely, whatever is admirable" (Phil. 4:8) through the work of His Holy Spirit, these should be for us the signs of the coming glory. "The firstfruits" were always "holy to the Lord" (Lev. 23:20 KJV), and thus our new nature, along with all its powers and gifts, is a consecrated thing.

Yet the new life is not ours to the extent that we should attribute its excellence to our own merit, for it is the creation of Christ, it has been made in His image, and it is ordained for His glory. And remember, the firstfruits were not the harvest itself, in the same way that the works of the Holy Spirit in us at this time are not the ultimate consummation, for perfection is yet to come. So we must not boast that we have attained perfection. Instead, we must "hunger and thirst for righteousness" (Matt. 5:6) and yearn for "the day of [complete] redemption" (Eph. 4:30).

Dear reader, even now, "Open wide your mouth and [God] will fill it" (Ps. 81:10). Let the blessings of what you currently possess create in you a sacred "greed" for more grace. Groan deeply within yourself for higher levels of consecration, and your Lord will grant them to you, for He "is able to do immeasurably more than all we ask or [even] imagine" (Eph. 3:20).

From the pen of Jim Reimann:

As Spurgeon said, "The firstfruits were not the harvest itself." Paul stated it this way: "Not that I have already obtained all this, or have already been made perfect, but I press on to take hold of that for which Christ Jesus took hold of me" (Phil. 3:12). And in another letter he directly addressed the gift of Christ Himself as our firstfruits, saying,

> If only for this life we have hope in Christ, we are to be pitied more than all men. But Christ has indeed been raised from the dead, the firstfruits of those who have fallen asleep.... For as in Adam all die, so in Christ all will be made alive. But each in his own turn: Christ, the firstfruits; then, when he comes, those who belong to him.
> 1 Corinthians 15:19 – 20, 22 – 23

Not only is Christ our firstfruits, but thankfully, we are His as well, for James declared: "He chose to give us birth through the word of truth, that we might be a kind of firstfruits of all he created" (James 1:18).

AUGUST 17

This sickness will not end in death.

John 11:4

From the pen of Charles Spurgeon:

From our Lord's words here we learn there is a limit to sickness, for it is restrained by Him, and there is thus an ultimate end beyond which it can go. In this passage, Lazarus might pass through death, but death was not to be the ultimate end of his sickness. In fact, in all sickness, the Lord says to the "waves" of pain, "This far you may come and no farther; here is where your proud waves halt" (Job 38:11). His unchanging purpose is not the *destruction*, but the *instruction* of His people. His wisdom hangs the thermometer at the furnace door, and He regulates the heat. So what may we learn regarding God's limit?

1. The limit is comprehensive. We should be encouraged to know that our sovereign God has limited the time, type, intensity, repetition, and effects of all our sicknesses. Each throb of pain is decreed, each sleepless hour predestined, each relapse ordained, each depression of our spirit foreknown, and each sanctifying result eternally purposed by Him. Nothing large or small escapes the ordaining hand of Him who says, "Even the very hairs of your head are all numbered" (Matt. 10:30).

2. The limit is adjusted by God's wisdom according to our strength, to the designed purpose, and to the amount of grace extended. Afflictions do not come in a haphazard way, but the intensity of every stroke of "the rod" (Prov. 22:15) is precisely measured. He who made no mistakes in apportioning the clouds or in meting out the heavens commits no errors in prescribing the ingredients that comprise the medicine of our souls. We cannot suffer too much or be relieved too late.

3. The limit is tenderly ordained. The scalpel of the heavenly Surgeon never cuts deeper than absolutely necessary, "For he does not willingly bring affliction or grief to the children of men" (Lam. 3:33). A mother's heart will cry, "Spare my child!"; but no mother is more compassionate than our gracious God. And when we consider how "strong-mouthed" we are, it is a wonder that we are not bridled by a sharper bit.

What a consoling thought that He who has fixed the limits of our *habitation* has also fixed the limits of our *tribulation*.

From the pen of Jim Reimann:

Some believers today would have had Lazarus "claim" his illness away. Yet even if that were possible, think of what we would have missed seeing — the power of Jesus to raise the dead! Jesus Himself said, "This sickness ... is for God's glory so that God's Son may be glorified through it" (John 11:4). And in the story of the "man ... born blind" (John 9:2), Jesus said, regarding his blindness, "This happened so that the work of God might be displayed in his life" (v. 3).

Thus, when it comes to sickness, we must keep in mind there may be a purpose greater than our own — that God may be glorified! May the words of Paul become mine: "If I must boast, I will boast of the things that show my weakness" (2 Cor. 11:30). And may I also remember these words of Peter, who wrote:

> For a little while you may have had to suffer grief in all kinds of trials. These have come so that your faith ... may be proved genuine and may result in praise, glory and honor when Jesus Christ is revealed.
>
> 1 Peter 1:6 – 7

AUGUST 18

Then they offered [Jesus] wine mixed with myrrh,
but he did not take it.

Mark 15:23

From the pen of Charles Spurgeon:

A precious truth is expressed in the fact that the Savior refused to take the cup of "wine mixed with myrrh" to His lips. In eternity past the Son of God looked down upon our globe from the heights of heaven and considered His future deep descent to the utmost depths of human misery. He weighed the vast total of all the agony His atonement for sin would require, yet He refused to shrink from even one "jot" ["the smallest letter" (Matt. 5:18)] of suffering. He solemnly determined that to offer a sufficient atoning sacrifice, He must go the whole way — from the highest to the lowest — from the throne of highest glory to the cross of deepest woe.

The cup of myrrh, with its numbing properties, would have offered Him a little relief from the severity of His extreme misery, which is why He refused it. He would not stop short of all He had undertaken to suffer for His people. Yet how many of us have longed for relief from our suffering when that very relief would have been damaging to us.

Dear reader, do you ever pray to be relieved from some difficult place of service or severe suffering with an irritable and willful eagerness? If our sovereign God were to answer your plea, He would be removing your deepest desire with one swift stroke. Christian, allow me to ask, "If you desire for your loved one to live, but God will be dishonored as a result, could you put away the temptation to ask for healing and simply pray, 'May your will be done'" (Matt. 26:42)?

Oh, how sweet it would be for us to pray:

My Lord, although I would rather not suffer, if I can honor You more by suffering, and if the loss of everything I have on earth would bring You glory, then may it be. I refuse the comfort, if it gets in the way of Your honor.

Oh, that we would walk more in the footsteps of our Lord, that we would cheerfully endure trials for His sake, and that we would willingly and promptly put away the thought of living for ourselves and for comfort when it interferes with finishing the work He has given us to do.

Of course, great grace would be needed. But great grace has been provided!

From the pen of Jim Reimann:

Many misunderstand why Jesus was offered "the wine mixed with myrrh" on the cross, assuming it was simply another act of cruelty. Yet it was actually one of the few compassionate deeds extended to Him. Myrrh, when ingested, is an intoxicant, and is still used to this day to reduce pain, especially in parts of the Middle and Far East. By refusing the myrrh, Jesus refused any shortcut in His mission to "make atonement for the sins of the people" (Heb. 2:17). When it comes to suffering, we should remember His words uttered shortly before He went to the cross: "I have set you an example that you should do as I have done for you" (John 13:15).

May I remember these words of His: "What good will it be for a man if he gains the whole world, yet forfeits his soul?" (Matt. 16:26). And may this prayer of the psalmist David be the pure expression of my heart today:

"You are my Lord; apart from you I have no good thing" (Ps. 16:2).

AUGUST 19

Pull me out of the net which they have secretly laid for me,
for You are my strength.

Psalm 31:4 NKJV

From the pen of Charles Spurgeon:

Our spiritual foes are of the serpent's brood — those who seek to ensnare us through subtle deception. And the prayer of our text indicates the possibility of a believer being trapped like a bird. Also, the fact that the satanic fowler does his work so skillfully shows that naïve believers are often quickly caught in his net. This verse, however, asks that the captive be delivered even from Satan's trap. Certainly this is an appropriate petition and one that can be granted, for eternal Love can rescue a saint even "from the lion's mouth" (2 Tim. 4:17) and "from the depths of the grave" (Jonah 2:2).

It may require a swift tug to save a soul from the net of temptations and a mighty pull to extricate a person from the snares of malicious cunning, but the Lord is equal to any and every emergency, and even the most skillfully placed nets of the hunter will never be able to hold His chosen ones. Yet woe to those who are so clever at the laying of nets, for they who tempt others will be destroyed themselves.

"For You are my strength." What an inexpressible sweetness is found in these few words. How joyfully may we encounter difficult tasks, or cheerfully endure great suffering, when we can lay hold of the Lord's heavenly strength. His divine power will confound the politics of our enemies, frustrate their deceitful tricks, and, in fact, render all their work totally useless. Happy is the person who has such matchless might employed on his side. Our own strength would be of little use once we are embarrassed by becoming entrapped in the nets of such hellish cunning, but the Lord's strength is always available. We have only to invoke it, and we will find it close at hand.

If, by faith, we are depending solely on the strength of the mighty God of Israel, we may use our holy reliance *upon* Him to plead our case *before* Him in prayer.

> Lord, evermore Your face we seek:
> Tempted we are, and poor, and weak;
> Keep us with lowly hearts, and meek.
> Let us not fall. Let us not fall.
>
> Mary Bowly Peters, 1813 – 56

From the pen of Jim Reimann:

The prophet Jeremiah had many enemies, and, like Jesus, even his friends turned against him. As you read his complaint below, be sure to notice his focus on the Lord's protection and his resulting praise:

All my friends are waiting for me to slip, saying, "Perhaps he will be deceived; then we will prevail over him and take our revenge on him." But the LORD is with me like a mighty warrior; so my persecutors will stumble and not prevail. They will fail and be thoroughly disgraced; their dishonor will never be forgotten. *O LORD Almighty, you who examine the righteous and probe the heart and mind, let me see your vengeance upon them, for to you I have committed my cause.* Sing to the LORD! Give praise to the LORD! He rescues the life of the needy from the hands of the wicked.

Jeremiah 20:10 – 13

AUGUST 20

They restored Jerusalem as far as the Broad Wall.

Nehemiah 3:8

From the pen of Charles Spurgeon:

Well-fortified cities of old had broad walls, as did Jerusalem in her glory. Likewise, "the new Jerusalem" (Rev. 3:12) must be surrounded and protected by "the Broad Wall" of nonconformity to the world and of separation from its customs and spirit. Yet the tendency today is to break down that holy barrier and thereby make the distinction between the church and the world merely nominal at best. Professing Christians are no longer strict and puritanical, for questionable books are pervasive, frivolous pursuits are indulged, and a general carelessness threatens to deprive the Lord's "peculiar people" (1 Peter 2:9 KJV) of the sacred distinctives which separate them from sinners. It will not be a good day for the church or the world once their proposed merger is complete — once "the sons of God" and "the daughters of men" (Gen. 6:2) become one — for then another flood of the Lord's wrath will be ushered in.

Therefore, beloved reader, make it your aim — in heart, in speech, in dress, in action — to maintain "the Broad Wall," remembering "that friendship with the world is hatred toward God" (James 4:4).

"The Broad Wall" provided a pleasant place of recreation for the inhabitants of Jerusalem, for it offered commanding views of the surrounding countryside. What a beautiful picture this is of the Lord's "broad" commandments, in which we walk in liberty in communion with Jesus, overlooking the scenes of earth while also looking farther out to the glories of heaven. Separated from the world and denying ourselves all ungodliness and "sinful desires" (1 Peter 2:11), we are nevertheless not in prison or restricted within narrow limits. No! "I … walk about in freedom, for I have sought out your precepts" (Ps. 119:45).

Dear reader, determine today "to live by [God's] decrees" (1 Kings 8:61). And, just as friends met friends on "the Broad Wall," meet with your Lord through holy prayer and meditation. You have the right to walk the "wall" of salvation, for you are "the Lord's freedman" (1 Cor. 7:22) of His royal city — a citizen of the city of heaven.

From the pen of Jim Reimann:

Spurgeon quotes one phrase today from Solomon's advice to the citizens of Jerusalem at the dedication of the temple. Let us obey his words, as Christians whose "citizenship is in heaven" (Phil. 3:20) — so the world may know we are indeed a "peculiar people" whose "God is God" (Deut. 10:17).

Praise be to the LORD, who has given rest to his people Israel just as he promised. Not one word has failed of all the good promises he gave through his servant Moses. May the LORD our God be with us as he was with our fathers; may he never leave us nor forsake us. *May he turn our hearts to him, to walk in all his ways and to keep the commands, decrees and regulations he gave our fathers.* And may these words of mine, which I have prayed before the LORD, be near to the LORD our God day and night, that he may uphold the cause of his servant and the cause of his people Israel according to each day's need, so that all the peoples of the earth may know that the LORD is God and that there is no other. *But your hearts must be fully committed to the LORD our God, to live by his decrees and obey his commands.*

1 Kings 8:56 – 61

AUGUST 21

I have not said to Jacob's descendants,
"Seek me in vain."

Isaiah 45:19

From the pen of Charles Spurgeon:

We can receive much comfort by considering what God has *not* said. What He *has* said is inexpressibly full of comfort and delight, but what He has *not* said is no less rich in consolation. For example, it was one of these "not saids" which preserved the kingdom of Israel in the days of "Jeroboam son of Jehoash," for "the LORD *had not said* he would blot out the name of Israel from under heaven" (2 Kings 14:27).

Our text gives us the assurance God will answer prayer, because He has "*not said* to Jacob's descendants, 'Seek me in vain.'" Those of you who expect only the worst in life, let your doubts and fears say what they will, but God has not cut you off from His mercy. Thus, there is no room for despair, for even the voice of your own conscience carries little weight if it is not seconded by His voice. It is only what God *has said* that will cause you to tremble, so never allow your hopeless thoughts to overwhelm you with despondency and sinful despair.

Many fearful people have been troubled by their suspicion that there may be something in God's decree that shuts them out from hope, but today's verse is a complete refutation to that troublesome fear, because no true seeker can be condemned to His wrath. Our text also says, "I have not spoken in secret, from somewhere in a land of darkness" — not even the secret depths of God's unsearchable decree — "I have not said ... 'Seek me in vain.'"

The Lord has clearly revealed He will hear the prayer of "all who call on him" (Ps. 145:18), and that declaration cannot be broken. He has spoken so firmly, truthfully, and righteously that there can be no room for doubt; and He does not reveal His mind in unintelligible words, but speaks plainly and directly, saying, "Ask and you *will* receive" (John 16:24).

Therefore, O fearful one, believe this sure truth: your prayer must and will be heard; and never, even in the secrets of eternity, has the Lord ever said to any living soul, "Seek me in vain."

From the pen of Jim Reimann:

It may seem contradictory to read: "The LORD looks down from heaven ... to see if there are any who understand, any who seek God.... There is no one who does good, not even one" (Ps. 14:2 – 3), and "Seek the LORD while he may be found; call on him while he is near" (Isa. 55:6).

So how may we reconcile this seeming discrepancy? The truth is that mankind, left to his own devices, will never seek the Lord on his own. Thus, those who appear to be seeking Him are doing so only through God's gracious act of drawing them to Himself. Let us remember these words of His: "I revealed myself to those who did not ask for me; I was found by those who did not seek me" (Isa. 65:1). Jesus Himself said, "There are some of you who do not believe.... This is why I told you that no one can come to me unless the Father has enabled him" (John 6:64 – 65).

Therefore, I once thought I was seeking the Lord, but I learned that in reality, like David, "He reached down from on high and took hold of me; he drew me out of deep waters" (2 Sam. 22:17).

"Salvation is of the LORD" (Jonah 2:9 KJV).

AUGUST 22

The unsearchable riches of Christ ...

Ephesians 3:8

From the pen of Charles Spurgeon:

My Master has riches beyond the counting of numbers, the measuring stick of reason, the ability to dream or imagine, or the eloquence of mere words. His riches are unsearchable! You may carefully examine and study Him, but Jesus is a greater Savior than you think Him to be, even when your thoughts are at their highest. My Lord is more "ready to pardon" (Neh. 9:17 KJV) than you are to sin, more able to forgive than you are to transgress, and more willing to "meet all your needs" (Phil. 4:19) than you are to confess them. So never tolerate thoughts of meagerness regarding my Lord Jesus.

When you place the crown on His head, you are only able to do so with one of silver, while He deserves gold. My Master, however, has abundant riches of happiness to bestow on you, for He can make you "lie down in green pastures" and lead you "beside quiet waters" (Ps. 23:2). There is no music as beautiful as the music of His flute when He is your Shepherd and you are His sheep, lying at His feet. There is no love like His, for nothing on earth nor in heaven can equal it. "Knowing Christ ... and [to] be found in him" (Phil. 3:8 – 9) — oh, this is life and joy, "the best of meats and the finest of wines" (Isa. 25:6).

My Master is never miserly with His servants, but gives to them as a king gives to another king. He gives them two heavens — one here below in which to serve Him in this life, and another one above in which to delight in Him forever. Yet not until eternity will we truly understand the full extent of His unsearchable riches. On the way to heaven, He will give you all you need, for your "refuge will be the mountain fortress. [Your] bread will be supplied, and water will not fail [you]" (Isa. 33:16). But it is there in heaven, where you will hear the song of those who triumph, the shout of those who feast, and will have a "face to face" (1 Cor. 13:12) view of the glorious and beloved One. Oh, "the unsearchable riches of Christ." This is *the* song for the musicians of earth and *the* song for the harpists of heaven.

Lord, teach us more and more of Jesus, and we will spread the good news of Him to others.

From the pen of Jim Reimann:

Spurgeon, quoting a portion of Philippians 3, writes: "Knowing Christ ... and [to] be found in him" is life. This is consistent with the teaching of Jesus, who said, "Now this is eternal life: that they may know you, the only true God, and Jesus Christ" (John 17:3). Notice that Jesus' definition of eternal life is not rendered in terms of time, which is typically how mankind views it. Instead, the Lord views eternal life in terms of relationship, saying, in essence, that eternal life is knowing Him. John obviously understood this truth, for later in life he penned the following teaching: "We are in him who is true — even in his Son Jesus Christ. He is the true God and eternal life" (1 John 5:20). Particularly notice John's final thought, for he equates Jesus with eternal life itself.

This is why Paul could say, "I consider everything a loss compared to the surpassing greatness of knowing Christ Jesus my Lord.... I want to know Christ" (Phil. 3:8, 10).

AUGUST 23

I pray that ...
Christ may dwell in your hearts through faith.
Ephesians 3:16 – 17

From the pen of Charles Spurgeon:

A blessing to be desired beyond measure is for us, as believers, to have the person of Jesus constantly before us in order to ignite our love for Him and to increase our knowledge of Him. I desire before God that each of my readers would enroll as diligent scholars in Jesus' "college," that they be students of Corpus Christi (Latin for "the body of Christ"), and that they resolve to attain a "degree" in the "school" of the cross. But to have Jesus always near, the heart must be full of Him — in fact, overflowing with His love — which is why the apostle Paul "pray[s] that ... Christ may dwell in your hearts."

See how near Paul desires Jesus to be to us, for nothing is closer than having Jesus within our heart. Notice his words: "That ... Christ *may dwell*," not that He *may visit* as a traveler stays overnight on occasion, but that He "*may dwell*" — that Jesus may become the Lord and Tenant of our inmost being, never to leave.

Also notice Paul says: "That ... Christ may dwell *in your hearts*" — the best "room" of the house of mankind. Christ is to dwell not only in our thoughts, but also in our affections; not merely in the mind's meditations, but also in the heart's emotions. Thus, we should yearn for a love for Christ of the most abiding quality, not a love that quickly flares up and just as quickly dies down into the darkness of a few embers, but a constant flame supplied by sacred fuel, like the fire on the altar of the temple that never went out (see Lev. 6:12 – 13). This type of love, however, cannot be accomplished except by faith. And faith must be strong or love will not be fervent, just as the root of a plant must be healthy for its flower to be pretty. Faith is the root while love is the flower.

Dear reader, Jesus cannot be in your heart's love if you don't have a firm hold on Him by your heart's faith. So pray that you will always trust Christ in order that you will always love Him, for if your love is cold, you may be sure your faith has faded.

From the pen of Jim Reimann:

Almighty God has chosen to dwell with His people and has made it possible for us to dwell with Him. But, of course, it is only those He has made righteous who may do so, for David prayed, "*With you the wicked cannot dwell. The arrogant cannot stand in your presence.... But I, by your great mercy, will come into your house; in reverence will I bow down toward your holy temple*" (Ps. 5:4 – 5, 7). And though David also wrote the following words, they find their perfect fulfillment in Jesus: "My eyes will be on the faithful in the land, that they may dwell with me; *he whose walk is blameless will minister to me. No one who practices deceit will dwell in my house*" (Ps. 101:6 – 7).

Later, David's son Solomon, at the dedication of the temple that he himself had constructed, was in awe that the Lord would indwell a building, for he prayed, "Will God really dwell on earth with men? The heavens, even the highest heavens, cannot contain you. How much less this temple I have built!" (2 Chron. 6:18). How much more amazing, then, that the Creator of the universe has chosen to indwell the human hearts of His chosen ones!

I praise You Lord that "the dwelling of God is with men" (Rev. 21:3).

AUGUST 24

If a fire breaks out and spreads into thornbushes
so that it burns shocks of grain or standing grain or the whole field,
the one who started the fire must make restitution.

Exodus 22:6

From the pen of Charles Spurgeon:

Restitution can be made for the above mistake, but what restitution can be made by someone who scatters the flames of heresy or the coals of evil that set souls ablaze with the fires of hell? His guilt is beyond measure, and the result is irretrievable. And if such an offender is ultimately forgiven, what great remorse it will cause him, since he cannot undo the mischief he created.

One bad action may kindle a flame that years of changed character cannot quench. Burning someone's food is bad, but how much worse to destroy his soul! Perhaps it would be useful to reflect on past guilty actions and to ask whether, in the present, there is some evil in us that has a tendency to cause damage to the souls of relatives, friends, or neighbors.

The fire of strife is a terrible evil when it breaks out in God's church, for wherever converts are multiplying, and the Lord is being glorified, jealousy and envy do the Devil's work. Where God's golden grain is being stored, as a reward to the redeeming work of the great "Boaz" (or Jesus), the fires of enmity enter in, leaving little else but smoke and a heap of ashes. "But woe to that person through whom they come" (Luke 17:1). May they never come through us, for since we cannot make restitution, we will certainly be those who suffer the most if we are the chief offenders. Those who fuel the fire deserve their just punishment, but he who first set the fire is the most to blame.

Although discord usually takes hold first among the "weeds" or "thorns" of the church, it is then nurtured along by the hypocrites and minimal professors of the faith. But ultimately it finds its way to the righteous, blown by the winds of hell, and no one knows where it may end.

O Lord of peace, make us peacemakers; and never let us aid and abet the people of strife or even unintentionally cause the least division among Your people.

From the pen of Jim Reimann:

The New Testament places great emphasis on loving others, especially other believers, for how can we extend love to the lost if we don't love those in the family. Jesus said to His followers, "A new command I give you: Love one another. As I have loved you, so you must love one another. By this all men will know that you are my disciples, if you love one another" (John 13:34 – 35). Paul put it like this: "Now about brotherly love we do not need to write to you, for you yourselves have been taught by God to love each other.... Yet we urge you, brothers, to do so more and more" (1 Thess. 4:9 – 10). He also wrote: "There should be no division in the body, but that its parts should have equal concern for each other" (1 Cor. 12:25).

With these truths in mind, imagine how the world must view divisions in the family of the Lord Jesus. When a church fellowship splits over some triviality, imagine how our message of reconciliation with God must sound like a "clanging cymbal" (1 Cor. 13:1) in the ears of unbelievers.

"Blessed are the peacemakers, for they will be called sons of God" (Matt. 5:9).

AUGUST 25

If you believe with all your heart,
you may [be baptized].

Acts 8:37 NKJV

From the pen of Charles Spurgeon:

If you are a devout believer, dear reader, perhaps this verse will answer any hesitation you may have regarding the sacred ordinances. Do you say to yourself, "I should be afraid to be baptized, for it is such a solemn thing to acknowledge my death and burial with Christ. I should not feel at liberty to come to the Master's table, for I should be afraid of eating and drinking 'without recognizing the body of the Lord,' and thereby bring 'judgment on [myself]'" (1 Cor. 11:29)?

O fearful one, Jesus has given you liberty — don't be afraid! When a stranger comes to your house, he waits at the door, never intruding into your bedroom, for he is not at home. Yet your child is free to roam the house. And so it is with a child of God. When the Holy Spirit gives you the assurance of adoption, you may come to Christian ordinances without fear. The same rule holds true for a believer's inner privileges.

Poor believer, you may think as you seek the Lord that you are not allowed to rejoice "with an inexpressible and glorious joy" (1 Peter 1:8), and that if you were only permitted inside Christ's door or allowed to sit at the foot of His table, you would be content. Oh, you will not have fewer privileges than His very greatest, for God loves each of His children the same. A child is a child to Him, and He will never make a child "like one of [His] hired men" (Luke 15:19). No, His son will dine on "the fattened calf" and will "feast and celebrate" (v. 23) with "music and dancing" (v. 25) as though he had never gone astray. When Jesus comes into a heart, He issues a certificate of permission to "be glad in the LORD" (Ps. 32:11 KJV). No chains are worn in the court of King Jesus, and though our admission into full privileges may be gradual, it is certain.

Perhaps you are saying, "I wish I could enjoy His promises and walk in liberty in my Lord's commands." "If you believe with all your heart, you may"! "Free yourself from the chains on your neck, O captive Daughter of Zion" (Isa. 52:2), for Jesus has made you free.

From the pen of Jim Reimann:

Any hesitation believers have in sharing in the holy ordinances should be overcome by remembering: it is not what we do that makes us worthy to partake in them, but who we are — a child of God! In the same way that our works did not save us, our works do not make us worthy to share in the sacraments. Or course, we are to partake of them in the proper way, confessing our sins before doing so. "A man ought to examine himself before he eats of the bread and drinks of the cup" (1 Cor. 11:28).

As Christians, we have a right to partake — but again, not due to our works, but due to Christ's work on the cross, which made us a child of God. "To all who received him, to those who believed in his name, he gave the right to become children of God" (John 1:12). Notice again the emphasis on the necessity of believing.

"If you believe with all your heart, you may...." So "let the righteous rejoice in the LORD and take refuge in him" (Ps. 64:10).

AUGUST 26

As soon as all the people saw Jesus,
they were overwhelmed with wonder and ran to greet him.

Mark 9:15

From the pen of Charles Spurgeon:

What a difference between the people's re-action to Moses and to Jesus! When Moses, the prophet of Sinai, had been on the mountain forty days, he underwent a transfiguration, for "his face was radiant, and they were afraid to come near him" (Ex. 34:30). Moses "put a veil over his face" (v. 33), for people could not endure to look upon Moses' glory. But not so with our Savior. On the Mount of Transfiguration, Jesus had been transfigured to a greater glory than that of Moses on Mount Sinai, yet we do not read that the people were blinded by the blazing radiance of His countenance. On the contrary — "They were overwhelmed with wonder and ran to greet him."

The glory of the law repels, while the greater glory of Jesus attracts. Although the Lord is holy and just, His purity is blended with so much "grace and truth" (John 1:17) that sinners run to Him. Amazed by His goodness and fascinated by His love, they "greet him," become His disciples, and take Him to be their Lord and Master.

Dear reader, perhaps you are blinded by the stunning brightness of the law of God. You feel its claims on your conscience, but you are un-able to obey it in your life. Not that you find fault with the law, for, in fact, it commands your profoundest esteem. Yet you find that in no way does it draw you to God. Instead, you find your heart being hardened, and you are on the verge of desperation.

O poor heart, turn your eyes from Moses, with all his repelling splendor, and look to Jesus, who is radiant with a milder, welcoming glory. Behold His bleeding wounds and His thorn-crowned head. Not only is He greater than Moses, because He is the Son of God, but He is also the Lord of love and is thus more tender than the lawgiver. Jesus bore the wrath of God, and in His death re-vealed more of God's justice than if all of Sinai were set ablaze. By His death God's justice is now vindicated, and that justice is forevermore the guardian of believers in Jesus.

Look, O sinner, to the bleeding Savior, and as you feel the attraction of His love, run to His arms, and "you will be saved" (Rom. 10:9).

From the pen of Jim Reimann:

Moses was simply a "shadow" of the Messiah, for he wrote: "The LORD your God will raise up for you a prophet like me from among your own brothers. You must listen to him" (Deut. 18:15). And, as Hebrews declares: "Jesus has been found worthy of greater honor than Moses" (Heb. 3:3). Paul too described the difference between the ministry of Moses and the ministry of the Spirit of Jesus as follows:

> Now if the ministry that brought death, which was engraved in letters on stone, came with glory, so that the Israelites could not look steadily at the face of Moses because of its glory, fading though it was, will not the ministry of the Spirit be even more glori-ous? If the ministry that condemns men is glorious, how much more glorious is the ministry that brings righteousness! ... And we, who with unveiled faces all reflect the Lord's glory, are being transformed into his likeness with ever-increasing glory, which comes from the Lord, who is the Spirit.

2 Corinthians 3:7 – 9, 18

AUGUST 27

Into Your hand I commit my spirit;
You have redeemed me, O Lord God of truth.

Psalm 31:5 NKJV

From the pen of Charles Spurgeon:

These words often have been used by saints of God at their hour of departure from this life. So let us consider their value to us. The primary concern during life and at death for a person of faith is not his body or his estate, but his spirit — his choicest treasure — and if it is safe, all is well. What is our earthly condition when compared to that of the soul? A believer commits his soul to the hand of His God, for it came from Him, belongs to Him, is sustained by Him, is kept safe by Him, and thus it is most fitting that He should receive it.

All things are safe in Jehovah's hand — whatever we entrust to Him now, and whatever we entrust to Him for that Day of days that is quickly approaching. To rest in the care of heaven is to have peaceful living and glorious dying. At all times, we should commit our all to Jesus' faithful hand; and though life may be hanging by a thread, and adversities may be multiplying like the sands of the sea, our "soul shall dwell at ease" (Ps. 25:13 KJV) and delight itself in quiet resting places.

"You have redeemed me, O Lord God of truth." Redemption is a solid foundation for confidence. David did not know Calvary as we do, but even the temporary moments of redemption of this life cheered him. So shouldn't our eternal redemption bring us even sweeter comfort? Past deliverances are great reasons to make strong appeals for present assistance, for what the Lord has done He will do again, because "He ... does not change" (Ps. 15:4 NKJV). He is faithful to His promises and gracious to His saints — He will not turn away from His people.

> Though You slay me I will trust,
> Praise You even from the dust,
> Prove, and tell it as I prove,
> Your unutterable love.
> You may chasten and correct,
> But You never can neglect;
> Since the ransom price is paid,
> On Your love my hope is stayed.
>
> John Samuel Bewley Monsell, 1811 – 75

From the pen of Jim Reimann:

No matter what we must face in this life, our eternal future is safe in God's hands. Consider this great truth as taught by Paul, and then Peter:

> Join with me in suffering for the gospel.... I know whom I have believed, and am convinced that he is able to guard what I have entrusted to him for that day.
>
> 2 Timothy 1:8, 12

> God ... has given us new birth ... into *an inheritance that can never perish, spoil or fade — kept in heaven for you, who through faith are shielded by God's power....* In this you greatly rejoice, though now for a little while you may have had to suffer grief in all kinds of trials ... for you are receiving the goal of your faith, the salvation of your souls.
>
> 1 Peter 1:3 – 6, 9

O Lord, "Though [You] slay me, yet will I trust in [You]" (Job 13:15 KJV).

AUGUST 28

Sing, O barren woman,
… burst into song, shout for joy.

Isaiah 54:1

From the pen of Charles Spurgeon:

Although we have produced some fruit for Christ and have the joyful hope we are "a planting of the Lord" (Isa. 61:3), there are times when we feel quite barren. At those times our prayers are lifeless, our love is cold, our faith is weak, and each of God's gifts in the garden of our heart seems to languish and wilt. We are like flowers in the hot sun, needing rain. So what are we to do?

Today's text addresses this situation: "Sing, O barren woman,… burst into song, shout for joy." But what am I to sing about? If I sing about the present or the past, they seem full of barrenness. Yes, but I can sing of Jesus Christ! I can sing of past visits the Redeemer has made to me, or I can focus on the great love He has shown His people when He left the heights of heaven for our redemption. I will go to His cross again. "Come," my soul, and remember that once you were "weary and burdened" (Matt. 11:28), but that you lost your burden there.

I will go to Calvary again. Perhaps that very cross that gave me life will give me fruitfulness. What is my barrenness, if not the foundation for His fruit-producing power? What is my wilderness, if not the dark setting for the radiant sapphire of His everlasting love? I will go in all my poverty, helplessness, shame, and backsliding. I will tell the Lord I am still His child, and in the confidence of His faithfulness, I — the barren one — will "burst into song [and] shout for joy"!

Sing, believer, for it will cheer your heart and the hearts of others in desolation. Sing, for now that you are truly ashamed of being barren, you will soon be fruitful. Sing, for now that God has caused you to loathe being fruitless, He will soon cover you with clusters of fruit.

Indeed, experiencing barrenness is painful, whereas time with the Lord is a delight. Yet it is a sense of our own poverty that drives us to Christ, and that is where we need to be, for it is in Him that our fruit is found.

From the pen of Jim Reimann:

In biblical times, a barren woman was considered unloved and disgraced. Perhaps this is why we are told: "When the Lord saw that Leah was not loved [by Jacob], he opened her womb, but Rachel was barren" (Gen. 29:31). Of course, later Rachel's womb was opened as well, for "God remembered Rachel; he listened to her and opened her womb. She became pregnant and gave birth to a son and said, 'God has taken away my disgrace'" (Gen. 30:22 – 23).

Isaiah 54, from which our text is taken, shows us the fruitfulness that comes only from God. Left to our own power, we are hopeless to produce fruit or a godly heritage. But by His power, although barren or desolate, His people will be fruitful. Here's what the Lord said:

> More are the children of the desolate woman than of her who has a husband.… You will spread out to the right and to the left; your descendants will dispossess nations and settle in their desolate cities.
>
> Isaiah 54:1, 3

In closing, let us remember these words of Jesus: "If a man remains in me and I in him, he will bear much fruit; apart from me you can do nothing" (John 15:5).

AUGUST 29

As long as he is a Nazirite,
he must not eat anything that comes from the grapevine,
not even the seeds or skins.

Numbers 6:4

From the pen of Charles Spurgeon:

Among the vows of the Nazirites is one that prohibited them from partaking of wine. In order not to violate the obligation in any way, they were forbidden from drinking the vinegar of wine or strong liquor; and in order to make the rule even more clear, they were forbidden even to touch unfermented grape juice or to eat the fruit itself, whether fresh or dried. Furthermore, in order to secure the integrity of the vow, they were not even allowed anything whatsoever that had to do with a vine or a vineyard — in fact, they were to avoid "all appearance of evil" (1 Thess. 5:22 KJV).

Surely there is a lesson in this for us, the Lord's separated ones, teaching us to separate ourselves from sin in any and every form. Not only should we avoid those sins that are obviously grievous in nature, but we also should avoid anything that even hints of the spirit or likeness of sin. Walking in such strictness is greatly despised today, but rest assured, dear reader, it is both the safest and happiest way to live. Whoever takes a step or two in the ways of the world is in a fearful, dangerous place, for whoever eats the grapes of Sodom will soon drink the wine of Gomorrah. A small crack in the seawall in Holland would be disastrous, for the gap would quickly grow until the entire country would be flooded and the people drowned.

Likewise, any degree of worldly conformity is a snare to the soul and makes us more likely to commit sins of arrogance. Just as a Nazirite who drank grape juice could not be totally sure whether the grapes may have become somewhat fermented — and consequently could not be sure in his heart if his vow was intact — a Christian who yields ever so slightly to a temptation cannot have a conscience totally clear of all offense, but must feel that his inner monitor is causing him some doubt. Those things that cause us doubt, however, should do so no longer, for anything causing us doubt is wrong for us. We must never trifle with any temptation that comes our way, but should quickly flee from it.

Better to be sneered at as a Puritan than to be despised as a hypocrite. Careful living may involve much self-denial, but it brings pleasures of its own that are more than sufficient reward.

From the pen of Jim Reimann:

Spurgeon said that "whoever eats the grapes of Sodom will soon drink the wine of Gomorrah." His words are reminiscent of this passage, speaking of Israel's enemies:

Their vine comes from the vine of Sodom and from the fields of Gomorrah. Their grapes are filled with poison, and their clusters with bitterness. Their wine is the venom of serpents, the deadly poison of cobras.

Deuteronomy 32:32 – 33

No doubt this is why the church is later told, regarding unbelievers: "Come out from them and be separate, says the Lord. Touch no unclean thing" (2 Cor. 6:17).

Dear Lord, I thank You for "our great God and Savior, Jesus Christ, who gave himself for us to redeem us from all wickedness and to purify for himself a [peculiar (KJV)] people that are his very own, eager to do what is good" (Titus 2:13 – 14).

AUGUST 30

Heal me, O LORD, and I will be healed.

Jeremiah 17:14

I have seen his ways, but I will heal him.

Isaiah 57:18

From the pen of Charles Spurgeon:

It is the sole prerogative of God to remove spiritual disease. Physical diseases may be healed by the methods of doctors, but even then the honor belongs to God who gives the healing qualities to the medicine and who bestows the power to the body to fight disease. But as for spiritual sicknesses, they remain under the control of the great Physician alone. He claims it as His prerogative, saying, "I put to death and I bring to life, I have wounded and I will heal" (Deut. 32:39). One of the Lord's greatest titles is Jehovah-Rapha — "the LORD, who heals you" (Ex. 15:26); and one of the promises that could never come from man, but only from the mouth of "the eternal God" (Deut. 33:27), is: "I will restore you to health and heal your wounds" (Jer. 30:17).

This is why David cried to the Lord, "Heal me, for my bones are in agony" (Ps. 6:2), and "Heal me, for I have sinned against you" (Ps. 41:4). Because only God can heal, the godly praise Him, saying, "Praise the LORD, O my soul,... who ... heals all your diseases" (Ps. 103:2 – 3). He who made mankind can restore mankind. What an awe-inspiring comfort to know that in Jesus "all the fullness of the Deity lives in bodily form" (Col. 2:9).

Dear soul, whatever your disease may be, this great Physician can heal you, for since He is God, there is no limit to His healing power. So come to Him with your blind eyes of darkened understanding, your limping feet of totally spent energy, your withered hands of weak faith, your fever of an angry temper, or your chills of shivering despondency. Come just as you are. He who is God can restore you from your plague, for no one can restrain the healing power that flows from Jesus our Lord. Legions of demons have been made to yield to the power of the beloved Physician, and never once has He been unsure or baffled. All His patients have been cured in the past and will be in the future. And you will be among them if you will rest yourself in Him today.

From the pen of Jim Reimann:

Indeed, all healing comes from God, but only spiritual healing from sin has eternal consequences. In fact, one of today's texts focuses on the spiritual healing needed for salvation. Here is the verse in its context:

O LORD,... those who turn away from you will be written in the dust because they have forsaken the LORD, the spring of living water. Heal me, O LORD, and I will be healed; save me and I will be saved, for you are the one I praise.

Jeremiah 17:13-14

Today's second text also speaks of the spiritual healing and peace that comes only through salvation. Here is its context:

"I have seen his ways, but I will heal him; I will guide him and restore comfort to him, creating praise on the lips of the mourners in Israel. Peace, peace, to those far and near," says the LORD. "And I will heal them." But the wicked are like the tossing sea, which cannot rest, whose waves cast up mire and mud. "There is no peace," says my God, "for the wicked."

Isaiah 57:18 – 21

Once I am a believer, however, I still need the Lord's ongoing healing from sin. Thus, may David's prayer become mine:

"O LORD, have mercy on me; heal me, for I have sinned against you" (Ps. 41:4).

AUGUST 31

If we walk in the light,
as he is in the light …
1 John 1:7

From the pen of Charles Spurgeon:

"As he is in the light …" Will we ever be able to walk as clearly in the light as He whom we call "Our Father" (Matt. 6:9) and of whom it is written: "God is light; in him there is no darkness at all" (1 John 1:5)? Certainly this is the goal set before us, for the Savior Himself said, "Be perfect … as your heavenly Father is perfect" (Matt. 5:48). Although we may feel we can never rival the perfection of God, we are to seek after it and never be satisfied until we attain it. A young artist painting with his first brush can hardly hope to equal Michelangelo, yet if he never has a high ideal in mind, he will only attain something quite ordinary.

So exactly what is meant by the expression that a Christian is to "walk in the light, as he is in the light"? I believe it conveys the idea of likeness — not degree — for although I am as actually and sincerely "in the light, as he is in the light," I cannot be there in the same measure. I cannot dwell on the sun, for it is too bright to be my residence, but I can walk in the light of the sun. Although I cannot attain the level of perfection of purity and truth that belongs to the Lord Almighty by virtue of His nature as He who is infinitely good, I still can set the Lord always before me and seek after conformity to His image through the help of His indwelling Spirit.

Bible commentator John Trapp (1601 – 69) once said, "We may be in the light as God is in the light for quality, but not for equality." We are to have the same light, and are as truly to walk in it as God does. However, when it comes to equality with Him in His holiness and purity, we must wait on that until we cross the Jordan and enter into the perfection of the Most High. Until then, we should take note that the blessings of sacred fellowship and perfect cleansing are tied to "walk[ing] in the light."

From the pen of Jim Reimann:

What Spurgeon encourages us to "take note" of regarding "sacred fellowship and perfect cleansing" comes from the context of today's verse. As you read, take note that fellowship and cleansing are conditional — dependent on our action — since they are preceded by a number of "ifs."

This is the message we have heard from him and declare to you: God is light; in him there is no darkness at all. If we claim to have fellowship with him yet walk in the darkness, we lie and do not live by the truth. But if we walk in the light, as he is in the light, we have fellowship with one another, and the blood of Jesus, his Son, purifies us from all sin. If we claim to be without sin, we deceive ourselves and the truth is not in us. If we confess our sins, he is faithful and just and will forgive us our sins and purify us from all unrighteousness. If we claim we have not sinned, we make him out to be a liar and his word has no place in our lives.
1 John 1:5 – 10

So let us go to the Lord and pray,

"Have mercy on me, O God, according to your unfailing love; according to your great compassion blot out my transgressions. Wash away all my iniquity and cleanse me from my sin.… Cleanse me with hyssop, and I will be clean" (Ps. 51:1 – 2, 7).

September

SEPTEMBER 1

Trust in [God] at all times

Psalm 62:8

From the pen of Charles Spurgeon:

We are to exercise faith as much in the temporal life as in the spiritual — to have as much faith in God for our earthly concerns as we do for our heavenly matters — for it is only as we learn to trust Him to supply all our daily needs that we will live above the world. Yet we are not to be idle, which does not show trust in God who "is always at his work to this very day" (John 5:17); for idleness, instead, shows trust in the Devil who is the father of idleness. Nor are we to be rash or imprudent, as though we were trusting in chance rather than trusting the living God, who is a God of order and reason. Acting in righteousness and with judgment, we are to rely simply and entirely upon the Lord "at all times."

Allow me to recommend to you a life of trust in God in all temporal things, for when you truly are trusting in God, you will never have to grieve over having used sinful means to grow rich. If you will serve Him with integrity, even if you never achieve worldly success, at least you will have no sin troubling your conscience. By trusting God, you will never be guilty of self-contradiction, while whoever trusts in his own craftiness sails this way today and that way tomorrow, like a boat tossed by the fickle wind. Whoever trusts in the Lord is like a ship powered by steam that slices through the waves, defies the wind, and cuts a silvery and straightforward path toward her designated haven.

Be a person with God's living principles within, never bowing to the changing customs of worldly wisdom. Walk in your path of integrity with steadfast steps, showing you are invincibly strong in the strength that confidence in God alone can bestow. Only then will you be delivered from anxious cares, nor will you be troubled by evil news, for your heart will be steadfast — trusting in the Lord.

How pleasant it is to float on the stream of God's providence. There is no more blessed way of living than that of a life of dependence upon a covenant-keeping God. We have no anxiety "because he cares for [us] (1 Peter 5:7); we have no troubles because we "cast [our] cares on the LORD" (Ps. 55:22).

From the pen of Jim Reimann:

Jesus gave His disciples the prescription for a troubled heart: "Do not let your hearts be troubled. *Trust in God; trust also in me*" (John 14:1). Then He proceeded to share with them that soon He was going to His "Father's house ... to prepare a place for [them]" (v. 2). Believing in that place, however, required trust in God and seeing — with spiritual eyes — something unnatural and difficult for mankind.

The Promised Land of the Old Testament was only a shadow of that heavenly place. Yet, regarding it, the Lord said to Moses, "*I have let you see it with your eyes*, but you will not cross over into it" (Deut. 34:4). Later in Hebrews, however, we read that Moses was blessed because "he persevered because *he saw him who is invisible*" (Heb. 11:27).

Trust requires seeing the invisible, seeing not with my physical eyes, but with the eyes of my heart. No doubt this is why Paul wrote: "I pray ... that the eyes of your heart may be enlightened" (Eph. 1:18).

SEPTEMBER 2

Unless you people see miraculous signs and wonders …
you will never believe.

John 4:48

From the pen of Charles Spurgeon:

Yearning for miracles was a symptom of the sickly state of people's minds in our Lord's day, for they hungered after things of mere wonder more than true spiritual nourishment. The gospel they so greatly needed, they rejected; but the miracles Jesus did not always choose to give, they eagerly demanded. It is often the same today, for many demand "signs and wonders" or they will not believe.

Still others have said in their heart that they must experience some deep horror of their soul or they will not believe in Jesus. If you are one of those, what if you never feel such horror, as you probably never will? Will you go to hell out of spite against God simply because He will not treat you like someone else? Others have said that if they would have a particular dream or would experience some sudden shock, they would believe. If you are saying this, are you — an undeserving mortal — presuming that my Lord is to have conditions dictated to Him by you? You are a beggar at His gate, asking for mercy, and you think you can draft the rules and regulations as to how He is to dispense that mercy? Do you truly think He will submit to you? My Master has a generous spirit, but He also has a righteous, royal heart. He spurns all dictation and maintains His sovereignty in His every action.

If this way of thinking describes you, dear reader, why do you yearn for "signs and wonders"? Isn't the gospel its own sign and wonder? Isn't this the miracle of miracles: "God so loved the world that he gave his one and only Son, that whoever believes in him shall not perish but have eternal life" (John 3:16). Surely this precious verse, "Whoever wishes, let him take the free gift of the water of life" (Rev. 22:17), and the following solemn promise, "Whoever comes to me I will never drive away" (John 6:37) are better than "signs and wonders."

A truthful Savior ought to be believed, for He is truth itself. Why would you dare ask for proof of the truthfulness of the One who "cannot lie" (Titus 1:2 KJV)? Remember — the demons themselves declared Him to be the Son of God (see Luke 4:41). Will *you* believe Him?

From the pen of Jim Reimann:

If today's devotion strikes at your heart, perhaps you still are walking in unbelief toward Jesus and do not know Him as Lord and Savior. If this describes you, please know that believing is much more than simply giving mental assent to Jesus, for, as we have seen, even the demons do that. True belief adds trust to the equation. For example, the Amplified Bible defines "believes in" as "trusts in, clings to, relies on" (John 3:16 Amplified).

There are many today who trust in church attendance, rituals, or a prayer once prayed, rather than truly trusting in Christ Jesus Himself. Churches are filled with "tares among the wheat" (Matt. 13:25 KJV), which is why Paul wrote the church in Corinth, declaring: "Examine yourselves to see whether you are in the faith; test yourselves. Do you not realize that Christ Jesus is in you — unless, of course, you fail the test?" (2 Cor. 13:5).

Dear reader, are you "trust[ing] in, cling[ing] to, rely[ing] on" Jesus to be your "all in all" (1 Cor. 15:28)?

SEPTEMBER 3

The LORD tests the righteous.
Psalm 11:5 NKJV

From the pen of Charles Spurgeon:

Everything is under the control of Providence; consequently all the trials of life can be traced back to the great "First Cause." From the golden gate of God's decree, the armies of trials march forth in formation, clad in their armor, and armed with the weapons of war. Each of the Lord's providential works are doors to trials, for even His mercies, like roses, have their thorns. For instance, people can be drowned in seas of prosperity as well as in rivers of affliction. Our mountains are not too high nor our valleys too low to avoid temptations. Trials lurk on every road, whether high or low, for we are surrounded with dangers and always subject to attack. Yet no drop of rain falls unordained from a threatening cloud, for each has its purpose as it falls to earth.

The trials God sends are sent to establish and confirm the gifts of His grace, to illustrate the power of that grace, to test the genuineness of our virtues, and to strengthen each one. In His infinite wisdom and superabundant love, our Lord sets so high a premium on His people's faith that He will not shield them from the very trials by which their faith is strengthened. You never would have possessed the precious faith that supports you today if your faith never had been tested by fire. You are a tree that never would have become so well rooted if the wind had not forced you to and fro and thereby made you take hold of the precious truths of God's covenant grace.

Worldly ease in reality is a great foe to faith, for it loosens the joints of holy valor and snaps the sinews of sacred courage. A balloon never rises until its string is cut, and it is affliction that performs this service for the believer. While the wheat sleeps comfortably in its husk, it is useless to mankind; it must be threshed from its resting place before its value can be determined.

Therefore, it is good "the LORD tests the righteous," for it causes them to grow rich toward God.

From the pen of Jim Reimann:

Today Spurgeon shares the principle of wheat having no value until it is threshed. Jesus taught this very truth in these words:

> I tell you the truth, unless a kernel of wheat falls to the ground and dies, it remains only a single seed. But if it dies, it produces many seeds. The man who loves his life will lose it, while the man who hates his life in this world will keep it for eternal life. Whoever serves me must follow me; and where I am, my servant also will be. My Father will honor the one who serves me. Now my heart is troubled, and what shall I say? "Father, save me from this hour"? No, it was for this very reason I came to this hour.
>
> John 12:24 – 27

Of course, Jesus was referring to His impending suffering and death. Shortly thereafter, He followed up this teaching by saying, "Remember the words I spoke to you: 'No servant is greater than his master.' If they persecuted me, they will persecute you also" (John 15:20).

So, dear reader, "Consider it pure joy ... whenever you face trials of many kinds, because you know that the testing of your faith develops perseverance. Perseverance must finish its work so that you may be mature and complete, not lacking anything" (James 1:2 – 4).

SEPTEMBER 4

Use honest scales and honest weights,
an honest ephah and an honest hin.

Leviticus 19:36

From the pen of Charles Spurgeon:

We see from today's text that scales, weights, and measures were to be according to an honest standard of justice. Surely no Christian needs to be reminded of this in business, for even if righteousness were completely banished from the unbelieving world, it should find a shelter in believers' hearts. However, there are other scales that weigh moral and spiritual things, and these often need to be examined as well.

Are the scales we use to weigh our own and other people's character completely accurate? Don't we often turn our own ounces of goodness into pounds while turning the other person's bushels of excellence into pecks? Dear Christian, we must be careful here. Also, are the scales we use to measure our trials and troubles according to standard? The apostle Paul, who had more to suffer than we have, considered his afflictions to be "light" (2 Cor. 4:17), while we often consider ours to be heavy. Surely something must be wrong with our standard of measure. Thus, we must look into this matter, lest we get reported to the court above for unjust dealing.

Furthermore, are the scales by which we measure our doctrinal beliefs completely fair? For example, the doctrines of grace should carry the same weight with us as other precepts of God's Word — no more and no less — but I fear that one teaching or another is given unfair weight by many people. It is of great importance that we be just in our measuring of truth, so, dear believer, be careful here.

Finally, we must be especially careful when it comes to measuring our own obligations and responsibilities, for we tend to think of them as rather small. But when a rich person gives no more to the cause of God than the poor contribute, is that "an honest ephah and an honest hin"? When ministers are half-starved, is that honest dealing? When the poor are despised while ungodly rich people are admired, is that using "honest scales"?

Dear reader, I could continue with this list, but I prefer to leave you with this assignment: search and destroy all your unrighteous scales, weights, and measures.

From the pen of Jim Reimann:

There is much truth to the teaching that we tend to judge others by a much different standard than we judge ourselves. Jesus condemned this imbalance when He declared:

> Why do you look at the speck of sawdust in your brother's eye and pay no attention to the plank in your own eye? How can you say to your brother, "Let me take the speck out of your eye," when all the time there is a plank in your own eye? You hypocrite, first take the plank out of your own eye, and then you will see clearly to remove the speck from your brother's eye.

Matthew 7:3-5

Paul too condemned such unequal judging by saying, "You ... have no excuse, you who pass judgment on someone else, for at whatever point you judge the other, you are condemning yourself, because you who pass judgment do the same things" (Rom. 2:1).

Remember — whether physical or spiritual: "The LORD abhors dishonest scales, but accurate weights are his delight" (Prov. 11:1).

SEPTEMBER 5

Have you journeyed to the springs of the sea.

Job 38:16

From the pen of Charles Spurgeon:

Some things in nature will remain a mystery even to the most intelligent and enterprising scientists, for human knowledge has its limits. Some knowledge is for God alone, and if this is true in the things that are seen and temporal, you may rest assured it is even more true in matters that are spiritual and eternal.

Why then do we torture ourselves with speculation about predetermination versus free will, and providence versus human responsibility? We are no more able to comprehend these deep, profound truths than we are to search out the depths of the deepest oceans and thereby discover where they draw their watery supplies. Why are we so curious to know the reasons behind our Lord's providential works, the motives of His actions, and the purposes of His visitations among mankind?

Will I ever be able to grasp the sun in my fist or hold the universe in the palm of my hand? Yet these are only a drop in the bucket compared to what the Lord my God can do. So let me not strive to understand the infinite, but instead use my energy for love, for what I cannot gain through intellect I can possess through affection. Let me be content in that. I cannot penetrate the heart of the sea, but I can enjoy the warm, healthy breezes that sweep across its body, and I can sail over its blue waves, powered by its promising winds.

Even if I could journey "to the springs of the sea," the feat would serve no useful purpose for me or others. It would not save one sinking ship or return a drowned sailor to his mourning wife and children. My solving of these deep mysteries would not accomplish one thing, whereas even the least amount of love for God, as well as the simplest act of obedience to Him, are better than the most profound knowledge.

My Lord, I therefore leave the infinite to You. And I pray that You would drive far from me any love for "the tree of … knowledge" that might keep me from "the tree of life" (Gen. 2:9).

From the pen of Jim Reimann:

The Scriptures teach us that "the secret things belong to the LORD our God" (Deut. 29:29). But aren't we also taught that "He reveals the deep things of darkness and brings deep shadows into the light" (Job 12:22) and that "the Spirit searches all things, even the deep things of God" (1 Cor. 2:10)?

In light of this, what areas of knowledge are worthy of a believer's pursuit? Paul explained his mission to Titus by saying that he was "a servant of God and an apostle of Jesus Christ for the faith of God's elect and *the knowledge of the truth that leads to godliness — a faith and knowledge resting on the hope of eternal life*" (Titus 1:1 – 2). He also said that God "made his light shine in our hearts to give us *the light of the knowledge of the glory of God in the face of Christ*" (2 Cor. 4:6).

"Oh, the depth of the riches of the wisdom and knowledge of God! How unsearchable his judgments, and his paths beyond tracing out!" (Rom. 11:33). And though the Lord's knowledge is infinite, we can take comfort in the fact that someday "the earth will be filled with *the knowledge of the glory of the LORD*, as the waters cover the sea" (Hab. 2:14).

SEPTEMBER 6

If you are led by the Spirit,
you are not under law.

Galatians 5:18

From the pen of Charles Spurgeon:

Whoever views his own character and standing from a legal point of view not only will despair when he comes to the end of judging himself but also, if he is wise, will despair from the beginning — for if we are judged on the basis of the law, "no one will be declared righteous" (Rom. 3:20). Thus, how blessed we are to know that we dwell in the domain of grace rather than that of law.

When considering my standing before God, the question I should ask is not, "Am I perfect before the law?" but, "Am I 'perfect in Christ'(Col. 1:28)?" for that is a different matter. We need not ask, "Am I without sin through some natural means?" but, "Have I been washed in the fountain the Lord opened for sin and uncleanness?" The question is not, "Am I, in and of myself, pleasing to God?" but, "Am I 'accepted in the beloved' (Eph. 1:6 KJV)?"

When a Christian views the evidence of his salvation from the top of Sinai, he will be alarmed; consequently, it would be much better to consider his position in light of Calvary. Upon viewing his faith he will say, "My faith is mixed with unbelief and is unable to save me." If, however, he will view the *object* of his faith, rather than his faith itself, he will say, "Since there is no failure in Christ, I am safe." Or a believer may be concerned regarding his hope, saying his hope is flawed and dimmed by anxiety and worry. But had he considered the foundation of his hope, he would have seen that the promise of God stands firm, and that whatever doubts may come, God's oath and promise never fail.

Believer, it is always safer to be led by the Spirit into gospel liberty than to wear the chains of the law. Judge yourself by who Christ is, not by who you are. Satan will attempt to destroy your peace by reminding you of your sinfulness and imperfections, and only you will be able to counter his accusations by faithfully adhering to the gospel and refusing to wear the yoke of bondage.

From the pen of Jim Reimann:

We begin today with Paul's teaching that "no one will be declared righteous" on the basis of the law. Reiterating this, Paul also said: "Know that a man is not justified by observing the law, but by faith in Jesus Christ. So we, too, have put our faith in Christ Jesus that we may be justified by faith in Christ and not by observing the law, because by observing the law no one will be justified" (Gal. 2:16). Thus, let us heed Spurgeon's great advice "to judge yourself by who Christ is, rather than by who you are." Next let us remember that Paul also taught: "Those who are led by the Spirit of God are sons of God. For you did not receive a spirit that makes you a slave again to fear, but you received the Spirit of sonship" (Rom. 8:14 – 15).

Finally, regarding this sonship and our hope in Christ, let us remember:

> Because God wanted to make the unchanging nature of his purpose very clear to the heirs of what was promised, he confirmed it with an oath. God did this so that … we who have fled to take hold of the hope offered to us may be greatly encouraged. We have this hope as an anchor for the soul, firm and secure.

Hebrews 6:17 – 19

SEPTEMBER 7

There is sorrow on the sea;
it cannot be quiet.
Jeremiah 49:23 KJV

From the pen of Charles Spurgeon:

We have no idea what sorrow there may be on the sea at this very moment. Safe in our quiet homes, we are far from the sea and the hurricanes that may be cruelly seeking the lives of sailors. But listen how the fiends of death howl across the rigging, and how the timbers of the ships shudder as the waves beat them like battering rams. May the great Lord of the sea and the land calm your storm, and may He deliver you safely to your desired haven.

Yet I should not only pray for them, but also should try to do something to further benefit these hardy souls who constantly risk their lives. What have I ever done for them? What can I do? Just think of how often the stormy seas swallow up the mariner. Thousands of corpses lie with the pearls at the bottom of the deep, while the death-sorrow of the sea echoes in the long wail of widows and orphans. The salt of the sea is in many an eye of mothers and wives, for remorseless, billowing waves have devoured the love of women and the primary support of households.

Imagine what an amazing resurrection there will be from the caverns of the deep when the sea gives up her dead. Until then, however, "there is sorrow on the sea." As though in sympathy with the woes of earth, the sea is forever fretting along a thousand shores, wailing with the sorrowful cry of her shore birds, booming with the hollow crash of restless waves, ranting with uproarious discontent, roaring with raging wrath, or rattling with the voices of untold thousands of complaining pebbles.

Yet the roar of the sea may be a joyous sound to a rejoicing spirit. To a son of sorrow, however, the wide, wide ocean is even more depressing than the wide, wide world. Thankfully, the sea is not our final place of rest, as the restless billows declare to us. We are headed to a land of which our Lord has spoken — one where there is no more sea — and our faces are steadfastly set toward it. Until then, let us cast our sorrows on Him who walked upon the sea of old and "who made a road in the depths of the sea" (Isa. 51:10) for His redeemed.

From the pen of Jim Reimann:

John wrote of the coming judgment, detailing for us how "the sea gave up the dead that were in it" (Rev. 20:13). We can only imagine how many souls that will be, but since the days of Spurgeon — especially in light of two world wars — those numbers have increased greatly.

Thus, it can be no wonder, as Paul wrote, "that the whole creation has been groaning as in the pains of childbirth right up to the present time" (Rom. 8:22). Of course, the greater import of Paul's words is what follows, describing how the saved should face the future, for he went on to say: "Not only so, but we ourselves, who have the firstfruits of the Spirit, groan inwardly as we wait eagerly for our adoption as sons, the redemption of our bodies. For in this hope we were saved" (vv. 23 – 24).

Yet, Father, even believers often walk in doubt. Therefore, I pray that those on the seas of unbelief today would "believe and not doubt, because he who doubts is like a wave of the sea, blown and tossed by the wind" (James 1:6).

SEPTEMBER 8

I pray also ... that you may know ... his incomparably great power for us who believe.
That power is like the working of his mighty strength,
which he exerted in Christ when he raised him from the dead.

Ephesians 1:18 – 20

From the pen of Charles Spurgeon:

In the resurrection of Christ, just as in our salvation, there was nothing short of God's divine power at work. So what shall we say to those who think conversion is the result of the free will of mankind and is due to their own betterment of their nature? Only when we see the dead rise from the grave by their own power may we expect to see ungodly sinners turn to Christ by their own free will. It is not the result of the Word being read or preached by itself, for all life-giving power proceeds from the Holy Spirit Himself — and His power is unstoppable and irresistible.

All the Roman soldiers and the Jewish high priests could not keep the body of Christ in the tomb, nor could Death himself hold Jesus in His bonds. And that same power at work when a believer is raised to "walk in newness of life" (Rom. 6:4 KJV) is likewise irresistible. No sin, no corruption, no demons in hell, no sinners on earth can stop the hand of God's grace when He intends to convert someone. When omnipotent God says, "You will," mere man will not say, "I will not."

Not only was the power that raised Christ from the dead irresistible, it was also glorious, for it reflected honor upon God and brought dismay to the hosts of evil. Likewise, there is great glory to God in the conversion of every sinner.

This power is everlasting power, "For we know that since Christ was raised from the dead, he cannot die again; death no longer has mastery over him" (Rom. 6:9). Thus, we also having been "raised from the dead" do not go back to our dead works or our old corruption, but we "live for God" (Gal. 2:19). Jesus said, "Because I live, you also will live" (John 14:19). "You died, and your life is now hidden with Christ in God" (Col. 3:3). "Just as Christ was raised from the dead through the glory of the Father, we too may live a new life" (Rom. 6:4).

Finally, notice in today's verse the union of the new life to Jesus, for the same power that raised the Head works life into the members of His body. What a blessing to be made alive together with Christ.

From the pen of Jim Reimann:

Along with today's text, Paul also taught that *"Christ [Himself is] the power of God"* (1 Cor. 1:24) and that "the gospel ... is *the power of God* for the salvation of everyone who believes" (Rom. 1:16). "For the message of the cross is foolishness to those who are perishing, but to us who are being saved it is *the power of God*" (1 Cor. 1:18). And, as we have seen today, we live by that same power which brought Christ back from the dead. "For to be sure, he was crucified in weakness, yet *he lives by God's power*. Likewise, we are weak in him, yet *by God's power we will live with him*" (2 Cor. 13:4).

If we don't recall anything else, let us remember that salvation is by the power *of God* — not us! We can claim no part in our salvation, for as Paul said: "*All this is from God*, who reconciled us to himself through Christ" (2 Cor. 5:18). "So do not be ashamed to testify about our Lord.... But join with me in suffering for the gospel, *by the power of God*" (2 Tim. 1:8).

SEPTEMBER 9

Surrounding the throne were twenty-four other thrones,
and seated on them were twenty-four elders.
They were dressed in white.

Revelation 4:4

From the pen of Charles Spurgeon:

These twenty-four representatives of the saints in heaven are said to be "surrounding the throne." In Song of Songs 1:12, where Solomon sings of "the king … at his table," various translators have rendered it as "a round table." From this, some Bible expositors, without straining the meaning, have said this indicates "equality among the saints." That idea is also conveyed by the equal proximity to the throne of the twenty-four elders. Thus, the position of the glorified saints in heaven is that of nearness to Christ, complete with a full view of His glory, constant access to His court, and personal fellowship with Him. Nor is there any difference in any of these blessings between one saint or another, for all the people of God — whether apostles, martyrs, ministers, or unknown private Christians — will be seated near His throne, where they will gaze forever upon their exalted Lord and be satisfied by His love. All will be close to Christ, all overwhelmed by His love, all eating and drinking at His table, and all equally loved as His closest friend, even if not all will be rewarded equally as His servants.

With this in mind, may each believer on earth imitate the saints in heaven in their nearness to Christ. May each of us be as the elders in heaven, sitting around His throne. May Christ be the object of our every thought — the very center of our lives — for how could we endure to live far from our Beloved?

Lord Jesus, draw us closer to You. Say to us, "Remain in me, and I will remain in you"

(John 15:4), *and cause us to sing, "His left arm is under my head, and his right arm embraces me"* (Song 2:6).

O lift me higher, nearer Thee,
And as I rise more pure and meet,
O let my soul's humility
Make me lie lower at Thy feet;
Less trusting self, the more I prove
The blessed comfort of Thy love.

John Samuel Bewlay Monsell, 1811 – 75

From the pen of Jim Reimann:

In support of Song of Songs 1:12 conveying the idea of the king's table being *round*, Young's Literal Translation renders the phrase as follows: "The king is in his *circle*." Don't we often speak of someone's "circle of friends"? What a beautiful image to consider — that Jesus will be fellowshipping with us around His table, as His friends, forever and ever! In that light, let us recall these glorious words of His: "I no longer call you servants, because a servant does not know his master's business. Instead, I have called you friends, for everything that I learned from my Father I have made known to you" (John 15:15). Especially notice from these words that He spoke in the past tense, meaning we don't have to wait for heaven to fellowship with Him as His friends, for we are His friends today!

Therefore, let us praise "God, who has called [us] into fellowship with his Son Jesus Christ our Lord" (1 Cor. 1:9), for "our fellowship is with the Father and with his Son, Jesus Christ" (1 John 1:3).

SEPTEMBER 10

… fiercer than wolves at dusk.

Habakkuk 1:8

From the pen of Charles Spurgeon:

A wolf at sundown, especially when angered and frustrated by a day without food, is fiercer and more ravenous than he would have been in the morning. But may this furious creature not represent our doubts and fears after a long day of frustrations, losses in business, or perhaps unfriendly ridicule from those around us. Yet how often our thoughts howl in our ears, saying, "Where is [your] God?" (Ps. 115:2). How ravenous and greedy are our thoughts, swallowing up any suggestion of comfort and remaining as hungry as ever.

Great Shepherd, slay these evening wolves and call Your sheep to "lie down in green pastures" (Ps. 23:2), undisturbed by insatiable unbelief.

The fiends of hell are much like these evening wolves, for when Christ's flock experiences a cloudy and dark day, and the sun begins to set, they quickly move in to destroy and devour. Seldom will they attack a Christian in the daylight of faith, but will wait for the gloominess of conflict within a believer's soul before pouncing.

O Lord, who has laid "down [Your] life for the sheep" (John 10:15), protect them from the fangs of the wolf.

False teachers who craftily and busily hunt for precious lives, devouring people by their falsehoods, are as dangerous and detestable as evening wolves. Darkness is their habitat, deceit is their character, and destruction is their end. We are most in danger from them when they wear sheep's skin. Thus, blessed is he who is kept from them, for thousands become the prey of dreadful wolves who enter the sheepfold of the church. Yet what a miracle of God's grace when those fierce persecutors of believers are converted, for then "the wolf … live[s] with the lamb" (Isa. 11:6), and people with cruel, unteachable spirits become gentle and teachable.

O Lord, my prayer today is that You would convert many such "wolves."

From the pen of Jim Reimann:

There are several warnings in the Scriptures regarding false prophets. In one of them, referred to by Spurgeon today, Jesus calls these false teachers "ferocious wolves." Here is His warning: "Watch out for false prophets. They come to you in sheep's clothing, but inwardly they are ferocious wolves. By their fruit you will recognize them" (Matt. 7:15 – 16). Later Peter warned of false teachers as well, saying, "There will be false teachers among you. They will secretly introduce destructive heresies, even denying the sovereign Lord who bought them — bringing swift destruction on themselves. Many will follow their shameful ways and will bring the way of truth into disrepute" (2 Peter 2:1 – 2).

The prevalence of false teachers today also makes John's words as relevant today as when they were written. Here is what he taught:

Dear friends, do not believe every spirit, but test the spirits to see whether they are from God, because many false prophets have gone out into the world. This is how you can recognize the Spirit of God: Every spirit that acknowledges that Jesus Christ has come in the flesh is from God, but every spirit that does not acknowledge Jesus is not from God. This is the spirit of the antichrist, which you have heard is coming and even now is already in the world.

1 John 4:1 – 3

SEPTEMBER 11

Lead me, O LORD, in your righteousness
because of my enemies.

Psalm 5:8

From the pen of Charles Spurgeon:

The world's hatred for the people of Christ is very bitter. They will forgive a thousand faults among each other, but will exaggerate the most trivial offense in the followers of Jesus. Yet instead of vainly lamenting this, let us find some good in it. Since so many people are watching for our every stumble, let this be a special incentive to walk carefully before God. If we live carelessly, the eagle-eyed world will quickly see it and will spread the story with a hundred tongues, exaggerating and emblazoning it with slanderous zeal. They will shout triumphantly, "Aha! See how these Christians act! They are all hypocrites."

Much damage is done to the cause of Christ in this way, and great insult is brought to His name. The cross of Christ itself is an offense to the world, so let us be careful not to add any offense of our own. It is "a stumbling block to Jews," so let us be careful not to place another where there are enough already; and it is "foolishness to Gentiles" (1 Cor. 1:23), so let us not through our folly add another reason for scorn that the world will use to ridicule the gospel.

How watchful we should be of ourselves! How strict with our own consciences! In plain view of adversaries who will misrepresent our best deeds and impugn our motives when they cannot criticize our actions, how cautious we should be. Christian pilgrims are considered suspect by the world as they travel through Vanity Fair. [Editor's note: In *The Pilgrim's Progress* by John Bunyan (1628 – 1688), Vanity Fair is a city through which the King's Highway passes.] Not only are we under surveillance, but there are more spies than we know; espionage is everywhere, whether we are at home or abroad. And if we fall into the enemy's hands, we should expect generosity from a wolf or mercy from a demon sooner than expecting anything even approaching patience and understanding for our shortcomings from those who fuel their infidelity toward God with scandals against His people.

Forever "lead me, O LORD," lest my enemy trip me up!

From the pen of Jim Reimann:

Never be surprised that those who are enemies of Jesus are our enemies. Let us recall His warning to us:

If the world hates you, keep in mind that it hated me first. If you belonged to the world, it would love you as its own. As it is, you do not belong to the world, but I have chosen you out of the world. That is why the world hates you. Remember the words I spoke to you: "No servant is greater than his master." If they persecuted me, they will persecute you also. If they obeyed my teaching, they will obey yours also. They will treat you this way because of my name, for they do not know the One who sent me.

John 15:18 – 21

Let us also be mindful of these hopeful words of Paul: "Many live as enemies of the cross of Christ. Their destiny is destruction, their god is their stomach, and their glory is in their shame. Their mind is on earthly things. But our citizenship is in heaven. And we eagerly await a Savior from there, the Lord Jesus Christ" (Phil. 3:18 – 20).

After all, as Spurgeon says in a later devotion: "It is a very bad omen to hear a wicked world clap its hands and shout 'Well done!' to the Christian man."

SEPTEMBER 12

I will sing of your love and justice;
to you, O Lord, I will sing praise.

Psalm 101:1

From the pen of Charles Spurgeon:

Faith triumphs in trials. When reason is thrust into an "inner cell," with her feet "fastened … in the stocks" (Acts 16:24), faith makes the dungeon walls ring with her joyous songs, proclaiming, "I will sing of your love and justice; to you, O Lord, I will sing praise." Faith pulls the mask from the face of trouble and discovers the angel underneath. Faith gazes toward an ominous cloud, but finds that it:

'Tis big with mercy and shall break
In blessings on her head.

William Cowper, 1731 – 1800

Thus we discover a number of reasons for singing can be found even in the justice of God toward us. First, we see our trial is not as heavy as it might have been; next, our trouble is not as severe as we deserved; and finally, our affliction is not as crushing a burden as many others have to bear. Faith sees that even in her worst sorrow, there is nothing punitive — there is not one drop of God's wrath in it — that it is all sent in love. Faith discerns love, gleaming like a jewel on the breast of an angry God, and thereby says of her grief, "This is my badge of honor, for a true child will experience 'the rod of discipline'" (Prov. 22:15). Then Faith sings of the sweet result of her sorrows, because she knows they work to her spiritual good. Even more, Faith says, "These 'light and momentary troubles are achieving for [me] an eternal glory that far outweighs them all'" (2 Cor. 4:17). Faith rides her dark horse victoriously forward, trampling down fleshly, carnal reason, singing of victory amid the heat of battle.

All I meet I find assists me
In my path to heavenly joy:
Where, though trials now attend me,
Trials never more annoy.
Blest there with a weight of glory,
Still the path I'll ne'er forget,
But, exulting, cry, it led me
To my blessed Savior's seat.

Isaac Watts, 1674 – 1748

From the pen of Jim Reimann:

Today Spurgeon alludes to an example of true faith that found a reason to sing. Here is the context:

The magistrates ordered [Paul and Silas] to be stripped and beaten. After they had been severely flogged, they were thrown into prison, and the jailer was commanded to guard them carefully. Upon receiving such orders, he put them in the inner cell and fastened their feet in the stocks. About midnight Paul and Silas were praying and singing hymns to God.

Acts 16:22 – 25

O God, grant me faith like theirs!

SEPTEMBER 13

This man welcomes sinners.

Luke 15:2

From the pen of Charles Spurgeon:

Notice the great humility of Jesus in this verse. "This man"—He who towers above all others and who is holy, harmless, undefiled, and separate from sinners—"welcomes sinners." "This man"—He who is none other than the eternal God and before whom angels veil their faces—"welcomes sinners." Only the tongue of an angel could adequately describe such a mighty humiliation of love.

That any of us would be willing to seek the lost is not that amazing, for they are of our own human race. But that He—the offended God and He against whom the transgressions have been committed—would take upon Himself "the very nature of a servant" (Phil. 2:7) and bear "the sin of many" (Isa. 53:12) and would be willing to welcome the vilest of the vile—this is a miracle!

"This man welcomes sinners," but not that they may remain sinners. He welcomes them so He may pardon their sins, justify them by His righteousness, cleanse their hearts by His purifying Word, preserve their souls by the indwelling of the Holy Spirit, and enable them to serve Him, to offer Him praise, and to have fellowship with Him. Furthermore, "this man welcomes sinners" into His heart's love, lifting them "out of the dunghill" (Ps. 113:7 KJV), wearing them "like jewels in [His] crown" (Zech. 9:16), snatching them like "a burning stick ... from the fire" (Zech. 3:2) and preserving them as costly monuments of His mercy.

None are as precious in Jesus' sight as those sinners for whom He died. Thus, when Jesus "welcomes sinners," He doesn't receive them just anywhere—not some casual, outdoor place, where someone might greet a passing beggar. No, He opens the golden gates of His royal heart, welcoming the sinner into Himself. He receives the humble penitent into a personal union, making the penitent a member of His body—His flesh and His bones. Never was there such a glorious reception as this!

And this fact is true today: Jesus is still welcoming sinners. Oh, that sinners would welcome Him!

From the pen of Jim Reimann:

John describes Jesus as "the Word [who] became flesh and made his dwelling among us" (John 1:14). And it was Jesus — the Word — who said, "The Son of Man came to seek and to save what was lost" (Luke 19:10). John also said, "He came to that which was his own, but his own did not receive him. Yet to all who received him, to those who believed in his name, he gave the right to become children of God — children born not of natural descent, nor of human decision or a husband's will, but born of God" (John 1:11 – 13).

Therefore, woe be to those who reject Jesus the Word! Let us remember the warning of Samuel to King Saul: "Because you have rejected the word of the LORD, he has rejected you as king" (1 Sam. 15:23); and these words of Jeremiah: "The wise will be put to shame; they will be dismayed and trapped. Since they have rejected the word of the LORD, what kind of wisdom do they have?" (Jer. 8:9).

If you do not know Jesus as Savior and Lord, remember: "This man welcomes sinners." In fact, He lovingly declared, "Come to me, all you who are weary and burdened, and I will give you rest" (Matt. 11:28).

SEPTEMBER 14

I acknowledged my sin to you and did not cover up my iniquity.
I said, "I will confess my transgressions to the LORD" —
and you forgave the guilt of my sin.

Psalm 32:5

From the pen of Charles Spurgeon:

As we see from this psalm, David's grief was bitter. In fact, sin's effects were visible in his outer frame, for he said, "My bones wasted away" (v. 3), and, "My strength was sapped as in the heat of summer" (v. 4). Yet he could find no remedy until he made a full confession before the throne of heavenly grace. He said that for a time he "kept silent" (v. 3), and thus his heart became more and more filled with grief. Like a mountain pool whose outlet is blocked, his soul became swollen with torrents of sorrow. He made excuses for himself and endeavored to divert his thoughts, but it was all to no avail. Like a festering sore, his anguish grew, and since he would not use the "lance" of confession, his spirit was full of torment and he found no rest.

At last it came to this: he must return to his God in humble repentance — or die. So he hurried to God's "mercy seat" (Ex. 25:17 KJV), and once there, unrolled his list of iniquities before the all-seeing One, acknowledging all the evil of his ways in words such as we see in Psalm 51 and other psalms of repentance. And once having done this, an act so simple — yet so difficult to one's pride — he immediately received the sign of God's divine forgiveness: his bones that had been crushed were now made to rejoice (see Ps. 51:8), and he rose from his prayer closet to sing, "Blessed is he whose transgressions are forgiven" (Ps. 32:1).

Notice the great value of a grace-produced confession of sin! In every situation where there is genuine, gracious confession, God's mercy is freely given. This happens, however, not because repentance and confession deserve mercy, but for the sake of Christ Himself. Praise the Lord that there is always healing for the brokenhearted — that His fountain is forever flowing to cleanse us from our sins!

Truly, O Lord, "you are a God ready to forgive (Neh. 9:17 ESV). *Therefore, I will acknowledge all my iniquities.*

From the pen of Jim Reimann:

David also wrote the following psalm, which is in strong agreement with Psalm 32:

The righteous cry out, and the LORD hears them; he delivers them from all their troubles. The LORD is close to the brokenhearted and saves those who are crushed in spirit. A righteous man may have many troubles, but the LORD delivers him from them all; he protects all his bones, not one of them will be broken.

Psalm 34:17 – 20

Another psalmist, one who also understood the importance of confession and openness before the Lord, wrote the following beautiful words. As you read, allow these words to lead you to an attitude of praise for all He has done for you.

Come and listen, all you who fear God; let me tell you what he has done for me. I cried out to him with my mouth; his praise was on my tongue. If I had cherished sin in my heart, the Lord would not have listened; but God has surely listened and heard my voice in prayer. Praise be to God, who has not rejected my prayer or withheld his love from me!

Psalm 66:16 – 20

I thank You, Lord, that in Christ I am now "holy in [Your] sight, without blemish and free from accusation" (Col. 1:22).

SEPTEMBER 15

… the people close to his heart.
Psalm 148:14

From the pen of Charles Spurgeon:

The topic of distance was a prominent feature in the giving of the old covenant. When God appeared to Moses, He said, "Do not come any closer.… Take off your sandals" (Ex. 3:5); and when He revealed Himself on Mount Sinai to His chosen people, one of His first commands was, "Put limits for the people around the mountain" (Ex. 19:12). And in worship in both the tabernacle and the temple, the idea of distance was important. For example, most of the people did not enter even the outer court, and only the priests entered the inner court. Only the high priest could enter the innermost place, known as the Holy of Holies or "the Most Holy Place" (Ex. 26:33), and then only "once a year" (Ex. 30:10).

It was as though the Lord in the early ages sought to teach the Israelites that sin was utterly loathsome to Him. He would treat them as lepers, even meeting with Moses "outside the camp" (Ex. 33:7). When the Lord did come close to His people, He made sure they felt the distance between a holy God and an impure sinner.

When the gospel came, however, we were placed on quite another footing. The word *Go* was exchanged with *Come*, distance gave way to nearness, and we "who once were far away have been brought near through the blood of Christ" (Eph. 2:13). "Come to me, all you who are weary and burdened, and I will give you rest" (Matt. 11:28) is the joyful proclamation of God as He appears in human flesh. No longer does He teach the sinner of his "leprosy" by putting him at a distance, but by suffering the penalty of the sinner's defilement. Thus, what glorious safety and privilege there is in nearness to God through Jesus.

Dear reader, have you experienced this blessing? If so, are you living in the fullness of its power? Yet, as wonderful as this nearness is, it will someday be followed by the giving of an even greater nearness, when it will be said, "Now the dwelling of God is with men, and he will live with them" (Rev. 21:3).

May it be soon, O Lord!

From the pen of Jim Reimann:

Psalm 148, from which our text is taken, is akin to David's thought: "When I consider your heavens, the work of your fingers, the moon and the stars, which you have set in place, what is man that you are mindful of him, the son of man that you care for him?" (Ps. 8:3 – 4). Here is a portion of Psalm 148, setting forth the miraculous truth that the God of the heavens desires closeness to us:

Praise the Lord. Praise the Lord from the heavens, praise him in the heights above. Praise him, all his angels, praise him, all his heavenly hosts.… Praise the Lord from the earth, you … kings of the earth and all nations, you princes and all rulers on earth, young men and maidens, old men and children. Let them praise the name of the Lord, for his name alone is exalted; his splendor is above the earth and the heavens. He has raised up for his people a horn, the praise of all his saints, of Israel, the people close to his heart. Praise the Lord.

Psalm 148:1 – 2, 7, 11 – 14

I praise you, O God, for Jesus who "has destroyed the barrier, the dividing wall of hostility" (Eph. 2:14), that once kept me "outside the camp."

SEPTEMBER 16

Am I the sea, or the monster of the deep,
that you put me under guard?

Job 7:12

From the pen of Charles Spurgeon:

This was a strange question for Job to ask the Lord. Job felt he was too insignificant to be watched so closely and to be chastened, and he hoped that he was not so disobedient as to need to be restrained in this way. His question was only natural from someone besieged by seemingly undeserved miseries, but it comes with a humbling answer. It is true that man is not the sea, yet in some respects man is even more troublesome and unruly. For example, the sea respects its boundary, seldom jumping across its limit, even though that boundary is simply a belt of sand. As mighty as it is, it hears God's divine decree, and even when raging in a storm, it ultimately respects that decree and returns to its place.

Self-willed man, however, defies heaven and oppresses earth, and has no end to his rebellious rage. Restless beyond his limits, man also sleeps while on duty, being idle when he should be active. A self-willed man will neither come nor go at God's divine command, but would rather do what he should not do and leave undone that which is required of him. By contrast, every drop of water, bubble of foam, and every shell and pebble feel the power of God's law, yielding or moving at once. Oh, that our nature were even one thousandth as conformed to the will of God.

We say the sea is fickle, but how constant it is. Since the days of old, the sea has remained where it was, beating on the same cliffs to the same tune. We know where to find it, for it never forsakes its bed and never changes even in its ceaselessness. But where is vain and fickle man?

Can even the wisest of men guess by what folly he will next be seduced and thereby turn from his obedience? Thus, we need more watching than the billowing sea, for we are far more rebellious.

Lord, rule us for Your own glory. Amen.

From the pen of Jim Reimann:

In yesterday's devotion, we read David's question of God: "What is man that you are mindful of him?" (Ps. 8:4). David's question was asked in a much different spirit than today's text, posed by Job as part of an angry rant. As you read more of his rant, notice how Job asks the Lord the same basic question as David asked:

Let me alone; my days have no meaning. *What is man that you make so much of him*, that you give him so much attention, that you examine him every morning and test him every moment? Will you never look away from me, or let me alone even for an instant? If I have sinned, what have I done to you, O watcher of men? Why have you made me your target? Have I become a burden to you? Why do you not pardon my offenses and forgive my sins?

Job 7:16–21

Thankfully, we ultimately hear Job confess to his sovereign Lord: "I know that you can do all things; no plan of yours can be thwarted.... Surely I spoke of things I did not understand, things too wonderful for me to know. My ears had heard of you but now my eyes have seen you. Therefore I despise myself and repent in dust and ashes" (Job 42:2–3, 5–6).

SEPTEMBER 17

The LORD ... said [to Moses] ...,
"Encourage him."
Deuteronomy 1:37 – 38

From the pen of Charles Spurgeon:

God uses His people to encourage one another. Notice in today's Scripture that He did not say to an angel, such as Gabriel, "My servant Joshua is about to lead My people into Canaan. Go and 'encourage him.'" The Lord never works needless miracles, so if His purposes can be accomplished through ordinary means, He will not use miraculous ones. Gabriel would not have been half as well suited for this work of encouragement as Moses. A brother's sympathy is always more precious than the dutiful work of an angel.

Although swift of wing, angels understood much more about doing the Master's bidding than they understood the people's circumstances. No angel had ever experienced the difficulty of the road, "fiery serpents" (Num. 21:6 KJV), or led "a stiff-necked people" (Ex. 32:9) in the wilderness as Moses had done. We should be thankful that God usually works for mankind by using mankind, for doing so forms a bond of brotherhood. And, thus, since we are mutually dependent on one another, we are fused more completely into one family.

Believer, take today's verse as God's personal message to you to work to help others, especially striving to encourage them. Cheerfully speak to the young and curious enquirer regarding the things of God and lovingly attempt to remove stumbling blocks out of his way. When you find a spark of grace in someone's heart, kneel down and blow it into a flame. And when it comes to a new believer, allow him to discover the roughness of the road by degrees, but tell him of the strength that dwells in God, of the certainty of His promises, and of the blessings of fellowship with Christ. Make it your goal to comfort the sorrowful and to revitalize the despondent. "Speak a word in season to him that is weary" (Isa. 50:4 KJV) and encourage those who are fearful to go joyfully along their way.

Remember — God encourages you through His promises, Christ encourages you as He points to the heaven He has won for you, and the Spirit encourages you as He "works in you to will and to act according to his good purpose" (Phil. 2:13). So imitate God's wisdom and encourage others, as directed by today's verse.

From the pen of Jim Reimann:

We are introduced to Barnabas in the New Testament with the following account: "Joseph, a Levite from Cyprus, whom the apostles called Barnabas (which means Son of Encouragement), sold a field he owned and brought the money and put it at the apostles' feet" (Acts 4:36 – 37). What an encouragement that must have been to the apostles. No wonder his name was changed to Barnabas! A thoughtful act or a kind word always lifts our spirits, which is no doubt why we are instructed to encourage each other. For example, we are told: "Encourage one another daily" (Heb. 3:13); "Preach the Word; be prepared in season and out of season; correct, rebuke and encourage — with great patience and careful instruction" (2 Tim. 4:2).

But let us remember the true source of all encouragement:

Everything that was written in the past was written to teach us, so that through endurance and the encouragement of the Scriptures we might have hope. May the God who gives endurance and encouragement give you a spirit of unity.

Romans 15:4 – 5

SEPTEMBER 18

… and they follow me.
John 10:27

From the pen of Charles Spurgeon:

We should follow our Lord as unhesitatingly as sheep follow their shepherd, for He has a right to lead us wherever He pleases. "[We] are not [our] own; [we] were bought at a price" (1 Cor. 6:19 – 20) — so let us recognize the rights of Him whose blood redeemed us. A soldier follows his captain and a servant obeys his master. How much more should we follow our Redeemer, to whom we are a "purchased possession" (Eph. 1:14 KJV).

We are untrue to our confession of being a Christian, if we question the bidding of our Leader and Commander. Submission is our duty, and trivial objections our folly. Our Lord has every right to say to us, as He did to Peter, "What is that to you? You must follow me" (John 21:22). And wherever Jesus may lead us, He goes before us, so even if we do not know where we are going, we know with whom we go. With such a companion, who should fear the perils of the road? The journey may be long, but His "everlasting arms" (Deut. 33:27) will carry us to the end. The presence of Jesus is the assurance of eternal salvation, for "because [He] live[s], [we] also will live" (John 14:19).

We should follow Christ in simplicity and faith, because every path in which He leads will end in glory and immortality. It is true His paths may not be smooth, for they may be covered with painfully difficult trials, but they ultimately lead to "the city with foundations, whose architect and builder is God" (Heb. 11:10). "All the paths of the LORD are steadfast love and faithfulness, for those who keep his covenant" (Ps. 25:10 ESV).

So let us put our full trust in our Leader, since we know that whether we experience prosperity or adversity, sickness or health, popularity or contempt, His purpose will be accomplished, and that purpose will be pure, unmitigated good to every heir of His mercy. May we find it a blessing to go up the unsheltered side of the hill with Christ, and when the rain and snow blow in our faces, may His dear love make us far more blessed than those who sit at home, warming their hands by the world's fire. To "the crest of Amana," (Song 4:8) we will follow our Beloved!

Precious Jesus, "Draw me away! We will run after you" (Song 1:4 NKJV).

From the pen of Jim Reimann:

The prayer of Psalm 63, where David says, *"My soul follows close behind You,"* was used by the early church for daily prayers. May it be our closing prayer today:

"O God, You are my God; early will I seek You; my soul thirsts for You; my flesh longs for You in a dry and thirsty land where there is no water. So I have looked for You in the sanctuary, to see Your power and Your glory. Because Your lovingkindness is better than life, my lips shall praise You. Thus I will bless You while I live; I will lift up my hands in Your name. My soul shall be satisfied as with marrow and fatness, And my mouth shall praise You with joyful lips. When I remember You on my bed, I meditate on You in the night watches. Because You have been my help, therefore in the shadow of Your wings I will rejoice. My soul follows close behind You; Your right hand upholds me" (Ps. 63:1 – 8 NKJV).

SEPTEMBER 19

I prayed for this child.

1 Samuel 1:27

From the pen of Charles Spurgeon:

Devout believers delight in looking at the mercies they have received in answer to their prayers, for they see God's special love in them. And when we can name our blessings "Samuel," meaning "asked of God," they will be as precious to us as Hannah's son was to her. Elkanah's other wife, Peninnah, had many children, but they came to her as common blessings not sought by prayer. Thus, Hannah's one heaven-given child was far more precious to her because he was the fruit of earnest pleadings. And how sweet was the water miraculously provided for Samson at "the spring . . . called En Hakkore" (Judg. 15:19), meaning "the spring of him who called." Quassia cups, or blossoms, make any water bitter, but cups of prayer give a sweetness to every drink they bring.

Did you pray for the conversion of your children? If so, how doubly sweet, once they were saved, to see your petitions fulfilled in them. Isn't rejoicing over them as the fruit of your pleadings even better than rejoicing over them as the fruit of your body?

Have you sought the Lord for a special spiritual gift? When it came to you, wrapped in the gold cloth of His faithfulness and truth, wasn't it doubly precious? Have you petitioned Him for success in His work? Then how joyful was the blessing that came flying on the wings of prayer! Isn't it always best to receive blessings in the most legitimate way — through the door of prayer? Then they are blessings indeed — not temptations. And even when the answers may seem slow in coming, the blessings grow even richer for the delay. Surely the boy Jesus, left behind in

Jerusalem, was all the more lovely to Mary after "anxiously searching for [Him]" (Luke 2:48).

Blessings won by prayer should be dedicated to God, as Hannah dedicated Samuel. The gift came from heaven — let it go to heaven. Prayer brought it, gratitude sang over it, let devotion consecrate it. Each blessing provides a special opportunity to pray, "We have given you only what comes from your hand" (1 Chron. 29:14).

Dear reader, is prayer a source of power or one of weariness in your life?

From the pen of Jim Reimann:

Often we grow weary in prayer by not knowing how to pray. Yet God's Word offers us many beautiful examples of godly prayer. One of these, quoted briefly by Spurgeon today, is that of David as the people gave to build the temple. As you read more of that prayer below, why not make it your offering of praise to God?

"Praise be to you, O Lord, God of our father Israel, from everlasting to everlasting. Yours, O Lord, is the greatness and the power and the glory and the majesty and the splendor, for everything in heaven and earth is yours. Yours, O Lord, is the kingdom; you are exalted as head over all. Wealth and honor come from you; you are the ruler of all things. In your hands are strength and power to exalt and give strength to all. Now, our God, we give you thanks, and praise your glorious name. But who am I, and who are my people, that we should be able to give as generously as this? Everything comes from you, and we have given you only what comes from your hand" (1 Chron. 29:10 – 14).

SEPTEMBER 20

At evening let not your hands be idle.

Ecclesiastes 11:6

From the pen of Charles Spurgeon:

Ministry opportunities are plentiful in the evening as people return home from work. A zealous soul-winner will find this a wonderful time to share the love of Jesus, so let me no longer withhold my hand from the Lord's service, which needs much work. Sinners are perishing for a lack of spiritual knowledge, thus he who is idle may find himself crimson-stained with the blood of souls. Jesus gave both His hands to the nails of the cross, so how can I withhold one of mine from His blessed work? Up, idle heart! Stretch out your hand to work or lift it up in prayer. Heaven and hell are in earnest, so let me be in earnest as well, and this evening sow good seed for the Lord my God.

The evening of life — our latter years — also has its spiritual calling. Typically, a life is characterized by a morning of vigor and an evening of decay. Life seems long for some, but even a fourpence coin is a great sum to a poor man. In fact, life is so brief that no one can afford to lose a day. Someone once said that if a wealthy king gave us an entire day to take from his treasury of gold, letting us take as much as we could on that day, we would make a long day of it. We would begin early in the morning and would not allow our hands to be idle in the evening. Yet isn't winning souls a far nobler work? Then how is it that we so quickly withdraw from it?

Some of us will survive to a long evening of old age, but one still green with life. If such is my case, may I use whatever talents I still retain to serve my blessed and faithful Lord to the very last hour, laying down my calling only when I lay down my body. The aged can instruct the young, cheer the fainthearted, and encourage the despondent. And although the evening years may have less vigor and energy, they should have more calm spiritual wisdom.

Therefore, "at evening" I will "let not [my] hands be idle."

From the pen of Jim Reimann:

Indeed, Spurgeon fulfilled today's commitment. As evidence of his lifelong goal of sharing the gospel, he spoke these words in 1874:

In a little while, there will be a gathering of people in the streets. I can hear someone enquiring, "What are all these people waiting for?" "Do you not know? He is to be buried today." "And who is that?" "It is Spurgeon." "What! The man who preached at the Tabernacle?" "Yes, he is to be buried today." That will happen very soon, and when you see my coffin carried to the silent grave, I should like every one of you, whether converted or not, to be constrained to say, "He did earnestly urge us, in plain and simple language, not to put off the consideration of eternal things. He did entreat us to look to Christ. Now he is gone, our blood is not at his door if we perish." God grant that you may not have to bear the bitter reproach of your own conscience! But, as I feel "the time is short," I will stir you up as long as I am in this Tabernacle.

Lord, like Spurgeon, may my hands never "be idle" — but be used to share Your gospel as long as I am able.

SEPTEMBER 21

Do not take away my soul along with sinners.

Psalm 26:9

From the pen of Charles Spurgeon:

Fear prompted this prayer of David. Although he may have whispered it, he feared that at death his soul would be lost like those of sinners. That fear, tied to unbelief, arises primarily from a holy anxiety over the remembrance of past sin. Even a forgiven person might ask, "What if, at the end of my life, my sins are remembered and I am left off the list of the saved?" He thinks of his current unfruitfulness — so little grace, love, and holiness — that when he considers the future, along with his weakness and the many temptations that plague him, he fears he may fall and become prey to the enemy. Thus, a sense of his current sin, evil, and corruption — which he feels powerless to overcome — compels him to pray, in fear and trembling, "Do not take away my soul along with sinners."

Dear reader, if you have prayed this prayer and if your character is like that described in Psalm 26, you need not be afraid that you will be taken away as sinners will be. Do you have the two virtues David had: the outward walking in integrity and the inward trusting in the Lord? (See v. 1.) Are you resting solely upon Christ's sacrifice, and can you circle the altar of God with humble hope? If so, rest assured you will never be taken away with the wicked, for that calamity is impossible. When the Lord gathers people together at the judgment, he will gather like kind with like kind, for Jesus said, "First collect the weeds and tie them in bundles to be burned; then gather the wheat and bring it into my barn" (Matt. 13:30).

If you are like God's people, you will be with God's people. You cannot be gathered with the wicked, for you have been bought at too high a price. Redeemed by the blood of Christ, you are His forever, and where He is, there His people must be (see John 14:3). You are loved too much to be cast away with those who are reprobates.

Will one soul dear to Christ perish? Impossible! Hell cannot hold you, for heaven claims you. Trust in your Guarantor (see Heb. 7:22) and fear not!

From the pen of Jim Reimann:

Sheep and goats have some characteristics in common, but they are easy to distinguish from one another. Thus, on judgment day, a true believer need not fear being mistaken for a goat. Much akin to Jesus' teaching on the wheat and weeds that Spurgeon quoted today is the following account by Jesus of His second coming:

All the nations will be gathered before [the Son of Man], and he will separate the people one from another as a shepherd separates the sheep from the goats. He will put the sheep on his right and the goats on his left. Then the King will say to those on his right, "Come, you who are blessed by my Father; take your inheritance, the kingdom prepared for you since the creation of the world...." Then he will say to those on his left, "Depart from me, you who are cursed, into the eternal fire prepared for the devil and his angels."

Matthew 25:32 – 34, 41

Believer, don't fear, but take careful note of this: "'The Lord knows those who are his' and, 'Everyone who confesses the name of the Lord must turn away from wickedness'" (2 Tim. 2:19).

SEPTEMBER 22

I call as my heart grows faint;
lead me to the rock that is higher than I.

Psalm 61:2

From the pen of Charles Spurgeon:

Most of us know how it feels for our heart to be overwhelmed, to have a sinking feeling, like a boat tossed at the mercy of a storm. Discovering our true inner corruption will cause this. Disappointment and heartbreak will cause this as well, when wave after wave rolls over us, tossing us like a broken shell in the surf.

Yet blessed be the Lord that at such times we are not without an all-sufficient comfort, for God Himself is the harbor of weather-beaten sails and the inn for forlorn pilgrims. The Lord is higher than we are — His mercy higher than our sins, His love higher than our thoughts. Our confidence is fixed upon an exceedingly high and glorious Lord. He is a Rock because He never changes, a High Rock because the storms that overwhelm us rage far beneath His feet. He is not disturbed by them, but sovereignly rules them by His will. And if we will get under the shelter of this lofty Rock, we may defy a hurricane, for all is calm under the protection of the One who is a towering cliff. Unfortunately, however, our troubled minds are often thrown into such confusion that we need piloting to the Lord's divine shelter. No doubt this is why David prayed, "Lead me to the rock that is higher than I."

O Lord our God, by Your Holy Spirit, teach us the way of faith and lead us into Your rest. The wind blows us out to sea, but the rudder doesn't respond to our weak hand. You, and You alone, can steer us between hidden, destructive reefs, taking us safely to Your calm port. How dependent we are on You! We need You to bring us to Yourself, for to be wisely directed and steered into safety and peace is a gift from You, and only You. Even this day, may You be pleased to deal in this manner with Your servants.

From the pen of Jim Reimann:

Thankfully, there is One who is higher than we are, for as David said, "Each man is but a breath" (Ps. 39:11). Thus, one of the most powerful lessons we can learn is to always keep in perspective who God is — and who we are in relation to Him. With that in mind, let us heed these words from Isaiah:

> Seek the LORD while he may be found; call on him while he is near. Let the wicked forsake his way and the evil man his thoughts. Let him turn to the LORD, and he will have mercy on him, and to our God, for he will freely pardon. "For my thoughts are not your thoughts, neither are your ways my ways," declares the LORD. "As the heavens are higher than the earth, so are my ways higher than your ways and my thoughts than your thoughts."
>
> Isaiah 55:6 – 9

May it never take for us what it took for the children of Israel in the wilderness to remember the Lord. Here is a portion of the psalmist's account:

> In spite of his wonders, they did not believe. So he ended their days in futility and their years in terror. Whenever God slew them, they would seek him; they eagerly turned to him again. They remembered that God was their Rock, that God Most High was their Redeemer.
>
> Psalm 78:32 – 35

SEPTEMBER 23

Jesus said to him,
"If you can believe ..."
Mark 9:23 NKJV

From the pen of Charles Spurgeon:

The man to whom Jesus was speaking had a son "who [was] possessed by a spirit that ... robbed him of speech" (v. 17). The father, having seen the futile efforts of Jesus' disciples to cast the demon from his child, had little faith in Christ. Therefore, when he took his son to Jesus, he said, "If you can do anything, take pity on us and help us" (v. 22).

The poor, trembling father had placed an "if" in his question, but he had put it in the wrong place. Thus, Jesus, without commanding the man to retract the "if," compassionately placed it in its legitimate position. The Lord seemed to be saying, in essence, "There should be no 'if' about My power or My willingness. The 'if' belongs somewhere else"—"*If* you can believe, all things are possible to him who believes" (Mark 9:23 NKJV). Suddenly the man's trust was strengthened, and he offered a humble prayer for an increase of faith. Then Jesus immediately spoke the word — casting out the demon and commanding it never to return.

There is a lesson here we need to learn. Like this man, we often use an "if," but we are perpetually placing it in the wrong place. We say, "*If* Jesus can help me ..."; "*If* He can give me the grace to overcome temptation ..."; "*If* He can forgive me ..."; or "*If* He can make me successful ..."

No! You have misplaced your "if," for "*If* you can believe," He both can and will. If you can confidently trust, just as "all things are possible with God" (Mark 10:27), all things will be possible for you. Faith stands on God's power, is robed in His majesty and royal apparel, and rides the King's horse, for it is the gift of His grace that the King delights in honoring. Arming itself with the glorious might of the all-powerful Spirit, faith becomes, through the omnipotence of God, mighty to do, to dare, and to suffer. Without limit, "all things are possible to him who believes."

Dear soul, can you believe your Lord today?

From the pen of Jim Reimann:

Another important aspect to this story is what followed the healing of the demon-possessed boy. We are told, "When [Jesus] had come into the house, His disciples asked Him privately, 'Why could we not cast it out?' So He said to them, 'This kind can come out by nothing but prayer and fasting.'" (Mark 9:28 – 29 NKJV).

Jesus also was saying, in essence, "'This kind' *of faith* comes about 'by nothing but prayer and fasting.'" Faith is a gift of God, but it is strengthened through these spiritual disciplines. Remember, however, the Lord is under no obligation to answer, no matter how great our faith, *if* our request is not in compliance with His will. This is precisely where so many professing believers run amok today, for many believe they can "name and claim" all disease, hardship, and suffering away. Instead, may we heed the words of Peter, who said, "*Those who suffer according to God's will* should commit themselves to their faithful Creator and continue to do good" (1 Peter 4:19).

Father, help me to know Your will and to come to You with confident, mature faith. But when my faith falters, humble me that I may pray, like the man in today's story, "I do believe; help me overcome my unbelief!" (Mark 9:24).

September 24

I slept
but my heart was awake.
Song of Songs 5:2

From the pen of Charles Spurgeon:

Paradoxes abound in Christendom, and this is one, for the beloved spouse was asleep, yet awake. But not everyone can understand a paradox; you must have experienced it, for, as Samson said, "If you had not plowed with my heifer, you would not have solved my riddle" (Judg. 14:18). With that in mind, the two main points of today's text are a mournful sleepiness and a hopeful wakefulness.

"I slept." Through sin that dwells in me, I may have become lax in holy duties, lazy in Christian disciplines, dull to spiritual joys, and completely apathetic and passive. This is a shameful condition for someone in whom the life-giving Spirit dwells, and it is dangerous to the highest extent. Even wise virgins sometimes sleep (see Matt. 25:7), but it is high time for every believer to shake off the chains of laziness. We should be greatly concerned that believers will lose their strength, just as Samson lost his hair (see Judg. 16:19), while sleeping on the lap of carnal security. With the world dying around us, to sleep is cruel; and with eternity so close at hand, it is sheer madness. Yet none of us are as fully awake as we should be, and thus a few claps of thunder would do us all some good. And it just may be, unless we wake ourselves, those thunderclaps will come in the form of war, pestilence, or personal bereavements and losses. Oh, that we would rise forever from our couch of fleshly ease and march forth with flaming torches to meet the coming Bridegroom.

"But my heart was awake." This is a wonderful sign! Life is not extinct, although it is sadly smothered. When our renewed heart struggles against our natural sleepiness, we should be grateful to God's sovereign grace for keeping a little vitality within our body of death. Jesus will hear, help, and visit our hearts, for the voice of the wakeful heart is actually the voice of our Beloved, saying, "Open to me" (Song 5:2). Then holy zeal surely will unlock the door.

Oh lovely attitude! He stands
With melting heart and laden hands;
My soul forsakes her every sin;
And lets the heavenly Stranger in.
Joseph Grigg, 1843 – 1909?

From the pen of Jim Reimann:

The church in Sardis is a good example of believers who had fallen asleep and who appeared as dead. May Jesus' wake-up call to them be a warning to us to promptly prepare for His coming. Here is what the Lord said:

I know your deeds; you have a reputation of being alive, but you are dead. Wake up! Strengthen what remains and is about to die, for I have not found your deeds complete in the sight of my God. Remember, therefore, what you have received and heard; obey it, and repent. But if you do not wake up, I will come like a thief, and you will not know at what time I will come to you.... He who has an ear, let him hear what the Spirit says to the churches.

Revelation 3:1 – 3, 6

O Lord, "Who will rescue me from this body of death? Thanks be to God — through Jesus Christ our Lord!" (Rom. 7:24 – 25).

SEPTEMBER 25

Christ Jesus ...
has become for us wisdom from God.

1 Corinthians 1:30

From the pen of Charles Spurgeon:

Mankind's intellect seeks after rest, but by nature seeks it apart from the Lord Jesus Christ. The well-educated are apt, even once converted, to look at the simplicities of the cross with too little reverence and love. They are trapped in the same old net by which the Greeks were taken: that of trying to mix man's philosophy with God's revelation. The temptation of a person of refined thinking and advanced education is to depart from the simple truth of "Christ crucified" (1 Cor. 1:23), and to formulate a more intellectual doctrine. Yet it was this very thing that led some in the early church into Gnosticism, inundating believers with all sorts of heresies. In fact, this is the root of many errors, including Neology (rationalist theology, appealing to reason as a source of knowledge or justification), which was so popular in Germany in the recent past and is still ensnaring some Christian thinkers today.

Reader, whoever you are and whatever your education level, if you are the Lord's, be assured you will never find true rest by philosophizing Divinity. You may receive the dogma of one great thinker or the dream of another profound intellectual, but as chaff is to wheat is what their teachings will be compared to the pure Word of God. All that reasoning, even when guided by the most brilliant minds, can only discover the ABCs of truth — and even that lacks certainty. But in Christ Jesus "are hidden all the treasures of wisdom and knowledge" (Col. 2:3). Any attempt on the part of Christians to be content with systems such as those who promote liberalism or universalism would approve are doomed to failure.

The true heirs of heaven must come back to the amazingly simple reality that causes a poor plowboy's eyes to brighten with joy, and that gladdens a devoted pauper's heart: "Christ Jesus came into the world to save sinners" (1 Tim. 1:15). Jesus satisfies even the most elevated intellect when He is believingly received, but apart from Him, the mind of the regenerated believer will never find rest.

"The fear of the LORD is the beginning of knowledge" (Prov. 1:7). "All who follow his precepts have good understanding" (Ps. 111:10).

From the pen of Jim Reimann:

Gnosticism, referred to by Spurgeon today, was confronted by Paul in several of his letters. Derived from the Greek word *gnosis*, meaning "knowledge," Gnosticism taught that salvation was achieved not by faith in Christ, but by special knowledge. And, paradoxically, although a person's body was considered evil, Gnosticism led to the throwing off of all moral restraints. To this day, mankind continues to pervert the gospel in this way. But let us be reminded of the simple message of the cross of Christ — one so simple that even a child can go to Him. Here is how Paul stated it:

I did not come with eloquence or superior wisdom as I proclaimed to you the testimony about God. For I resolved to know nothing while I was with you except Jesus Christ and him crucified.... My message and my preaching were not with wise and persuasive words, but with a demonstration of the Spirit's power, so that your faith might not rest on men's wisdom, but on God's power.

1 Corinthians 2:1 – 2, 4 – 5

SEPTEMBER 26

Wail, O pine tree,
for the cedar has fallen.

Zechariah 11:2

From the pen of Charles Spurgeon:

When the crash of a large tree is heard in the forest, it is typically a sign that loggers are at work, and thus every tree may tremble lest tomorrow the sharp edge of the axe should discover it. We are all like trees marked for the axe, and the fall of one should remind us that for each of us — whether as great as a cedar or as humble as a pine — the appointed hour is fast approaching. Yet I hope we do not become callous to death because we hear of it so often. May we regard death as the most weighty of all events and be sobered by its approach.

It does not behoove us to take death lightly when our eternal destiny hangs by a thread. Death's sword has been unsheathed — let us take it seriously; its edge has been polished and sharpened — let us not play with it. He who does not prepare for death is more than a fool — he is a madman! So when "the sound of the LORD God" is heard "among the trees of the garden" (Gen. 3:8) let each tree hear Him, whether fig or sycamore, elm or cedar.

Be ready, servant of Christ, for your Master will come suddenly, when the ungodly world least expects Him. Make sure to be faithful in His work, for the grave will soon be dug for you. Be ready, parents, rearing your children in the fear of God, for they soon will be orphans. Be ready, businessman, taking care to be honest in all your dealings and making sure to serve God with all your heart. The days of your earthly service will soon be ended, and you will be called to "give an account" (Rom. 14:12) for the deeds done in the body, whether good or evil. May we all prepare for our judgment by the great King with such care that we will be rewarded with the gracious commendation: "Well done, good and faithful servant!" (Matt. 25:21).

From the pen of Jim Reimann:

Trees often are symbolic of people in the Scriptures. In today's text, they represent the ungodly, doomed for the fire (see Zech. 11:1). But trees are also symbolic of the godly, as in the following: "He is like a tree planted by streams of water, which yields its fruit in season and whose leaf does not wither. Whatever he does prospers" (Ps. 1:3).

Today's verse mentions pine and cedar, both used by Solomon in the building of the temple. "He lined its interior walls with cedar boards, paneling them from the floor of the temple to the ceiling, and covered the floor of the temple with planks of pine" (1 Kings 6:15). And although both trees were honored by being used in such a holy and beautiful building, believers are later referred to as marble pillars in the temple, symbolizing eternal life. Here is how Jesus Himself described His people, along with an admonition to be prepared for His coming:

> I am coming soon. Hold on to what you have, so that no one will take your crown. Him who overcomes I will make a pillar in the temple of my God. Never again will he leave it. I will write on him the name of my God and the name of the city of my God, the new Jerusalem, which is coming down out of heaven from my God; and I will also write on him my new name.

> Revelation 3:11 – 12

September 27

My beloved put his hand by the latch of the door,
and my heart yearned for him.

Song of Songs 5:4 NKJV

From the pen of Charles Spurgeon:

"My beloved [was] knocking" (v. 2 ESV), yet knocking was not enough, for my heart was too soundly asleep, too cold and ungrateful to rise and open the door. But the touch of His powerful, effective grace has made my soul stir itself. Oh, the compassion of my Beloved, to tarry when He found Himself shut out and saw me fast asleep upon my bed of laziness. Oh, the greatness of His patience to knock and knock again and add His voice, imploring me by saying, "Open to me" (v. 2). How could I have refused Him! O wicked heart, blush in amazement for His ultimate kindness, that He becomes His own doorman and unlocks the door Himself! How blessed is His hand that humbly condescends to lift the latch and turn the key.

Now I see that nothing but my Lord's own power can save such a sinful heap of wickedness as I am. His law fails me, and even the gospel has no effect on me until His hand is extended to me. Now I also perceive that His hand is good when everything else is unsuccessful, for He alone can open the door when nothing else will. Blessed be His name, for I feel His gracious presence even now. May "my heart [yearn] for him" when I think of all He has suffered for me, and then consider my unfaithfulness. I have allowed my affections to wander, setting up rivals to Him, and thereby have grieved Him.

O my Beloved, the sweetest and dearest of all, I have treated You as an unfaithful wife treats her husband. Oh, my cruel sins — my cruel being itself! What can I do? Tears are a poor show of my repentance. What a wretched person I am to treat my Lord, my "all in all" (1 Cor. 15:28), *my greatest joy, as though You were a stranger. Jesus, You forgive so freely, but this is not enough — prevent my unfaithfulness in the future. Kiss away my tears and purge my heart, perfectly binding it to Yourself, never to wander again.*

From the pen of Jim Reimann:

Two primary truths should be gleaned from today's devotion. The first is that unless the Lord reaches out to the unbeliever and unlatches the door of his heart, he remains in a hopeless situation. Jonah, finally recognizing his helpless condition inside the belly of the great fish, proclaimed, "Salvation comes from the Lord" (Jonah 2:9). And, of course, Jesus confirmed this truth, saying, "No one can come to me unless the Father who sent me draws him" (John 6:44), and again, "No one can come to me unless the Father has enabled him" (John 6:65).

The second truth is that once saved, continuing in sin greatly grieves our Lord. Let us remember this admonition from the apostle Paul:

Do not grieve the Holy Spirit of God, with whom you were sealed for the day of redemption. Get rid of all bitterness, rage and anger, brawling and slander, along with every form of malice. Be kind and compassionate to one another, forgiving each other, just as in Christ God forgave you.

Ephesians 4:30 – 32

"Shall we go on sinning so that grace may increase? By no means! We died to sin; how can we live in it any longer?" (Rom. 6:1 – 2). May we never cheapen God's grace in this way, but let us remember what our sin cost Him — His precious Son!

SEPTEMBER 28

"Go and look toward the sea," [Elijah] told his servant....
Seven times Elijah said,
"Go back."
1 Kings 18:43

From the pen of Charles Spurgeon:

Success is certain when the Lord has promised it. And though you may have pleaded with Him for months without evidence of an answer, it is impossible for the Lord to be deaf when His people are earnest in a matter concerning His glory. The prophet Elijah continued to wrestle with God on the top of Mount Carmel, but never for a moment gave way to the fear that perhaps he was unsuited to approach Jehovah's court. Six times his servant returned, but each time nothing was said except, "Go back."

We must never dream of giving in to unbelief, but hold to our faith "seventy times seven" (Matt. 18:22 KJV). Faith sends expectant hope to look from Carmel's summit, and if nothing is seen, she sends it back again and again. And far from being crushed by repeated disappointment, faith is inspired to plead even more fervently with God. She may be humbled, but not destroyed. Her groans and sighs simply grow stronger, but she never relaxes her hold or removes her hand.

Of course, flesh and blood prefer a speedy answer, but believing souls have learned to be submissive and to discover that it is good to wait for, and upon, the Lord. Delayed answers often cause the heart to begin searching itself, and thus lead us to contrition and spiritual reformation. In this way, death blows strike our areas of corruption, and the chambers of our sinful heart are cleansed. The great danger is that we would give up in weakness and miss the blessing.

Reader, don't give in to that sin, but continue to pray and watch, for in today's story a small cloud — the sure forerunner of torrents of rain — was finally seen. And it will be the same with you. The sign of coming good will surely be given, and you will rise as a conquering prince to enjoy the mercy you have sought. Elijah was a person with emotions like us, thus his power with God did not lie in his own merits. And if his prayer of faith produced so much, why shouldn't yours? Plead "the precious blood of Christ" (1 Peter 1:19) with great insistence, and it will be yours just as you desire.

From the pen of Jim Reimann:

Part of the beauty of God's Word is that it doesn't hide the frailties of those whom the Lord used in the greatest ways. Elijah was a human being — one like us — but one whom the Lord used in mighty ways. In fact, the apostle James, writing about prayer, used Elijah as an example, but did not fail to remind us that he was human. He wrote: "The prayer of a righteous man is powerful and effective. Elijah was a man just like us. He prayed earnestly that it would not rain, and it did not rain on the land for three and a half years. Again he prayed, and the heavens gave rain, and the earth produced its crops" (James 5:16 – 18).

Perhaps, like Elijah, you have not experienced the blessing of "rain" for three and a half years or more, but continue to "go back" by the path of the prayer of faith. Remember — even before Elijah prayed, he said by faith, "There is the sound of a heavy rain" (1 Kings 18:41)!

"May [God] fulfill every good purpose of yours and every act prompted by your faith" (2 Thess. 1:11).

September 29

I found the one my heart loves.
I held him and would not let him go.

Song of Songs 3:4

From the pen of Charles Spurgeon:

Does Christ receive us when we come to Him in spite of our past sinfulness? Does He rebuke us for having tried every other place of refuge first?

Certainly there is no one on earth like Jesus. Isn't He the very best of all who are good and the most beautiful of all? Oh, then let us praise Him! "Daughters of Jerusalem" (v. 5), exalt Him with "tambourine and harp" (Ps. 149:3). Down with our idols and up with the Lord Jesus. Let our banners of vanity and pride be trampled underfoot; let the cross of Jesus, which the world frowns and scoffs at, be lifted on high. Oh, for a "great throne inlaid with ivory" (1 Kings 10:18) for our eternal King "Solomon." May He be set on high forever, and may my soul sit at His footstool, kiss His feet, and wash them with my tears (see Luke 7:37 – 38). Oh, how precious is Christ! Yet how can it be that I have thought so little of Him? How is it that I searched everywhere but in Him for joy and comfort, when He is so full, so rich, so satisfying?

Believer, make a covenant with your heart that you will never depart from Him, and ask your Lord to confirm it. Ask Him to make you like a signet ring on His finger and a bracelet on His wrist. Ask Him to bind you to Himself, "as a bridegroom adorns his head like a priest, and as a bride adorns herself with her jewels" (Isa. 61:10).

I desire to live in Your heart, dear Christ; "in the clefts of [that] rock" (Song 2:14) may my soul eternally live. "Even the sparrow has found a home, and the swallow a nest for herself, where she may have her young — a place near your altar, O LORD Almighty, my King and my God" (Ps. 84:3). I too desire to make my nest — my home — in You. May my soul, as Your dove, never leave again; but may I nestle close to You, O Jesus, my true — my only — rest.

When my precious Lord I find,
All my ardent passions glow;
Him with cords of love I bind,
Hold and will not let Him go.

Author unknown

From the pen of Jim Reimann:

The things of the world have a tempting allure to the best of us. But the closer we get to Jesus, the more His brilliance dims the glow of worldly temptations. Yet at one point in His ministry, "many of his disciples turned back and no longer followed him" (John 6:66), due to the "hard teaching" (v. 60) He shared with them. Then Jesus asked His twelve, "You do not want to leave too, do you?" (v. 67); at which Peter declared, "Lord, to whom shall we go? You have the words of eternal life" (v. 68).

As Spurgeon urged, let us covenant never to turn away again. "To whom shall we go"!

"No one is like you, O LORD; you are great, and your name is mighty in power. Who should not revere you, O King of the nations? This is your due. Among all the wise men of the nations and in all their kingdoms, there is no one like you" (Jer. 10:6 – 7).

SEPTEMBER 30

Even a live dog is better off than a dead lion!

Ecclesiastes 9:4

From the pen of Charles Spurgeon:

Life is precious — even in its humblest form it is better than death. And this is eminently true in spiritual things, for it is better to be the "least in the kingdom of heaven" (Matt. 11:11) than the greatest outside it. Even the lowest degree of grace is superior to the highest level of the unregenerate nature. Where the Holy Spirit implants God's divine life in a soul, there is a precious deposit that none of the refinements produced by education can equal. The thief on the cross (see Luke 23:39 – 43) outshines the greatest Caesar on his throne; the beggar Lazarus, even when "the dogs came and licked his sores" (Luke 16:21), was better off than the Roman senator and statesman Cicero (106 – 43 BC); and even the most illiterate Christian is superior to the Greek philosopher Plato (c. 424 – 348 BC) in the sight of God. In the spiritual realm, life is the badge of nobility, and those without it are simply either coarser or finer specimens of the same lifeless material. They need to "be made alive" (1 Cor. 15:22), for they are "dead in ... transgressions and sins" (Eph. 2:1).

Likewise, a living, loving gospel sermon, regardless of how uneducated the preacher or uncultured his style, is better than the finest discourse devoid of the Spirit's anointing and power. The worst speaker, yet someone who is a spiritual preacher, is infinitely better than the most eloquent orator who has no wisdom but that of words and no power but that of sound. And the same holds true for our prayers and other Christian activities; if we are empowered in them by the Holy Spirit, they are acceptable to God through Jesus Christ. But when we think of them as worthless things, or when we make them grand performances in which our hearts are absent, they are "a dead lion" — the mere rotting flesh of a dead animal in the sight of the living God.

Oh, for *living* sighs, *living* groans, *living* despondencies rather than lifeless songs and dead calms. Better anything than death. What greater curse can we have than a dead faith, and thus a dead proclamation of our faith?

"Revive us," O Lord. "Revive us"! (Ps. 80:18)

From the pen of Jim Reimann:

The prayer *"Revive us"* is taken from a beautiful psalm of God's people, pleading with Him to restore them to life. As you read the following excerpt, be reminded that this psalm finds its ultimate fulfillment in Jesus:

"Let your hand rest on the man at your right hand, the son of man you have raised up for yourself. Then we will not turn away from you; revive us, and we will call on your name. Restore us, O LORD God Almighty; make your face shine upon us, that we may be saved" (Ps. 80:17 – 19).

The Messiah was sent to answer their prayer and proclaimed His mission in these words: "I have come that they may have life" (John 10:10); and "I tell you the truth, whoever hears my word and believes him who sent me has eternal life and will not be condemned; he has crossed over from death to life. I tell you the truth, a time is coming and has now come when the dead will hear the voice of the Son of God and those who hear will live" (John 5:24 – 25).

October

OCTOBER 1

The LORD will give grace and glory.

Psalm 84:11 KJV

From the pen of Charles Spurgeon:

Abundant generosity is Jehovah's nature; to give is His delight. His gifts are precious beyond measure and are as freely given as the light of the sun. He gives grace to His elect because He wills it, to His redeemed because of His covenant, to the called because of His promise, to believers because they desire it, and to sinners because they need it. And He gives that grace abundantly, constantly, readily, sovereignly, and always in a timely fashion, greatly enhancing the value of the blessing even in the way He bestows it. He also freely renders grace to His people in all its forms: comforting, preserving, sanctifying, guiding, instructing, and assisting grace. He generously pours into their souls without ceasing, and He will always do so whatever may occur. Sickness may strike, but the Lord will give grace; poverty may happen, but grace will surely be afforded; death must come, but grace will light a candle at the darkest hour.

Dear reader, how blessed it will be as the years roll by, as the leaves begin to fade and fall, to enjoy such an unfading promise as "The LORD will give grace." Yet the little conjunction *and* in today's verse is a diamond rivet binding the present to the future, for "grace *and* glory" always go together. God has married them, and no one can divorce them. Thus, the Lord will never deny glory to a soul whom He has freely given His grace to live. In fact, glory is nothing more than grace robed in its Sabbath best, grace in full bloom, grace like autumn fruit — ripe, mellow, perfected.

How soon we will experience glory no one can say. It may be before this present month of October is over that we will see "the Holy City" (Rev. 21:2), but whether the time seems short or long, we will soon be glorified. Glory — the glory of heaven, the glory of eternity, the glory of Jesus, the glory of the Father — is what the Lord will surely give His chosen. Oh, the extraordinary promise of a faithful God!

> Two golden links of one celestial chain:
> Who owneth grace shall surely glory gain.
> Author unknown

From the pen of Jim Reimann:

Indeed, "The LORD [promised] grace and glory," and He has done it! "The Word became flesh and made his dwelling among us. We have seen his glory, the glory of the One and Only, who came from the Father, full of grace and truth" (John 1:14). "Therefore, since we have been justified through faith, we have peace with God through our Lord Jesus Christ, through whom we have gained access by faith into this grace in which we now stand. And we rejoice in the hope of the glory of God" (Rom. 5:1 – 2). Thus, may the following verses be our benediction and closing prayer:

> "*The God of all grace, who called you to his eternal glory in Christ, after you have suffered a little while, will himself restore you and make you strong, firm and steadfast*" (1 Peter 5:10). "*But grow in the grace and knowledge of our Lord and Savior Jesus Christ. To him be glory both now and forever! Amen*" (2 Peter 3:18).

OCTOBER 2

... a man greatly beloved.

Daniel 10:11 KJV

From the pen of Charles Spurgeon:

Child of God, do you hesitate to appropriate this title for yourself? Has your unbelief made you forget that you are "greatly beloved" too? Must you not have been greatly beloved to have been bought "with the precious blood of Christ, a lamb without blemish or defect" (1 Peter 1:19)? When God struck down "his only begotten Son" (John 3:16 KJV) for you, was it not you being "greatly beloved"? You not only lived in sin, you reveled in it; must you not have been "greatly beloved" for God to have been so patient with you? You were called by grace and led to the Savior and were, thereby, made a child of God and an heir of heaven. Doesn't all this prove His great love?

Since that time, whether your path has been rough with troubles or smooth with mercies, it has been filled with proof that you are someone "greatly beloved." When the Lord has disciplined you, it has not been done in anger; when you have been made poor, you still have been rich in grace. And the more unworthy you feel yourself to be, the more evidence you have that nothing but the Lord Jesus' inexpressible love could have led Him to save a soul such as you. The more lacking in merit you feel, the clearer the display of God's abounding love in having chosen you, called you, and made you an heir of His blessings.

Therefore, if there is such great love between God and us, let us live in its influence and sweetness, taking advantage of the privilege of our position. Let us not approach our Lord as though we were strangers to Him, as though He were unwilling to hear us, for we are "greatly beloved" by our loving Father. "He who did not spare his own Son, but gave him up for us all — how will he not also, along with him, graciously give us all things?" (Rom. 8:32).

O believer, come boldly to Him, for despite the murmurings of Satan and even the doubting of your own heart, you are "greatly beloved." Meditate on the exceeding greatness and faithfulness of His divine love, going throughout your day in peace.

From the pen of Jim Reimann:

Today's text describes God's people as "greatly beloved." Indeed, "God *so loved* the world that he gave his one and only Son, that whoever believes in him shall not perish but have eternal life" (John 3:16). "Because of his great love for us, God, who is rich in mercy, made us alive with Christ even when we were dead in transgressions — it is by grace you have been saved" (Eph. 2:4 – 5).

God's love is so great that Paul said, in essence, we as finite people cannot fully comprehend its infinite greatness. His prayer in that regard was this: "I pray that you, being rooted and established in love, may have power, together with all the saints, to grasp how wide and long and high and deep is the love of Christ, and to know this love that surpasses knowledge" (Eph. 3:17 – 19). "How great is the love the Father has lavished on us"? So great "that we should be called children of God! And that is what we are!" (1 John 3:1). Therefore, "Whoever is wise, let him heed these things and consider the great love of the LORD" (Ps. 107:43).

In gratitude for His love, I pray,

"I love you, O LORD" (Ps. 18:1).

OCTOBER 3

[Jesus] himself suffered when he was tempted.

Hebrews 2:18

From the pen of Charles Spurgeon:

Although it is common biblical knowledge, it nevertheless tastes like nectar to a weary heart to know that Jesus was "tempted … just as we are" (Heb. 4:15). No doubt you have heard that truth many times, but have you truly grasped it? He was tempted to commit the very same sins into which we fall, so do not separate Jesus from the personhood we share with Him. Temptation is a dark room we go through, but Jesus went through it before us. It is a fierce battle we wage, but Jesus stood toe-to-toe with the very same enemy. So let us take heart, knowing that Christ has carried the burden before us and that the blood-stained footsteps of the King of glory can be seen along the road we travel at this very moment.

Yet there is something even better — Jesus was tempted, but He never sinned. Thus, my soul, it is not necessary for you to sin, for Jesus was a man; and if He — a man — endured these temptations and never sinned, then in His power the members of His body may also cease from sin. Some who are new to the Christian life think they cannot be tempted without sinning, but they are mistaken. There is no sin in being tempted; the sin is in yielding to temptation. This should be a great comfort to those who are severely tempted.

There is still more to encourage new believers — the Lord Jesus, though tempted, gloriously triumphed. And just as He overcame, His followers will as well, for Jesus is the representative for His people; the Head has triumphed, and thus the members of His body share in the victory. Therefore, fear is needless, for Christ is with us and is armed for our defense, and our place of safety is in the loving embrace of the Savior.

Perhaps we are facing temptation even now, but doing so in order to drive us closer to Him. So blessed be any wind that blows us into the port of our Savior's love. Blessed be the wounds that cause us to seek the beloved Physician. O tempted ones, come to your tempted Savior, for He can be touched with the feeling of your infirmities and will comfort every tried and tempted soul.

From the pen of Jim Reimann:

As Spurgeon said, "There is no sin in being tempted; the sin is in yielding to temptation." We must remember to "take up the shield of faith, with which you can extinguish all the flaming arrows of the evil one" (Eph. 6:16). These flaming arrows are often tempting thoughts that enter our minds. Thus, having the thought is not a sin, but dwelling on it and, of course, acting on it are indeed sinful.

The battle begins in your mind, which is why the apostle Paul taught: "We demolish arguments and every pretension that sets itself up against the knowledge of God, and we take captive every thought to make it obedient to Christ" (2 Cor. 10:5). Victory is won through "the renewing of your mind" (Rom. 12:2), and that is accomplished only by spending time in God's Word — filling your mind with it.

Therefore, "whatever is true, whatever is noble, whatever is right, whatever is pure, whatever is lovely, whatever is admirable — if anything is excellent or praiseworthy — think about such things" (Phil. 4:8).

OCTOBER 4

If anybody does sin,
we have one who speaks to the Father in our defense —
Jesus Christ, the Righteous One.
1 John 2:1

From the pen of Charles Spurgeon:

If we sin, we still have Jesus. Notice John did not say, "'If anybody does sin,' he forfeits someone to speak in his defense"; but said, in essence, "Although we sin, 'we have one who speaks to the Father in our defense.'" All the sin a believer has ever committed or will commit in the future cannot destroy His claim to the Lord Jesus Christ as his advocate.

The name "Jesus" in today's text is indicative of this truth. He is the perfect advocate for us, for His name — the sweetest of all names — is that of one whose work and delight it is to save. Joseph was told, "You are to give him the name Jesus, because he will save his people from their sins" (Matt. 1:21).

In today's text He is also called Christ, or *Khristos* in Greek, meaning "the anointed." This shows His authority to plead our case. The Christ has the right to represent us because He is the Father's own appointed advocate and ordained priest. Someone of our choosing might fail, but since God has designated Him who is almighty, we may safely lay our troubles before Him upon whom God has laid His all-powerful help. Jesus is Christ and is therefore authorized; He is Christ, and therefore is qualified, for His anointing has fully entitled Him for His work. Thus He can plead to move the heart of God and prevail. Oh, what words of tenderness, what sentences of persuasion the Anointed One will use when He stands to plead my case!

He is also called "the Righteous One" in today's verse. This describes not only His character but also His plea. Of course, it is His character, and if "the Righteous One" is my advocate, then my case is good or He would not have taken it. But it is His plea as well, for He counters the charge of unrighteousness against me by the plea that He is righteous. He declares Himself to be my substitute and places His obedience on my account.

My soul, you have a Friend well suited to be your advocate and to plead your case. He cannot help but succeed, so trust yourself entirely to His hands.

From the pen of Jim Reimann:

In the original Greek, today's text conveys the meaning that Jesus is our defense attorney. With that in mind, let us consider the many words we see in the various translations of the Scriptures that are legal terms, such as *judge, justice, witness, testimony,* and *impute* or *imputation,* just to name a few.

Even the word *counselor* is a legal term. Yet more often than not, we think of a counselor as someone who gives advice for emotional issues or difficult circumstances, but its original meaning is a legal one, synonymous with *attorney.* In that light, let us consider the following words of Jesus and take courage that God the Son, and God the Holy Spirit, are our Advocate before God's throne and our Counselor in the world.

"The Counselor, the Holy Spirit, whom the Father will send in my name, will teach you all things and will remind you of everything I have said to you" (John 14:26). "When you are brought before synagogues, rulers and authorities, do not worry about how you will defend yourselves or what you will say, for the Holy Spirit will teach you at that time what you should say" (Luke 12:11 – 12).

OCTOBER 5

Whoever believes and is baptized will be saved.

Mark 16:16

From the pen of Charles Spurgeon:

John MacDonald once asked the people of St. Kilda how a person must be saved. [Editor's note: MacDonald, an itinerate preacher, took the gospel to the remote Scottish island of St. Kilda from 1822 to 1844.] An old man replied, "We will be saved if we repent, forsake our sins, and turn to God." One woman added, "Yes, but we must do it with a sincere heart." Another said, "It must be done with a prayer," while a fourth person said, "But a prayer of the heart." Finally a fifth added, "And we must be diligent in keeping God's commandments."

Thus, each having contributed his "two cents' worth," the parishioners looked up and listened for the preacher's approval. Instead they had aroused his pity. The sinful mind always maps out for itself a way in which self can work and become great, but the Lord's way is the reverse. Believing and being baptized are not matters of personal merit for us to take glory in; God's gift of grace alone deserves the credit.

Dear reader, perhaps you are unsaved. If so, what is the reason? Do you think the way of salvation as presented in today's verse is uncertain? But how can that be when God Himself has pledged His own word for its certainty? Do you think it is too easy? Then why not do it? The very fact that it is so easy leaves people who neglect to follow it without excuse. To believe simply means to trust and depend upon Christ Jesus. And to be baptized is simply to submit to the ordinance that our Lord Himself fulfilled at the Jordan River (see Matt. 3:13 – 17), that to which those converted at

Pentecost submitted (see Acts 2:41), and that to which the Philippian jailer yielded his obedience on the very night of his conversion (see Acts 16:33). Of course, baptism is an outward sign that does not save us, but it does set before us our death, burial, and resurrection in Jesus (see Rom. 6:3 – 4) and, like the Lord's Supper, is not to be neglected (see Luke 22:19 and Matt. 28:19).

Reader, do you believe in Jesus? Then, dear friend, dismiss your fears, you will be saved. Or are you still an unbeliever? If so, remember, there is only one door, and if you will not enter through it, you will perish in your sins.

From the pen of Jim Reimann:

Some people use today's verse to teach that baptism is essential for salvation. But they fail to read the second part of the verse, which says, " ... *but whoever does not believe will be condemned*" (Mark 16:16). Therefore, what is it that condemns? The sin of unbelief! Remember the words of Jesus: "If you do not believe that I am the one I claim to be, you will indeed die in your sins" (John 8:24). Also know that the "one door" of salvation referred to today is Jesus, who said, "I am the gate; whoever enters through me will be saved" (John 10:9), and "I am the way and the truth and the life. No one comes to the Father except through me" (John 14:6).

Unbeliever, the world may tell you otherwise, but Solomon, the wisest man who ever lived once said, "There is a way that seems right to a man, but in the end it leads to death" (Prov. 14:12). Jesus is "*the* way"!

OCTOBER 6

[Moses] had married an Ethiopian woman.

Numbers 12:1 NKJV

From the pen of Charles Spurgeon:

The choice of an Ethiopian wife was a strange choice for Moses, who was Jewish, but how much more strange is the choice of Him who is a prophet like Moses — only greater! Our Lord, who is as fair as a lily, has united Himself in a marriage with those who have been stained by the darkness of sin. It is the wonder of angels that the love of Jesus should be placed on poor, lost, and guilty people. When filled with a sense of His love, every believer should be overwhelmed and astonished that such love would be lavished on someone so utterly unworthy of it. Knowing as we do our hidden darkness, guiltiness, and unfaithfulness, our hearts should be softened in grateful admiration for the matchless love of Jesus and the sovereignty of His grace. Yet He must have found the motive for His love in His own heart, for He could not have found it in us because it is not there.

Even since our conversion, a certain darkness has remained within us, although grace has made us beautiful in God's eyes. The godly Samuel Rutherford (Scottish Presbyterian preacher, 1600? – 1661) once said of himself what each of us should believe: "Christ's relationship to me is: I am sick, and He is the physician I need. But alas! How often I play fast and loose with Him! He binds, I loose; He builds, I tear down; I argue with Him, and He agrees with me twenty times a day!"

O most tender and faithful Husband of our souls, continue Your gracious work of conforming us to Your image until You finally present even us poor "Ethiopians" to Yourself "without stain or wrinkle or any other blemish" (Eph. 5:27).

Moses faced opposition because of his marriage, and both he and his wife became the targets of evil scrutiny. Is it any wonder then that the vain world of today opposes Jesus and His spouse, especially when notorious sinners are converted? Don't today's Pharisees continue to object on the following basis: "This man welcomes sinners" (Luke 15:2). Aren't they simply reviving the original cause: "Miriam and Aaron spoke against Moses *because of the Ethiopian woman whom he had married*" (Num. 12:1 NKJV)?

From the pen of Jim Reimann:

In the Old Testament we see the relationship between Israel and their God as one of marriage, just as in the New Testament we see the church as the bride of Jesus. We can take comfort in this relationship, for even though we still sin, the Lord sees us as His bride, and is patient and always willing to take us back. Here is how this precious truth was expressed through Isaiah, the prophet of God:

"Your Maker is your husband — the LORD Almighty is his name — the Holy One of Israel is your Redeemer; he is called the God of all the earth. The LORD will call you back as if you were a wife deserted and distressed in spirit — a wife who married young, only to be rejected," says your God. "For a brief moment I abandoned you, but with deep compassion I will bring you back. In a surge of anger I hid my face from you for a moment, but with everlasting kindness I will have compassion on you," says the LORD your Redeemer.

Isaiah 54:5 – 8

OCTOBER 7

Now in whom do you trust?

Isaiah 36:5 NKJV

From the pen of Charles Spurgeon:

This is an important question. As you read the following — which is how a true Christian should respond — see if it agrees with your beliefs:

"Whom do I trust? I trust in the Triune God. I trust the Father, believing He has chosen me 'before the creation of the world' (Eph. 1:4); I trust Him to provide for me through His providence, to teach me, to guide me, to correct me when I need it, and one day to take me home to his house where there 'are many rooms' (John 14:2).

"I trust the Son — 'very God of very God' (The Nicene Creed) — the man Christ Jesus. I trust Him to take away all my sins by His own sacrifice, and to clothe me with His perfect righteousness. I trust Him to be my Intercessor, to present my prayers and desires before His Father's throne; and I trust Him to be my Advocate on that last great day, to plead my case and to justify me. I trust Him for who He is, for what He has done, and for what He has promised yet to do.

"Finally, I trust the Holy Spirit — He who has begun to save me from my inborn sins. I trust Him to drive them all away; I trust Him to curb my temper, to subdue my will, to enlighten my understanding, to restrain my passions, to comfort my despair, to help my weaknesses, and to illuminate my darkness. I trust Him to dwell in me as my very life; to reign in me as my King; to sanctify me completely, in spirit, soul, and body; and then to take me heavenward to live with the saints in light forever."

Oh, blessed trust! To trust Him whose power will never be exhausted, whose love will never grow cold, whose kindness will never change, whose faithfulness will never fail, whose wisdom can never be challenged, and whose perfect goodness can never be diminished.

And blessed are you, dear reader, if this type of trust is yours. For if you trust in this way, you will enjoy the blessing of peace here and now, and the blessing of glory forever — and the foundation of your trust will never be shaken or removed.

From the pen of Jim Reimann:

My friend, how *did* you answer today's question? If your answer was not in agreement with the thoughts of Spurgeon, may you heed the following words: "Pay attention and listen to the sayings of the wise; apply your heart to what I teach, for it is pleasing when you keep them in your heart and have all of them ready on your lips. So that your trust may be in the LORD" (Prov. 22:17 – 19). And may the following prayer of David become the prayer of your heart, now and forever:

> "To you, O LORD, I lift up my soul; in you I trust, O my God…. Show me your ways, O LORD, teach me your paths; guide me in your truth and teach me, for you are God my Savior, and my hope is in you all day long" (Ps. 25:1 – 2, 4 – 5).

"May the God of hope fill you with all joy and peace as you trust in him, so that you may overflow with hope by the power of the Holy Spirit" (Rom. 15:13). "Trust in the LORD forever, for the LORD, the LORD, is the Rock eternal" (Isa. 26:4).

OCTOBER 8

Pray in the Holy Spirit.
Jude 20

From the pen of Charles Spurgeon:

This is the characteristic of true prayer — "In the Holy Spirit." The seed of acceptable devotion must come from heaven's storehouse, for only a prayer that comes from God can go to God. We must shoot the Lord's "arrows" back to Him, for the desire He writes upon our heart moves His heart to bring down a blessing, while the desires of the flesh have no power with Him whatsoever.

"Pray[ing] in the Holy Spirit" is praying with fervency, whereas offering cold prayers is equal to asking the Lord not to hear them. Those who do not plead fervently do not plead at all; those who have a lukewarm fire in their heart offer lukewarm prayers. So it is essential we be red hot and that we pray perseveringly. A true believer offering true prayer actually gathers force as he proceeds, growing more fervent even when God delays His answer. The longer the door is closed, the more vehemently he knocks, and the longer the angel lingers, the more resolved he is that he will not let him go without a blessing (see Gen. 32:26). Tearful, agonizing, and unconquerable insistence is beautiful in God's sight, but it means praying humbly, for the Holy Spirit never puffs us up with pride. It is His role to convict us of sin, and thereby to humble us in contrition and brokenness of spirit. After all, we will never sing "Gloria in excelsis Deo" (Latin for "Glory to God in the highest," Luke 2:14) until we pray to God "*de profundis*" (Latin for "out of the depths," Ps. 130:1). We must cry "out of the depths" or we will never behold God's "glory … in the highest."

"Pray[ing] in the Holy Spirit" is loving prayer. True prayer should be perfumed and saturated with love — love for our fellow saints and love for Christ. True prayer must be a prayer full of faith, for a person will prevail in prayer only as long as he believes. The Holy Spirit is the author of faith and is He who strengthens it so that we may pray believing God's promises.

Oh, that all these blessed attributes of prayer, as priceless as "all the spices of the merchant" (Song 3:6), might be fragrant within us because the Holy Spirit is in our hearts.

O blessed Comforter, exert Your mighty power within us, overcoming our weaknesses in prayer.

From the pen of Jim Reimann:

Oh, how quickly we give up when praying to God! Yet Jesus had much to say about persevering in prayer. For example, He taught:

Suppose one of you has a friend, and he goes to him at midnight and says, "Friend, lend me three loaves of bread…." I tell you, though he will not get up and give him the bread because he is his friend, yet because of the man's boldness [or *persistence*, NIV footnote] he will get up and give him as much as he needs. So I say to you: Ask and it will be given to you; seek and you will find; knock and the door will be opened to you. For everyone who asks receives; he who seeks finds; and to him who knocks, the door will be opened.

Luke 11:5, 8 – 10

Remember, believer, "The effective, fervent prayer of a righteous man avails much" (James 5:16 NKJV). "Will not God bring about justice for his chosen ones, who cry out to him day and night?" (Luke 18:7).

OCTOBER 9

Jesus did not answer [her] a word.
Matthew 15:23

From the pen of Charles Spurgeon:

Believers who are genuinely seeking a blessing, but who have not yet obtained it, should take comfort from today's story (see Matt. 15:21 – 28). The Savior did not immediately bestow the blessing even though the woman had great faith in Him. He intended to give it, but He waited for a while. "Jesus did not answer a word."

Was her prayer not good? No, there is not a better prayer anywhere. Was she not truly in need? No, she was sorrowfully needy. Did she not feel her need sufficiently? No, she was overwhelmed by it. Was she not earnest enough? No, she was very intense. Did she not have any faith? No, in fact, she had such a high degree of faith that even Jesus was in awe, saying, "Woman, you have great faith!" (v. 28).

Let us learn from this that although it is true that faith brings peace, it does not always bring it instantaneously. There may be certain reasons calling for the trial of faith rather than the reward of faith. Genuine faith may be in our soul like a hidden seed, but may not have budded and blossomed into joy and peace. A painful silence by the Savior is the extremely difficult trial of many a seeking soul, but far worse is the affliction of a harsh, cutting reply such as: "It is not right to take the children's bread and toss it to their dogs" (v. 26).

Many people waiting on the Lord find immediate delight, but this is not the case with everyone. Some, like the Philippian jailer, are turned in a moment from darkness to light (see Acts 16:22 – 34), while others are plants with slower growth. Perhaps a deeper sense of sin, instead of a sense of pardon, will be given to you, and you will need great patience to sustain the heavy blow.

O poor heart, though Christ may beat and bruise you or even "though he slay [you],... trust in him" (Job 13:15 KJV); and though He may speak an angry word to you, believe in the love of His heart. No matter what, I implore you, never give up seeking and trusting your Master just because you have not yet obtained the joy for which you yearn. Throw yourself in complete dependence upon Him and determine to persevere even when you cannot rejoice in hope.

From the pen of Jim Reimann:

Jesus' words to this Canaanite woman, "It is not right to take the children's bread and toss it to their dogs," is somewhat softer in the Greek, for it conveys the idea of "little dogs," such as a pet dog. But whether harsh or not, this woman understood the essence of His words: He was sent first to the people of Israel. Yet here was a Gentile, expressing such faith in Him that Jesus referred to her faith as "great faith" — something He never said of anyone in Israel. In fact, the only other time Jesus mentioned "great faith" was in regards to another Gentile, the Roman centurion who asked Jesus to heal his servant (see Matt. 8:5 – 10).

Jesus was seemingly harsh with His own disciples at times. Immediately after He calmed the storm on the sea, He chastened them, saying, "Why are you so afraid? Do you still have *no faith*?" (Mark 4:40). Consider this amazing contrast: Gentiles with "great faith," and Jewish disciples of Jesus with "no faith"!

Dear Christian, how would Jesus describe your faith?

OCTOBER 10

I will deliver you from the hand of the wicked,
and I will redeem you from the grip of the terrible.

Jeremiah 15:21 NKJV

From the pen of Charles Spurgeon:

Notice how the Lord Jehovah personally makes this promise, for He says, "I will … I will…." He steps in to deliver and redeem His people, personally pledging to rescue them. Notice that not a word is mentioned of any effort on our part. In fact, neither our strength nor our weakness is taken into account, but simply the word *I*. Why then do we evaluate our strength and consult with flesh and blood (see Gal. 1:15 – 16) to our own great detriment? O you unbelieving thoughts, "Peace, be still" (Mark 4:39 KJV) and know "the LORD reigns!" (1 Chron. 16:31).

Also notice there is no hint of a secondary means or cause. The Lord undertakes the work alone and feels no need of human arms to aid Him. Thus it is a vain exercise for us to look to our family and friends for help, for they become like broken reeds when we lean on them — often unwilling when able, and unable when willing. Since the promise comes from God alone, it would be good to wait solely upon Him; and when we do so, our expectation never fails us.

So who are "the wicked" in today's text that we should fear them? The Lord will consume them — they are to be pitied rather than feared. And who are "the terrible"? They are only a terror to those who have no God, for when the Lord is on our side, "whom shall [we] fear?" (Ps. 27:1). If we run to sin in order to please the wicked, we have reason to be afraid; but if we will hold fast to our integrity, the rage of tyrants will be overcome for our good.

Remember — when the fish swallowed Jonah, he found him to be a mouthful he could not digest (see Jonah 2:10); and when the world attempts to devour the church, it is glad to be rid of it again. At all times, in every "fiery trial" (1 Peter 4:12 KJV), "by standing firm you will gain life" (Luke 21:19).

From the pen of Jim Reimann:

David is a great example of one who stood firm in each "fiery trial" and looked to the Lord for help. For example, when captured by the Philistines he prayed, "Record my lament; list my tears on your scroll — are they not in your record? Then my enemies will turn back when I call for help. By this I will know that God is for me" (Ps. 56:8 – 9). And when David fled from his son Absalom, he sang the following psalm, which reiterates the truth of today's text from Jeremiah. May it be our prayer of faith and may we rejoice in the Lord Jehovah, our deliverer!

"O LORD, how many are my foes! How many rise up against me! Many are saying of me, 'God will not deliver him.' But you are a shield around me, O LORD; you bestow glory on me and lift up my head. To the LORD I cry aloud, and he answers me from his holy hill. I lie down and sleep; I wake again, because the LORD sustains me. I will not fear the tens of thousands drawn up against me on every side. Arise, O LORD! Deliver me, O my God! Strike all my enemies on the jaw; break the teeth of the wicked. From the LORD comes deliverance. May your blessing be on your people" (Ps. 3:1 – 8).

October 11

Those he predestined,
he also called.

Romans 8:30

From the pen of Charles Spurgeon:

Paul said to Timothy, "God … has saved us and called us to a *holy* life" (2 Tim. 1:8 – 9). These words are a standard by which we can test our calling. It is a *holy* calling — "not because of anything we have done but because of his own purpose and grace" (v. 9). It is a calling that forbids all trust in our own works, taking us to Christ alone for salvation, and which after salvation purges us from dead works "to serve the living and true God" (1 Thess. 1:9). Therefore, "just as he who called you is holy, so be holy in all you do" (1 Peter 1:15). But know this: if you are living in sin, you are not called; yet if you are truly Christ's, you will say, "Nothing hurts me as much as sin, and thus I yearn to be rid of it. *Lord, help me to be holy.*" Is this the desire of your heart? Does holiness characterize your life with God? Isn't this His divine will for you?

In Philippians, Paul tells of "the *high* calling of God in Christ Jesus" (Phil. 3:14 KJV). Is your calling a *high* calling? Has it lifted your heart, setting it on heavenly things? Has it elevated your hopes, your thoughts, and your desires? Has it raised your constant focus so that you spend your life with God and for God?

In Hebrews we find another test of our calling, for we are referred to as those "who share in the *heavenly* calling" (Heb. 3:1). We share in a calling from *heaven*; so if your call is simply from mankind, you are not called. Is your calling of God? Is it a call *to* heaven as well as *from* heaven? Unless you are a stranger here on earth and consider heaven to be your home, you have not been called with a "heavenly calling," for those called in this way boldly declare they are "looking forward to the city with foundations, whose architect and builder is God" (Heb. 11:10), and they see themselves as strangers and pilgrims on earth.

With this in mind, is your calling holy, high, and heavenly? If so, beloved, you have been called of God, for this describes the calling God uses to call His people.

From the pen of Jim Reimann:

Even unbelievers often quote from Romans, saying, "All things work together for good" (Rom. 8:28 KJV), as though these words apply to everyone. But they have plucked the phrase from its context, for this precious promise only applies to "those who love him, who have been *called* according to his purpose" (v. 28).

Again, it is only the *called* of God — "those who are called to belong to Jesus Christ … and called to be saints" (Rom. 1:6 – 7) — who may claim this promise. And, as we have seen today, we must remember that those who are called are "called … by the grace of Christ" (Gal. 1:6). Thus, we did nothing to merit our calling. So as we consider God's grace in our calling, let us not forget to live in such a way as to glorify Him through it. Remember — it is holy, high, and heavenly!

"The God of all grace, *who called you to his eternal glory in Christ,* after you have suffered a little while, will himself restore you and make you strong, firm and steadfast. *To him be the power for ever and ever. Amen*" (1 Peter 5:10 – 11).

OCTOBER 12

The Comforter …,
the Holy Spirit …
John 14:26 Amplified

From the pen of Charles Spurgeon:

The time in which we live is distinguished by the fact that it is the age of the Holy Spirit — an age in which Jesus encourages us, not by His personal presence, as He will soon do, but by the indwelling and constant abiding of the Holy Spirit, who is forever the Comforter of God's church. As Comforter, His role is to console the hearts of God's people, but He also convicts of sin and instructs us in God's Word. Yet His primary work lies in gladdening the hearts of the renewed, in restoring the weak, and in lifting up all those He has humbled.

How does He do this? By revealing Jesus to them, for the Holy Spirit consoles, but Christ Himself is the consolation. Consider this analogy: the Holy Spirit is the Physician, but Jesus is the medicine. The Spirit heals the wound, but it is by applying the holy ointment of Christ's name and grace, for the Spirit does not apply His own work, but the work of Christ.

Therefore, if we give the Holy Spirit the Greek name *Paraclete* (one who consoles), as sometimes we do, then our heart also must confer on our blessed Lord Jesus the title of *Paraklesis* ("the consolation of Israel" [Luke 2:25]). In other words, if the Spirit is the Comforter, Jesus is the Comfort. With such rich provision for our needs, why should any Christian be sad and despondent? The Holy Spirit is at work to be your Comforter. Do you honestly think, O weak and fearful believer, that He will neglect His sacred trust? Do you really believe He has begun a work He cannot or will not perform? If it is His exclusive work to strengthen you and to comfort you, do you truly assume He has forgotten His work or that He will fail in carrying out His task when it comes to you?

No! Never think so negatively of the gentle and blessed Spirit whose name is "the Comforter." He delights in giving you "the oil of gladness instead of mourning, and a garment of praise instead of a spirit of despair" (Isa. 61:3). Trust in Him and He will surely comfort you until the "house of mourning" (Eccl. 7:2) is closed forever and the marriage feast has begun (see Rev. 19:7).

From the pen of Jim Reimann:

Seven hundred years before the coming of the Messiah, Isaiah described Jesus' spiritual anointing with the following words: "The Spirit of the LORD will rest on him — the Spirit of wisdom and of understanding, the Spirit of counsel and of power, the Spirit of knowledge and of the fear of the LORD" (Isa. 11:2). Thus in this one verse alone we see the Holy Spirit's attributes of wisdom, understanding, counsel, power, knowledge, and fear or reverence!

Then in the New Testament the Spirit is given the following titles, among others: "the Spirit of truth" (John 14:17), "the Spirit of holiness" (Rom. 1:4), "the Spirit of life" (Rom. 8:2), "the Spirit of sonship" (Rom. 8:15), "the Spirit of wisdom and revelation" (Eph. 1:17), "the Spirit of grace" (Heb. 10:29), and "the Spirit of glory" (1 Peter 4:14).

So, believer, what is it you lack? Remember: "If the Spirit of him who raised Jesus from the dead is living in you, he who raised Christ from the dead will also give life to your mortal bodies through his Spirit, who lives in you" (Rom. 8:11). What an amazing gift of God's grace!

OCTOBER 13

Love is as strong as death.

Song of Songs 8:6

From the pen of Charles Spurgeon:

Whose love is this verse describing — a love as mighty as a conqueror of kings, or "as strong as death," the destroyer of the human race? Wouldn't it sound ridiculous to apply this verse to my poor, weak, and barely living love for Jesus my Lord? Yes, I love Him, and perhaps, by His grace, I would even die for Him, but as for my love by itself, it could scarcely endure scoffing ridicule, much less a cruel death.

Thus there can be no doubt it is my Beloved's love that is spoken of here — the love of Jesus, the matchless lover of souls. His love is indeed stronger than the most terrible death, for it triumphantly endured the cross. His death was a slow, torturous one, but His love survived the torment; a shameful death, but a love that dismissed the shame; a punishing death, but a love that freely bore our iniquities; a forsaken, lonely death, from which the eternal Father hid His face, but a love that endured the curse and gloried over it all. There was never such a death. But also — never such love! His death was a desperate duel, but His love conquered all. So what about my own heart? What emotions arise within me when I consider such heavenly affection?

Yes, O Lord, I yearn; I pant to experience Your love like a flaming furnace within me. Jesus, I invite You to come and ignite the passion of my spirit.

For every drop of crimson blood
Thus shed to make me live,

O Lord, if only I could have
A thousand lives to give!

James Shirley, 1596 – 1666

Why should I ever agonize over loving Jesus with a love "as strong as death"? He deserves it, and I desire it. If the martyrs of the faith felt such love, and they were flesh and blood, then why not I? Certainly, they grieved over their weakness, and yet out of their weakness they were made strong. It was God's grace that gave them their unflinching courage, and that same grace is available to me.

Jesus, lover of my soul, pour Your love into my heart even now (see Rom. 5:5).

From the pen of Jim Reimann:

Hebrews tells us of many martyrs. As you read their stories, notice, as Spurgeon noted, that their weakness was transformed by our loving God into strength.

I do not have time to tell about … [all those] whose *weakness was turned to strength*; and who became powerful in battle and routed foreign armies. Women received back their dead, raised to life again. Others were tortured and refused to be released, so that they might gain a better resurrection. Some faced jeers and flogging, while still others were chained and put in prison. They were stoned; they were sawed in two; they were put to death by the sword.… The world was not worthy of them.

Hebrews 11:32, 34 – 38

OCTOBER 14

Do not conform any longer to the pattern of this world.

Romans 12:2

From the pen of Charles Spurgeon:

If a Christian can be saved while conforming "to the pattern of this world," it will be "only as one escaping through the flames" (1 Cor. 3:15). Yet such a bare-minimum salvation should be dreaded more than anything.

Dear reader, would you truly desire to leave this world from the darkness of a despondent death bed, entering heaven like a shipwrecked mariner clinging to the rocks of his country's coastline? If so, then be worldly. Be friends with those trusting in worldly wealth, and refuse to "go ... outside the camp, bearing the disgrace [Jesus] bore" (Heb. 13:13).

Or do you desire to have a heaven here below as well as one above? Do you desire, "together with all the saints, to grasp how wide and long and high and deep is the love of Christ, and to know this love that surpasses knowledge" (Eph. 3:18–19)? Do you desire to "share your master's happiness" (Matt. 25:21)? If so, then "come out from [unbelievers] and be separate.... Touch no unclean thing" (2 Cor. 6:17). Do you desire to attain the "full assurance of faith" (Heb. 10:22)? If so, you cannot reach it while continuing to fellowship with sinners. Do you desire a flaming, passionate love for Christ? The drenching "rain" of a godless society will only serve to dampen your flame of love. You can remain a baby in grace, but you cannot become a great Christian — one who is "mature, attaining to the whole measure of the fullness of Christ" (Eph. 4:13) — while yielding to the teachings or the methods of business of those in the world. Just as it looks bad for a king's emissary to be too friendly with the king's enemies, it is wrong for the heirs of heaven to be close friends with the heirs of hell. In fact, even small inconsistencies are dangerous, for even little thorns cause large blisters; even little moths destroy fine garments; and even little mischievous acts can rob your faith of a thousand joys.

Oh, professing Christian — you who are too little separated from sinners — you have no idea how much you are losing by conforming "to the pattern of the world"! It severs the tendons of your strength, causing you to crawl when you should be able to run. So for your own comfort's sake and for the sake of your growth in grace, if you are truly a Christian — be a Christian, but one determined to be distinctly different!

From the pen of Jim Reimann:

Spurgeon warns us that "even small inconsistencies are dangerous." This is much akin to the teaching of Solomon who once wrote of "the little foxes that ruin the vineyards" (Song 2:15). The idea was that Solomon did not want anything, small or large, to come between himself and his beloved. In the same way, we as those who love Christ must not let even little things come between Him and us to destroy our fellowship with Him. We must be vigilant, not simply paying attention to the so-called "big" sins, but being sensitive to even what we may consider to be trivial. Remember — all our sins are an offense to Him who atoned for those sins through the price of His shed blood.

"Search me, O God, and know my heart; test me and know my anxious thoughts. See if there is any offensive way in me, and lead me in the way everlasting" (Ps. 139:23–24).

OCTOBER 15

Redeem the firstborn donkey with a lamb,
but if you do not redeem it, break its neck.

Exodus 34:20

From the pen of Charles Spurgeon:

The Lord said, "The first offspring of every womb belongs to me, including all the firstborn males of your livestock" (v. 19), but since the donkey was unclean, it could not be presented to Him as a sacrifice. Because it was unclean, should it then be exempt from God's law? By no means! God allows no exceptions. The donkey was owed to Him, but He would not accept it; He will not abandon His claim, although He cannot be pleased with a donkey as the sacrificial victim. Thus there was no way around this dilemma except through redemption — the animal had to be saved by the substitution of a lamb in its place — or, if not redeemed, it must die.

My soul, there is a lesson here for you. That unclean animal is you, for you are legally the property of the Lord who made and sustains you. But you are so sinful that He will not, in fact cannot, accept you. So it has come to this — "the Lamb of God" (John 1:29) must stand in your place or you will die eternally. So if you have been redeemed, let the world know of your gratitude for that perfect Lamb who shed His blood for you and who thereby redeemed you from the fatal curse of the law.

Among the Israelites, surely there were times when they questioned which one should die, the donkey or the lamb. Wouldn't it be only natural for a good man to hesitate and compare the two? However, there is no comparison between the value of the soul of mankind and the life of the Lord Jesus. Yet the Lamb dies, while the man — the unclean "donkey" — is spared!

With great admiration, my soul, consider the limitless love of God to you and others of the human race in this. We — mere "worms" — are bought with the blood of the Son of the Highest! "Though I am nothing but dust and ashes" (Gen. 18:27), I have been redeemed by a price far above silver and gold! What a dreadful judgment was mine, if not for Jesus' abundant redemption! The breaking of the donkey's neck was but a momentary penalty, for who can fully measure God's eternal wrath against sin? Nor can we measure how precious is the glorious Lamb who has redeemed us from such a dreadful eternal death!

From the pen of Jim Reimann:

May Spurgeon's thoughts compel each of us to consider the great cost to our heavenly Father for our redemption. "For you know that it was not with perishable things such as silver or gold that you were redeemed from the empty way of life handed down to you from your forefathers, but with the precious blood of Christ, a lamb without blemish or defect" (1 Peter 1:18 – 19).

Let us keep in mind that God's plan of redemption was no afterthought on His part or something He devised along the way in His dealings with mankind. No! He chose to send His Son for us even before there was an "us." "For he chose us in him before the creation of the world" (Eph. 1:4), and John described Him as "the Lamb that was slain from the creation of the world" (Rev. 13:8).

Therefore, "'Do not be afraid, O worm Jacob, O little Israel, for I myself will help you,' declares the LORD, your Redeemer, the Holy One of Israel" (Isa. 41:14).

OCTOBER 16

With you [the Lord] is the fountain of life.

Psalm 36:9

From the pen of Charles Spurgeon:

There are times in our spiritual lives when human counsel or sympathy, or even the ordinances of our faith, fail to comfort or help us. Why does our gracious God permit this? Perhaps it is because all too often we attempt to live without Him, and thus, in order to drive us to Himself, He takes everything from us upon which we have been in the habit of depending.

It is a blessing, however, to live at the source of "the fountain of life." Doing so keeps our "bottles" of flesh full, but when we run dry, nothing will help us, except calling to the Lord, as Hagar later did, saying, "You are the God who sees me" (Gen. 16:13). We are like the prodigal son (see Luke 15:11 – 32), for we are prone to love the pig troughs and their husks and to forget our Father's house. Remember, we can turn even our various Christian rituals and ordinances into pig troughs; they are blessed things, but once we put them in place of God, they have no value. Anything becomes an idol when it keeps us from God. Even "the bronze snake" should be despised as "Nehushtan" (2 Kings 18:4) if we worship it instead of God. [NIV footnote: "Nehushtan sounds like the Hebrew for *bronze* and *snake* and *unclean thing*."]

The prodigal son was never safer than when he was driven to his father's embrace, because his needs could be met nowhere else. Our Lord blesses us with "a famine through the land" (Amos 8:11) in order to make us seek after Him all the more. The best place for a Christian is one of living wholly and directly on God's grace — abiding where he stood at first — "having nothing, and yet possessing everything" (2 Cor. 6:10). And may we never think, even for a moment, that our standing before God is the result of our works of holiness, our self-denying discipline, our talents, or our feelings; but let us know that we are saved only because Christ offered full atonement and that we are complete only in Him. Then, trusting in nothing of our own, but resting solely on the merits of Jesus, His passion and holy life provide for us the only solid ground of confidence.

Beloved, when we are brought to the point of true thirst, we are sure to turn to "the fountain of life" with eagerness.

From the pen of Jim Reimann:

God's prophets looked forward to the coming eternal "Fountain." For example, Zechariah pictured the Messiah as "a fountain … to cleanse [His people] from sin and impurity" (Zech. 13:1). Joel also wrote of "a fountain [that] will flow out of the LORD's house" (Joel 3:18), and Solomon described the Beloved as "a garden fountain, a well of flowing water streaming down" (Song 4:15). With that in mind, consider the consistency of God's Word — and His flowing fountain of grace — in the following:

"All you who are thirsty, come to the waters" (Isa. 55:1); "If anyone is thirsty, let him come to me and drink" (John 7:37); "To him who is thirsty I will give to drink without cost from the spring of the water of life" (Rev. 21:6); and, finally, "Whoever is thirsty, let him come; and whoever wishes, let him take the free gift of the water of life" (Rev. 22:17).

OCTOBER 17

The Sovereign LORD ... gathers the lambs in his arms
and carries them close to his heart.

Isaiah 40:10 – 11

From the pen of Charles Spurgeon:

We, the sheep of "the good shepherd" (John 10:11), are at various stages in our faith. Some are "strong in the Lord" (Eph. 6:10), while others are weak in their faith. Yet He is totally impartial in caring for His sheep, for the weakest lamb is as dear to Him as the most mature of His flock. Lambs are prone to lag behind, to wander, and to grow weary, but our Shepherd protects them from all the dangers arising from their weaknesses by His arm of strength. He finds newborn souls who, like newborn lambs, are close to perishing and then nourishes them until their life becomes strong and vigorous. And He finds those with emotional weakness of mind — those who are ready to faint and die — and consoles them and renews their strength.

Our Shepherd gathers all "these little ones," for our "Father in heaven is not willing that any of [them] should be lost" (Matt. 18:14). Oh, how amazingly quick must be His vision to see them all! What a tender heart He must have to care for them all! And what a far-reaching and powerful arm He must have to gather them all! Jesus, during His life on earth, was a great gatherer of the weaker ones, and now that He dwells in heaven, His loving heart still yearns toward the meek and contrite, the timid and feeble, the fearful and fainting here below.

Oh, how gently He gathered me to Himself, to His truth, to His blood, to His church! And with what amazing, effective grace He compelled me to come to Him! And since He first converted me, how often He has restored me from my wanderings and again and again taken me into the loving embrace of His "everlasting arms" (Deut. 33:27).

Best of all, however, is that He does this Himself — personally. He does not delegate the task of love, but humbles Himself to rescue and preserve *me* — His most unworthy servant. How then can I love Him enough or serve Him in a worthy manner? I eagerly desire to proclaim His great name to the very ends of the earth, but what can my feebleness do for Him?

O great Shepherd, please add this to Your gifts of mercy: a heart to love You more faithfully, as I should.

From the pen of Jim Reimann:

The context of today's verse is one of the most beautiful and most often quoted chapters of Scripture. Here is just a portion of how Isaiah described our loving Shepherd in this passage:

The Sovereign LORD comes with power, and his arm rules for him. See, his reward is with him, and his recompense accompanies him. He tends his flock like a shepherd: He gathers the lambs in his arms and carries them close to his heart; he gently leads those that have young.... The LORD is the everlasting God, the Creator of the ends of the earth. He will not grow tired or weary, and his understanding no one can fathom. He gives strength to the weary and increases the power of the weak. Even youths grow tired and weary, and young men stumble and fall; but those who hope in the LORD will renew their strength. They will soar on wings like eagles; they will run and not grow weary, they will walk and not be faint.

Isaiah 40:10 – 11, 28 – 31

OCTOBER 18

To obey is better than sacrifice.
1 Samuel 15:22

From the pen of Charles Spurgeon:

King Saul had been commanded to kill every single Amalekite and all their cattle. Instead of obeying, however, he returned with King Agag and allowed his men to take "the best of the sheep and cattle" (v. 15). When called to account for his actions, Saul explained that he did this in order to offer a sacrifice to God, but Samuel immediately confronted him with the truth that sacrifices are no excuse for an act of deliberate rebellion.

Today's text is worthy of being printed in letters of gold and to be hung before the eyes of this current idolatrous generation — those who are quite fond of the rituals of self-worship and who thereby totally neglect the laws of God. May you always remember that strictly obeying your Savior's commands is better than any outward ritual of faith, and to heed His precepts with an attentive ear is better than to offer "the fat of rams" (v. 22) or any other precious thing you might lay upon His altar.

Therefore, if you are failing to keep even the least of Christ's commands given to His disciples, I pray you will be disobedient no longer. Remember — all your assertions of closeness to your Master and all the devout actions you may perform are no compensation for disobedience. "To obey" — even in the slightest and smallest thing — "is better than sacrifice" — regardless of how great. Don't even bother to speak of Gregorian chants, costly robes, incense, and worship banners, for the first thing God requires of His children is obedience. And though you may "give all [you] possess to the poor and surrender [your] body to the flames" (1 Cor. 13:3), if you do not heed the Lord's precepts, all your formalities will profit you nothing.

It is a blessed thing to be as teachable as a little child, but it is even more blessed, once the lesson has been learned, to obey it to the letter. How many people richly decorate their churches and robe their pastors, but refuse to obey the Word of the Lord!

My soul, let me not follow their way.

From the pen of Jim Reimann:

Earlier Saul had been guilty of the same sin — that of attempting to excuse his deliberate disobedience by blaming it on his "religious" actions. Again confronted by Samuel, he gave the prophet this excuse: "When I saw ... that you did not come at the set time ... I thought, 'Now the Philistines will come down against me at Gilgal, and I have not sought the LORD's favor.' *So I felt compelled to offer the burnt offering*" (1 Sam. 13:11 – 12). But listen to Samuel's rebuke: "You acted foolishly.... You have not kept the command the LORD your God gave you; if you had, he would have established your kingdom over Israel for all time" (v. 13). And in today's story, Samuel also said to Saul, "Although you were once small in your own eyes, did you not become the head of the tribes of Israel? ... The LORD has torn the kingdom of Israel from you today and given it ... to one better than you" (1 Sam. 15:17, 28). What a terrible price he paid for his deliberate wickedness!

Lord Jesus, let this be a warning to me. Keep me "small in [my] own eyes." "[You] must become greater; I must become less" (John 3:30).

OCTOBER 19

God my Maker …
gives songs in the night.
Job 35:10

From the pen of Charles Spurgeon:

Anyone can sing in the day. When our cup is full, we draw inspiration from it. And when wealth rolls in like the waves of the sea, anyone can praise God who provides such bounty. It is easy for a wind harp to whisper its music when the wind blows; the difficulty is for the music to rise when no wind is stirring. It is easy to sing when we can read the notes by daylight, but only someone skilled can sing when there is no ray of light by which to read — for then one must sing from the heart.

No one can make "songs in the night" by himself — they must be divinely inspired. When everything is going well, I can weave songs together, fashioning them wherever I go from the flowers growing along my path. But put me in a desert, where nothing green is growing, and what will I use to compose a hymn of praise to God? How can mortal man make a crown for the Lord where no jewels are found? When my voice is strong and my body is healthy, I can sing God's praise, but when my tongue is silenced and I am languishing on my sickbed, how will I be able to lift His praises on high unless God Himself gives me the song?

Again, it is not within our power to sing when all is bad unless "a live coal … from [God's] altar" (Isa. 6:6) should touch our lips. A good example is the divine song Habakkuk sang in the night: "Though the fig tree does not bud and there are no grapes on the vines, though the olive crop fails and the fields produce no food, though there are no sheep in the pen and no cattle in the stalls, yet I will rejoice in the LORD, I will be joyful in God my Savior" (Hab. 3:17 – 18). Therefore, since

"God my Maker … gives songs in the night," let me wait upon Him for the music.

O Chief Musician, let me not remain song-less when I am suffering afflictions, but tune my lips to Your melody of thanksgiving.

From the pen of Jim Reimann:

The psalmists of old confirm the truth of Job's words in today's text, for they too wrote of singing during the dark night of the soul. Here is how they expressed it:

Why are you downcast, O my soul? Why so disturbed within me? Put your hope in God, for I will yet praise him, my Savior and my God. My soul is downcast within me; therefore I will remember you from the land of the Jordan, the heights of Hermon. Deep calls to deep in the roar of your waterfalls; all your waves and breakers have swept over me. By day the LORD directs his love, *at night his song is with me* — a prayer to the God of my life.

Psalm 42:5 – 8

"When I was in distress, I sought the Lord; at night I stretched out untiring hands and my soul refused to be comforted. I remembered you, O God, and I groaned; I mused, and my spirit grew faint. You kept my eyes from closing; I was too troubled to speak. I thought about the former days, the years of long ago; *I remembered my songs in the night*" (Ps. 77:2 – 6).

Therefore, "I will sing of your love and justice; to you, O LORD, I will sing praise" (Ps. 101:1).

OCTOBER 20

I will say ... to the south,
"Do not hold them back."

Isaiah 43:6

From the pen of Charles Spurgeon:

Although this message was said to the nations of the south to hold back no longer the dispersed descendants of Israel, the following may be a valuable summons to personally apply to ourselves as well: "Do not hold ... back." It is only natural to attempt to hold onto the good things of the past, but one lesson of God's grace is to learn to go forward in His ways instead.

Dear reader, are you still unconverted, but have a desire to trust in the Lord Jesus? Then, "Do not hold ... back." Love invites you, God's promises guarantee your success, and Christ's precious blood prepares your way. Do not allow your sins or fears to hinder you, but come to Jesus just as you are. Do you yearn to pray to Him — to pour out your heart before the Lord? Then again, "Do not hold ... back." His "mercy seat" (Ex. 25:17 KJV) stands ready for such a need as yours — mercy — and a sinner's cries will prevail with God. You are invited — no, you are commanded — to pray; therefore "approach the throne of grace with confidence" (Heb. 4:16).

Dear friend, are you already saved? Then, "Do not hold ... back" from union with the Lord's people. Do not neglect the ordinances of baptism and the Lord's Supper. Perhaps you have a timid personality, but you must fight against it, lest it lead you into disobedience. There is a blessed promise made to those who confess Christ, so by no means miss it, lest you come under the same condemnation of those who deny Him. If you have been blessed with talents, don't hold back from using them. Neither hoard your wealth, waste your time, let your abilities rust, nor let your influence be unused. Jesus did not hold back, so imitate Him by leading in self-denials and self-sacrifices. Don't hold back from close communion with God, from boldly appropriating His covenant blessings, from advancing in His divine life, and from searching into the precious mysteries of the love of Christ.

Beloved friend, do not be guilty of holding others back by your coldness, harshness, or doubts. For His sake, go forward with Jesus and encourage others to do the same. Hell and its besieging armies of false doctrine and unfaithfulness never cease from marching forward to the battle.

Therefore, O soldiers of the cross, "Do not hold ... back."

From the pen of Jim Reimann:

Spurgeon ends today's devotion by referring to believers as "soldiers of the cross," which is a very biblical way to view ourselves. In fact, Paul told Timothy to "endure hardship with us like a good soldier of Christ Jesus" (2 Tim. 2:3). And, of course, a "good soldier" does not "hold back," but like Paul, "Forgetting what is behind ... press[es] on toward the goal" (Phil. 3:13 – 14). Thus, as soldiers of the cross, may the words of this hymn, composed in 1865 by the English pastor Sabine Baring-Gould (1834 – 1924), be our battle cry today:

> Onward, Christian soldiers, Marching as to war,
> With the cross of Jesus, Going on before;
> Christ, the royal Master, Leads against the foe;
> Forward into battle, See, His banners go.

OCTOBER 21

Why are you troubled,
and why do doubts rise in your minds?
Luke 24:38

From the pen of Charles Spurgeon:

"Why do you say, O Jacob, and complain, O Israel, 'My way is hidden from the LORD; my cause is disregarded by my God'?" (Isa. 40:27). The Lord cares for all things, for even the smallest of creatures share in His universal providence, but His particular providence is over His saints. "The angel of the LORD encamps around those who fear him" (Ps. 34:7); "Precious is their blood in his sight" (Ps. 72:14); "Precious in the sight of the LORD is the death of his saints" (Ps. 116:15); and "We know that in all things God works for the good of those who love him, who have been called according to his purpose" (Rom. 8:28). May this truth cheer and comfort you, that although He is "the Savior of all men," He is "especially [the Savior] of those who believe" (1 Tim. 4:10).

You are the Lord's particular care, His "treasured possession" (Ex. 19:5), which He guards as "the apple of his eye" (Deut. 32:10); you are "the vineyard of the LORD Almighty" (Isa. 5:7), which He watches over day and night. "Even the very hairs of your head are all numbered" (Matt. 10:30). Therefore allow the thoughts of His special love for you to be a spiritual "pain-killer" — an end to your sense of woe. God says the following as much to you as He did to any saint of old: "Never will I leave you; never will I forsake you" (Heb. 13:5), and "I am your shield, your very great reward" (Gen. 15:1). We miss much of God's comfort by being in the habit of reading His promises as being for the whole church, but forgetting to apply them personally to ourselves.

Dear believer, don't forget to grasp God's divine Word with a personal, appropriating faith. Hear Jesus say to you, "I have prayed for you … that your faith may not fail" (Luke 22:32). See Him walking on the waves of your trouble, for He is there, and He is saying to you, "It is I. Don't be afraid" (Matt. 14:27). Forget others for a moment and accept the voice of Jesus as addressed to you and proclaim: "Jesus whispers comfort to me and I cannot refuse it. 'I [will] delight to sit in his shade'" (Song 2:3).

From the pen of Jim Reimann:

God said through the prophet Jeremiah that "Israel … will be *my* people" (Jer. 31:1). In this we see a personal Savior, and thus we should be grateful for the opportunity of a personal relationship with Him. And as we have seen today, personalizing Scripture is a wonderful way to strengthen our faith and to realize the impact of God's promises in our own spiritual life. As you read the following prayer of David, notice its personal emphasis. Why not make it your *personal* prayer today?

"The LORD is **my** *shepherd,* **I** *shall not be in want. He makes* **me** *lie down in green pastures, he leads* **me** *beside quiet waters, he restores* **my** *soul. He guides* **me** *in paths of righteousness for his name's sake. Even though* **I** *walk through the valley of the shadow of death,* **I** *will fear no evil, for you are with* **me**; *your rod and your staff, they comfort* **me**. *You prepare a table before* **me** *in the presence of* **my** *enemies. You anoint* **my** *head with oil;* **my** *cup overflows. Surely goodness and love will follow* **me** *all the days of* **my** *life, and* **I** *will dwell in the house of the LORD forever"* (Ps. 23:1 – 6).

OCTOBER 22

The Spirit will take from what is mine
and make it known to you.

John 16:15

From the pen of Charles Spurgeon:

There are times when all the promises and doctrines of the Bible are of no benefit to us unless God's gracious hand applies them to our life. We may be thirsty but too faint to crawl to the stream of water. Or we may be like a soldier wounded in battle, for it is of little use to him to know there are people at the hospital who can dress his wounds and medicines there to ease his pain, when what he needs is to be taken there and to have the remedies applied.

It is the same with our soul, for to meet our needs there is Someone — "the Spirit of truth" (John 14:17) — who takes the things of Jesus and applies them to us. Never think that Christ has placed the love He provides on the shelves of heaven, expecting us to climb there to receive it. No, He draws near to us and "has poured out his love into our hearts by the Holy Spirit" (Rom. 5:5).

Dear Christian, if you are working under the pressure of deep distress today, your Father has not given you His promises expecting you to draw them up from His Word like buckets from a well. Instead, the promises He has written in His Word He will write once more on your heart (see Jer. 31:33). He will reveal His love to you, and through the work of His blessed Spirit will dispel your cares and troubles.

And, you who mourn, know that it is God's prerogative to "wipe away every tear from [His people's] eyes" (Rev. 7:17). The good Samaritan did not say, "Here is the oil and wine for you"; he poured the oil and wine onto the man's wounds (see Luke 10:34). And Jesus not only gives you the sweet wine of His promise but also holds the golden chalice to your lips and pours the life-giving blood into your mouth. A poor, sick, way-weary pilgrim is not merely strengthened to walk, but is "carried ... on eagles' wings" (Ex. 19:4).

What a glorious gospel — one which provides everything the helpless need, one which draws close to us when we cannot reach for it, and one which brings us grace before we seek it. We see as much glory in the way the gift is given as in the gift itself. How blessed are those who have the Holy Spirit to bring Jesus to them.

From the pen of Jim Reimann:

As Spurgeon said, what the Spirit teaches is useless to us unless applied to our hearts. And, yes, it is God's sovereign work by the power of His Spirit that brings it to life in us. Yet let us never forget our responsibility to obey what has already been applied. He gave this warning in Isaiah regarding His disobedient people:

> They have chosen their own ways, and their souls delight in their abominations; so I also will choose harsh treatment for them and will bring upon them what they dread. For when I called, no one answered, when I spoke, no one listened. They did evil in my sight and chose what displeases me.
>
> Isaiah 66:3 – 4

In contrast, however, let us take special note of these words which went before: "This is the one I esteem: he who is humble and contrite in spirit, and trembles at my word" (Isa. 66:2). And let us take comfort in this great promise of God from Jeremiah: "I am watching to see that my word is fulfilled" (Jer. 1:12).

OCTOBER 23

"Why are you sleeping?" [Jesus] asked them.
"Get up and pray so that you will not fall into temptation."

Luke 22:46

From the pen of Charles Spurgeon:

When is a Christian most likely to sleep? Isn't it when his current temporal circumstances are prospering? Haven't you found this to be true in your own life? When you experienced troubles that took you to God's throne of grace, weren't you wider awake than you are now? The truth is: roads of ease make for sleepy travelers.

Another dangerous time for a believer is when all is going pleasantly in his spiritual life. In *The Pilgrim's Progress* by John Bunyan (1628 – 88), Christian did not fall asleep when lions were in his way, or when he was wading through the river, or when fighting Apollyon, the lord of the City of Destruction. But once he had climbed halfway up the Hill Difficulty, representing the right road for him, he came to a delightful arbor, sat down, and quickly fell asleep, much to his own sorrow and loss. That enchanted place was one of balmy breezes filled with lovely fragrances, lulling pilgrims to sleep. Bunyan described it as follows: "Then they came to an arbor — warm, and promising much refreshment to the pilgrims, for it was beautifully covered overhead with greenery, and was furnished with long benches. It also had a soft couch where the weary might rest.... This arbor was known as The Slothful's Friend, and was purposely designed to allure weary travelers."

Therefore, you can be sure of this: it is in the easy places that people shut their eyes and wander into the dreamy land of forgetfulness. Ralph Erskine (Scottish preacher and hymnist, 1685 – 1752) once remarked, "I like a roaring devil better than a sleeping one." In other words,

there is no temptation half as dangerous as not being tempted. A distressed soul does not sleep, for it is only after we enter into peaceful confidence and full assurance that we are in danger of sleeping.

In today's text the disciples had fallen asleep in Gethsemane — *after* their mountaintop experience of seeing Jesus transfigured (see Matt. 17:1 – 2). So take heed, joyful Christian, good times are close neighbors to temptations. Be as happy as you wish — but be watchful.

From the pen of Jim Reimann:

Pay close attention to Jesus' remedy for falling into temptation. First, He said, "Get up," meaning, "Wake up"! Remember His words to the church in Sardis: "Wake up! Strengthen what remains and is about to die.... Remember ... what you have received and heard; obey it, and repent. But if you do not wake up, I will come like a thief, and you will not know at what time I will come to you" (Rev. 3:2 – 3). Paul too warned of spiritual sleep: "The hour has come for you to wake up from your slumber.... The night is nearly over; the day is almost here. So let us put aside the deeds of darkness and put on the armor of light" (Rom. 13:11 – 12); and "Wake up, O sleeper, rise from the dead, and Christ will shine on you" (Eph. 5:14).

Next, Jesus said, "Pray" — a reiteration of what He had previously warned: "Be always on the watch, and pray that you may be able to escape all that is about to happen, and that you may be able to stand before the Son of Man" (Luke 21:36).

What great advice — "Get up and pray"!

OCTOBER 24

[Jesus] ... began to wash his disciples' feet.

John 13:5

From the pen of Charles Spurgeon:

The Lord Jesus loves His people so much that each and every day He continues to do for them many things that are comparable to washing their dirty feet. For example, He accepts their poorest actions, feels their deepest sorrows, hears their slightest wishes, and forgives their every transgression. He is still their Servant as well as their Friend and Master. He not only performs majestic deeds for them, such as pleading their case while wearing the priestly garments, including the sacred turban on His head, and the precious jewels glittering on His breastpiece (see Ex. 28:4), but He also humbly and patiently moves among His people with His foot-washing bowl and towel. And He does this while continuing day by day to take our constant infirmities and sins and cast them far from us.

Just yesterday, on your knees, you mournfully confessed that much of your conduct was not worthy of your profession of being a Christian; today you must mourn anew that you have fallen again into the same foolishness and sin from which His glorious grace delivered you long ago. Yet Jesus still has great patience with you, listens to your confessions of sin, and continues to say, "I am willing [to make you clean].... Be clean!" (Matt. 8:3). He will continue to apply His "sprinkled blood" (Heb. 12:24) to you, speak peace to your conscience, and remove every defect from you. It is a great act of His eternal love when Christ absolves a sinner once for all time, putting him into the family of God. Yet what humble and great patience the Savior exhibits when He bears the often recurring foolishness of His wayward disciple, washing away the multiple transgressions of His erring but beloved child, day after day, hour after hour.

To dry up a flood of rebelliousness is truly miraculous, but then to endure the continual dripping of repeated offenses is divine indeed! While we find comfort and peace in our Lord's daily cleansing, its primary effect should be to increase our watchfulness and to enliven our desire to walk in holiness.

Is this true in your life?

From the pen of Jim Reimann:

From the Old Testament to the New Testament, we see the Messiah at His first coming as a humble servant. But how different it will be when Jesus finally appears in the glory of His second coming! At His first coming, He came as a baby; He will return as the conquering "KING OF KINGS AND LORD OF LORDS" (Rev. 19:16)! His first coming was announced to a lowly few, but when He returns "every eye will see him" (Rev. 1:7)! At His first coming He was "wrapped ... in swaddling clothes, and [lying] ... in a manger" (Luke 2:7 KJV), but He will return "dressed in a robe ... with a golden sash around his chest" (Rev. 1:13), "standing in the center of [His] throne" (Rev. 5:6)! At His first coming "He was despised and rejected by men" (Isa. 53:3), but when He returns "every knee [will] bow ... and every tongue confess that Jesus Christ is Lord, to the glory of God the Father" (Phil. 2:10 – 11)!

Once we are in glory with Jesus, we will sing to Him, "Holy, holy, holy is the Lord God Almighty, who was, and is, and is to come" (Rev. 4:8). Why don't we begin that song even now, and honor Him by walking in holiness today?

OCTOBER 25

[Ruth] went out and began to glean in the fields behind the harvesters.
As it turned out, she found herself working in a field belonging to Boaz,
who was from the clan of Elimelech.

Ruth 2:3

From the pen of Charles Spurgeon:

"As it turned out ..." Yes, it seemed to be nothing but an accident, but oh, how God's sovereignty ruled! Ruth had entered the fields to do humble yet honorable work, doing so with Naomi's blessing and under the care of her mother-in-law's God, but the providence of God was guiding her every step. Little did she know that among the sheaves she would find a husband, that he would make her joint owner of his many acres, and that she — a poor foreigner — would become one of the direct ancestors of the Messiah of God.

The Lord is very good to those who trust in Him and often surprises them with unlooked-for blessings. Little do we know what may happen to us tomorrow, but may this sweet truth cheer us: "No good thing does he withhold from those whose walk is blameless" (Ps. 84:11). The idea of chance is removed from the faith of Christians, for they see the hand of God in everything. They know that the seemingly trivial events of today or tomorrow may lead to consequences of the greatest importance.

This is a weary world when we are far from Jesus. Our souls know the virtue that dwells in Jesus, and we can never be content without Him. Thus, we will wait in prayer today until it "turns out" that we find ourselves in the field belonging to Jesus — where He will reveal Himself to us.

From the pen of Jim Reimann:

Because God is sovereign, there is no such thing as "just by chance" or "just by accident." As Spurgeon said, what an amazing work of God that Ruth, "a poor foreigner" — not to mention a Gentile — should end up in the genealogy of the Jewish Messiah! So as we pray today that we would find ourselves in Jesus' field, where we may enjoy close fellowship with Him, let us first read the following words of Paul and reflect on the fact that we can actually commune with the sovereign God of the universe: "In him we were also chosen, having been predestined according to the plan of him who works out everything in conformity with the purpose of his will" (Eph. 1:11).

O Lord, deal as graciously with Your servants today as You did with Ruth. What a blessing it would be if, while wandering through the fields of meditation today, it would "turn out" that the place we travel is where our glorious Kinsman Redeemer will reveal Himself to us! O Spirit of God, guide us to Him. We would rather glean in His field than own the entire harvest of any other. Guide the footsteps of Your flock, that we may find the "green pastures" (Ps. 23:2) where He dwells!

Our prayer is to You, "God, the blessed and only Ruler, the King of kings and Lord of lords, who alone is immortal and who lives in unapproachable light, whom no one has seen or can see. To him be honor and might forever. Amen" (1 Tim. 6:15 – 16). "Not to us, O Lord, not to us but to your name be the glory, because of your love and faithfulness. Why do the nations say, 'Where is their God?' Our God is in heaven; he does whatever pleases him" (Ps. 115:1 – 3).

OCTOBER 26

All streams flow into the sea, yet the sea is never full.
To the place the streams come from, there they return again.

Ecclesiastes 1:7

From the pen of Charles Spurgeon:

Everything in the heavens is on the move, for time knows nothing of rest. Even the seemingly solid earth is a rolling ball, and our huge sun is a star, obediently following its path across the universe. Tides move great seas, winds stir vast oceans of air, and friction wears away solid rock, for change and death rule everywhere in the material world. But as we see from today's text, the sea is not some miser's storehouse for his wealth of water, for just as by one force the water flows into it, by another it is lifted from the sea again.

People are born only to die, and in the meantime everything is hurry, worry, and an anxious spirit. But, friend of the unchanging Jesus, what a joy it is to reflect on our changeless heritage. Our sea of joy will be forever full, since God Himself will pour eternal rivers of pleasure into it. May today's verse teach us to be eternally grateful, for God our Father is a great receiving "ocean," but also a generous giver. What the rivers bring to Him, He returns to us in the form of clouds and rain. And mankind should not be unlike His universe, which receives but gives back again, for, in fact, giving to others is sowing seeds for ourselves. A wise steward who willingly uses his assets for his Lord will be entrusted with more (see Matt. 25:29).

Friend of Jesus, are you returning to Him according to what you have received? Much has been given you, but how much fruit has been produced? Have you done all you can? Can't you do more? To be selfish is to be wicked. Suppose the oceans never gave up any of their watery treasure — it would bring ruin to the human race. Jesus did not live to please Himself. In Him, "all the fullness of the Deity lives" (Col. 2:9), but from that "fullness ... we have all received" (John 1:16). Oh, may that same trait of Jesus be in us; from this point onward may we not live for ourselves!

From the pen of Jim Reimann:

John once commended his friend Gaius for being generous with other believers even though he did not know them personally. He wrote, "You are faithful in what you are doing for the brothers, even though they are strangers to you" (3 John 5). It is one thing to do for those we know, but quite another to do for people we have never met. So let us take to heart the words of Jesus, who shared the following regarding the end times:

"I was a stranger and you invited me in, I needed clothes and you clothed me, I was sick and you looked after me, I was in prison and you came to visit me." Then the righteous will answer him, "Lord, when did we see you hungry and feed you, or thirsty and give you something to drink? When did we see you a stranger and invite you in, or needing clothes and clothe you? When did we see you sick or in prison and go to visit you?" The King will reply, "I tell you the truth, whatever you did for one of the least of these brothers of mine, you did for me."

Matthew 25:35 – 40

O Lord, may I never be like the Dead Sea — always receiving but never giving!

OCTOBER 27

All of us have become like one who is unclean,
and all our righteous acts are like filthy rags.

Isaiah 64:6

From the pen of Charles Spurgeon:

As believers, we are "a new creation" (2 Cor. 5:17); we are part of "a holy nation, a people belonging to God" (1 Peter 2:9); the Spirit of God is in us, and in every respect we are far removed from the natural man. However, in spite of all that, we are still sinners due to the imperfection of our nature, which will continue till the end of our earthly life. Sin mars our repentance even before the great Potter has perfected it on His potter's wheel. Selfishness defiles our tears, while unbelief tampers with our faith. The best deed we ever did apart from the merit of Jesus serves to actually increase the number of our sins, for when we think we are the most pure in our own eyes, we are not pure in God's sight at all. Just as He charged His heavenly angels with foolishness, how much more will He hold us accountable, even during what we consider to be our most "angelic" times.

Our best song rising to heaven still has human disharmony in it. And a prayer — one that moves the arm of God — is still a bruised and battered prayer, moving His arm solely because the sinless One, the great Mediator, has intervened to take away the sin of our supplication. Standing on its own human merits, even the most golden degree of faith, or even the purest level of sanctification a Christian has ever attained on earth, has so much dross in it as to be worthy only of flames. Every day, as we look in a mirror, we see a sinner and should confess: "All of us have become like one who is unclean, and all our righteous acts are like filthy rags" (Isa. 64:6).

Oh, how precious is the blood of Christ to hearts such as ours! How priceless is the gift of His perfect righteousness! And how bright the hope of our perfect holiness in eternity! Even now, though sin still dwells in us, its power is broken. It has no dominion over us, for it is like a snake whose back has been snapped; we are still in bitter conflict with it, but we are dealing with a vanquished foe.

Remember — in just a little while, in complete victory, we will enter the city where nothing will ever defile us again.

From the pen of Jim Reimann:

In the Old Testament, Israel is a picture of God's church to come. And just as the Israelites were defiled by the pagans around them, God's people today are stained by the spiritual pollution surrounding us. Yet, as we have just seen, we are to be "a holy nation." The Jewish exiles of Ezra's day, finally coming to this understanding, prayed the following prayer. May it be our prayer today, and may we recognize just how far short our righteousness falls compared to God's perfect measure — His glorious Son.

> "O LORD, God of Israel, you are righteous!... Here we are before you in our guilt, though because of it not one of us can stand in your presence" (Ezra 9:15).

And in light of the gift of God's righteousness to us in Jesus, let us praise Him with these words of David:

> "I will give thanks to the LORD because of his righteousness and will sing praise to the name of the LORD Most High" (Ps. 7:17).

OCTOBER 28

His head is purest gold;
his hair is wavy and black as a raven.

Song of Songs 5:11

From the pen of Charles Spurgeon:

All comparisons are insufficient to fully describe the Lord Jesus, but in today's text the bride does the best she can, using terms from her own experience. Simply mentioning His head is a recognition of His deity, for "the head of Christ is God" (1 Cor. 11:3); describing it of "purest gold" is the best possible metaphor, although the description still falls short of one so precious, pure, and glorious. Jesus is not a mere grain of gold, but a vast globe of it — a priceless treasure such as earth nor heaven can surpass. Created beings, however, are mere iron and clay and will perish like "wood, hay or straw" (1 Cor. 3:12); but the ever-living Head of God's creation will shine on forever and ever. In Him is no hint of a mixture of alloy or the slightest taint of dross, for He is eternally and infinitely holy and altogether divine.

The description of His wavy hair depicts His manly vigor and strength. There is nothing effeminate in our Beloved, for He is the manliest of men — "bold as a lion" (Prov. 28:1), strong as an ox, swift as an eagle. Every conceivable — and inconceivable — beauty is found in Him, although once "He was despised and rejected by men" (Isa. 53:3).

> His head the finest gold;
> With secret sweet perfume,
> His curled locks hang all as black
> As any raven's plume.
> Michael Drayton, 1563 – 1631

The glory of the Lord Jesus' head is not shorn away, for He is eternally crowned with matchless majesty. And the blackness of His hair indicates youthful vitality, for Jesus forever has "the dew of [His] youth" (Ps. 110:3) upon Him. Others lack vigor and energy with age, but He is "a priest forever, in the order of Melchizedek" (Ps. 110:4); others come and go, but He abides as God upon His throne — "for ever and ever!" (Eph. 3:21).

Let us behold Jesus even now. Angels are gazing upon Him, thus His redeemed should not turn away their adoring eyes from Him. Where else is there such a Beloved? Oh, for just an hour of fellowship with Him! Away, distracting worldly cares. Jesus draws me closer — I will run after Him.

From the pen of Jim Reimann:

On earth Jesus set His beauty and glory aside, for "He had no beauty or majesty to attract us to him, nothing in his appearance that we should desire him" (Isa. 53:2). Yet throughout eternity He is "all beautiful" (Song. 4:7). In fact, David asked "one thing ... of the LORD: ... that I may dwell in the house of the LORD all the days of my life, to gaze upon the beauty of the LORD" (Ps. 27:4); and Isaiah prophesied that fulfillment: "Your eyes will see the king in his beauty" (Isa. 33:17).

Therefore, as our beautiful Savior draws us to Himself, let us "give unto the LORD the glory due unto his name [and] worship the LORD in the beauty of holiness" (Ps. 29:2 KJV); "and let the beauty of the LORD our God be upon us" (Ps. 90:17 KJV).

OCTOBER 29

They were kept from recognizing him.

Luke 24:16

From the pen of Charles Spurgeon:

The two disciples on the road to Emmaus should have known Jesus. They had heard His voice so often and had gazed on His now-marred face so frequently, it is a wonder they did not recognize Him. Perhaps this is true of you as well. You have not seen Jesus recently. Although you have eaten at His table, you have not met Him there. You are in deep trouble today, and though He clearly says to you, "It is I. Don't be afraid" (Matt. 14:27), you cannot discern His presence.

Unfortunately, like these disciples, at times we are unable to recognize Him. We know His voice, have looked in His face, and have leaned our head on His shoulder, yet although Christ is very close to us, we continue to say, "If only I knew where to find him" (Job 23:3). We should know Jesus, for we have the Scriptures to reflect His image. How is it possible for us to open that precious Book and catch no glimpse of our Beloved.

Dear child of God, do you find yourself in this condition today? Jesus "browses among the lilies" (Song 2:16) — the very lilies you walk among — and yet you do not see Him. It is His custom to walk through the meadows of Scripture and to commune with His people, just as His Father did with Adam "in the garden in the cool of the day" (Gen. 3:8). How is it that you are in the garden of Scripture but cannot see Him, even though He is always there?

Our inability to see Jesus must be attributed to unbelief. But the same was true for these disciples, for they evidently did not expect to see Him and thus did not recognize Him. To a great extent in spiritual things, we get exactly what we expect of the Lord. Faith is the only thing that can cause us to recognize Jesus.

May this then be my prayer: "Open my eyes that I may see" (Ps. 119:18) my Savior who is always with me. It is a blessed thing to desire to see Him — but oh, how much better to actually gaze upon Him. To disciples who seek Him, He is kind, but to those who find Him, He is precious beyond words!

From the pen of Jim Reimann:

Not only is it proper to pray: "Open *my* eyes that I may see," but it is also fitting to pray that the *Lord's* eyes remain open. Consider this prayer of Solomon at the dedication of the temple: "*May your eyes be open* toward this temple night and day, this place of which you said, 'My Name shall be there,' so that you will hear the prayer your servant prays toward this place" (1 Kings 8:29). Of course, we are told in Scripture: "He who watches over you will not slumber; indeed, he who watches over Israel will neither slumber nor sleep" (Ps. 121:3 – 4). Thus the question then arises: Why ask God to do something He is already committed to do?

Remember, believer, prayer doesn't change God — it changes us, aligning us with His will and ultimately strengthening our faith. This is why, although God cannot fail to fulfill His Word, we may pray with David: "*Do as you promised,* so that your name will be great forever" (2 Sam. 7:25 – 26).

O Lord, "My eyes stay open through the watches of the night, that I may meditate on your promises" (Ps. 119:148).

OCTOBER 30

You who dwell in the gardens with friends in attendance,
let me hear your voice!

Song of Songs 8:13

From the pen of Charles Spurgeon:

Our sweet Lord Jesus well remembers the Garden of Gethsemane, and although He has left that garden, He now dwells in the garden of His church where He discloses Himself to those who share in blessed fellowship with Him. And the voice of love with which He speaks to His beloved is more beautiful than the harps of heaven, for there is a depth of melodious love within it that leaves all human music far behind. Even now, tens of thousands on earth, and untold millions above, are treated to its rapturous harmonies. In fact, some souls I know well, and whom I greatly envy, are at this very moment listening to His beloved voice. Some of them are poor, some are bedridden, and some of them are near the gates of death. Oh, that I knew their joy!

But, O my Lord, I would cheerfully starve with them, yearn with them, even die with them, if I might only hear Your voice! I used to hear it often, but I have grieved Your Spirit (see Eph. 4:30). In Your compassion, return to me, and say to me again, "I am your salvation" (Ps. 35:3). No other voice can satisfy; I know Your voice and cannot be deceived by another. Let me hear You, I pray. I do not know what You will say, nor do I place any condition upon You, "O my beloved" (Song 7:13 KJV). All I ask is that You let me hear You speak, and if it is a rebuke, I will bless You for it. Perhaps it will take a severe wound to my flesh to cleanse my deaf ears, but whatever the cost, may I not turn from my all-consuming desire to hear Your voice. Today, grant Your unworthy servant my great desire: pierce my eardrums anew with even Your harshest notes, only do not permit me to continue deaf to Your calls, "for I am yours" (Ps. 119:94) —

You have bought me with Your blood (see 1 Peter 1:18 – 19). *You have opened my eyes to see You, and the glorious sight has saved me. Lord, open my ears. I have read Your heart, now let me hear Your voice.*

From the pen of Jim Reimann:

In yesterday's devotion, we saw the two disciples walking to Emmaus. Of course, it was not until "their eyes were opened" (Luke 24:31) by Jesus Himself that they were able to recognize Him. By way of contrast, today we are considering the blessing of *hearing* the Lord, truly recognizing His voice. And although that too is a work of His grace, He invites us be involved in the process.

The Lord says, "Listen and hear my voice; pay attention and hear what I say" (Isa. 28:23), clearly indicating our responsibility to be engaged in active listening. Thus, we would be wise to heed the following words, spoken to God's people in the wilderness:

See, I am sending an angel ahead of you to guard you along the way and to bring you to the place I have prepared. *Pay attention to him and listen to what he says.* Do not rebel against him; he will not forgive your rebellion, since my Name is in him. *If you listen carefully* to what he says and do all that I say, I will be an enemy to your enemies and will oppose those who oppose you.

Exodus 23:20 – 22

O Lord, let me hear Your voice, but may my response be akin to that of Isaiah, who in active, listening obedience said, "I heard the voice of the Lord saying, 'Whom shall I send? And who will go for us?' And I said, 'Here am I. Send me!'" (Isa. 6:8).

OCTOBER 31

I knew you in the wilderness,
in the land of great drought.

Hosea 13:5 NKJV

From the pen of Charles Spurgeon:

Yes, Lord, You did indeed know me in my fallen condition, and yet, even then, You chose me for Yourself. When I was loathsome and self-hating, You received me as Your child and satisfied all my deepest yearning needs. May Your name be blessed forever for this free, rich, and limitless mercy. Since then, my inner experience has often been a wilderness, but You have continued to possess me as Your beloved and have poured streams of love and grace into me to gladden my heart and make me fruitful. Yes, even when my outward circumstances have been at their worst — when I have wandered through a land of drought — Your sweet presence has comforted me. Others have turned from me when scorn has awaited me, but You have known my soul through adversities, for no affliction dims the luster of Your love.

Most gracious Lord, I exalt You for Your faithfulness to me during trying circumstances. But I deplore the fact that at times I have forgotten You and instead have exalted myself in my heart, especially since I owe everything to Your gentleness and love. "Have mercy on me ... your servant" (Ps. 86:16) in this sin.

My dear soul, if Jesus acknowledged you in this way while you were in your fallen condition, be sure that you claim Him and His cause as your own now that you have been given such riches. Never be so lifted up by your worldly success as to be ashamed of the truth — or ashamed of the poor church of which you are now associated.

Follow Jesus into the wilderness, willing to bear the cross with Him when the heat of persecution grows hot. He claimed you, "O my soul" (Ps. 103:2), in your poverty and shame; so never be so disloyal as to be ashamed of Him. Oh, for more shame at even the thought of being ashamed of my best Beloved.

Jesus, my soul clings to You.

I'll turn to Thee in days of light,
As well as nights of care,
Thou brightest amid all that's bright!
Thou fairest of the fair!

John Samuel Bewley Monsell, 1811 – 75

From the pen of Jim Reimann:

Let us revisit the fact that Jesus died for us while we were in a fallen condition. Notice how Paul stated this: "*When we were still powerless, Christ died for the ungodly.* God demonstrates his own love for us in this: *While we were still sinners, Christ died for us*" (Rom. 5:6, 8). Thus, we should not be surprised that Paul also said, "*I am not ashamed of the gospel*, because it is the power of God for the salvation of everyone who believes" (Rom. 1:16).

God forbid we ever be ashamed of Jesus and His Word! Our Lord Himself said, "If anyone is ashamed of me and my words in this adulterous and sinful generation, the Son of Man will be ashamed of him when he comes in his Father's glory" (Mark 8:38). He also said, "If anyone would come after me, he must deny himself and take up his cross daily and follow me" (Luke 9:23).

November

November 1

They knew nothing about what would happen
until the flood came and took them all away.
That is how it will be at the coming of the Son of Man.

Matthew 24:39

From the pen of Charles Spurgeon:

The doom of the flood was universal, for except for Noah and his family, no one escaped — whether rich or poor, educated or illiterate, admired or hated, religious or blasphemous, young or old — all sank in one common ruin. No doubt some of them had ridiculed the patriarch Noah, but where are their cheerful jestings now? Others had threatened him for his zeal, which they considered madness — where are their cruel boastings and harsh words now? The detractors who judged the old man's work were drowned in the same sea that covered their scoffing friends. Those who spoke patronizingly of the good man's faithfulness to his convictions, but who did not share in them, sank to rise no more. Even the paid workers who helped build the amazing ark are all lost. The flood swept them all away, not making a single exception.

In the same way, except for those in Christ, final destruction will come to every "man born of woman" (Job 14:1), for no position, possession, or quality will suffice to save a single soul who has not believed in the Lord Jesus. Dear soul, behold this widespread judgment and tremble at it.

How stunning was the apathy in Noah's time! "For in the days before the flood, people were eating and drinking, marrying and giving in marriage" (Matt. 24:38), until that awful morning dawned. However, there was not one wise person who drowned, for foolishness had duped the entire human race — the folly of trusting in self-preservation, the most foolish of all follies. It was the folly of doubting the one true God — the most evil and deadly of all follies. Isn't it strange, dear soul, how negligent people are in thinking of their own soul until God's grace gives them true reason? Only then do they leave their madness behind and act like rational beings — but not until then.

Blessed be God, however, that all within the ark were safe, for no devastation entered it. All were safe, from the huge elephant to the tiny mouse; even the timid, helpless bunny was equally secure with the courageous lion and the powerful ox. Likewise, all are safe in Jesus.

Dear soul, are you in Him?

From the pen of Jim Reimann:

An important lesson to know is that Noah and his family were not spared because they were perfect. On the contrary, all mankind since Adam has been born with a sin nature. Although we are told, "Noah was a righteous man, blameless among the people of his time" (Gen. 6:9), it is the previous verse that explains how that was possible: "Noah found grace in the eyes of the LORD" (Gen. 6:8 KJV).

Like Noah in the ark, only those in Christ are "holy and blameless in his sight" (Eph. 1:4), and "salvation is found in no one else" (Acts 4:12). Thus, there can be no doubt that Noah would agree with these precious words of David:

The salvation of the righteous comes from the LORD; he is their stronghold in time of trouble. The LORD helps them and delivers them; he delivers them from the wicked and saves them, because they take refuge in him.
Psalm 37:39-40

Remember — God alone saved Noah, for "the LORD shut him in" (Gen. 7:16).

November 2

Indignation grips me because of the wicked,
who have forsaken your law.

Psalm 119:53

From the pen of Charles Spurgeon:

Dear soul, do you share this righteous anger and holy shuddering at the sins of others? If not, you lack inner holiness. David's face was wet with rivers of tears due to the wickedness of his day, Jeremiah desired his eyes be "a fountain of tears" (Jer. 9:1) to lament the iniquities of Israel, and Lot was distraught over the evil plans of the men of Sodom (see Gen. 19:4 – 7). And in Ezekiel's vision, the prophet was told, "Go throughout the city of Jerusalem and put a mark on the foreheads of those who grieve and lament over all the detestable things that are done in it" (Ezek. 9:4).

It cannot help but grieve compassionate souls to see what great pains others are taking to enter hell. These gracious saints know from their own experience the evil of sin and, as a result, are alarmed to see others flying like moths to sin's flame. Sin makes the righteous shudder because it violates God's holy law that is in everyone's best interest to obey, and thus sin serves to destroy the structure of society. Sin in others should horrify a believer, because it should remind him of the corruptness of his own heart. When he sees someone sin, he should cry, "He fell today, and I may fall tomorrow" (Italian proverb, possibly from St. Bernard, 923 – 1008). And because it crucified the Savior, a true believer views sin as horrible, seeing the cruel nails and spear in every iniquity.

Dear heart, it is an awful thing to insult God to His face. Our *good* God deserves better treatment, our *great* God claims it, and our *just* God will have it, or else He must repay His adversary to his face. A truly saved and awakened heart trembles at the audacity of sin and is alarmed at the very thought of its punishment. How monstrous is rebellion, and how dreadful the doom prepared for the ungodly. So never laugh at sin's foolishness, lest you ultimately come to smile at sin itself. Sin is your enemy — and your Lord's enemy — so view it as detestable. Only then will you exhibit the possession of holiness — and "without holiness no one will see the Lord" (Heb. 12:14).

From the pen of Jim Reimann:

"Holy, holy, holy is the LORD Almighty" (Isa 6:3). And because God is holy, He must judge sin. This is why He warned the Israelites in Moses' day of persisting in sin, saying: "I will destroy your high places, cut down your incense altars and pile your dead bodies on the lifeless forms of your idols, and I will abhor you" (Lev. 26:30). Yet He would not forget His promise to Abraham, and would maintain a remnant of saved souls, for He continued, "Yet in spite of this, when they are in the land of their enemies, I will not reject them or abhor them so as to destroy them completely, breaking my covenant with them" (Lev. 26:44).

Obadiah echoed these words of judgment on God's enemies and the promise of the ultimate blessing of His people:

The day of the LORD is near for all nations. As you have done, it will be done to you; your deeds will return upon your own head. But on Mount Zion will be deliverance; it will be holy, and the house of Jacob will possess its inheritance.

Obadiah 15, 17

Lord, thank You for Your deliverance, but may I abhor all sin — the sins of others and mine.

NOVEMBER 3

Their prayer reached heaven,
his holy dwelling place.

2 Chronicles 30:27

From the pen of Charles Spurgeon:

Prayer is the fail-proof course of action for a Christian, regardless the situation. When you cannot use "the sword of the Spirit," you can use the weapon of "all kinds of prayers" (Eph. 6:17 – 18). Your powder may not be dry nor your bowstring taut, but the weapon of "all kinds of prayer" is never out of order. "Leviathan" (Ps. 74:14) laughs at a javelin, but he trembles at prayer. Swords and spears must be polished and sharpened, but prayer never rusts, and even when we may think it may be the most dull, it cuts the best.

Prayer is an open door no one can shut. Devils may surround you on every side, but the way upward is always open, and as long as that road is unobstructed, you will not fall into the enemy's hand. We can never be defeated by blockades, land mines, scaling of walls, or surprise attacks as long as the comfort of heaven can come down to us on Jacob's ladder (see Gen. 28:12), providing relief in our time of greatest need.

Prayer is never out of season, for its merchandise is always priceless. It gains us an audience with heaven in the dead of night, in the middle of a business transaction, in the heat of the day, and in the shade of the late afternoon. And in every condition, whether poverty, sickness, slander, or doubt, your covenant God welcomes your prayer and answers it from His holy place.

Prayer is never futile, for true prayer always has true power. You may not always receive what you request, but you will always have your real needs supplied. When God does not answer His children to the letter of their prayer, He answers according the spirit of their prayer. If you ask for coarse-ground meal, will you be angered because He provides you with the finest flour? If you seek health for your body, should you complain if He uses your sickness to bring about the healing of your spiritual problems instead? Isn't it better to have your cross sanctified rather than removed?

Dear soul, do not forget to offer your petition and request today, for the Lord stands ready to grant your desires.

From the pen of Jim Reimann:

"The prayer of a righteous man is powerful and effective" (James 5:16). So let us examine our hearts and then pray these words of David to the Lord with thanksgiving for His righteousness applied to us:

> "O LORD, hear my prayer, listen to my cry for mercy; in your faithfulness and righteousness come to my relief. Do not bring your servant into judgment, for no one living is righteous before you.... Answer me quickly, O LORD; my spirit fails. Do not hide your face from me or I will be like those who go down to the pit. Let the morning bring me word of your unfailing love, for I have put my trust in you. Show me the way I should go, for to you I lift up my soul. Rescue me from my enemies, O LORD, for I hide myself in you. Teach me to do your will, for you are my God; may your good Spirit lead me on level ground. For your name's sake, O LORD, preserve my life; in your righteousness, bring me out of trouble. In your unfailing love, silence my enemies; destroy all my foes, for I am your servant" (Ps. 143:1 – 2, 7 – 12).

November 4

In your light we see light.

Psalm 36:9

From the pen of Charles Spurgeon:

No one can speak the love of Christ into the human heart until Jesus Himself speaks it to us. Every attempt even to describe it falls flat unless the Holy Spirit fills it with life and power, for until our Immanuel reveals Himself within us, the soul cannot see Him. If you desire to see the sun, would you gather all your lamps together, seeking in that way to behold the globe of the day? Of course not. The sun must reveal itself.

It is the same with Christ, as He said to Peter, "Blessed are you, Simon son of Jonah, for this was not revealed to you by man, but by my Father in heaven" (Matt. 16:17). Try as you may to purify flesh and blood through any means of education you may select, or try to elevate your mental faculties to the highest degree of intellectual power — none of these will reveal Christ. The Spirit of God must come with power and overshadow the person with His wings, and then in that mysterious Holy of Holies, the Lord Jesus will reveal Himself to sanctified eyes, something He will never do for the spiritually blind of mankind.

Christ must be His own mirror, for the great masses of this bleary-eyed world can see nothing of the indescribable glories of Immanuel. He stands before them "like a root out of dry ground," with "no beauty or majesty to attract [them] to him," "despised [by the proud] and rejected" by the vain (Isa. 53:2 – 3). Only once the Spirit has touched one's eyes with His healing touch, has given divine life to one's heart, and has trained one's soul to know the taste of heaven — only then is He understood. "To you who believe, this stone is precious. [To you He] has become the capstone" (1 Peter 2:7), "the Rock of [y]our salvation" (Ps. 95:1), your "all in all" (1 Cor. 15:28); but to others He is "a stone that causes men to stumble and a rock that makes them fall" (1 Peter 2:8). How blessed is he to whom our Lord chooses to reveal Himself, for His promise is that He and His Father "will come to him and make [their] home with him" (John 14:23).

O Jesus my Lord, my heart is open. Come in, never to leave again. Reveal Yourself to me even now! Favor me with a glimpse of Your all-conquering character qualities, especially Your powerful love.

From the pen of Jim Reimann:

Not only is our Lord willing to give us a glimpse of His character traits, but also He is willing to share those very qualities with us. For example, Paul told Timothy: "The grace of our Lord was poured out on me abundantly, along with the faith and love that are in Christ Jesus. I was shown mercy so that in me, the worst of sinners, Christ Jesus might display his unlimited patience as an example for those who would believe on him and receive eternal life" (1 Tim. 1:14, 16). And leaving no doubt as to the source of these qualities, he also wrote: "We know that suffering produces perseverance; perseverance, character; and character, hope. And hope does not disappoint us, *because God has poured out his love into our hearts by the Holy Spirit, whom he has given us*" (Rom. 5:3 – 5).

Lord, "every good and perfect gift is from above, coming down from [You —]the Father of the heavenly lights" (James 1:17).

NOVEMBER 5

Give thanks to him and praise his name.

Psalm 100:4

From the pen of Charles Spurgeon:

Our Lord desires that all His people be filled with high and blessed thoughts regarding Him and His greatness. Jesus is not content for those who are His promised bride to have lowly thoughts of Him, for it is His pleasure and desire that they be delighted with His beauty. We are not to think of Him as a bare necessity, like bread and water, but as a luxurious delicacy — a rare and beautiful delight. To this end He has revealed Himself as the "pearl of great price" (Matt. 13:46 KJV) in its matchless beauty, as the "sachet of myrrh" (Song 1:13) in its refreshing fragrance, as the "rose of Sharon" in its lasting perfume, and as the "lily of the valleys" (Song 2:1) in its perfect purity.

A help in having high thoughts of Christ is to think of how He is regarded in heaven, where everything is measured by the proper standard. Think how the Father esteems His "only begotten" (John 1:14 KJV) — "his indescribable gift!" (2 Cor. 9:15). Consider what the angels think of Him as they count it their highest honor to veil their faces before Him. Consider what the blood-washed saints in glory think of Him as they sing His well-deserved praises.

High thoughts of Christ will enable us to act consistently in our relationship with Him. The higher we picture Him enthroned, and the more lowly we see ourselves when bowing before the foot of His throne, the more truly we will be prepared to conduct ourselves properly toward Him. Our Lord Jesus desires we think well of Him in order that we cheerfully will submit to His authority. High thoughts of Him increase our love, for esteem and love go together.

Therefore, believer, think often of your Master's greatness. Study His glory in eternity past, before He took your nature upon Himself. Think of His almighty love that drew Him from His throne to die on the cross for you. Admire Him as He conquers the powers of hell. See Him risen, crowned, and glorified. Bow before Him as the "Wonderful," the "Counselor," the "Mighty God" (Isa. 9:6), for only then will your love for Him be what it should be.

From the pen of Jim Reimann:

Indeed, we are to exalt the Lord for His greatness, yet in the following passage from Zephaniah, notice how the Lord will praise and honor His people. Truly, this is something for which we should "give thanks to him and praise his name."

Sing, O Daughter of Zion; shout aloud, O Israel! Be glad and rejoice with all your heart, O Daughter of Jerusalem! The Lord has taken away your punishment, he has turned back your enemy. The Lord, the King of Israel, is with you; never again will you fear any harm. On that day they will say to Jerusalem, "Do not fear, O Zion; do not let your hands hang limp. The Lord your God is with you, he is mighty to save. *He will take great delight in you,* he will quiet you with his love, *he will rejoice over you with singing. I will give them praise and honor* in every land where they were put to shame. At that time I will gather you; at that time I will bring you home. *I will give you honor and praise among* all the peoples of the earth when I restore your fortunes before your very eyes," says the Lord.

Zephaniah 3:14 – 17, 19 – 20

NOVEMBER 6

[Moses] said,
"This is the blood of the covenant,
which God has commanded you to keep."
Hebrews 9:20

From the pen of Charles Spurgeon:

There is an unusual power even in the mention of blood, and the sight of it always seems to affect us. A tender heart cannot bear to see a sparrow bleed, and unless a person sees it often, he will turn away with horror at the slaughter of any animal. And when it comes to the blood of mankind, it is sacred; consequently, shedding it in anger is murder, and squandering it in war is a dreadful crime. I think this solemn view arises from the fact that "the blood is the life" (Deut. 12:23), so the loss of it is the sign of death.

Moving higher, to the contemplation of the blood of the Son of God, our awe is even more increased. We should shudder to think of the guilt of sin and its terrible penalty, which Jesus, the Sin-bearer, endured. Blood is all the more priceless when it flows from Immanuel's side. The blood of Jesus sealed God's covenant of grace, guaranteeing it forever. Covenants of old were struck by sacrifice, and this everlasting covenant was ratified in the same manner.

Oh, the delight of being saved upon the sure foundation of God's divine agreements that cannot be dishonored. Salvation by works of the law is a frail and leaky boat whose shipwreck is certain, but the ship of the covenant fears no storms, for Jesus' blood ensures it from stem to stern. His blood made His testimony valid, for a will has no power until the testator dies. In this regard, the soldier's spear became a blessed aid to our faith, since it proved our Lord to be truly dead. Therefore, as to the matter of whether He was really dead, there can be no doubt; as a result we may boldly appropriate the inheritance He left to His people.

Happy are we who have our title to heavenly blessings guaranteed to us by a Savior who died. But doesn't His blood continue to speak to us? Doesn't it call us to sanctify ourselves unto Him through whom we have been redeemed? Doesn't it call us to "walk in newness of life" (Rom. 6:4 KJV), and to motivate us to complete consecration to the Lord?

Oh, that the power of Christ's blood might be known and felt in us today!

From the pen of Jim Reimann:

As Spurgeon said, "The blood of Jesus sealed God's covenant of grace." This was foreshadowed by the Lord walking through the blood when He struck the covenant with Abraham. God walked through the blood in the form of "a smoking firepot with a blazing torch" (Gen. 15:17), while Abraham had fallen "into a deep sleep" (v. 12), indicating the Lord was willing to uphold both ends of the agreement. So as God stepped into the blood, He condemned His Son to death — death for us!

Spurgeon also said, "His blood made His testimony valid," which is confirmed by these words of John: "This is the one who came by water and blood — Jesus Christ…. There are three that testify: the Spirit, the water and the blood; and the three are in agreement. And this is the testimony: God has given us eternal life, and this life is in his Son" (1 John 5:6 – 8, 11).

"To him who loves us and has freed us from our sins by his blood … be glory and power for ever and ever! Amen" (Rev. 1:5 – 6).

NOVEMBER 7

You will be my witnesses.

Acts 1:8

From the pen of Charles Spurgeon:

In order to learn how to perform your duty as a witness for Christ, look at His example. He was always witnessing, whether at the well in Samaria (see John 4:4 – 29), the temple in Jerusalem, the Lake of Gennesaret (see Luke 5:1 – 3), or on a mountaintop. He witnessed day and night, even through His powerful prayers, which spoke of God as powerfully as His daily work. He witnessed under all circumstances; the scribes and Pharisees could not shut His mouth, and even before Pilate He declared His kingship (see Matt. 27:11). He witnessed so clearly and distinctly that no mistake could be found in Him.

In the same way, dear Christian, make your life a clear testimony. Be like a mountain stream where every pebble on the bottom may be seen, not like a muddy creek where only the surface is visible. Let your heart be clear and transparent so that your love for God and for others may be visible to all. Never say, "I am faithful" — simply be faithful. Never boast of your integrity — just be truthful. Then others cannot help but see your testimony. Never compromise your witness for fear of feeble man, but remember that your lips have been warmed by a "live coal … from [God's] altar" (Isa. 6:6), so let them speak like heaven-touched lips should do. "Sow your seed in the morning, and at evening let not your hands be idle" (Eccl. 11:6). Don't watch the clouds or consult the wind, but witness for your Savior "in season and out of season" (2 Tim. 4:2). And if it should happen that you must endure suffering of any kind for the sake of Christ and His gospel, don't cower in fear, but rejoice in the honor thereby conferred upon you — that you have

been "counted worthy of suffering" (Acts 5:41) with your Lord. Also rejoice in this — that your sufferings, losses, and persecution will make you a better platform from which you may more vigorously and powerfully witness for Christ Jesus.

Diligently study your great Example, and "be filled with [His] Spirit" (Eph. 5:18). Also remember that you need much teaching of His Word, much upholding in prayer, much grace, and much humility if your witnessing is to be to your Master's glory.

From the pen of Jim Reimann:

John refers to Jesus Christ as "the faithful witness" (Rev. 1:5), a description later used by the Lord Himself when He said, "These are the words of the Amen, the faithful and true witness" (Rev. 3:14). Thus, as we have seen today, let us imitate Jesus, especially when it comes to sharing the gospel. In that regard, let us remember His instructions shortly before His death: "I have set you an example that you should do as I have done for you. I tell you the truth, no servant is greater than his master, nor is a messenger greater than the one who sent him" (John 13:15 – 16). Furthermore, let us remember the message is His — not ours. As Paul acknowledged: "He has committed to us the message of reconciliation. *We are therefore Christ's ambassadors,* as though God were making his appeal through us" (2 Cor. 5:19 – 20).

Finally, let us immerse our efforts in prayer, just as Paul prayed "that God may open a door for our message, so that we may proclaim the mystery of Christ. [And] pray that [we] may proclaim it clearly, as [we] should" (Col. 4:3 – 4).

November 8

The Teacher asks:
Where is my guest room,
where I may eat the Passover with my disciples?
Mark 14:14

From the pen of Charles Spurgeon:

At Passover time Jerusalem was one large inn, for each homeowner invited his family and friends from other towns, hosting them in his home. But no one had invited the Savior, and He had no house of His own. And the fact that He found an upper room in which to observe the feast was a result of His own supernatural power.

It is the same even to this day, for Jesus is not received by mankind except where He remakes their hearts by a work of His supernatural power and grace. Many doors are open to the prince of darkness, but Jesus must clear a way for Himself or sleep on the street. It was through the mysterious power exerted by our Lord that this homeowner raised no objection or asked any questions, but at once cheerfully and joyfully opened his guest room (see vv. 15 – 16). Who he was and what he did we don't know, but he readily accepted the honor the Redeemer offered to confer on him.

The Lord's chosen, and those who are not His chosen, are still revealed in this way today. When the gospel comes to those who are not chosen, they fight against it and refuse it; but when people warmly receive it, this is a sure indication that there is a secret work occurring in the soul, and that God has chosen them for eternal life.

Dear reader, are you willing to receive Christ? If so, then there is no difficulty in your way — Christ will be your guest, for His power is at work in you, making you willing. What an honor to entertain the Son of God! "The heavens, even the highest heavens, cannot contain him" (2 Chron. 2:6), and yet He humbles Himself to find a house within our hearts! We are not worthy that He should come under our roof, but what an inexpressible privilege that He humbly enters our hearts! And once He enters, He throws a feast, causing us to feast with Him on "delicacies fit for a king" (Gen. 49:20). We sit at a banquet where the food is immortal, and is food which gives immortality to those who feed upon it.

Blessed are the children of Adam chosen to entertain the Lord of angels!

From the pen of Jim Reimann:

Today, once again, Spurgeon writes of God's electing grace. We see God has chosen some for salvation — and then by definition — has not chosen others. In other words, some people were created for glory, while others were created for destruction — no doubt a difficult teaching for us to grasp. Thus, often the question arises: Why would a loving Lord create some people for destruction? Paul, obviously knowing this question ultimately would come, answers by saying, "What if God, choosing to show his wrath and make his power known, bore with great patience the objects of his wrath — prepared for destruction? What if he did this to make the riches of his glory known to the objects of his mercy, whom he prepared in advance for glory — even us, whom he also called" (Rom. 9:22 – 24).

Indeed, this is a difficult teaching, but as Paul also said, "Does not the potter have the right to make out of the same lump of clay some pottery for noble purposes and some for common use?" (v. 21). Therefore, let us rest in this fact: "The LORD is righteous in all his ways and loving toward all he has made" (Ps. 145:17).

November 9

He who walks righteously ... is the man who will dwell on the heights,
whose refuge will be the mountain fortress.
His bread will be supplied, and water will not fail him.

Isaiah 33:15 – 16

From the pen of Charles Spurgeon:

Dear Christian, do you doubt God will fulfill this promise? Will "the mountain fortress" be blown away by a storm? Will God's storehouses of bread and water be emptied? Do you think your heavenly Father, although He knows you need food and clothing, will forget you? (See Luke 12:30.) If a sparrow does not "fall to the ground apart from the will of your Father," and if "even the very hairs of your head are all numbered" (Matt 10:29 – 30), will you mistrust and doubt Him?

Whatever affliction you are suffering, it may continue until you have the courage to trust your God. Surely there are many people who have been driven by sheer desperation to exercise faith in God, but only after being severely tried and tested. And, in fact, the moment of their deliverance was the very moment they believed by faith that God would keep His promise.

Oh, I plead with you, doubt Him no longer! Don't please Satan by continuing to have thoughts of doubt. Never think it is a trivial matter to doubt Jehovah. It is a sin — and not a little one either. Angels never doubt Him, nor even demons; we alone, out of all the beings God created, tarnish His honor through unbelief and mistrust.

Our God does not deserve to be treated in such a humiliating fashion, for throughout our lives He has proven to be faithful to His Word. With the many instances of His love and kindness we have received from His hand, and continue to receive each day, it is inexcusable for us to allow one doubt to remain in our hearts. Therefore, let us wage constant war against doubts of our God, which are truly enemies of His honor and our peace. With unfaltering faith, let us believe that what He has promised He will perform.

Lord, "I do believe; help me overcome my unbelief!" (Mark 9:24).

From the pen of Jim Reimann:

Worry and fear are sins of unbelief that accomplish nothing. This is why our Lord had much to say about them. Let us consider the following passage, alluded to by Spurgeon today, and let us be determined to trust the Lord.

Jesus said to his disciples: "Therefore I tell you, do not worry about your life, what you will eat; or about your body, what you will wear. Life is more than food, and the body more than clothes. Consider the ravens: They do not sow or reap, they have no storeroom or barn; yet God feeds them. And how much more valuable you are than birds! Who of you by worrying can add a single hour to his life? Since you cannot do this very little thing, why do you worry about the rest? ... And do not set your heart on what you will eat or drink; do not worry about it. For the pagan world runs after all such things, and your Father knows that you need them. But seek his kingdom, and these things will be given to you as well. Do not be afraid, little flock, for your Father has been pleased to give you the kingdom."

Luke 12:22 – 26, 29 – 32

Father, "I have put my trust in the Lord GOD, that I may declare all Your works" (Ps. 73:28 NKJV).

NOVEMBER 10

It is enough for the student to be like his teacher.

Matthew 10:25

From the pen of Charles Spurgeon:

Who would dispute this statement, for wouldn't it be inappropriate for the student to be exalted above his teacher? Yet when our Lord was on earth, what kind of treatment did He receive? Were His claims acknowledged, His instructions followed, and His perfection worshiped by those He came to bless? No! "He was despised and rejected by men" (Isa. 53:3). His place was "outside the camp" (Heb. 13:13), and His occupation was cross-bearer. Did the world provide Him comfort and rest? No, for He said, "Foxes have holes and birds of the air have nests, but the Son of Man has no place to lay his head" (Matt. 8:20). This inhospitable world offered Him no shelter, but instead cast Him aside and crucified Him.

Likewise, if you are a follower of Jesus who maintains a consistent, Christlike walk and conversation, you must expect your spiritual lot in life — at least in its visible, outward development — to come under the scrutiny of others. They will treat you as they treated the Savior — they will despise you. Never imagine the world will admire you, or that the more holy and Christlike you are, the more peaceably people will act toward you. If they didn't treasure the polished Gem, do you honestly believe they will value the jewel still in the rough? "If the head of the house has been called Beelzebub, how much more the members of his household!" (Matt. 10:25). The more like Christ we are, the more His enemies will hate us. Thus, it is a sad dishonor for a child of God to be the world's favorite.

It is a bad omen to hear a wicked world clap its hands and shout "Well done!" to the Christian man. When the unrighteous give their approval, he should take a long look at his character, wondering if he has been doing wrong. Let us be true to our Teacher, having no friendship with a blind, wicked world who scorns and rejects Him. Far be it from us to seek a crown of honor where our Lord found one of thorns.

From the pen of Jim Reimann:

Why do we care what the world thinks of us? This world is temporary, while our Creator is eternal. Jeremiah, the faithful prophet of God, stood alone against the world for many years, but even he needed this warning from the Lord: "Your brothers, your own family — even they have betrayed you; they have raised a loud cry against you. Do not trust them, *though they speak well of you*" (Jer. 12:6). And, as students of the Lord, let us remember these great words of our Teacher:

Blessed are you when men hate you, when they exclude you and insult you and reject your name as evil, because of the Son of Man. Rejoice in that day and leap for joy, because great is your reward in heaven. For that is how their fathers treated the prophets. *Woe to you when all men speak well of you*, for that is how their fathers treated the false prophets. But I tell you who hear me: Love your enemies, do good to those who hate you, bless those who curse you, pray for those who mistreat you. Do to others as you would have them do to you.

Luke 6:22 – 23, 26 – 28, 31

Jesus, my prayer is that one day I will hear You alone say, "Well done, good and faithful servant!" (Matt. 25:21).

NOVEMBER 11

The great King over all the earth
chose our inheritance for us.

Psalm 47:2, 4

From the pen of Charles Spurgeon:

Dear believer, if your earthly inheritance or lot in life is lowly, you still should be satisfied, for you may rest assured that it is what is best for you. God's unerring wisdom ordained your lot, selecting the safest and best condition for you.

Life is like a ship of great tonnage being navigated up the river. In some areas there are sandbars, so that someone might ask, "Why does the captain steer through the deep part of the channel and deviate so much from a straight line?" His answer would be, "If I do not keep the ship in the deepest channel, I will not get it to the harbor at all." And it may be the same in your case — you may run aground and suffer shipwreck if your divine Captain does not steer you into the depths of affliction, where wave after wave of trouble follow each other in quick succession.

Some plants die from getting too much sunshine, and it may be you are planted where you get very little sun. But you have been planted there by your loving Gardener because it is only in that situation you will produce fruit to perfection. So remember this: if any other condition had been better for you than the one in which you find yourself, then divine Love would have placed you there. You have been placed by God in the most suitable circumstances for you, and if you had been given a lot in life of your own choosing, you would soon be crying, "Lord, choose my inheritance for me, for when I choose my own way, I am 'pierced ... through with many sorrows'" (1 Tim. 6:10 KJV). "Be content with what you have" (Heb. 13:5), for the Lord has ordained all things for your good. "Take up [your own] cross daily" (Luke 9:23), for it is the burden best suited for your shoulder. Ultimately it will prove to be the most effective way to "equip you with everything good for doing his will" (Heb. 13:21) to the glory of God.

Down with my busy self and my own proud impatience. It is not for me to choose my lot in life — the choice belongs to the Lord of love!

> Trials must and will befall —
> But with humble faith to see
> Love inscribed upon them all;
> This is happiness to me.
>
> William Cowper, 1731 – 1800

From the pen of Jim Reimann:

If we will be honest with ourselves, we will admit there is a certain peace and confidence that comes from knowing God is sovereign in all things — even our lot in life. Dear Christian, learn to rest in the fact that you are the sheep, while Jesus is the Shepherd. All we must do is follow — not lead. Remember, each of us has a personal "race marked out for us" (Heb. 12:1), and we must run our race, not the race of someone else. With that in mind, we also should remember that comparing our race with that of others will serve only to make us dissatisfied, untrusting, or covetous.

O Lord, You are "the great King over all the earth." Therefore, "I will trust in you" (Ps. 56:3).

November 12

Jesus went out to a mountainside to pray,
and spent the night praying to God.

Luke 6:12

From the pen of Charles Spurgeon:

If there were ever one "born of woman" (Job 14:1) who might have been able to live without prayer, it was our spotless, perfect Lord; yet no one was as much in prayer as He! His love was so great for His Father that He loved to commune continually with Him, and His love is so great for His people that He desires to intercede continually for them. Notice the high priority Jesus gave to prayer, for it is a wonderful lesson for us, "leaving [us] an example, that [we] should follow in his steps" (1 Peter 2:21).

Also notice the time our Lord often chose for prayer. It was a time of quiet and inactivity when crowds would not disturb Him, when everyone but He had ceased their work, and when, due to being asleep, people ceased coming to Him for help. So while others found rest in sleep, He refreshed Himself with prayer.

We should note Jesus' place of prayer as well. He chose a place where no one could intrude, and where no one could observe Him. Thus He was free from rude interruptions and Pharisaic ostentation. Those dark and silent mountains became a fitting chapel of prayer for the Son of God. In the stillness of midnight, heaven and earth heard the groans and sighs of the mysterious Being in whom both worlds came together.

Next, let us consider the remarkable duration of His times of prayer. Although long, His watches of prayer were not too long, for the cold wind never chilled His devotion, the gloomy darkness never darkened His faith, nor did the loneliness ever weaken His perseverance. We cannot "keep watch for one hour" (Mark 14:37) with Him, but He watched entire nights for us.

Finally, notice what precipitated the Lord's time of prayer in today's text. It was after His enemies "were furious and began to discuss ... what they might do to Jesus" (Luke 6:11), revealing prayer was His refuge and comfort. And this occasion was before He "called his disciples to him and chose twelve of them, whom he also designated apostles" (v. 13), illustrating prayer was the starting gate of His endeavor — the herald of His new work. Therefore, shouldn't we learn from Jesus to have special times of prayer when we are under a difficult trial or when we are contemplating new endeavors for the Master's glory?

"Lord, teach us to pray" (Luke 11:1).

From the pen of Jim Reimann:

Jesus answered the above request by giving us this beautiful discourse:

> When you pray, say: "Father, hallowed be your name, your kingdom come. Give us each day our daily bread. Forgive us our sins, for we also forgive everyone who sins against us. And lead us not into temptation." ... Ask and it will be given to you; seek and you will find; knock and the door will be opened to you. For everyone who asks receives; he who seeks finds; and to him who knocks, the door will be opened. Which of you fathers, if your son asks for a fish, will give him a snake instead? Or if he asks for an egg, will give him a scorpion? If you then, though you are evil, know how to give good gifts to your children, how much more will your Father in heaven give the Holy Spirit to those who ask him!

Luke 11:2 – 4, 9 – 13

NOVEMBER 13

Jesus told his disciples ...
that they should always pray and not give up.

Luke 18:1

From the pen of Charles Spurgeon:

If Jesus said His disciples "should always pray and not give up," how much more should we as Christians in today's society? Jesus has sent His church into the world on the same mission for which He came, and that mission includes intercession. What if I shared with you that the church is the world's priest? When it comes to prayer, God's creation is mute, so the church has to speak for it.

The church's greatest privilege is to pray, knowing that her prayer will be heard and accepted. God's door of grace is always open for her petitions, and she never returns empty-handed. "The curtain of the temple was torn in two" (Matt. 27:51) for her, "the blood" was "sprinkled on the altar" (Ex. 24:6) for her, and thus God continually invites her to "ask whatever [she] wish[es]" (John 15:7). So will she refuse the privilege for which angels might envy her? Is she not the bride of Christ? May she not enter the presence of her King at any hour? Will she truly allow the precious privilege to go unused?

The church always has a reason to pray, for there are those in her midst who are declining in health or who are falling into open sin. There also are lambs to be prayed for, that they may be carried on Christ's shoulders; the strong, lest they become presumptuous; and the weak, lest they yield to despair. Even if we kept our prayer meetings going 24 hours a day, 365 days a year, we would never lack something special for which to pray. Are we ever without the sick, the poor, the troubled, or those wavering in their faith? Are we ever without those who desire the conversion of relatives, the reclaiming of backsliders, or the salvation of the wicked?

Of course not! In cities and towns, congregations are continually gathering, ministers are always preaching, yet millions of sinners are lying "dead in [their] transgressions and sins" (Eph. 2:1). In a country over which the darkness of Roman Catholicism is certainly descending, and in a world full of idols, cruelty, and devilry, if the church does not pray, how can she possibly excuse her appalling neglect of the commission of her loving Lord?

Therefore, let the church be ever vigil, with every believer throwing in their "small copper coins ... into [God's] treasury" of prayer (Mark 12:42 – 43).

From the pen of Jim Reimann:

When Israel was in Babylonian captivity during the time of Daniel, King Darius decreed that "anyone who prays to any god or man during the next thirty days ... shall be thrown into the lions' den" (Dan. 6:7). But look at Daniel's amazing response to the edict: "When Daniel learned that the decree had been published, he went home to his upstairs room where the windows opened toward Jerusalem. Three times a day he got down on his knees and prayed, giving thanks to his God, *just as he had done before*" (v. 10).

The time may come — and in some countries is already here — that prayer to the one true God will be illegal. So let the church be the church. Let us "pray without ceasing" (1 Thess. 5:17 KJV). Remember what Jesus said: "As long as it is day, we must do the work of him who sent me. Night is coming, when no one can work" (John 9:4).

NOVEMBER 14

Laban replied,
"It is not our custom here to give the younger daughter in marriage
before the older one."
Genesis 29:26

From the pen of Charles Spurgeon:

Although we cannot excuse Laban for his dishonesty in dealing with Jacob, there is a lesson we can learn from the custom he cited as his excuse. Some things must be taken in the proper order, and if we hope to win the second, we must initially secure the first. The second may be more lovely in our eyes, but the rule of God's heavenly country must stand — that the elder be married first.

In other words, many men desire the "lovely in form, and beautiful" *Rachel* of joy and peace of faith, but they must first be married to the "weak-eyed" *Leah* of repentance (see v. 17). Everyone falls in love with happiness, and many would cheerfully serve "fourteen years" (Gen. 31:41) to enjoy it, but according to the rule of the Lord's kingdom, the Leah of true holiness must be the beloved of our soul before the Rachel of true happiness can be attained. Heaven comes second — not first — thus only by persevering to the end will we win our heavenly inheritance (see Heb. 10:36). We must carry our cross before we can wear our crown; we must follow our Lord in His humiliation, or we will never rest with Him in glory.

Dear soul, how will you respond to this? Are you so vain as to think you can elude God's heavenly rule? Do you hope for reward without labor, or honor without work? If so, dismiss your futile expectation and learn to be content to accept the ill-favored things for the sake of the sweet love of Jesus, which will more than compensate for it all. It is only in that spirit, through hard work and suffering, that the bitterness of life will become sweet and the difficult things will become easy. Then, like Jacob, your years of service will seem "like only a few days" (Gen. 29:20) because of your love for Jesus, for once the sweet hour of the wedding feast finally has come, all your work will be as though it had never been.

One hour with Jesus will more than offset an entire lifetime of pain and labor.

> Jesus, to win Thyself so fair,
> Thy cross I will with gladness bear:
> Since so the rules of heaven ordain,
> The first I'll wed the next to gain.
>
> Author unknown

From the pen of Jim Reimann:

Chronologically, the Christian's earthly life comes first and was never meant to be easy, for we must be sanctified for heavenly life, which comes second. Knowing that, Paul wrote the following to encourage us:

> When the perishable has been clothed with the imperishable, and the mortal with immortality, then the saying that is written will come true: "Death has been swallowed up in victory. Where, O death, is your victory? Where, O death, is your sting?" The sting of death is sin, and the power of sin is the law. But thanks be to God! He gives us the victory through our Lord Jesus Christ. *Therefore, my dear brothers, stand firm. Let nothing move you. Always give yourselves fully to the work of the Lord, because you know that your labor in the Lord is not in vain.*
>
> 1 Corinthians 15:54 – 58

NOVEMBER 15

Show us your strength, O God,
as you have done before.

Psalm 68:28

From the pen of Charles Spurgeon:

Not only is it wise to continually beseech God to strengthen that which He has created in us — it is a necessity. And because of neglecting to do so, many Christians must blame themselves for those inner spiritual trials and afflictions that arise from unbelief. It is true that Satan seeks to flood the beautiful garden of the heart, making it a scene of total desolation; but it is also true that many Christians leave the floodgates open themselves, letting in the dreadful deluge by their own carelessness and lack of prayer to their strong Helper. We often forget that "the author ... of our faith" (Heb. 12:2) is the Preserver of it as well.

The lamp of the temple in Jerusalem was never allowed to go out, but it had to be replenished daily with new oil. In the same way, our faith can live only by being sustained by the oil of grace, which can be obtained only from God Himself. Just as He who built the world sustains it — keeping it from falling in one tremendous crash — He who made us Christians must sustain us by His Spirit, or our ruin would be fast and final.

So let us not be like the foolish virgins who failed to secure the needed oil for their lamps (see Matt. 25:1 – 13). Let us go to our Lord each and every day for the grace and strength we need. We have a strong argument to plead before Him, for it is His own work of grace we ask Him to strengthen — "as [He has] done before." If you will let your faith take hold of His strength, all the powers of darkness led by the master fiend of hell will be unable to cast even a cloud or shadow over your joy and peace.

Why be weak when you can be strong? Why suffer defeat when you can conquer? Take your wavering faith and weakened gifts to Him who can revive and replenish them. Then earnestly pray,

"Show us your strength, O God, as you have done before."

From the pen of Jim Reimann:

Today's text says, "Show us ...," indicating, as Paul once said, "Jews request a sign" (1 Cor. 1:22 NKJV). Although it is perfectly correct to ask the Lord to "show us," there are some things we — His people — should not ask. For example, Philip, one of Jesus' disciples, asked, "Lord, show us the Father and that will be enough for us." [But] Jesus answered: "Don't you know me, Philip, even after I have been among you such a long time? Anyone who has seen me has seen the Father. How can you say, 'Show us the Father'?" (John 14:8 – 9).

One psalmist asked the following of the Father: "Show us your unfailing love, O Lord, and grant us your salvation" (Ps. 85:7). But notice the responsibility the writer felt after asking something of the Lord, for he immediately wrote: "I will listen to what God the Lord will say; he promises peace to his people, his saints — but let them not return to folly" (v. 8).

Finally, notice David's response after having asked the Lord to "Show us your strength, O God" in today's verse. May it be the prayer of our heart today.

"Proclaim the power of God, whose majesty is over Israel, whose power is in the skies. You are awesome, O God, in your sanctuary; the God of Israel gives power and strength to his people. Praise be to God!" (Ps. 68:34 – 35).

NOVEMBER 16

Your eyes will see the king in his beauty.

Isaiah 33:17

From the pen of Charles Spurgeon:

The better you know Christ, the less you will be satisfied with superficial views of Him. And the more deeply you study His work in the eternal covenant, His dealings on your behalf as its everlasting guarantee, and the fullness of His grace that shines in all His roles, the more you "will see the king in his beauty" to the fullest extent possible.

Meditation on His Word and diligent study of it become the windows through which we often behold our Redeemer. This meditation puts the telescope to our eye, actually enabling us to see Jesus in a better way than we could have seen Him even if we had lived when He walked this earth. If we would meditate more on our incarnate Lord, His beauty would shine on us with greater glory.

Beloved, if we get to know Jesus in this way, it is quite probable that when it is time for us to die, we will have such a sight of our glorious King — one unlike anything we have ever experienced. When dying, many saints have looked up from their stormy sea only to see Jesus "walking on the water" and have heard Him say, "It is I; don't be afraid" (John 6:19 – 20).

Yes! Even when the house begins to shake, the plaster begins to shatter, and the roof is blown apart, we will see Christ through the cracks, and between the rafters the sunlight of heaven will come streaming through. But for this to be true for us — if we truly desire to see "the king in his beauty" face to face, either we must go to heaven for the sight or the King must come to us in person.

Oh, that He would come "on the wings of the wind" (Ps. 104:3). He is our Husband (see Isa. 54:5), and thus we are widowed by His absence; He is our Brother, precious and beautiful, and we are lonely without Him. Thick clouds now veil our souls from their true life (see Job 22:14). Oh, how long "until the day breaks and the shadows flee" (Song 2:17)? O long-awaited day, begin!

From the pen of Jim Reimann:

If I not only desire to see "the king in his beauty" but also yearn to see His beauty reflected in my life, my life's goal will be akin to that of Paul's, who said, "I want to know Christ and the power of his resurrection and the fellowship of sharing in his sufferings, becoming like him in his death" (Phil. 3:10). My heart's prayer also will be that of Paul's, who prayed, "I keep asking that the God of our Lord Jesus Christ, the glorious Father, may give you the Spirit of wisdom and revelation, so that you may know him better" (Eph. 1:17), and "I pray that out of his glorious riches he may strengthen you with power through his Spirit in your inner being, so that Christ may dwell in your hearts through faith. And I pray that you, being rooted and established in love, may have power, together with all the saints, to grasp how wide and long and high and deep is the love of Christ" (Eph. 3:16 – 18). Lastly, I must remember God's promise to His people — made only to those who are His — even me: "If … you seek the LORD your God, you will find him if you look for him with all your heart and with all your soul" (Deut. 4:29).

Only then will I long for my beautiful King.

"Come, Lord Jesus" (Rev. 22:20).

November 17

Whoever splits logs may be endangered by them.

Ecclesiastes 10:9

From the pen of Charles Spurgeon:

Those who oppress the poor and needy may get their way with them as easily as a woodsman splits a log, but they should keep in mind that it is dangerous business, for many woodsmen have been killed by splitting a tree. When God's saint is being injured, Jesus within him is persecuted, and He is mighty to avenge His beloved ones. Thus, success in trampling the poor and needy is something over which we should tremble, for even if no immediate danger is apparent, we can be sure great danger will be the eventual result.

Dear reader, there too are dangers connected to your calling and daily life, and it would be wise for you to beware of them. I am not referring to hazards such as floods, wild animals, disease, or accidental death. I am referring to perils of a spiritual nature, and although your occupation may be humble, the Devil can still tempt you in it. Perhaps you are a domestic servant and are greatly screened from temptations we may consider greater vices, yet some secret sin may cause you harm. Even those who work at home may be threatened by their very seclusion. In fact, no place is safe for him who thinks himself to be safe; for pride may enter the heart, greed may reign in the homemaker's soul, and uncleanness may dare to enter even the most tranquil house. Anger, envy, and malice may find their way into the most rural of homes. We may sin simply in speaking a few words to an employee; a small purchase at a store may be the first link in a chain of temptations; merely looking out a window may be the beginning of evil.

O Lord, how exposed we are! How will we be secure! Protecting ourselves is a task too difficult for us, for You alone are able to preserve us in this world of evil. Spread Your wings over us — and may we, like "chicks under [Your] wings" (Matt. 23:37), humble ourselves beneath You and feel safe.

From the pen of Jim Reimann:

We must remember that it is only in Jesus we will feel — and be — safe. It is He who keeps us — not us — for His Word says, "*He who keeps Israel will neither slumber nor sleep*" (Ps. 121:4 Amplified). Peter grasped this great truth, for he wrote:

Praise be to the God and Father of our Lord Jesus Christ! In his great mercy he has given us new birth into a living hope through the resurrection of Jesus Christ from the dead, and into an inheritance that can never perish, spoil or fade — *kept in heaven for you, who through faith are shielded by God's power.*

1 Peter 1:3 – 5

All this is a fulfillment of the words of the blessing initially given to Aaron, Israel's first high priest, for he was told, "This is how you are to bless the Israelites. Say to them: '*The Lord bless you and keep you*; the Lord make his face shine upon you and be gracious to you; the Lord turn his face toward you and give you peace'" (Num. 6:23 – 26). Now, however, we see Jesus as our eternal high priest and "Keeper," for Luke tells us: "When he had led them out to the vicinity of Bethany, *he lifted up his hands and blessed them.* While he was blessing them, he left them and was taken up into heaven" (Luke 24:50 – 51).

NOVEMBER 18

You are from all eternity.

Psalm 93:2

From the pen of Charles Spurgeon:

Christ is eternal. Thus, we may sing with the psalmist: "Your throne, O God, will last for ever and ever" (Ps. 45:6). So rejoice, believer, in "Jesus Christ ... the same yesterday and today and forever" (Heb. 13:8). Jesus always was. The baby born in Bethlehem "was the Word, and ... was with God in the beginning. [And] through him all things were made" (John 1:1–3). The title Jesus used when revealing Himself to John on Patmos was: "[He] who is, and who was, and who is to come" (Rev. 1:4). If He were not God from eternity past, we could not love Him as deeply, nor could we believe He had any role in the eternal love that is the source of all covenant blessings. But since He is from all eternity with the Father, we can trace the stream of divine love equally as much to Him as we can to the Father and His blessed Spirit.

As our Lord always was, He is "for ever and ever!" (Rev. 1:18). Jesus is not dead — "He always lives to intercede for [us]" (Heb. 7:25). So turn to Him in your time of need, for He is waiting to bless you even now. Jesus our Lord will always be. If God should spare your life so that "the length of [y]our days is seventy years — or eighty" (Ps. 90:10), you will discover that His cleansing fountain is still open, that His precious blood has not lost its power, and that the Priest who filled the healing fountain with His own blood ever lives to purge you from all iniquity. When you face your final battle, the living Savior will comfort His dying saint. As you enter heaven, you will find Him there, still displaying "the dew of [His] youth" (Ps. 110:3), for throughout eternity the Lord Jesus will remain the perennial fountain of joy,

life, and glory for His people. And it is from this sacred "well of living waters" (Song 4:15 KJV) that we may draw!

Jesus always was, He always is, He always will be. He is eternal in all His attributes, in all His roles, in all His power, and in all His willingness to bless, comfort, guard, and crown His chosen people.

From the pen of Jim Reimann:

May this psalm of Moses, briefly cited by Spurgeon today, be our prayer:

"Lord, you have been our dwelling place throughout all generations. Before the mountains were born or you brought forth the earth and the world, from everlasting to everlasting you are God. You turn men back to dust, saying, 'Return to dust, O sons of men.' For a thousand years in your sight are like a day that has just gone by, or like a watch in the night.... The length of our days is seventy years — or eighty, if we have the strength; yet their span is but trouble and sorrow, for they quickly pass, and we fly away.... Teach us to number our days aright, that we may gain a heart of wisdom. Relent, O Lord! How long will it be? Have compassion on your servants. Satisfy us in the morning with your unfailing love, that we may sing for joy and be glad all our days. Make us glad for as many days as you have afflicted us, for as many years as we have seen trouble. May your deeds be shown to your servants, your splendor to their children. May the favor of the Lord our God rest upon us; establish the work of our hands for us — yes, establish the work of our hands" (Ps. 90:1–4, 10, 12–17).

NOVEMBER 19

If only I knew where to find him;
if only I could go to his dwelling!
Job 23:3

From the pen of Charles Spurgeon:

Job's entire being was crying out to the Lord, for the longing desire of an afflicted child of God is to once again see his Father's face. Notice that his initial prayer was not, "Oh, that I might be healed of the disease that is now plaguing every part of my body!" or even, "Oh, that I might see my children returned from the jaws of the grave and my property restored from the hand of the spoiler." No! His first and highest cry was: "If only I knew where to find him; if only I could go to his dwelling!"

God's children run home when the storm begins to rage, for it is the heaven-born instinct of a soul blessed by His grace to seek shelter from all troubles beneath the wings of Jehovah. A true believer should be known as one who has made the Lord his refuge. A hypocrite, however, when afflicted by God, resents his circumstances and thus he runs from the Master. But not so with a true heir of heaven, for he actually kisses the Hand that strikes him and seeks shelter from "the rod of discipline" (Prov. 22:15) in the embrace of God who frowned on him.

Job's desire to commune with the Lord was intensified by the failure of all other sources of comfort. The patriarch turned away from his pitifully inadequate friends, looking instead to God's celestial throne, just as a thirsty hiker turns away from his empty canteen and heads straight toward a stream of water. Job bid farewell to earthborn hopes and cried out, "If only I knew where to find him!" Nothing teaches us the preciousness of our Creator as much as learning the emptiness of everything else. So let us rejoice in Him whose faithful Word is "sweeter than honey, than honey from the comb" (Ps. 19:10). In every trouble, let us first seek to recognize God's presence, for when we enjoy His smile we are able, with willing hearts, to "take up [our] cross daily" (Luke 9:23) for His blessed sake.

From the pen of Jim Reimann:

There are times when we, like Job, don't know where to go, especially when we have sinned. Yet the answer is always to turn back to God in humility and repentance. Joel wrote of this by saying, "'Even now,' declares the LORD, 'return to me with all your heart, with fasting and weeping and mourning.' Rend your heart and not your garments. Return to the LORD your God, for he is gracious and compassionate, slow to anger and abounding in love" (Joel 2:12 – 13).

Old or New Testament, the message is the same: "Let the wicked forsake his way and the evil man his thoughts. Let him turn to the LORD, and he will have mercy on him, and to our God, for he will freely pardon" (Isa. 55:7), and "If we confess our sins, he is faithful and just and will forgive us our sins and purify us from all unrighteousness" (1 John 1:9).

Job said, "If only I could go to his dwelling!" But, dear believer, you can! "If you make the Most High your dwelling — even the LORD, who is my refuge — then no harm will befall you, no disaster will come near your tent" (Ps. 91:9 – 10).

"How lovely is your dwelling place, O LORD Almighty!" (Ps. 84:1).

November 20

Coneys are creatures of little power,
yet they make their home in the crags.
Proverbs 30:26

From the pen of Charles Spurgeon:

The coney, a distant cousin of the rabbit, is conscious of its own natural defenselessness, so it burrows into the crags of rocks to be secure from its enemies. Thus, dear heart, may you be willing to learn a lesson from this weak creature.

You are as weak and exposed to peril as the timid coney, so be as wise as it is in seeking shelter. Your best security is within the fortress of an immutable Jehovah, where His unalterable promises stand like giant walls of rock. It will go well with you if you always will hide yourself within the fortification of His glorious attributes, all of which guarantee safety for those who put their trust in Him.

"Blessed be the name of the Lord" (Ps. 113:2 KJV), for I have done this, and have found myself to be like David who "escaped to the cave of Adullam" (1 Sam. 22:1) — safe from the cruelty of my enemy. I don't need to rediscover the blessedness of the person who puts his trust in the Lord, for long ago, when Satan and my own sins pursued me, I fled to the "cleft in the rock" (Ex. 33:22) — Christ Jesus — and in His torn side found the most wonderful of all resting places.

Dear one, why don't you run to Him afresh today, whatever your present trouble may be, for Jesus cares for you, Jesus comforts you, Jesus will help you. No king in the most impregnable fortress is more secure than a coney in his "cleft in the rock." In Jesus the weak are strong and the defenseless safe; they could not be more strong if they were giants, nor more safe if they were in heaven itself.

It is faith that gives those on earth the protection of the God of heaven. There is nothing more they need or nothing more for which to wish. A coney cannot build a castle, but simply avails itself to what is there already. Likewise, I cannot make a refuge for myself, but I have one; for Jesus provided it, His Father has given it, and His Spirit has revealed it. Once again, I enter it, and I am safe from every foe.

From the pen of Jim Reimann:

When Paul felt weak, God said to him, "My grace is sufficient for you, for my power is made perfect in weakness," leading Paul to respond, "Therefore I will boast all the more gladly about my weaknesses, so that Christ's power may rest on me. That is why, for Christ's sake, I delight in weaknesses, in insults, in hardships, in persecutions, in difficulties. For when I am weak, then I am strong" (2 Cor. 12:9 – 10).

Oh, if only each of us in the church would take this attitude as our own. And may this prayer of David's be our prayer as well:

"Hear my cry, O God; listen to my prayer. From the ends of the earth I call to you, I call as my heart grows faint; lead me to the rock that is higher than I. For you have been my refuge, a strong tower against the foe. I long to dwell in your tent forever and take refuge in the shelter of your wings. For you have heard my vows, O God; you have given me the heritage of those who fear your name" (Ps. 61:1 – 5).

NOVEMBER 21

Lazarus was among those reclining
at the table with [Jesus].

John 12:2

From the pen of Charles Spurgeon:

Lazarus should be envied. While it is good to be a Martha and serve, it is better to be a Lazarus and commune with Jesus. Certainly there are appropriate times to serve and to fellowship, but no plant in the garden yields more abundant clusters than the vine of fellowship. To sit with Jesus, hear His voice, witness His works, and receive His smiles was such a blessing that it must have made Lazarus as happy as the angels of heaven.

Lazarus should be imitated. It would have been strange if he had not been at the table with the Lord, for Jesus had raised him from the dead. For the one raised from the dead to be absent when the Lord who gave him life was at his house would have been ungrateful indeed. Yet we were once dead as well, and like Lazarus we were stinking in the grave of sin. Then Jesus raised us to life, and by His life we live. So how could we ever be content to live far away from Him? But don't we cruelly forget to remember Him at His table where He humbles Himself to feast with His brothers and sisters? Thus it behooves us to repent and to do as He has instructed, for even His least wish should be as law to us.

For Lazarus to have lived without constant fellowship with the One of whom the Jews said, "See how he loved him!" (John 11:36) would have been a disgrace. Isn't it as inexcusable in us whom Jesus has loved "with an everlasting love" (Jer. 31:3)? To have coldly snubbed Him who wept over his lifeless corpse would have shown great insensitivity in Lazarus. So what would it say of us over whom the Savior has not only wept but shed His own blood?

Dear brothers and sisters, as we read this today, let us return to our heavenly Bridegroom. And let us ask for His Spirit that we may have closer intimacy with Him, sitting at His table from this point forward.

From the pen of Jim Reimann:

A sign of a growing relationship with Jesus is the deep desire to fellowship with Him. With that in mind, hear the words of the psalmist: "Those who are far from you will perish; you destroy all who are unfaithful to you. But *as for me, it is good to be near God.* I have made the Sovereign LORD my refuge; I will tell of all your deeds" (Ps. 73:27 – 28). But let us also be sure that our fellowship with Him is indeed sincere, taking to heart this warning from Isaiah:

The Lord says: "These people come near to me with their mouth and honor me with their lips, but their hearts are far from me. Their worship of me is made up only of rules taught by men. Therefore once more I will astound these people with wonder upon wonder; the wisdom of the wise will perish, the intelligence of the intelligent will vanish." Woe to those who go to great depths to hide their plans from the LORD, who do their work in darkness and think, "Who sees us? Who will know?"

Isaiah 29:13 – 15

"Therefore, brothers, since we have confidence to enter the Most Holy Place by the blood of Jesus ... let us draw near to God with a sincere heart" (Heb. 10:19, 22).

NOVEMBER 22

The power of his resurrection ...
Philippians 3:10

From the pen of Charles Spurgeon:

The doctrine of a risen Savior is exceedingly precious, for the resurrection is the cornerstone of the entire building of Christianity and the keystone of the arch of our salvation. It would take a massive book to record all the streams of living water that flow from this one sacred source: the resurrection of our precious Lord and Savior Jesus Christ. Yet knowing that He has risen and having fellowship and communion with the risen Savior by personally possessing a risen life — by leaving the tomb of worldliness ourselves — is even more precious. The doctrine of the resurrection is the basis of our experience, but just as a flower is more lovely than the root of a plant, the personal experience of fellowship with the risen Savior is more beautiful than the doctrine.

I do desire that you believe Christ rose from the dead so you will share the message and will derive all the comfort possible from this well-witnessed and well-documented fact. But I implore you not to be content with that. Although you cannot physically see Him as the disciples did, I urge you to aspire to see Christ Jesus through the eyes of faith. Although you cannot touch Him as Mary Magdalene did, you personally can converse with Him, know that He is risen, and be raised to "newness of life" (Rom. 6:4 KJV).

To know that a *crucified* Savior has crucified *my* sins is truly wonderful knowledge. Even more amazing, however, is to know that a *risen* Savior has justified *me*, and to realize that He has bestowed new life on *me*, making *me* "a new creation" (2 Cor. 5:17). This is indeed the highest level of living and, short of it, no believer should ever be satisfied.

Thus, may you not only "know Christ" (Phil. 3:10) but also know "the power of his resurrection." Why should souls who have been made alive with Jesus continue to wear the grave clothes of worldliness and unbelief? Rise, believer, for the Lord *is* risen!

From the pen of Jim Reimann:

Imagine the impact on your faith if Jesus had not risen from the dead. Imagine as well, then, that our earthly life is all there is. What would be the point of continuing to strive to move forward? Pretty depressing even to consider, isn't it?

Yet this is exactly where those who deny our risen Savior live. In spite of all the evidence to the contrary, they argue against the fact of the resurrection. This is why Paul addressed the issue, saying:

> If there is no resurrection of the dead, then not even Christ has been raised. And if Christ has not been raised, our preaching is useless and so is your faith. More than that, we are then found to be false witnesses about God, for we have testified about God that he raised Christ from the dead. But he did not raise him if in fact the dead are not raised. For if the dead are not raised, then Christ has not been raised either. And if Christ has not been raised, your faith is futile; you are still in your sins.... If only for this life we have hope in Christ, we are to be pitied more than all men.
>
> 1 Corinthians 15:13 – 17, 19

Yet thankfully, Paul did not stop there, for he declared: "*But Christ has indeed been raised from the dead*" (v. 20). "The Lord is risen indeed" (Luke 24:34 KJV)!

NOVEMBER 23

Go up on a high mountain.

Isaiah 40:9

From the pen of Charles Spurgeon:

Every believer should thirst for God, yearning to "ascend the hill of the LORD" (Ps. 24:3) and see Him face to face. We should never rest content in the mists of the valley when the summit of the Mount of Transfiguration awaits us. "My soul thirsts for God, for the living God" (Ps. 42:2), to drink deeply of the cup reserved for those who reach the mountain's top and who, as a result, bathe their brow in heaven. How pure the dew of the hills, how fresh the mountain air, how rich the food of those who dwell above — those whose windows open onto "the new Jerusalem" (Rev. 3:12).

Yet many people are content to live like men in coal mines who cannot see the sun. They "eat dust" (Gen. 3:14) like the serpent, when they could savor the ambrosia of angels; they are content to wear the work clothes of miners, when they could wear the robes of kings; and tears stain their faces, when they could be anointed with celestial oil instead. I am convinced that many a believer pines away in a dungeon, when he could walk on the palace roof to view "the good land beyond the Jordan" (Deut. 3:25).

Awake, O believer, from your lowly condition! Cast aside your laziness, your lethargy, your apathy, or whatever interferes with your perfect, pure love for Christ, your soul's Husband. Make Him the source, the center, and the circumference of your entire soul's delight. What captivates you so much to be foolish enough to remain in a pit when you could sit on a throne? Don't live in the lowlands of bondage now that mountain liberty has been conferred upon you. Don't be satisfied any longer with meager attainments, but press forward to things more awe-inspiring and heavenly. Desire a higher, nobler, and fuller life. Upward to heaven! Nearer to God!

> When will You come unto me, Lord?
> Oh come, my Lord most dear!
> Come near, come nearer, nearer still,
> I'm blessed when You are near.
>
> Thomas Shepherd, 1665 – 1739

From the pen of Jim Reimann:

In Jesus' parable of the talents, the master harshly scolded the servant who wasted the opportunity afforded him. Notice how he is described in these words from his master:

> You *wicked, lazy* servant! … Take the talent from him and give it to the one who has the ten talents. For everyone who has will be given more, and he will have an abundance. Whoever does not have, even what he has will be taken from him. And throw that *worthless* servant outside.
>
> Matthew 25:26, 28 – 30

He's called wicked, lazy, and worthless! Yes, he is still referred to as a servant, but a wicked, lazy, and worthless one.

What lesson should I learn from this? It's not easy being a good servant of Christ, but it is worth it. This is why Paul wrote: "I press on toward the goal to win the prize for which God has called me heavenward in Christ Jesus" (Phil. 3:14).

Lord, help me to "press on" — and to climb the "high mountain" for Your glory!

NOVEMBER 24

A little sleep, a little slumber, a little folding of the hands to rest —
and poverty will come on you like a bandit
and scarcity like an armed man.

Proverbs 24:33 – 34

From the pen of Charles Spurgeon:

Even the worst of sluggards only asks for "a little sleep" — being indignant if accused of complete idleness. "A little folding of the hands to rest" is all he craves, and he has a host of excuses to show that his indulgence is quite proper. Thus, his day wastes away little by little until the time for work is over and, ultimately, his field is overgrown with thorns.

It is by little procrastinations that people ruin their soul. They had no intention to delay year after year. They thought, "I will attend to spiritual things in a few more months, when it's more convenient," or "Tomorrow will be a better time to think about this, for I'm too busy with other things. Right now is just not a suitable time." In this way they beg to be excused for doing nothing, but like sand in an hourglass, time passes and life is wasted, grain by grain. Long seasons of grace are lost by these "little slumber[s]."

Oh, to be wise, to catch the fleeting hour, to make use of every moment on the fly. May the Lord teach us this holy wisdom, for otherwise poverty of the worst order awaits us — an eternal spiritual poverty that will lack for even one drop of water and beg for it in vain. Like a traveler steadily pursuing his destination, poverty overtakes the slothful and ruin overthrows those who lack direction. Each wasted hour brings that dreaded pursuer closer, for he does not pause along the way. Just as an armed man demands power and authority, poverty will come to the slothful and death to the unrepentant — there will be no escape.

Oh, that people were wise moment by moment, that they would seek the Lord Jesus diligently before that solemn day dawns when it will be too late to repent and believe. Once the day of harvest arrives, it is futile to lament the fact that seedtime was neglected.

It is not too late, but faith and holy decisions won't linger. May we possess them today.

From the pen of Jim Reimann:

The book of Hebrews carries a stern warning to believers, particularly warning against procrastination. A portion of the warning is a quote of David's from Psalm 95, again stressing obedience "Today." Here is the passage, written to the Hebrew Christians of the early church. As you read, remember — it applies to us as well.

See to it, brothers, that none of you has a sinful, unbelieving heart that turns away from the living God. *But encourage one another daily, as long as it is called Today,* so that none of you may be hardened by sin's deceitfulness. We have come to share in Christ if we hold firmly till the end the confidence we had at first. As has just been said: "*Today,* if you hear his voice, do not harden your hearts as you did in the rebellion."

Hebrews 3:12 – 15

Let us also pay close attention to these words of Paul to Timothy, so that we will not be tempted to lapse into laziness: "Be diligent in these matters; give yourself wholly to them, so that everyone may see your progress. Watch your life and doctrine closely. Persevere in them, because if you do, you will save both yourself and your hearers" (1 Tim. 4:15 – 16).

November 25

For [God] says to Moses,
"I will have mercy on whom I have mercy,
and I will have compassion on whom I have compassion."

Romans 9:15

From the pen of Charles Spurgeon:

With these words, in the plainest way possible, the Lord claims the right to give or to withhold His mercy according to His own sovereign will. Just as the prerogative of life and death is vested in a worldly king with absolute power, the Judge of all the earth has a right to spare or condemn the guilty as He sees best. Due to their sins, mankind has forfeited all claim to God and deserves to perish for those sins. And if all should perish, they have no grounds for complaint. If the Lord steps in to save anyone, He may do so as long as His justice is not thwarted. But if He judges it best to leave the condemned to suffer a just sentence of death, no one may bring legal charges against Him.

The arguments of those who place the rights of mankind on the same footing as those of the Lord are nothing short of foolish and impudent. And their contentions against God's discriminating grace are simply ignorant, if not worse.

Once we are brought to the point of seeing our own utter ruin and spiritual desert, and recognize the justice of God's divine verdict against sin, we will no longer quibble over the fact that the Lord is not obligated to save us. Nor will we complain if He chooses to save others, as though He were doing us an injustice; but we will feel that if He deigns to look upon us, it will be a free act of His own undeserved goodness, for which we will forever bless His name.

Yet how will those who are the objects of divine election sufficiently adore the grace of God?

They have no room for boasting, for the Lord's sovereignty most effectively excludes it. His will alone is glorified, and the very notion of human merit is cast aside into everlasting contempt. There is no more humbling doctrine in Scripture than that of election, none which should prompt more gratitude and, consequently, none more sanctifying. Thus, believers should not be afraid of it, but should adoringly rejoice in it.

From the pen of Jim Reimann:

In his "A Defense of Calvinism," Spurgeon once wrote: "Had a man been an Arminian in those days [of Augustine, Calvin, Whitefield, or the Puritans], he would have been accounted the vilest heretic breathing, but now *we* are looked upon as the heretics, and they as the orthodox. *We* have gone back to the old school; *we* can trace our descent from the apostles." In the same article Spurgeon said: "In my own private opinion, there is no such thing as preaching 'Christ and Him crucified' (1 Cor. 2:2), unless we preach what today is called Calvinism. It is a nickname to call it Calvinism, but *it is the gospel, and nothing else.* I do not believe we can preach the gospel, if we do not preach justification by faith, without works; nor unless we preach the sovereignty of God in His dispensing of grace."

No doubt Spurgeon, who spent his entire adult life "contend[ing] for the faith" (Jude 3), could relate to these words of Paul to Timothy: "I endure everything for the sake of the elect, that they too may obtain the salvation that is in Christ Jesus" (2 Tim. 2:10).

NOVEMBER 26

Who despises the day of small things?
Men will rejoice when they see the plumb line in the hand of Zerubbabel.
Zechariah 4:10

From the pen of Charles Spurgeon:

Small things marked the beginning of the work in Zerubbabel's hands, but no one could despise it, for the Lord had raised up someone who would persevere until the capstone would be brought forth with great cheering. The plumb line was in good hands — a foreshadowing of the comfort every believer has in the Lord Jesus. No matter how small His work of grace may be in the beginning, the plumb line is in good hands, for a Master Builder "greater than Solomon" (Matt. 12:42) has undertaken to build the heavenly temple, and He will not fail nor be discouraged until the uppermost pinnacle is set in place. If the plumb line were in the hands of any mere human being, we might fear for the completion of the building, but the purpose of the Lord definitely will succeed in Jesus' hands.

In Zerubbabel's case, the rebuilding of the temple did not proceed randomly or without careful scrutiny, for he was a competent builder using a good instrument. If its walls had been hurriedly built without proper supervision, they might not have been perpendicular, but the plumb line was used by God's chosen overseer. And Jesus is even more watchful of the erecting of His spiritual temple, that it be built securely and well. We humans are all for haste, but Jesus is all for judgment. He will use His plumb line, and any part of His building that is out of plumb must come down — every stone of it — hence the failure of many spiritual works that look wonderful on the outside, and the overthrow of many glittering, yet false, professions of faith. Yet it is not for us to measure the Lord's church. Jesus

has a steady hand, a keen eye, and can use the plumb line well. And shouldn't we rejoice to see judgment left to Him? Furthermore, in today's text we see the plumb line in active use, for it is in the Builder's hand — a sure indication that He means to push the work through to completion.

O Lord Jesus, how joyful we would be if only we could see You at Your great work. O Zion the beautiful, Your walls are still in ruins! Rise, O glorious Builder, and make her desolation rejoice at Your coming.

From the pen of Jim Reimann:

Lest Zerubbabel be tempted to take personal credit for the rebuilding of the temple, the Lord gave him this message, "'Not by might nor by power, *but by my Spirit*,' says the LORD Almighty" (Zech. 4:6). Then our sovereign God, knowing the mountain of opposition Zerubbabel was about to face, added these words of encouragement, "What are you, O mighty mountain? Before Zerubbabel you will become level ground. Then he will bring out the capstone to shouts of 'God bless it! God bless it!'" (v. 7).

Finally, in an effort to show Zerubbabel that He always brings His work to completion, the Lord continued, "The hands of Zerubbabel have laid the foundation of this temple; his hands will also complete it. Then you will know that the LORD Almighty has sent me to you" (v. 9).

Lord God, may I never despise "the day of small things." And may I always trust "that [You] who began a good work in [me] will carry it on to completion" (Phil. 1:6).

NOVEMBER 27

In [Jesus Christ] we have ... the forgiveness of sins,
in accordance with the riches of God's grace.

Ephesians 1:7

From the pen of Charles Spurgeon:

Could there be a sweeter word in any language than the word *forgiveness* as it resounds in a guilty sinner's ear like the joyous songs of jubilee to a captive Israelite? Forever blessed is that glorious star of pardon that shines into the prison of the condemned, giving those who are perishing a gleam of hope amid the midnight of despair. Can it really be possible that sin — sin such as mine — can be forgiven, completely forgiven, forever? Hell is my inevitable destiny as a sinner, and there is no possibility of escaping it while sin remains on me. Can my load of guilt truly be lifted and the crimson stain of sin removed? Can the diamond-hard stones of my prison wall ever be loosened from their mortar or my cell doors be removed from their hinges?

Yet Jesus tells me I am already clean. Forever blessed is the revelation of His atoning love that not only tells me pardon is possible but that it is already secured for all who rest in Him. I have believed in His preordained propitiation — which is "Christ crucified" (1 Cor. 1:23) — and therefore my sins are this very moment, and forever, forgiven by virtue of His substitutionary suffering and death. How blessed am I — to be a perfectly pardoned soul!

Thus my soul dedicates all its strength to Him who, of His own free love, became my guarantee of life, buying my "redemption through His blood" (Eph. 1:7). What amazing riches of His grace does this free forgiveness exhibit. How amazing to forgive at all, to forgive fully, to forgive freely, to forgive forever! This is a constellation of heavenly wonders, and when I think of how many sins I had, the more prized to me are those precious drops of blood that cleansed me from them all. And the more I realize how gracious was His work that sealed my pardon, the more I find myself in a state of awe and adoring affection. I bow before the throne that forgives me; I cling to the cross that delivers me; and all my days I will forever serve the Incarnate God through whom I am a pardoned soul today.

From the pen of Jim Reimann:

Spurgeon mentioned Jesus'"preordained propitiation." The word *propitiation* is a term meaning: "a sacrifice that fully satisfies the wrath of God on sin." And by using the word *preordained* with it, Spurgeon is saying that the sacrifice of God's Son was determined well in advance. This is why Peter wrote, regarding Jesus as God's choice as the sacrificial lamb: "He was chosen before the creation of the world, but was revealed in these last times" (1 Peter 1:20). This is also why Paul could say, "He chose us in him before the creation of the world" (Eph. 1:4).

The writer of Hebrews reminds us of the Old Testament teaching that "without the shedding of blood there is no forgiveness" (Heb. 9:22). But he goes on to say that Christ "has appeared once for all at the end of the ages to do away with sin by the sacrifice of himself" (Heb. 9:26). Shouldn't His selfless love and precious sacrifice motivate us to greater love and service for Him?

"In this is love: not that we loved God, but that He loved us and sent His Son to be the propitiation (the atoning sacrifice) for our sins" (1 John 4:10 Amplified).

NOVEMBER 28

Mordecai ... sought the welfare of his people.

Esther 10:3 Amplified

From the pen of Charles Spurgeon:

Mordecai was a true patriot and, once promoted to be "second in rank to King Xerxes" (v. 3), he used his high position to promote the prosperity of Israel. By doing this he was a type of Christ, for Jesus — seated on His throne of glory — seeks not His own welfare, but exercises His power for the benefit of His people. And it would be good if every Christian were a Mordecai to the church, striving with all his strength for the church's prosperity. Some believers are placed in positions of affluence and influence, so may they honor their Lord in the lofty places on earth and testify for Jesus before the world's powerful people.

Other believers have what is far better, namely, close fellowship with "the King of kings" (1 Tim. 6:15), so let them daily plead the case of the weak, the doubting, the tempted, and the comfortless of the Lord's people. It will result to their honor if they intercede on behalf of those who are in darkness — those who themselves dare not draw near to God's "mercy seat" (Ex. 25:17 KJV). Well-taught believers serve their Master well when they spend their talents teaching others the things of God.

The very least of our "Israel" can seek the welfare of His people, and even if all he can offer is his desire to serve, that will be acceptable before the Lord. Ceasing to live for himself is not only the most Christlike but also the happiest path for a believer to walk, for he who blesses others cannot fail to be blessed himself. On the other hand, seeking our own personal greatness is a wicked and unhappy way of life, for it is the path of disaster, and its end will be fatal.

Therefore I ask you, dear friend, are you seeking the welfare of the church to the best of your strength where God has placed you? Or are you doing damage to the church through bitterness and scandal or weakening it by your neglect? Friend, unite with the Lord's poor and bear their cross, doing them all the good you can, and you will receive your promised reward.

From the pen of Jim Reimann:

As we have seen today, there is indeed a blessing attached to spending ourselves for the sake of others — and not a blessing just for the next life. For example, listen to what Paul said regarding Epaphroditus, whom he was sending back to the church in Philippi: "Welcome him in the Lord with great joy, and honor men like him, because he almost died for the work of Christ" (Phil. 2:29 – 30). How much greater will it be to be welcomed into glory by the Lord Himself with these words: "Well done, good and faithful servant! You have been faithful with a few things; I will put you in charge of many things. Come and share your master's happiness!" (Matt. 25:21). After all, "It was he who gave some to be apostles, some to be prophets, some to be evangelists, and some to be pastors and teachers, *to prepare God's people for works of service, so that the body of Christ may be built up*" (Eph. 4:11 – 12). With this in mind, may this be our closing prayer today:

"May the God of peace ... equip you with everything good for doing his will, and may he work in us what is pleasing to him, through Jesus Christ, to whom be glory for ever and ever. Amen" (Heb. 13:20 – 21).

November 29

... spices for the anointing oil.

Exodus 35:8

From the pen of Charles Spurgeon:

God's law prescribed a number of uses for this anointing oil, and the Holy Spirit, which it symbolizes, is of primary importance in the gospel itself. The Holy Spirit anoints us for all holy service and is thus indispensable to us if we desire to serve the Lord in an acceptable way. Without His help, our service to God would be nothing but a vain ritual, and our inner spiritual experience would be dead. Whenever our visible ministry lacks His anointing, how miserable it becomes. Nor are our private prayers, praises, meditation, or other efforts one bit better.

A holy anointing is the soul and life of faith, and its absence is the worst of all calamities. To go before the Lord without His anointing is like a common Levite thrusting himself into the priest's office, resulting in our ministry efforts becoming sin, not service. Therefore, may we never venture out to do our sacred duties without God's sacred anointing. The Spirit's anointing falls upon us from our glorious Head, for from His anointing we who are "the skirts of his garments" (Ps. 133:2 KJV) partake of His abundant unction. According to God's law, select spices were to be mixed with the careful skill of a pharmacist to create the perfect anointing oil, indicating for us the rich and perfect powers of the Holy Spirit.

All good things are found in the divine Comforter. Matchless consolation, infallible instruction, immortal life, spiritual power, and divine sanctification are all mixed together with other excellencies of God in that sacred salve — the heavenly anointing oil of the Holy Spirit. His anointing imparts a delightful fragrance to the character and person of the one upon whom it is poured, and nothing as wonderful can be found in all the treasuries of the rich or in the deepest secrets of the wise.

The Spirit's anointing is not to be imitated. It comes only from God and is freely given through Jesus Christ to every waiting soul. So let us seek it, for we may have it — even this very moment.

O Lord, anoint Your servants.

From the pen of Jim Reimann:

In the Old Testament, the Spirit would come upon a person for a particular work and then depart. For example, we are told that before leading God's people into battle "the Spirit of the LORD came upon Gideon" (Judg. 6:34). David is the only person in the Old Testament, however, upon whom the Spirit came, never to leave again, for the Scripture tells us: "Samuel took the horn of oil and anointed him in the presence of his brothers, and *from that day on the Spirit of the LORD came upon David in power*" (1 Sam. 16:13). No doubt, this is why David, upon being confronted with his sins of adultery and murder, prayed, "Do not ... take your Holy Spirit from me" (Ps. 51:11).

Then in the New Testament we see God giving His Spirit to those He saves, sealing them in Christ and reconfirming the truth: "Never will I leave you; never will I forsake you" (Heb. 13:5). And Paul addressed the Spirit's anointing of us by saying, "He anointed us, set his seal of ownership on us, and put his Spirit in our hearts as a deposit, guaranteeing what is to come" (2 Cor. 1:21 – 22).

So, believer — "be filled with the Spirit" (Eph. 5:18).

NOVEMBER 30

There was war in heaven.
Michael and his angels fought against the dragon,
and the dragon and his angels fought back.

Revelation 12:7

From the pen of Charles Spurgeon:

War will continue to rage between the two great powers until one or the other is crushed. Peace between good and evil is impossible, for, in fact, the very pretense of it would be a triumph for the power of darkness. Michael will always fight because his holy soul is greatly troubled by sin and will not tolerate it. And Jesus will always be the Dragon's foe — and not quietly, but actively, vigorously, and with the determination to exterminate evil completely. Thus, all Jesus' servants, whether angels in heaven or messengers on earth, will and must fight. They have been created to be warriors, for at the cross they enter into a covenant never to make a truce with evil, becoming a warlike unit that stands firm in defense and fierce in offense. The duty of every soldier in the army of the Lord is to fight against the Dragon with all his heart, soul, and strength each day.

Yet "the dragon and his angels" will not run from the fight. They are incessant in their onslaughts and will spare no weapon, legal or not. Therefore it is foolish for us to expect to serve God without opposition, and the more zealous we are for Him, the more certain we are to be attacked by the minions of hell. The church may grow lazy, but not so her great Enemy. His restless spirit never will allow a pause in the war and would gladly devour the church if he could.

But glory be to God that we know the end of the war! "The great dragon" (Rev. 12:9) will be cast down and forever destroyed, while Jesus — and those who are with Him — "will receive the crown of life" (James 1:12). So let us sharpen our swords even now and pray for the Holy Spirit to strengthen our arms for the conflict. We will never face a battle so important or receive a crown so glorious. Everyone to your post, O warriors of the cross, and may the Lord soon trample Satan under your feet!

From the pen of Jim Reimann:

As you read the following passage from Isaiah, notice in these brief words of Lucifer that he says "I will" five times:

How you have fallen from heaven, O morning star, son of the dawn! You have been cast down to the earth, you who once laid low the nations! You said in your heart, "*I will* ascend to heaven; *I will* raise my throne above the stars of God; *I will* sit enthroned on the mount of assembly, on the utmost heights of the sacred mountain. *I will* ascend above the tops of the clouds; *I will* make myself like the Most High."

Isaiah 14:12 – 14

Yet, just as we see Satan's ultimate downfall in Revelation, we see it in Isaiah, for the Lord goes on to prophesy: "But you are brought down to the grave, to the depths of the pit" (v. 15).

O Lord, may I never be so boastful as to say "I will," but may I be like Jesus, who, although Himself is God the Son, prayed, "Not my will, but yours be done" (Luke 22:42), and "Your will be done on earth as it is in heaven" (Matt. 6:10). And, Father, may I be fully engaged to "fight the good fight of the faith" (1 Tim. 6:12) to bring You great glory!

December

DECEMBER 1

Let them give thanks to the LORD for his unfailing love
and his wonderful deeds for men.

Psalm 107:8

From the pen of Charles Spurgeon:

If we complained less and praised more, we would be much happier and God would be more glorified. So let us daily praise Him for common, everyday mercies — common, as we frequently call them, yet so priceless that when deprived of them we are ready to perish. Let us bless the Lord for the eyes with which we behold the sun, for the health and strength to walk, for the bread we eat, and for the clothing we wear. Let us praise Him that we are not wandering among the homeless and the hopeless, or deprived of our freedom with the guilty. Let us thank Him for liberty, for friends and family relationships, and for creature comforts. Let us praise Him, in fact, for everything we receive from His generous hand, for we deserve so little and yet are so abundantly blessed.

Yet, beloved, our sweetest and loudest songs of praise should be of God's redeeming love. His act of redemption for His chosen ones should be the favorite theme of our praise forever. So if we know what redemption means, let us not withhold our psalms of thanksgiving. We have been redeemed from the power of our own corruption and raised from the depth of sin into which we were plunged by our own sin nature. We have been led to the cross of Christ, our shackles of guilt have been broken, and we are no longer slaves, but are "the children of the living God" (Rom. 9:26 KJV). Thus, we look back to the cross as well as forward to the day we will be presented before the throne "without stain or wrinkle or any other blemish" (Eph. 5:27). Even now by faith we wave "palm branches" (John 12:13) of praise and robe ourselves with "fine linen" (Rev. 19:8). Shouldn't we also give unceasing thanks to the Lord our Redeemer?

Child of God, can you be silent? "Wake up, wake up, break out in song!" (Judg. 5:12), you inheritors of glory. And cry out with David, "Praise the LORD, O my soul; all my inmost being, praise his holy name" (Ps. 103:1). May this new month begin with new songs of praise.

From the pen of Jim Reimann:

Luke describes Jesus' Palm Sunday entry into Jerusalem in the following manner:

> When he came near the place where the road goes down the Mount of Olives, the whole crowd of disciples began joyfully to praise God in loud voices for all the miracles they had seen: "Blessed is the king who comes in the name of the Lord!" "Peace in heaven and glory in the highest!" Some of the Pharisees in the crowd said to Jesus, "Teacher, rebuke your disciples!" "I tell you," he replied, "if they keep quiet, the stones will cry out."

Luke 19:37 – 40

Isaiah had prophesized that the Messiah would come "to comfort all who mourn, and provide for those who grieve in Zion — to bestow on them a crown of beauty instead of ashes, the oil of gladness instead of mourning, and a garment of praise instead of a spirit of despair" (Isa. 61:2 – 3). Thus, as Spurgeon asked: "Can you be silent?" with so great a Savior! If so, "the stones will cry out," and we will miss the blessing of offering praise to Him who alone is worthy.

"And they sang a new song: 'You are worthy to take the scroll and to open its seals, because you were slain, and with your blood you purchased men for God from every tribe and language and people and nation'" (Rev. 5:9).

DECEMBER 2

I have seen all the things that are done under the sun;
all of them are meaningless.

Ecclesiastes 1:14

From the pen of Charles Spurgeon:

Nothing can satisfy the entire man but the Lord's love and the Lord Himself. Saints have tried to anchor their souls in other ports of shelter, but ultimately have been driven from such fatal places of refuge. In fact, Solomon, the wisest man of all time, was permitted to make experiments for us all, doing for us what we must not dare do for ourselves. Here is his testimony in his own words:

> I became greater by far than anyone in Jerusalem before me. In all this my wisdom stayed with me. I denied myself nothing my eyes desired; I refused my heart no pleasure. My heart took delight in all my work, and this was the reward for all my labor. Yet when I surveyed all that my hands had done and what I had toiled to achieve, everything was meaningless, a chasing after the wind; nothing was gained under the sun.
>
> Ecclesiastes 2:9 – 11

"Utterly meaningless! Everything is meaningless" (Eccl. 1:2). What! All of this is meaningless? O favored King Solomon, does your wealth mean nothing? Is there nothing in your entire domain, from the Jordan to the sea, that has any meaning? Nothing in your palaces? Nothing in all your music and dancing, wine and luxury? After having traveled the road of pleasure from end to end, Solomon replied, in essence, "Nothing, but 'a weariness of the flesh'" (Eccl. 12:12 KJV). But to embrace our Lord Jesus, to dwell in His love, and to be fully assured of our union with Him — this is "all in all" (1 Cor. 15:28).

Dear reader, you need not try other paths of life in order to see whether they are better than the Christian path. If you travel the world over, you will never see a sight as wonderful as the Savior's face. If you had all the comforts of life but lost your Savior, you would be hopeless. If you have Christ, you could be rotting in a dungeon but find it to be a paradise; you could die in obscurity or in famine but be satisfied with the full favor and goodness of the Lord.

From the pen of Jim Reimann:

Unfortunately, many teens do not heed their parents' advice, only to discover for themselves the destructive power of sin. Oh, if only they would listen. Think of all the pain and suffering they and others would be spared. And if only we as believers would heed what we have read today, for Spurgeon tells us that Solomon "was permitted to make experiments for us all, doing for us what we must not dare do for ourselves." Oh, if only we would heed his findings!

Doesn't the Bible tell us: "These things happened to [our forefathers] as examples and were written down as warnings for us" (1 Cor. 10:11). Is it possible that our children not listening to us is God's way of showing us how we ignore His advice? Is it possible that if we were more obedient to God's Word our children would follow our example?

Thus, may we, and our children, obey our Savior, who said, "*I have set you an example that you should do as I have done for you.* I tell you the truth, no servant is greater than his master, nor is a messenger greater than the one who sent him. Now that you know these things, *you will be blessed if you do them*" (John 13:15 – 17).

DECEMBER 3

Who is this King of glory?
The Lord strong and mighty,
the Lord mighty in battle.

Psalm 24:8

From the pen of Charles Spurgeon:

Our God should be viewed as glorious by His people due to the miracles He has worked for them, in them, and through them. *For them,* the Lord Jesus routed every foe at Calvary, breaking all the weapons of the Enemy into pieces by His finished work of perfect, fully sufficient obedience. By His triumphant resurrection and ascension, He overturned the hopes of hell, "led captives in his train" (Eph. 4:8), and "made a public spectacle of them, triumphing over them by the cross" (Col. 2:15). Every arrow of guilt that Satan might have shot at us is broken, for "who will bring any charge against those whom God has chosen?" (Rom. 8:33). Thus, the continual swinging of the sharp swords of evil and the perpetual waging of war against the church by the Serpent's seed are nothing but vain pursuits, for even the most crippled of God's saints overcomes his prey, and even the weakest warrior is crowned victorious.

The saved of God should greatly adore their Lord for His conquests *in them* as well, since the arrows of their natural-born hatred for Him, and the weapons of their rebellion toward Him, have been broken. What great victories God's grace has won in our evil hearts. And how glorious is our view of Jesus once our will has been subdued and sin dethroned. But as for our remaining corruption, it will sustain an equally certain defeat, and every temptation, doubt, and fear will be utterly destroyed. In the Salem of our now peaceful hearts, the name of Jesus is great beyond compare. He has victoriously won our love and will be crowned with it.

With the same certainty, the saved should look for victories *through them.* "We are more than conquerors through him who loved us" (Rom. 8:37). We will dethrone the powers of darkness in this world through our faith, zeal, and holiness. We will win sinners to Jesus, we will overturn false systems of belief, we will convert nations, "for God is with us" (Isa. 8:10), and thus no strategy against us will stand.

Even now, Christian warrior, sing the battle song and prepare for war. "The one who is in you is greater than the one who is in the world" (1 John 4:4).

From the pen of Jim Reimann:

Our text is taken from a psalm of David, one of the greatest warriors ever known. Yet notice how he fully recognized the source of victory: "*The Lord* mighty in battle." And this recognition was something that came to him early in life, for even as a boy confronting Goliath, he declared: "The battle is the Lord's." The following is that statement in its context. As you read, notice David's total confidence in the coming victory and that he gave the glory to God *before* the victory was won.

David said to the Philistine, "You come against me with sword and spear and javelin, but I come against you in the name of the Lord Almighty, the God of the armies of Israel, whom you have defied. This day the Lord will hand you over to me ... and *the whole world will know that there is a God in Israel.* All those gathered here will know that it is not by sword or spear that the Lord saves; for *the battle is the Lord's,* and he will give all of you into our hands."

1 Samuel 17:45 – 47

DECEMBER 4

We ourselves ... groan inwardly
as we wait eagerly for our adoption as sons,
the redemption of our bodies.

Romans 8:23

From the pen of Charles Spurgeon:

This groaning is universal among God's saints, for to a greater or lesser extent, we all feel it. It is not the groan of grumbling or distress, but rather the groan of a deep desire. Having received the "deposit guaranteeing our inheritance" (Eph. 1:14), we desire the remainder. We groan to see our entire personhood — in its trinity of spirit, soul, and body — set free from the last vestige of the fall. We yearn to put off "the perishable," weakness, and dishonor and to be "clothed with the imperishable," "immortality" (1 Cor. 15:54), glory, and the spiritual body the Lord Jesus will bestow to His people. We long for the complete manifestation of "our adoption as sons."

"We ... groan," but notice that it is done "inwardly." It is not the groan of a hypocrite, which would only serve to make people believe we are saints because we appear so wretchedly miserable. Our groaning is sacred — something too holy for us to share with the world — so we keep our longings for our Lord alone.

Next we see that we who groan "wait." From this we learn that we are not to be impulsive, like Elijah and Jonah, who prayed, "Take my life" (1 Kings 19:4 and Jonah 4:3). Nor are we to whine and cry for the end of our life because we have become weary of the work, nor wish to escape our present sufferings until the will of the Lord is ultimately done. Yes, we are to groan for our glorification, but are to wait patiently for it, knowing that what the Lord ordains is best. Waiting, however, also implies being ready. We are to stand at the door eagerly expecting our Beloved to open it and take us to be with Him.

Finally, we see that this groaning is a test, for a person is judged by what he "groans for" or "groans about." Some people groan for wealth, thus worshiping money; others groan about the troubles of life, thereby revealing their impatience. But the person who groans after God, never being satisfied until he is made like Christ, is a blessed person indeed. May God Himself help us to groan for the coming of the Lord and the resurrection He will bring to us.

From the pen of Jim Reimann:

Regarding the second coming, Matthew wrote: "As Jesus was sitting on the Mount of Olives, the disciples came to him privately. 'Tell us,' they said, 'when will this happen, and what will be the sign of your coming and of the end of the age?'" (Matt. 24:3). From this we see that for 2,000 years, God's people have wondered about the timing of our Lord's return. Although we don't know when He will return, we know where He will return — the very place the disciples asked this question — the Mount of Olives. More than 500 years before Christ, the prophet Zechariah predicted the following regarding the Messiah: "On that day his feet will stand on the Mount of Olives, east of Jerusalem, and the Mount of Olives will be split in two from east to west, forming a great valley, with half of the mountain moving north and half moving south" (Zech. 14:4).

Seismologists have proven that the only east-west fault line in Israel lies across the Mount of Olives. God and every detail of His Word can be trusted. So take heart, believer, "This same Jesus ... *will* come back" (Acts 1:11).

DECEMBER 5

The LORD showed me four craftsmen.
Zechariah 1:20

From the pen of Charles Spurgeon:

In his vision, Zechariah also saw four fearsome horns. They were pushing this way and that, throwing down the strong. The prophet asked, "What are these?" The answer: "These are the horns that scattered Judah, Israel and Jerusalem" (v. 19). What Zechariah saw was also a foreshadowing of the powers that would someday oppress God's church. There were "four horns" (v. 18), representing the fact that the church is attacked from all directions. This vision might have caused Zechariah to become dismayed, but suddenly "the LORD showed [him] four craftsmen." And the prophet asked, "What are these coming to do?" to which the Lord responded, "The craftsmen have come to terrify [the four horns] and throw down these horns of the nations" (v. 21).

God will always find people for His work — and will always find them at the right time. Notice that Zechariah did not see the craftsmen first, when there was no work to do. He only saw them after he had seen the horns. Notice also that the Lord always finds enough people to do His work, for Zechariah did not see only three craftsmen, but four; there were "four horns," thus "four craftsmen" were needed. Finally, notice that God finds the right people for the work. In this case He didn't send four people with pens for writing or four architects to draw plans. He sent "four craftsmen" to do rough work.

Rest assured, you who fear for the ark of God — His church — for when the horns cause trouble, the craftsmen will be found. You need never fret over the apparent weakness of God's church, for, growing up in obscurity, there may be a valiant reformer who will shake the nations. Another Chrysostom (c. 347 – 407, early church leader) or Augustine (354 – 430, early church leader) may appear from the thickest darkness of poverty. The Lord knows where to find His servants. He has a multitude of mighty men waiting to ambush His foes, and at His word they will rise to war. "The battle is the LORD'S" (1 Sam. 17:47), and He will take the victory for Himself. So let us remain faithful to Christ, trusting that He — at the perfect time — will mount a defense for us, whether it is at a moment of our personal need or in a season of danger to His church.

From the pen of Jim Reimann:

John Chrysostom, mentioned today, has been referred to as "the greatest preacher in the early church." But there can be no doubt that Spurgeon, known as "the prince of preachers," became one of those the Lord raised up at a time when the church and the gospel came under attack. He took a stand for truth, boldly living up to the following words of Jude. May each of us be determined to do the same.

Dear friends, although I was very eager to write to you about the salvation we share, I felt I had to write and urge you to *contend for the faith* that was once for all entrusted to the saints. For certain men whose condemnation was written about long ago have secretly slipped in among you. They are godless men, who change the grace of our God into a license for immorality and deny Jesus Christ our only Sovereign and Lord. Though you already know all this, I want to remind you that the Lord delivered his people out of Egypt, but later destroyed those who did not believe.

Jude 3 – 5

DECEMBER 6

In the middle of the lampstands I saw one like a son of man,
clothed in a robe reaching to the feet,
and girded across His chest with a golden sash.

Revelation 1:13 NASB

From the pen of Charles Spurgeon:

"One like a son of man" appeared to John on Patmos, and "the disciple whom Jesus loved" (John 13:23) noted that Jesus was "girded ... with a golden sash." And just as Jesus never was unprepared while on earth, but always stood ready for service, He now stands serving before the eternal throne, "girded" as the priests of old were girded with the "skillfully woven waistband ... of one piece with the ephod and made with gold" (Ex. 28:8).

How blessed we are that Jesus has not ceased to fulfill this glorious and loving role, since this is one of our great safeguards — "because he always lives to intercede for [us]" (Heb. 7:25). Jesus never is idle, with His sash untied or loose as though His work were ended, but He diligently carries on the cause of His people. He wears "a golden sash," revealing to us His royalty, the superiority of His service, the dignity of His state, and the glory of His reward. He pleads our case with the authority of a King and a Priest. Thus, our cause is safe in the hands of our enthroned "Melchizedek" (see Heb. 6:20).

This view of Jesus should be an example for us. We must never untie our sash or loosen our belt, for this is the time for service and warfare. We need "the belt of truth [tightly] buckled around [our] waist" (Eph. 6:14). Ours too is "a golden sash," and thus should be our most prized piece of armor. We greatly need it, for a believer's heart that is not firmly girded with the truth of Jesus and with the faithfulness produced by the Spirit will be easily entangled with the things of this life and snared by temptation. It is meaningless for us to have the Scriptures unless we gird them around us like a belt or a sash. They are to surround our entire nature, keeping each part of our character in order and bringing a firmness to our entire person.

If Jesus, in heaven, is still "girded ... with a golden sash," how much more do we, on earth, need to remain girded? "Stand firm then, with the belt of truth buckled around your waist" (Eph. 6:14).

From the pen of Jim Reimann:

The fact that John in his vision saw Jesus wearing a sash should not be a surprise to us. Jesus said, "Do not think that I have come to abolish the Law or the Prophets; I have not come to abolish them but to fulfill them" (Matt. 5:17). And how beautifully He has done just that!

More than 1,400 years before Christ, the Lord told Moses: "These are the garments they are to make: a breastpiece, an ephod, a robe, a woven tunic, a turban *and a sash*. They are to make these sacred garments for your brother Aaron and his sons, so they may serve me as priests" (Ex. 28:4). Approximately 700 years later, Isaiah described the coming Messiah with these words: "Righteousness will be his belt and faithfulness *the sash around his waist*" (Isa. 11:5).

Should we be surprised that these three men, Moses, Isaiah, and John, all described the same sash? After all, "Prophecy never had its origin in the will of man, but men spoke from God as they were carried along by the Holy Spirit" (2 Peter 1:21).

DECEMBER 7

I have become all things to all men
so that by all possible means I might save some.
1 Corinthians 9:22

From the pen of Charles Spurgeon:

Paul's primary objective was not merely to improve people or to instruct them, but to save them. Anything short of salvation would have disappointed him, for his desire was to see people forgiven and sanctified with their hearts renewed — in fact, to see them saved. Has the aim of our Christian work been anything less than this great goal? If so, let us change our ways, for what benefit will there be on the last "great Day" (Jude 6) to have simply taught people morals if they then stand before God unsaved? Our clothes will be stained with blood if throughout this life we have lesser goals, forgetting that people need to be saved. Paul knew the ruin of mankind's natural condition and did not attempt to educate people, but to save them. He watched people sinking into hell and did not speak of refining them, but of saving them "from the coming wrath" (1 Thess. 1:10).

Therefore, to bring about their salvation, Paul totally gave himself with untiring zeal to share the gospel far and wide, warning and imploring people to "be reconciled to God" (2 Cor. 5:20). His prayers were persistent and his work relentless, for the salvation of souls was his all-consuming passion, objective, and calling. He became a servant "to all men," feeling: "Woe to me if I do not preach the gospel!" (1 Cor. 9:16). Paul set aside his personal preferences to prevent prejudice, submitting his will in things of lesser importance. If people would simply receive the gospel, he raised no objections over form or ritual, for the gospel itself was the all-important issue with him. If he "might save some," Paul would be content, for this was the crown for which he strove — the sole and sufficient reward of all his labor and self-denial.

Dear reader, ask yourself: "Have I lived to win souls? Do I possess the same all-consuming desire? If not, why not?" Remember — Jesus died for sinners. Can't we then live for them? Where is our compassion? Where is our love for Christ if we do not seek His honor through the salvation of others?

O Lord, saturate us through and through
with an undying zeal for the souls of mankind.

From the pen of Jim Reimann:

Some believers excuse their lack of soul-winning by quoting the following verse, thereby attempting to prove not everyone is called to evangelism: "It was [Christ] who gave some to be apostles, some to be prophets, some to be evangelists, and some to be pastors and teachers" (Eph. 4:11). Although it is true not everyone's primary gift is evangelism, we must remember we are to be like Christ. After all, Paul reminded Timothy, a pastor: "Christ Jesus came into the world to save sinners" (1 Tim. 1:15).

The Lord has chosen to work through His people to save souls, which is why Paul also said, "We are therefore Christ's ambassadors, as though God were making his appeal through us" (2 Cor. 5:20). Believer, don't miss the crown rewarded to those who win souls, for Paul wrote these words to those who had come to Christ through his work: "What is our hope, our joy, or the crown in which we will glory in the presence of our Lord Jesus when he comes? *Is it not you? Indeed, you are our glory and joy*" (1 Thess. 2:19 – 20).

DECEMBER 8

From your bounty, O God,
you provided for the poor.
Psalm 68:10

From the pen of Charles Spurgeon:

All God's gifts are from His prepared bounty stored up for our future needs. He anticipates our needs and out of the fullness of that bounty, which He has treasured up in Christ Jesus, He "provide[s] for the poor." You can trust Him for every necessity that may occur, for He infallibly has foreknown each one of them. Only God can say that He knows exactly what each of us will face. We may plan to take a journey across a desert and, after traveling for a day and then pitching our tent, discover we forgot to pack a number of necessities or items of comfort. We do not foresee such things, and if we had it to do all over again, would pack those things so necessary for our comfort.

God, however, perfectly foresees all the requirements of His poor wandering children, and thus when needs arise, His supplies are ready. Yet it is only goodness He has prepared in advance for the poor in heart — goodness and only goodness. And He says to us: "My grace is sufficient for you" (2 Cor. 12:9), and "Your strength will equal your days" (Deut. 33:25).

Dear reader, is your heart heavy today? If so, God knew it would be, and the comfort your heart needs is treasured up in the sweet assurance of today's text. You are poor and needy, but He has not forgotten you; He has in His bounty the exact blessing you require. So plead the promise of today's verse in prayer, believe it, and obtain its fulfillment.

Do you feel you were never as consciously aware of your vileness as you are at this moment? Then behold — the crimson fountain is still open, with all its past effectiveness to wash your sin away. Remember, you will never be in such a place that Jesus Christ cannot help you. You will never face an emergency in your spiritual life where He is unequal to the task, for your entire history has been foreseen — and provided for — in Jesus.

From the pen of Jim Reimann:

David personally experienced the Lord's provision time and time again. After you read today's verse in its following context, why not take a moment to praise the Lord — as David does in this psalm — for all the ways He has continued to meet your needs?

> Sing to God, sing praise to his name, extol him who rides on the clouds — his name is the LORD — and rejoice before him. A father to the fatherless, a defender of widows, is God in his holy dwelling. God sets the lonely in families, he leads forth the prisoners with singing; but the rebellious live in a sun-scorched land. When you went out before your people, O God, when you marched through the wasteland, the earth shook, the heavens poured down rain, before God, the One of Sinai, before God, the God of Israel. You gave abundant showers, O God; you refreshed your weary inheritance. Your people settled in it, and from your bounty, O God, you provided for the poor. . . . The chariots of God are tens of thousands and thousands of thousands; the Lord has come from Sinai into his sanctuary. When you ascended on high, you led captives in your train; you received gifts from men, even from the rebellious — that you, O LORD God, might dwell there. Praise be to the Lord, to God our Savior, who daily bears our burdens.

Psalm 68:4 – 10, 17 – 19

DECEMBER 9

My people will live in peaceful dwelling places ...
in undisturbed places of rest.

Isaiah 32:18

From the pen of Charles Spurgeon:

Peace and rest do not belong to the unregenerate, for those blessings are the unique possession of the Lord's people. "The God of peace" (Rom. 15:33) gives "perfect peace" to those "whose mind is stayed on [Him]" (Isa. 26:3 KJV). Before man fell, God gave him the beautiful "Garden of Eden" (Gen. 2:15) as his quiet resting place. Alas, how quickly sin blighted that lovely home of innocence.

Yet even in the day of universal wrath, when the flood swept away a guilty race, the chosen family of Noah was peacefully secure in the resting place of the ark (see Gen. 7:7). And that ark, which floated them from the old condemned world to the new earth of the rainbow and God's covenant (see Gen. 9:13), is a type of Jesus — the ark of our salvation. Later Israel rested safely behind blood-painted doorposts while the destroying angel struck the firstborn of Egypt (see Ex. 12:29), and then in the wilderness the "pillar of cloud" (Ex. 13:21) and the "water out of the rock" (Num. 20:8) provided sweet rest for the weary pilgrims.

Likewise, we who are His today rest in the promises of our faithful God this very moment. His words are full of truth and power and are a comfort themselves. We rest in the doctrines of His Word, such as the covenant of His grace, which has become for us a haven of delight. Thus we are more highly blessed than David in the safety of "the cave of Adullam" (1 Sam. 22:1) and better protected than Jonah beneath his gourd (see Jonah 4:6 KJV), for no one can invade or destroy our shelter. The person of Jesus Himself is the quiet resting place of His people, and when we draw near to Him in "the breaking of bread" (Acts 2:42), in hearing the preaching of the Word, in studying the Scriptures, or through prayer and praise, we find that any of these ways of approaching Him are the way of return to peace in our spirit.

I hear the words of love, I gaze upon the
blood,
I see the mighty sacrifice, and I have peace
with God.
'Tis everlasting peace, sure as Jehovah's name,
'Tis stable as His steadfast throne,
forevermore the same:
The clouds may go and come, and storms
may sweep my sky,
This blood-sealed friendship changes not,
the cross is ever nigh.

Horatius Bonar, 1808 – 89

From the pen of Jim Reimann:

Regarding true "places of rest," God warns us not to be as the unbelieving Israelites in the wilderness, saying, "I declared on oath in my anger, 'They shall never enter my rest'" (Ps. 95:11). Much later those words are echoed in Hebrews, with the early Jewish believers being warned: "Since *the promise of entering his rest still stands*, let us be careful that none of you be found to have fallen short of it. For we also have had the gospel preached to us, just as they did; but the message they heard was of no value to them, *because those who heard did not combine it with faith*" (Heb. 4:1 – 2). He continues, however, with this glorious truth: "*We who have believed enter that rest*" (v. 3).

But let us remember the true source of "that rest," for Jesus said, "Come to me ... and *I will give you rest*" (Matt. 11:28).

DECEMBER 10

The Lord opened [Lydia's] heart
to respond to Paul's message.

Acts 16:14

From the pen of Charles Spurgeon:

In the story of Lydia's conversion, there are a number of interesting points. First, we see it was brought about through providential circumstances. She was "a dealer in purple cloth from the city of Thyatira" (v. 14), but at just the right moment to hear Paul, she is at Philippi. God's providence, the handmaiden of His grace, led her to the perfect spot. Grace was preparing her soul for the blessing of grace. And though she did not know the Savior, she was "a worshiper of God" (v. 14), indicating she was a convert to Judaism. Thus she knew many truths that became excellent stepping-stones to the knowledge of Jesus.

Another interesting point is the time and place of Lydia's conversion. Luke tells us: "On the Sabbath we went ... to find a place of prayer" (v. 13). So at a time and place where prayers were common, her prayer was heard. So never neglect the means of God's grace, for though He may bless us when we are not in His house, don't we have a greater reason to hope He will bless us when we are communing with His saints?

Also notice: "The Lord opened her heart" — she didn't open her own heart. Her prayers didn't do it, nor did Paul. Only the Lord Himself can open a heart to receive what brings us peace. He alone can place the key in the lock, open it, and gain admittance for Himself. He is the heart's master, because He is the heart's maker. Notice too that the first evidence of her opened heart was obedience, for as soon as Lydia believed in Jesus, she was baptized. This is a sure sign of a humble and broken heart, that a child of God is willing to obey a command not essential to her salvation nor something forced upon her by a selfish fear of condemnation, but something that is a simple act of obedience and communion with her Master. The next evidence was that of love, revealed in acts of grateful kindness to the apostles (see v. 15). Love for the saints has always been a mark of a true convert, and those who do nothing for Christ or His church are sorry evidence of an "opened heart."

Lord, forevermore give me an opened heart.

From the pen of Jim Reimann:

Spurgeon begins with the important fact of Lydia's conversion being wrought "through providential circumstances." No doubt Paul recognized God's sovereignty at work in her life, for he is the one who wrote these words every believer loves to quote: "We know that *in all things God works for the good of those who love him*, who have been called according to his purpose" (Rom. 8:28). If this is true — and it is — why am I so quick to complain about my circumstances? And why would I ever say, "Things just aren't going my way"?

If I truly have faith in God, I will not want things to go my way — I will want His way! It is the Lord who said, "As the heavens are higher than the earth, *so are my ways higher than your ways*" (Isa. 55:9). May my heart sing this psalm: "As for God, *his way is perfect*" (Ps. 18:30), and may I submit my will and my ways to Him.

Lord, "All my ways are known to you" (Ps. 119:168). May they be Your ways!

DECEMBER 11

It is the Lord Christ you are serving.

Colossians 3:24

From the pen of Charles Spurgeon:

Were these words spoken to the elite of society? Or to kings who proudly boast a divine right to serve? No! For all too often these people serve themselves — or Satan — totally forgetting the true God whose very patience permits them to tout their false majesty for their few minutes of glory.

Or were these words of the apostle spoken to the so-called "right reverend fathers of God" or "the venerable archbishops and archdeacons" of His church? No! For Paul knew nothing of these mere inventions of man. Nor were these words spoken even to pastors and teachers or to the wealthiest and most esteemed among believers. No! They were said to servants — actually, to slaves! (See v. 22.)

Among the working multitudes, the common workers, the day laborers, the domestic servants, and the menial kitchen workers, Paul found — as we still do today — some of the Lord's chosen. It was to them the apostle said, "Whatever you do, work at it with all your heart, as working for the Lord, not for men, since you know that you will receive an inheritance from the Lord as a reward. It is the Lord Christ you are serving" (vv. 23 – 24). These words ennoble even the most weary routines of earthly employment and shine a halo over the most humble of occupations.

The washing of feet may be the work of a servant, but to wash the feet of Jesus makes it royal work (see John 12:3). Untying someone's sandals is dirty work, but to untie the great Master's sandals is a princely privilege (see Mark 1:7). A workshop, a barn, a kitchen, and a factory all become temples when men and women "do ... all for the glory of God" (1 Cor. 10:31). In this way, divine service for God is not simply a matter of a few hours in a few places here and there, but all of life becomes holy unto the Lord, and thus every place and every thing is just as consecrated unto Him as the tabernacle and its "lampstand of pure gold" (Ex. 25:31).

Teach me, my God and King, in all things
> Thee to see;
And what I do in anything to do it as to Thee.
All may of Thee partake, nothing can be so
> low,
With Thy holy view, for Thy sake, will not
> soon brightly glow.
A servant with Thine eyes makes drudgery
> divine;
Who sweeps a room, as for Thy laws, makes
> that, and the action fine.

George Herbert, 1593 – 1633

From the pen of Jim Reimann:

The Old Testament teaches: "Nothing that a man owns and devotes to the LORD — whether man or animal or family land — may be sold or redeemed; *everything so devoted is most holy to the LORD*" (Lev. 27:28). Later, as Ezra led the Jews back from captivity, he said to the priests, "*You are holy to the LORD, and the vessels are holy*" (Ezra 8:28 ESV).

Do you ask, "What does this have to do with me? I'm not a priest!" But remember, believer, Jesus "*has made us to be a kingdom and priests to serve his God and Father*" (Rev. 1:6). So, again, "do ... all for the glory of God"!

DECEMBER 12

They are unfaithful to the LORD.

Hosea 5:7

From the pen of Charles Spurgeon:

What a sorrowful truth! Believer, you are "the beloved of the LORD" (Deut. 33:12), "redeemed … with the precious blood of Christ" (1 Peter 1:18 – 19), "kept by Jesus Christ" (Jude 1), "accepted in the beloved" (Eph. 1:6 KJV), and on your way to heaven. Yet you have been "unfaithful to the LORD," your best Friend; unfaithful to Jesus, to whom you belong; and unfaithful to the Holy Spirit, by whom you have been raised from death to eternal life.

Think how unfaithful you have been in fulfilling your vows and promises. Do you remember the love you had when you were first betrothed to Christ, during the joyous springtime of your spiritual life? Oh, how closely you clung to your Master then, saying, "He will never be able to accuse me of indifference. I will never slow in my service to Him. I will never allow my heart to wander after other loves, for in Him is more than I could possibly imagine. I surrender everything for my Lord Jesus' glory."

How have you done? Unfortunately, if your conscience were to speak, wouldn't it say, "You who promised so well have performed quite badly. Your prayers often have been superficial at best; short, but not sweet; brief, but not fervent. Your communion with Christ has been forgotten, and instead of being heavenly minded, you have been consumed with carnal cares, worldly vanities, and evil thoughts. Instead of service, there has been disobedience; instead of fervency, lukewarmness; instead of patience, restlessness; instead of faith, confidence in 'the arm of flesh' (2 Chron. 32:8); and as a soldier of the cross there has been cowardice, defiance, and desertion to a shamefully great degree."

I have been unfaithful — unfaithful to Jesus! But what words shall I use to denounce it? Mere words will avail little, so let my repentant thoughts begin to loathe and expose the egregious sins deep within me. *Unfaithful to Your wounds, O Jesus! Forgive me, and let me not sin again!* How shameful it is to be unfaithful to Him who never forgets us, but who this very day stands before His eternal throne with our names engraved on His breastplate (see Ex. 28:11 – 12).

From the pen of Jim Reimann:

In yesterday's devotion, we saw that Jesus "*has made us to be a kingdom and priests* to serve his God and Father" (Rev. 1:6). Therefore, these words from the context of today's verse from Hosea apply to God's church as much as they once applied to Israel: "Hear this, you priests! Pay attention, you Israelites! Listen, O royal house! This judgment is against you: You have been a snare at Mizpah, a net spread out on Tabor. The rebels are deep in slaughter. I will discipline all of them" (Hos. 5:1 – 2).

Dear church, we are to take our unfaithfulness seriously. Thankfully, we have a God who indeed will discipline us. But wouldn't it be better for us to repent on our own initiative, heeding these words of Jesus to the church in Ephesus — a church filled with believers whose love had cooled toward their Savior:

> I hold this against you: You have forsaken your first love. Remember the height from which you have fallen! Repent and do the things you did at first. If you do not repent, I will come to you and remove your lampstand from its place.
>
> Revelation 2:4 – 5

DECEMBER 13

I will make your windows and pinnacles of [sparkling] agates or rubies.

Isaiah 54:12 Amplified

From the pen of Charles Spurgeon:

Here we see God's church symbolized by a building designed by divine skill and constructed by heavenly power. A spiritual house like this could not be dark inside, for the Israelites had windows to allow light into their homes; and thus this house too must have windows not only to let light inside, but also to permit the inhabitants to gaze outside. The windows are described as precious "agates or rubies," which is how the church should view heaven and the Lord Himself, for He, heaven, and all spiritual truth in general, should be held in the highest esteem. Yet agates and rubies are not the most transparent of gems, for they simply allow light to pass through them at best.

> Our knowledge of that life is small,
> Our eye of faith is dim
>
> Richard Baxter, 1615 – 91

Faith is one of those precious agate or ruby windows, but unfortunately, our faith is often covered with mist or fog so that we see rather poorly at times, even mistaking much of what we do see. Although we cannot gaze through windows as clear as diamonds and "know fully, even as [we are] fully known" (1 Cor. 13:12), it is a glorious thing to behold Him who is "altogether lovely" (Song 5:16), even if the window may be as hazy as "agates or rubies."

Experience is another of these clouded but precious windows, yielding a subdued spiritual light to us, but light through which we view the sufferings of the "man of sorrows" (Isa. 53:3) through our own afflictions. Our weak human eyes could not endure viewing the Master's glory through fully transparent glass, but when our eyes are clouded with tears, the rays of "the sun of righteousness" (Mal. 4:2) are tempered, shining through the windows of agates and rubies with a soft radiance that is inexpressibly soothing to tempted souls.

Sanctification, the process of conforming us to the image of our Lord, is another of those beautiful windows. Only as we become heavenly can we fully comprehend heavenly things, for it is "the pure in heart" (Matt. 5:8) who can see a pure God. Those who are like Jesus "see him as he is" (1 John 3:2). Because we are so little like Him, the window is made of "agates or rubies" — and because we are somewhat like Him, it is "agates or rubies." So we thank God for what we have and yearn for more. We look for the day when "we shall see" God and Jesus, heaven and truth, "face to face" (1 Cor. 13:12).

From the pen of Jim Reimann:

As we have seen, the building the Lord describes in today's text is a foreshadowing of what God is doing today: building His church. "You are … God's building…. God's temple is sacred, and you are that temple" (1 Cor. 3:9, 17). "And in him you too are being built together to become a dwelling in which God lives by his Spirit" (Eph. 2:22). "You also … are being built into a spiritual house to be a holy priesthood, offering spiritual sacrifices" (1 Peter 2:5).

Therefore, with our holy God and our sanctification in mind, let "each one … be careful how he builds" (1 Cor. 3:10).

DECEMBER 14

I have been crucified with Christ.

Galatians 2:20

From the pen of Charles Spurgeon:

What the Lord Jesus Christ did He did as the great visible representative of His people, and His death on the cross essentially was the death of them all. In this way, in essence, His saints rendered what was due unto God's justice and made atonement to divine vengeance for all their sins. This is why Paul, "the apostle to the Gentiles" (Rom. 11:13), rejoiced to believe that as one of Christ's chosen people, he too died on the cross of Christ. He not only believed this doctrinally but accepted it confidently and based his eternal hope on it. He believed that by virtue of Christ's death, he had satisfied divine justice and had been reconciled to God.

Beloved, what a blessed thing when a soul can stretch itself upon the cross of Christ and proclaim: "I am dead, for the law has slain me. Therefore I am now free from its power, because through my Guarantor I have borne its curse. And in the person of my Substitute, all the power of the law to condemn has been fully executed upon me, for 'I have been crucified with Christ.'"

Yet Paul meant even more than this. He not only believed in Christ's death and trusted in it, but he actually felt its power in himself, causing the crucifixion of his old corrupt nature. So when he saw "the pleasures of sin" (Heb. 11:25), he said, in effect, "I cannot enjoy these, for I am dead to them." And such is the experience of every true Christian. Having received Christ, he is utterly dead to this world. And yet, while conscious of his death to the world, he still can exclaim with Paul, "Nevertheless I live" (Gal. 2:20 KJV). He is fully "alive to God" (Rom. 6:11).

Therefore, the Christian life is a matchless riddle. No person of the world can comprehend it, and even a believer himself cannot understand it. Dead — but alive! "Crucified with Christ," yet at the same time "raised from the dead" with Him to "live a new life" (Rom. 6:4)! Oh, what soul-cheering blessings: union with the suffering, bleeding Savior and death to the world and sin. Oh, may we enjoy them more!

From the pen of Jim Reimann:

One of the world's great ironies is that the lost often view us as being deprived of the so-called "good life," not realizing that believers are the only ones *with* life. "He who has the Son has life; he who does not have the Son of God does not have life" (1 John 5:12). Nor are they able to grasp the fact that true joy, peace, contentment, and the ongoing enjoyment of life are possessed by the children of God alone.

Yet before we grow smug over our exclusive blessings, let us remember we were "chosen by God" (1 Peter 2:4) through no merit of our own. And let us also remember that a true believer has a desire to share the blessings of eternal life with the unsaved, especially those closest to him. Paul said, for example, "I speak the truth in Christ — I am not lying, my conscience confirms it in the Holy Spirit — I have great sorrow and unceasing anguish in my heart. For I could wish that I myself were cursed and cut off from Christ for the sake of my brothers" (Rom. 9:1 – 3). What an amazing testimony of selfless love!

Lord, increase my desire to share Your message of grace.

December 15

I will build … your foundations with sapphires.
Isaiah 54:11

From the pen of Charles Spurgeon:

This verse reveals that not only what is seen of God's church is beautiful and precious, but also what is unseen. A building's foundations are unseen, so as long as they are strong, no one would expect them to be made of precious materials. But when it comes to Jehovah's work, everything is made of materials of great value, for He uses nothing of inferior quality. Thus, the deep foundations of the work of God's grace are as precious as sapphires, with no human mind able to comprehend their full radiance and glory. We have the covenant of grace upon which to build, and that foundation is harder than diamonds and is as enduring as other precious jewels the passing of time attempts to erode in vain. Sapphire foundations are eternal, and the covenant will abide throughout the eternity of Almighty God.

Another foundation is the person of the Lord Jesus Himself. He has perfect clarity, is flawless, is everlasting, and is as beautiful as sapphire, blending together the deep blue of earth's ever-rolling ocean with the azure of its overarching sky. When He died, covered in His own blood, He might have been likened to a ruby, but now we see Him radiant with the soft blue hue of love — love deep, limitless, eternal.

Our eternal hope is also built upon the justice and faithfulness of God, which are as clear and cloudless as a sapphire. We are not saved by mere compromise, by mercy defeating justice, or by law being suspended. No! I defy even an eagle's eye to detect a single flaw in the foundation of our confident assurance, for it is one of sapphire — one which will endure the "refiner's fire" (Mal. 3:2).

The Lord Himself has laid the foundation of His people's hope. And thus we come to a gravely serious question: Is *my* hope built upon *that* foundation? Good works and religious ceremonies are not a foundation of sapphire, but are "wood, hay [and] straw" (1 Cor. 3:12); they are not one laid by God, but one built by our own prideful conceit. One day soon every foundation will be tested, and woe to him whose lofty tower, built only on quicksand, comes down with a crash. Yet he whose eternal assurance is built on sapphires can face storms or fires with calm confidence, for he will withstand the test.

From the pen of Jim Reimann:

We return today to Isaiah 54 (see devotion for December 13) and the topic of the Lord building His church. We have seen how God is building His people into His temple, and that He is the one who has laid the perfect foundation. With those truths in mind, let us pay particular attention to the following familiar teaching from Paul. But may each of us examine our own life anew as we read.

No one can lay any foundation other than the one already laid, which is Jesus Christ. If any man builds on this foundation using gold, silver, costly stones, wood, hay or straw, his work will be shown for what it is, because the Day will bring it to light. It will be revealed with fire, and the fire will test the quality of each man's work. If what he has built survives, he will receive his reward. If it is burned up, he will suffer loss; he himself will be saved, but only as one escaping through the flames.

1 Corinthians 3:11 – 16

DECEMBER 16

You have neither heard nor understood;
from of old your ear has not been open.

Isaiah 48:8

From the pen of Charles Spurgeon:

It is painful to think that, to a certain degree, this accusation can be laid at the feet of believers, for we are all too often spiritually insensitive and unresponsive. We would do well to mourn the fact that we often do not hear the voice of God as we should. "You have [not] heard." There are gentle workings of the Holy Spirit in our soul that we ignore and soft whisperings of God's divine commands and heavenly love that also go unheeded by our sluggish minds.

Sadly, we have been ignorant as well. "You have [not] ... understood." There are things within us we should have seen: inner corruptions making headway in our lives completely unnoticed, precious affections blighted like flowers by the frost all unintended by us, and glimpses of God's divine face we might have seen if the windows of our soul had not been closed. But we missed them — we have not understood.

So as we think of what we have missed, we are humbled to the deepest level of self-humiliation. We learn from the context of today's verse that all of our foolish ignorance was foreknown by God, and that, in spite of His foreknowledge, He has been pleased to be merciful to us. Let us glory in His wondrous, sovereign grace that has chosen us in spite of all this. Let us be in awe at the price Christ paid for us even though He knew what we would be. He who hung upon the cross foresaw us as unbelieving, backsliding, cold-hearted, indifferent, careless, and lazy when it comes to prayer, yet He said, "I am the LORD, your God, the Holy One of Israel, your Savior.... Since you are precious and honored in my sight, and because I love you, I will give men in exchange for you, and people in exchange for your life" (Isa. 43:3 – 4).

O Redemption, how wondrously glorious do You shine when we think how sinfully dark we are! O Holy Spirit, give us from this point forward hearing ears and understanding hearts!

From the pen of Jim Reimann:

As Spurgeon said today, we should "glory in [God's] wondrous, sovereign grace," especially in light of the context of today's verse, for it is this context that reveals the Lord's foreknowledge of our spiritual deafness and lack of understanding. Here is more of what God said through Isaiah, along with its New Testament fulfillment:

You have neither heard nor understood; from of old your ear has not been open. Well do I know how treacherous you are; you were called a rebel from birth. For my own name's sake I delay my wrath; for the sake of my praise I hold it back from you, so as not to cut you off. See, I have refined you, though not as silver; I have tested you in the furnace of affliction. For my own sake, for my own sake, I do this. How can I let myself be defamed? I will not yield my glory to another. Listen to me, O Jacob, Israel, whom I have called: I am he; I am the first and I am the last.

Isaiah 48:8 – 12

"I am the Alpha and the Omega, the First and the Last, the Beginning and the End." "He who has an ear, let him hear what the Spirit says to the churches" (Rev. 22:13; 2:7).

December 17

I am the gate;
whoever enters through me will be saved.
He will come in and go out, and find pasture.

John 10:9

From the pen of Charles Spurgeon:

Jesus, the great "I AM" (Ex. 3:14), is the door into the true church and the way of access to God Himself. And He gives to everyone who comes to God through Him these special privileges:

1. He "will be saved." In ancient Israel, a killer could flee to a city of refuge and be safe once he entered the gate (see Num. 35:6), just as Noah entered the door of "the ark to escape the waters of the flood" (Gen. 7:7). Likewise, no one can be lost who takes Jesus as his soul's door of faith. Jesus, the door into peace, is also the guarantee of entering — by the same door — into heaven. He is the only door, and blessed is he who places his hope on the crucified Redeemer for admission into glory.

2. "He will come in." He will be privileged to "come in" to God's family, share the children's bread, and participate in all their honors and enjoyment. He will "come in" to the inner rooms of communion and the storehouses of the promises. He will "come in" to "the King of kings" (1 Tim. 6:15) "by the power of the Holy Spirit" (Rom. 15:13), and the Lord Himself will confide in him (see Ps. 25:14).

3. "He will ... go out." This blessing is often forgotten. We "go out" into the world to serve and to suffer in the name and the power of Jesus. Like Him, we are called "to testify to the truth" (John 18:37), to cheer the downhearted, to warn the careless, to win souls, and to glorify God. And as the Lord said to Gideon, we must "Go in the strength [we] have" (Judg. 6:14), for the Lord desires we "go out" as His messengers in His name, depending on His strength.

4. "He will ... find pasture." He who knows Jesus will not be in need. Going in, or going out, will be helpful to him, for when he is in close fellowship with God, he will grow, and by going out to provide water to others, he will be provided water. Having made Jesus his "all in all" (1 Cor. 15:28), he will have all he needs. "[He] will be like a well-watered garden, like a spring whose waters never fail" (Isa. 58:11).

From the pen of Jim Reimann:

Jesus came to earth to be our Shepherd, a fulfillment of prophecies such as this from Micah: "He will stand and shepherd his flock in the strength of the LORD, in the majesty of the name of the LORD his God. And they will live securely, for then his greatness will reach to the ends of the earth. And he will be their peace" (Mic. 5:4 – 5). Yet the Shepherd of all shepherds humbly referred to Himself simply as "the good shepherd," as we see from the context of today's verse. Let us always remember — He is the Shepherd, we are the sheep!

I tell you the truth, I am the gate for the sheep. All who ever came before me were thieves and robbers, but the sheep did not listen to them. I am the gate; whoever enters through me will be saved. He will come in and go out, and find pasture. The thief comes only to steal and kill and destroy; I have come that they may have life, and have it to the full. I am the good shepherd. The good shepherd lays down his life for the sheep.

John 10:7 – 11

DECEMBER 18

Be sure you know the condition of your flocks,
give careful attention to your herds.

Proverbs 27:23

From the pen of Charles Spurgeon:

Just as a wise shepherd knows the condition of his flock, every wise merchant takes an inventory of his stock at least annually to ascertain whether his business is prospering or declining. Likewise, a person who is wise in the kingdom of heaven will cry out: "Search me, O God, and … test me" (Ps. 139:23) and will set aside frequent times of self-examination to discover whether things are right between his soul and God.

The Lord we worship is the great Heart-Searcher, and since the days of old His servants have known Him to be "the LORD [who] search[es] the heart and examine[s] the mind" (Jer. 17:10). So allow me to stir you to action in His name to make a solemn test of yourself and your spiritual condition lest you fall short of His promised rest. That which every wise person does, and that which God Himself does with us all, I exhort you to do with yourself today. May even the oldest of saints examine the fundamentals of his faith, for gray hair may be covering the darkness of his heart. And may the youngest professing believer not despise this word of warning, for the greenness of youth is sometimes united with the rottenness of hypocrisy.

Every now and then even a mighty cedar falls in our midst, for the Enemy continues to sow "weeds among the wheat" (Matt. 13:25). Know, however, my purpose here is not to raise doubts and fears in your mind. To the contrary! My hope is that the powerful wind of self-examination will help drive doubts away. It is not security, but a carnal false security I desire to see killed; not confidence, but fleshly confidence I desire to put to death; not peace, but false peace I wish to see destroyed. I implore you by "the precious blood of Christ" (1 Peter 1:19) — blood shed not to make you a hypocrite, but to make you a sincere soul who may glorify Him — search yourself, lest in the final analysis it be said of you: "You have been weighed on the scales and found wanting" (Dan. 5:27).

From the pen of Jim Reimann:

So often people will say, "Before I obey God, I need to see the handwriting on the wall." Yet, as we see from the context of Spurgeon's quote from Daniel, once the handwriting is seen, it may be too late to repent. Here is what Daniel told the king of Babylon:

> O king, the Most High God gave your father Nebuchadnezzar sovereignty and greatness and glory and splendor.… But when his heart became arrogant and hardened with pride, he was deposed from his royal throne and stripped of his glory … until he acknowledged that the Most High God is sovereign over the kingdoms of men and sets over them anyone he wishes. But you his son, O Belshazzar, have not humbled yourself, though you knew all this. Instead, you have set yourself up against the Lord of heaven. You did not honor the God who holds in his hand your life and all your ways. Therefore he sent the hand that wrote the inscription.

Daniel 5:18, 20 – 24

May this be a lesson to us! "Examine yourselves to see whether you are in the faith; test yourselves. Do you not realize that Christ Jesus is in you — unless, of course, you fail the test?" (2 Cor. 13:5).

DECEMBER 19

There was no longer any sea.

Revelation 21:1

From the pen of Charles Spurgeon:

Who would rejoice over the thought of losing our glorious oceans? The "new heavens and a new earth" (Isa. 65:17) don't seem so beautiful to us if there will be no great, wide seas with their glistening waves and shell-covered shores. But isn't today's text to be understood as a metaphor — one tainted by the human bias of how we have thought of the sea since days of old? Indeed, a physical world without a sea is a sad thing to imagine, for it would be like a ring without the sapphire that once made it so beautiful.

Consequently, there must be a deeper spiritual meaning here. In the age to come there will be no division, for seas separate nations and people from each other. For example, the deep waters were like prison walls to John on "the island of Patmos" (Rev. 1:9), shutting him out from his brothers and his ministry. Thus, there will be no such barriers in the world ahead. In the glorious world to come, we will enjoy unbroken fellowship with every member of our redeemed family. So it is in this sense that there will be no more sea.

Furthermore, the sea is a symbol of change, always ebbing and flowing, going from glassy smoothness to mountainous waves, and quickly changing its gentle breezes into tumultuous roaring. So the sea, a slave of the changing moon and fickle winds, is the perfect metaphor of instability, something we have too much of in this mortal life. This earth is constant only in her constant change, but in heaven all mournful change will be unknown, along with all fear of storms to wreck our hopes and drown our joys. And heaven's "sea of glass" (Rev. 4:6) will glow with a glory unbroken by any waves, for no tempest howls along the peaceful shores of paradise. Soon we will reach that blessed land where separations, changes, and storms will be ended forever. Jesus Himself will waft us there. Are you in Him, or not?

This is the great question.

From the pen of Jim Reimann:

As Spurgeon said, our text is to be understood spiritually, not literally. After all, we are told, "Before the throne there was what looked like a sea of glass, clear as crystal" (Rev. 4:6), and "There was no longer any sea." Indeed, some passages of Scripture are difficult to understand, but surely the context of today's text is quite clear. As we read from that context, let us rejoice in what is to come, for we as believers "will inherit all this" (Rev. 21:7):

I saw a new heaven and a new earth, for the first heaven and the first earth had passed away, and there was no longer any sea. I saw the Holy City, the new Jerusalem, coming down out of heaven from God, prepared as a bride beautifully dressed for her husband. And I heard a loud voice from the throne saying, "Now the dwelling of God is with men, and he will live with them. They will be his people, and God himself will be with them and be their God. He will wipe every tear from their eyes. There will be no more death or mourning or crying or pain, for the old order of things has passed away." He who was seated on the throne said, "I am making everything new!"

Revelation 21:1 – 5

DECEMBER 20

Call the workers and pay them their wages.

Matthew 20:8

From the pen of Charles Spurgeon:

God is a wonderful paymaster, for He pays His servants while they are at work and after they have finished their work. And one of His payments is this: a clear conscience. For example, if you faithfully share the gospel of Jesus with just one person today, you can go to bed tonight with joy, thinking, "Today I have freed my conscience of that person's blood." Consequently, we learn there is great comfort in doing something for Jesus.

There is also great reward in seeing the very first budding of the conviction of a soul. What a blessing to be able to say of someone, "She has a tender heart. I believe the Lord is at work within her." Or what a blessing it is to return home and pray for someone who earlier in the day made a statement that indicated he was beginning to grasp more of God's truth than you had hoped. Oh, the joy of hope! But even more the joy of success, for that joy is inexpressible.

To be a soul-winner is the happiest thing in the world, for with every soul you bring to Christ, you also bring a new heaven to earth. But who can imagine the happiness that awaits us above. Oh, how precious are the words: "Enter into the joy of your lord" (Matt. 25:21 NKJV). Do you know how much joy Christ has over one sinner being saved? This is the very joy you will possess in heaven. When He ascends to His throne, you will be with Him, and when the heavens resound with the words "Well done" (Matt. 25:21), you will share in that reward. You have served with Him, you have suffered with Him, and you will reign with Him. You have sown seeds with Him, and you will reap the harvest with Him. Your face has been covered with sweat like His. And your soul has grieved for the sins of man as His soul did. But in glory your face will be bright with heaven's splendor like His countenance and your soul will be filled to overflowing with perfect happiness and inner peace — just as His soul is.

From the pen of Jim Reimann:

Today we have seen that when we share our faith, the Lord, who is heaven's paymaster, "pays" us with a clear conscience. But Paul taught that we also are "paid" in another way when he said, "I pray that you may be active in sharing your faith, *so that you will have a full understanding of every good thing we have in Christ*" (Philem. 6). What an amazing thought, that "a full understanding" will only be gained through sharing our faith! But, oh, how often we want to fully understand before we are willing to obey!

"Full understanding" ultimately will be ours, but we must be patient and we must have endurance. So let us heed Paul's words to the early church when he exhorted them to "never tire of doing what is right" (2 Thess. 3:13), and when he said, "Let us not become weary in doing good, for at the proper time we will reap a harvest if we do not give up" (Gal. 6:9). "This calls for patient endurance on the part of the saints who obey God's commandments and remain faithful to Jesus" (Rev. 14:12). But remember — "Patient endurance [is] ours in Jesus" (Rev. 1:9).

DECEMBER 21

I clothed you with an embroidered dress and put leather sandals on you.
I dressed you in fine linen and covered you with costly garments.

Ezekiel 16:10

From the pen of Charles Spurgeon:

Notice the matchless generosity the Lord exhibits in providing garments for His people. Each of His children is elaborately dressed, clothed in such a way as to reveal God's unequaled embroidery — into which every attribute and aspect of His beauty are woven and thereby disclosed. No human art compares to the art displayed in our salvation, nor is any craftsmanship equal to that seen in the righteousness of His saints.

Justification has been the theme of the pens of learned men throughout the ages of the church, and it will be the subject of our admiration in eternity as well. Like us, our justification was "secret[ly] ... woven together" (Ps. 139:15) by God. Yet with all its elaborate intricacies, mingled in are usefulness and durability, such as our being shod with "leather sandals." As to which animal the leather is from, we do not know, but we do know it was this animal's skin that was used as the covering for the tabernacle, producing one of the finest and strongest leathers ever known. [Editor's note: Today's text in the KJV has "badgers' skin," rather than "leather sandals." Regarding the covering for the tabernacle, Moses was instructed, "Make for the tent a covering of ram skins dyed red, and over that a covering of hides of sea cows" (Ex. 26:14). The KJV for this verse again has "badgers' skins," rather than "hides of sea cows."] Likewise, "the righteousness that comes from God and is by faith" (Phil. 3:9) endures forever, and whoever is shod with it will safely traverse deserts and may even "trample the great lion and the serpent" (Ps. 91:13).

The purity and dignity of our holy garments are signified by the "fine linen" of today's verse, for when the Lord sanctifies His people, they are dressed like priests in white so pure that even snow itself cannot surpass it. They are so beautiful that neither men, angels, nor God Himself can find any "stain or wrinkle" (Eph. 5:27) in them. And this delicate royal apparel of ours ultimately is described as "costly garments," for no expense is spared, beauty withheld, nor elegance denied.

So how will I respond? Surely there is gratitude to be felt and joy to be expressed. Come, my heart, break forth with hallelujahs! Sing God's praises!

Strangely, my soul, are you arrayed
By the Great Sacred Three!
In sweetest harmony of praise
Let all your powers agree.

Isaac Watts, 1674 – 1748

From the pen of Jim Reimann:

O Lord, "May [we] your priests be clothed with righteousness; may [we] your saints sing for joy" (Ps. 132:9). And may these be the words of our song:

"'Hallelujah! For our Lord God Almighty reigns. Let us rejoice and be glad and give him glory! For the wedding of the Lamb has come, and his bride has made herself ready. Fine linen, bright and clean, was given her to wear.' (Fine linen stands for the righteous acts of the saints.) Then the angel said to me, 'Write: "Blessed are those who are invited to the wedding supper of the Lamb!"'" (Rev. 19:6 – 9).

DECEMBER 22

Their spot is not the spot of his children.

Deuteronomy 32:5 KJV

From the pen of Charles Spurgeon:

What is this special "spot" that is the unmistakable sign of a child of God? It would be meaningless for us to determine this based on our own judgment, for God's Word reveals it to us, and we may always walk securely where we have His revelation as our guide. With this is mind, we see that His Word tells us concerning our Lord: "To all who received him, to those who believed in his name, he gave the right to become children of God" (John 1:12). Based on this, if I have received Christ Jesus into my heart, I am a child of God. And that "reception of Him," is described in the same verse, in essence, as "believing in the name of Jesus Christ." So if I "believe in his name" — simply meaning, that in my heart I trust myself to the crucified but now exalted Redeemer, I am a member of the family of "God Most High" (Gen. 14:18). And from that point forward, whatever else I may or may not have, I have this: the privilege to be a child of God.

Our Lord Jesus sums up the matter in another way: "My sheep listen to my voice; I know them, and they follow me" (John 10:27). Christ is seen as a shepherd to His own sheep — not to others — and as soon as He appears, His sheep recognize Him, trust Him, and are prepared to follow Him. There is mutual knowledge and a constant connection between them, for He knows them, and they know Him. Therefore the one "spot" — the true, infallible sign — of regeneration and adoption by God is a living faith in the God-ordained Redeemer.

Dear reader, are you in doubt as to whether or not you bear the special mark of God's chil-

dren? Then don't let an hour pass until you have said, "Search me, O God, and know my heart" (Ps. 139:23). I implore you not to quibble over your petty objections. Regarding your soul — your never-dying soul and its eternal destiny — I plead with you to take this seriously. Make your eternity certain.

From the pen of Jim Reimann:

Once we believe, the Lord desires we walk in assurance. Here is how the writer of Hebrews addressed this issue: "Since we have confidence to enter the Most Holy Place by the blood of Jesus, by a new and living way opened for us through the curtain, that is, his body, and since we have a great priest over the house of God, *let us draw near to God with a sincere heart in full assurance of faith.*... Let us hold unswervingly to the hope we profess, for he who promised is faithful" (Heb. 10:19 – 23).

Paul taught this as well, saying, "You did not receive a spirit that makes you a slave again to fear, but you received the Spirit of sonship. And by him we cry, 'Abba, Father.' *The Spirit himself testifies with our spirit that we are God's children*" (Rom. 8:15 – 16). Finally, John, in complete agreement, wrote:

> This is the testimony: God has given us eternal life, and this life is in his Son. He who has the Son has life; he who does not have the Son of God does not have life. *I write these things to you who believe in the name of the Son of God so that you may know that you have eternal life.*
>
> 1 John 5:11 – 13

DECEMBER 23

The day is yours, and yours also the night;
you established the sun and moon.

Psalm 74:16

From the pen of Charles Spurgeon:

Yes, Lord, You do not abdicate Your throne when the sun goes down. Nor do You abandon the world through these long wintry nights of December, leaving us to be the prey of evil; for Your eyes, like stars, watch us; and Your arms, like the constellations that belt the sky, surround us. The dew of blessed sleep and all the soft influences of the moon upon the earth are in Your hands, just as all the serious alarms and troubles of the night are under Your sovereign control.

This truth is quite important to me, especially when wide awake and tossing to and fro in anguish through the midnight hours. I must remember that there are precious fruits provided by the light of the moon as well as by the sun. May my Lord favor me to be a partaker of them, for the night of affliction is as much under the design and control of the Lord of love as are the bright summer days when all is bliss and happiness. Jesus is in the darkest stormy night, His love wrapping the night around itself as a robe, and to the eye of faith, that robe appears as a beautiful sable cloak, hardly a fearful disguise. From the first watch of the night to the first light of day, our eternal Watcher observes His saints, overruling the darkness and dew of midnight for His people's greatest good. Therefore we do not view night following day as rival deities of evil and good contending with one another for control, but we hear the voice of Jehovah saying, "I form the light and create darkness.... I, the LORD, do all these things" (Isa. 45:7).

Gloomy seasons of spiritual indifference and

the dark sin of neglecting fellowship with the Lord are not exempt from His divine purpose. When the altar of truth is defiled and the ways of God forsaken, the Lord's servants ultimately will weep with bitter sorrow. But they should not despair, for even the darkest times are governed by Him and will come to an end at His decree. What may appear as defeat to us may be victory to Him.

> Though enwrapped in gloomy night,
> We perceive no ray of light;
> Since the Lord Himself is here,
> 'Tis not fit that we should fear.
>
> Thomas Kelly, 1769 – 1855

From the pen of Jim Reimann:

Regardless of how dark your circumstances, you can take comfort in the fact that your God knows no darkness and forever watches over His children. If your heart is troubled by a season of gloom and despair, let His Word minister to you even now.

> The LORD watches over you — the LORD is your shade at your right hand; the sun will not harm you by day, nor the moon by night. The LORD will keep you from all harm — he will watch over your life.
>
> Psalm 121:5 – 7

"If I go up to the heavens, you are there; if I make my bed in the depths, you are there.... If I say, 'Surely the darkness will hide me and the light become night around me,' even the darkness will not be dark to you; the night will shine like the day, for darkness is as light to you" (Ps. 139:8, 11 – 12).

DECEMBER 24

And the glory of the Lord will be revealed,
and all mankind together will see it.

Isaiah 40:5

From the pen of Charles Spurgeon:

I look forward to the joyous day when the whole world will be converted to Christ; when the gods of the heathen will be thrown to moles and bats; when Roman Catholicism will be exploded, and the crescent of Islam will fade, never again to cast their sinister rays upon the nations; and when kings will bow before the "Prince of Peace" (Isa. 9:6) and all nations will call their Redeemer blessed. Yet some people despair to think of this, for they see the world as a ship being broken to pieces never to float again. I know that one day this world and everything in it will burn, and that afterwards we will see "new heavens and a new earth" (Isa. 65:17), but we cannot read our Bibles without the conviction that

> Jesus shall reign where'er the sun
> Does His successive journeys run.
>
> Isaac Watts, 1674 – 1748

Yet I am not discouraged by His lengthy delays nor disheartened by the long period He has allotted to the church to struggle with little success and many defeats. I believe God will not allow this world, which has once seen Christ's blood shed upon it, to be the Devil's stronghold forever. After all, Christ came to deliver this world from the detestable control of "the dominion of darkness" (Col. 1:13). What a glorious sound it will be when men and angels alike will shout, "Hallelujah! For our Lord God Almighty reigns" (Rev. 19:6). And what satisfaction there will be on that day to have participated in the battle, to have helped break "the arrows of the enemy" (Ps. 76:3 NLT), to have aided in winning the victory for our Lord!

How happy are they who trust themselves to this conquering Lord and who fight side by side with Him, doing however little they do, but doing it in His name and by His strength. But how unhappy are they on the side of evil. It is the losing side, and this is a matter where losing is to be lost forever.

Whose side are you on?

From the pen of Jim Reimann:

Jesus said, "He who is not with me is against me" (Matt. 12:30), and it is only those who are "with Him" who will enjoy "the new heavens and the new earth." According to God's Word, His people are to "look forward" to His coming again. In that regard, notice Peter's precise wording in this passage:

> The day of the Lord will come like a thief. The heavens will disappear with a roar; the elements will be destroyed by fire, and the earth and everything in it will be laid bare. Since everything will be destroyed in this way, what kind of people ought you to be? You ought to live holy and godly lives as you *look forward* to the day of God and speed its coming. That day will bring about the destruction of the heavens by fire, and the elements will melt in the heat. But in keeping with his promise we are *looking forward* to a new heaven and a new earth, the home of righteousness. So then, dear friends, since you are *looking forward* to this, make every effort to be found spotless, blameless and at peace with him.
>
> 2 Peter 3:10 – 14

DECEMBER 25

When a period of feasting had run its course, Job would send and have them purified.
Early in the morning he would sacrifice a burnt offering for each of them, thinking,
"Perhaps my children have sinned and cursed God in their hearts."
This was Job's regular custom.

Job 1:5

From the pen of Charles Spurgeon:

What Job did "early in the morning" after "a period of feasting" would be wise for each believer to do for himself before resting tonight. Amid the cheerfulness of family gatherings, it is easy to slide into sinfulness, forgetting our character as Christians. Though it should not be so, days of feasting are very seldom filled with *holy* enjoyment, but frequently degenerate into *unholy* fun. It is possible to have joyful festivities, pure and sanctifying as though a person were bathed in the rivers of Eden, and holy gratitude should be just as purifying as grief. Yet, for our heart, "It is better to go to a house of mourning than to go to a house of feasting" (Eccl. 7:2).

Believer, have you sinned during this season? Have you forgotten your high calling? Have you been careless, using idle words and loose speech? Confess your sin and flee to the sacrifice that sanctifies. The precious blood of "the Lamb, who was slain" (Rev. 5:12) rids us of guilt and the defilement of our sins of ignorance and carelessness. Isn't this the best way to end this Christmas — to wash anew in the cleansing fountain? Christian, come to this sacrifice continually, for if it is worthwhile today, it is worthwhile every day. To live before God's altar is the privilege of His royal priesthood, and for us, sin — as great as it is — is still no cause for despair, because we may draw near again to the sin-atoning Victim to purge our soul from dead works.

Gladly I close this festive day,
Grasping the altar's hallowed horn;
My sins and faults are washed away,
The Lamb has all my trespass borne.

Author unknown

From the pen of Jim Reimann:

As suggested by this devotion, Spurgeon was not an avid proponent of celebrating Christmas. The following is from his sermon, December 24, 1871:

We have no superstitious regard for times and seasons. Certainly we do not believe in the present ecclesiastical arrangement called *Christmas:* because we do not believe in the *mass* at all, but abhor it … ; and because we find no Scriptural warrant whatever for observing any day as the birthday of the Savior. Consequently, its observance is a superstition, because not of divine authority.… It was not till the middle of the third century that any part of the church celebrated the nativity of our Lord.… Where is the method in the madness of this superstition? Probably the fact is that the holy days were arranged to fit in with heathen festivals.… Yet, since it is lawful, and even laudable, to meditate upon the incarnation of the Lord any day of the year, it cannot be in the power of other men's superstitions to render such a meditation improper for today. Regarding not the day, let us, nevertheless, give God thanks for the gift of his dear son.

Let us consider Paul's words as well: "You are observing special days and months and seasons and years! I fear for you, that somehow I have wasted my efforts on you" (Gal. 4:10 – 11).

"Lord, what do You desire me to do?"
(Acts 9:6 Amplified).

DECEMBER 26

Surely I am with you always.
Matthew 28:20

From the pen of Charles Spurgeon:

The Lord Jesus is in the midst of His church, He "walks among the seven golden lampstands" (Rev. 2:1), and His promise is: "Surely I am with you always." He is as surely with us now as He was with the disciples beside the Sea of Galilee, when "they saw a fire of burning coals there with fish on it, and some bread" (John 21:9). Not physically, but still in actual truth, Jesus is with us. And what a blessed truth it is, for where Jesus is, love is set ablaze.

Even a quick glimpse of Him overwhelms us. Even the smell of His robe, "fragrant with myrrh and aloes and cassia" (Ps. 45:8) wafting from it, causes the sick and the weak to grow strong. Give us even a brief moment of "reclining next to him" (John 13:23), leaning our head upon His gracious shoulder, and receiving His divine love into our poor, cold heart, and suddenly we are cold no longer, but glow like seraphim, becoming equal to every task, and capable of enduring great suffering.

If we know that Jesus is with us, every power within us is intensified, every gift is strengthened, and we will throw ourselves into the Lord's service with "all [our] heart and with all [our] soul and with all [our] strength" (Deut. 6:5). Therefore the presence of Christ is to be desired above all things. But His presence will be most realized by those who are most like Him. So if you desire to see Jesus, you must grow in conformity to Him. Through the power of the Holy Spirit, bring yourself into oneness with Christ's desires, motives, and plans of action, and then you are likely to be favored with His presence.

Remember — His presence is possible. His promise is as true now as ever. He delights to be with us. Thus, if He does not come, it is because we have hindered Him by our indifference. He will reveal Himself in answer to our earnest prayers, graciously allowing Himself to be detained by our passionate pleas and by our tears, for these are the golden chains that bind Jesus to His people.

From the pen of Jim Reimann:

Ironically, the promise Jesus made to His disciples in today's text — "Surely I am with you always" — was said just before He left them, ascending into heaven. Luke describes the scene as follows: "When he had led them out to the vicinity of Bethany, he lifted up his hands and blessed them. While he was blessing them, *he left them and was taken up into heaven*. Then they worshiped him and returned to Jerusalem with great joy. And they stayed continually at the temple, praising God" (Luke 24:50 – 53).

But why were they now so joyful? Jesus had left them! The answer is simple — they believed His preceding promise: "I am going to send you what my Father has promised" (v. 49). He had already declared,

> The Counselor, the Holy Spirit, whom the Father will send in my name, will teach you all things and will remind you of everything I have said to you. Peace I leave with you; my peace I give you. I do not give to you as the world gives. Do not let your hearts be troubled and do not be afraid.
>
> John 14:26 – 27

And Jesus kept His promise!

DECEMBER 27

The LORD will guide you always.

Isaiah 58:11

From the pen of Charles Spurgeon:

Jehovah Himself, not an angel, "will guide you." God did not tell Moses that He would lead His people through the wilderness; instead He said, "My angel will go before you" (Ex. 32:34). But "then Moses said to him, 'If your Presence does not go with us, do not send us up from here'" (Ex. 33:15).

Christian, God has not left your earthly pilgrimage to the guidance of an angel — He Himself leads you. You may not see the "pillar of cloud" or the "pillar of fire" (Ex. 13:21), but Jehovah "will never ... forsake you" (Deut. 31:6). Notice in today's text the word *will* — "The LORD *will* guide you," indicating its certainty. His precious word — *will* — is far superior to the promises of men. "God has said, 'Never will I leave you; never will I forsake you'" (Heb. 13:5).

Next notice the word *always* — "The LORD will guide you *always*." He does not merely guide us *sometimes*, for we have an eternal Guide. He does not occasionally leave us to "lean ... on [our] own understanding" (Prov. 3:5), making us wander; we *always* have the guiding voice of the Great Shepherd. If we will follow closely behind, we will never go wrong, but will be led on the proper path to a safe place to dwell.

If you have to change your life's vocation, if you have to emigrate to a distant land, if you find yourself thrown into poverty, if you suddenly are promoted to a more responsible position than you have today, if you find yourself surrounded by strangers or enemies, don't be afraid, for — "The LORD will guide you always." There is no difficulty out of which you will not be delivered if you live close to God, keeping your heart warmed by His holy love, for he who continually follows Him will never go astray. Like Enoch, walk with God (see Gen. 5:24), and you will never take the wrong road, even by mistake. You have His infallible wisdom to direct you, His immutable love to comfort you, and His eternal power to defend you. It is Jehovah — again, Jehovah God, the LORD — who "will guide you always."

From the pen of Jim Reimann:

Spurgeon mentions a number of life-changing events, the first being a change in vocation. A biblical example is the call of Peter. As he was pursuing his career as a fisherman, Jesus said to him and his brother Andrew, "Come, follow me" (Matt. 4:19). To their credit, "*At once* they left their nets and followed him" (v. 20). After Jesus' resurrection, however, we hear impetuous Peter declare, "I'm going out to fish" (John 21:3), returning to what he knew best. As happened at his initial call, he was unsuccessful in catching fish until Jesus worked a miracle. Of course, Jesus restored Peter to his calling, doing so with the very words of his first call: "Follow me!" (John 21:19). The call of Jesus is permanent, which is why He once said, "No one who puts his hand to the plow and looks back is fit for service in the kingdom of God" (Luke 9:62). But, thankfully, we have a God who forgives and restores.

So regardless of the difficulties of your calling, remember God's promise: "Be strong and courageous. Do not be afraid or terrified ... for the LORD your God goes with you; *he will never leave you nor forsake you*" (Deut. 31:6).

DECEMBER 28

I did not come to bring peace, but a sword.

Matthew 10:34

From the pen of Charles Spurgeon:

A Christian will make enemies. Although it will not be his objective, simply believing the truth and doing what is right will cause him to lose every earthly friend. But he will consider it a small loss, since his great Friend in heaven will reveal Himself more graciously than ever. You who have taken up His cross, have you forgotten what your Master said: "I have come to turn 'a man against his father, a daughter against her mother, a daughter-in-law against her mother-in-law — a man's enemies will be the members of his own household'" (Matt. 10:35 – 36)? Christ is the great Peacemaker, but before He makes peace, He brings war. Where the light shines, darkness must retreat, and where truth is, falsehood must flee. Yet where falsehood attempts to hold its ground, there will be a fierce battle, for the truth cannot and will not lower its standard, and untruths must be trampled underfoot.

If you follow Christ, all the dogs of the world will be nipping at your heels. If you desire to live in such a way as to withstand the test of the final judgment, know that the world will not speak well of you. "Anyone who chooses to be a friend of the world becomes an enemy of God" (James 4:4). But if you are true and faithful to "God Most High" (Gen. 14:18), people will resent your unflinching faithfulness because it will be a testimony against their own iniquities.

You must do what is right, unafraid of any consequences. Yet to unhesitatingly pursue a course that will turn your best friend into your fiercest foe, you will need the courage of a lion. You must be willing to risk your reputation and other people's affection for the sake of God's truth, but doing so continually will require a level of moral principle that only the Spirit of God can build into you. So don't turn and run like a coward, but be strong, boldly following in your Master's footsteps, for He has walked this rough road before you. Isn't it better to experience brief warfare followed by eternal rest, than false peace followed by everlasting torment?

From the pen of Jim Reimann:

The context of today's verses from Matthew is actually Jesus quoting the prophet Micah, who said, "Do not trust a neighbor; put no confidence in a friend. Even with her who lies in your embrace be careful of your words. For a son dishonors his father, a daughter rises up against her mother, a daughter-in-law against her mother-in-law — a man's enemies are the members of his own household" (Mic. 7:5 – 6). But the prophet continued with these comforting words: "But as for me, I watch in hope for the LORD, I wait for God my Savior; my God will hear me. Do not gloat over me, my enemy! Though I have fallen, I will rise. Though I sit in darkness, the LORD will be my light" (vv. 7 – 8).

Believer, are you willing to obediently follow Jesus and wait patiently for His vindication, even if it means He will be your only friend? Remember His words:

> Woe to you when all men speak well of you, for that is how their fathers treated the false prophets. But I tell you who hear me: Love your enemies, do good to those who hate you, bless those who curse you, pray for those who mistreat you.
>
> Luke 6:26 – 28

DECEMBER 29

What do you think about the Christ?
Matthew 22:42

From the pen of Charles Spurgeon:

The great measure of your soul's health is: "What do you think about the Christ?" Is He more beautiful to you than "the most excellent of men" (Ps. 45:2), the most "outstanding among ten thousand" (Song 5:10), and "altogether lovely" (Song 5:16)? Whenever Christ is esteemed in this way, all the faculties of the spiritual man are greatly energized. So I judge your faith by this: Is Christ highly or lowly esteemed by you? If you give Him little thought and are content to live without His presence, if you give little care to honoring Him, if you neglect His laws, then I know your soul is sick. May God grant that it be a "sickness [that] will not end in death" (John 11:4).

But if the first thought of your spirit is to say, "How can I honor Jesus?" or if the desire of your soul is, "If only I knew where to find him!" (Job 23:3), then you may have a thousand infirmities and scarcely know whether you are a child of God, yet I am persuaded beyond doubt that you are safe, since Jesus is greatly esteemed by you. Your clothing of rags doesn't matter. What do you think of His royal apparel? Your wounds are not the issue, regardless of how grievous they may be. What do you think of His wounds? Are they like priceless rubies to you? I don't think less of you even if you are like Lazarus, lying on a dunghill "covered with sores" (Luke 16:20) that the dogs are licking, for I am not judging you by your poverty, but by what you think of "the king in his beauty" (Isa. 33:17). Is He highly enthroned in your heart? Would you lift His throne even higher if you could? Are you willing to die if only you could add another trumpet to His chorus of praise?

If so, all is well with you. Whatever you may think of yourself, if you highly esteem Christ, then before long you will dwell with Him in glory.

> Though all the world my esteem deride,
> Yet Jesus shall my portion be;
> For I am pleased with none beside,
> The fairest of the fair is He.
> Gerhard Tersteegen, 1697 – 1769

From the pen of Jim Reimann:

Isaiah prophesied of Christ: "We esteemed him not" (Isa. 53:3), a prophecy precisely fulfilled. So life's great question is: "What do you think about the Christ?" Jesus Himself asked, "Who do people say the Son of Man is?" (Matt. 16:13), but He quickly made it personal, asking, "But what about you? Who do you say I am?" (v. 15). Our eternity hangs in the balance on our answer to that question, but ultimately it is a matter of faith. Either we believe God's Word and Jesus' testimony, or we do not. The Bible is quite clear, for Peter declared: "You are the Christ, the Son of the living God" (v. 16). When standing before Pilate, Jesus was asked, "Are you the king of the Jews?" to which He replied, "Yes, it is as you say" (Matt. 27:11). The truth is this: One day "every tongue [will] confess that Jesus Christ is Lord" (Phil. 2:11) — either in this life or on judgment day.

But — "If you confess with your mouth, 'Jesus is Lord,' and believe in your heart that God raised him from the dead, you will be saved" (Rom. 10:9) — today!

DECEMBER 30

Don't you realize that this will end in bitterness?

2 Samuel 2:26

From the pen of Charles Spurgeon:

Dear reader, if you merely *profess*, but do not *possess* faith in Christ Jesus, the following is a true summary of your tragic existence from beginning to end:

Your beginning is that you are a respected churchgoer, but you go because others go, not because your heart is right with God. I suppose that for the next twenty to thirty years, if the Lord spares your life, you will continue as you do now, professing faith through your outward church attendance, while inwardly denying God's grace and having no heart for it. But I warn you to tread carefully here, and I feel compelled to show you the deathbed of someone such as you.

Gazing gently on him, we see clammy sweat on his brow as he wakes up crying, "O God, it's hard to die! Send for my pastor." Then, once the minister arrives, the dying man says, "Sir, I am afraid I'm dying!" to which the minister asks, "Do you have any hope?" The man confesses, "I don't. I'm afraid to stand before God. Pray for me!" A prayer is offered with sincere earnestness, and the way of salvation is shared with him for the ten-thousandth time, but just before he grasps his only hope, I see him sink. I close his eyelids, for they will never see anything here again. But where is he now, and what do his spiritual eyes see?

Of the rich, but lost, man in the Scriptures, we read: "In hell, where he was in torment, he looked up" (Luke 16:23). Oh, why didn't he lift up his eyes before! It was because he was so accustomed to hearing the gospel that his soul slept through

it. Unfortunately, dear reader, if you wait until then to lift up your eyes, how bitter will be your cries! The rich man's own words from hell, as told by the Savior, reveal his great woe: "Father Abraham, have pity on me and send Lazarus to dip the tip of his finger in water and cool my tongue, because I am in agony in this fire" (Luke 16:24). There is dreadful meaning in those words. May you never have to utter them while experiencing Jehovah's fiery wrath.

From the pen of Jim Reimann:

Jesus said, "Not everyone who says to me, 'Lord, Lord,' will enter the kingdom of heaven, but only he who does the will of my Father who is in heaven. Many will say to me on that day, 'Lord, Lord, did we not prophesy in your name, and in your name drive out demons and perform many miracles?' Then I will tell them plainly, 'I never knew you. Away from me, you evildoers!' Therefore everyone who hears these words of mine and puts them into practice is like a wise man who built his house on the rock" (Matt. 7:21 – 24).

Have you built your spiritual "house on the rock" of Jesus? As yet another year ends, examine your relationship — or lack of relationship — with Him. "Examine yourselves to see whether you are in the faith" (2 Cor. 13:5). Then pray, "Search me, O God, and know my heart; test me and know my anxious thoughts. See if there is any offensive way in me, and *lead me in the way everlasting*" (Ps. 139:23 – 24).

Jesus is "*the way*" (John 14:6). "Believe on him and receive eternal life" (1 Tim. 1:16).

DECEMBER 31

The harvest is past, the summer has ended,
and we are not saved.

Jeremiah 8:20

From the pen of Charles Spurgeon:

"Not saved"! Dear reader, is this your sad predicament? You have been warned of "the judgment to come" (Acts 24:25) and cautioned to "flee for your [life]" (Gen. 19:17). You know "the way to be saved" (Acts 16:17), for you have read it in the Bible and heard it preached. Still you ignore it — still you are "not saved"! You will be "without excuse" (Rom. 1:20) when the Lord "will judge the living and the dead" (2 Tim. 4:1). Year after year have followed one another into eternity, and soon your final year will be here.

Will you ever be saved? Every method has failed with you, even the best of methods done with great perseverance and affection. What more can be done for you? Neither prosperity nor affliction have made an impression on you. Tears, prayers, and sermons have been wasted on your barren heart. Isn't it quite likely that you will stay just as you are now until death forever slams the door of hope? Isn't it logical to assume that you will never "find it convenient" (Acts 24:25) until you find yourself in hell? But take a moment to consider what hell actually is.

If you die unsaved, there are no words adequate to describe your doom. Your dreaded situation can only be written with tears and blood, with groanings and "gnashing of teeth" (Matt. 8:12). "[You] will be punished with everlasting destruction and shut out from the presence of the Lord" (2 Thess. 1:9). Be wise, and before another year begins, believe in Jesus "who is able to save" (James 4:12) completely and forever.

Dedicate these final hours of the year to your inner thoughts. If deep repentance is born in you, it will be good. And if it leads to a humble faith in Jesus, it will be the best of all. Believe and live — now, now, NOW!

From the pen of Jim Reimann:

Unbeliever, if you ignore what you have just read, those very words will be called as a witness against you one day. In fact, God will "call heaven and earth as witnesses against you" (Deut. 4:26). Hebrews warns: "If the message spoken by angels was binding, and every violation and disobedience received its just punishment, *how shall we escape if we ignore such a great salvation*?" (Heb. 2:2 – 3).

But remember — God is gracious and has promised: "In the time of my favor I will answer you, and in the day of salvation I will help you" (Isa. 49:8). Heed Paul's warning: "Now is the time of God's favor, now is the day of salvation" (2 Cor. 6:2).

And believer, if you truly love Jesus, make a renewed commitment to walk in obedience this coming year, for "this is love: that we walk in obedience to his commands" (2 John 6). "Do not merely listen to the word, and so deceive yourselves. Do what it says" (James 1:22).

As this year comes to a close, "Let us bow down in worship, let us kneel before the LORD our Maker; for he is our God and we are the people of his pasture, the flock under his care. Today, if you hear his voice, do not harden your hearts" (Ps. 95:6 – 8).

"Hear my voice; pay attention and hear what I say" (Isa. 28:23).

Scripture Index

Old Testament

Genesis

New Testament

Index: page 15

SUBJECT INDEX

About the Author

Jim Reimann has more than five million books in print in more than twelve languages, including the updated editions of *Streams in the Desert* and *My Utmost for His Highest*. He is a former retail executive and past chairman of the Christian Booksellers Association. Jim is an ordained minister, Bible teacher, author, and Israel tour host, having led numerous Bible-teaching tours to Israel and other Bible lands, which he offers through his website: *www.JimReimann.com*

Jim and his wife, Pam, have three married children and six granddaughters. They make their home in Atlanta, Georgia.

The companion volume to *Evening by Evening: The Devotions of Charles Spurgeon* is also available from Zondervan:

Morning by Morning: The Devotions of Charles Spurgeon
Expanded, Indexed, and Updated in Today's Language by Jim Reimann

Other Classic Devotionals Updated by Jim Reimann:

My Utmost for His Highest by Oswald Chambers, Updated Edition
Published by Discovery House Publishers

Streams in the Desert by L. B. Cowman, Updated Edition
Published by Zondervan

Streams for Teens by L. B. Cowman, Updated Edition
Published by Zondervan

Streams in the Desert for Graduates by L. B. Cowman, Updated Edition
Published by Zondervan

Streams in the Desert®

366 Daily Devotional Readings

L. B. Cowman.
Edited by Jim Reimann,
Editor of My Utmost for His Highest, Updated Edition

For years, the beloved classic devotional *Streams in the Desert* has sustained and replenished God's weary desert travelers. Now, bursting forth like a sparkling clear river of wisdom, encouragement, and inspiration, this updated edition of *Streams in the Desert* promises to revive and refresh today's generation of faithful sojourners, providing daily Scripture passages from the popular, readable New International Version—and modern, easy-to-understand language that beautifully captures the timeless essence of the original devotional. Filled with insight into the richness of God's provision and the purpose of his plan, this enduring classic has encouraged and inspired generations of Christians.

James Reimann, editor of the highly acclaimed, updated edition of *My Utmost for His Highest* by Oswald Chambers, again brings us the wisdom of the past in the language of today by introducing this updated edition of *Streams in the Desert*.

Day by day, *Streams in the Desert* will lead you from life's dry, desolate places to the waters of the River of Life—and beyond, to their very Source.

Available in stores and online!

ZONDERVAN®
.com

Morning by Morning

The Devotions of Charles Spurgeon

Jim Reimann,
Editor of the Updated Editions of Streams in the Desert® & My Utmost for His Highest

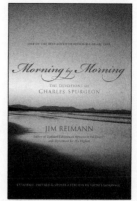

What can *Morning by Morning* do for you?

A lot! Especially if you're a serious Christian or a Bible student who wants to be challenged to think differently about how to apply God's Word to your life.

Jim Reimann, inspired interpreter of such classics as *Streams in the Desert* and *My Utmost for His Highest*, gives *Morning by Morning*—the powerful devotions of Charles Spurgeon—a new spin.

Reimann carefully maintains the strength and dignity of the original edition, but broadens the appeal by adding:

- *Updated language and precise NIV text*
- *Contemporary applications and prayers*
- *Scripture references for every Bible quote*
- *Easy-to-use Scripture and subject indexes*
- *Scriptures selected from every book of the Bible*

These additions are designed to make *Morning by Morning* ideal for personal use as well as for sharing in study groups. But it's the author's thoughtful "From the pen of Jim Reimann" segments that really make this devotional shine.

The author's daily commentary complements Spurgeon's writing perfectly. Each day, Reimann includes personal reflections and shares thought-provoking ideas gleaned from his extensive travel and studies in Israel and other Bible lands. The result is a day-by-day opportunity for Christians to pause, reflect, learn, and grow.

Whether you're mature in your faith or new to the journey, this stimulating devotional delivers a daily dose of just what you need.

Available in stores and online!

Share Your Thoughts

With the Author: Your comments will be forwarded to the author when you send them to *zauthor@zondervan.com*.

With Zondervan: Submit your review of this book by writing to *zreview@zondervan.com*.

Free Online Resources at www.zondervan.com

Zondervan AuthorTracker: Be notified whenever your favorite authors publish new books, go on tour, or post an update about what's happening in their lives at www.zondervan.com/authortracker.

Daily Bible Verses and Devotions: Enrich your life with daily Bible verses or devotions that help you start every morning focused on God. Visit www.zondervan.com/newsletters.

Free Email Publications: Sign up for newsletters on Christian living, academic resources, church ministry, fiction, children's resources, and more. Visit www.zondervan.com/newsletters.

Zondervan Bible Search: Find and compare Bible passages in a variety of translations at www.zondervanbiblesearch.com.

Other Benefits: Register yourself to receive online benefits like coupons and special offers, or to participate in research.

ZONDERVAN

ZONDERVAN.com/
AUTHORTRACKER
follow your favorite authors